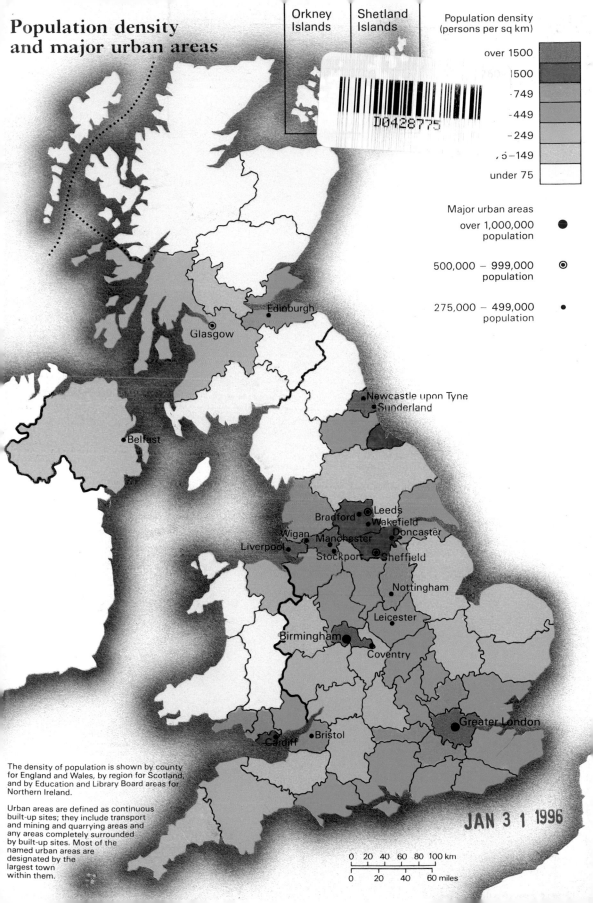

Population density and major urban areas

Orkney Islands

Shetland Islands

D0428775

Population density (persons per sq km)

- over 1500
- 1500
- -749
- -449
- -249
- 5-149
- under 75

Major urban areas

over 1,000,000 population ●

500,000 – 999,000 population ◉

275,000 – 499,000 population •

Edinburgh

Glasgow

Newcastle upon Tyne

Sunderland

Belfast

Bradford · Leeds
Wakefield
Wigan Doncaster
Liverpool Manchester
Stockport Sheffield

Nottingham

Leicester

Birmingham
Coventry

Cardiff · Bristol

Greater London

The density of population is shown by county for England and Wales, by region for Scotland, and by Education and Library Board areas for Northern Ireland.

Urban areas are defined as continuous built-up sites; they include transport and mining and quarrying areas and any areas completely surrounded by built-up sites. Most of the named urban areas are designated by the largest town within them.

JAN 3 1 1996

0 20 40 60 80 100 km

0 20 40 60 miles

BRITAIN
1996
AN OFFICIAL HANDBOOK

Prepared by the Central Office of Information
London: HMSO

Applications for reproduction should be made to HMSO, Copyright Unit, St. Crispins, Norwich NR3 1PD

First published 1995

ISBN 0 11 702024 9

Contents

List of Illustrations

Photographs

Acknowledgments for the use of photographs appear on p. 554.

Foreword

Britain 1996 is the 47th in the series of annual Handbooks prepared by the Central Office of Information (COI). Drawing on a wide range of official and other authoritative sources, it provides a factual and up-to-date overview of government policy and other recent developments in Britain.

Handbook is widely recognised as an established work of reference, not only in Britain itself, but also overseas, where it is an important element of the information service provided by British diplomatic posts. It is sold by HMSO and its agents throughout the world.

Features

The text has, of course, been fully updated and revised. There are more pages and more charts, tables and graphs.

To mark COI's fiftieth anniversary, we have included a selection of COI pictures highlighting people, places and events over the past five decades.

And, in response to many requests, we have provided a calendar of events for 1996, featuring not only famous fixtures like Wimbledon and Trooping the Colour, but also many smaller, traditional local events that are not so well known.

Coverage

Every effort is made to ensure that the information given in *Handbook* is accurate at the time of going to press. The text, generally, is based on information available up to September 1995.

As far as possible, *Handbook* presents information that applies to Britain as a whole. However, this is not always possible. Care should be taken when using Handbook to note whether the information given refers to:

- Britain, formally the United Kingdom of Great Britain and Northern Ireland;
- Great Britain, which comprises England, Wales and Scotland;
- England and Wales, which are grouped together for many administrative and other purposes; or, in some instances,
- England alone.

Aspects of Britain

COI also produces the Aspects of Britain series of paperbacks, which cover in depth Britain's political, economic and social structure, and its place in the international community. Appropriate titles are given in the list of further reading at the end of most chapters. For further information please write to COI Publishing Services or phone 0171 261 8310.

Acknowledgments

Britain 1996 has been compiled with the co-operation of around 250 organisations, including other government departments and agencies. The editor would like to thank all those whose careful comments have contributed once more to *Handbook*'s high standards of accuracy.

Readers' Comments

We welcome readers' comments and suggestions on *Handbook*. These should be sent to:

The Editor
Britain: An Official Handbook
Publishing Services
Central Office of Information
Hercules Road
London SEI 7DU.

Britain and its People

1 Introduction

Britain comprises Great Britain (England, Wales and Scotland) and Northern Ireland, and is one of the member states of the European Union (EU). Its full name is the United Kingdom of Great Britain and Northern Ireland.

Physical Features

Britain constitutes the greater part of the British Isles. The largest of the islands is Great Britain. The next largest comprises Northern Ireland and the Irish Republic. Western Scotland is fringed by the large island chain known as the Hebrides and to the north east of the Scottish mainland are the Orkney and Shetland Islands. All these have administrative ties with the mainland, but the Isle of Man in the Irish Sea and the Channel Islands between Great Britain and France are largely self-governing, and are not part of the United Kingdom.

With an area of about 242,000 sq km (93,000 sq miles), Britain is just under 1,000 km (about 600 miles) from the south coast to the extreme north of Scotland and just under 500 km (around 300 miles) across in the widest part.

The climate is generally mild and temperate. Prevailing winds are south-westerly and the weather from day to day is mainly influenced by depressions moving eastwards across the Atlantic. The weather is subject to frequent changes. In general, there are few extremes of temperature; it rarely rises above 32°C (90°F) or falls below –10°C (14°F).

Average annual rainfall is more than 1,600 mm (over 60 inches) in the mountainous areas of the west and north but less than 800 mm (30 inches) over central and eastern parts. Rain is fairly well distributed throughout the year, but, on average, March to June are the driest months and September to January the wettest. During May, June and July (the months of longest daylight) the mean daily duration of sunshine varies from five hours in northern Scotland to eight hours in the Isle of Wight; during the months of shortest daylight (November, December and January) sunshine is at a minimum, with an average of an hour a day in northern Scotland and two hours a day on the south coast of England.

Geographical Facts

- Highest mountain: Ben Nevis, in the highlands of Scotland, at 1,343 m (4,406 ft)
- Longest river: the Severn, 354 km (220 miles) long, which rises in central Wales and flows through Shrewsbury, Worcester and Gloucester in England to the Bristol Channel
- Largest lake: Lough Neagh, Northern Ireland, at 396 sq km (153 sq miles)
- Highest waterfall: Eas a'Chual Aluinn, from Glas Bheinn, in the highlands of Scotland, with a drop of 200 m (660 ft)
- Deepest cave: Ogof Ffynnon Ddu, Wales, at 308 m (1,010 ft) deep
- Most northerly point on the British mainland: Dunnet Head, north-east Scotland
- Most southerly point on the British mainland: Lizard Point, Cornwall

Historical Outline

The name 'Britain' derives from Greek and Latin names probably stemming from a Celtic original. Although in the prehistoric timescale the Celts were relatively late

Britain

Shetland Islands

Orkney Islands

SCOTLAND

SCOTLAND

| 0 | 50 | 100 | 150 km |

| 0 | 50 | 100 miles |

Hebrides

Outer Hebrides

Western Isles

Inner Hebrides

Highland

Grampian

Tayside

Fife

Central

Edinburgh

Lothian

Strathclyde

Borders

Atlantic Ocean

Dumfries and Galloway

Northumberland

NORTHERN IRELAND

Belfast

Tyne and Wear

Cumbria

Durham

Cleveland

North Sea

North Yorkshire

ENGLAND

Isle of Man

Lancashire

West Yorkshire

Humberside

Irish Sea

Merseyside

South Yorkshire

IRISH REPUBLIC

Clwyd

Cheshire

Derbyshire

Lincolnshire

Gwynedd

Staffordshire

Norfolk

Leicester

WALES

Powys

Cambridge

Suffolk

Hereford and Worcester

Essex

Dyfed

Oxford

Gwent

Gloucestershire

Cardiff

London

Avon

Berkshire

Wiltshire

Surrey

Kent

Somerset

Hampshire

West Sussex

East Sussex

Strait of Dover

BELGIU

Devon

Dorset

Isle of Wight

Cornwall

English Channel

FRANCE

Isles of Scilly

International boundaries

Country boundaries

County boundaries (regional boundaries in Scotland)

1. Greater Manchester
2. Nottinghamshire
3. Shropshire
4. West Midlands
5. Warwickshire
6. Northamptonshire
7. Bedfordshire
8. Hertfordshire
9. Buckinghamshire
10. Greater London
11. West Glamorgan
12. Mid Glamorgan
13. South Glamorgan

Note: This map is correct at time of going to press.
New local government boundaries will be introduced
in Scotland, Wales and parts of England in April 1996.

Channel Islands

arrivals in the British Isles, only with them does Britain emerge into recorded history. The term 'Celtic' is often used rather generally to distinguish the early inhabitants of the British Isles from the later Anglo-Saxon invaders.

After two expeditions by Julius Caesar in 55 and 54 BC, contact between Britain and the Roman world grew, culminating in the Roman invasion of AD 43. Roman rule was gradually extended from south-east England to include Wales and, for a time, the lowlands of Scotland. The final Roman withdrawal in 409 followed a period of increasing disorder during which the island began to be raided by Angles, Saxons and Jutes from northern Europe. It is from the Angles that the name 'England' derives. The raids turned into settlement and a number of small English kingdoms were established. The Britons maintained an independent existence in the areas now known as Wales and Cornwall. Among these kingdoms more powerful ones emerged, claiming overlordship over the whole country, first in the north (Northumbria), then in the midlands (Mercia)

and finally in the south (Wessex). However, further raids and settlement by the Vikings from Scandinavia occurred, although in the 10th century the Wessex dynasty defeated the invading Danes and established a wide-ranging authority in England.

Dates of some of the main events in Britain's history are given on p. 4. The early histories of England, Wales, Scotland and Northern Ireland are included in Chapters 2 to 5, which also deal with the main aspects of their social, economic and political life. Additional material is included on the political situation in Northern Ireland. Table 1.1 gives a selection of some of the main statistics for each of the four lands.

Wildlife

Britain is home to a great variety of wildlife, with an estimated 30,000 animal species, as well as marine, microscopic and less well-known groups, about 2,800 species of 'higher' plants, and many thousands of mosses, fungi and algae.

Table 1.1: General Statistics

	England	Wales	Scotland	Northern Ireland	United Kingdom
Population (1994) ('000)	48,707	2,913	5,132	1,642	58,395
Area (sq km)[a]	130,423	20,766	77,080	13,483	241,752
Population density (persons per sq km)	373	140	67	122	242
Gross domestic product (£ per head, 1993)	9,404	7,831	9,104	7,574	9,248
Employees in employment ('000, June 1995)	18,417	981	1,944	567	21,909
Percentage of employees (June 1995) in:					
services	76.2	70.4	73.9	73.4	75.7
manufacturing	17.9	23.3	16.4	18.0	18.0
construction	3.6	3.2	5.8	4.1	3.8
mining, energy and water supply	1.0	1.1	2.1	1.2	1.1
agriculture, forestry and fishing	1.3	2.0	1.9	3.4	1.4
Unemployment rate (per cent, seasonally adjusted, July 1995)	8.2	8.4	8.0	11.7	8.3

Sources: *Regional Trends, Annual Abstract of Statistics,* Office of Population Censuses and Surveys, Central Statistical Office
[a]Figures for area are not on a strictly comparable basis; those for England and Wales include inland water, while those for Scotland and Northern Ireland are for the land area only.

Significant Dates

55 and 54 BC: Julius Caesar's expeditions to Britain

AD 43: Roman conquest begins under Claudius

122–38: Hadrian's Wall built

c409: Roman army withdraws from Britain

450s onwards: foundation of the Anglo-Saxon kingdoms

597: arrival of St Augustine to preach Christianity to the Anglo-Saxons

664: Synod of Whitby opts for Roman Catholic rather than Celtic church

789–95: first Viking raids

832–60: Scots and Picts merge under Kenneth Macalpin to form what is to become the kingdom of Scotia

860s: Danes overrun East Anglia, Northumbria and eastern Mercia

871–99: reign of Alfred the Great in Wessex

1066: William the Conqueror defeats Harold Godwinson at Hastings and takes the throne

1215: King John signs Magna Carta to protect feudal rights against royal abuse

1301: Edward of Caernarvon (later Edward II) created Prince of Wales

1314: battle of Bannockburn ensures survival of separate Scottish kingdom

1337: Hundred Years War between England and France begins

1348–49: Black Death (bubonic plague) wipes out a third of England's population

1381: Peasants' Revolt in England

1455–87: Wars of the Roses between Yorkists and Lancastrians

1477: first book to be printed in England, by William Caxton

1534–40: English Reformation; Henry VIII breaks with the Papacy

1536–42: Acts of Union integrate England and Wales administratively and legally and give Wales representation in Parliament

1547–53: Protestantism becomes official religion in England under Edward VI

1553–58: Catholic reaction under Mary I

1558: loss of Calais, last English possession in France

1558–1603: reign of Elizabeth I; moderate Protestantism established

1588: defeat of Spanish Armada

c1590–c1613: plays of Shakespeare written

1603: union of the two crowns under James VI of Scotland

1642–51: Civil Wars between King and Parliament

1649: execution of Charles I

1653–58: Oliver Cromwell rules as Lord Protector

1660: monarchy restored under Charles II

1688: Glorious Revolution; accession of William and Mary

1707: Act of Union unites England and Scotland

c1760s–c1830s: Industrial Revolution

1761: opening of the Bridgewater Canal ushers in Canal Age

1775–83: American War of Independence leads to loss of the Thirteen Colonies

1793–1815: Revolutionary and Napoleonic Wars

1801: Act of Union unites Great Britain and Ireland

1825: opening of the Stockton and Darlington Railway, the world's first passenger railway

1829: Catholic emancipation

1832: First Reform Act extends the franchise

1914–18: First World War

1921: Anglo-Irish Treaty establishes the Irish Free State; Northern Ireland remains part of the United Kingdom

1939–45: Second World War

1952: accession of Elizabeth II

1973: Britain enters European Community (now the European Union)

Channel Islands and Isle of Man

Although the Channel Islands and the Isle of Man are not part of the United Kingdom, they have a special relationship with it. The Channel Islands were part of the Duchy of Normandy in the 10th and 11th centuries and remained subject to the English Crown after the loss of Normandy to the French. The Isle of Man was under the nominal sovereignty of Norway until 1266, and eventually came under the direct administration of the British Crown in 1765. Today the territories have their own legislative assemblies and systems of law. The British Government is responsible for their international relations and external defence.

2 England

England is predominantly a lowland country, although there are upland regions in the north (the Pennine Chain, the Cumbrian mountains and the Yorkshire moorlands) and in the south west, in Cornwall, Devon and Somerset. The greatest concentrations of population (see Table 2.1) are in London and the South East, the West Yorkshire and north-west industrial cities, the Midlands conurbation around Birmingham, the north-east conurbations on the rivers Tyne and Tees, and along the Channel coast.

Early History

In 1066 the last successful invasion of England took place. Duke William of Normandy defeated the English at the Battle of Hastings. Normans and others from France came to settle. French became the language of the nobility for the next three centuries, and the legal and social structures were influenced by those prevailing across the Channel.

With the final loss of the English Crown's possessions in France during the late Middle Ages, and the union of England and Scotland in 1707, England's position as the most populous part of the British nation state was established.

Government

England has no government minister or department exclusively responsible for its central administration, in contrast to Wales, Scotland and Northern Ireland. Instead, there are a number of government departments, whose responsibilities in some cases also cover aspects of affairs in Wales and Scotland (see Appendices).

There are currently 524 English parliamentary constituencies represented in the House of Commons. The changes approved following the recent boundary review (see p. 72) will increase this to 529 after the next general election. In September 1995 England had 314 Conservative Members of Parliament, 195 Labour, 14 Liberal Democrat and the Speaker of the House of Commons. Conservative support tends to be strongest in suburban and rural areas, and the Conservatives have a large majority of the parliamentary seats in the southern half of England and in East Anglia. The Labour Party derives its main support from urban industrialised areas. Liberal Democrat support in England is particularly strong in the South West, where the party holds seven of its 14 English seats.

Local government is mainly administered through a two-tier system of counties

8

Table 2.1: Population and Population Density Mid-1994

	Population	People per sq km		Population	People per sq km
North	**3,099,900**	**201**	Greater London	6,966,800	4,415
Cleveland	560,100	938	Hampshire	1,605,800	425
Cumbria	490,200	72	Hertfordshire	1,005,300	613
Durham	607,900	250	Isle of Wight	124,700	328
Northumberland	307,700	61	Kent	1,545,900	414
Tyne and Wear	1,134,000	2,100	Oxfordshire	590,400	227
Yorkshire and Humberside	**5,025,800**	**326**	Surrey	1,043,800	622
Humberside	889,500	254	West Sussex	722,200	363
North Yorkshire	726,900	87	**South West**	**4,795,700**	**201**
South Yorkshire	1,305,400	837	Avon	978,700	735
West Yorkshire	2,104,000	1,034	Cornwall and Isles of Scilly	478,900	135
East Midlands	**4,102,500**	**263**	Devon	1,051,300	157
Derbyshire	954,100	363	Dorset	672,300	253
Leicestershire	916,900	359	Gloucestershire	549,600	207
Lincolnshire	605,800	102	Somerset	477,500	138
Northamptonshire	594,800	251	Wiltshire	587,500	169
Nottinghamshire	1,030,900	477	**West Midlands**	**5,295,000**	**407**
East Anglia	**2,105,600**	**168**	Hereford and Worcester	700,000	178
Cambridgeshire	687,800	202	Shropshire	416,400	119
Norfolk	768,500	143	Staffordshire	1,054,500	388
Suffolk	649,300	171	Warwickshire	496,300	251
South East	**17,870,600**	**656**	West Midlands (Metropolitan County)	2,627,800	2,923
Bedfordshire	543,200	439	**North West**	**6,412,100**	**873**
Berkshire	768,400	610	Cheshire	975,700	419
Buckinghamshire	658,400	351	Greater Manchester	2,578,000	2,005
East Sussex	726,400	405	Lancashire	1,424,000	464
Essex	1,569,400	427	Merseyside	1,434,400	2,190
			England	**48,707,500**	**373**

Source: Office of Population Censuses and Surveys

(see map, p. 4) subdivided into districts. However, there are some single-tier authorities. The structure of local government in England is being reformed following its review by the Local Government Commission (see p. 72).

The English legal system comprises on the one hand a historic body of conventions known as 'common law' and 'equity', and, on the other, parliamentary and European Community (EC) legislation. In the formulation of common law since the Norman Conquest, great reliance has been placed on precedent. Equity law derives from the practice of petitioning the King's Chancellor in cases not covered by common law.

The Church of England, which was separated from the Roman Catholic Church at the time of the Reformation, is the Established Church; the Sovereign must always be a member of the Church and appoints its two archbishops and 42 other diocesan bishops.

The Economy

Considerable changes in the economy of England have occurred during the 20th century. In the second half of the century, jobs in service industries have grown and now account for 74 per cent of employees in employment, with expansion having been particularly noticeable in financial and business services. Services account for three-quarters of gross domestic product (GDP) in London and the South East, and over a fifth of employees in Greater London work in financial services. London is one of the world's leading centres of banking, insurance and other financial services.

Manufacturing, although declining as a proportion of the employment base, remains important in a number of areas. In terms of GDP, it is most significant in the West Midlands (where manufacturing accounted for 30 per cent of the region's GDP in 1992) and the North. The region with the highest proportion of employment in manufacturing is the East Midlands, followed by the West Midlands, Yorkshire and Humberside and the North. East Anglia has been the fastest-growing English region in terms of both population and employment since the 1960s, although in the recession of the early 1990s the unemployment rate rose faster there than in most other regions. Once largely agricultural, high-technology industry has in recent years developed in the region.

In agriculture, dairying is most common in the west of England; sheep and cattle are reared in the hilly and moorland areas of the North and South West. Arable farming, pig and poultry farming and horticulture are concentrated in the east and south.

Tourism and leisure now form one of England's biggest industries, worth over £36,000 million in 1994 and contributing 5 per cent of gross domestic product. Tourism and leisure also provide about 1.5 million jobs.

Table 2.2: Percentage Change in Population, Employment and Housing Stock

	Population 1981–92	Employment[a] 1981–93	Dwelling stock 1981–92
North	−0.6	−0.9	6.6
Yorkshire and Humberside	1.7	2.5	7.6
East Midlands	5.4	5.4	11.9
East Anglia	10.3	20.3	16.6
South East	4.1	−0.2	12.4
South West	8.3	11.8	15.7
West Midlands	1.7	0.6	8.3
North West	−0.9	−2.9	5.7
England	**3.3**	**2.0**	**10.6**

Source: *Regional Trends*
[a]Employees in employment plus self-employed.

Table 2.3: Attendances at English Tourist Attractions, 1994		
		millions
Blackpool Pleasure Beach	F	7.2*
British Museum	F	5.9
National Gallery	F	4.3
Palace Pier, Brighton	F	3.5*
Alton Towers	P	3.0
Madame Tussaud's	P	2.6
St Paul's Cathedral	P	2.6**
Funland and Laserbowl, Trocadero, London	F	2.5*
Tower of London	P	2.4
Canterbury Cathedral	F	2.3*
Tate Gallery	F	2.2
Westminster Abbey	F	2.2*
Pleasure Beach, Great Yarmouth	F	2.0*
York Minster	F	2.0*
Pleasureland, Southport	F	2.0*
Natural History Museum	P	1.6

Source: British Tourist Authority
F   Free admission
P   Paid-for admission
*   Estimated visitor numbers
** Including some free admissions

Transport

The motorway network comprises four long-distance routes linking London and the cities of the Midlands, the North and North West, and the South West; the London orbital route (M25); and over 30 shorter motorways. In all, there are about 3,200 km (2,000 miles) of motorway in England, plus about 14,400 km (9,000 miles) of other trunk roads.

Further Reading

Regional Trends, annual report. HMSO.

On the railways a major development was the official opening in May 1994 of the Channel Tunnel, which links Britain with the European rail system.

Cultural and Social Affairs

London has a wealth of cultural centres, including four major art galleries and many renowned museums, together with theatres, ballet and opera houses and concert halls. Other major cities and towns also have a broad range of cultural interests. Many theatres outside London are used for touring by the national theatre, dance and opera companies. Further large arts projects are likely to benefit from the proceeds of the National Lottery. Numerous regions and towns have associations with great English writers and artists, such as William Shakespeare (Stratford-upon-Avon), William Wordsworth (Lake District), Arnold Bennett (Stoke-on-Trent), the Brontë sisters (Yorkshire), Thomas Hardy (Dorset) and John Constable (Essex and Suffolk).

Despite the relatively high population density and degree of urbanisation, there are still many unspoilt rural and coastal areas. There are seven National Parks, six forest parks, 36 designated 'areas of outstanding natural beauty', 22 environmentally sensitive areas, almost 200 country parks approved by the Countryside Commission, 800 km (500 miles) of designated heritage coastline, and about 2,000 historic buildings and some 3,600 gardens open to the public. Safari, wildlife and theme parks all offer family activities and entertainment.

3 Northern Ireland

About half of the 1.6 million people in Northern Ireland are settled in the eastern coastal region, the centre of which is the capital, Belfast. Most industry is situated in this eastern part of the province. Northern Ireland is at its nearest point only 21 km (13 miles) from Scotland. It has a 488-km (303-mile) border with the Irish Republic.

According to the 1991 Census, 50.6 per cent of the people regarded themselves as Protestants and 38.4 per cent as Roman Catholics. Most of the Protestants are descendants of Scots or English settlers who crossed to north-eastern Ireland; they are British by culture and tradition and committed to remaining part of the United Kingdom. The Roman Catholic population is mainly Irish by culture and history, and the majority of them favour a united Ireland.

History

During the tenth century Ireland was dominated by the Vikings. In 1169 Henry II of England launched an invasion of Ireland since he had been granted its overlordship by the English Pope Adrian IV, who was anxious to bring the Irish Church into full obedience to Rome. Although a large part of the country came under the control of Anglo-Norman magnates, little direct authority was exercised from England during the Middle Ages.

The Tudor monarchs showed a much greater tendency to intervene in Ireland. During the reign of Elizabeth I, a series of campaigns was waged against Irish insurgents. The main focus of resistance was the northern province of Ulster. After the collapse of this resistance in 1607 and the flight of its leaders, Ulster was settled by immigrants from Scotland and England.

The English civil wars (1642–51) led to further risings in Ireland which were crushed by Oliver Cromwell. More fighting took place after the overthrow of James II, a Roman Catholic, in 1688. In 1690 during the Battle of the Boyne the forces of James II were defeated by those of the Protestant William of Orange, who became the British King.

Throughout most of the 18th century there was an uneasy peace. In 1782 the Irish Parliament (dating from medieval times) was given legislative independence; the only constitutional tie with Great Britain was the crown. The Parliament, however, represented only the privileged Anglo-Irish minority, and Roman Catholics were excluded from it. An abortive rebellion led by Wolfe Tone's United Irishmen movement took place in 1798, and in 1801 Ireland was unified with Great Britain, its separate Parliament being abolished. Ireland was henceforth represented in the British Parliament in London.

The Irish question was one of the major issues of British politics during the 19th century and after. In 1886 the Liberal Government introduced a Home Rule Bill designed to give an Irish Parliament devolved authority over most internal matters while reserving control over foreign policy to Britain. This led to a split in the Liberal Party and the failure of the Bill. In 1893 a second Home Rule Bill was approved by the House of Commons but rejected by the House of Lords.

The issue returned to the political agenda in 1910 because Asquith's Liberal administration was dependent on support from the pro-home rule Irish Parliamentary Party. The controversy intensified as unionists and nationalists in Ireland formed private armies. In 1914 home rule was approved in the Government of Ireland Act. Implementation, however, was delayed by the outbreak of the First World War.

A nationalist rising in Dublin in 1916 was suppressed and its leaders executed. Two years later the nationalist Sinn Fein party won a large majority of the Irish seats in elections to the Westminster Parliament. Its members refused to attend the House of Commons and, instead, formed the *Dail Eireann* in Dublin. A nationalist guerrilla force called the Irish Republican Army began operations against the British administration in 1919.

The 1920 Government of Ireland Act provided for the establishment of two home rule parliaments, one in Dublin and the other in Belfast. The Act was implemented in 1921 in Northern Ireland, comprising six of the nine counties of the province of Ulster; in addition, Northern Ireland was represented in, and subject to, the supreme authority of the British Parliament.

In the South the guerillas continued to fight for independence. A truce was agreed in June 1921, followed by negotiations between the British Government and Sinn Fein. These concluded with the December 1921 Treaty establishing the Irish Free State, which became a republic in 1949.

From its creation in 1921, Northern Ireland's Parliament had a consistent unionist majority from which government ministers were drawn. The nationalist minority resented this persistent domination and their effective exclusion from political office and influence. Although an active and articulate civil rights movement emerged during the 1960s, reforms made in response were unable to forestall the development of serious

sectarian rioting. This led to the introduction in 1969 of British Army support for the police. These sectarian divisions were subsequently exploited by terrorists from both sides, most notably by the Provisional Irish Republican Army (IRA), which claimed to be protecting the Roman Catholic minority.

Because of increased terrorism and inter-communal violence, the British Government took over responsibility for law and order in 1972. The Northern Ireland unionist Government resigned in protest at this decision, and direct rule from London began.

Government

Under the system of direct rule, the British Parliament approves all laws, and Northern Ireland's government departments are controlled by the Secretary of State — a Cabinet minister — and his ministerial team.

Seventeen members are elected to the House of Commons. In the most recent general election in April 1992 the Ulster Unionists won 9 seats, the Democratic Unionists 3, the Ulster Popular Unionists 1 and the nationalist Social Democratic and Labour Party (SDLP) 4. The Alliance Party, offering an alternative to unionists and nationalists, did not obtain a seat. Sinn Fein also fought the election but lost its only seat to the SDLP.

Northern Ireland elects three members of the European Parliament.

Efforts to Achieve Devolved Government

Throughout the period of direct rule, successive British governments have favoured a devolved administration widely acceptable to both unionist and nationalist political traditions. In 1974 a unionist-nationalist coalition Executive was formed but collapsed after a short period as a result of a protest strike by those unionists opposed to power sharing. In 1982 an Assembly was elected by proportional representation but was dissolved four years later because no agreement could be reached between the parties on a devolved administration.

Following another government initiative, the four main constitutional parties (Ulster

Unionists, Democratic Unionists, Alliance Party and SDLP) held a series of talks in 1991 and 1992 to see whether they could reach an agreement taking into account three sets of relationships relevant to the Northern Ireland problem—those within Northern Ireland, within the island of Ireland and between the British and Irish governments. The talks ended in November 1992 without agreement.

Since then, the British Government has been engaged in a series of bilateral talks with the Northern Irish parties in order to explore the basis on which they might come together for further dialogue. Intensive discussions were also held with the Irish Government. The aim of all these discussions was to produce a settlement attracting widespread agreement among the two political traditions in the North.

Relations with the Irish Republic

The British and Irish governments have worked closely together in order to bring peace to Northern Ireland. The 1985 Anglo-Irish Agreement created an Intergovernmental Conference, in which both governments discuss issues such as improved cross-border co-operation and security. The Irish Government can put forward views and proposals on matters related to Northern Ireland provided that these are not the responsibility of a devolved administration in Belfast. Each government retains full sovereign responsibility for decisions and administration within its own jurisdiction.

The Downing Street Declaration

Signed in December 1993 by the British and Irish governments, the Downing Street Declaration is a statement of fundamental principles which made clear that the consent of a majority of people in Northern Ireland would be required before any constitutional change could come about. On this basis the British Government reiterated that it had no selfish strategic or economic interest in Northern Ireland and that, were a majority in Northern Ireland to wish it, the Government would introduce legislation to bring about a united Ireland. The Irish Government accepted that it would be wrong to attempt to impose a uni`.ed Ireland without the freely given consent of the majority of people in Northern Ireland.

Paramilitary Ceasefires

In August 1994 the IRA announced a complete cessation of its military operations. This was followed in October by a similar cessation by the loyalist paramilitary organisations. In December 1994 British officials started a separate exploratory dialogue with Sinn Fein and with the Progressive Unionist and Ulster Democratic parties in order to explore the basis on which they could be admitted to the talks process. In 1995 British ministers joined this dialogue, stressing the need for the decommissioning of illegally held arms before these parties could take part in wider political talks.

Joint Framework Document

In February 1995 the British and Irish governments published their Joint Framework Document, reaffirming the need for self-determination in the North, the employment of democratic and exclusively peaceful means in the search for a settlement, and protection for the rights of the unionist and nationalist political traditions. The British Government undertook to propose changes to its constitutional legislation in order to incorporate its continuing willingness to accept the will of a majority of the people in Northern Ireland and to exercise its jurisdiction there with rigorous impartiality. The Irish Government stated that it would introduce and support proposals for changes in the Irish constitution so that no territorial claim over Northern Ireland contrary to the will of a majority of its people is asserted; it also recognised the legitimacy of any choice freely exercised by the people of Northern Ireland regarding their constitutional status.

The Document also proposed a new North-South body comprising elected representatives from, and accountable to, a new elected Northern Ireland Assembly (see below) and the Irish Parliament, which would deal with matters designated by the two governments in agreement with the parties; all decisions within this body would be by agreement between the two sides. It envisages, for example, that the new body should have an important role, in consultation with the two governments, in developing an agreed approach for the whole of Ireland regarding the challenges and opportunities of the European Union.

Both governments also envisage the creation of a parliamentary forum, with representatives from new political institutions in Northern Ireland and from the Irish Parliament to consider matters of mutual interest.

These proposals do not provide for joint authority by the two governments over Northern Ireland.

Accountable Government in Northern Ireland

Alongside the British–Irish Framework Document, the British Government set out its own proposals providing for:

- a single-chamber Northern Ireland Assembly of about 90 members elected by proportional representation for a fixed term, with legislative and executive responsibilities;

- a system of Assembly committees, constituted broadly in proportion to party strengths in the Assembly; and

- a system of detailed checks and balances intended to sustain the confidence in the new institutions by both parts of the community in Northern Ireland.

These proposals closely reflect discussions with the four main parties in the 1992 talks process and subsequently. The British Government has pointed out that any settlement will have to be approved by Parliament and by the people of Northern Ireland in a referendum.

Human Rights

Economic and social deprivation exist on both sides of the Northern Ireland community. However, on all major social and economic indicators, Roman Catholics generally experience higher levels of disadvantage than Protestants. These different experiences lead to feelings of discrimination and alienation, which in turn influence attitudes to political and security issues. Government guidelines aim to promote fair treatment by ensuring that policies and programmes do not discriminate unjustifiably against particular sections of the community—for example, people of different religious beliefs or political opinions, women, disabled people, ethnic minorities and people of different sexual orientation. The Standing Advisory Commission for Human Rights advises the Secretary of State for Northern Ireland on the effectiveness of anti-discrimination laws and measures.

The aim is to encourage a more pluralistic and tolerant society with equal esteem for unionist and nationalist traditions. Through the Community Relations Council, the Government helps finance organisations promoting cross-community contact and reconciliation. In addition, it provides grant aid to local government programmes designed to encourage mutual understanding and appreciation of cultural diversity. Support is also given to the Cultural Traditions Programme, which aims to show that different cultures do not have to lead to division.

Direct or indirect discrimination in employment on grounds of religious belief or political opinion is unlawful. Legislation requires all public authorities and all those private employers with more than ten employees to register with the Fair Employment Commission; it also provides for compulsory monitoring of the religious composition of workforces, review of recruitment, training and promotion procedures and affirmative action if fair employment is not provided. There are criminal penalties and economic sanctions for defaulting employers, and the Fair Employment Tribunal deals with individual complaints about discrimination.

An independent Chief Electoral Officer maintains the accuracy of the electoral register, while electoral boundaries for parliamentary constituencies are determined by impartial statutory procedures conducted by the Boundary Commission for Northern

Ireland. The Northern Ireland Ombudsman and Commissioner for Complaints deal with complaints against government departments and local authorities. An independent commission supervises police investigations into the more serious complaints against police officers and, at its discretion, the investigation of other matters (see p. 85).

Security Policy

In order to protect the public, the Northern Ireland (Emergency Provisions) Act 1991 gives the authorities exceptional powers to deal with and prevent terrorist activities. These powers include special powers of arrest for those suspected of certain serious terrorist offences, non-jury courts to try terrorist offences (see p. 91) and the banning of terrorist organisations. The legislation is subject to annual independent review and to annual approval by Parliament. Although ceasefires have been implemented by republican and loyalist paramilitary organisations, the legislation remains in force, pending a political settlement. The 1991 Act reaches the end of its life in August 1996. The Government hopes that, once a lasting peace is established, there will be no need for these exceptional powers and is keeping the requirement for such powers under continuing review.

An independent Commissioner observes and reports on the conditions under which terrorist suspects are detained by the security forces in police offices known as holding centres. The Commissioner submits an annual report to the Secretary of State which is published.

Statutory codes of practice have been published relating to the detention, treatment, questioning and identification of suspects. Any breach of the codes by a police officer is a disciplinary offence.

The Economy

Trends in output and employment tend to reflect overall trends in Britain. However, unemployment (11.6 per cent in August 1995) is higher because a relatively high birth rate leads to a higher natural rate of population increase than in any other region in Britain.

Some 74 per cent of employees work in service industries and 18 per cent in manufacturing. The largest industrial employer is Short Brothers, owned by the Canadian company Bombardier, with some 6,600 employees engaged on the manufacture of aircraft and their components, guided missiles and related products and services. Another large undertaking is the shipbuilders Harland and Wolff, with 1,175 employees. Two-thirds of output from companies in Northern Ireland is exported—50 per cent to Great Britain, 35 per cent to other European Union countries and 15 per cent to the rest of the world.

Agriculture accounts for 4 per cent of gross domestic product or 7 per cent if ancillary industries are included. Some 10.5 per cent of the workforce is employed in agriculture, forestry, fishing and ancillary industries.

Tourism is promoted throughout the world by the Northern Ireland Tourist Board and generates about 11,000 jobs. Over 1.29 million people visited Northern Ireland in 1994 and it hopes to attract 1.5 million in 1995.

Overseas and other companies are important investors. Northern Ireland attracted 9 per cent of all new investment jobs in Britain in 1993–94 even though it accounted for only 2.8 per cent of the British population. Nearly 200 externally owned companies employ almost 44,500 people—nearly half the manufacturing labour force. Many overseas companies use the region as a base for operations in the ever-increasing European market.

The Industrial Development Board encourages industrial development and new international investment. In 1994–95, 6,000 new jobs were created by new and established companies. The Local Enterprise Development Unit assists the establishment and growth of small businesses as well as 36 local enterprise agencies run by people with business skills and expertise. The Training and Employment Agency is responsible for training the workforce. The Industrial Research and Technology Unit manages programmes aimed at increasing the quality and level of innovation and research.

Considerable public expenditure has been devoted to improving conditions in urban and rural areas. The percentage of unfit houses in

Belfast has been reduced from 25 per cent to 8 per cent in the last 16 years or so. Other government schemes include the £89 million cross-harbour rail and road bridges, which have transformed Belfast's infrastructure. The telecommunications firm BT is investing £30 million in its new Laganbank headquarters, and another important Laganside development is the Belfast City Council's new concert hall and conference centre. More than 200 economic, social and environmental projects in the city's disadvantaged areas have been supported in a bid to improve education, training for adults, and job-finding services for unemployed people.

In Londonderry major private and public sector developments recently completed or under way include a new £65 million shopping centre and car park development in the city centre, construction of a new terminal building and access roads at the City of Derry Airport, the relocation of the port of Londonderry downstream on the River Foyle and the construction of a new science and technology park.

Northern Ireland has parity with England, Scotland and Wales on taxation and services. The British Government makes a contribution of nearly £3,500 million a year to maintain social services at the level of those in Great Britain, to meet the cost of security measures and to compensate for the natural disadvantages of geography and lack of resources.

In 1986 the British and Irish governments established the International Fund for Ireland. Some three-quarters of its resources is spent in Northern Ireland, the rest going to border areas in the Irish Republic. Programmes cover business enterprise, tourism, community relations, urban development, agriculture and rural development. Donors include the United States, the European Union, Canada and New Zealand.

Cultural and Social Affairs

Northern Ireland's cultural heritage is preserved and portrayed by the Ulster Museum in Belfast, the Ulster Folk and Transport Museum in County Down and a number of smaller museums. The Ulster-American Folk Park in Omagh specialises in the history of Irish emigration to America; it has an extensive database on emigrants which is available for use by the public.

Local arts festivals are an important feature of the arts calendar, the highlight being the Belfast festival based at Queen's University. The Ulster Orchestra has a notable reputation. Government support for the arts is channelled through the Arts Council of Northern Ireland, which gives financial help and advice to opera and drama companies, orchestras and festivals, arts centres, galleries, theatres, writers and artistic groups.

Local district councils provide leisure facilities, including leisure centres and swimming pools. The Government finances the Sports Council for Northern Ireland, which promotes sport and physical recreation.

Health and personal social services correspond fairly closely to those in the rest of Britain.

Although publicly-financed schools must be open to children from all religions, in practice Roman Catholic and Protestant children are mainly educated in separate schools. There are 28 integrated schools for both Protestant and Roman Catholic children, and this process is being encouraged by the Government (see p. 429).

Most housing is owner-occupied. The Housing Executive (see p. 343) allocates public housing to those in greatest need.

Local television and radio programmes are broadcast and there is a local press (see p. 495). National television and radio broadcasts are received, and the national press is sold widely.

Further Reading

A History of Ulster. Bardon, Jonathon. Blackstaff Press, 1992.

Northern Ireland. Aspects of Britain series, HMSO, 1995.

Northern Ireland Expenditure Plans and Priorities. The Government's Expenditure Plans 1995–96 to 1997–98. HMSO, 1995.

4 Scotland

Three-quarters of the population of Scotland and most of the industrial towns are in the central lowlands. The chief cities are Edinburgh (the capital), Glasgow, Aberdeen and Dundee. Just over half of Scotland consists of the sparsely populated highlands and islands in the north.

Scotland contains large areas of unspoilt and wild landscape, and the majority of Britain's highest mountains—nearly 300 peaks over 913 m (3,000 ft). The Grampians in the central highlands contain Ben Nevis (1,343 m, 4,406 ft), the highest peak in Britain.

Early History

At the time of the Roman invasion of Britain, what is now Scotland was mainly inhabited by the Picts. Despite a long campaign, Roman rule was never permanently extended to most of Scotland. In the sixth century, the Scots from Ireland settled in what is now Argyll, giving their name to the present-day Scotland. Lothian was populated by the Angles, while Britons moved north to Strathclyde. In the ninth century parts of Scotland were subject to raids by the Vikings; a united Scottish kingdom was established at this time.

The powerful English monarchy threatened Scottish independence in the Middle Ages, particularly under Edward I, and war between the two kingdoms was frequent. There were also, however, strong links with England; several Scottish kings held land and titles in England and there was intermarriage between the Scottish and English royal families. Cultural influences on Scotland were also strong. Despite reverses such as the defeat of William Wallace's uprising in 1298, Robert the Bruce's victory over Edward II of England at Bannockburn ensured the survival of a separate kingdom of Scotland.

The two crowns were eventually united when Elizabeth I of England was succeeded in 1603 by James VI of Scotland (James I of England), who was her nearest heir. Even so, England and Scotland remained separate political entities during the 17th century, apart from an enforced period of unification under Oliver Cromwell in the 1650s. The religions of the two kingdoms had also developed in different directions, with England retaining an Episcopalian church (governed by bishops) and Scotland embracing a Presbyterian system (see p. 452). In 1707 both countries, realising the benefits of closer political and economic union, agreed on a single parliament for Great Britain. Scotland retained its own system of law and church settlement.

Government

There are special arrangements for the conduct of Scottish affairs within the British system of government and separate Acts of Parliament are passed for Scotland where appropriate. There are 72 Scottish seats in the House of Commons. In August 1995 there were 49 Labour Members of Parliament, 10 Conservative, 9 Liberal Democrat and 4 Scottish Nationalist.

Scottish administration is the responsibility of the Secretary of State for Scotland, a member of the Cabinet, working through The Scottish Office, which has its headquarters in Edinburgh and an office in London.

Review of Scottish Government

In 1993 the Government issued a White Paper, *Scotland in the Union: A Partnership for Good*, following a wide-ranging examination of Scotland's place in Britain and the role of Parliament in Scottish affairs. Changes to improve the parliamentary arrangements for handling Scottish business are being implemented. The range of business handled by the Scottish Grand Committee (which consists of all 72 Scottish MPs) is being widened and the Committee now meets in Scotland as well as at Westminster. Other changes include improved scrutiny of Scottish legislation through special standing committees; and greater accountability of Scottish Office ministers through parliamentary question time (see p. 57).

Certain functions have been transferred from Whitehall departments to The Scottish Office. For example, responsibility for the Scottish Arts Council was transferred from the Department of National Heritage in April 1994. To increase the responsiveness of The Scottish Office to the people of Scotland, a central enquiry unit and information points are being established in many towns.

Local Government Reform

The structure of local government is due to change from April 1996. Under the Local Government etc. (Scotland) Act 1994, a

Table 4.1: Population, June 1994

	Population	Population density (people per sq km)
Regions:		
Borders	105,700	23
Central	273,400	104
Dumfries and Galloway	147,800	23
Fife	352,100	269
Grampian	532,500	61
Highland	207,500	8
Lothian	758,600	432
Strathclyde	2,287,800	169
Tayside	395,000	53
Islands:		
Orkney Islands	19,810	20
Shetland Islands	22,880	16
Western Isles	29,310	10
Scotland	**5,132,400**	**67**

Source: General Register Office for Scotland.

single-tier structure of 29 councils will replace the 62 regional and district councils. The three islands councils—Orkney, Shetland and the Western Isles—will be largely unchanged. Edinburgh, Glasgow, Dundee and Aberdeen will each have its own council. Elections for the new councils were held in April 1995 and the councils are operating in shadow form alongside the existing councils until the change of responsibility. The new councils will be required to devise plans by April 1997 to decentralise their administration and services, with the intention of enhancing local democracy and encouraging public participation.

Legal System

The principles and procedures of the Scottish legal system differ in many respects from those of England and Wales. These differences stem, in part, from the adoption of elements from other European legal systems, based on Roman law, during the 16th century. One difference is in the verdicts which a jury may give—in Scotland a jury can give a verdict of 'not proven' when, as with a 'not guilty' verdict, the accused is acquitted.

Following a wide-ranging review of the criminal justice system in Scotland, the Criminal Justice (Scotland) Act 1995 has been introduced (see Chapter 8). The Act is intended to:

- implement major procedural reforms designed to make the criminal justice system more responsive to the needs of victims, witnesses and jurors; and

- increase the capacity of the system to deal with offenders and strengthen the powers available to prevent crime and reduce re-offending.

The Economy

Scotland has experienced the same pressure on its traditional industries as Wales and the north of England. However, since 1987 economic growth in Scotland has on average been greater than in Britain as a whole and it was less affected by the recession in the early 1990s than were other areas.

The most significant development has been the discovery in the early 1970s of oil and gas under the North Sea. Up to about 100,000 jobs are estimated to have arisen directly or indirectly as a result of North Sea activities.

Industry

As traditional industries such as coal, steel and shipbuilding have declined, there has been growth in high technology industries such as chemicals, electronic engineering and lighter forms of mechanical and instrument engineering. Scotland has one of the biggest concentrations of the electronics industry in Western Europe. The industry, which includes many of the world's leading companies in this field, provides nearly 13 per cent of jobs in manufacturing and about 19 per cent of manufacturing output.

Some traditional industries, such as high-quality tweeds and other textiles, and food and drink products, remain important. There are over 100 whisky distilleries, mostly in the north-east. Whisky exports, valued at £2,191 million in 1994, represent about one-fifth of Scotland's manufacturing exports.

Industrial Development

Government measures have helped to attract firms to Scotland, and investment by overseas companies has helped to make a significant contribution to the growth of modern technologically based industries.

Government support for enterprise and training is channelled through Scottish Enterprise and Highlands and Islands Enterprise, which both have general functions in economic development, training and environmental improvement in the Scottish lowlands and the Highlands and Islands respectively. They contract with 22 Local Enterprise Companies (led by the private sector), which arrange the provision of training and business support.

Services

A marked expansion has occurred in services, which now employ over 70 per cent of the workforce. Financial and business services are of growing importance, and over 200,000 people are employed in the sector. There are four Scottish-based clearing banks and they have limited rights to issue their own banknotes. About one-third of investment funds in Britain are managed from Scotland, which is also a base for a large number of insurance companies.

Tourism and leisure also make a significant contribution to the economy, directly providing over 180,000 jobs. In 1993, 10.9 million visitors spent over £2,000 million in Scotland. In November 1994 the Government launched a strategic plan for the development of the tourism industry, including targets for raising tourist expenditure and the number of jobs in the industry. The plan aims to build on Scotland's strengths, such as scenery, culture, historic buildings and opportunities for leisure, while spreading tourism throughout Scotland and increasing tourism in off-peak periods.

Agriculture, Forestry and Fishing

About 75 per cent of the land area of Scotland is devoted to agriculture. Most of this is rough grazing for cattle and sheep. Scotland's cattle industry has a worldwide reputation, both for the quality of meat and for pedigree breeds. Arable farms are highly productive, and the principal crop is barley, which is used in the making of whisky.

Scotland accounts for over half of Britain's forest area and for just under half of timber production. Forestry is continuing to expand and many new woodlands are being created, including native pine forests.

Fishing remains important, particularly in the north-east and the islands. Scotland accounts for 73 per cent by weight and 62 per cent by value of the fish landed in Britain by British vessels.

Energy and Water Resources

Nuclear and hydro-electric generation supply a higher proportion of energy than in any other part of Britain. Over 40 per cent of Scotland's electricity comes from nuclear power, with hydro-power and other renewables contributing over 10 per cent.

With abundant rainfall, there is an extensive supply of water from upland sources. As a result of the changes in local government, three new public water authorities will be set up in April 1996 to take over responsibility for water and sewerage services from the regional and islands councils.

Transport

Communications, both domestic and international, have improved in many parts of Scotland. Electrification of the Edinburgh to London railway was completed in 1991.

The road construction programme includes completion of the Central Scotland motorway network and the extension of the M74 from Carlisle to Glasgow. Proposals to improve public and private transport services around the Firth of Forth are being considered. A public inquiry is planned to examine proposals for a second Forth Road Bridge and associated road links.

Environment

Scotland's countryside contains a rich variety of wildlife, with some species not found elsewhere in Britain. There are 71 national nature reserves and 1,381 Sites of Special Scientific Interest. Four regional parks and 40 national scenic areas have been designated, covering 13 per cent of the land surface. Four of the 11 forest parks in Great Britain are in Scotland, and a fifth spans the border between Scotland and England.

In all, 43 Special Protection Areas have been designated in Scotland under the European Community (EC) directive on wild birds. In March 1995 the Government announced that more than 100 wildlife sites of international importance would be consulted on for possible designation as Special Areas of Conservation under the EC's directive on habitats.

Housing and Urban Regeneration

The tenure pattern is somewhat different from that in the rest of Britain. Home ownership is increasing but, at 56 per cent, is still lower than in other areas of Britain. Some 34 per cent of housing is rented from the public sector, compared with 20 per cent for Britain as a whole. Projects to tackle the problems in inner city areas and some peripheral housing estates include a series of partnerships between The Scottish Office and other groups, such as local communities and the private sector (see p. 350).

Health

There has been a general improvement in the health of people in Scotland, but for certain diseases, such as lung cancer and heart disease, the health record is not as good as elsewhere in Britain. In 1992 the Government issued a policy statement with a range of initiatives to improve health in Scotland and meet the targets for the year 2000 which had been announced in 1991. Progress is being made towards meeting some of these targets, with falls in mortality in coronary heart disease, and lower levels of cigarette smoking among those aged 25 to 64.

Education

The concept of universal education was accepted in Scotland as early as the 16th century. The Scottish education system has a number of distinctive features, for example, in examinations (see p. 436). Four of the 12 universities—St Andrews, Glasgow, Aberdeen and Edinburgh—were established in the 15th century. Record numbers of students are entering higher education; in 1993–94 about 143,000 students (full-time equivalents) were taking higher education courses, 45 per cent more than in 1989–90.

Cultural and Social Affairs

Gaelic, a language of ancient Celtic origin, is spoken by some 70,000 people; the greatest concentration of Gaelic speakers is in the islands of the Hebrides. The Government is encouraging people to learn more about the Gaelic language and culture. Government support for Gaelic—which amounted to £11.3 million in 1994–95—covers three main areas: education, Gaelic organisations and television broadcasting.

Many Scots have achieved eminence in arts and sciences. The annual Edinburgh International Festival is one of the world's leading cultural events. Held in August and September, it is the largest of its kind in the world. Edinburgh and the Mayfest international arts festival in Glasgow are the two largest arts festivals in Britain. Scotland possesses a number of major collections of the fine and applied arts, such as the Burrell Collection in Glasgow. A new Museum of Scotland is to be built in Edinburgh to house the National Museums' Scottish collection. Each spring Edinburgh hosts the International Science Festival, the world's biggest science festival in a single city.

The predominant Church of Scotland is a Protestant church which is Presbyterian in form; it is governed by a hierarchy of church courts, each of which includes lay people.

The sport of golf originated in Scotland, and there are over 400 golf courses, including St Andrews, Gleneagles, Turnberry, Muirfield, Troon and Prestwick, which are internationally renowned. A wide range of outdoor activities, such as mountaineering, hill walking and fishing, are also pursued. Winter sports are becoming increasingly popular in the Cairngorm Mountains, Glencoe and a number of other areas.

Further Reading

Scotland. Aspects of Britain series, HMSO, 1993.

Scotland in the Union: A Partnership for Good. Cm 2225. HMSO, 1993.

Serving Scotland's Needs: The Government's Expenditure Plans 1995–96 to 1997–98. Departments of the Secretary of State for Scotland and the Forestry Commission. Cm 2814. HMSO, 1995.

5 Wales

Two-thirds of the population of Wales live in the southern valleys and the lower-lying coastal areas. The chief urban centres are Cardiff (with a population of 300,000), Swansea, Newport and Wrexham. However, much of Wales is hilly or mountainous. The highest mountains are in Snowdonia and the tallest peak is Snowdon (1,085 m, 3,560 ft).

Wales is a principality; Prince Charles, the heir to the throne, was invested by the Queen with the title of Prince of Wales at Caernarfon Castle in 1969, when he was 20. The Welsh name of the country is Cymru.

Early History

After the collapse of Roman rule in Britain (see p. 5), Wales remained a Celtic stronghold, although often within the English sphere of influence. For much of the period, it was divided into a number of separate principalities, and unity was achieved only sporadically. In 1267 Llywelyn ap Gruffudd, who had achieved control over a large portion of Wales, was recognised as Prince of Wales by the English. However, on his death in 1282, Edward I launched a successful campaign to bring Wales under English rule. The series of great castles that he had built in north Wales remain among Britain's finest historic monuments (see p. 357). Edward I's eldest son—later Edward II—was born at Caernarfon in 1284 and was given the title Prince of Wales, which continues to be borne by the eldest son of the reigning monarch to this day.

Continued strong Welsh national feeling culminated in the rising led by Owain Glyndŵr at the beginning of the 15th century. The Tudor dynasty, which ruled England from 1485 to 1603, was of Welsh ancestry. The Acts of Union of 1536 and 1542 united England and Wales administratively, politically and legally.

Language

At the time of the 1991 census Welsh speakers made up 19 per cent of the population. In much of the rural north and west, Welsh remains the first language of most of the population. There is some evidence that the decline in the number of Welsh speakers is being halted, with greater numbers of children and young people able to speak Welsh, and a revival in the largely anglicised areas of south-east and north-east Wales.

The Government has reaffirmed its commitment to enhancing Welsh culture and developing greater use of the Welsh language. Bilingual education in schools is encouraged (see p. 435), and there has been an extended use of Welsh for official purposes and in broadcasting. There are now many more bilingual publications and most road signs are bilingual. Expenditure of £6.3 million in support of the language is planned in 1995–96. The Welsh Language Act 1993 establishes the principle that, in the context of public business and the administration of justice in Wales, Welsh and English should be treated on an equal basis.

The Act also put the Welsh Language Board (formerly an advisory body) on a statutory basis. Its aim is to promote and facilitate the use of the Welsh language. One of its main tasks is to help public bodies which provide services in Wales to prepare Welsh language schemes setting out their commitments to provide services through the medium of Welsh.

Government

The country returns 38 Members of Parliament to the House of Commons. For the last 60 years the industrial communities have tended to support the Labour Party in elections, ensuring a Labour majority of seats. In August 1995 Wales had 27 Labour Members of Parliament, 6 Conservative, 4 Plaid Cymru (Welsh Nationalist) and 1 Liberal Democrat. Special arrangements exist for the discussion of Welsh affairs in the parliamentary Welsh Grand Committee, whose function is to consider matters relating exclusively to Wales; Bills are referred to it for consideration as to whether they should be given a second reading (see p. 57).

The Secretary of State for Wales, who is a member of the Cabinet, has wide-ranging responsibilities relating to the economy, education, welfare services and the provision of amenities. The headquarters of the administration is the Welsh Office in Cardiff; it also has an office in London. The legal system is identical to the English one.

Under the Local Government (Wales) Act 1994, local government is being reorganised, with the abolition of the two-tier structure of eight county councils and 37 district councils. Elections for the 22 new unitary authorities were held in May 1995 and the authorities are operating on a 'shadow' basis until they replace the existing councils in April 1996.

The Economy

Recent decades have seen fundamental changes in the basis of the Welsh economy, with the dependence on refined fuels and coalmining considerably reduced. The most notable features have been expansion in service industries and the development of a more diverse range of manufacturing industries, including many at the forefront of technology. About 800 new plants have been created since 1980, providing around 55,000 new employment opportunities. Wales is now an important centre for consumer electronics, information technology, automotive components, chemicals and materials, and food and drink. About 16,000 people are employed by around 100 companies in electronics and telecommunications.

In the service sector the most marked growth has been in financial and business

Table 5.1: Population Mid-1994

	Population	Population density (people per sq km)
Clwyd	417,400	172
Dyfed	352,300	61
Gwent	452,300	328
Gwynedd	240,400	62
Mid Glamorgan	544,600	535
Powys	120,200	24
South Glamorgan	414,800	997
West Glamorgan	371,000	452
Wales	**2,913,000**	**140**

Source: Welsh Office

services, and leisure services. Annual earnings from tourism, for example, are estimated at about £1,300 million and the industry employs about 95,000 people. The Wales Tourist Board seeks to develop tourism in ways which will yield the optimum economic benefit for the people of Wales.

> The traditional industry of steelmaking remains important, and Wales accounts for about a third of steel production in Britain. British Steel has invested £1,200 million over the last ten years in its plants in Wales, and there have been significant improvements in productivity. About £22 million is to be invested in the steelworks at Llanwern (Gwent), increasing hot rolling capacity by a third.

Although south Wales remains the principal industrial area, new industries and firms have been introduced in north-east Wales and light industry attracted to the towns in the rural areas of mid- and north Wales.

Inward Investment

Wales has been particularly successful in attracting investment from overseas companies. Through its International Division, the Welsh Development Agency (WDA) seeks to attract investment into Wales and co-ordinates the approach for responding to the needs of investors. Since 1983 it has recorded over 1,400 projects, promising a total of over 84,000 new jobs and capital investment of £7,200 million.

Economic Development

The economic programmes of the Welsh Office are complemented by the work of the WDA and the Development Board for Rural Wales, which have wide powers to promote economic, industrial and environmental change. Planned expenditure by these bodies in 1995–96 totals £153 million and £18 million respectively. One of the main areas of activity is providing accommodation for

business, increasingly in partnership with the private sector. The WDA has also undertaken the largest land reclamation programme in Europe, and all the significant remaining industrial dereliction in Wales is expected to have been removed by the end of the 1990s.

The south Wales valleys are one of the main areas to have been affected by the decline in traditional industries. A second five-year Programme for the Valleys was launched in 1993. While retaining the most successful features of the earlier programme, the emphasis of the new programme has moved away from centralised initiatives towards stronger partnerships between the Welsh Office, development agencies, local councils and the private and voluntary sectors. In September 1994 the Secretary of State for Wales announced plans to attract £1,000 million of private sector investment to the valleys. During 1995 this economic development and private finance initiative is being extended to the rest of Wales.

A development corporation has been set up to stimulate the regeneration of the Cardiff Bay area. A new barrage is being built across the harbour mouth and should be completed in 1998. It is expected that more than 23,000 new jobs will be created in the Cardiff Bay area, 4,400 new homes built and over £1,200 million of private sector investment attracted. As well as commercial and residential development, a new centre for the Welsh National Opera is proposed.

Agriculture and Forestry

Agriculture occupies about 82 per cent of the land area. The main activities are sheep and cattle rearing in the hill regions and dairy farming in the lowlands. About 12 per cent of Wales is covered by woodland.

Transport

Improvements to road and rail links, such as the upgrading of the north Wales coast road, have helped the Welsh economy in recent years. In the south there are motorway links across the Severn Bridge to southern England and the Midlands, and high-speed rail services to a number of destinations in

England. A second major motorway crossing of the Severn and associated approach motorways are under construction. The bridge, scheduled for completion in 1996, is being built and financed by a private sector company, Severn River Crossing plc.

> Passenger traffic at Cardiff Wales airport at Rhoose has nearly doubled since 1991, to over 1 million passengers in 1994. The airport was privatised in April 1995.

Environment

About one-quarter of Wales is designated as a National Park or Area of Outstanding Natural Beauty (see p. 363). As well as three National Parks—Snowdonia, the Brecon Beacons and the Pembrokeshire Coast—and five Areas of Outstanding Natural Beauty, there are two national trails, 31 country parks and large stretches of heritage coast. There are 52 National Nature Reserves and about 890 Sites of Special Scientific Interest. Nearly all of the rivers and canals are classified as having water of good or fair quality, and a significant improvement has been achieved in the quality of bathing waters.

Cultural and Social Affairs

Welsh literature is one of the oldest and richest in Europe. The Welsh people also have strong musical traditions; the country is well known for its choral singing and the Welsh National Opera has an international reputation. Special festivals, known as eisteddfodau, encourage Welsh literature and music. The largest is the annual Royal National Eisteddfod, consisting of competitions in music, singing, prose and poetry entirely in Welsh. Artists from all over the world come to the town of Llangollen for the annual International Musical Eisteddfod. New galleries and a permanent Evolution of Wales exhibition were opened at the National Museum of Wales in Cardiff in 1993. Work on a third building at the National Library of Wales, costing some £11 million, started in 1994 and is expected to be completed in 1998.

There is no established church, the Anglican church in Wales having been disestablished in 1920 following decades of pressure from adherents of the Methodist and Baptist churches. Methodism in particular spread rapidly in Wales in the 18th century, assuming the nature of a popular movement among Welsh speakers and finding strong support later in industrial communities.

An active local press includes a number of Welsh language publications. The fourth television channel, Sianel Pedwar Cymru (S4C), broadcasts most of its programmes in Welsh during peak viewing hours and is required to see that a significant proportion of programmes are in Welsh.

The education system is similar to that in England. Welsh and English are both used as media of instruction. Most Welsh-medium schools are situated in the traditionally Welsh-speaking, largely rural, areas, although there are also bilingual schools in the anglicised, mainly industrial areas to cater for children whose parents want them to be educated through the medium of both languages. Welsh is a core subject in Welsh-speaking schools and a foundation subject elsewhere under the National Curriculum (see p. 435). The collegiate University of Wales, founded in 1893, comprises six member institutions.

Among many sporting activities, there is particular interest in rugby union football, which has come to be regarded as the Welsh national game. The provision of sports facilities, such as indoor sports halls and swimming pools, has increased in recent years.

Further Reading

The Government's Expenditure Plans 1995–96 to 1997–98. A Report by the Welsh Office and the Office of Her Majesty's Chief Inspector of Schools in Wales. Cm 2815. HMSO, 1995.
Wales. Aspects of Britain series, HMSO, 1993.

6 The Social Framework

Among the main social changes during the second half of the 20th century are longer life expectancy and a lower birth rate, reflected in a growing proportion of elderly people; a higher divorce rate; wider educational opportunities; technological progress and a higher standard of living.

POPULATION

According to mid-1994 estimates, Britain's population is 58.4 million, the 17th largest in the world. Statistics are derived from the census (taken every ten years), with allowance made for subsequent births and deaths (obtained from compulsory registration), and migration.

The population has been growing slowly since the early 1980s, thanks to increased longevity. On mid-1992-based projections, the population in Britain is forecast to rise to 59.8 million in 2001 and 61.3 million in 2011.

Birth Rates

In 1994 there were 751,000 live births in Britain, compared with 762,000 in 1993. The total period fertility rate (an indication of average family size) remains below 2.1, the level leading to the long-term replacement of the population, although it is projected that it will increase from 1.75 in 1994 to 1.9 for women born in or after 1980.

Contributory factors to the relatively low birth rate in recent years (12.9 live births per 1,000 population in 1994) include:

- the trends towards later marriage and towards postponing having children, which have led to an increase in the average age of women giving birth—28.4 years in England and Wales in 1994, compared with 26.8 in 1981;

- a preference for smaller families than in the past, which has led to a significant decline in the proportion of families with four or more children;[1] and

- more widespread and effective contraception, making it easier to plan families, and the greater prevalence of voluntary sterilisation for both men and women.

Mortality

At birth the expectation of life for a man is about 73 years and for a woman 78 years, compared with 49 years for men and 52 years for women in 1901. There has, however,

---

[1] In 1993 20 per cent of households in Great Britain consisted of a married couple with one or two dependent children, compared with 5 per cent of households consisting of a married couple with three or more dependent children.

been only a small increase in life expectancy in the older age groups.

There were provisionally estimated to be 626,000 deaths in 1994, a death rate of 10.7 per 1,000 population. There has been a decline in mortality at most ages, particularly among children. The infant mortality rate (deaths of infants under one year old per 1,000 live births) was 6.3 in 1993; neonatal mortality (deaths of infants under four weeks old per 1,000 live births) was 4.2; and maternal mortality is about 0.07 per 1,000 total births. The decline in the mortality rate reflects better nutrition, rising standards of living, the advance of medical science, the increased availability of medical facilities, improved health measures, better working conditions, education in personal hygiene and the smaller size of families.

Deaths caused by circulatory diseases (including heart attacks and strokes) now account for nearly half of all deaths, and mortality from heart disease in England and Wales remains high compared with that of other developed countries. The next largest cause of death is cancer, which is responsible for nearly one-quarter of deaths.

Cigarette smoking is the greatest preventable cause of illness and death in Britain. However, there has been a significant decline in the prevalence of smoking, with 29 per cent of adult males and 28 per cent of adult females smoking cigarettes in 1992, compared with 52 and 41 per cent respectively in 1972.

Between 1990 and 1992 the Government set out strategies for continuing the overall improvement in health, emphasising disease prevention and health promotion (see p. 402). A number of government priorities, aimed at supporting the overall goals of improving the country's health and providing high-quality care for those who need it, have been listed. The Government is also pursuing a comprehensive strategy against drug misuse in Britain. Initiatives are aimed at reducing both the supply of, and demand for, drugs.

From 1991 onwards, annual surveys have been carried out in England to monitor trends in health.

Marriage and Divorce

Britain has one of the highest marriage and divorce rates in the European Union. In 1993 there were 341,600 marriages in Britain, of which 38.4 per cent were remarriages of one or both parties. Some 36.2 per cent of marriages were remarriages where one or both parties had been divorced. Of the population aged 16 or over in England and Wales in 1992, 57 per cent were married, 27 per cent single, 9 per cent widowed and 7 per cent divorced. The average age for first marriages in England and Wales is now about 28.2 for men and 26.2 for women.

With the coming into force of the Marriage Act 1994, couples in England and Wales who choose a register office marriage are no longer restricted to having the ceremony in the register office for the area in which they live. Ceremonies may also now be held at other buildings, such as hotels and stately homes, approved for marriages by the local authority for the area.

In 1993 there were 13.9 divorces for every 1,000 married couples in England and Wales. The rates for Scotland and Northern Ireland are lower than that for England and Wales. In 1993 180,400 divorces were granted in Britain. The average age of people at the time of divorce in England and Wales is now about 39.3 for men and 37.6 for women.

Another feature, common to many other Western European countries, has been an increase in cohabitation, and 18 per cent of non-married men and women aged 16–59 in Great Britain were cohabiting in 1992. Between 1979 and 1992 the proportion of non-married women aged 18–49 who were cohabiting rose from 11 to 21 per cent. Cohabitation is particularly high (25 per cent) among divorced women, but recently the largest increase has been for single women.

There is some evidence of a growing number of stable non-married relationships. Roughly half of all births outside marriage (which accounted for 32 per cent of live births in Britain in 1994) are registered by both parents giving a single address as their place of residence.

Age and Sex Structure

The most significant changes in the age structure of the population have been the growing numbers of elderly people and the decline in the proportion of young people. The proportion of young people aged under 16 fell from 25.5 per cent in 1971 to 20.6 per cent in 1993. During the same period the proportion of elderly people (those aged 65 and over) increased from 13.2 to 15.8 per cent, while 18.3 per cent of the population were over the normal retirement ages (65 for men and 60 for women), compared with 16.3 per cent in 1971.

There is a ratio of about 104 females to every 100 males in the population as a whole. There are about 3 per cent more male than female births every year. However, because of the higher mortality of men at all ages, there is a turning-point, at about 50 years of age, beyond which the number of women exceeds the number of men. This imbalance increases with age so that there are many more women among the elderly.

Distribution of Population

The population density is about 241 inhabitants per sq km, which is well above the EU average of about 153 per sq km. Of the four lands, England is the most densely populated, with 373 people per sq km. Scotland is the least densely populated, with 67 people per sq km. Wales and Northern Ireland have 140 and 122 people per sq km respectively.

Since the 19th century there has been a trend, especially in London, for people to move away from congested urban centres into the suburbs. Between the 1981 and 1991 censuses, all metropolitan counties (with the exception of West Yorkshire) experienced small decreases in population, the largest being in Merseyside (5 per cent). There has also been a geographical redistribution of the population, away from Scotland and the northern regions of England. The regions with the highest rates of increase in

population between 1981 and 1991 were East Anglia (10 per cent) and the South West (8 per cent). Retirement migration is also a feature of population movement, the main recipient areas being the south coast of England and East Anglia (where in some towns the retired constitute over one-quarter of the population).

Migration

From 1989 to 1993 some 1.1 million people left Britain (excluding the Channel Islands and the Isle of Man) to live abroad. About 1.2 million came from overseas to live in Britain, so that net immigration increased the population by about 94,000. These figures exclude migration to and from the Irish Republic, and are also likely to exclude people admitted as visitors who were subsequently granted an extension of stay for a year or more.

In 1993 the total inflow of people intending to stay in Britain for one year or more was 209,000, some 3 per cent less than in 1992. The outflow of people leaving to live abroad, at 213,000, was 6 per cent lower than in 1992.

Of the 213,000 departing residents in 1993:

- 29 per cent left for EU countries;
- 24 per cent for Australia, Canada, New Zealand or South Africa;
- 15 per cent for other Commonwealth countries;
- 15 per cent for the United States;
- 4 per cent for the Middle East; and
- 12 per cent for other countries.

Of the 209,000 new residents in 1993:

- 21 per cent came from Australia, Canada, New Zealand or South Africa;
- 22 per cent from other Commonwealth countries;
- 24 per cent from EU countries;
- 11 per cent from the United States;
- 4 per cent from the Middle East; and
- 17 per cent from other countries.

Nationality

Under the British Nationality Act 1981 there are three main forms of citizenship:

- British citizenship for people closely connected with Britain;
- British Dependent Territories citizenship for people connected with the dependent territories (see p. 117); and
- British Overseas citizenship for those citizens of the United Kingdom and Colonies who did not acquire either of the other citizenships when the 1981 Act came into force.

British citizenship is acquired automatically at birth by a child born in Britain if his or her mother or father is a British citizen or is settled in Britain. A child adopted in Britain by a British citizen is a British citizen. A child born abroad to a British citizen born, adopted, naturalised or registered in Britain is generally a British citizen by descent. The Act safeguards the citizenship of a child born abroad to a British citizen in Crown service, certain related services, or in service under a European Union institution.

British citizenship may also be acquired:

- by registration for certain children, including those born in Britain who do not automatically acquire such citizenship at birth, or who have been born abroad to a parent who is a citizen by descent;
- by registration for British Dependent Territories citizens, British Overseas citizens, British subjects under the Act, British Nationals (Overseas) and British protected persons after five years' residence in Britain, except for people from Gibraltar, who may be registered without residence;
- by registration for stateless people and those who have previously renounced British nationality; and
- by naturalisation for all other adults aged 18 or over.

Naturalisation is at the Home Secretary's discretion. Requirements include five years' residence, or three years if the applicant's spouse is a British citizen. Those who are not married to a British citizen are also required to have a sufficient knowledge of English, Welsh or Scottish Gaelic; they must also intend to have their main home in Britain or be employed by the Crown, by an international organisation of which Britain is a member, or by a company or association established in Britain.

Legislation passed in 1983 conferred British citizenship on Falkland Islanders who did not acquire it under the 1981 Act. Special arrangements covering the status of British Dependent Territories citizens connected with Hong Kong when the territory returns to the People's Republic of China in 1997 are made by the Hong Kong (British Nationality) Order 1986. Under this, such citizens are entitled, before 1997, to acquire a status known as British National (Overseas) and to hold a passport in that status. In addition, the British Nationality (Hong Kong) Act 1990 made provision for the registration as British citizens before 30 June 1997 of up to 50,000 people who are able to meet certain criteria and who are recommended by the Governor, together with their spouses and children who are still minors.

In 1994, 44,000 people were granted British citizenship.

Immigration

Immigration into Britain is largely governed by the Immigration Act 1971 and the Immigration Rules made under it. The Rules set out the requirements to be met by those who are subject to immigration control and seek entry to or leave to remain in Britain. New Immigration Rules came into effect in October 1994. British citizens and those Commonwealth citizens who had the right of abode before January 1983 maintain the right of abode and are not subject to immigration control.

Under the Immigration Rules nationals of certain specified countries or territorial entities must obtain a visa before they can enter Britain. Other nationals subject to immigration control require entry clearance when coming to work or settle in Britain. Visas and other entry clearances are normally obtained from the nearest or other specified British diplomatic post in a person's home country.

Nationals of the European Economic Area (EEA)—EU member states plus Norway, Iceland and Liechtenstein—are not subject to substantive immigration control. They may work in Britain without restriction. Provided that they are working or able to support themselves financially, EEA nationals have a right to reside in Britain.

Britain respects its obligations under the United Nations Convention and Protocol relating to the Status of Refugees. These provide that refugees lawfully resident should enjoy treatment as least as favourable as that accorded to other foreign nationals.

In 1994 9.2 million foreign and Commonwealth nationals (excluding EEA nationals) were admitted to Britain. About 55,000 people were accepted for settlement.

Table 6.1: Acceptances for Settlement 1984–1994

	1984	1994
Pakistan	5,510	6,240
India	5,140	4,780
United States	3,750	3,990
Nigeria	320	3,090
Bangladesh	4,180	3,050
Japan	1,100	2,060
Turkey	530	1,870
Sri Lanka	760	1,860
Australia	3,590	1,740
Ghana	690	1,620
Hong Kong	1,040	1,490
Somalia	20	1,410
Jamaica	290	1,280
South Africa	690	1,260
New Zealand	2,460	1,080

Source: Home Office

LANGUAGE

English is the main language spoken in Britain, and is also one of the most widely used in the world.[2] Recent estimates suggest that 310 million people speak it as their first language, with a similar number speaking it as a second language. It is an official language in a large number of overseas countries, and is widely used internationally as the main

[2]For the Welsh language see p. 23; for Gaelic see p. 22.

language for purposes such as air traffic control and academic gatherings.

Modern English derives primarily from one of the dialects of Anglo-Saxon. However, it has been very greatly influenced by other languages, particularly, following the Norman conquest, by French. French was the language of the nobility and the law courts for many years after 1066. The re-emergence of English as the universal language of England was signified by such events as the Statute of Pleadings in 1362, which laid down that English was to be used in court. The 14th century also saw the first major English literature since Anglo-Saxon days, with the writing of works such as *Piers Plowman* by William Langland and *The Canterbury Tales* by Geoffrey Chaucer. However, there remained great regional variations in the language, and spellings were not always standardised.

The 16th and early 17th centuries saw a considerable flowering of English literature, with writers such as William Shakespeare, Edmund Spenser and Christopher Marlowe. Cranmer's prayerbook and the Authorised ('King James') Version of the Bible, which have had a profound effect on literature down to modern times, also date from this period. About this time, too, translations of Latin, Italian and other European works into English vastly expanded the English language. The work of early lexicographers, of whom the most famous was Samuel Johnson (1709–84), also led to greater standardisation in matters such as spelling.

ETHNIC AND NATIONAL MINORITIES

For centuries people from overseas have settled in Britain, either to escape political or religious persecution or in search of better economic opportunities.

The Irish have long formed a large section of the population. Jewish refugees who came to Britain towards the end of the 19th century and in the 1930s were followed by other European refugees after 1945. Substantial immigration from the Caribbean and the South Asian sub-continent dates principally from the 1950s and 1960s. In recent years, the number of people coming from the South

Asian sub-continent has remained roughly stable, but there has been a rise in immigration from some African countries, such as Ghana, Nigeria and Somalia (see Table 6.1).

The 1991 census included for the first time a question on ethnic grouping. This found that 94.5 per cent of the population belonged to the 'white' group, while just over 3 million people (5.5 per cent) described themselves as belonging to another ethnic group (see Table 6.2). Members of other ethnic groups were heavily concentrated in industrial and urban areas, and over half lived in the South East. The highest proportion was in the London borough of Brent: nearly 45 per cent of the population. Ethnic minority groups also accounted for over a third of the population in the London boroughs of Newham, Tower Hamlets and Hackney.

Outside London the main concentrations were in Leicester, Slough, Luton, Bradford, the West Midlands and the Pennine conurbation. Regional concentrations varied among the ethnic groups. About three-fifths of people from black ethnic groups lived in London, compared with about two-fifths of Indians and 18 per cent of Pakistanis, who were concentrated in other metropolitan areas such as West Yorkshire.

Overall, 47 per cent of the ethnic minority population were born in Britain. A higher proportion is under 16 than for the white group (33 per cent and 19 per cent respectively), but a much lower proportion is over pensionable age (3 per cent and about 17 per cent respectively).

According to the Labour Force Survey, economic activity rates for men of working age in Great Britain tend to be similar to those for the white groups. In spring 1994 they were 79 per cent for the black group, 80 per cent for the Indian group, 75 per cent for the Pakistani/Bangladeshi population and 86 per cent for the white group. The variations are much greater for women: 67 per cent of those from the black ethnic group were economically active, compared with 62 per cent in the Indian group, 72 per cent in the white group and only 26 per cent in the Pakistani/Bangladeshi group.

Alleviating Racial Disadvantage

Although many members of the black and Asian communities are concentrated in the inner cities, where there are problems of deprivation and social stress, progress has been made over the last 20 years in tackling racial disadvantage in Britain.

Many individuals have achieved distinction in their careers and in public life, and the proportion of ethnic minority members occupying professional and managerial positions is increasing. There are at present six ethnic minority Members of Parliament, and the number of ethnic minority councillors in local government is growing. There has also been an expansion of commercial enterprise, and numerous self-help projects in ethnic minority communities have been established. Black competitors have represented Britain in a range of sporting activities (such as athletics and football), and ethnic minority talents in the arts and in entertainment have increasingly been recognised.

The principal means of combating disadvantage is through the economic, environmental, educational and health programmes of central government and local authorities. There are also special allocations, mainly through Home Office and Department of the Environment grants, which channel extra resources into projects of specific benefit to ethnic minorities. These include, for example, the provision of specialist teachers for children needing English language tuition. Cultural and

Table 6.2: Population by Ethnic Group, 1991, Great Britain

	Number of People (000s)	Per cent
White	51,874	94.5
Other groups	3,015	5.5
of whom:		
Black	891	1.6
Indian	840	1.5
Pakistani	477	0.9
Bangladeshi	163	0.3
Chinese	157	0.3
Other	488	0.9

Source: Office of Population Censuses and Surveys

recreational schemes and the health and personal social services also take account of the particular needs of ethnic minorities.

The Government is promoting equal opportunities for ethnic minorities through training programmes, including greater provision for unemployed people who need training in English as a second language.

In recognition of the tensions that can arise between the police and ethnic minorities, there is statutory consultation between the police and the community. Liaison work is also undertaken with children in schools.

Race Relations Legislation

The Race Relations Act 1976 strengthened previous legislation passed in the 1960s. It makes discrimination unlawful on grounds of colour, race, nationality or ethnic or national origin in the provision of goods, facilities and services, in employment, in housing, in education and in advertising. The 1976 Act also gave complainants direct access to civil courts and, for employment complaints, to industrial tribunals. The Race Relations (Remedies) Act 1994 removed the ceiling on industrial tribunal awards in race discrimination cases. It is a criminal offence to incite racial hatred under the provisions of the Public Order Act 1986.

Commission for Racial Equality

The Commission for Racial Equality was established by the 1976 Act. It has power to investigate unlawful discriminatory practices and to issue non-discrimination notices, requiring such practices to cease. It has an important educational role and has issued codes of practice in employment, education, health care, maternity services and housing. It also provides advice to the general public about the Race Relations Act and may help individuals with their complaints about racial discrimination. In 1994 the Commission registered 1,937 applications for assistance and handled successfully 137 litigation cases. It can also undertake or fund research.

The Commission supports the work of over 90 racial equality councils. These are autonomous voluntary bodies set up in most areas with a significant ethnic minority population to promote equality of opportunity and good relations at the local level. The Commission helps pay the salaries of the racial equality officers employed by the councils, most of whom also receive funds from their local authorities. It also gives grants to ethnic minority self-help groups and to other projects run by or for the benefit of the minority communities.

THE ECONOMIC AND SOCIAL PATTERN

Marked improvements in the standard of living have taken place during the 20th century. According to a United Nations report on human development published in 1994, Britain ranked tenth out of 173 countries on a human development index that combines life expectancy, education levels and basic purchasing power.

Britain has also performed well economically. Growth between 1980 and 1990 was higher than in all other major EU countries except Spain. Subsequently, following the recession of the early 1990s, Britain has been one of the first countries to experience recovery. Gross domestic product in Britain grew by 3.9 per cent in 1994—well above the EU and Organisation for Economic Co-operation and Development averages of 3.3 per cent. Inflation has recently been around 3 per cent a year, with the underlying level of inflation in 1994 the lowest since 1964.

Income and Wealth

Wages and salaries remain the main source of household income for most people, although the proportion they contribute of household income (56 per cent in 1993, compared with 68 per cent in 1971) has been declining. Sources which have become more important include private pensions and annuities (11 per cent, up from 5 per cent in 1971) as the number of people who have made such provision has grown. Disposable income in 1992 was nearly 80 per cent higher than in 1971 after allowing for inflation.

The proportion of household income that is paid in income tax and National Insurance contributions by a two-children family with a father on average earnings was 21.8 per cent in 1994–95. This figure has not changed significantly in recent years. The top 20 per cent of households by income received 43 per cent of income in 1991–92. Wealth is less evenly distributed, with the richest 10 per cent of the population having 49 per cent of marketable wealth in 1992. The inclusion of 'non-marketable' wealth, such as rights in occupational and state pension schemes, reduces this share substantially, to 33 per cent. Since the mid-1970s there has been little change in the distribution of marketable wealth.

A large proportion of personal wealth—30 per cent in 1993—is in dwellings, down quite sharply from the level of immediately preceding years as house prices have fallen.

The proportion of net wealth held in shares declined up to 1984, but has since increased. The Government's privatisation programme has contributed to the growth in share ownership. In 1993 about 10 million people— 22 per cent of the adult population in Great Britain—owned shares, compared with 7 per cent in 1979.

Eating and Drinking Habits

The general level of nutrition remains high. There has been a significant shift in eating patterns over the last decade, reflecting greater emphasis on health, frozen and convenience foods. Changes in household consumption of selected foods between 1983 and 1994 are shown in the diagram below. Consumption of several items, such as packet sugar, eggs, fresh potatoes and fresh green vegetables, has declined substantially. Other changes include:

Availability of Certain Durable Goods

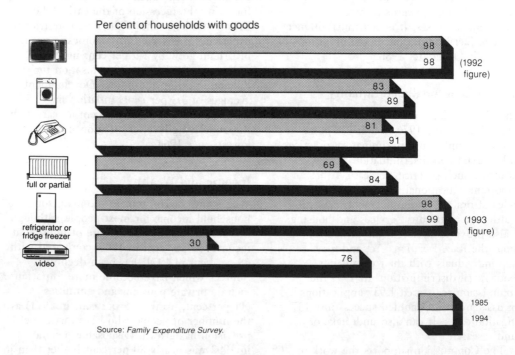

Per cent of households with goods

98
98 (1992 figure)

83
89

81
91

full or partial
69
84

refrigerator or fridge freezer
98
99 (1993 figure)

video
30
76

1985
1994

Source: *Family Expenditure Survey.*

Changes in Average Household Food Consumption 1984–1994

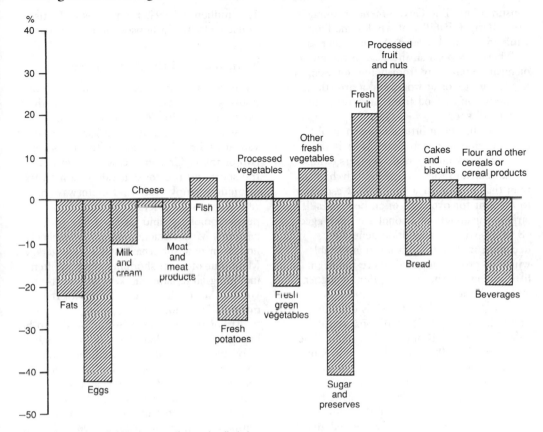

Note: Average household food consumption may be affected by the decline in household size as well as changes in eating habits.

Source: *National Food Survey*, MAFF.

- a decline in consumption of beef, lamb and pork—this has been partly offset by a continuing increase in poultry consumption, which is now at a record level;

- an increase in purchases of semi-skimmed milk, with skimmed milk now constituting more than half of the total household consumption of liquid milk;

- a decline in the total consumption of cooking and spreading fats, with large falls in butter and lard usage being partly offset by rapid rises in the consumption of vegetable and salad oils and reduced-fat spreads;

- an increase in the consumption of rice and pasta, which may be partly responsible for the decline in the consumption of fresh potatoes;

- a trend away from consumption of some fresh green vegetables such as cabbages and beans towards leafy salads and cauliflowers;

- a large increase in purchases of fruit juice; and

- a switch in fish consumption away from fresh white fish towards canned fish and shellfish.

Average mineral and nutrient intakes are generally above the daily amounts recommended by the Department of Health. There has been a steady fall in fat intakes, and a small increase in the intake of fibre. There is some evidence that health considerations influence food consumption, for example, the move away from whole milk and in the growth in low fat spread consumption. The Government encourages the widest availability of wholesome food, while giving high priority to consumer safety.

There has been an increase in the number of meals eaten away from home, for example, in restaurants or at work, and a growth in the consumption of food from 'take-away' and 'fast food' shops.

There has been little change in alcohol consumption in recent years. Beer is the most popular drink among male drinkers, whose overall consumption is significantly higher than that of women. Lager is now estimated to account for over half of all beer sales. The largest consumers of alcohol are those aged 18 to 24, with consumption generally declining with age. Consumption of table wine has grown, although there has been little change in the consumption of higher strength wines such as sherry and port.

A high proportion of beer is drunk in public houses ('pubs'), traditional social centres for many people, and in clubs. The Licensing Act 1988 relaxed restrictions on the opening hours of public houses, but this has not resulted in a significant increase in alcohol consumption. There are signs that they are becoming more popular with families: more meals are being served and the consumption of non-alcoholic drinks is increasing. Under the Deregulation and Contracting Out Act 1994, pubs can now apply for a children's certificate. This allows children under 14 into designated areas if accompanied by an adult.

Households

The average size of households in Great Britain has fallen from over four people in 1911 to three in 1961 and 2.4 in 1993. The fall reflects a greater number of people living on their own (14 per cent of adults in 1993), or in one-parent families, the increasing number of old people (more of whom are living alone) and the preference for smaller families.

A large proportion of households—67 per cent—own their own homes. Owner-occupation is higher for married couples than for single, divorced or widowed household heads. The number of owner-occupied dwellings rose from over 4 million in 1951 to

15.8 million in 1994. Four-fifths of British households live in houses rather than flats.

Transport and the Environment

An important influence on the planning of housing and services has been the growth of car ownership; in 1993, 68 per cent of households had the use of at least one car or van, including 23 per cent with the use of two or more. Greater access to motorised transport and the construction of a network of modern trunk roads and motorways have resulted in a considerable increase in personal mobility and changed leisure patterns. Most detached or semi-detached houses in new suburban estates have garages. Many out-of-town shopping centres, often including large supermarkets and do-it-yourself stores, have been built with the motorist in mind.

Although the growth in car ownership has brought benefits, there have been a number of problems, notably increased congestion, noise and air pollution arising from motor vehicle emissions. Cars, taxis and motor cycles accounted for 87 per cent of all passenger transport in Great Britain in 1994, compared with 57 per cent in 1961. To relieve road congestion, the Government regards carefully targeted improvements to the road system as essential. The Government is also seeking to use the planning system (see p. 353) to reduce people's need to travel without inhibiting their freedom to do so. To help meet the British target for reducing carbon dioxide emissions (see p. 373), it is increasing fuel duty by 5 per cent a year in real terms.

Women

The economic and domestic lives of women have been transformed in the 20th century. These changes are due partly to women obtaining many political and legal rights previously open only to men. A major feature has been the rise in the number of women, especially married women, at work. Women now make up nearly 46 per cent of the workforce in employment. The growth of part-time and flexible working patterns, and training and retraining schemes, increases employment opportunities, allowing more women to combine raising a family with paid employment. About 800,000 women run their own businesses, 27 per cent more than in 1984.

Responsibility for co-ordinating policy on women's issues was strengthened in 1992, when a ministerial group was upgraded to a Cabinet Sub-committee for Women's Issues. A working group advises on practical measures to extend equal opportunities for women in the workplace and elsewhere. The Women's National Commission, an official advisory committee, represents the views of women to the Government and other public bodies. About 50 of the main national women's organisations are represented on the Commission.

In 1991 the Government launched an initiative to increase the proportion of public appointments held by women. The proportion has subsequently risen from 23 to 30 per cent. Nearly half of the appointments made by public bodies in 1994 went to women.

The Government supports the 'Opportunity 2000' campaign, an employer-led initiative to increase the quantity and quality of women's participation in the workforce. Membership stands at over 280 employers, with organisations employing about a quarter of the workforce being committed to the campaign. Many member organisations are adopting improvements to their equal opportunities policies and practices, such as offering job share arrangements and flexible working hours to employees. Within the civil service, the proportion of posts at the top seven grades filled by women rose from 7.2 per cent to 17.2 per cent between 1984 and 1994.

The Government is trying to maximise the options available to working parents by increasing childcare provision. It is spending £45 million to help set up over 50,000 out-of-school and holiday childcare places in Great Britain. By June 1995, over 33,250 childcare places had been created.

Equal Opportunities

The Sex Discrimination Acts 1975 and 1986 make discrimination between men and women unlawful, with certain limited exceptions, in employment, education, training and the provision of housing, goods, facilities and services. Discriminatory job recruitment advertisements are unlawful. Complaints of discrimination concerning employment are dealt with by industrial tribunals; other complaints are taken before county courts in England and Wales or the Sheriff Court in Scotland. Under the Equal Pay Act 1970, as amended in 1984, women in Great Britain are entitled to equal pay with men when doing work that is the same or broadly similar, or work which is rated as equivalent or work which is of equal value. Parallel legislation on sex discrimination and equal pay is in operation in Northern Ireland.

The Equal Opportunities Commission has powers to enforce some parts of the Sex Discrimination and Equal Pay Acts. Its statutory duties are to work towards the elimination of sex discrimination, to promote equality of opportunity, and to keep legislation on sex discrimination and equal pay under review, submitting proposals for amending it to the Government. The Commission may advise people of their rights under the Acts and may give financial or other assistance to help individuals conduct a case before a court or tribunal. It is empowered to carry out formal investigations and issue notices requiring discriminatory practices to stop. The Commission carries out research on the causes, nature and effects of discrimination. It runs an 'Equality Exchange', which enables employers to exchange information on good practice.

The Voluntary Sector

There is a long tradition in Britain of voluntary service to the community. There are hundreds of thousands of voluntary organisations, ranging from national bodies to small local groups. One area of rapid expansion in the last 20 years or so has been 'self-help' groups. Examples include bodies which provide playgroups for pre-school children, or help their members to cope with a particular disability.

Voluntary organisations may be staffed by professional workers, but many rely on the efforts of volunteers at some level. It has been estimated that up to half of all adults take part in some form of organised voluntary work in the course of a year. Many volunteers are involved in work which improves the quality of life in their local communities or, more widely, give their time to help organise events or groups in areas as diverse as social welfare, education, sport and the arts. A very large number of volunteers are involved in activities to protect or improve the environment, working, for example, for the National Trust, which has over 2 million members (see p. 359). The Government greatly values the voluntary sector's contribution to society and, as a result, is keen to encourage productive partnerships between the statutory and voluntary sectors. For example, voluntary organisations are important providers of government-supported employment and training services for unemployed people.

'Make a Difference' Initiative

The Home Office Voluntary Services Unit co-ordinates government policy towards the voluntary sector throughout Britain. It also aims to support a healthy and cost-effective voluntary sector and to promote volunteering. Its 'Make a Difference' initiative, launched in 1994, brings together the business, voluntary and public sectors to develop effective local voluntary action. As one aspect of the initiative, a nationwide telephone helpline was set up in March 1995. This aims to provide callers throughout Britain with information on how to get involved with local voluntary initiatives.

The report of a team responsible for drawing up a national strategy on volunteering was published in June 1995. The Government is considering its recommendations.

Funding

Voluntary organisations receive income from several sources, including contributions from individuals, businesses and trusts; central and local government grants; and earnings from commercial activities and investments. They also receive fees (from central and local government) for those services which are provided on a contractual basis. In 1993–94 direct grants to voluntary organisations from government amounted to £612 million.

Tax changes in recent budgets have helped the voluntary sector secure more funds from industry and individuals. The Gift Aid scheme provides tax relief on single cash donations of more than £250. By March 1995 charities had received donations of more than £1,000 million under the scheme and had claimed tax repayments of £340 million on them. Employees can also make tax-free donations to charity from their earnings. The Payroll Giving scheme provides tax relief on donations of up to £900 a year.

Charities

In England and Wales nearly 178,700 charities are registered with the Charity Commission. The Commission also gives advice to trustees of charities on their administration. Organisations may qualify for charitable status if they are established for exclusively charitable purposes such as the relief of poverty, the advancement of education or religion, or the promotion of certain other purposes of public benefit. These may include good community relations, the prevention of racial discrimination, the protection of health and the promotion of equal opportunity. The Charity Commission also has a statutory responsibility to ensure that charities make effective use of their resources.

By August 1995, National Lottery proceeds available to the distributing body for charities, the National Lottery Charities Board, had reached £172 million. In its initial grants programme, the Board will concentrate on people in Britain disadvantaged by poverty. Charities are also eligible to apply to the other distributing bodies to support projects that meet the criteria of those bodies.

Table 6.3: Income of the Top Fund-raising Charities 1993–4

Charity	£ million total income	Voluntary income[a]
National Trust	151.3	78.7
Save the Children Fund	112.8	53.9
Oxfam	78.9	59.0
Barnardo's	76.5	36.5
Royal National Lifeboat Institution	72.1	56.2
Salvation Army	66.8	32.3
Imperial Cancer Research Fund	55.7	48.4
Cancer Research Campaign	52.2	45.4
National Society for the Prevention of Cruelty to Children	40.2	30.8
Help the Aged	37.1	33.1
Royal Society for the Prevention of Cruelty to Animals	36.5	28.3

Source: Charities Aid Foundation
[a] Mostly donations but also includes other funds such as legacies and proceeds of charity shops.

The Charities Acts 1992 and 1993 strengthened the Commissioners' power to investigate and supervise, so increasing their accountability. For example, new measures to protect charities and donors from bogus fund-raisers came into force in March 1995. The changes will enable people who buy goods in aid of charity to know how much of what they pay will go to that charity.

The Charities Aid Foundation, an independent body, is one of the main organisations that aid the flow of funds to charity from individuals, companies and grant-making trusts.

Umbrella Organisations

The National Council for Voluntary Organisations is one of the main co-ordinating bodies in England, providing close links between voluntary organisations, government departments, local authorities, the European Commission and the private sector; around 650 national voluntary organisations are members. It also protects the interests and independence of voluntary agencies, and provides them with advice, information and other services. Councils in Scotland, Wales and Northern Ireland perform similar functions. The National Association of Councils for Voluntary Service is another umbrella organisation providing resources, with over 230 local councils for voluntary service throughout England. Their role is to encourage the development of local voluntary action, mainly in urban areas. The rural equivalent is Action with Communities in Rural England, representing 38 rural community councils.

Leisure Trends

About 14 per cent of total household expenditure went on leisure goods and services in 1993. The most common leisure activities are home-based, or social, such as visiting relatives or friends. Television viewing is by far the most popular leisure pastime, and nearly all households have a television set, with 96 per cent in 1992 having a colour set. Average viewing time is nearly 27 hours a week. Around 73 per cent of households now have at least one video recorder, compared with 30 per cent in 1985.

Listening to radio has been increasing, and averages over 10 hours a week. Purchases of compact discs have risen very rapidly, and in 1992 for the first time exceeded the sales of audio cassettes. The proportion of households with a compact disc player has grown considerably, from 15 per cent in 1989 to 46 per cent in 1994.

Other popular pursuits include: reading, do-it-yourself home improvements, gardening and going out for a meal, for a drink or to the cinema. About half of households have a pet, the most common being dogs and cats, with roughly 7 million of each in Britain.

Holidays

In 1994, 60 per cent of the adult population took at least one long holiday of four or more nights away from home. The number of long holidays taken by British residents was 58 million, of which 31.5 million were taken in Britain. The most frequented free attraction was Blackpool Pleasure Beach (Lancashire), with an estimated 7.2 million visitors. The most popular destinations for summer holidays are the West Country, Scotland and Wales.

In 1994 the most popular destinations for overseas holidays by British residents were:

- France (12 per cent);
- mainland Spain (11 per cent);
- the United States (8 per cent); and
- mainland Greece (1 per cent).

In all, British residents took 26.3 million long holidays overseas in 1994, of which 57 per cent involved 'package' arrangements. About 77 per cent of all holidays abroad are taken in Europe, although more people are taking holidays further afield, for example to the United States. The proportion of adults taking two or more holidays a year was 26 per cent in 1994.

Further Reading

Ethnic Minorities. Aspects of Britain series, HMSO, second edition in preparation.

Immigration and Nationality. Aspects of Britain series, HMSO, 1992.

Population. Aspects of Britain series, HMSO, 1995.

Women. Aspects of Britain series, HMSO, second edition in preparation.

Annual Reports

Family Spending. HMSO.

General Household Survey. HMSO.

Social Trends. HMSO.

Women and Men in Britain. Equal Opportunities Commission.

Government and Administration

7 Government

The system of parliamentary government in Britain is not based on a written constitution, but is the result of gradual evolution over many centuries. The Monarchy is the oldest institution of government, dating back to at least the ninth century. Parliament is one of the oldest representative assemblies in the world. In government among the most significant recent developments have been the steps taken to improve management. New management structures—such as the creation of executive agencies—have been developed; competition has been introduced or extended; and arrangements for pay are changing. The aim of all these changes is to safeguard and improve the standards of the public services.

Development of the British System of Government

The growth of political institutions in England can be traced back to the period of Saxon rule, which lasted from the fifth century AD until the Norman Conquest in 1066 (see p. 6). This period saw the origins of the institution of kingship, and of the idea that the king should seek the advice of a council of prominent men.

The period of Norman rule after 1066 saw a considerable strengthening of royal power. However, the monarchy eventually experienced difficulties in controlling the growing machinery of government. The actions of King John (1199–1216) led to opposition from the nobility and leading figures in the Church. In 1215 the barons forced the King to agree to a series of concessions embodied in a charter which became known as Magna Carta. The charter, which provided for the protection of the rights of freemen against the abuse of royal power, came to be regarded as the key expression of the rights of the community against the Crown.

The first known occurrence of the term 'Parliament' to describe the meetings of nobles to advise the king is in 1236; by the late 13th century representatives of counties and towns were also occasionally being summoned at the same time, usually to express political support, but increasingly to give consent to taxation. By the end of the 15th century Parliament existed in a form virtually recognisable today: as a body whose function was to agree to taxes and to legislate, and which consisted of two separate chambers—the House of Commons and the House of Lords.

Although the influence of government in

Parliament was considerable, the body was always an area for political conflict; one such clash led to the outbreak of the Civil War in 1642 between Crown and Parliament. Following the defeat of the royalist armies and the execution of Charles I in 1649, the Monarchy and the House of Lords were abolished and the country was proclaimed a republic. However, the republican experiment came to an end in 1660, two years after the death of the 'Lord Protector', Oliver Cromwell. Charles I's son was restored to the throne as Charles II.

Charles II's successor, James II (James VII of Scotland: 1685–88), sought both to bypass Parliament and to make it more amenable. As a result, in 1688 a group of leading men invited William of Orange (a grandson of Charles I and the husband of Mary, James's eldest daughter) to 'secure the infringed liberties' of the country. James fled into exile. Following the success of the revolution of 1688, Parliament in 1689 passed the Bill of Rights, which defined the rights and privileges of Parliament.

Increasingly thereafter parliamentary control of national finance made it impracticable for the Sovereign to ignore the wishes of Parliament. Ministers were appointed by the Sovereign, but they had to have sufficient support in the House of Commons to enable them to persuade Parliament to pass legislation and vote for taxation. The development of 'party' during the 18th and 19th centuries provided them with the machinery for securing that support, while the personal involvement of the Monarch in policy and the day-to-day business of administration declined, leaving government in the hands of the cabinet, presided over by a 'Prime' Minister.

Since the mid-19th century the Prime Minister has normally been the leader of the party with a majority in the House of Commons.

The Reform Act of 1832 altered the medieval system of parliamentary representation and standardised the qualifications for the right to vote. Subsequent reforms gave the vote to virtually all adults—women were finally enfranchised in 1918, but not on the same terms as men until 1928.

The British Constitution

The British constitution is to a large extent a product of the historical events described above. Unlike the constitutions of most other countries, it is not set out in any single document. Instead it is made up of statute law, common law and conventions. (Conventions are rules and practices which are not legally enforceable but which are regarded as indispensable to the working of government.)

The constitution can be altered by Act of Parliament, or by general agreement, and is thus adaptable to changing political conditions.

The organs of government overlap but can be clearly distinguished. Parliament is the legislature and the supreme authority. The executive consists of:

- the Government—the Cabinet and other ministers responsible for national policies;
- government departments and agencies, responsible for national administration;
- local authorities, responsible for many local services; and
- public corporations, responsible for operating particular nationalised industries or other bodies, subject to ministerial control.

The judiciary (see Chapter 8) determines common law and interprets statutes.

The Monarchy

The Monarchy is the oldest institution of government, going back to at least the ninth century. Queen Elizabeth II is herself directly descended from King Egbert, who united England under his rule in 829. The only interruption in the history of the Monarchy was the republic which lasted from 1649 to 1660 (see above).

Today the Queen is not only head of State, but also an important symbol of national unity. The royal title in Britain is: 'Elizabeth the Second, by the Grace of God of the United Kingdom of Great Britain and Northern Ireland and of Her other Realms and Territories Queen, Head of the Commonwealth, Defender of the Faith'.

In the Channel Islands and the Isle of

The Royal Family from the Reign of Queen Victoria to August 1995

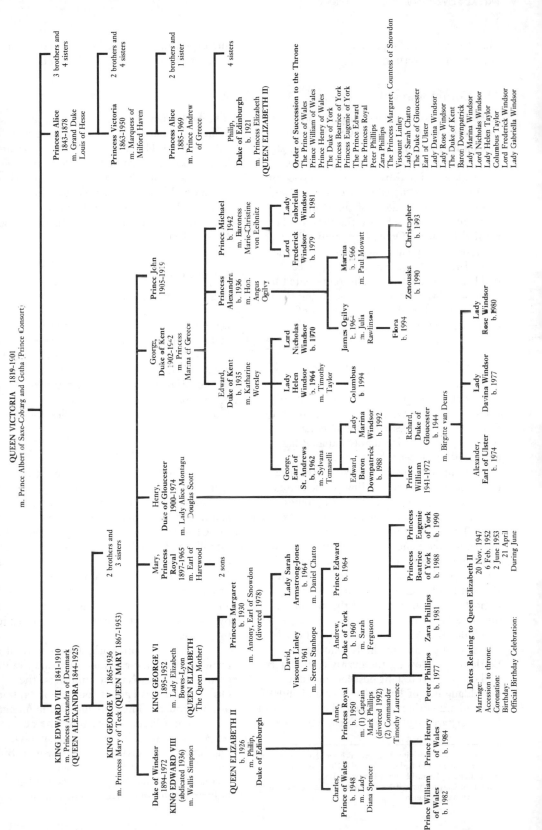

Man the Queen is represented by a Lieutenant-Governor.

The Commonwealth

Although the seat of the Monarchy is in Britain, the Queen is also head of state of a number of Commonwealth states[1]. In each such state the Queen is represented by a Governor-General, appointed by her on the advice of the ministers of the country concerned and completely independent of the British Government. In each case the form of the royal title varies. Other Commonwealth states are republics or have their own monarchies.

In British dependent territories (see p. 117) the Queen is usually represented by governors, who are responsible to the British Government for the administration of the countries concerned.

Succession

The title to the Crown is derived partly from statute and partly from common law rules of descent. Despite interruptions in the direct line of succession, the hereditary principle upon which it was founded has always been preserved.

Sons of the Sovereign have precedence over daughters in succeeding to the throne. When a daughter succeeds, she becomes Queen Regnant, and has the same powers as a king. The consort of a king takes her husband's rank and style, becoming Queen. The constitution does not give any special rank or privileges to the husband of a Queen Regnant, although in practice he fills an important role in the life of the nation, as does the Duke of Edinburgh.

Under the Act of Settlement of 1700, which formed part of the Revolution Settlement following the events of 1688 (see p. 44), only Protestant descendants of a granddaughter of James I of England and VI of Scotland (Princess Sophia, the Electress of Hanover) are eligible to succeed. The order of

succession can be altered only by common consent of the countries of the Commonwealth.

Accession

The Sovereign succeeds to the throne as soon as his or her predecessor dies: there is no interregnum. He or she is at once proclaimed at an Accession Council, to which all members of the Privy Council (see p. 63) are summoned. The Lords Spiritual and Temporal (see p. 50), the Lord Mayor and Aldermen and other leading citizens of the City of London are also invited.

Coronation

The Sovereign's coronation follows the accession after a convenient interval. The ceremony takes place at Westminster Abbey in London, in the presence of representatives of the Houses of Parliament and of all the great public organisations in Britain. The Prime Ministers and leading members of the other Commonwealth nations and representatives of other countries also attend.

The Monarch's Role in Government

The Queen personifies the State. In law, she is head of the executive, an integral part of the legislature, head of the judiciary, the commander-in-chief of all the armed forces of the Crown and the 'supreme governor' of the established Church of England. As a result of a long process of evolution, during which the Monarchy's absolute power has been progressively reduced, the Queen acts on the advice of her ministers. Britain is governed by Her Majesty's Government in the name of the Queen.

Within this framework, and in spite of a trend during the past hundred years towards giving powers directly to ministers, the Queen still takes part in some important acts of government. These include summoning, proroguing (discontinuing until the next session without dissolution) and dissolving Parliament; and giving Royal Assent to Bills passed by Parliament. The Queen also formally appoints many important office holders, including government ministers,

---

[1]The other Commonwealth states of which the Queen is head of state are: Antigua and Barbuda, Australia, Bahamas, Barbados, Belize, Canada, Grenada, Jamaica, New Zealand, Papua New Guinea, St Christopher and Nevis, Saint Lucia, St Vincent and the Grenadines, Solomon Islands and Tuvalu.

judges, officers in the armed forces, governors, diplomats, bishops and some other senior clergy of the Church of England. She is also involved in pardoning people convicted of crimes; and in conferring peerages, knighthoods and other honours.[2] An important function is appointing the Prime Minister (see p. 61). In international affairs the Queen, as head of State, has the power to declare war and make peace, to recognise foreign states and governments, to conclude treaties and to annex or cede territory.

With rare exceptions (such as appointing the Prime Minister), acts involving the use of 'royal prerogative' powers are now performed by government ministers, who are responsible to Parliament and can be questioned about particular policies. Parliamentary authority is not required for the exercise of these prerogative powers, although Parliament may restrict or abolish such rights.

The Queen continues to play a role in the working of government. She holds Privy Council meetings, gives audiences to her ministers and officials in Britain and overseas, receives accounts of Cabinet decisions, reads dispatches and signs state papers. She must be consulted on every aspect of national life, and must show complete impartiality.

Provision has been made to appoint a regent to perform these royal functions should the Queen be totally incapacitated. The regent would be the Queen's eldest son, the Prince of Wales, then those, in order of succession to the throne, aged 18 or over. In the event of her partial incapacity or absence abroad, the Queen may delegate certain royal functions to the Counsellors of State (the Duke of Edinburgh, the four adults next in line of succession, and the Queen Mother). However, Counsellors of State may not, for instance, dissolve Parliament (except on the Queen's instructions), nor create peers.

Ceremonial and Royal Visits

Ceremonial has always been associated with the British monarchy, and, in spite of

changes in the outlook of both the Sovereign and the people, many traditional ceremonies continue to take place. Royal marriages and royal funerals are marked by public ceremony, and the Sovereign's birthday is officially celebrated in June by Trooping the Colour on Horse Guards Parade. State banquets take place when a foreign monarch or head of State visits Britain; investitures are held at Buckingham Palace and the Palace of Holyroodhouse in Scotland to bestow honours; and royal processions add significance to such occasions as the state opening of Parliament.

Each year the Queen and other members of the Royal Family visit many parts of Britain. They are also closely involved in the work of many charities. For example, the Prince of Wales is actively involved in the Youth Business Trust, set up to encourage small firms and self employment in inner cities, while the Princess Royal is President of the Save the Children Fund and takes an active interest in third world development issues. The Queen pays state visits to foreign governments, accompanied by the Duke of Edinburgh. She also tours the other countries of the Commonwealth. Other members of the Royal Family pay official visits overseas, occasionally representing the Queen.

Royal Income and Expenditure

Until 1760 the Sovereign had to provide for payment of all government expenses, including the salaries of officials and the expenses of the royal palaces and households. These were met from hereditary revenues, mainly income from Crown lands, and income from some other sources granted to the Monarch by Parliament. The income from these sources eventually proved inadequate and in 1760 George III turned over to the Government most of the hereditary revenue. In return he received an annual grant (Civil List), from which he continued to pay royal expenditure of a personal character, the salaries of government officials, the costs of royal palaces, and certain pensions. The latter charges were removed from the Civil List in 1830.

---

[2]Although most honours are conferred by the Queen on the advice of the Prime Minister, a few are granted by her personally—the Order of the Garter, the Order of the Thistle, the Order of Merit and the Royal Victorian Order.

Present Arrangements

Today the expenditure incurred by the Queen in carrying out her public duties is financed from the Civil List and from government departments—which meet the cost of, for example, the Royal Yacht and the aircraft of No. 32 (the Royal) Squadron. All such expenditure is approved by Parliament. In 1991 Civil List payments were fixed at £7.9 million a year for ten years. About three-quarters of the Queen's Civil List provision is required to meet the cost of staff. They deal with, among other things, state papers and correspondence, and the organisation of state occasions, visits and other public engagements undertaken by the Queen in Britain and overseas. The Queen's private expenditure as Sovereign is met from the Privy Purse, which is financed mainly from the revenue of the Duchy of Lancaster;[3] her expenditure as a private individual is met from her own personal resources.

Under the Civil List Acts, other members of the Royal Family also receive annual parliamentary allowances to enable them to carry out their public duties. The Prince of Wales, however, receives no such allowance, since as Duke of Cornwall he is entitled to the income of the estate of the Duchy of Cornwall. Each year the Queen refunds the government for all annuities paid to members of the Royal Family except the Queen Mother and the Duke of Edinburgh.

Since April 1993 the Queen has voluntarily paid income tax on all her personal income and on that part of the Privy Purse income which is used for private purposes. The Queen also pays tax on any realised capital gains on her private investments and on the private proportion of assets in the Privy Purse. Inheritance tax will not, however, apply to transfers from one sovereign to his or her successor, although any personal bequests other than to the successor will be subject to inheritance tax. In line with these changes the Prince of Wales pays income tax on the income from the Duchy of Cornwall to the extent that it is used for private purposes.

Parliament

Origins of Parliament

The medieval kings were expected to meet all royal expenses, private and public, out of their own revenue. If extra resources were needed for an emergency, such as a war, the Sovereign would seek to persuade his barons, in the Great Council—a gathering of leading men which met several times a year—to grant aid. During the 13th century several kings found the private revenues and baronial aids insufficient to meet the expenses of government. They therefore summoned not only the great feudal magnates but also representatives of counties, cities and towns, primarily to get their assent to extraordinary taxation. In this way the Great Council came to include those who were summoned by name (those who, broadly speaking, were to form the House of Lords) and those who were representatives of communities—the commons. The two parts, together with the Sovereign, became known as 'Parliament' (the term originally meant a meeting for parley or discussion).

Over the course of time the commons began to realise the strength of their position. By the middle of the 14th century the formula had appeared which in substance was the same as that used nowadays in voting supplies to the Crown—that is, money to the government—namely, 'by the Commons with the advice of the Lords Spiritual and Temporal'. In 1407 Henry IV pledged that henceforth all money grants should be approved by the House of Commons before being considered by the Lords.

A similar advance was made in the legislative field. Originally the King's legislation needed only the assent of his councillors. Starting with the right of individual commoners to present petitions, the Commons as a body gained the right to submit collective petitions. Later, during the 15th century, they gained the right to participate in giving their requests—their 'Bills'—the form of law.

---

[3]The Duchy of Lancaster is an inheritance which, since 1399, has always been enjoyed by the reigning Sovereign. It is kept quite apart from his or her other possessions and is separately administered by the Chancellor of the Duchy of Lancaster.

The subsequent development of the power of the House of Commons was built upon these foundations. The constitutional developments of the 17th century (see p. 44) led to Parliament securing its position as the supreme legislative authority.

The Powers of Parliament

The three elements which make up Parliament—the Queen, the House of Lords and the elected House of Commons—are constituted on different principles. They meet together only on occasions of symbolic significance such as the state opening of Parliament, when the Commons are summoned by the Queen to the House of Lords. The agreement of all three elements is normally required for legislation, but that of the Queen is given as a matter of course.

Parliament can legislate for Britain as a whole, or for any part of the country. It can also legislate for the Channel Islands and the Isle of Man, which are Crown dependencies and not part of Britain. They have local legislatures which make laws on island affairs (see p. 7).

As there are no legal restraints imposed by a written constitution, Parliament may legislate as it pleases, subject to Britain's obligations as a member of the European Union. It can make or change any law, and overturn established conventions or turn them into law. It can even prolong its own life beyond the normal period without consulting the electorate.

In practice, however, Parliament does not assert its supremacy in this way. Its members bear in mind the common law and normally act in accordance with precedent. The House of Commons is directly responsible to the electorate, and in this century the House of Lords has recognised the supremacy of the elected chamber. The system of party government helps to ensure that Parliament legislates with its responsibility to the electorate in mind.

The European Union

As a member of the European Union, Britain recognises the various types of Community legislation and wider policies. It sends 87 elected members to the European Parliament (see p. 114).

The Functions of Parliament

The main functions of Parliament are:

- to pass laws;
- to provide, by voting for taxation, the means of carrying on the work of government;
- to scrutinise government policy and administration, including proposals for expenditure; and
- to debate the major issues of the day.

In carrying out these functions Parliament helps to bring the relevant facts and issues before the electorate. By custom, Parliament is also informed before all important international treaties and agreements are ratified. The making of treaties is, however, a royal prerogative exercised on the advice of the Government and is not subject to parliamentary approval.

The Meeting of Parliament

A Parliament has a maximum duration of five years, but in practice general elections are usually held before the end of this term. The maximum life has been prolonged by legislation in rare circumstances such as the two world wars. Parliament is dissolved and writs for a general election are ordered by the Queen on the advice of the Prime Minister.

The life of a Parliament is divided into sessions. Each usually lasts for one year—normally beginning and ending in October or November. There are 'adjournments' at night, at weekends, at Christmas, Easter and the late Spring Bank Holiday, and during a long summer break usually starting in late July. The average number of 'sitting' days in a session is about 165 in the House of Commons and about 140 in the House of Lords. At the start of each session the Queen's speech to Parliament outlines the Government's policies and proposed legislative programme. Each session is ended by prorogation. Parliament then 'stands prorogued' for about a week until the new session opens. Prorogation brings to an end nearly all parliamentary business: in particular, public Bills which have not been passed by the end of the session are lost.

The House of Lords

The House of Lords consists of the Lords Spiritual and the Lords Temporal. The Lords Spiritual are the Archbishops of Canterbury and York, the Bishops of London, Durham and Winchester, and the 21 next most senior diocesan bishops of the Church of England. The Lords Temporal consist of:

- all hereditary peers of England, Scotland, Great Britain and the United Kingdom (but not peers of Ireland);

- life peers created to assist the House in its judicial duties (Lords of Appeal or 'law lords')[4]; and

- all other life peers.

Hereditary peerages carry a right to sit in the House provided holders establish their claim and are aged 21 years or over. However, anyone succeeding to a peerage may, within 12 months of succession, disclaim that peerage for his or her lifetime. Disclaimants lose their right to sit in the House but gain the right to vote and stand as candidates at parliamentary elections. When a disclaimant dies, the peerage passes on down the family in the usual way.

Peerages, both hereditary and life, are created by the Sovereign on the advice of the Prime Minister. They are usually granted in recognition of service in politics or other walks of life or because one of the political parties wishes to have the recipient in the House of Lords. The House also provides a place in Parliament for people who offer useful advice, but do not wish to be involved in party politics.

Peers who attend the House (the average daily attendance is some 360) receive no salary for their parliamentary work, but can claim for expenses incurred in attending the House (for which there are maximum daily rates) and certain travelling expenses.

Officers of the House of Lords

The House is presided over by the Lord Chancellor, who takes his place on the woolsack[5] as ex-officio Speaker of the House. In his absence his place is taken by a deputy. The first of the deputy speakers is the Chairman of Committees, who is appointed at the beginning of each session and normally chairs Committees of the Whole House and some domestic committees. The Chairman and the Principal Deputy Chairman of Committees are the only Lords who receive salaries as officers of the House.

In mid-1995 there were 1,194 members of the House of Lords, including the two archbishops and 24 bishops. The Lords Temporal consisted of 754 hereditary peers who had succeeded to their titles, 15 hereditary peers who had had their titles conferred on them (including the Prince of Wales), and 399 life peers, of whom 24 were 'law lords'.

The potential membership of the House of Lords is about 1,200, but this number is reduced by about 75 by a scheme which allows peers who do not wish to attend to apply for leave of absence for the duration of a Parliament. In addition some hereditary peers do not establish their claim to succeed and so do not receive a writ of summons entitling them to sit in the House; there were around 77 such peers in mid-1995.

The Clerk of the Parliaments is responsible for the records of proceedings of the House of Lords and for the text of Acts of Parliament. He is the accounting officer for the cost of the House, and is in charge of the administrative staff of the House, known as the Parliament Office. The Gentleman Usher of the Black Rod, usually known as 'Black Rod', is responsible for security, accommodation and services in the House of Lords' part of the Palace of Westminster.

---

[4]The House of Lords is the final court of appeal for civil cases in Britain and for criminal cases in England, Wales and Northern Ireland.

[5]The woolsack is a seat in the form of a large cushion stuffed with wool from several Commonwealth countries; it is a tradition dating from the medieval period, when wool was the chief source of the country's wealth.

The House of Commons

The House of Commons is elected by
universal adult suffrage (see below) and
consists of 651 Members of Parliament
(MPs). In mid-1995 there were 63 women,
three Asian and three black MPs. Of the 651
seats, 524 are for England, 38 for Wales, 72
for Scotland, and 17 for Northern Ireland.

General elections are held after a
Parliament has been dissolved and a new one
summoned by the Queen. When an MP dies
or resigns,[6] or is given a peerage, a by-
election takes place. Members are paid an
annual salary of £33,189 and an office costs
allowance of up to £41,308. There are also
a number of other allowances, including
travel allowances, a supplement for
London members and, for provincial
members, subsistence allowances and
allowances for second homes. (For ministers'
salaries see p 62.)

Officers of the House of Commons

The chief officer of the House of Commons
is the Speaker, elected by MPs to preside
over the House. Other officers include the
Chairman of Ways and Means and two
deputy chairmen, who act as Deputy
Speakers. They are elected by the House on
the nomination of the Government but are
drawn from the Opposition as well as the
government party. They, like the Speaker,
neither speak nor vote other than in their
official capacity. Responsibility for the
administration of the House rests with the
House of Commons Commission, a statutory
body chaired by the Speaker.

Permanent officers (who are not MPs)
include the Clerk of the House of Commons,
who is the principal adviser to the Speaker
on its privileges and procedures. The Clerk's
departmental responsibilities relate to the
conduct of the business of the House and its
committees. The Clerk is also accounting
officer for the House. The Serjeant-at-Arms,
who waits upon the Speaker, carries out

certain orders of the House. He is also the
official housekeeper of the Commons' part
of the building, and is responsible for
security. Other officers serve the House in
the Library, the Department of the Official
Report (*Hansard*), the Finance and
Administration Department and the
Refreshment Department.

Parliamentary Electoral System

For electoral purposes Britain is divided
into constituencies, each of which returns
one member to the House of Commons.
To ensure that constituency electorates are
kept roughly equal, four permanent
Parliamentary Boundary Commissions, one
each for England, Wales, Scotland and
Northern Ireland, keep constituencies
under review. They recommend any
adjustment of seats that may seem
necessary in the light of population
movements or other changes. Reviews are
conducted every eight to 12 years. Elections
are by secret ballot.

The last general review of
constituencies began in 1991. The
reports of the Commissions for
Scotland and for Wales were
approved by Parliament in April 1995,
the report for England was approved
in June 1995, and that for Northern
Ireland was submitted in June 1995.
Following this review, the number
of seats will increase from 651 to
659: England will get an extra five
seats. Wales two and Northern
Ireland one. The new boundaries
will come into effect after the
dissolution of Parliament at the next
general election.

Voters

British citizens, together with citizens of
other Commonwealth countries and citizens
of the Irish Republic resident in Britain,
may vote provided they are:
● aged 18 or over;

[6]An MP who wishes to resign from the House can do so only by
applying for an office under the Crown as Crown Steward or
Bailiff of the Chiltern Hundreds, or Steward of the Manor of
Northstead.

- included in the annual register of electors for the constituency; and
- not subject to any disqualification.

People not entitled to vote include members of the House of Lords, patients detained under mental health legislation, sentenced prisoners and people convicted within the previous five years of corrupt or illegal election practices. Members of the armed forces, Crown servants and staff of the British Council employed overseas (together with their wives or husbands if accompanying them) may be registered for an address in the constituency where they would live but for their service. British citizens living abroad may apply to register as electors for a period of 20 years after they have left Britain.

Voting Procedures

Each elector may cast one vote, normally in person at a polling station. Electors whose circumstances on polling day are such that they cannot reasonably be expected to vote in person at their local polling station—for example, electors away on holiday—may apply for an absent vote at a particular election. Electors who are physically incapacitated or unable to vote in person because of the nature of their work or because they have moved to a new area may apply for an indefinite absent vote. People entitled to an absent vote may vote by post or by proxy, although postal ballot papers cannot be sent to addresses outside Britain.

Voting is not compulsory; 76.6 per cent of a total electorate of 43.3 million people voted in the general election in April 1992. The simple majority system of voting is used. Candidates are elected if they have more votes than any of the other candidates (although not necessarily an absolute majority over all other candidates).

Candidates

British citizens and citizens of other Commonwealth countries, together with citizens of the Irish Republic, may stand for election as MPs provided they are aged 21 or over and are not disqualified. Those disqualified include undischarged bankrupts;

people sentenced to more than one year's imprisonment; clergy of the Church of England, Church of Scotland, Church of Ireland and Roman Catholic Church; peers; and holders of certain offices listed in the House of Commons Disqualification Act 1975. A candidate's nomination for election must be proposed and seconded by two electors registered as voters in the constituency and signed by eight other electors.

Candidates do not have to be backed by a political party. A candidate must also deposit £500, which is returned if he or she receives 5 per cent or more of the votes cast.

The maximum sum a candidate may spend on a general election campaign is £4,642 plus 3.9 pence for each elector in a borough constituency, or 5.2 pence for each elector in a county constituency. Higher limits have been set for by-elections in order to reflect the fact that they are often regarded as tests of national opinion in the period between general elections. The maximum sum is £18,572 plus 15.8 pence for each elector in borough seats, and 20.8 pence for each elector in county seats. A candidate may post an election communication to each elector in the constituency free of charge. All election expenses, apart from the candidate's personal expenses, are subject to the statutory limit.

The Political Party System

The party system, which has existed in one form or another since the 18th century, is an essential element in the working of the constitution. The present system depends upon the existence of organised political parties, each of which presents its policies to the electorate for approval. The parties are not registered nor formally recognised in law, but in practice most candidates in elections, and almost all winning candidates, belong to one of the main parties.

For the last 150 years a predominantly two-party system has existed. Since 1945 either the Conservative Party, whose origins go back to the 18th century, or the Labour Party, which emerged in the last decade of the 19th century, has held power. A new party—the Liberal Democrats—was formed in 1988 when the Liberal Party, which traced its origins to the 18th century, merged with the Social Democratic Party, formed in 1981. Other parties include two nationalist parties, Plaid Cymru (founded in Wales in 1925) and the Scottish National Party (founded in 1934). In Northern Ireland there are a number of parties. They include the Ulster Unionist Party, formed in the early part of this century; the Ulster Democratic Unionist Party, founded in 1971 by a group which broke away from the Ulster Unionists; and the Social Democratic and Labour Party, founded in 1970.

Since 1945 eight general elections have been won by the Conservative Party and six by the Labour Party; the great majority of members of the House of Commons have belonged to one of these two parties. The results of the general election of April 1992 are shown in Table 7.1.

The party which wins most seats (although not necessarily the most votes) at a general election, or which has the support of a majority of members in the House of Commons, usually forms the Government. By tradition, the leader of the majority party is asked by the Sovereign to form a government. About 100 of its members in the House of Commons and the House of Lords receive ministerial appointments (including appointment to the Cabinet—see p. 62) on the advice of the Prime Minister. The largest minority party becomes the official Opposition, with its own leader and 'shadow cabinet'.

The Party System in Parliament

Leaders of the Government and Opposition sit on the front benches of the Commons with their supporters (the backbenchers) sitting behind them.

Similar arrangements for the parties also apply to the House of Lords; however, a significant number of Lords do not wish to be associated with any political party, and sit on the 'cross-benches'.

The effectiveness of the party system in Parliament rests largely on the relationship between the Government and the opposition parties. Depending on the relative strengths of the parties in the House of Commons, the Opposition may seek to overthrow the Government by defeating it in a vote on a 'matter of confidence'. In general, however, its aims are to contribute to the formulation of policy and legislation by constructive criticism; to oppose government proposals it considers objectionable; to seek amendments to government Bills; and to put forward its own policies in order to improve its chances of winning the next general election.

The detailed arrangements of government business are settled, under the direction of the Prime Minister and the Leaders of the two Houses, by the Government Chief Whip in consultation with the Opposition Chief Whip. The Chief Whips together constitute the 'usual channels' often referred to when the question of finding time for a particular item of business is discussed. The Leaders of the two

Table 7.1: Results of the April 1992 General Election

Party	Members elected	Number of votes cast	% of votes cast
Conservative	336	14,094,116	41.9
Labour	271	11,557,134	34.4
Liberal Democrats	20	5,998,446	17.8
Plaid Cymru (Welsh Nationalist)	4		
Scottish National	3		
Ulster Unionist (Northern Ireland)	9	1,960,703	5.9[a]
Ulster Democratic Unionist (Northern Ireland)	3		
Ulster Popular Unionist (Northern Ireland)	1		
Social Democratic and Labour (Northern Ireland)	4		
Total	651	33,610,399	100.0

[a]These figures include votes for other parties whose candidates were unsuccessful.

Houses are responsible for enabling the Houses to debate matters about which they are concerned.

Outside Parliament, party control is exercised by the national and local organisations. Inside, it is exercised by the Chief Whips and their assistants, who are chosen within the party. Their duties include keeping members informed of forthcoming parliamentary business, maintaining the party's voting strength by ensuring members attend important debates, and passing on to the party leadership the opinions of backbench members. Party discipline tends to be less strong in the Lords than in the Commons, since Lords have less hope of high office and no need of party support in elections.

The formal title of the Government Chief Whip in the Commons is Parliamentary Secretary to the Treasury. Of the other Government Whips, three are officers of the Royal Household (one of these is Deputy Chief Whip), five hold titular posts as Lords Commissioners of the Treasury and five are Assistant Whips. The Opposition Chief Whips in both Houses and two of the Opposition Assistant Whips in the Commons receive salaries. The Government Whips in the Lords hold offices in the Royal Household; they also act as government spokesmen.

Financial Assistance to Parties

Annual assistance from public funds helps opposition parties carry out parliamentary work at Westminster. It is limited to parties which had at least two members elected at the previous general election or one member elected and a minimum of 150,000 votes cast. The amount for the period 1 April 1995 to 31 March 1996 is £3,442.5 for every seat won at the 1992 general election, plus £6.89 for every 200 votes.

Parliamentary Procedure

Parliamentary procedure is based on custom and precedent, partly codified by each House in its Standing Orders. The system of debate is similar in both Houses. Every subject starts off as a proposal or 'motion' by a member. After debate, in which each member may speak only once, the motion may be withdrawn: if it is not, the Speaker or Chairman 'puts the question' whether to agree with the motion or not. The question may be decided without voting, or by a simple majority vote. The main difference of procedure between the two Houses is that the Speaker or Chairman in the Lords has no powers of order; instead such matters are decided by the general feeling of the House.

In the Commons the Speaker has full authority to enforce the rules of the House and must guard against the abuse of procedure and protect minority rights. The Speaker has discretion on whether to allow a motion to end discussion so that a matter may be put to the vote and has powers to put a stop to irrelevance and repetition in debate, and to save time in other ways. In cases of grave disorder the Speaker can adjourn or suspend the sitting. The Speaker may order members who have broken the rules of behaviour of the House to leave the Chamber or can initiate their suspension for a period of days.

The Speaker supervises voting in the Commons and announces the final result. In a tied vote the Speaker gives a casting vote, without expressing an opinion on the merits of the question. The voting procedure in the House of Lords is broadly similar, although the Lord Chancellor does not have a casting vote.

Financial Interests

The Commons has a public register of MPs' financial interests. Members with a financial interest in a debate in the House must declare it when speaking. If the interest is direct, immediate and personal, the member cannot vote on the issue. In other proceedings of the House or in dealings with other members, ministers or civil servants, MPs must also disclose any relevant financial interest.

There is no register of financial interests in the Lords, but Lords speaking in a debate in which they have a direct interest are expected to declare it.

Public Access to Parliamentary Proceedings

Proceedings of both Houses are normally public. The minutes and speeches (transcribed verbatim in *Hansard,* the official report) are published daily.

The records of the Lords from 1497 and of the Commons from 1547, together with the parliamentary and political papers of a number of former members of both Houses, are available to the public through the House of Lords Record Office.

The proceedings of both Houses of Parliament may be broadcast on television and radio, either live or, more usually, in recorded or edited form. Complete coverage is available on cable television.

The Law-making Process

Statute law consists of Acts of Parliament and delegated legislation made by ministers under powers given to them by Act (see p. 57). While the law undergoes constant refinement in the courts, changes to statute law are made by Parliament.

Draft laws take the form of parliamentary Bills. Proposals for legislation affecting the powers of particular bodies (such as local authorities) or the rights of individuals (such as certain proposals relating to railways, roads and harbours) are known as Private Bills, and are subject to a special form of parliamentary procedure. Bills which change the general law and which constitute the significant part of the parliamentary legislative process are Public Bills.

Public Bills can be introduced into either House, by a government minister or by an ordinary ('private' or 'backbench') member. Most Public Bills that become Acts of Parliament are introduced by a government Minister and are known as 'Government Bills'. Bills introduced by other members of Parliament are known as 'Private Members' Bills.'

The main Bills which constitute the Government's legislative programme are announced in the Queen's Speech at the State opening of Parliament, which usually takes place in November, and the Bills themselves are introduced into one or other of the Houses over the succeeding weeks.

Before a government Bill is drafted, there may be consultation with professional bodies, voluntary organisations and other agencies interested in the subject, and interest and pressure groups which seek to promote specific causes. Proposals for legislative changes are sometimes set out in government 'White Papers', which may be debated in Parliament before a Bill is introduced. From time to time consultation papers, sometimes called 'Green Papers', set out government proposals which are still taking shape and seek comments from the public.

Private Members' Bills

Early in each session backbench Members of the Commons hold a ballot (draw lots) for the opportunity to introduce a Bill on one of the Fridays during the session on which such Bills have precedence over government business. The first 20 Members whose names are drawn win this privilege, but it does not guarantee that their Bills will pass into law. Members may also present a Bill on any day without debate, and on most Tuesdays and Wednesdays on which the Commons is sitting there is also an opportunity to seek leave to present a Bill under the 'ten minute rule', which provides an opportunity for a brief speech by the Member proposing the Bill (and by one who opposes it). Few of these Bills make further progress or receive any debate, but in most sessions a few do become law. Recent examples include the Marriage Act 1994, the Sale and Supply of Goods Act 1994 and the Building Societies (Joint Account Holders) Act 1995. Private Members' Bills do not often call for the expenditure of public money; but if they do they cannot proceed to committee stage unless the Government decides to provide the necessary money resolution. Peers may introduce Private Members' Bills in the House of Lords at any time. A Private Members' Bill passed by either House will not proceed in the other House unless it is taken up by a member of that House.

Passage of Public Bills

Public Bills must normally be passed by both Houses. Bills relating mainly to financial matters are almost invariably introduced in the Commons. Under the provisions of the Parliament Acts 1911 and 1949, the powers of the Lords in relation to 'money Bills' are very restricted. The Parliament Acts also provide for a Bill to be passed by the Commons without consent of the Lords in certain (very rare) circumstances.

The process of passing a Public Bill is similar in each House. On presentation the Bill is considered, without debate, to have been read a first time and is printed (although a substantial number of Private Members' Bills are never printed). After an interval, which may be between one day and several weeks, a Government Bill will receive its second reading debate, during which the general principles of the Bill are discussed. If it obtains a second reading in the Commons, a Bill will normally be committed to a standing committee (see p. 57) for detailed examination and amendment. In the Lords, the committee stage usually takes place on the floor of the House, and this procedure may also be followed in the Commons if that House so decides (usually in cases where there is a need to pass the Bill quickly or where it raises matters of constitutional importance). The Commons may also decide to divide the committee stage of a Bill between a standing committee and a committee of the whole House (which is commonly the case with the annual Finance Bill).

The committee stage is followed by the report stage ('consideration') on the floor of the House, during which further amendments may be made. In the Commons, this is usually followed immediately by the third reading debate, where the Bill is reviewed in its final form. In the Lords, a Bill may be further amended at third reading.

After passing its third reading in one House a Bill is sent to the other House, where it passes through all the stages once more, and where it is, more often than not, further amended. Amendments made by the second House must be agreed by the first, or a compromise agreement reached, before a Bill can go for Royal Assent.

In the Commons, the House may vote to limit the time available for consideration of a Bill. This is done by passing a 'timetable' motion proposed by the Government, commonly referred to as a 'guillotine'.

There are special procedures for Public Bills which consolidate existing legislation or which enact private legislation relating to Scotland.

Royal Assent

When a Bill has passed through all its parliamentary stages, it is sent to the Queen for Royal Assent, after which it is part of the law of the land and known as an Act of Parliament. Royal Assent takes the form of an announcement rather than any signature or mark on a copy of the Bill. The Royal Assent has not been refused since 1707. (A list of the main Public Bills receiving Royal Assent since autumn 1994 is given on p. 537.)

Limitations on the Power of the Lords

Most Government Bills introduced and passed in the Lords pass through the Commons without difficulty, but a Lords Bill which was unacceptable to the Commons would not become law. The Lords, on the other hand, do not generally prevent Bills insisted upon by the Commons from becoming law, though they will often amend them and return them for further consideration by the Commons. By convention the Lords pass Bills authorising taxation or national expenditure without amendment. Under the Parliament Acts 1911 and 1949, a Bill that deals only with taxation or expenditure must become law within one month of being sent to the Lords, whether or not they agree to it, unless the Commons directs otherwise. If no agreement is reached between the two Houses on a non-financial Commons Bill the Lords can delay the Bill for a period which, in practice, amounts to at least 13 months. Following this the Bill may be submitted to the Queen for Royal Assent, provided it has been passed a second time by the Commons. The Parliament Acts make one important exception: any Bill to lengthen the life of a Parliament requires the full assent of both Houses in the normal way.

The limits to the power of the Lords, contained in the Parliament Acts, are based on the belief that nowadays the main legislative function of the non-elected House is to act as a chamber of revision, complementing but not rivalling the elected House.

Delegated Legislation

In order to reduce unnecessary pressure on parliamentary time, primary legislation often gives ministers or other authorities the power to regulate administrative details by means of 'delegated' or secondary legislation. To minimise any risk that delegating powers to the executive might undermine the authority of Parliament, such powers are normally only delegated to authorities directly accountable to Parliament. Moreover, the Acts of Parliament concerned usually provide for some measure of direct parliamentary control over proposed delegated legislation, by giving Parliament the opportunity to affirm or annul it. Certain Acts also require that organisations affected must be consulted before rules and orders can be made.

A joint committee of both Houses reports on the technical propriety of these 'statutory instruments'. In order to save time on the floor of the House, the Commons uses standing committees to debate the merits of instruments; actual decisions are taken by the House. The House of Lords has appointed a delegated powers scrutiny committee which examines the appropriateness of the powers to make secondary legislation in Bills as they come before that House.

Private Legislation

Private Bills are promoted by people or organisations outside Parliament (often local authorities) to give them special legal powers. They go through a similar procedure to Public Bills, but most of the work is done in committee, where procedures follow a semi-judicial pattern. The promoter must prove the need for the powers sought and the objections of opposing interests are heard. Both sides may be legally represented. Hybrid Bills are Public Bills which may affect private rights. As with Private Bills, the passage of hybrid Bills through Parliament is governed by special procedures which allow those affected to put their case.

Parliamentary Committees

Committees of the Whole House

Either House may pass a resolution setting itself up as a committee of the whole House to consider Bills in detail after their second reading. This permits unrestricted discussion: the general rule that an MP or Lord may speak only once on each motion does not apply in committee.

Standing Committees

House of Commons standing committees debate and consider Public Bills at the committee stage. The committee considers the Bill clause by clause, and may amend it before reporting it back to the House. The standing committees include two Scottish standing committees, and the Scottish, Welsh and Northern Ireland Grand Committees. Ordinary standing committees do not have names but are referred to simply as Standing Committee A, B, C, and so on; a new set of members is appointed to them to consider each Bill. Each committee has between 16 and 50 members, with a party balance reflecting as far as possible that in the House as a whole.

The Scottish Grand Committee comprises all 72 Scottish members (and may be convened anywhere in Scotland as well as at Westminster). It may consider the principles of Scottish Bills referred to it at second reading stage. It also debates Scottish public expenditure estimates and other matters concerning Scotland. Since July 1994 these have included questions tabled for oral answer, ministerial statements and other debates in addition to statutory instruments referred to it.

The Welsh Grand Committee, with all 38 Welsh members and up to five others, considers Bills referred to it at second reading stage, and matters concerning Wales only. Similarly, the Northern Ireland Grand Committee debates matters relating specifically to Northern Ireland. It includes all 17 Northern Ireland members and up to 25 others.

There are also standing committees to

debate proposed European legislation, and to scrutinise statutory instruments made by the Government.

The Lords' equivalent to a standing committee, a Public Bill Committee, is rarely used; instead the committee stage of a Bill is taken by the House as a whole.

Select Committees

Select committees are appointed for a particular task, generally one of enquiry, investigation and scrutiny. They report their conclusions and recommendations to the House as a whole; in many cases their recommendations invite a response from the Government, which is also reported to the House. A select committee may be appointed for a Parliament, or for a session, or for as long as it takes to complete its task. To help Parliament with the control of the executive by examining aspects of public policy, expenditure and administration, 17 committees, established by the House of Commons, examine the work of the main government departments and their associated public bodies. The Foreign Affairs Select Committee, for example, 'shadows' the work of the Foreign & Commonwealth Office. The committees are constituted on a basis which is in approximate proportion to party strength in the House.

Other regular Commons select committees include those on Public Accounts, European Legislation, Members' Interests, and the Parliamentary Commissioner for Administration (the 'Parliamentary Ombudsman'—see p. 60). 'Domestic' select committees also cover the internal workings of Parliament.

In their examination of government policies, expenditure and administration, committees may question ministers, civil servants, and interested bodies and individuals. Through hearings and published reports, they bring before Parliament and the public an extensive body of fact and informed opinion on many issues, and build up considerable expertise in their subjects of inquiry.

In the House of Lords, besides the Appeal and Appellate Committees, in which the bulk of the House's judicial work is transacted,

there are two major select committees (along with several sub-committees), on the European Community and on Science and Technology. *Ad hoc* committees may also be set up to consider particular issues, and 'domestic' committees—as in the Commons—cover the internal workings of the House.

Joint Committees

Joint committees, with a membership drawn from both Houses, are appointed in each session to deal with Consolidation Bills and delegated legislation. The two Houses may also agree to set up joint select committees on other subjects.

Party Committees

In addition to the official committees of the two Houses there are several unofficial party organisations or committees. The Conservative and Unionist Members' Committee (the 1922 Committee) consists of the backbench membership of the party in the House of Commons. When the Conservative Party is in office, ministers attend its meetings by invitation and not by right. When the party is in opposition, the whole membership of the party may attend meetings. The then leader appoints a consultative committee, which acts as the party's 'shadow cabinet'.

The Parliamentary Labour Party comprises all members of the party in both Houses. When the Labour Party is in office, a parliamentary committee, half of whose members are elected and half of whom are government representatives, acts as a channel of communication between the Government and its backbenchers in both Houses. When the party is in opposition, the Parliamentary Labour Party is organised under the direction of an elected parliamentary committee, which acts as the 'shadow cabinet'.

Other Forms of Parliamentary Control

House of Commons

In addition to the system of scrutiny by select committees, the House of Commons offers a number of opportunities for the examination of government policy by both the Opposition and the Government's own backbenchers. These include:

1. Question time, when for 55 minutes on Monday, Tuesday, Wednesday and Thursday, ministers answer MPs' questions. The Prime Minister's question time is every Tuesday and Thursday when the House is sitting. Parliamentary questions are one means of seeking information about the Government's intentions. They are also a way of raising grievances brought to MPs' notice by constituents. MPs may also put questions to ministers for written answer; the questions and answers are published in *Hansard*. There are some 50,000 questions every year.

2. Adjournment debates, when MPs use motions for the adjournment of the House to raise constituency cases or matters of public concern. There is a half-hour adjournment period at the end of the business of the day, while immediately before the adjournment for each recess (Parliament's Christmas, Easter, Whitsun and summer breaks) a full day is spent discussing issues raised by private members. There are also adjournment debates following the passage, three times a year, of Consolidated Fund[7] or Appropriation Bills.[8]

   In addition, an MP wishing to discuss a 'specific and important matter that should have urgent consideration' may, at the end of question time, seek leave to move the adjournment of the House. On the very few occasions when leave is obtained, the matter is debated for three hours in what is known as an emergency debate, usually on the following day.

3. Early day motions (EDMs) provide a further opportunity for backbench MPs to express their views on particular issues. A number of EDMs are tabled each sitting day; they are very rarely debated but can be useful in gauging the degree of support for the topic by the number of signatures of other MPs which the motion attracts.

4. The 20 Opposition days each session, when the Opposition can choose subjects for debate. Of these days, 17 are at the disposal of the Leader of the Opposition and three at the disposal of the second largest opposition party.

5. Debates on three days in each session on details of proposed government expenditure, chosen by the Liaison Committee.

Procedural opportunities for criticism of the Government also arise during the debate on the Queen's speech at the beginning of each session; during debates on motions of censure for which the Government provides time; and during debates on the Government's legislative and other proposals.

House of Lords

Similar opportunities for criticism and examination of government policy are provided in the House of Lords at daily question time and during debates.

Control of Finances

The main responsibilities of Parliament, and more particularly of the House of Commons, in overseeing the revenue of the State and public expenditure, are to authorise the raising of taxes and duties, and the various objects of expenditure and the sum to be spent on each. It also has to satisfy itself that the sums granted are spent only for the purposes which Parliament intended. No payment out of the central government's public funds can be made and no taxation or loans authorised, except by Act of Parliament. However, limited interim payments can be made from the Contingencies Fund.

The Finance Act is the most important of the annual statutes, and authorises the raising of revenue. The legislation is based on the Chancellor of the Exchequer's Budget statement. This includes a review of the public finances of the previous year, and proposals for future expenditure (see p. 159).

---

[7] At least two Consolidated Fund Acts are passed each session authorising the Treasury to make certain sums of money available for the public service.
[8] The annual Appropriate Act fixes the sums of public money provided for particular items of expenditure.

Scrutiny of public expenditure is carried out by House of Commons select committees (see p. 58).

European Union Affairs

To keep the two Houses informed of EU developments, and to enable them to scrutinise and debate Union policies and proposals, there is a select committee in each House (see p. 58), and two Commons standing committees debate specific European legislative proposals. Ministers also make regular statements about Union business.

The Commons' Ability to Force the Government to Resign

The final control is the ability of the House of Commons to force the Government to resign by passing a resolution of 'no confidence'. The Government must also resign if the House rejects a proposal which the Government considers so vital to its policy that it has declared it a 'matter of confidence' or if the House refuses to vote the money required for the public service.

Parliamentary Commissioner for Administration

The post of Parliamentary Commissioner for Administration (the 'Parliamentary Ombudsman') was established under the Parliamentary Commissioner Act 1967. The Ombudsman is independent of government and reports to a Select Committee of the House of Commons. He investigates complaints from members of the public (referred through MPs) alleging that they have suffered injustice arising from maladministration. The Ombudsman's jurisdiction covers central government departments and a large number of non-departmental public bodies. He cannot investigate complaints about government policy, the content of legislation or relations with other countries. In making his investigations, the Commissioner has access to all departmental papers, and has powers to summon those from whom he wishes to take evidence. When an investigation is completed, he sends a report with his findings to the MP who referred the complaint (with a copy report for the complainant). In reports of justified cases, the Ombudsman normally recommends that the department provides redress (which can include a financial remedy for the complainant in appropriate cases). His recommendations are almost always put into practice. He submits an annual report to Parliament, and also publishes selected cases three times a year.

> In 1994 the Ombudsman received a record 1,332 new complaints. He completed 226 investigations; of these he found 200 wholly or partly justified and 26 unjustified.

The Parliamentary Ombudsman also monitors the Code of Practice on Access to Official Information, which came into force in 1994. He investigates complaints, referred through MPs, that government departments or bodies have wrongly refused access to official information. If he finds a complaint justified, he can recommend that the information is released.

Parliamentary Privilege

Each House of Parliament has certain rights and immunities to protect it from obstruction in carrying out its duties. The rights apply collectively to each House and to its staff and individually to each member.

For the Commons the Speaker formally claims from the Queen 'their ancient and undoubted rights and privileges' at the beginning of each Parliament. These include freedom of speech; first call on the attendance of its members, who are therefore free from arrest in civil actions and exempt from serving on juries, or being compelled to attend court as witnesses; and the right of access to the Crown, which is a collective privilege of the House. Further privileges include the rights of the House to control its own proceedings (so that it is able, for instance, to exclude 'strangers'[9] if it wishes);

---

[9] All those who are not members or officials of either House.

to decide upon legal disqualifications for membership and to declare a seat vacant on such grounds; and to punish for breach of its privileges and for contempt. Parliament has the right to punish anybody, inside or outside the House, who commits a breach of privilege—that is, offends against the rights of the House.

The privileges of the House of Lords are broadly similar to those of the House of Commons.

Her Majesty's Government

Her Majesty's Government is the body of ministers responsible for the conduct of national affairs. The Prime Minister is appointed by the Queen, and all other ministers are appointed by the Queen on the recommendation of the Prime Minister. Most ministers are members of the Commons, although the Government is also fully represented by ministers in the Lords. The Lord Chancellor is always a member of the House of Lords.

The composition of governments can vary both in the number of ministers and in the titles of some offices. New ministerial offices may be created, others may be abolished, and functions may be transferred from one minister to another.

Prime Minister

The Prime Minister is also, by tradition, First Lord of the Treasury and Minister for the Civil Service. The Prime Minister's unique position of authority derives from majority support in the House of Commons and from the power to appoint and dismiss ministers. By modern convention, the Prime Minister always sits in the House of Commons.

The Prime Minister presides over the Cabinet, is responsible for the allocation of functions among ministers and informs the Queen at regular meetings of the general business of the Government.

The Prime Minister's other responsibilities include recommending a number of appointments to the Queen. These include:

- Church of England archbishops, bishops and deans and some 200 other clergy in Crown 'livings';
- senior judges, such as the Lord Chief Justice;
- Privy Counsellors; and
- Lord-Lieutenants.

They also include certain civil appointments, such as Lord High Commissioner to the General Assembly of the Church of Scotland, Poet Laureate, Constable of the Tower, and some university posts; and appointments to various public boards and institutions, such as the BBC (British Broadcasting Corporation), as well as various royal and statutory commissions. Recommendations are likewise made for the award of many civil honours and distinctions and of Civil List pensions (to people who have achieved eminence in science or the arts and are in financial need). The Prime Minister also selects the trustees of certain national museums and institutions.

The Prime Minister's Office at 10 Downing Street (the official residence in London) has a staff of civil servants who assist the Prime Minister. The Prime Minister may also appoint special advisers to the Office to assist in the formation of policies.

Departmental Ministers

Ministers in charge of government departments are usually in the Cabinet; they are known as 'Secretary of State' or 'Minister', or may have a special title, as in the case of the Chancellor of the Exchequer.

Non-departmental Ministers

The holders of various traditional offices, namely the Lord President of the Council, the Chancellor of the Duchy of Lancaster, the Lord Privy Seal, the Paymaster General and, from time to time, Ministers without Portfolio, may have few or no departmental duties. They are thus available to perform any duties the Prime Minister may wish to give them. In the present administration, for example, the Lord President of the Council is Leader of the House of Commons and the

Chancellor of the Duchy of Lancaster is Minister for Public Service.

Lord Chancellor and Law Officers

The Lord Chancellor holds a special position, as both a minister with departmental functions and the head of the judiciary (see p. 105). The four Law Officers of the Crown are: for England and Wales, the Attorney General and the Solicitor General; and for Scotland, the Lord Advocate and the Solicitor General for Scotland.

Ministers of State and Junior Ministers

Ministers of State usually work with ministers in charge of departments. They normally have specific responsibilities, and are sometimes given titles which reflect these functions. More than one may work in a department. A Minister of State may be given a seat in the Cabinet and be paid accordingly.

Junior ministers (generally Parliamentary Under-Secretaries of State or, where the senior minister is not a Secretary of State, simply Parliamentary Secretaries) share in parliamentary and departmental duties. They may also be given responsibility, directly under the departmental minister, for specific aspects of the department's work.

Ministerial Salaries

The salaries of ministers in the House of Commons range from £47,987 a year for junior ministers to £67,819 for Cabinet ministers. In the House of Lords salaries range from £41,065 for junior ministers to £55,329 for Cabinet ministers. The Prime Minister receives £82,003 and the Lord Chancellor £126,138. (The Leader of the Opposition receives £64,257 a year; two Opposition whips in the Commons and the Opposition Leader and Chief Whip in the Lords also receive salaries.)

The Cabinet

The Cabinet is composed of about 20 ministers (the number can vary) chosen by the Prime Minister and may include departmental and non-departmental ministers.

The functions of the Cabinet are to initiate and decide on policy, the supreme control of government and the co-ordination of government departments. The exercise of these functions is vitally affected by the fact that the Cabinet is a group of party representatives, depending upon majority support in the House of Commons.

Cabinet Meetings

The Cabinet meets in private and its proceedings are confidential. Its members are bound by their oath as Privy Counsellors not to disclose information about its proceedings, although after 30 years Cabinet papers may be made available for inspection in the Public Record Office at Kew, Surrey.

Normally the Cabinet meets for a few hours each week during parliamentary sittings, and rather less often when Parliament is not sitting. To keep its workload within manageable limits, a great deal of work is carried on through the committee system. This involves referring issues either to a standing Cabinet committee or to an *ad hoc* committee composed of the ministers directly concerned. The committee then considers the matter in detail and either disposes of it or reports upon it to the Cabinet with recommendations for action.

The membership and terms of reference of all ministerial Cabinet committees are published by the Cabinet Office. Where appropriate, the Secretary of the Cabinet and other senior officials of the Cabinet Office attend meetings of the Cabinet and its committees.

Diaries published by several former ministers have given the public insight into Cabinet procedures in recent times.

The Cabinet Office

The Cabinet Office is headed by the Secretary of the Cabinet (a civil servant who is also Head of the Home Civil Service) under the direction of the Prime Minister. It comprises the Cabinet Secretariat and the Office of Public Service (OPS).

The Cabinet Secretariat serves ministers collectively in the conduct of Cabinet business, and in the co-ordination of policy at the highest level.

The Chancellor of the Duchy of Lancaster is in charge of the Office of Public Service and is a member of the Cabinet. The OPS is responsible for:

- raising the standard of public services across the public sector through the Citizen's Charter (see p. 66);
- promoting openness in government; and
- improving the effectiveness and efficiency of central government, through, among other things, the establishment of executive agencies and the market testing programme (see p. 69).

The Historical and Records Section is responsible for Official Histories and managing Cabinet Office records.

Ministerial Responsibility

'Ministerial responsibility' refers both to the collective responsibility for government policy and actions, which ministers share, and to ministers' individual responsibility for their departments' work.

The doctrine of collective responsibility means that the Cabinet acts unanimously even when Cabinet ministers do not all agree on a subject. The policy of departmental ministers must be consistent with the policy of the Government as a whole. Once the Government's policy on a matter has been decided, each minister is expected to support it or resign. On rare occasions, ministers have been allowed free votes in Parliament on government policies involving important issues of principle. In February 1994, for example, free votes were allowed on lowering the age of consent to homosexual sex from 21 to 18.

The individual responsibility of ministers for the work of their departments means that they are answerable to Parliament for all their departments' activities. They bear the consequences of any failure in administration, any injustice to an individual or any aspect of policy which may be criticised in Parliament, whether personally responsible or not. Since most ministers are members of the House of Commons, they must answer questions and defend themselves against criticism in person. Departmental ministers in the House of Lords are represented in the Commons by someone qualified to speak on their behalf, usually a junior minister.

Departmental ministers normally decide all matters within their responsibility. However, on important political matters they usually consult their colleagues collectively, either through the Cabinet or through a Cabinet committee. A decision by a departmental minister binds the Government as a whole.

On assuming office ministers must resign directorships in private and public companies, and must ensure that there is no conflict between their public duties and private interests.

The Privy Council

The Privy Council was formerly the chief source of executive power in the State; its origins can be traced back to the King's Court, which assisted the Norman monarchs in running the government. As the system of Cabinet government developed in the 18th century, however, much of the role of the Privy Council was assumed by the Cabinet, although the Council retained certain executive functions. Some government departments originated as committees of the Privy Council.

Nowadays the main function of the Privy Council is to advise the Queen on the approval of Orders in Council, including those made under prerogative powers, such as Orders approving the grant of royal charters of incorporation and those made under statutory powers. Responsibility for each Order, however, rests with the minister answerable for the policy concerned, regardless of whether he or she is present at the meeting where approval is given.

The Privy Council also advises the Sovereign on the issue of royal proclamations, such as those summoning or dissolving Parliament. The Council's own statutory responsibilities, which are independent of the powers of the Sovereign in Council, include supervising the registration authorities of the medical and allied professions.

Membership of the Council (retained for life, except for very occasional removals) is accorded by the Sovereign on the recommendation of the Prime Minister (or occasionally, Prime Ministers of Commonwealth countries) to people eminent in public life—mainly politicians and judges—in Britain and the independent monarchies of the Commonwealth. Cabinet ministers must be Privy Counsellors and, if not already members, are admitted to membership before taking their oath of office at a meeting of the Council. There are about 450 Privy Counsellors. A full Council is summoned only on the accession of a new Sovereign or when the Sovereign announces his or her intention to marry.

Committees of the Privy Council

There are a number of Privy Council committees. These include prerogative committees, such as those dealing with legislation from the Channel Islands and the Isle of Man, and with applications for charters of incorporation. Committees may also be provided for by statute, such as those for the universities of Oxford and Cambridge and the Scottish universities. Membership of such committees is confined to members of the current administration. The only exceptions are the members of the Judicial Committee and the members of any committee for which specific provision authorises a wider membership.

Administrative work is carried out in the Privy Council Office under the Lord President of the Council, a Cabinet minister.

The Judicial Committee of the Privy Council is the highest court of appeal for certain independent members of the Commonwealth, the British dependent territories, the Channel Islands and the Isle of Man. It also hears appeals from the disciplinary committees of the medical and allied professions and certain ecclesiastical appeals. In 1994 69 appeals were registered and 58 were heard.

Government Departments

Government departments and their agencies, staffed by politically impartial civil servants, are the main instruments for implementing

government policy when Parliament has passed the necessary legislation, and for advising ministers. They often work alongside local authorities, statutory boards, and government-sponsored organisations operating under various degrees of government control.

A change of government does not necessarily affect the number or general functions of government departments, although major changes in policy may be accompanied by organisational changes.

The work of some departments (for instance, the Ministry of Defence) covers Britain as a whole. Other departments, such as the Department of Social Security, cover England, Wales and Scotland, but not Northern Ireland. Others, such as the Department of the Environment, are mainly concerned with affairs in England. Some departments, such as the Department of Trade and Industry, maintain a regional organisation, and some which have direct contact with the public throughout the country (for example, the Department of Social Security) also have local offices.

Departments are usually headed by ministers. In some departments the head is a permanent official, and ministers with other duties are responsible for them to Parliament. For instance, ministers in the Treasury are responsible for HM Customs and Excise, the Inland Revenue, the National Investment and Loans Office and a number of other departments as well as executive agencies such as the Royal Mint. Departments generally receive their funds directly out of money provided by Parliament and are staffed by members of the Civil Service.

The functions of the main government departments are set out on pp. 525–33.

Non-departmental Public Bodies

There are bodies which have a role in the process of national government, but are not government departments nor parts of a department (in April 1994 there were 1,345, employing 110,200 staff). There are three kinds of non-departmental public bodies: executive bodies, advisory bodies and tribunals. The last of these are a specialised group of bodies whose functions are essentially judicial (see p. 104).

Executive Bodies

Executive bodies normally employ their own staff and have their own budget. They are public organisations whose duties include executive, administrative, regulatory or commercial functions. They normally operate within broad policy guidelines set by departmental ministers, but are in varying degrees independent of government in carrying out their day-to-day responsibilities. Examples include the Legal Aid Board, the Police Complaints Authority, the Countryside Commission and the Human Fertilisation and Embryology Authority.

Advisory Bodies

Many government departments are assisted by advisory councils or committees which undertake research and collect information, mainly to give ministers access to informed opinion before they come to a decision involving a legislative or executive act. In some cases a minister must consult a standing committee, but advisory bodies are usually appointed at the discretion of the minister. Examples include the British Overseas Trade Board and the Theatres Trust.

The membership of advisory councils and committees varies according to the nature of the work involved, but normally includes representatives of the relevant interests and professions.

In addition to standing advisory bodies, there are committees set up by the Government to examine specific matters and make recommendations. For example, the Committee on Standards in Public Life (the Nolan Committee) was set up in October 1994, reporting directly to the Prime Minister. The Committee issued its first report in May 1995, recommending, among other things, independent scrutiny of the conduct of MPs and ministers and of how ministers make appointments to public bodies. The Government has accepted the broad thrust of its recommendations.

For certain important inquiries, Royal Commissions, whose members are chosen for their wide experience, may be appointed. Royal Commissions examine evidence from government departments, interested organisations and individuals, and submit recommendations; some prepare regular reports. Examples include the standing Royal Commission on Environmental Pollution, set up in 1970, and the Royal Commission on Criminal Justice, which issued its report in 1993 (see Chapter 8). Inquiries may also be undertaken by departmental committees.

Government Information Services

Each of the main government departments has its own information division, public relations branch or news department. These are normally staffed by professional information officers responsible for communicating their department's activities to the news media and the public (sometimes using publicity services provided by the Central Office of Information—see p. 530). They also advise their departments on the public's reaction.

The Lobby

As press adviser to the Prime Minister, the Prime Minister's Press Secretary and other staff in the Prime Minister's Press Office have direct contact with the parliamentary press through regular meetings with the Lobby correspondents. The Lobby correspondents are a group of political correspondents who have the special privilege of access to the Lobby of the House of Commons, where they can talk privately to government ministers and other members of the House. The Prime Minister's Press Office is the accepted channel through which information about parliamentary business is passed to the media.

Administration of Scottish, Welsh and Northern Ireland Affairs

Scotland

Scotland has its own system of law and wide administrative autonomy. The Secretary of

State for Scotland, a Cabinet minister, has responsibility in Scotland (with some exceptions) for a wide range of policy matters (see p. 532). Following an examination of Scotland's place in Britain which began after the general election in April 1992, a number of changes to the responsibilities of The Scottish Office have been made. These make it responsible for more areas of policy.

The distinctive conditions and needs of Scotland and its people are also reflected in separate Scottish legislation on many domestic matters. Special provisions applying to Scotland alone are also inserted in Acts which otherwise apply to Britain generally.

British government departments with significant Scottish responsibilities have offices in Scotland and work closely with The Scottish Office.

Wales

Since 1964 there has been a separate Secretary of State for Wales, who is a member of the Cabinet and is responsible for many aspects of Welsh affairs. (For further details see p. 533.)

Northern Ireland

Since the British Government's assumption of direct responsibility for Northern Ireland in 1972 (see p. 13), the Secretary of State for Northern Ireland, with a seat in the Cabinet, has been in charge of the Northern Ireland Office, which governs the province. The Secretary of State is directly responsible for political and constitutional matters, security policy, broad economic questions and other major policy issues. A team of ministers share responsibility for the Departments of Agriculture, Economic Development, Education, Environment, Finance and Personnel, and Health and Social Services.

Citizen's Charter

The Citizen's Charter was launched by the Prime Minister in 1991. The Charter's aim is to raise the standard of all public services and make them more responsive to their users. It is closely linked to other reforms, including the Next Steps programme, efficiency measures and the Government's contracting out and market testing programmes (see p. 69). The Citizen's Charter is a ten-year programme which is intended to be at the heart of the Government's policy-making throughout the 1990s.

The Charter applies to all public services, at both national and local levels, and the privatised utilities. Most major public services have now published separate charters (by mid-1995 40 had been issued). In many cases separate charters have been published for services in Northern Ireland, Scotland and Wales. (Details of many of the charters can be found in the relevant chapters; a full list, together with information on how to obtain them, appears on p. 538.)

The Principles of Public Service

The Charter sets out a number of key principles which users of public services are entitled to expect:

Standards

Setting, monitoring and publishing explicit standards for the services that individual users can reasonably expect. Publication of actual performance against these standards.

Information and Openness

Full and accurate information should be readily available in plain language about how public services are run, their cost and performance, and who is in charge.

Choice and Consultation

There should be regular and systematic consultation with those who use services. Users' views about services, and their priorities for improving them, should be taken into account in final decisions about standards.

Courtesy and Helpfulness

Courteous and helpful service from public servants, who will normally wear name badges. Services available equally to all who are entitled to them and run to suit their convenience.

Putting Things Right

If things go wrong, an apology, a full explanation and a swift and effective remedy should be given. Well publicised and easy to use complaints procedures, with independent review wherever possible, should be available.

Value for Money

Efficient and economical delivery of public services within the resources the nation can afford, and independent validation of performance against standards.

Implementing the Charter

A Cabinet minister, the Chancellor of the Duchy of Lancaster, is responsible for the Charter programme. The Chancellor of the Duchy is supported by the Citizen's Charter Unit within the OPS (see p. 62). The Prime Minister also receives advice on the Charter from an Advisory Panel drawn from business, consumer affairs and education. The Panel works with the Citizen's Charter Unit and officials in all the departments to implement and develop the Citizen's Charter programme. The Prime Minister holds regular Citizen's Charter seminars with Advisory Panel members and Cabinet ministers to report on progress and plan further action.

Executive agencies (see p. 69) are expected to comply fully with the principles of the Citizen's Charter, and the pay of agency chief executives is normally directly related to their agency's performance. Performance-related pay is being introduced throughout the public service.

Progress on the Charter

Projects to ensure that the Charter becomes an integral part of all public services and that members of the public are aware of the standards of service to which they are entitled include:

Charter Mark Awards

The Charter Mark Scheme has been introduced to reward excellence in delivering public services: winners are judged by the Prime Minister's Citizen's Charter Advisory Panel. Applicants have to demonstrate that they have achieved measurable improvements in the quality of services over the previous two years, and that their customers are satisfied with their services.

In 1994 awards were made to 98 of over 520 public service organisations and privatised utilities which had applied. Winners ranged from schools and colleges, hospitals and health services, and executive agencies, such as the Benefits Agency and the Employment Service, to Victoria Coach Station. Award winners can use the Charter Mark on their products and equipment, and on stationery, vehicles and promotional material for up to three years.

Complaints Task Force

A task force set up in June 1993 reviews and recommends improvements to public service complaints procedures.

Charter Forums and Quality Networks

A programme of Charter Forums has been held around the country, providing an opportunity for local service providers to exchange information about best practice in implementing the Citizen's Charter. Following this, a series of Citizen's Charter Quality Networks was announced in July 1994. These offer public service managers the opportunity to discuss lessons of good practice on a regular basis.

Open Government

In line with Citizen's Charter principles, the Government has a general policy of increasing the openness and accountability of public administration. In 1994 it introduced a code of practice on access to government information. This commits the Government to release certain information as a matter of course and also to respond to requests for other factual information which it holds. The code is policed by the Parliamentary Ombudsman. Similar codes of practice have been proposed to cover the health service and local authorities.

As part of the same openness, the Government is also to propose legislation to provide rights of access to health and safety information and personal records. These rights would add to a number of existing rights of access to information in specific areas such as environmental information.

The Civil Service

The Civil Service is concerned with the conduct of the whole range of government activities as they affect the community. These range from policy formulation to carrying out the day-to-day duties of public administration.

Civil servants are servants of the Crown. Fc. all practical purposes the Crown in this context means, and is represented by, the Government of the day. In most circumstances the executive powers of the Crown are exercised by, and on the advice of, Her Majesty's ministers, who are in turn answerable to Parliament. The Civil Service as such has no constitutional personality or responsibility separate from that of the Government of the day. The duty of the individual civil servant is first and foremost to the minister of the Crown who is in charge of the department in which he or she is serving. A change of minister, for whatever reason, does not involve a change of staff. Ministers sometimes appoint special advisers from outside the Civil Service. The advisers are normally paid from public funds, but their appointments come to an end when the Government's term of office finishes, or when the minister concerned leaves the Government or moves to another appointment.

Following publication in July 1994 of a White Paper on the role and future of the Civil Service—*The Civil Service: Continuity and Change*—a new Civil Service code has been drawn up. This describes the duties and responsibilities of civil servants and their relationship with ministers and the Government. The code, which will have an independent line of appeal, is designed to protect the political impartiality and professional standards of all civil servants.

The number of civil servants fell from 732,000 in April 1979 to 520,000 in March 1995, reflecting the Government's policy of controlling the cost of the Civil Service and of improving its efficiency.

About half of all civil servants are engaged in the provision of public services. These include paying sickness benefits and pensions, collecting taxes and contributions, running employment services, staffing prisons, and providing services to industry and agriculture. A quarter are employed in the Ministry of Defence. The rest are divided between central administrative and policy duties; support services; and largely financially self-supporting services, for instance, those provided by the Department for National Savings and the Royal Mint. Four-fifths of civil servants work outside London.

Equality of Opportunity

The Government is committed to achieving equality of opportunity for all its staff. In support of this commitment, the Civil Service, which recruits and promotes on the basis of merit, is actively pursuing policies to develop career opportunities for women, ethnic minorities and people with disabilities:

● women now represent 51.3 per cent of all non-industrial civil servants, and since 1987 the proportion of women in the top three grades of the service has more than doubled to 9.3 per cent;

● representation of ethnic minority staff among non-industrial civil servants has increased from 5.2 per cent in 1993 to 5.3 per cent in 1994 and compares well with 4.9 per cent, which is the ethnic minority representation in the working population.

- 1.6 per cent of civil servants are registered as disabled, which is just above the proportion of registered disabled people in the workforce as a whole and twice the proportion employed in the private sector.

Progress is monitored and reported on regularly by the Cabinet Office (OPS).

Management Reforms

Civil Service reforms are being implemented to ensure improved management performance, in particular through the increased accountability of individual managers, based on clear objectives and responsibilities. These reforms include performance-related pay schemes and other incentives.

Executive Agencies: Next Steps Programme

The Next Steps Programme, launched in 1988, aims to deliver government services more efficiently and effectively within available resources for the benefit of taxpayers, customers and staff. This has involved setting up, as far as is practicable, separate units or agencies to perform the executive functions of government. Agencies remain part of the Civil Service but under the terms of individual framework documents they enjoy greater delegation of financial, pay and personnel matters. Agencies are headed by chief executives who are accountable to ministers but who are personally responsible for the day-to-day operations of the agency.

No agency can be established until the 'prior options' of abolition, privatisation and contracting out have been considered and ruled out. These 'prior options' are reconsidered when agencies are reviewed after three to three-and-a-half years of operation. The Government announced in its White Paper *The Civil Service: Continuity and Change* in July 1994 that the normal period between agency reviews would in future be five, rather than three, years.

By April 1995 over 100 agencies had been set up, together with 23 Executive Units of Customs and Excise and 29 Executive Offices of the Inland Revenue. Over 369,000 civil servants—66 per cent of the total—work in organisations run on Next Steps lines. In April 1995 a further 65 agency candidates— employing over 84,000 staff—had been identified as suitable for agency status.

In 1993–94 agencies met around 80 per cent of their key performance targets—a small improvement on the previous year because, in general, targets will have been made progressively tougher.

Competing for Quality

In 1991 the Government announced further proposals to extend competition and choice in the provision of public services. Value for money improvements in public expenditure are being sought through a range of techniques, including market testing the in-house operation against external competition and, where appropriate, contracting out. Between April 1992 and September 1994:

- £2,000 million worth of government services had been market tested or otherwise examined;

- annual savings of at least £410 million had been identified;

- £1,100 million of work had been awarded to external suppliers; and

- there had been a reduction of 26,900 posts in the areas reviewed; 10,600 staff had transferred to external suppliers; and 3,300 redundancies had been made, divided evenly between voluntary and compulsory.

Central Management and Structure

Responsibility for central co-ordination and management of the Civil Service is divided between the Cabinet Office (OPS) and the Treasury.

The OPS, which is under the control of the Prime Minister, as Minister for the Civil Service, oversees organisation, senior civil service pay, pensions and allowances, recruitment, retirement and redundancy policy, personnel management and statistics, and the overall efficiency of the Service.

Following the fundamental expenditure review of the Treasury's running costs during 1994 (see p. 159), that department's responsibilities for the effective and efficient management of the public sector have been narrowed down to the basic objective of maintaining a financial control system which delivers continuing improvements in the efficiency of government.

The function of official Head of the Home Civil Service is combined with that of Secretary of the Cabinet.

At the senior levels, where management forms a major part of most jobs, there are common grades throughout the Civil Service. These unified grades 1 to 7 are known as the Open Structure and cover grades from Permanent Secretary level to Principal level. Within the unified grades each post is filled by the person best qualified, regardless of the occupational group to which he or she previously belonged.

Below this the structure of the non-industrial Civil Service is based on a system of occupational groups. These groups assist the recruitment and matching of skills to posts and offer career paths in which specialist skills can be developed. Departments and agencies are being encouraged to develop their own pay and grading arrangements. They are expected to produce value-for-money benefits which are greater than those available through centrally controlled negotiation. From April 1996 all departments and agencies will take responsibility for implementing their own systems of pay and grading of staff below senior levels.

The Diplomatic Service

The Diplomatic Service, a separate service of some 6,000 people, provides the staff for the Foreign & Commonwealth Office (see p. 111) and for British diplomatic missions abroad.

The Diplomatic Service has its own grade structure, linked to that of the Home Civil Service. Terms and conditions of service are comparable, but take into account the special demands of the Service, particularly the requirement to serve abroad. Home civil servants, members of the armed forces and individuals from the private sector may also serve in the Foreign & Commonwealth Office and at overseas posts on loan or attachment.

Civil Service Recruitment

Recruitment is based on the principle of selection on merit by fair and open competition. Independent Civil Service Commissioners are responsible for approving the selection of people for appointment to Grade 5 and above. Recruitment of all other staff is the responsibility of departments and executive agencies. Departments and agencies can choose whether to undertake this recruitment work themselves, to employ a private sector recruitment agency or to use the Recruitment and Assessment Services Agency to recruit on their behalf.

People from outside the Civil Service may be recruited directly to all levels, particularly to posts requiring skills and experience more readily found in the private sector. The exchange of staff between the Civil Service and industry is also encouraged.

Since May 1995 departments and agencies have been required to publish information about their recruitment systems.

Training

Individual government departments and agencies are responsible for the performance of their own staff. They provide training and development to meet their business needs, to improve performance, and to help staff respond effectively to changing demands. Most training and development takes place within departments and agencies. In addition, the Civil Service College provides management and professional training, mainly for those who occupy, or hope to occupy, relatively senior positions. Considerable use is made of other providers in the private and public sectors.

Civil servants aged under 18 may continue their general education by attending courses, usually for one day a week ('day release' schemes). All staff may be entitled to financial support to continue their education, mainly in their own time. There are also opportunities for civil servants to undertake research and study in areas of interest to them and to their department or agency.

Promotion

Departments are responsible for promotion up to and including Grade 4. Promotion or appointment to Grades 1 and 2 and all transfers between departments at these levels are approved by the Prime Minister, who is advised by the Head of the Home Civil Service. Promotions and appointments to Grade 3 are approved by the Cabinet Office.

Political and Private Activities

Civil servants are required to perform loyally the duties assigned to them by the Government of the day, whatever its political persuasion. It is essential that ministers and the public should have confidence that the personal views of civil servants do not influence the performance of their official duties, given the role of the Civil Service in serving successive governments formed by different parties. The aim of the rules which govern political activities by civil servants is to allow them, subject to these fundamental principles, the greatest possible freedom to participate in public affairs consistent with their rights and duties as citizens. The rules are therefore concerned with activities liable to give public expression to political views rather than with privately held beliefs and opinions.

The Civil Service is divided into three groups for the purposes of deciding the extent to which individuals may take part in political activities:

- those in the 'politically free' group, consisting of industrial staff and non-office grades, are free to engage in any political activity outside official time, including adoption as a prospective candidate for the British or the European Parliament (although they would have to resign from the Service before giving their consent to nomination).

- those in the 'politically restricted' group, which comprises staff in Grade 7 and above as well as Administration Trainees and Higher Executive Officers (D), may not take part in national political activities but may apply for permission to take part in local political activities; and

- the 'intermediate' group, which comprises all other civil servants, may apply for permission to take part in national or local political activity, apart from candidature for the British or the European Parliament.

Where required, permission is granted to the maximum extent consistent with the Civil Service's reputation for political impartiality and the avoidance of any conflict with official duties. A code of discretion requires moderation and the avoidance of embarrassment to ministers

Generally, there are no restrictions on the private activities of civil servants, provided that these do not bring discredit on the Civil Service, and that there is no possibility of conflict with official duties. For instance, a civil servant must comply with any departmental instruction on the need to seek authority before taking part in any outside activity which involves official experience.

Security

Each department is responsible for its own internal security. As a general rule the privately-held political views of civil servants are not a matter of official concern. However, no one may be employed on work which is vital to the security of the State who is, or has been, involved in, or associated with, activities threatening national security. Certain posts are not open to people who fall into this category, or to anyone whose reliability may be in doubt for any other reason.

The Security Commission may investigate breaches of security in the public service and advise on changes in security procedure if requested to do so by the Prime Minister after consultation with the Leader of the Opposition.

Local Government

Although the origins of local government in England can be traced back to Saxon times, the first comprehensive system of local councils was established in the late 19th century.

Local Government Reform

A major reform of local government took place in 1974 in England and Wales and in 1975 in Scotland. This created two main tiers of local authority throughout England and Wales: counties and the smaller districts. Local government in London had been reorganised along the same lines in 1965. In Scotland functions were allocated to regions and districts on the mainland; single-tier authorities were introduced for the three Islands areas. In Northern Ireland changes were made in 1973 which replaced the two-tier county council and urban/rural council system with a single-tier district council system.

The Local Government Act 1985 abolished the Greater London Council and the six metropolitan county councils in England. Most of their functions were transferred to the London boroughs and metropolitan district councils respectively in 1986 (see below).

Local Government Commission

The Local Government Act 1992 made provision for the establishment of a Local Government Commission to review the structure, boundaries and electoral arrangements of local government in England. The Commission, set up in 1992, has reviewed the structure of local government in non-metropolitan England. The reviews considered whether the two-tier structure should be replaced by single-tier ('unitary') authorities in each area; for the most part the Commission recommended the retention of two-tier government, but suggested unitary authorities for some areas, especially the larger cities. Most of these recommendations have been accepted by the Secretary of State for the Environment. In some areas he has asked the Commission to conduct fresh reviews of individual districts. The first

changes, on the Isle of Wight, were implemented in April 1995. Other changes will follow in April 1996 and April 1997. The Commission will also be looking at the boundaries of metropolitan areas, probably starting in 1996. The Government is looking at ways of improving the internal management of local authorities.

Scotland and Wales

The Local Government etc. (Scotland) Act 1994 provides for 29 new unitary councils to replace the present system of nine regional and 53 district councils. The three islands councils will remain. The new authorities will take over in April 1996. In Wales, under the Local Government (Wales) Act 1994, 22 unitary authorities will replace the existing eight county councils and 37 district councils, again from April 1996. The first elections for the new councils took place in April 1995 for Scotland and May 1995 for Wales.

Local Authorities' Powers

Local authorities derive their power from legislation. Although local authorities are responsible for administering certain services, ministers have powers in some areas to secure a degree of uniformity in standards to safeguard public health or to protect the rights of individual citizens.

Relations with Central Government

The main link between local authorities and central government in England is the Department of the Environment. However, other departments such as the Department for Education and Employment and the Home Office are also concerned with various local government functions. In the rest of Britain the local authorities deal with the Scottish or Welsh Offices or the Department of the Environment for Northern Ireland, as appropriate.

Principal Types of Local Authority

Before the recent reforms, England outside Greater London was divided into counties, sub-divided into districts. All the districts and the non-metropolitan counties had locally elected councils with separate functions. County councils provided large-scale services such as education and social services, while district councils were responsible for the more local ones (see p. 74). These arrangements will broadly continue in areas where two-tier local government will remain.

Greater London is divided into 32 boroughs and the City of London, each of which has a council responsible for local government in its area. In the six metropolitan counties there are 36 district councils; there are no county councils. A number of services, however, require a statutory authority over areas wider than the individual boroughs and districts. These are:

- waste regulation and disposal (in certain areas);
- the fire services, including civil defence; and
- (outside London) public transport.

These are run by joint authorities composed of elected councillors nominated by the borough or district councils. Local councils also provide many of the members of the police authorities (see p. 83).

In addition to the two-tier local authority system in England, over 8,000 parish councils or meetings provide and manage local facilities such as allotments and village halls, and act as agents for other district council functions. They also provide a forum for discussion of local issues. In Wales over 700 community councils have similar functions, and provision is made for local community councils in Scotland.

The boundaries and electoral arrangements of local authorities in Wales and Scotland are kept under review by the Local Government Boundary Commissions for Wales and Scotland respectively. In 1992 the responsibilities of the former Local Government Boundary Commission for England passed to the Local Government Commission (see p. 72).

In Northern Ireland 26 district councils are responsible for local environmental and certain other services. Statutory bodies, such as the Northern Ireland Housing Executive and area boards, are responsible to central government departments for administering other major services (see p. 531).

Election of Councils

Local councils consist of elected councillors. Councillors are paid a basic allowance but may also be entitled to additional allowances and expenses for attending meetings or taking on special responsibilities. Parish and community councillors cannot claim allowances for duties undertaken within their own council areas. In Scotland community councillors are not eligible for any form of allowance.

In England and Wales each council elects its presiding officer annually. Some districts have the ceremonial title of borough, or city, both granted by royal authority. In boroughs and cities the presiding officer is normally known as the Mayor. In the City of London and certain other large cities, he or she is known as the Lord Mayor. In Scotland the presiding officer of the district council of each of the four cities is called the Lord Provost. In other councils he or she is known as a convenor or provost. District councils in Northern Ireland are presided over by mayors. In Wales the presiding officer of the new authorities is called chairman in the case of counties and mayor in the case of county boroughs.

Councillors are elected for four years. All county councils in England, London borough councils, and about two-thirds of non-metropolitan district councils are elected in their entirety every four years. In the remaining districts (including all metropolitan districts) one-third of the councillors are elected in each of the three years when county council elections are not held. Where new unitary authorities are to be set up in England, Parliamentary Orders make the necessary provisions regarding elections. In Scotland local elections will now be held every three years, with the next elections due in 1999. Each election covers the whole council. In Wales elections will continue to be held every four years, again with the next due in 1999.

Voters

Anyone may vote at a local government election in Britain provided he or she is:

- aged 18 years or over;
- a citizen of Britain or of another Commonwealth country, or of the Irish Republic, or (from 1996) a citizen of the European Union;
- not legally disqualified; and
- on the electoral register.

To qualify for registration a person must be resident in the council area on the qualifying date. In Northern Ireland there are slightly different requirements.

Candidates

Most candidates at local government elections stand as representatives of a national political party, although some stand as independents. Candidates must be British citizens, other Commonwealth citizens or citizens of the European Union, and aged 21 or over. In addition, they must either:

- be registered as local electors in the area of the relevant local authority; or
- have occupied (as owner or tenant) land or premises in that area during the whole of the preceding 12 months; or
- have had their main place of work in the area throughout this 12-month period.

No one may be elected to a council of which he or she is an employee, and there are some other disqualifications. All candidates for district council elections in Northern Ireland are required to make a declaration against terrorism.

Electoral Divisions and Procedure

Counties in England are divided into electoral divisions, each returning one councillor. Districts in England and Northern Ireland are divided into wards, returning one councillor or more. In Scotland the electoral areas in the new councils are called wards and in Wales they are called electoral divisions; each returns one or more councillors. Parishes (in England) and communities (in Wales) may be divided into wards. Wards return at least one councillor. The minimum parish/community council size is five councillors.

The procedure for local government voting in Great Britain is broadly similar to that for parliamentary elections. In Northern Ireland local government elections are held by proportional representation, and electoral wards are grouped into district electoral areas.

Council Functions and Services

At present in England county councils are responsible for strategic planning, transport planning, highways, traffic regulation, education,[10] consumer protection, refuse disposal, police,[11] the fire service, libraries and the personal social services. District councils are responsible for services such as environmental health, housing, decisions on most local planning applications, and refuse collection. Both tiers of local authority have powers to provide facilities such as museums, art galleries and parks; arrangements depend on local agreement. Where unitary authorities are created in non-metropolitan areas, they will be responsible for both county and district level functions.

In the metropolitan counties the district councils are responsible for all services apart from the police, the fire service and public transport and, in some areas, waste regulation and disposal (see p. 367). In Greater London the boroughs and the Corporation of the City of London have similar functions, but London's metropolitan police force is responsible to the Home Secretary. Responsibility for public transport lies with London Transport (see p. 298).

In Wales the division of responsibilities between districts and counties is broadly the same as in England up to April 1996, when the new unitary councils will take over.

In mainland Scotland the functions of regional and district authorities are at present divided up in a broadly similar way to the

---

[10] Schools may, however, 'opt out' of local education authority control by obtaining grant-maintained status—see p. 428.
[11] In many areas, police forces cover more than one county, and in these cases a joint board is set up to act as police authority.

The 1946 Victory Parade:
members of the
Women's Land Army
pass the saluting base.

On a Welsh hill farm the
tenant farmer begins
spring planting (1951).

50 YEARS OF PHOTOGRAPHS AT COI

The 1950s were marked by emigration and immigration to and from Commonwealth countries. Emigration reached 87,000 in 1952 and peaked again in 1956-57, when there was a surge in emigration to Canada; the total gross figure for that period is estimated at about 230,000, with immigration in the same year thought to be at least as high.

West Indian immigrants arriving in Britain.

Emigrants on the deck of a ship at Southampton, bound for Australia.

The coronation of Queen Elizabeth II at Westminster Abbey on 2 June 1953.

1963: the Beatles take the music world by storm.

50 YEARS OF PHOTOGRAPHS AT COI

Britain joins the European Community in 1973, under the premiership of Edward Heath.

Jayne Torvill and Christopher Dean skate to Ravel's *Bolero* in the 1984 Winter Olympics in Sarajevo, former Yugoslavia, where they won a gold medal.

counties and districts in England and Wales. As in Wales, new unitary councils come into being in April 1996, taking over all local government functions.

In Northern Ireland local environmental and certain other services, such as leisure and the arts, are administered by the district councils. Responsibility for planning, roads, water supply and sewerage services is exercised in each district through a divisional office of the Department of the Environment for Northern Ireland. Area boards, responsible to central departments, administer education, public libraries and the health and personal social services locally. The Northern Ireland Housing Executive, responsible to the Department of the Environment for Northern Ireland, administers housing.

Changes in Local Government

There have been numerous changes in recent years in the way that local authorities approach their responsibilities. Many of these can be encapsulated under the term 'the enabling authority'. It is used to describe the general shift away from local authorities providing services directly and towards them arranging for services to be provided, or carrying out functions in partnership with other bodies. For example, councils often have nomination rights to housing association properties (see p. 341), so that they are acting not as provider but as 'gatekeeper'. Likewise, under the community care reforms, councils with social services responsibilities draw up care plans for those who need them (see p. 407), but the care is often provided by the private or voluntary sectors funded by the council, rather than directly by the local authority itself.

Internal Organisation of Local Authorities

Local authorities have considerable freedom to make arrangements for carrying out their duties; these are set out in standing orders. Some decisions are made by the full council; many other matters are delegated to committees composed of members of the council. A council may delegate most functions to a committee or officer, although certain powers are legally reserved to the council as a whole. The powers and duties of local authority committees are usually laid down in the terms of reference. Parish and community councils in England and Wales are often able to do their work in full session, although they appoint committees from time to time as necessary.

In England and Wales committees generally have to reflect the political composition of the council (although the legislation governing this specifically excludes parish or community councils). In practice, this is often also the case in Scotland, although it is not enforced by legislation. People who are not members of the council may be co-opted onto decision-making committees and can speak and take part in debates; they cannot normally vote. Legislation also prevents senior officers and others in politically sensitive posts from being members of another local authority or undertaking public political activity. Some of these provisions have not been introduced in Northern Ireland.

Public Access

The public (including the press) are admitted to council, committee and sub-committee meetings, and have access to agendas, reports and minutes of meetings and certain background papers. Local authorities may exclude the public from meetings and withhold these papers only in limited circumstances.

Employees

About 1.4 million people[12] are employed by local authorities in England. These include administrative, professional and technical staff, teachers, firefighters, and manual workers, but exclude those in law and order services. Education is the largest service, employing some 40 per cent of all local government workers. Councils are individually responsible, within certain national legislative requirements, for deciding the structure of their workforces.

---

[12]Whole-time equivalents.

Senior staff appointments are usually made by the elected councillors. More junior appointments are made by heads of departments. Pay and conditions of service are usually a matter for each council, although there are scales recommended by national negotiating machinery between authorities and trade unions, and most authorities follow these.

Authorities differ in the degree to which they employ their own permanent staff to carry out certain functions or use private firms under contract. The Government's policy of promoting value for money is encouraging the use of private firms where savings can be made. Many local government functions, such as refuse collection and leisure management, must be put out to tender ('compulsory competitive tendering'—CCT), although the local authority's own workforce can put up an in-house bid. Between 1989 and 1992, CCT achieved average cost savings of 6 to 7 per cent. CCT is currently being extended to local authorities' provision of a range of professional services. The metropolitan districts and London boroughs will need to have new arrangements in place during 1996–97 for most of these services.

Local Authority Finance

Local government expenditure accounts for about 25 per cent of public spending. The Government has sought to influence local government spending as part of a general policy of controlling the growth of public expenditure. Since 1984 the Government has had powers to limit or 'cap' local authority budgets (local authority taxation in Scotland) by setting a maximum amount for local authorities which have, in its view, set budgets which are excessive.

In 1994–95 expenditure by local authorities in Britain was about £73,300 million. Current expenditure amounted to £62,100 million; capital expenditure, net of capital receipts, was £6,900 million; and debt interest £4,300 million. Local government capital expenditure is financed primarily by borrowing within limits set by central government and from capital receipts from the disposal of land and buildings.

Local authorities in Great Britain raise revenue through the council tax, which replaced the community charge system in April 1993 (see p. 166). However, their revenue spending is financed primarily by grants from central government and by the redistribution of revenue from the national non-domestic rate, a property tax levied on businesses and other non-domestic properties.

District councils in Northern Ireland continue to raise revenue through the levying of a domestic rate.

Financial Safeguards

Local councils' annual accounts must be audited by independent auditors appointed by the Audit Commission in England and Wales, or by the Commission for Local Authority Accounts in Scotland. In Northern Ireland this role is exercised by the chief local government auditor, who is appointed by the Department of the Environment for Northern Ireland.

Local Government Complaints System

Local authorities are encouraged to resolve complaints through internal mechanisms, and members of the public will often ask their own councillor for assistance in this. Local authorities must also appoint a monitoring officer, whose duties include ensuring that the local authority acts lawfully in the conduct of its business.

Allegations of local government maladministration may be investigated by statutory independent Commissioners for Local Administration, often known as 'local government ombudsmen'. There are three of these in England, and one each in Wales and Scotland. A report is issued on each complaint fully investigated and, if injustice caused by maladministration is found, the local ombudsman normally proposes a remedy. The council must consider the report and reply to it.

An independent review of the local government ombudsman service began in July 1995.

In Northern Ireland a Commissioner for Complaints deals with complaints alleging injustices suffered as a result of maladministration by district councils and certain other public bodies.

Pressure Groups

Pressure groups are informal organisations which aim to influence Parliament and Government in the way decisions are made and carried out, to the benefit of their members and the causes they support. There is a huge range, covering politics, business, employment, consumer affairs, ethnic minorities, aid to developing countries, foreign relations, education, culture, defence, religion, sport, transport, social welfare, animal welfare and the environment. Some have over a million members, others only a few dozen. Some exert pressure on a number of different issues; others are concerned with a single issue. Some have come to play a recognised role in the way Britain is governed; others seek influence through radical protest.

While political parties seek to win political power, pressure groups aim to influence those who are in power, rather than to exercise the responsibility of government and to legislate.

Pressure Groups and Policy

Pressure groups operating at a national level have a number of methods for influencing the way Britain is governed. Action by them may highlight a particular problem, which is then acknowledged by the Government. Groups whose scale of membership indicates that they are broadly representative in their field may then be consulted by a government department, or take part in Whitehall working groups or advisory councils. If the Government considers that legislation is necessary, then proposals are drafted, which are circulated to interested groups for their comments. Legislation is then put before Parliament, and at various times during the passage of a Bill— especially at the committee stage—pressure groups have opportunities to influence its content. If the Act includes delegated legislation (see p. 57), pressure groups may be consulted and have the opportunity to provide information and express their views.

Pressure Groups and Government

The principle of consultation to gain the consent and co-operation of as wide a range of organisations as possible, and to ensure the smooth working of laws and regulations, plays an important part in the relationship between government departments and interested groups.

In some instances a department is under legal obligation to consult interested groups. The Government has a duty to consult organised interests, providing the pressure groups involved have a broad enough membership for them to represent a majority view, and that they observe confidentiality about their discussions with the department. Members of pressure groups have direct expertise, and an awareness of what is practicable, and can give advice and information to civil servants engaged in preparing policy or legislation. In return, the pressure groups have the opportunity to express their opinions directly to the Government. The contacts between civil servants and pressure group representatives may be relatively informal— by letter or telephone—or more formal, through involvement in working parties or by giving evidence to committees of inquiry.

Administration by Pressure Groups

As well as providing information and opinions, pressure groups can also be involved in administering government policy. The Law Society—the representative body for solicitors— administered the Government's Legal Aid scheme until that function was taken over in 1989 by the Legal Aid Board (see p. 106). The Government also makes grants to pressure groups which, as well as speaking on behalf of their members or for an issue, also provide a service. Relate: National Marriage Guidance has received grants for the advice centres it runs, and government departments make grants to a number of pressure groups for research relating to public policy.

Pressure Groups and Parliament

Lobbying—the practice of approaching MPs or Lords, persuading them to act on behalf of a cause, and enabling them to do so by providing advice and information—is a form of pressure group activity which has increased substantially in recent years.

A common pressure group tactic is to ask members of the public to write to their MP about an issue—for example, the Sunday trading laws, or the plight of political prisoners in particular countries—in order to raise awareness and persuade the MP to support the cause.

Raising Issues in Parliament

Other ways through which pressure groups may exert influence include:

- suggesting to MPs or Lords subjects for Private Members' Bills (see p. 55); many pressure groups have ready-drafted legislation waiting to be sponsored;

- approaching MPs or Lords to ask parliamentary questions as a means of gaining information from the Government and of drawing public attention to an issue;

- suggesting to MPs subjects for Early Day Motions (see p. 59); and

- orchestrating public petitions as a form of protest against government policy, or to call for action. If the petition is to be presented in Parliament, it must be worded according to Commons or Lords rules, and be presented by an MP or Lord in his or her own House.

Parliamentary Lobbyists

Many pressure groups employ full-time parliamentary workers or liaison officers, whose job is to develop contacts with MPs and Lords sympathetic to their cause, and to brief them when issues affecting the group are raised in Parliament.

There are also public relations and political consultancy firms specialising in lobbying Parliament and Government. Such firms are employed by pressure groups—as well as by British and overseas companies and organisations—to monitor parliamentary business, and to promote their clients' interests where they are affected by legislation and debate.

Further Reading

The British System of Government. Aspects of Britain series, HMSO, 1994.

The Civil Service. Aspects of Britain series, HMSO, 1995.

The Civil Service: Taking Forward Continuity and Change. Cm 2748, HMSO, 1995.

History and Function of Government Departments. Aspects of Britain series, HMSO, 1993.

Open Government. Cm 2290, HMSO, 1993.

Organisation of Political Parties. Aspects of Britain series, HMSO, 1994.

Parliament. Aspects of Britain series, HMSO, 1994.

Parliamentary Elections. Aspects of Britain series, HMSO, 1995.

Pressure Groups. Aspects of Britain series, HMSO, 1994.

Renewing Local Government in the English Shires: A Final Report on the 1992–95 Structural Review. Local Government Commission, HMSO, 1995.

8 Justice and the Law

A new independent Criminal Cases Review Commission will investigate the safety of criminal convictions in England, Wales and Northern Ireland following the enactment of the Criminal Appeal Act in July 1995.

In Scotland the Criminal Justice (Scotland) Act, which also received the Royal Assent in July 1995, will reinforce the powers available to crack down on crime and reduce offending. The bulk of the Act's provisions are being implemented on 1 April 1996.

England and Wales, Scotland, and Northern Ireland all have their own legal systems, with considerable differences in law, organisation and practice. All three have separate prosecution, prison and police services. Crime prevention policy and non-custodial treatment for offenders are similar throughout Britain. There are different civil court and civil law systems in England and Wales and in Scotland; Northern Ireland's system is in many ways similar to the English and Welsh model.

Common Law and Statute Law

One of the main sources of law in England and Wales and in Northern Ireland is common law, which has evolved over centuries from judges' decisions. It forms the basis of the law except when superseded by legislation. In Scotland, too, the doctrine of legal precedent has been more strictly applied since the end of the 18th century.

Much of the law, particularly that relating to criminal justice, is statute law passed by Parliament. If a court reaches a decision which is contrary to the intentions of Parliament, then Parliament must either accept the decision or pass amending legislation. Some Acts create new law, while others are passed to draw together existing law on a given topic. Parliament can repeal a statute and replace it with another.

European Community Law

European Community law, deriving from Britain's membership of the European Union, is confined mainly to economic and social matters; in certain circumstances it takes precedence over domestic law. It is normally applied by the domestic courts, but the most authoritative rulings are given by the European Court of Justice (see p. 114).

Certain changes to United Kingdom law have been made to bring it into line with rulings of the European Court of Human Rights (see p. 129).

Branches of the Law

There are two main branches of the law—criminal and civil. Criminal law is concerned with acts punishable by the State. Civil law covers:

● disputes between individuals about their rights, duties and obligations; and

● dealings between individuals and companies, and between one company and another.

Criminal Justice

Crime Statistics

Differences in the legal systems, police recording practices and statistical classifications make it impracticable to analyse in detail trends in crime for Britain as a whole. Nevertheless, there has, as in Western Europe generally, been a substantial increase in crime since the early 1950s. Annual official statistics cover crime recorded by the police and can be affected by changes in unreported crime.

Recorded crimes in England and Wales in 1994 are detailed in Table 8.1. In 1994 the Scottish police recorded 527,064 crimes, of which 195,745 were cleared up. In Northern Ireland, of the 67,886 recorded crimes in 1994, 24,342 were cleared up.

Most crime is committed by young males, is opportunist and is not planned by hardened professional criminals, although these do exist.

Crime tends to be concentrated in large cities and urban areas. About 93 per cent of offences recorded by the police in England and Wales are directed against property but only 6 per cent involve violence. Rising affluence has provided more opportunities for casual property crime. In 1957, for example, car crime was only one-tenth of total crime but this has risen to about 28 per cent. The demand for, and supply of, illegal drugs has been an increasing factor in the incidence of crime in recent years.

Regular crime surveys are undertaken in England and Wales and in Scotland. These indicate that many crimes go unrecorded by the police, mainly because not all victims report what has happened to them. The surveys confirm that the majority of crimes are against property, in the form of theft and vandalism.

Crime Prevention

National publicity campaigns are a regular feature of the Government's crime prevention programmes. The Home Office provides support to the police effort through its Crime Prevention Centre, which offers training and advice, and promotes best practice. Other government departments are brought together with the Home Office to formulate prevention strategies.

Crime Concern, a national independent organisation, encourages local initiatives and business participation in crime prevention.

Local crime prevention panels (including mainly school-based youth panels) assist the

Table 8.1: Notifiable Crimes Recorded by the Police in England and Wales 1994

Offence Group	Recorded crimes	Crimes cleared up	Per cent
Violence against the person	219,270	169,361	77
Sexual offences	32,494	24,882	77
Burglary	1,257,960	268,393	21
Robbery	59,771	13,032	22
Theft and handling stolen goods	2,559,023	604,863	24
Fraud and forgery	145,845	75,525	52
Criminal damage[a]	708,070	119,944	17
Other	48,569	45,717	94
Total	5,031,002	1,321,718	26

Source: Home Office.
[a]Excludes criminal damage of £20 or under.

police in preventing crime through publicity, marking goods and equipment, and fund-raising to buy security devices.

A major initiative promoting co-operation between the public and the police—Partners Against Crime—was launched by the Government in September 1994. It is based on a three-tier approach:

1. Neighbourhood Watch schemes, of which there are 142,000 in England and Wales covering over 5 million households (and also 3,600 schemes in Scotland);

2. Street Watch, in which local people, in agreement with the police, work out specific routes and regularly walk the chosen area; and

3. The Neighbourhood Constable scheme, which is a variation of the existing special constabulary (see p. 83). Neighbourhood constables have the same status, powers and training as special constables, but they work in their own neighbourhood.

In 1994 the Home Office issued a booklet on best practice in the use of closed-circuit television (CCTV) for the prevention and investigation of crime; the Government has actively encouraged the setting up of CCTV schemes across the country.

The Safer Cities Programme tackles crime and the fear of crime in inner city and urban areas in England through joint crime prevention action by local government, private businesses, the police and voluntary agencies. Twenty locally-based projects had, by October 1994, supported 3,600 schemes with funding of over £22 million. The second phase of the programme has seen the establishment of 32 new projects, including some in Wales.

There is a Safer Cities programme in Scotland, and similar projects are being funded by the Government in Northern Ireland.

The National Board for Crime Prevention advises the Government about ways of involving all sections of the community in the development and delivery of crime prevention in England and Wales. There is also a Scottish Crime Prevention Council and a Northern Ireland Crime Prevention Panel.

Helping the Victim

The Government has emphasised the importance of victims' interests within the criminal justice system.

There are some 365 victim support schemes —with some 12,000 volunteer visitors, covering the whole of England and Wales— providing practical help and emotional support to victims of crime. They are co-ordinated by a national organisation, Victim Support, which receives a government grant (£10.8 million in 1995–96). Similar schemes operate in Scotland and Northern Ireland.

In England and Wales the Witness Service, run by Victim Support with Home Office funding, provides support for victims and witnesses attending the Crown Court. About 55 witness schemes have been set up to help victims through the stress of giving evidence; the Witness Service is being extended to all 78 main Crown Court centres by the end of 1995.

A new offence of witness intimidation was introduced by the Criminal Justice and Public Order Act 1994 to protect victims who are also witnesses. The same legislation provides for the abolition of committal proceedings (see p. 90), so that victims no longer have to give evidence and be cross-examined twice over.

The Government accepted all the recommendations made by the Royal Commission on Criminal Justice in 1993 on help for the victims of crime, such as giving them better information about the progress of investigations or court proceedings and improving facilities for them at court. Most of these have now been implemented, and the 50 standards of treatment set out in the Victims' Charter (published by the Government in 1990) have been or are well on the way to being met (see also Courts Charter—p. 90).

In September 1994 the Government announced that reports prepared on offenders before sentencing would include a section about the effects of the crime on the victim (see p. 93).

Blameless victims of violent crime in England, Wales and Scotland, including foreign nationals, may be eligible for compensation from public funds. In 1994–95 £170 million was paid out under the Criminal Injuries Compensation Scheme. In Northern Ireland there are separate statutory arrangements for compensation for criminal injuries, and for malicious damage to property, including any resulting loss of profits.

Strengthening the Law

Important measures to strengthen the criminal justice system have been taken in recent years. The courts, for instance, have powers to trace, freeze and confiscate the proceeds of drug trafficking. A court can require an offender to pay an amount equal to the full value of the proceeds arising from the trafficking. Following a conviction, the onus is on the offender to prove that property does not represent the proceeds of trafficking. Offenders may not opt to serve a period of imprisonment in default of paying a confiscation order. Restraint and confiscation orders made by courts can be enforced against assets held overseas, and vice versa, if a bilateral confiscation agreement has been made between Britain and another state.

A court in England, Wales and Northern Ireland may also confiscate the proceeds of offences such as robbery, fraud, blackmail and insider dealing in shares. These powers are being strengthened under the provisions in the Proceeds of Crime Act 1995. The Criminal Justice (Scotland) Act 1995 introduces powers for the courts in Scotland to order confiscation of the proceeds of general crime and widens their powers for ordering forfeiture.

New powers to clamp down on money launderers[1] came into force in 1994, with heavy penalties for those who launder money gained from any sort of serious crime.

There are strict legislative controls on firearms. The police license the possession of firearms and have powers to regulate their

safekeeping and movement. The private ownership of certain highly dangerous types of weapon, such as machine guns, high-powered self-loading rifles and burst-fire weapons, is banned.

It is unlawful to manufacture, sell or import certain weapons such as knuckledusters or to carry a knife in a public place without good reason.

The Criminal Justice Act 1991 made a number of reforms to the criminal law in England and Wales, mainly concerning sentencing and the system for early release of prisoners (see p. 98). Similar reforms in Scotland took effect from October 1993.

The Police and Magistrates' Courts Act 1994 and the Criminal Justice and Public Order Act 1994 (mainly applicable in England and Wales, but also to some extent in Scotland) are designed to improve the organisation and management of the police, so that they are better able to combat crime, and to tilt the balance of the criminal justice system further against criminals.

The Criminal Justice (Scotland) Act 1995 increases the capacity of the criminal justice system in Scotland to deal with offenders, and increases the powers available to prevent crime and reduce re-offending.

Measures to Combat Terrorism

Certain special powers are available to help in preventing and investigating terrorist crime. The powers take account of the need to maintain a proper balance between the safety of the public and the rights of the individual. They must be renewed by Parliament each year and the use of the powers is reviewed annually by an independent person.

The Prevention of Terrorism (Temporary Provisions) Act 1989 applies throughout Britain. It makes it unlawful to support specified organisations involved in terrorism connected with the affairs of Northern Ireland, and enables the Government to exclude from all or part of Britain people who are believed to be involved in such terrorism. The legislation also gives the police wider powers to deal with suspected terrorists, including international terrorists, than are available under the general criminal

---

[1] Money laundering is the process by which illegally obtained property—from drugs or arms trafficking, terrorist activities or other serious crimes—is given the appearance of having originated from a legitimate source.

law. For example, the police may arrest terrorist suspects without warrant and hold them for up to 48 hours, and ministerial approval may be sought to extend detention for up to a further five days.

The legislation contains strong powers to deal with those who provide financial support for terrorism, or who launder terrorist funds, including powers to order the restraint or forfeiture of terrorist funds.

The Criminal Justice and Public Order Act 1994 gives the police new powers to stop and search for articles which may be used for terrorist purposes, and has created a new offence of possession of such articles.

Northern Ireland

The security forces in Northern Ireland have special powers to search, question and arrest under the Northern Ireland (Emergency Provisions) Act 1991. A person who is detained under emergency provisions is entitled to consult a solicitor privately.

The ceasefires declared by the paramilitary groupings in Northern Ireland in 1994 (see p. 14) have led to a new security situation, but the Government does not think it would be prudent to remove the protection of the emergency legislation from the statute book while illegal weaponry and explosives are still at large.

THE POLICE SERVICE

The Home Secretary and the Scottish and Northern Ireland Secretaries, together with police authorities and chief constables, are responsible for the provision of an effective and efficient police service in Britain.

Organisation

There are 52 police forces in Britain, mainly organised on a local basis: 43 in England and Wales, eight in Scotland and one (the Royal Ulster Constabulary) in Northern Ireland. The Metropolitan Police Force and the City of London force are responsible for policing London. The police service is financed by central and local government.

At the end of 1994 police strength in Britain was about 150,000, of which the Metropolitan Police numbered over 28,000. The establishment of the Royal Ulster Constabulary was around 8,500. Police strength in Scotland was about 14,300. Each force has volunteer special constables who perform police duties in their spare time, without pay, acting in support of regular officers. The Government is aiming to recruit a further 10,000 special constables by the end of 1996, so increasing the overall number by 50 per cent. In Northern Ireland there is a 5,000-strong part-time and full-time paid reserve.

Police forces are maintained in England and Wales by local police authorities (see below). The Home Secretary is responsible for London's Metropolitan Police Force. The police authorities in Scotland are the regional and islands councils, although new unitary councils will assume this role in April 1996. In Northern Ireland the police force is responsible to a police authority appointed by the Secretary of State for Northern Ireland.

Provincial forces are headed by chief constables. They are generally answerable to the police authorities for their force's competence, efficiency and conduct. The police authorities appoint the chief constable and assistant chief constable. They also fix the maximum strength of the force, and provide buildings and equipment.

London's Metropolitan Police Commissioner and immediate subordinates are appointed on the recommendation of the Home Secretary.

Police forces are inspected by independent inspectors of constabulary, whose reports to central government are published.

Police officers are not allowed to join a trade union or to go on strike. All ranks, however, have their own staff associations.

Reforms

The Police and Magistrates' Courts Act 1994 is designed to change the relationship between central government, police authorities and chief constables—to improve the management of the police and to reduce cumbersome central controls, devolving more power and decision-making to the local level.

The legislation provides for the appointment of independent members to police authorities in England and Wales outside London, in addition to local councillors and magistrates. The standard size of a police authority is set at 17 members, comprising nine locally elected councillors, three magistrates and five independent members. The Home Secretary may increase the size of a police authority beyond 17 if local circumstances make it desirable. The independent members are chosen by the other members of the police authority, from a list of ten names forwarded by the Home Secretary from a shortlist of 20 prepared by a local selection panel. A 12-member Metropolitan Police Committee assists the Home Secretary, who acts as police authority for the Metropolitan Police.

Police authorities in Scotland continue to be composed of elected councillors.

Other main provisions of the legislation include:

- setting key objectives for the police which give priority to fighting crime and protecting the public;

- placing a greater emphasis on community needs through local policing plans;

- strengthening the role of the Inspectorate of Constabulary, which has assumed a statutory responsibility to inspect the Metropolitan Police;

- ending detailed government controls on finance and manpower by giving chief constables freedom to manage police and civilian staff and to determine staff numbers; and

- introducing fixed-term appointments for senior police officers and abolishing the ranks of deputy chief constable and chief superintendent.

The duties of the police in Scotland have been set out in statute for many years.

Co-ordination of Police Operations

Certain police services are provided centrally either by the Government or through co-operation between forces. In England and Wales these include criminal intelligence, telecommunications, and research and development. In Scotland the main common services are centralised police training, the Scottish Crime Squad and the Scottish Criminal Record Office.

The National Criminal Intelligence Service, with a headquarters in London and five regional offices, co-ordinates and provides information to the police and HM Customs about major criminals and organised crime, including drug trafficking. The Service also liaises with the International Criminal Police Organisation (INTERPOL), which promotes international co-operation between police forces.

Britain has taken the lead in developing, with other European Union countries, a European police organisation (EUROPOL) designed to provide Union-wide intelligence about serious crime (see p. 130).

All British police forces have fraud squads responsible for investigating financial and commercial fraud.

Six regional crime squads in England and Wales deal with serious crime which goes beyond individual force, regional or national boundaries.

The Police National Computer provides all British police forces with rapid 24-hour-a-day access to operationally essential information. Phoenix—the Criminal Justice Record Service—is being implemented on the Police National Computer, and will give the police direct on-screen access to national records of arrests, bail decisions and convictions. This will gradually replace the manual record-keeping service currently operated by the National Identification Bureau (NIB), which is located at Metropolitan Police headquarters but financed by all police forces. Phoenix will eventually provide information direct to other agencies such as the courts, the Prison Service and the Crown Prosecution Service.

The Police National Network, a new communications network providing the full range of telecommunications services to forces throughout Britain, was officially opened in November 1994.

Scottish criminal records are held on computer at the Scottish Criminal Record

Office, which has an automatic national fingerprint record system; the initial implementation of a similar national system in England and Wales is planned for 1997–98.

The Police National Missing Persons Bureau, which comes under the NIB, is the first national database of missing people, holding information which all forces and international agencies can share.

Firearms

Officers in Great Britain do not normally carry firearms, although in an emergency they can be issued on the authority of a senior officer. Officers in armoured response vehicles in London can wear their sidearms in holsters at all times. In Northern Ireland police officers are issued with firearms for personal protection and other firearms are available for duty purposes.

Forensic Science Service

The Forensic Science Service (FSS) serves the administration of justice in England and Wales by providing scientific support in the investigation of crime, and by giving evidence to the courts. Its customers include the police, the Crown Prosecution Service (see p. 89), coroners and defence solicitors.

In February 1995 the Government announced that the FSS would merge with the Metropolitan Police Forensic Science Laboratory with effect from April 1996 to form a single agency serving all police forces in England and Wales through seven regional operational laboratories.

In Scotland forensic science services are provided by forces' own laboratories. Northern Ireland has its own forensic science laboratory.

Police Discipline

A police officer may be prosecuted if suspected of a criminal offence. Officers are also subject to a disciplinary code designed to deal with abuse of police powers and maintain public confidence in police impartiality. If found guilty of breaching the code, an officer can be dismissed from the force.

Revised disciplinary procedures for the police in Great Britain, similar to those in operation elsewhere in the public service, are being introduced. These provide for a more flexible system with greater line management involvement, the introduction of unsatisfactory performance procedures and changes in the appeals procedures which no longer involve the Home Secretary.

Members of the public have the right to make complaints against police officers if they feel that they have been treated unfairly or improperly. In England and Wales the investigation and resolution of complaints is scrutinised by the independent Police Complaints Authority. In Scotland complaints against police officers involving allegations of any form of criminal conduct are referred to the procurator fiscal for investigation (see p. 89). The Police and Magistrates' Courts Act 1994 empowers the Scottish Inspectorate of Constabulary to consider representations from complainants dissatisfied with the way the police have handled their complaints.

In Northern Ireland the Independent Commission for Police Complaints is required to supervise the investigation of a complaint regarding death or serious injury and has the power to supervise that of any other complaint. In certain circumstances, the Secretary of State may direct the Commission to supervise the investigation of matters that are not the subject of a formal complaint.

Community Relations

Police/community liaison consultative groups operate in every police authority; they consist of representatives from the police, local councillors and community groups.

Particular efforts are made to develop relations with young people through greater contact with schools. School governing bodies and head teachers have to describe in their annual reports the steps taken to strengthen their schools' links with the community, including the police.

The Government is committed to improving relations between the police and ethnic minorities. Central guidance recommends that all police officers should receive thorough training in community and race relations issues. Home Office and police service initiatives are designed to tackle racially motivated crime and to ensure that the issue is treated as a police priority. Forces' responses to racial incidents are monitored by the Inspectorate of Constabulary. Discriminatory behaviour by police officers, either to other officers or to members of the public, is an offence under the Police Discipline Code.

All police forces recognise the need to recruit women and members of the ethnic minorities in order to ensure that the police represent the community. At the end of 1993 there were 1,730 ethnic minority officers and 16,750 women police officers in England and Wales. Scottish police forces had 1,680 women officers. Every force has an equal opportunities policy.

Police Powers

The powers of a police officer in England and Wales to stop and search, arrest and place a person under detention are contained in the Police and Criminal Evidence Act 1984. The legislation and its accompanying codes of practice set out the powers and responsibilities of officers in the investigation of offences, and the rights of citizens.

An officer is liable to disciplinary proceedings if he or she fails to comply with any provision of the codes, and evidence obtained in breach of the codes may be ruled inadmissible in court. The codes must be readily available in all police stations for consultation by police officers, detained people and members of the public.

Stop and Search

A police officer in England and Wales has the power to stop and search people and vehicles if there are reasonable grounds for suspecting that he or she will find stolen goods, offensive weapons or implements that could be used for theft, burglary and other offences. The officer must, however, state and record the grounds for taking this action and what, if anything, was found.

The Criminal Justice and Public Order Act 1994 enables a senior police officer to authorise uniformed officers to stop and search people or vehicles for offensive weapons or dangerous implements where he or she has reasonable grounds for believing that serious incidents of violence may take place. The officer must specify the time scale and area in which the powers are to be exercised.

Arrest

In England and Wales the police have wide powers to arrest people suspected of having committed an offence with or without a warrant issued by a court. For serious offences, known as 'arrestable offences', a suspect can be arrested without a warrant. Arrestable offences are those for which five or more years' imprisonment can be imposed. This category also includes 'serious arrestable offences' such as murder, rape and kidnapping.

There is also a general arrest power for all other offences if it is impracticable or inappropriate to proceed by way of summons to appear in court, or if a police officer has reasonable grounds for believing that arrest is necessary to prevent the person concerned from causing injury to any other person or damage to property.

Detention, Treatment and Questioning

An arrested person must be taken to a police station (if he or she is not already at one) as soon as practicable after arrest. The suspect has a right to speak to an independent solicitor free of charge and to have a relative or other named person told of his or her arrest. Where a person has been arrested in connection with a serious arrestable offence, but has not yet been charged, the police in England and Wales may delay the exercise of these rights for up to 36 hours in the interests of the investigation if certain strict criteria are met.

A suspect may refuse to answer police questions or to give evidence in court. Changes to this so-called 'right to silence' have been made by the Criminal Justice and Public Order Act 1994 to allow courts in

England and Wales to draw inferences from a defendant's refusal to answer police questions or to give information during his or her trial. Reflecting this change in the law, a new form of police caution (which must precede any questions to a suspect for the purpose of obtaining evidence) is intended to ensure that people understand the possible consequences if they answer questions or stay silent.

Questions relating to an offence may not normally be put to a person after he or she has been charged with that offence or informed that he or she may be prosecuted for it.

The length of time a suspect is held in police custody before charge is strictly regulated. For lesser offences this may not exceed 24 hours. A person suspected of committing a serious arrestable offence can be detained for up to 96 hours without charge but beyond 36 hours only if a warrant is obtained from a magistrates' court. Reviews must be made of a person's detention at regular intervals—six hours after initial detention and thereafter every nine hours as a maximum—to check whether the criteria for detention are still satisfied. If they are not, the person must be released immediately.

The tape recording of interviews with suspected offenders at police stations must be used when the police are investigating indictable offences and in certain other cases. The police are not precluded from taping interviews for other types of offences. The taping of interviews is regulated by a code of practice approved by Parliament, and the suspect is entitled to a copy of the tape.

A person who thinks that the grounds for detention are unlawful may apply to the High Court in England and Wales for a writ of habeas corpus against the person who detained him or her, requiring that person to appear before the court to justify the detention. Habeas corpus proceedings take precedence over others. Similar procedures apply in Northern Ireland and a similar remedy is available to anyone who is unlawfully detained in Scotland.

Recognising that the use of DNA analysis has become a powerful tool in the investigation of crime, the Government has extended police powers to take body samples from suspects. The Criminal Justice and Public Order Act 1994 allows the police to take non-intimate samples without consent from anyone who is detained or convicted for a recordable offence, and to use the samples to search against existing records of convicted offenders or unsolved crimes. In time a national database will be built up.

Charging

Once there is sufficient evidence, the police have to decide whether a detained person should be charged with the offence. As an alternative, they can, for example, decide to defer charging or to take no further action and release the person on or without bail. They may also issue a formal caution (see p. 97), which will be recorded and may be taken into account if the person reoffends.

If charged, a person may be kept in custody if there is a risk that he or she might fail to appear in court or might interfere with the administration of justice. When no such considerations apply, the person must be released on or without bail. Where someone is detained after charge, they must be brought before a magistrates' court as soon as practicable. This is usually no later than the next working day.

Scotland

In Scotland the police have common law powers of arrest and may search an arrested person. A police officer may also search a person for stolen property if he or she has reasonable grounds for suspicion.

The police may detain and question a suspect for up to six hours. After this period the person must either be released or charged. Tape recording of interviews with suspects is common practice. A court will only allow as evidence statements fairly obtained by the police. Anyone arrested must be brought before a court on the first working day after arrest. In less serious cases the police may release a person who gives a written undertaking to attend court.

Where the charges involve serious crime, the accused is brought before the sheriff in private, either to be committed for a period not exceeding eight days to allow further enquiries to be made or to be committed for trial.

The Criminal Justice (Scotland) Act 1995 provides for an extension of the range of samples which the police in Scotland may take without warrant for DNA analysis.

Awaiting Trial

England and Wales

There are time limits on the period a defendant may be kept in custody awaiting trial in England and Wales. In cases tried before a magistrates' court these are generally 56 days from first appearance to trial or 70 days between first appearance to referral to trial in the Crown Court. The limit in Crown Court cases is 112 days from referral from the magistrates' court to taking of the plea. There are some cases where it is not possible to comply with the time limit and the courts have powers to extend limits if satisfied that there is a good reason and the prosecution has acted as quickly as possible.

Most accused people are released on bail pending trial. They are not remanded in custody except where strictly necessary. In England and Wales the court decides whether a defendant should be released on bail. Unconditional bail may be withheld only if the court believes that the accused would abscond, commit an offence, interfere with witnesses or otherwise obstruct the course of justice.

A court may also impose conditions before granting bail. If bail is refused, the defendant may apply to a High Court judge or to the Crown Court for bail. In certain circumstances the prosecution may appeal to a Crown Court judge against the granting of bail by magistrates. An application can also be made to the Crown Court for conditions imposed by a magistrates' court to be altered.

In some cases a court may grant bail to a defendant on condition that he or she lives in an approved bail or probation/bail hostel.

The probation service's bail information schemes provide the Crown Prosecution Service with information about a defendant which helps it to decide whether to oppose bail and enables the courts to take an

informed decision on whether to grant bail.

The Criminal Justice and Public Order Act 1994 gives the police powers of immediate arrest for breach of police bail and removes the presumption in favour of bail for people alleged to have offended while on bail. It also restricts the right to bail for someone charged with murder, manslaughter or rape if previously convicted of the same offence.

Scotland

When arrested, an accused person in Scotland may be released by the police to await summons, on an undertaking to appear at court at a specified time, or be held in custody to appear at court on the next working day. Following that appearance, the accused may be remanded in custody until trial or released by the court on bail. If released on bail, the accused must undertake to appear at trial when required, not to commit an offence while on bail, and not to interfere with witnesses or obstruct the course of justice. The court may also impose additional conditions on the accused as appropriate (for example, to keep away from certain people or locations).

There is a right of appeal to the High Court by an accused person against the refusal of bail, or by the prosecutor against the granting of bail, or by either against the conditions imposed.

The Criminal Justice (Scotland) Act 1995 gives the courts increased powers to sentence a person who commits an offence while on bail. A prison sentence may be increased by up to six months; a fine by up to £1,000. Bail will not be granted where an accused person is charged with murder, attempted murder, culpable homicide, rape or attempted rape and has a previous conviction for such a crime (in the case of culpable homicide involving a prison sentence).

If a person charged with a serious offence has been kept in custody pending trial, the trial must begin within 110 days of the date of full committal. The trial of a person released on bail on a serious offence must begin within 12 months of the first appearance in court on that charge. The trial of a person charged with a summary offence and held in custody must begin within 40 days of the date of first appearance in court.

Northern Ireland

In Northern Ireland bail may be granted by a resident magistrate except in cases dealt with under emergency provisions, where the decision is made by a judge of the High Court.

CRIMINAL COURTS

Prosecution

England and Wales

Once the police have instituted criminal proceedings against a person, the independent Crown Prosecution Service (CPS) takes control of the case, reviews the evidence and decides whether the case should be continued. The CPS is headed by the Director of Public Prosecutions, who is accountable to Parliament through the Attorney General. It is divided into 13 regional areas, each of which is headed by a Chief Crown Prosecutor.

A prosecution will proceed only if the prosecutor is satisfied that there is, on the evidence, a realistic prospect of conviction, and if so, that it is in the public interest for the prosecution to proceed. In nearly all cases the decision to prosecute is delegated to the lawyers in the area offices. However, some especially sensitive or complex cases, including terrorist offences and breaches of the Official Secrets Act, are dealt with by CPS headquarters.

Scotland

The Lord Advocate is responsible for prosecutions in the High Court of Justiciary, sheriff courts and district courts. There is no general right of private prosecution. The Lord Advocate is advised by the Crown Agent, who is head of the Procurator Fiscal Service and is assisted in the Crown Office by a staff of legally qualified civil servants.

Prosecutions in the High Court of Justiciary are prepared by procurators fiscal and Crown Office officials. They are conducted by the Lord Advocate, the Solicitor General for Scotland (the Lord Advocate's ministerial deputy) and advocate deputes, collectively known as Crown Counsel.

Crimes tried before the sheriff and district courts are prepared and prosecuted by procurators fiscal. The police and other law enforcement agencies investigate crimes and offences and report to the fiscal, who decides whether to prosecute, subject to the directions of Crown Counsel.

When dealing with minor crime, the fiscal can use alternatives to prosecution, such as formal warnings or diversion to social work. The Criminal Justice (Scotland) Act 1995 provides for an extension of fiscal fines for a wider range of minor offences.

The new legislation also strengthens the procedures for judicial examination of the accused before trial, and introduces an enhanced system of intermediate diets (sittings of the sheriff and district courts in advance of the trial) to establish the state of readiness of both the defence and the prosecution. These procedures should reduce inconvenience to both police and civilian witnesses, and should ensure that less time is wasted on trips to court that are not needed.

Northern Ireland

The Director of Public Prosecutions for Northern Ireland, appointed by the Attorney General, prosecutes all offences tried on indictment and may do so in other (summary) cases. Most summary offences are prosecuted by the police.

Prosecutions for Fraud

The Serious Fraud Office prosecutes the most serious and complex cases of fraud in England, Wales and Northern Ireland. Investigations are conducted by teams of lawyers, accountants, police officers and other specialists. In Scotland the Crown Office Fraud Unit, which is part of the public prosecution service, directs the investigation and preparation for prosecution of serious and complex fraud cases.

Courts

England and Wales

Very serious offences such as murder, manslaughter, rape and robbery can only be tried on indictment in the Crown Court, where all contested trials are presided over by a judge sitting with a jury. Summary offences—the less serious offences and the vast majority of criminal cases—are tried by unpaid lay magistrates or, in a few areas, by paid stipendiary magistrates; both sit without a jury.

Offences in a third category—such as theft, the less serious cases of burglary and some assaults—are known as 'either way' offences. They can be tried either by magistrates or by jury in the Crown Court. If magistrates are content to deal with the case, the accused has the right to choose trial by magistrates or trial by jury in the Crown Court.

All those charged with offences triable in the Crown Court must first appear before a magistrates' court, which decides whether to send them to the Court for trial. As recommended by the Royal Commission, a new administrative procedure for transferring cases to the Crown Court is replacing all committal proceedings under the provisions of the Criminal Justice and Public Order Act 1994. The defence can still argue that there is no case to answer and the magistrates' courts have a discretion to admit, on application, oral argument by the defence. No witnesses are called to give evidence. Existing procedures for transferring cases of serious or complex fraud or cases involving child evidence are not affected by the legislation.

A magistrates' court, which is open to the public and the media, usually consists of three lay magistrates—known as justices of the peace—who are advised by a legally qualified clerk or a qualified assistant. There are about 30,000 lay magistrates. The few full-time, legally qualified stipendiary magistrates may sit alone and usually preside in courts where the workload is heavy.

Most cases involving people under 18 are heard in youth courts. These are specialist magistrates' courts which either sit apart from other courts or are held at a different time. Restrictions are placed on access by ordinary members of the public. Media reports must not identify a young person concerned in the proceedings, whether as defendant, victim or witness.

Where a young person under 18 is charged jointly with someone of 18 or over, the case may be heard in an ordinary magistrates' court or the Crown Court. If the young person is found guilty, the court may transfer the case to a youth court for sentence.

An independent inspectorate has been set up to inspect the administration and management of magistrates' courts in order to improve performance and spread good practice. It does not comment on the judicial decisions of magistrates or their clerks in particular cases.

The Crown Court sits at 93 venues and is presided over by High Court judges, full-time circuit judges and part-time recorders.

Courts Charter

A Courts Charter, setting out the standards of service which apply in the higher courts in England and Wales, came into operation in January 1993. It outlines arrangements to help court users and ease the strains associated with court attendance. A new Charter, called the Charter for Court Users, was launched in July 1995. It gives more information about court systems and procedures and has new standards on, for example, the treatment of victims and witnesses and on complaints handling. It does not cover judicial decisions.

Scotland

The High Court of Justiciary tries the most serious crimes and has exclusive jurisdiction in cases involving murder, treason and rape. The sheriff court is concerned with relatively less serious offences and the district court with minor offences.

Criminal cases in Scotland are heard under solemn or summary procedure. In solemn procedure, an accused person's trial takes place before a judge sitting with a jury of 15 people. Details of the alleged offence are set out in a document called an indictment. In summary procedure the judge sits without a jury.

All cases in the High Court and the more serious ones in sheriff courts are tried by a judge and jury. Summary procedure is used in the less serious cases in the sheriff courts, and in all cases in the district courts. District court judges are lay justices of the peace. In Glasgow there are also stipendiary magistrates, who are full-time lawyers with the same powers as a sheriff in summary procedure.

Children under 16 who have committed an offence are normally dealt with by children's hearings (see p. 102).

The levels of service which citizens are entitled to expect from the main criminal justice agencies are set out in the Justice Charter for Scotland.

Northern Ireland

Cases involving minor summary offences are heard by magistrates' courts presided over by a full-time, legally qualified resident magistrate. Young offenders under 17 are dealt with by a juvenile court consisting of the resident magistrate and two specially qualified lay members, at least one of whom must be a woman.

The Crown Court deals with criminal trials on indictment. It is served by High Court and county court judges. Contested cases are heard by a judge and jury, although people charged with terrorist-type offences are tried by a judge sitting alone, because of the possibility of jurors being intimidated by terrorist organisations.

In non-jury Crown Court trials the onus remains on the prosecution to prove guilt beyond reasonable doubt and defendants have the right to be represented by a lawyer of their choice. The judge must set out in a written statement the reasons for convicting and there is an automatic right of appeal against conviction and sentence on points of fact as well as of law.

Trial

Criminal trials in Britain have two parties: the prosecution and the defence. The law presumes the innocence of an accused person until guilt has been proved by the prosecution. An accused person has the right to employ a legal adviser and may be granted legal aid from public funds (see p. 106). If remanded in custody, he or she may be visited by a legal adviser to ensure a properly prepared defence.

Disclosure to the Defence

In England and Wales, the prosecution in Crown Court cases must disclose to the defence all the statements from the witnesses on whom it proposes to rely. This duty does not apply to offences tried in the magistrates' court, except when advance information is requested by the defence in 'either way' cases (see p. 90).

There is also a general duty to disclose to the defence evidence, documents and information which might have a bearing on the defence case. In circumstances where the material attracts public interest immunity or is otherwise subject to a duty of confidentiality, the prosecution is obliged to place it before the court for a ruling.

In Scottish solemn cases the prosecution must give the defence advance notice of the witnesses it intends to call and of the documents and other items on which it will rely. In summary cases this is usually done as a matter of practice, although there is no obligation on the Crown to do so.

Trial Procedure

Criminal trials normally take place in open court and rules of evidence, which are concerned with the proof of facts, are rigorously applied. If evidence is improperly admitted, or excluded, a conviction can be quashed on appeal. In Scotland the Criminal Justice (Scotland) Act 1995 allows hearsay evidence to be admitted in particular circumstances.

During the trial the defendant has the right to hear and cross-examine prosecution witnesses. He or she can call his or her own witnesses who, if they will not attend voluntarily, may be legally compelled to do so. The defendant can also address the court in person or through a lawyer, the defence having the right to the last speech before the judge sums up.

The defendant cannot be questioned without consenting to be sworn as a witness in his or her own defence, although a court in England and Wales may, under recent legislation, draw inferences from a refusal to give evidence (see pp. 86–7). In Scotland, under the provisions of the Criminal Justice (Scotland) Act 1995, the prohibition on the prosecutor commenting on an accused person's failure to give evidence will be removed.

When a defendant does testify, he or she may be cross-examined about character or other conduct only in exceptional circumstances. Generally the prosecution may not introduce such evidence.

In Scotland cross-examination about the character or other conduct of the accused may be made in certain circumstances.

Child Witnesses

Legislation in 1988 abolished the presumption that children were incompetent as witnesses. It also introduced the system which allows children to give their evidence at court by means of a closed-circuit television link. Building on that, the Criminal Justice Act 1991 extended the closed-circuit television provisions, forbade the cross-examination of a child directly by the accused, and provided for a video-recorded interview with a child victim or witness to be admissible in court as his or her main evidence. The Criminal Justice and Public Order Act 1994 further clarified the law on child evidence, by requiring judges to admit the evidence of a child unless he or she is incapable of giving intelligible testimony. It is for the jury to decide what weight should be placed on a child's evidence.

In Scotland live television links installed in a number of criminal courts enable children to give their evidence without entering the courtroom. A child's evidence may also be given from behind a screen. Corroboration of a child's evidence is necessary to sustain a conviction.

Fraud Proceedings

In complex fraud cases the judge may order a preparatory Crown Court hearing to be held.

It is in open court but subject to restrictions on press reporting. This provides an opportunity for the judge to determine questions regarding admissibility of evidence and any other questions of law relating to the case. The judge also has the power to order the prosecution and the defence to serve on each other certain statements and to prepare the case in such a way that it is easier to understand. Appeals may be made to the Court of Appeal from certain decisions of the judge in the preparatory hearings.

The Jury

In jury trials the judge decides questions of law, sums up the evidence for the jury, and discharges or sentences the accused. The jury is responsible for deciding questions of fact. In England, Wales and Northern Ireland the verdict may be 'guilty' or 'not guilty', the latter resulting in acquittal. If the jury cannot reach a unanimous decision the judge may allow a majority verdict provided that, in the normal jury of 12 people, there are no more than two dissenters.

In Scotland the jury's verdict may be 'guilty', 'not guilty' or 'not proven'; the accused is acquitted if either of the last two verdicts is given. The jury consists of 15 people and a verdict of 'guilty' can only be reached if at least eight members are in favour. As a general rule no one may be convicted without corroborated evidence from at least two sources.

If the jury acquits the defendant, the prosecution has no right of appeal and the defendant cannot be tried again for the same offence.

A jury is independent of the judiciary. Any attempt to interfere with a jury is a criminal offence. Potential jurors are put on a panel before the start of the trial. In England and Wales the prosecution and the defence may challenge individual jurors on the panel, giving reasons for doing so. In Northern Ireland each defendant has the right to challenge up to 12 potential jurors without giving a reason. In Scotland, new legislation provides for improved procedures for the selection of juries, including the abolition of peremptory challenge.

People between the ages of 18 and 70 (65 in Scotland) whose names appear on the electoral register, with certain exceptions, are liable for jury service and their names are chosen at random. Ineligible people include, for example, judges and people who have within the previous ten years been members of the legal profession or the police, prison or probation services. People convicted of certain offences within the previous ten years cannot serve on a jury. Anyone who has received a prison sentence of five years or more is disqualified for life. Under the Criminal Justice and Public Order Act 1994, people on bail are also ineligible to sit on juries.

Sentencing

If a person is convicted, the magistrate or judge (or their Scottish equivalent) decides on the most appropriate sentence, taking into account the facts of the offence, the circumstances of the offender, any previous convictions or sentences and any statutory limits on sentencing. The defence lawyer may make a speech in mitigation.

The Criminal Justice Act 1991 places a requirement on the courts in England and Wales to obtain a 'pre-sentence' report from the probation service on offenders under the age of 18 in cases involving an offence triable either way before passing a custodial or more complex community sentence. In most other circumstances, such reports are discretionary. In England and Wales revised national standards for the supervision of offenders in the community require that pre-sentence reports include a new section in which the impact of the offence on the victim is explained to the court.

The Criminal Justice and Public Order Act 1994 provides for sentence discounts for those pleading guilty at an early stage in the court process in England and Wales.

In Scottish cases it is mandatory for a court to obtain a social enquiry report before imposing a custodial sentence if the accused is under 21 or has not previously served a custodial sentence. A report is also required before making a probation or community service order (see p. 96), or in cases involving people subject to supervision. In other cases the judge decides whether to obtain such a report.

The Criminal Justice (Scotland) Act 1995 makes provision for the High Court to issue guidelines on sentencing to the lower courts, encouraging consistency in sentencing in similar cases. The legislation also enables courts to take into account, when deciding the appropriate sentence, the fact that an accused person pleaded guilty, and the timing and circumstances in which the plea was made.

Appeals

England and Wales

A person convicted by a magistrates' court may appeal to the Crown Court against the sentence if he or she has pleaded guilty. An appeal may be made against both conviction and sentence, or sentence alone, if a 'not guilty' plea has been made. The High Court hears appeals on points of law and procedure—by either prosecution or defence—in cases originally dealt with by magistrates. If convicted by the Crown Court, a defendant may seek leave to appeal to the Court of Appeal (Criminal Division) against both the conviction and the sentence imposed. The House of Lords is the final appeal court, but it will only consider cases that involve a point of law of general public importance and where leave to appeal is granted.

The Attorney General (see p. 105) may seek a ruling of the Court of Appeal on a point of law which has been material in a case where a person is tried on indictment. The Court has power to refer the point to the House of Lords if necessary. The ruling will constitute a binding precedent, but an acquittal in the original case is not affected.

The Attorney General has the power to apply for leave to refer to the Court of Appeal for reconsideration a sentence imposed in the Crown Court if it is, in his or her view, unduly lenient. Originally, only a sentence imposed in respect of offences triable only on indictment could be reviewed. However, the Attorney General's power has been extended. Although any sentence must still have been passed by the Crown Court, certain offences triable either way are now covered. These are indecent assault, making threats to kill, and cruelty to, or neglect of, a child. The Attorney General's power has been further extended to cover certain types of serious or complex fraud. The Court of Appeal may, if it is minded to quash the original sentence, impose in its place any sentence which the original sentencing court had the power to impose.

On the basis of recommendations of the Royal Commission on Criminal Justice and subsequent consultations, new legislation has been passed on criminal appeals. The Criminal Appeal Act 1995 provides for the creation of a Criminal Cases Review Commission to operate in England, Wales and Northern Ireland. This body, independent of both Government and the courts, will examine possible miscarriages of justice in cases tried on indictment or summarily and decide whether to refer them to the courts on the grounds of sentence and conviction. It will direct and supervise investigations undertaken on its behalf and approve the appointment of investigating officers. Referral of a case will require some new argument or evidence not previously raised at the trial or on appeal.

The final decision on any case referred will rest with the respective Courts of Appeal in England and Wales and Northern Ireland (if the case was tried originally on indictment) or with the Crown Court following a referral in a summary case. The power of the Home Secretary (and the Secretary of State in Northern Ireland) to investigate and refer possible miscarriages of justice to the Court of Appeal will be relinquished.

Scotland

All appeal cases are dealt with by the High Court of Justiciary. In both solemn and summary procedure, the accused may appeal against conviction, or sentence, or both. The Court may authorise a retrial if it sets aside a conviction. There is no further appeal to the House of Lords. In summary proceedings the prosecutor may appeal on a point of law against acquittal or sentence. The Lord Advocate may seek the opinion of the High Court on a point of law in a case where a person tried on indictment is acquitted. The acquittal in the original case is not affected. The Crown has a right of appeal against lenient sentences in both solemn and summary procedure.

The Criminal Justice (Scotland) Act 1995 provides for the introduction of a requirement for leave to appeal. This will involve a single judge assessing whether there are arguable grounds for an appeal. The legislation will also reduce the number of High Court judges required to consider appeals against sentence only from three to two.

Northern Ireland

In Northern Ireland, appeals from magistrates' courts against conviction or sentence are heard by the county court. An appeal on a point of law alone can be heard by the Northern Ireland Court of Appeal, which also hears appeals from the Crown Court against conviction and/or sentence. Procedures for a further appeal to the House of Lords are similar to those in England and Wales.

A person convicted of a terrorist offence in a non-jury court has an automatic right of appeal against conviction and/or sentence.

The new Criminal Cases Review Commission (see above) will operate in Northern Ireland as well as in England and Wales.

Coroners' Courts

In England and Wales the coroner must hold an inquest if the deceased died a violent or unnatural death, a sudden death where the cause is unknown, or in prison or in other specified circumstances. In Northern Ireland in such circumstances the coroner investigates the matter to decide whether an inquest is necessary. The coroner's court establishes how, when and where the deceased died. A coroner may sit alone or, in certain circumstances, with a jury.

In Scotland the local procurator fiscal inquires privately into all sudden and suspicious deaths and may report the findings to the Crown Office. In a minority of cases a fatal accident inquiry may be held before the sheriff; this is mandatory in cases of death resulting from industrial accidents and of deaths in custody.

TREATMENT OF OFFENDERS

The Government believes that prison is the right response for the most serious, dangerous and persistent offenders. It also considers that there should be effective and demanding punishment within the community to deal with offenders for whom a prison sentence is not appropriate. Tough new national standards for community sentences were announced in March 1995. Fines continue to represent a proper penalty for other less serious offences.

Legislation sets the maximum penalties for offences, the sentence being entirely a matter for the courts, subject to these maxima. The Court of Appeal issues guidance on sentencing to the lower courts when points of principle have arisen on individual appeal cases.

In Scotland, where many offences are not created by statute, the penalty for offences at common law ranges from absolute discharge to life imprisonment.

Custody

England and Wales

A custodial sentence is the most severe penalty available to the courts. Under the Criminal Justice Act 1991, a custodial sentence can be imposed only where the offence is so serious that only such a sentence would be appropriate, or where there is a need to protect the public from a sexual or violent offender. A court is required to explain to the offender why it is passing a custodial sentence. The length of the sentence must reflect the seriousness of the offence.

A magistrates' court cannot impose a term of more than six months' imprisonment for an individual offence tried summarily. It can

impose consecutive sentences for 'either way' offences (see p. 90), subject to an overall maximum of 12 months' imprisonment. If an offence carries a higher maximum penalty, the court may commit the offender for sentence at the Crown Court. The Crown Court may impose a custodial sentence for any term up to life, depending on the seriousness of the offence and the maximum penalty available.

If a court decides that an offence is sufficiently serious to justify an immediate custodial sentence of not more than two years, the sentence may be suspended for a period of at least one year and not more than two years if exceptional circumstances justify the suspension. If the offender commits another imprisonable offence during the period of suspension, the court may order the suspended sentence to be served in addition to any punishment imposed for the second offence. When passing a suspended sentence, the court must consider whether it would also be appropriate to impose a fine or make a compensation order. The court may also order supervision of the offender by a probation officer if the suspended sentence is for more than six months.

There is a mandatory sentence of life imprisonment for murder throughout Britain. Life imprisonment is the maximum penalty for a number of serious offences such as robbery, rape, arson and manslaughter.

Northern Ireland

In Northern Ireland the position is generally the same as for England and Wales. A magistrates' court, however, cannot commit an offender for sentencing at the Crown Court if it has tried the case.

Scotland

In Scottish trials on indictment the High Court of Justiciary may impose a sentence of imprisonment for any term up to life, and the sheriff court any term up to three years. The latter may send any person to the High Court for sentence if the court considers its powers are insufficient. In summary cases the sheriff or stipendiary magistrate may normally impose up to three months' imprisonment or six months' for some repeated offences. The district court can impose a maximum term of imprisonment of 60 days.

Non-custodial Treatment

Non-custodial sentences include:

- fines;
- compensation orders;
- probation and supervision orders;
- community service orders; and
- a combination order, which includes elements of probation and community service.

Fines

About 80 per cent of offenders are punished with a fine. There is no limit to the fine which the Crown Court (and High Court of Justiciary and the sheriff court in Scotland under solemn procedure) may impose on indictment. The maximum fine that can be imposed by a magistrates' court in England and Wales (and a sheriff court in Scotland under summary procedure) is £5,000. When fixing the amount of a fine, courts are required to reflect the seriousness of the offence and to take into account the financial circumstances of the offender.

Probation

The locally organised probation service in England and Wales supervises offenders in the community under direct court orders and after release from custody. It also provides offenders in custody with help and advice.

A court probation order can last between six months and three years; if the offender fails to comply with any of the requirements of the order, he or she can be brought before the court again. A probation order can be combined with a community service order.

A probation order requires the offender to maintain regular contact with the probation officer, who is expected to supervise the offender and to confront him or her with the consequences of his or her offence. Special

conditions attached to the order may require the offender to attend a day centre for up to 60 days. Probation is intended as a punishment, although the time spent by offenders under supervision in the community offers an opportunity for constructive work to reduce the likelihood of reoffending.

In England and Wales the probation service also administers supervision orders, the community service scheme and supervises those released from prison on parole.

The statutory Probation Inspectorate monitors the work of the voluntary and private sectors with the probation service in addition to its inspection and advisory duties.

In Scotland local authority social work departments supervise offenders on probation, community service and other community disposals, and offenders subject to supervision on release from custody.

In Northern Ireland the service is administered by the government-funded Probation Board, whose membership is representative of the community.

Community Service

Offenders aged 16 or over convicted of imprisonable offences may, with their consent, be given community service orders. The court may order between 40 and 240 hours' unpaid service to be completed within 12 months. Examples of work done include decorating the houses of elderly or disabled people and building adventure playgrounds.

In England and Wales the court may make an order combining community service and probation. The maximum term for the probation element is the same as a probation order and the maximum period of community service is 100 hours (240 hours in Scotland).

Curfew Order

The Criminal Justice and Public Order Act 1994 provides for the use of curfew orders with electronic monitoring in trial areas. Courts in the trial areas can require offenders to remain at home for periods of between two and 12 hours a day. The order can be combined with probation or community service. A decision on whether to extend the order to courts throughout England and Wales will be taken in the light of the trials.

Compensation

The courts may order an offender to pay compensation for personal injury, loss or damage resulting from an offence. In England and Wales courts are required to give reasons for not awarding compensation to a victim. Compensation takes precedence over fines.

Other Measures

A court in England and Wales may discharge a person either absolutely or conditionally if it believes that it is not necessary to inflict punishment. If he or she is conditionally discharged, the offender remains liable to punishment for the offence if convicted of another offence within a period specified by the court (not more than three years).

Courts may also require an offender to keep the peace and/or be of good behaviour. If this requirement is not complied with, the offender is liable to forfeit a sum of money. Similar powers are available to courts in Northern Ireland.

Courts have the power to defer sentence, for the purpose of enabling the court, in dealing with the offender subsequently, to have regard to his or her conduct or any changes in his or her circumstances.

The police have discretion whether to charge an offender or formally to caution him or her. Cautioning is a form of warning and no court action is taken. New guidelines designed to stop the use of cautions for serious offences and to cut the number of repeated cautions were published by the Government in 1994. Cautioning is not available in Scotland.

Prisons

The Prison Service in England and Wales, the Scottish Prison Service and the Northern Ireland Prison Service are all executive agencies. Government ministers remain accountable for policy but the Chief Executives are responsible for the delivery of services.

Prisoners are housed in accommodation ranging from open prisons to high security establishments. In England, Scotland and Wales sentenced prisoners are classified into groups for security purposes. There are separate prisons for women. There are no open prisons in Northern Ireland, where the majority of offenders are serving sentences for terrorist offences. People awaiting trial in custody are entitled to privileges not granted to convicted prisoners. Those under 21 are, where possible, separated from convicted prisoners.

There are about 130 prison establishments in England and Wales and 22 in Scotland, many of which were built in the 19th century. Improvements are in progress to eliminate cells without access to integral sanitation, and a prison building programme is alleviating overcrowding.

In Northern Ireland there are four prisons and a young offenders' centre. Four of these establishments have been built since 1972.

The average prison population in 1994 was 48,000 in England and Wales, 1,920 in Northern Ireland, and 5,600 in Scotland.

Since 1991 the Government has been implementing a programme of reforms for the prison services in England and Wales and in Scotland. It is designed to provide a better prison system, with more effective measures for control, more constructive relationships between prisoners and staff, and more stimulating and useful programmes for prisoners.

In 1995–96 the key priority of the Prison Service in England and Wales is to strengthen physical security and security procedures, particularly at establishments holding high security prisoners.

Private Sector Involvement

Under the Criminal Justice Act 1991, the Home Secretary is empowered to contract out the management of prisons in England and Wales to the private sector, as well as escort and guarding functions.

The Court Escort and Custody Service is being progressively contracted out throughout the country. All escort services will be provided by the private sector by 1997, leaving police and prison officers free to concentrate on their own core duties.

Four prisons (which remain part of the Prison Service) are now managed by private contractors: The Wolds in Humberside opened in April 1992, Blakenhurst prison in Worcestershire opened in May 1993, and Doncaster prison and Buckley Hall prison in Rochdale opened in June and December 1994 respectively.

The Government has announced that six new prisons to be built will, for the first time, be designed, constructed, managed and financed by the private sector. The first two are expected to open in 1997–98 in Merseyside and South Wales.

The Prison Service is also continuing to contract out services both nationally and locally, including education services in prison and catering.

Provision for the further contracting out of prisons and prisoner escort services is included in the Criminal Justice and Public Order Act 1994.

Early Release of Prisoners

The Criminal Justice Act 1991 reformed the remission and parole systems in England and Wales, with revised arrangements for the early release of prisoners and for their supervision and liabilities after release. The Parole Board continues to advise the Home Secretary on the early release or recall of long-term prisoners.

Prisoners serving terms of less than four years may be released once they have served half of their sentences in custody. Long-term prisoners (those serving more than four years) may be released once they have served two-thirds of their sentence; the Parole Board may release them on licence half-way through their sentence if they are serving between four and seven years. The Home Secretary has to give final consent to such parole if the prisoner is serving more than seven years. All prisoners sentenced to a year or more may be supervised on release until three-quarters of their sentence has passed. Certain sex offenders may be supervised to the end of their sentence.

If convicted of another offence punishable with imprisonment and committed before the end of the original sentence, a released prisoner may be liable to serve all or part of the original sentence outstanding at the time the fresh offence was committed.

Similar changes have been adopted in Scotland.

Northern Ireland

In Northern Ireland prisoners serving a sentence of more than five days are eligible for remission of half their sentence. A prisoner serving a sentence of more than 12 months who is given remission is liable to be ordered to serve the remainder of this sentence if convicted of fresh imprisonable offences during this period.

Remission for those convicted of terrorist offences and serving sentences of five years or more is one-third. Any released prisoners convicted of another terrorist offence before the expiry of the original sentence must complete that sentence before serving any term for the second offence.

Life Sentence Prisoners

Arrangements for the early release of prisoners serving life sentences for offences other than murder are set out in the Criminal Justice Act 1991. The Home Secretary is required to release such prisoners after an initial period set by the trial judge if so directed by the Parole Board, which has to be satisfied that the protection of the public does not require their further confinement. These provisions conform with the requirements of the European Convention on Human Rights. Similar procedures have been adopted in Scotland.

The release on licence of prisoners serving mandatory life sentences for murder may only be authorised by the Home Secretary on the recommendation of the Parole Board. A similar policy applies in Scotland.

On release, life sentence prisoners remain on licence for the rest of their lives and are subject to recall if their behaviour suggests that they might again be a danger to the public.

People serving life sentences for the murder of police or prison officers, terrorist murders, murder by firearms in the course of robbery and the sexual or sadistic murder of children are normally detained for at least 20 years.

In Northern Ireland the Secretary of State reviews life sentence cases on the recommendation of an internal review body.

Repatriation

Sentenced prisoners who are nationals of countries which have ratified the Council of Europe Convention on the Transfer of Sentenced Persons or similar international arrangements may apply to be returned to their own country to serve the rest of their sentence there.

Independent Oversight of the Prison System

Every prison establishment has a Board of Visitors— a Visiting Committee in Scotland— drawn from the local community. In order to see that prisoners are being treated fairly, members may go to any part of the prison and interview any inmate at any time.

The independent Prisons Inspectorates report on the treatment of prisoners and prison conditions. Each establishment is visited about every three years.

Prison Industries

Prison industries aim to give inmates work experience which will assist them when released and to secure a return which will reduce the cost of the prison system. The main industries are clothing and textile manufacture, engineering, woodwork, laundering, farming and horticulture. In England and Wales most production caters for internal needs and for other public services, whereas in Scotland a greater proportion is sold to the private sector. A few prisoners are employed outside prison, some in community service projects.

Prison Education

Full-time education of 15 hours a week is compulsory for young offenders below school leaving age. For older offenders it is voluntary. Some prisoners study for public examinations, including those of the Open University. Competitive tendering for the provision of education services in prisons in England and Wales has taken place and contracts have been awarded, many to further and higher education establishments. In England, Wales and Scotland increased emphasis is being placed on the development and implementation of National and Scottish Vocational Qualifications (see p. 442) for inmates.

Physical education is voluntary for adult offenders but compulsory for young offenders. Practically all prisons have physical education facilities, some of which are purpose-built. Opportunities are given for inmates to obtain sporting proficiency awards. Inmates also compete against teams in the local community.

Health Care

The Health Care Service for Prisoners in England and Wales is responsible for the physical and mental health of all those in custody. A Health Advisory Committee provides independent medical advice to government ministers, the Prison Service Chief Executive and the Director of Health Care.

A greater emphasis is being placed on 'buying in' health care services either from the National Health Service (NHS— see p. 385) or the private sector. The Prison Service is also committed to transferring mentally disordered offenders to the care and treatment of the NHS and social services where possible.

In Scotland general medical services are provided mainly by visiting general practitioners. Psychiatric and psychological services are bought in from local health boards responsible for the NHS.

Privileges and Discipline

Prisoners may write and receive letters and be visited by relatives and friends, and those in all establishments in England, Wales and Scotland may make telephone calls. Privileges include a personal radio; books, periodicals and newspapers; watching television; and the opportunity to make purchases from the prison shop with money earned in prison. Depending on the facilities available, prisoners may be granted the further privileges of dining and recreation in association.

To maintain discipline, control and order the Prison Service in England and Wales is:

- developing incentive-based regimes, so that prisoners must earn privileges through responsible behaviour and will lose them for misbehaviour;
- increasing the penalties available to governors to deal with disciplinary offences;
- providing special units with facilities for dealing with violent or disruptive prisoners; and
- implementing a comprehensive strategy on drug misuse, including manadatory urine testing.

Breaches of discipline are dealt with by the prison governor. A Prisons Ombudsman for England and Wales has been appointed as a final appeal stage for prisoners' grievances.

In Scotland, prisoners who exhaust the internal grievance procedure may make application to the Scottish Prisons Complaints Commission, which is independent of the Scottish Prison Service.

Religion

Anglican, Church of Scotland, Roman Catholic and Methodist chaplains provide opportunities for worship and spiritual counselling, supported by visiting ministers of other denominations and faiths as required.

Preparation for Release

The prison services in England and Wales and in Scotland have a duty to prepare prisoners for release. Planning for safe release starts at the beginning of an offender's sentence and ties in with all the training, education and work experience provided. It is directed at equipping prisoners to fit back into society and to cope with life without reoffending. Risk assessment and confronting offending behaviour are essential elements of this process. Sentence planning is being extended progressively to all prisoners serving

substantial sentences, in conjunction with extended arrangements for aftercare.

Prisoners may be granted temporary licence for short periods, but they are subject to a rigorous risk assessment and are released only for very specific reasons.

The Pre-Release Employment Scheme in England and Wales and the Training for Freedom Scheme in Scotland enable selected long-term prisoners to spend their last six months before release in certain hostels attached to prisons in order to help them readapt to society. Hostellers work in the outside community and return to the hostel each evening. Frequent weekend leave allows hostellers to renew ties with their families.

In Northern Ireland prisoners serving fixed sentences may have short periods of leave near the end of their sentences and at Christmas. Life sentence prisoners are given a nine-month pre-release programme which includes employment outside the prison.

Aftercare

Professional support is given to offenders following their release. All young offenders and all adult offenders in England and Wales sentenced to 12 months' imprisonment and over are supervised on release by the probation service—or, in the case of certain young offenders, by local authority social services departments. In Scotland this support is provided by local authority social work services, although not all adult offenders are subject to supervision on release.

Young Offenders

England and Wales

Criminal proceedings cannot be brought against children below the age of 10 years. Offenders between the ages of 10 and 18 fall within the jurisdiction of youth courts. Sixteen- and 17-year-olds may be given the same probation, curfew and community service orders as older offenders; also available to the court are the same supervision orders or attendance centre orders as are given to younger offenders.

Under a supervision order—which may

remain in force for not more than three years—a child (10–13 years old) or young person (14–17 years old) normally lives at home under the supervision of a social worker or a probation officer. The order may require the offender to live in local authority accommodation and/or participate in specified activities at specified times.

Anyone under 21 years of age found guilty of an offence for which an adult may be imprisoned can be ordered to go to an attendance centre, as can an offender who refuses to comply with another order (for example, default in paying a fine or breach of a probation order). The maximum number of hours of attendance is 36 (or 24 if the offender is aged under 16) spread over a period; the minimum is 12 hours. The order aims to encourage offenders to make more constructive use of their leisure time.

Crown Court powers to order long periods of detention for young offenders who commit serious crimes are extended under the provisions of the Criminal Justice and Public Order Act 1994 to include 10- to 13-year-olds. The courts may detain 10- to 13-year-olds convicted of an offence for which an adult can be jailed for 14 years or more (including rape, arson, domestic burglary and robbery). Previously they could be given long terms of detention only if they had been convicted of murder or manslaughter. Courts may also detain any 10- to 15-year-old convicted of indecent assault on a woman, where previously only 16- and 17-year-olds could be detained for this offence. Any offender aged 14 or over who is convicted of causing death by dangerous or drunken driving may also be detained. Detention may be in a local authority secure residential unit, a centre managed by the Youth Treatment Service or a young offender institution.

The basic custodial sentence for those aged 15 to 21 is detention in a young offender institution. Alternatives include fines and compensation, attendance centre orders (for up to 36 hours) and community service orders (for between 40 and 240 hours).

In the area of parental responsibility, the Criminal Justice and Public Order Act 1994 extends the powers given to the courts by the Criminal Justice Act 1991. The 1991 Act:

- strengthened courts' powers to make parents attend hearings in cases involving offenders up to the age of 18;
- strengthened the liability on parents to pay fines and compensation arising from the crimes committed by their children;
- contained greater power for courts to order parents to take proper care and control of their children if necessary to prevent further offences; and
- allowed such orders to be imposed for up to three years, or until the offender's 18th birthday.

Where local authorities have assumed parental responsibility, the duty to attend court and pay any fines also applies.

Under the 1994 legislation, courts can order parents to ensure their children comply with community sentences. In every case when an offender aged between 10 and 15 years receives a community sentence, the court is under a duty to consider such an order. Courts have a power, as opposed to a duty, in the case of 16- and 17-year-olds. Courts are also empowered to impose a secure training order on persistent offenders aged between 12 and 14. The order means a period of detention in a secure training centre followed by a period of supervision; it is available for young offenders who have committed three or more imprisonable offences and who have failed to respond to punishment in the community. A further provision doubles the maximum sentence for 15- to 17-year-olds in a young offender institution from one to two years.

Scotland

Criminal proceedings may be brought against any child aged eight years or over, but the instructions of the Lord Advocate are necessary before anyone under 16 years of age is prosecuted.

Children under 16 who have committed an offence or are considered to be in need of care and protection may be brought before a children's panel. The panel, consisting of three lay people, determines in an informal setting whether compulsory measures of care are required and, if so, the form they should take. An official known as the reporter decides whether a child should come before a hearing. If the grounds for referral are not accepted by the child or parent, the case goes to the sheriff for proof. If he or she finds the grounds established, the sheriff remits the case to the reporter to arrange a hearing. The sheriff also decides appeals against a hearing's decision.

Young people aged between 16 and 21 serve custodial sentences in a young offender institution. Remission of part of the sentence for good behaviour, release on parole and supervision on release are available.

Northern Ireland

Those aged between 10 and 16 who are charged with a criminal offence are normally brought before a juvenile court. If found guilty of an offence punishable in the case of an adult by imprisonment, the court may order the offender to be placed in care, under supervision or on probation. The offender may also be required to attend a day attendance centre, be sent to a training school or committed to residence in a remand home. Non-custodial options are the same as in England and Wales.

Offenders aged between 16 and 24 who receive custodial sentences of less than three years serve them in a young offenders' centre.

Civil Justice

The Civil Law

The civil law of England, Wales and Northern Ireland covers business related to the family, property, contracts and torts (non-contractual wrongful acts suffered by one person at the hands of another). It also includes constitutional, administrative, industrial, maritime and ecclesiastical law. Scottish civil law has its own, broadly similar, branches.

CIVIL COURTS

England and Wales

Civil cases are heard in county courts and the High Court. Magistrates' courts have a concurrent jurisdiction with the county courts and the High Court in cases relating to children.

The jurisdiction of the 270 county courts covers:

- actions founded upon contract and tort;
- trust and mortgage cases;
- actions for the recovery of land;
- cases involving disputes between landlords and tenants;
- complaints about race and sex discrimination;
- admiralty cases (maritime questions and offences) and patent cases; and
- divorce cases and other family matters.

Specialised work is concentrated in certain designated courts. In some types of cases, for example admiralty cases, a county court is restricted to an upper financial limit.

For small claims, there are special arbitration facilities and simplified procedures. There are also special care centres and family hearing centres which deal with contested family matters involving children.

The High Court, which is divided into three divisions, deals with the more complicated civil cases. Its jurisdiction covers mainly civil and some criminal cases; it also deals with appeals from tribunals and from magistrates' courts in both civil and criminal matters. The three divisions are:

- the Family Division, which is concerned with family law, including adoption and wills;
- the Chancery Division, which deals with corporate and personal insolvency; disputes in the running of companies, between landlords and tenants and in intellectual property matters; and the interpretation of trusts and contested wills; and
- the Queen's Bench Division, which is concerned with contract and tort cases, and deals with applications for judicial review. Maritime law and commercial law are the responsibility of the Division's admiralty and commercial courts.

In the event of overlapping jurisdiction between the High Court and the county courts, cases of exceptional importance, complexity or financial substance are reserved or transferred for trial in the High Court.

Appeals

Appeals in matrimonial, adoption, guardianship and child care proceedings heard by magistrates' courts go to the Family Division of the High Court. Appeals from the High Court and county courts are heard in the Court of Appeal (Civil Division), and may go on to the House of Lords.

The Law Lords deal with cases submitted to the House of Lords. They are professional judges who have been given life peerages. In addition, peers who have held high judicial office are qualified to sit as Lords appeal judges. A group of five judges usually deals with cases. The Lord Chancellor is President of the House in its judicial capacity.

Scotland

The civil courts in Scotland are the Court of Session and the sheriff court, which have the same jurisdiction over most civil litigation, although cases with a value of less than £1,500 are dealt with only by the sheriff court. Appeals from the sheriff court may be made to the sheriff principal or directly to the Court of Session in ordinary actions.

In cases where the value of the claim is between £750 and £1,500, the case may be appealed to the sheriff principal on a point of law and to the Court of Session thereafter only if the sheriff principal certifies the case as suitable for such an appeal. In small claims cases where the value of the claim does not exceed £750 there may be an appeal to the sheriff principal on a point of law.

The Court of Session sits in Edinburgh, and in general has jurisdiction to deal with all kinds of action. It is divided into the Outer House (a court of first instance) and the Inner House (mainly an appeal court). Appeals to the Inner House may be made from the Outer House and from the sheriff court. From the Inner House an appeal may go to the House of Lords.

The Scottish Land Court deals exclusively with matters concerning agriculture. Its

chairman has the status and tenure of a judge of the Court of Session and its other members are lay specialists.

Northern Ireland

Civil cases up to a limited and specified monetary value are dealt with in county courts. The magistrates' court in Northern Ireland also deals with certain limited classes of civil case. The superior civil law court is the High Court of Justice, from which an appeal may be made to the Court of Appeal. The House of Lords is the final civil appeal court. Appeals from county courts are dealt with by the High Court or the Court of Appeal.

Civil Proceedings

England and Wales

Civil proceedings are started by the aggrieved person. Actions in the High Court are usually begun by a writ served on the defendant by the plaintiff, stating the nature of the claim. Before the case is tried, documents (pleadings) setting out the scope of the dispute are filed with the court; the pleadings are also served on the parties. County court proceedings are initiated by a summons, usually served on the defendant by the court. Child care cases are initiated by an application in the magistrates' courts.

In order to encourage parties to confine the issues in dispute, the High Court and the county courts have power to order pre-trial exchange of witness statements. Courts may impose penalties in costs on parties who unreasonably refuse to admit facts or to disclose documents before trial.

Civil proceedings, as a private matter, can usually be abandoned or ended by settlement between the parties at any time. Actions brought to court are usually tried without a jury, except in defamation, false imprisonment or malicious prosecution cases or where fraud is alleged, when either party may apply for trial by jury. The jury decides questions of fact and determines the damages to be paid to the injured party; majority verdicts may be accepted. The Court of Appeal is able to increase or reduce damages awarded by a jury if it considers them inadequate or excessive.

A decree of divorce must be pronounced in open court, but a procedure for most undefended cases dispenses with the need to give evidence in court and permits written evidence to be considered by the county court district judge.

In civil cases heard by a magistrates' court, the court issues a summons to the defendant setting out details of the complaint and the date on which it will be heard. Parties and witnesses give their evidence at the court hearing. Family proceedings are normally heard by not more than three lay justices, including both men and women. Members of the public are not allowed to be present. The court may make orders concerning residence, contact and supervision of children, and in some cases maintenance payments for spouses and children.

> A two-year review of rules and procedures of the civil courts of England and Wales began in March 1994, and an interim report was published in June 1995. The report recommends a fundamental transfer in the responsibility for the management of civil cases from litigants and their legal advisers to the courts.

Most judgments are for sums of money and may be enforced, in cases of non-payment, by seizure of the debtor's goods or by a court order requiring an employer to make periodic payments to the court by deduction from the debtor's earnings. Other court remedies may include an injunction restraining someone from performing an unlawful act. Refusal to obey a court order may result in a fine or imprisonment for contempt.

Normally the court orders the costs of an action to be paid by the party losing it, but, in the case of family law maintenance proceedings, a magistrates' court can order either party to pay the whole or part of the other's costs.

Scotland

Proceedings in the Court of Session or ordinary actions in the sheriff court are initiated by serving the defender with a summons—or, in sheriff court cases, an initial writ. A defender who intends to contest the action must inform the court; if he or she fails to do so, the court normally grants a decree in absence in favour of the pursuer. Where a case is contested, both parties must prepare written pleadings. Time is allowed for either party to adjust their pleadings in the light of what the other has said. At the end of this period a hearing will normally be arranged.

In cases involving sums between £750 and £1,500 in the sheriff court, a statement of claim is incorporated in the initial writ. The procedure is designed to enable most actions to be settled without the parties having to appear in court. Normally they, or their representatives, need appear only when an action is defended.

Northern Ireland

There are differences between proceedings in Northern Ireland and in England and Wales—for example, procedures in the county court start with the issue of a civil bill, which is served by the plaintiff on the defendant.

Tribunals

Tribunals exercise judicial functions separate from the courts and are intended to be more accessible, less formal and less expensive. They are normally set up under statutory powers, which also govern their constitution, functions and procedure. Tribunals often consist of lay people, but they are generally chaired by a legally qualified person.

Some tribunals settle disputes between private citizens. Industrial tribunals, for example, have a major role in employment disputes. Others, such as those concerned with social security, resolve claims by private citizens against public authorities. A further group, including tax tribunals, decide disputed claims by public authorities against private citizens. Tribunals usually consist of an uneven number of people so that a majority decision can be reached.

In the case of some tribunals a two-tier system operates, with an initial right of appeal to a lower tribunal and a further right of appeal, usually on a point of law, to a higher one, and in some cases to the Court of Appeal. Appeals from single-tier tribunals can usually be made only on a point of law to the High Court in England and Wales, to the Court of Session in Scotland, and to the Court of Appeal in Northern Ireland

The independent Council on Tribunals exercises general supervision over many tribunals. A Scottish Committee of the Council exercises the same function in Scotland.

Administration of the Law

GOVERNMENT RESPONSIBILITIES

England and Wales

The Lord Chancellor is the head of the judiciary and is responsible for the administration of all courts other than coroners' courts, and for a number of administrative tribunals. The highest judicial appointments are made by the Queen on the advice of the Prime Minister. The Lord Chancellor recommends all other judicial appointments to the Crown and appoints magistrates. He has general responsibility for the legal aid and advice schemes and for the administration of civil law reform.

The Home Secretary has overall responsibility for:

- criminal law;

- the police service;

- the prison system;

- the probation and after-care service; and

- advising the Queen on the exercise of the royal prerogative of mercy to pardon a person convicted of a crime or to remit all or part of a penalty imposed by a court.

The Attorney General and the Solicitor General are the Government's principal legal advisers and represent the Crown in appropriate domestic and international cases. They are senior barristers, elected members of the House of Commons and hold ministerial posts. The Attorney General is also Attorney General for Northern Ireland. As well as exercising various civil law functions, the Attorney General has final responsibility for enforcing the criminal law. The Solicitor General is the Attorney's deputy. As head of the Crown Prosecution Service, the Director of Public Prosecutions is subject to superintendence by the Attorney General, as are the Director of the Serious Fraud Office and the Director of Public Prosecutions for Northern Ireland.

Scotland

The Secretary of State for Scotland is responsible for Scottish criminal law, crime prevention, the police, the penal system and legal aid; he or she is advised on parole matters by the Parole Board for Scotland. He or she is also responsible for the substantive civil law.

The Secretary of State recommends the appointment of all judges other than the most senior ones, appoints the staff of the High Court of Justiciary and the Court of Session, and is responsible for the administration and staffing of the sheriff courts. (The district and islands local authorities are responsible for the district courts.)

The Lord Advocate and the Solicitor General for Scotland are the chief legal advisers to the Government on Scottish questions and the principal representatives of the Crown for the purposes of prosecutions and other litigation in Scotland. Both are government ministers.

Northern Ireland

Court administration is the responsibility of the Lord Chancellor, while the Northern Ireland Office, under the Secretary of State, deals with policy and legislation concerning criminal law, the police and the penal system. The Lord Chancellor has general responsibility for legal aid, advice and assistance.

JUDGES AND LAWYERS

Judges are not subject to ministerial direction or control. They are normally appointed from practising barristers, advocates (in Scotland), or solicitors (see below). Lay magistrates in England and Wales and Scottish district court justices are trained in order to give them sufficient knowledge of the law, including the rules of evidence, and of the nature and purpose of sentencing.

In Northern Ireland members of a lay panel who serve in juvenile courts undertake training courses; resident magistrates are drawn from practising solicitors or barristers.

The Legal Profession

The legal profession is divided into two branches: barristers (advocates in Scotland) and solicitors. Barristers and advocates advise on legal problems submitted through solicitors or other recognised professional bodies and present cases in all courts. Solicitors undertake legal business for individual and corporate clients; they can also, after appropriate training, present cases in all courts. Although people are free to conduct their own cases, most people prefer to be legally represented, especially in more serious cases.

Complaints systems against solicitors, barristers and licensed conveyancers are backed up by the Legal Services Ombudsman for England and Wales, who conducts investigations into the way the professional bodies handle these complaints. There is a separate Ombudsman for Scotland.

LEGAL AID

A person who needs legal advice, assistance or representation may be able to get help with his or her legal costs from the legal aid scheme. A person who qualifies for help may have all his or her legal costs paid for, or may be asked to make a contribution towards them, depending on his or her means.

Legal Advice and Assistance

Legal advice and assistance is available under the Green Form Scheme in England and Wales. People whose income and capital are within certain limits are entitled to free advice from a solicitor on certain legal matters. The scheme provides for up to three hours' work for matrimonial cases where a petition is drafted and two hours for other work. A similar scheme operates in Northern Ireland.

Legal Aid in Civil Proceedings

Civil legal aid may be available for most civil proceedings to those who satisfy the financial eligibility conditions. An applicant for legal aid must also show that he or she has reasonable grounds for taking, defending or being a party to proceedings. In England and Wales payments to lawyers are made through the Legal Aid Fund, administered by the Legal Aid Board. Scotland has a separate Legal Aid Fund, administered by the Scottish Legal Aid Board. Legal aid in Northern Ireland is administered by the Law Society for Northern Ireland.

In certain limited circumstances the successful unassisted opponent of a legally aided party may recover his or her costs in the case from the Legal Aid Board. Where the assisted person recovers or preserves money or property in the proceedings, the Legal Aid Fund will usually have a first charge on that money or property to recover money spent on the assisted person's behalf.

Legal Aid in Criminal Proceedings

In criminal proceedings in England, Wales and Northern Ireland legal aid may be granted by the court if it appears to be in the interests of justice and if a defendant is considered to require financial assistance. A legal aid certificate must be granted (subject to means) when a person is committed for trial on a murder charge or where the prosecutor appeals or applies for leave to appeal from the Court of Appeal to the House of Lords. In England and Wales a financial contribution may be payable.

The Legal Aid Board in England and Wales makes arrangements for duty solicitors to assist unrepresented defendants in the magistrates' courts. Solicitors are available, on a 24-hour basis, to give advice and assistance to those being questioned by the police. The services of a solicitor at a police station and of the duty solicitor at court are free.

Where legal aid is granted for criminal cases in Northern Ireland it is free. There is a voluntary duty solicitor scheme at the main magistrates' court in Belfast.

Scotland

A duty solicitor is available to represent people in custody on their first appearance in the sheriff courts and the district courts without enquiry into the person's means. In other cases, a person seeking legal aid in summary criminal proceedings must apply to the Scottish Legal Aid Board, which must be satisfied that the costs of the case cannot be met by the applicant without undue hardship, and that it is in the interests of justice that legal aid is awarded.

In solemn proceedings the court decides on the availability of legal aid and must be satisfied that the accused cannot meet the costs of the defence without undue financial hardship. Where legal aid is granted to the accused in criminal proceedings, he or she is not required to pay any contribution towards expenses.

Free Representation Unit

The Bar Council, the barristers' professional body, runs the Free Representation Unit in England and Wales for clients at a variety of tribunals for which legal aid is not available. Most of the representation in London is carried out by Bar students supported and advised by full-time case workers. Elsewhere the work is carried out by barristers.

Law Centres

In some urban areas law centres provide free legal advice and representation. They may employ a salaried lawyer and many have community workers. Much of their time is devoted to housing, employment, social security and immigration problems. Although there is a restriction on cases they will accept, most law centres will give preliminary advice.

Advice at minimal or no cost may be available in Citizens Advice Bureaux, consumer and housing advice centres and in specialist advice centres run by voluntary organisations.

Further Reading

Britain's Legal Systems. Aspects of Britain series, HMSO (second edition forthcoming).

Criminal Justice. Aspects of Britain series, HMSO (second edition forthcoming).

Home Office Annual Report. HMSO, 1995.

Report of the Royal Commission on Criminal Justice. HMSO, 1993.

External
Affairs

9 Overseas Relations

British foreign policy aims to make Britain more influential in the world and to contribute to a safer and fairer international order. To these ends, Britain is a member of some 120 international organisations, including the United Nations (UN), the Commonwealth, the North Atlantic Treaty Organisation (NATO) and the European Union (EU). Britain is pledged to increased co-operation among EU member states. It also plays an active part in maintaining international peace and security and has been fully involved in efforts to bring about peace in former Yugoslavia. Britain also protects the interests of its dependent territories, which include Hong Kong, the Falkland Islands and Gibraltar. The British aid programme is centred on the needs of the poorest countries.

ADMINISTRATION OF FOREIGN POLICY

Foreign & Commonwealth Office

The Foreign & Commonwealth Office (FCO) is in charge of overall foreign policy and is headed by the Foreign and Commonwealth Secretary, who is assisted by four ministers without Cabinet rank. One of these is the Minister for Overseas Development, who is responsible for the Overseas Development Administration (ODA). The FCO's Permanent Under-Secretary of State is a civil servant who is head of the Diplomatic Service and provides advice to the Foreign and Commonwealth Secretary on all aspects of foreign policy.

Of about 6,000 staff of the FCO's Diplomatic Wing appointed in the UK, some 2,500 serve overseas, of whom 167 are seconded from other government departments and other public and private organisations. British diplomatic missions also employ about 7,400 locally engaged staff.

Some 25 per cent of frontline staff overseas deal with political and economic work, while 30 per cent are engaged on commercial work, 14 per cent on entry clearance to Britain, 9 per cent on consular work, 5 per cent on aid administration, 9 per cent on information and 8 per cent on other activities, such as culture, science and technology.

The FCO administers pre-entry control

overseas for people wishing to enter Britain. Applications for entry clearance are dealt with by the visa section or consulate of a British mission.

Britain is committed to maintaining a worldwide diplomatic presence. Diplomatic or consular relations are maintained with 183 countries and there are missions at nine international organisations or conferences.

The FCO's only executive agency, Wilton Park International Conference Centre, contributes to the solution of international problems by organising conferences in Britain, attended by top politicians, officials, business people, academics and other professionals from all over the world. Its home is the Wilton House Conference Centre in West Sussex.

Other Departments

Other government departments, too, are concerned with overseas relations and foreign policy. The Ministry of Defence maintains military liaison with Britain's allies and with NATO, and also controls and administers the armed forces (see p. 138). The Department of Trade and Industry (DTI) has an important say on international trade policy and commercial relations with other countries, including EU member states. The FCO and DTI have a joint export promotion organisation—Overseas Trade Services (see p. 175). The Treasury is involved in British international economic policy and is responsible for Britain's relations with the World Bank and other international financial institutions.

When other departments are involved, the FCO decides policy in consultation with them. The department with the main interest usually takes the lead, particularly in EU matters and international economic policy. The FCO co-ordinates British EU policy through the Cabinet Office European Secretariat.

The British Council is responsible for British cultural relations with other countries (see p. 134). These are further enhanced by the BBC World Service (see p. 489), which is partly funded by the FCO.

INTERNATIONAL ORGANISATIONS

United Nations

Britain is a founder member of the United Nations and one of the five permanent members of the Security Council, along with China, France, Russia and the United States. In 1994 it was the sixth largest contributor to the UN regular budget. It is also one of the leading contributors to UN peacekeeping operations (see p. 122). Britain is fully committed to the purposes and principles of the UN Charter. Those purposes are the maintenance of international peace and security, the development of friendly relations among nations, the achievement of international co-operation on economic, social, cultural and humanitarian issues and the protection of human rights and fundamental freedoms.

European Union

Britain is a committed member of the European Union, which comprises the European Community (EC) and intergovernmental co-operation on foreign and security policy, and on justice and home affairs (see p. 118).

As one of the larger countries, Britain provides two of the 20 members of the European Commission, which puts forward policy proposals, executes decisions taken by the Council of the European Union and ensures that European Union rules are correctly observed. Britain is represented at each meeting of the Council, which is the main decision-making body. Each Council consists of government ministers from the 15 member states, representing national interests in the subjects under discussion— for example, trade, agriculture or transport. When a member state has the Presidency of the Union its ministers are responsible for chairing meetings of the Council. The Committee of Permanent Representatives, consisting of member states' ambassadors to the European Union, prepares the work of the Council.

The European Council, which meets at least twice a year, comprises the heads of state

The European Union

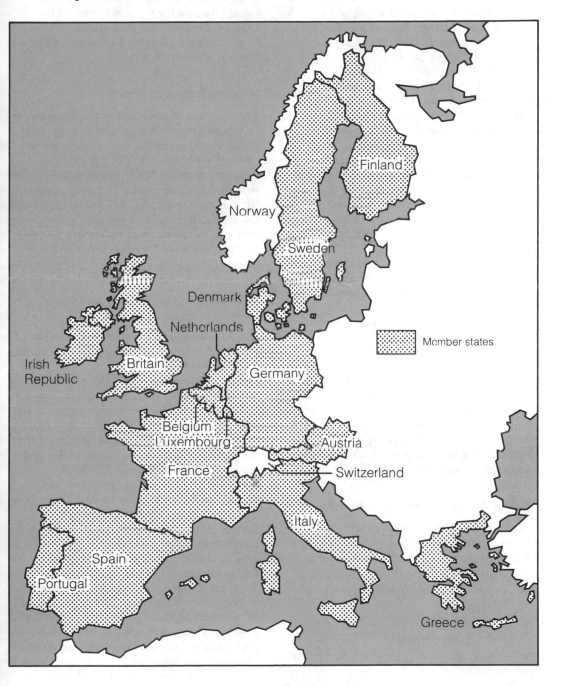

or government accompanied by their foreign ministers and the President of the Commission accompanied by one other Commissioner.

There are 626 members of the directly elected European Parliament, which is consulted about major decisions and has substantial shared power with the Council over the European Community budget. Britain has 87 seats. The fourth election to the Parliament took place in June 1994.

Each member state provides one of the judges to serve on the European Court of Justice, which is the supreme authority in the field of Community law. Its rulings must be applied by member states, and sanctions can be imposed on those failing to do so. The Court is assisted by a Court of First Instance, which handles certain cases brought by individuals and companies.

Britain is also represented on the Court of Auditors, which examines Community revenue and expenditure to see that it is legally received and spent.

European Community policies are implemented by various forms of Community legislation. The Community also enters into trade agreements with third countries and has a number of substantial aid programmes. Under the common foreign and security policy, member states agree common positions and take joint action on foreign policy issues. Member states also co-operate on justice and home affairs, including issues such as asylum, immigration and the fight against crime.

North Atlantic Treaty Organisation

Membership of NATO is the keystone of British defence policy (see p. 136). NATO is based on the principle of collective security and its core functions are:

- to provide a foundation for security in Europe;

- to deter aggression and defend member states against it; and

- to provide a forum for allied transatlantic consultation.

Each of the 16 member states has a permanent representative in NATO headquarters in Brussels. The main decision-taking body is the North Atlantic Council, at which foreign ministers meet at least twice a year. Permanent representatives meet on a weekly basis at the other meetings of the Council. Defence ministers attend meetings of the Defence Planning Committee and the Nuclear Planning Group.

Western European Union

Britain is one of ten members of the Western European Union (WEU), which is the main forum for co-operation and consultation on defence issues for NATO's European members. Current WEU members are Belgium, Britain, France, Germany, Greece, Italy, Luxembourg, the Netherlands, Portugal and Spain. Iceland, Norway and Turkey are associate members; Austria, Denmark, Finland, the Irish Republic and Sweden are observer members.

Organisation for Security and Co-operation in Europe (OSCE)

Britain is a signatory to the 1975 Helsinki Final Act, which established a framework for co-operation between OSCE states on European security (see p. 128), respect for human rights and economic matters. It was agreed that the Helsinki commitments should be reviewed at regular follow-up conferences.

The 1990 Charter of Paris committed the signatories to democracy, human rights and market economies. The OSCE has a Secretariat in Vienna, where Britain has a permanent delegation. Day-to-day business is conducted in the Permanent Council. A Prague office organises the twice-yearly meetings of senior officials.

The OSCE has 52 members, including every country in Europe (except the former Yugoslav Republic of Macedonia), the states of the former Soviet Union, and the United States and Canada. The Federal Republic of Yugoslavia was suspended in 1992. All states participate on an equal basis, and decisions are taken by consensus.

The main areas of OSCE work are:

- early warning of potential conflict through preventive diplomacy missions and the work of the OSCE High Commissioner on National Minorities;

- providing advice on human rights, democracy and law through the OSCE Office for Democratic Institutions and Human Rights, in Warsaw (see p. 129); and
- promoting security through arms control and military confidence building.

Council of Europe

Britain is a founding member of the Council of Europe, which is open to any European democracy accepting the rule of law and the protection of fundamental human rights and freedoms. The 36 member states co-operate on culture, education, sport, health, anti-crime policy, measures against drug trafficking, youth affairs and the improvement of the environment In 1950 the Council adopted its European Convention on Human Rights (see p. 129).

The Commonwealth

There are 52 members of the Commonwealth, including Britain. It is a voluntary association of states, nearly all of which were British territories but are now independent. The members are Antigua and Barbuda, Australia, Bahamas, Bangladesh, Barbados, Belize, Botswana, Britain, Brunei Darussalam, the Cameroon, Canada, Cyprus, Dominica, The Gambia, Ghana, Grenada, Guyana, India, Jamaica, Kenya, Kiribati, Lesotho, Malawi, Malaysia, Maldives, Malta, Mauritius, Namibia, Nauru, New Zealand, Nigeria, Pakistan, Papua New Guinea, St Kitts and Nevis, St Lucia, St Vincent and the Grenadines, Seychelles, Sierra Leone, Singapore, Solomon Islands, South Africa, Sri Lanka, Swaziland, Tanzania, Tonga, Trinidad and Tobago, Tuvalu, Uganda, Vanuatu, Western Samoa, Zambia and Zimbabwe. Nauru and Tuvalu are special members, entitled to take part in all Commonwealth meetings and activities, with the exception of the biennial Commonwealth heads of government meetings. South Africa rejoined in June 1994 after an absence of 33 years.

Consultation between member states takes place through:

- meetings of heads of government;
- specialised conferences of other ministers and officials;
- diplomatic representatives known as high commissioners; and
- non-governmental organisations.

The Queen is recognised as head of the Commonwealth and is head of state in Britain and 15 other member countries.

The Commonwealth Secretariat in London promotes consultation, disseminates information, and organises heads of government meetings, ministerial meetings and other conferences. It administers co-operative programmes agreed at these meetings, including the Commonwealth Fund for Technical Co-operation, which provides experts, consultancy services and training awards to Commonwealth developing countries

Membership of the Commonwealth enables Britain to play a responsible part alongside other nations in aiding the democratisation and development of the developing world. About 55 per cent of British direct aid (see p. 131) goes to Commonwealth countries. The British Government participates fully in all Commonwealth activities and welcomes it as a means of consulting and co-operating with peoples of widely differing cultures.

Other International Bodies

Britain is a member of many other international bodies, including the International Monetary Fund, which regulates the international financial system and provides a source of credit for member countries facing balance-of-payments difficulties.

In addition, Britain, along with 24 other industrialised countries, belongs to the Organisation for Economic Co-operation and Development (OECD), which promotes economic growth, support for less developed countries and worldwide trade expansion.

Other organisations to which Britain belongs or extends support include the regional development banks in Africa, the Caribbean, Latin America and Asia.

The Commonwealth

BRITAIN'S DEPENDENT TERRITORIES

Britain's dependent territories have a combined population of over 6 million, of whom 6 million live in Hong Kong. Most territories have considerable self-government, with their own legislatures. Governors appointed by the Queen are responsible for external affairs, internal security (including the police) and the public service. Certain responsibilities are delegated to locally elected ministers but the ultimate responsibility for all government affairs rests with the Foreign and Commonwealth Secretary. The British Indian Ocean Territory, the British Atlantic Territory, and South Georgia and the South Sandwich Islands have commissioners, not governors; a commissioner is not responsible for external affairs. Britain seeks to provide the territories with security and political stability, ensure efficient and honest government and help them achieve economic social development on a par with neighbouring countries.

The territories are:

- Anguilla;
- Bermuda;
- British Antarctic Territory;
- British Indian Ocean Territory;
- British Virgin Islands;
- Cayman Islands;
- Falkland Islands;
- Gibraltar;
- Hong Kong;
- Montserrat;
- Pitcairn, Ducie, Henderson and Oeno;
- St Helena and St Helena Dependencies (Ascension and Tristan da Cunha);
- South Georgia and the South Sandwich Islands; and
- Turks and Caicos Islands.

Few are rich in natural resources, and some are scattered groups of islands.

British policy is to help the inhabitants of the dependent territories to take independence if they want it and where it is practicable, and in accordance with treaty obligations, to do so. The reasonable needs of the dependent territories are a first call on the British aid programme.

Hong Kong

In 1984 Britain and China signed the Sino-British Joint Declaration on Hong Kong, 92 per cent of which is leased from China until 1997. Under this agreement, Britain is responsible for the administration of Hong Kong until 30 June 1997. After this date, the agreement says, Hong Kong will become a Special Administrative Region (SAR) of China, with its capitalist system and way of life remaining unchanged for at least 50 years. With the exception of foreign affairs and defence, the Hong Kong SAR will enjoy a high degree of autonomy and its government and legislature will be composed of Hong Kong people.

Britain is pledged to co-operate with China in bringing about a smooth transition to Chinese sovereignty in 1997. Recent agreements cover measures to set up a Court of Final Appeal and the financial arrangements for the new airport, one of the world's largest construction projects.

In September 1991 direct elections took place for the first time for 18 seats in the Legislative Council. Another 21 of the 60 seats were elected indirectly from functional constituencies. The remaining members were appointed. Elections have also been held for district boards and municipal councils under proposals which were discussed by the British and Chinese governments in 1993 and 1994, although no agreement was reached.

The most recent Legislative Council elections took place in September 1995, when 20 members were directly elected, 30 indirectly elected and the remaining ten chosen by an election committee.

Falkland Islands

The Falkland Islands are the subject of a territorial claim by Argentina but the inhabitants wish to remain under British sovereignty. The British Government does not accept the Argentine claim and is committed to defending the Islanders' right to live under a government of their own choice. This right of self-determination is set out in the 1985 Falkland Islands Constitution.

In 1982 Argentina invaded and occupied the Islands, but its forces were expelled by British troops following Argentina's failure to abide by United Nations resolutions requesting its forces to withdraw. Britain and Argentina, while sticking to their respective positions on sovereignty, maintain diplomatic relations and continue to discuss their common interests in the South Atlantic region, such as fisheries conservation and oil exploration.

Gibraltar

Gibraltar was ceded to Britain in 1713 by the Treaty of Utrecht. It is the subject of a territorial claim by Spain. Under the Treaty, Spain has the right of first refusal should Britain ever decide to relinquish sovereignty.

Britain is committed to honouring the wishes of the people of Gibraltar on their future, as set out in the 1969 Gibraltar Constitution.

Over the years, Spain has used pressure at the border with Gibraltar to pursue its national objectives. Strict controls, which caused severe delays and substantial damage to Gibraltar's economy, were applied, for example, in autumn 1994 and in spring/ summer 1995.

Gibraltar is part of the European Union, although it is outside the common customs system and does not participate in the Common Agricultural Policy.

Gibraltar has recently introduced strict anti-money laundering legislation and has taken action to combat drug smuggling from Morocco to Spain, although most of this has not involved Gibraltar.

Caribbean Territories

The Dependent Territories Regional Secretariat in Barbados administers aspects of British government policy towards the Caribbean territories. Jointly agreed country policy plans for each territory receiving British aid have been introduced.

An FCO minister chairs a ministerial group for the Caribbean territories, drawn from a number of government departments and agencies and benefiting from wider expertise than the FCO or the ODA alone can offer. It meets two or three times a year.

EUROPEAN UNION POLICY

As a European power, Britain is concerned first of all with the prosperity and security of this area of the world.

The main instrument for achieving European prosperity is the European Union, an association of 15 democratic nations—Austria, Belgium, Britain, Denmark, Finland, France, Germany, Greece, the Irish Republic, Italy, Luxembourg, the Netherlands, Portugal, Spain and Sweden.

> Britain is confident that new members will strengthen the European Union. It welcomed the accession of Austria, Finland and Sweden on 1 January 1995, and supports the opening of membership to the associated countries of Central and Eastern Europe. Cyprus and Malta will also be involved in the next phase of enlargement.

Britain regards the Union as a means of strengthening democracy and reinforcing political stability in Europe, and of increasing the collective strength of member states in international negotiations. The Government wants Britain to be at the heart of a Union in which member states work effectively together by pooling their ideas and resources for shared purposes, where such objectives cannot be achieved by member states acting on their own.

Background

The Union had its origins in the post-Second World War resolve by Western European nations, particularly France and Germany, to prevent wars breaking out again between themselves. The 1957 Rome Treaty, which established the European Community, defined its aims as the harmonious development of economic activities, a continuous and balanced economic expansion and an accelerated rise in the standard of living. These objectives were to be achieved by the creation of a common internal market and progressive harmonisation of economic policies, involving:

- the elimination of customs duties between member states;

- free movement of goods, people, services and capital;

- a common commercial policy towards other countries;

- the elimination of distortions in competition within the common market;

- the creation of a Social Fund to improve job opportunities for workers and raise their standard of living;

- the adoption of common agricultural and transport policies; and

- the association of overseas developing countries with the Community in order to increase trade and promote economic and social development.

These objectives were confirmed and augmented by the Single European Act of 1986 and the 1992 Maastricht Treaty on European Union.

Maastricht Treaty

The Maastricht Treaty amended the Rome Treaty and made other new commitments. It:

- established the European Union and introduced the concept of European Union citizenship as a supplement to national citizenship, provided some measure of institutional reform and strengthened control of the Community's finances;

- provided an intergovernmental basis for a common foreign and security policy (see p. 122) and for greater co-operation on issues concerned with interior/justice policy (see p. 130);

- clarified and codified Union competences in areas such as regional strategy, consumer protection, education and vocational training, the environment and public health;

- provided for moves towards economic and monetary union; and

- embodied the principle of subsidiarity, under which action is taken at the European level only if its objectives cannot be achieved by member states acting alone.

Under an agreement reached in 1992 a subsidiarity test is applied to all European Commission proposals for action.

The Treaty was ratified by Britain and the other member states and came into force in November 1993. An operational review will be undertaken by an intergovernmental conference beginning in 1996.

Economic and Monetary Union

During the negotiations on those parts of the Maastricht Treaty relating to economic and monetary union (EMU), the Government sought to ensure that:

- there would be no commitment by Britain to move to a single monetary policy or single currency;

- monetary matters would remain a national responsibility until the Union moved to a single currency and monetary policy;

- member states would retain primary responsibility for their economic policies; and

- there were clear and quantifiable convergence conditions which member states would have to satisfy before moving to a single currency.

The Maastricht Treaty provides for progress towards EMU in three stages: the first—completion of the single market— ended at the end of 1993. The second stage, which began on 1 January 1994, includes the establishment of a European Monetary Institute with a largely advisory and consultative role. Although the Institute will prepare for stage 3, monetary policy will still be a national responsibility. Member states will co-ordinate economic policies in the context of agreed non-binding policy guidelines. The British Government is participating in stage 2.

Under the Treaty, a single currency is

envisaged by 1 January 1999, although member states will have to satisfy certain criteria on inflation rates, government deficit levels, currency fluctuation margins and interest rates. A special protocol recognises that Britain is not obliged or committed to move to this final stage of EMU without a separate decision to do so by the Government and Parliament at the appropriate time.

The Community Budget

The Community's revenue consists of:

- levies on agricultural imports;
- customs duties;
- the proceeds of a notional rate of value added tax of up to 1.4 per cent on a standard 'basket' of goods and services; and
- contributions from member states based on gross national product (GNP).

Britain has an annual rebate worth some £2,000 million because of the fact that, without it, the British net contribution would be far greater than that justified by its share of Community GNP.

An agreement on future finance was reached at the European Council summit in Edinburgh in 1992. Under the agreement, the overall revenue ceiling was to be maintained at 1.2 per cent of Community GNP until 1995. It will then rise in steps, reaching 1.27 per cent in 1999. Agricultural spending will be less than half the budget by the end of the century, compared with 80 per cent in 1973 and 60 per cent at present. It was also agreed that more resources would be allocated to the poorer regions of the Union.

Single Market

The single market, providing for the free movement of people, goods, services and capital, is largely complete in legislative terms. It covers, among other benefits, the removal of customs barriers, the liberalisation of capital movements, the opening of public procurement markets and the mutual recognition of professional qualifications. The single market is designed to reduce business costs, stimulate efficiency, increase consumer choice and encourage the creation of jobs and wealth. The British Government is supporting continuing work on extending the single market to important areas such as telecommunications and energy.

Transport

The concept of a common transport policy was laid down in the Treaty of Rome, and Britain fully supports the extension of competition and deregulation in transport. Liberalisation measures relating to civil aviation, shipping, and road haulage and passenger services are described in Chapter 19.

Trans-European Networks

The EU is working towards the completion of trans-European networks in the fields of transport, energy and telecommunications. The aim is to improve the interconnection and interoperability of national networks. Of the 14 priority transport projects which have been endorsed by the European Council, Britain has an interest in four. One of these is the planned construction of a new rail link between London and the Channel Tunnel (see p. 302). Ten priority energy projects have been endorsed, but none with a British interest.

European Economic Area

The European Economic Area (EEA) Agreement, in force since 1 January 1994, has extended most of the single market measures beyond the EU member states to Iceland, Norway and Liechtenstein.

Trade

Britain is the world's fifth largest trading nation. EEA member states comprise the world's largest trading bloc, accounting for about 40 per cent of all trade. The British Government fully supports an open world trading system, on which EU member states depend for future economic growth and jobs.

Under the Rome Treaty, the European Commission speaks on behalf of Britain and the other member states in international trade negotiations, such as the recently concluded GATT Uruguay Round which led to the creation of the World Trade Organisation (WTO). The Commission negotiates on a mandate agreed by the Council. For further information on trade, see Chapter 12.

The Environment

European Union member states are at the forefront of many international measures on environmental issues, such as air quality standards and the depletion of the ozone layer. For further information, see p. 365.

Agriculture and Fisheries

The Common Agricultural Policy (CAP) is designed to secure food supplies and to stabilise markets. It has also, however, created overproduction and unwanted food surpluses, placing a burden on the Community's budget.

The Common Fisheries Policy is concerned with the rational conservation and management of fishery resources.

The operation of these policies, and Britain's advocacy of CAP reform, are described in Chapter 18.

Regional and Infrastructure Development

There are a number of Structural Funds designed to:
- promote economic development in underdeveloped regions;
- regenerate regions affected by industrial decline;
- combat long-term unemployment and facilitate the entry of young people into the labour market;
- help workers adapt to industrial changes and to advances in production systems;
- speed up the adjustment of production, processing and marketing structures in agriculture; and
- promote development in rural areas.

Infrastructure projects and productive investments are financed by the European Regional Development Fund. The European Social Fund supports training and employment measures for the unemployed and young people. The Guidance Section of the European Agricultural Guidance and Guarantee Fund supports agricultural restructuring and some rural development measures. The Financial Instrument of Fisheries Guidance supports the modernisation of the fishing industry.

A Cohesion Fund was set up under the Maastricht Treaty to reduce disparities between levels of development in the poorer and richer member states.

Other initiatives aim to assist the development of new economic activities in regions affected by the restructuring of traditional industries, such as steel, coal and shipbuilding.

The European Investment Bank, a non-profit making institution, lends at competitive interest rates to public and private capital investment projects. Lending is directed towards:
- less-favoured regions;
- transport infrastructure;
- protection of the environment;
- improving industrial competitiveness; and
- supporting loans to small and medium-sized enterprises.

The Bank also provides loans in support of the Community's policy of co-operation with the countries of the Mediterranean basin; Central and Eastern Europe; and the African, Caribbean and Pacific (ACP) states (see p. 174).

Employment and Social Affairs

In Britain's view, Community social policy should be primarily concerned with job creation and with maintaining a well-educated and trained workforce to ensure competitiveness in world markets.

The Government supports:
- measures to safeguard health and safety at work, freedom of movement for workers, mutual recognition of professional and vocational qualifications, and equal opportunities at work; and

- practical measures to increase jobs and cut unemployment which do not place more costs on employers.

At Maastricht the Government opposed the extension of Community social policy and qualified majority voting into new areas of social affairs on the grounds that the main responsibility for such policies should remain with individual member states. It negotiated the Social Protocol to the Maastricht Treaty, which allows other member states to agree social legislation in these areas which is not applicable in Britain.

Research and Development

Research collaboration among member states is promoted primarily through a series of framework programmes defining priorities and setting out the overall level of funding. The British Government actively encourages British companies and organisations to participate in collaborative research and development (R & D) with European partners.

The Fourth Framework Programme, adopted in April 1994, focuses on generic and precompetitive research which is of use to a number of industries. It covers information and communications technologies, industrial technologies, the environment, life sciences and technology, energy, transport and socio-economic research. The programme also provides for international co-operation, dissemination of research, and training and mobility of researchers.

Common Foreign and Security Policy

The common foreign and security policy (CFSP) was established by the Maastricht Treaty as an enhanced form of intergovernmental co-operation, distinct from the Community, covering all areas of common foreign and security policy.

The Treaty differentiates between security and defence policy, and confirms that defence issues are a matter for the Western European Union (see p. 114). There is, however, a commitment to 'the eventual framing of a common defence policy, which might in time lead to a common defence'.

The CFSP provides for EU member states to consult each other on issues of general interest and work together more effectively. Member states can agree common positions and take joint actions, and are obliged to respect agreed positions. All decisions are reached by consensus unless it is decided otherwise, again by consensus.

Examples of joint action taken under the CFSP include support for the Middle East peace process; the monitoring of elections in Russia and in South Africa; support for the delivery of humanitarian aid in Bosnia (see p. 123); and backing for the indefinite extension of the nuclear Non-Proliferation Treaty (see p. 128). Joint actions may be funded either by national contributions or from the European Community budget.

INTERNATIONAL PEACE AND SECURITY

Britain believes that states should not use, or threaten, force against other sovereign states and that they should resolve their disputes by peaceful means. The United Nations has the authority to seek to resolve disputes which threaten international peace and stability.

Britain believes that prevention of conflict is better than cure. It is, therefore, particularly active in looking for ways of enhancing the capacity of the UN and other international organisations to predict and prevent conflicts before they arise.

Britain and UN Peacekeeping

Britain fully supports UN efforts to increase the effectiveness of its peacekeeping and has pressed for the strengthening of the UN's Department of Peacekeeping Operations. Ten British officers are currently serving in the Department and are performing operational, financial and other specialist functions.

In 1994 Britain launched an initiative calling for a system of support running from early warning and preventive diplomacy through to humanitarian and peacekeeping operations on the ground. It has also taken the lead in the UN's efforts to reform the funding, administration and logistic support of peacekeeping operations. Together with the United States, Canada and other member states, Britain has made practical proposals for improving logistic support to UN missions and modernising the UN's procurement policies.

Britain pays its own assessed share of the costs of UN peacekeeping (nearly 6.6 per cent of the total), contributing about $250 million in 1994. By July 1995, Britain was contributing more troops to UN operations than any other country. There were nearly 9,000 British military personnel serving with the UN in former Yugoslavia, 600 in Angola, nearly 400 in Cyprus, 15 observers on the Iraq/Kuwait border and ten observers in Georgia.

British Contributions to UN Operations

Bosnia

Britain is committed to supporting efforts to establish a lasting peace in former Yugoslavia and is deeply involved in efforts to relieve suffering caused by the fighting in Bosnia and to prevent it spreading. Since the outbreak of inter-ethnic hostilities in mid-1991 the European Union and the UN have sought to bring peace to the area.

Britain is a major contributor to the UN Protection Force (UNPROFOR) in Bosnia. UNPROFOR seeks to support ceasefires, monitor military activity, safeguard UN-declared safe areas, such as Sarajevo, and escort humanitarian convoys. The British contribution to UNPROFOR consists of two infantry battalion groups, supported by logistic groups and a Royal Fleet Auxiliary based in Split, Croatia. Some 5,000 British troops are deployed as part of UNPROFOR's Rapid Reaction Force. In addition, a 70-strong mortar-locating radar troop is based in Sarajevo, and there are a number of British UN military observers.

The Royal Air Force contributes aircraft to the airlift of supplies to Sarajevo and to operations by NATO over former Yugoslavia. The Royal Navy is participating in NATO/WEU operations in the Adriatic.

Africa

In August 1994, Britain deployed a 600-strong logistic battalion to serve with the UN assistance mission in Rwanda for a period of three months. Its main task was to provide logistic support for the mission, including the repair of over 800 UN vehicles, the rebuilding of key access bridges and restoring utilities. Britain also sent a 600-strong logistic battalion to support the early stages of the recently expanded UN mission in Angola.

Cyprus

Britain continues to provide the largest contingent (nearly 400 strong) to the UN Force in Cyprus, which was established in 1974 to help prevent the recurrence of fighting on the island between Greek and Turkish Cypriots. Since the serious hostilities of 1974, when Turkish forces occupied the northern part of the island, the Force has been responsible for maintaining the ceasefire and control of a buffer zone between the two communities. It also carries out humanitarian missions.

Iraq/Kuwait

In 1991 a Security Council resolution established a demilitarised zone extending 10 km into Iraq and 5 km into Kuwait (see p. 141). Britain, along with the other permanent members of the Security Council, contributes 15 observers to the 1,000-strong UN Iraq/Kuwait observer mission, which was set up in April 1991 to deter violations of the boundary and to observe hostile or potentially hostile actions.

Georgia

Ten British officers are deployed as military observers in Georgia as part of a 136-strong UN observer mission there. The mission was established by the Security Council in August 1993 in order to observe and monitor the ceasefire established following violent conflict between the Georgian armed forces and the Abkhaz separatists.

CENTRAL AND EASTERN EUROPE AND THE FORMER SOVIET UNION

With the disintegration of the Warsaw Pact and the formation of democratically elected governments in Eastern and Central Europe and the former Soviet Union, the European security situation has been transformed.

In November 1990 NATO Allies and former Warsaw Pact states signed a joint declaration in Paris saying that:

- they were no longer adversaries and would build new partnerships;
- they would maintain only enough military forces to prevent war and provide for effective defence; and
- they would form the North Atlantic Co-operation Council to foster co-operation and understanding.

In January 1994 a NATO summit meeting invited the non-NATO states in Eastern and Central Europe and the former Soviet Union to join a Partnership for Peace in order to:

- develop a practical working relationship; and
- enlist the Partners' assistance in peacekeeping operations and guide their armed forces towards compatibility with those of NATO countries.

The Partnership is also monitoring matters such as the Partners' respect for international treaties, civilian control of the military and openness in defence budgeting.

Economic Help

Britain and other Western countries are taking action to help deal with the vast economic problems following the fall of Communism, and to promote the development of market economies. The European Bank for Reconstruction and Development is channelling Western investment to the region. The European Community's PHARE scheme is assisting Central and Eastern European countries in the process of reform and the development of infrastructure. Independent states of the former Soviet Union receive help through a parallel programme (TACIS), which concentrates on financial services, transport, energy (including nuclear safety) and humanitarian needs.

Know How Fund

The Know How Fund is Britain's programme of bilateral technical assistance to the countries of Central and Eastern Europe and the former Soviet Union. It aims to support their transition to pluralist democracy and a market economy by providing British skills and by encouraging British investment in the region.

In Central and Eastern Europe the Fund's main priorities are financial services, including banking, insurance, audit and privatisation; management training; small and medium-sized enterprise development; public administration; and employment services. Lesser priorities are agriculture, energy, industrial restructuring and the environment. In Russia and elsewhere in the former Soviet Union the Fund concentrates on energy, small businesses, financial services, privatisation and restructuring, agricultural reform and health management.

The Know How Fund also finances activities promoting good government and civil society, such as parliamentary exchanges, police training, development of legal services, media development and training.

Recent projects include:

- the establishment of four regional centres for management training and consultancy in Poland;
- helping to strengthen employment services in Russia, Poland, the Czech Republic and Slovakia; and
- advice on the development of a modern and efficient financial services industry throughout the former Soviet Union.

The Fund spent over £60 million in 1993–94 and since its inception in 1989 about £158 million has been allocated to some 2,000 projects.

Europe (Association) Agreements

The European Union has strengthened relations with Bulgaria, the Czech Republic, Estonia, Hungary, Latvia, Lithuania, Poland, Romania and Slovakia by signing Europe (Association) Agreements with these countries. The agreements envisage accession to the European Union when these countries are able to assume the obligations of membership. A strategy to prepare for this was adopted at the Essen European Council in December 1994. Negotiations for a similar agreement with Slovenia have been concluded.

In 1992 the EC agreed to negotiate Partnership and Co-operation Agreements with all the states of the former Soviet Union. Agreements have been signed with Russia, Ukraine, Moldova, Kazakhstan, Kyrgyzstan and Belarus. Trade and Co-operation Agreements are in force with Albania and Slovenia. Negotiations are under way with Georgia, Armenia and Azerbaijan.

The purpose of all these agreements is to reduce trade barriers, develop wide-ranging co-operation and increase political dialogue at all levels.

OTHER REGIONS

The Middle East

Middle East Peace Process

Britain warmly welcomed the breakthrough in the Middle East peace process in September 1993, when Israel and the Palestine Liberation Organisation (PLO) agreed to mutual recognition and signed a Declaration of Principles on interim self-government for the Palestinians in Israeli-held territories occupied in 1967. The first stage of the Declaration was implemented in May 1994, when the Palestinians adopted self-government in the Gaza Strip and the Jericho area. In October 1994 a peace treaty between Israel and Jordan was formally signed. Britain continues to encourage peace negotiations between Israel, Syria and Lebanon.

A further major advance was achieved in September 1995, when Israel and the PLO reached an interim agreement providing for a phased Israeli troop withdrawal from occupied Palestinian areas of the West Bank and for elections to a new Palestinian Council with legislative and executive powers. The British Government applauded the agreement, recognising the difficult compromises made on both sides.

Along with its other European Union partners, Britain has supported peace moves,

politically and economically, and is committing £85 million over three years on aid to the Palestinians and the peace process through bilateral and multilateral channels. Many programmes are already under way and are designed to support Palestinian administration, police training, the Palestinian Monetary Authority, legal structures and the judiciary, water management and health care.

The Gulf Conflict

As a permanent member of the UN Security Council, Britain strongly condemned Iraq's invasion of Kuwait in August 1990 and supported all the Council's resolutions designed to force Iraqi withdrawal and restore international legality. Because of Iraq's failure to withdraw, its forces were expelled in February 1991 by an international coalition led by the United States, Britain, France and Saudi Arabia, acting under a UN mandate.

UN Security Council Resolution 687, adopted in April 1991, formalised the ceasefire in the Gulf War and stipulated conditions for Iraqi acceptance, including measures to prevent the development of weapons of mass destruction, recognition of the border with Kuwait and the payment of compensation to those who suffered as a result of the invasion of Kuwait. The resolution, fully supported by Britain, imposed sanctions on Iraq which remain in force until the Security Council is satisfied that Iraq is fully in compliance with it.

As part of the agreement ending hostilities, the Security Council authorised the creation of a Special Commission (UNSCOM) to supervise the elimination of Iraq's weapons of mass destruction. Britain has provided considerable support to UNSCOM and the International Atomic Energy Authority in the form of personnel, equipment and information since the first inspection in May 1991.

The Security Council approved a separate resolution (688) in response to continued oppression by the Iraqi regime of the civilian population in northern Iraq and the marshes of southern Iraq. 'No fly' zones operate over both areas to monitor Iraqi actions and to deter air attacks. Britain takes an active part in both operations.

Iraqi troop movements threatening Kuwait in September/October 1994 were countered by swift military reinforcements by Britain and its coalition partners.

Sub-Saharan Africa

For many years, Britain has been concerned with the affairs of sub-Saharan Africa, where positive developments have included the abolition of apartheid and the establishment of a non-racial democracy in South Africa and free elections in Kenya, Malawi and Zambia.

The British Government has maintained close relations with all the main parties associated with political reform in South Africa and welcomed the first non-racial elections in April 1994. Britain helped to assist peacekeeping during the elections and allocated resources to the training of election officials and to the monitoring of election policing.

The British Government is working with President Mandela and his Government of National Unity to prepare black South Africans to play their full part in the government and the economy of their country. In addition to a £100 million aid package over the three years 1994–96, Britain is supporting South Africa's development through trade and investment, and with the backing of £1,000 million in official export credit guarantees. Britain is the largest overseas investor in South Africa, with a market value of between £8,000 million and £10,000 million. There is also a British investment promotion scheme designed to encourage more small and medium-sized businesses to invest in South Africa. In addition, young business people from Soweto are gaining management experience with British companies.

In spring 1995 the Queen paid a state visit to South Africa, thereby setting the seal on the revival of friendship between both countries.

Asia-Pacific Region

The dynamic growth of the East Asian economies has made the Asia-Pacific region more important in world affairs. There is also an encouraging trend towards political liberalisation.

Britain has a long association with the region and is giving it an even higher priority in its foreign policy. Close relations are maintained with Japan, China, India and Pakistan, the ASEAN countries (Brunei, Thailand, Malaysia, the Philippines and Singapore), Australia and New Zealand. Britain has defence links with some countries in the region. It is also contributing to the economic development of Vietnam.

The Indo-British Partnership initiative, established in 1993, has done much to encourage commercial and investment links between Britain and India.

Britain has stepped up political dialogue with countries in the region, developing British commercial activity through more trade and investment, and co-operating even more closely on international problem solving. It is also taking advantage of growing opportunities for English language teaching, co-operation in science and technology, and educational exchanges.

North and South America

Britain has long-established political, trade and cultural links with the United States. As founding members of NATO, both countries are deeply involved in Western defence arrangements (see p. 114) and, as permanent members of the UN Security Council, work closely together on major international issues. Strong links are also maintained with Canada, with whom Britain shares membership of the Commonwealth, NATO and other key international organisations. All three countries are members of the Group of Seven, which meets each year at the annual Economic Summit.

Important British connections with South America date from the participation of British volunteers in the wars of independence in the early 19th century. Britain has welcomed the fact that democratically elected governments are now the norm in the region; this, together with the trend towards more free market economies, presents many opportunities for Britain to strengthen its relations with Latin

American governments. The British Government is organising a three-year Latin American trade campaign—Link into Latin America—to promote trade and investment. There has been considerable British investment in Latin America as a result of the free market economic policies and economic growth of the last few years. There is a British diplomatic post in every Latin American country.

ARMS CONTROL

Britain and the other members of NATO are pledged to pursue further progress in arms control and confidence-building measures. Under recent agreements, nuclear forces in the former Soviet Union have been reduced and Russian forces have been withdrawn from Eastern Europe.

Nuclear Weapons

In 1991 the United States and the former Soviet Union signed the first Strategic Arms Reduction Treaty (START), under which an equal limit of 6,000 nuclear warheads on both sides was agreed, with an equal sub-limit of 4,900 ballistic missile warheads. The Treaty required the parties to reduce their strategic missiles and warheads by about 35 per cent over 15 years, including a cut of up to 50 per cent in the most destabilising systems.

In 1993 the United States and Russia signed a new treaty agreeing to reduce their strategic nuclear weapons by two-thirds within ten years.

Britain's position is that it would respond to the challenge of multilateral talks on the global reduction of nuclear arms in a world in which those of the US and Russian forces were counted in hundreds rather than thousands.

Britain is committed to early progress in the negotiations on a comprehensive nuclear test ban treaty. It supports a treaty of indefinite duration, with effective verification and the widest possible adherence, in order to prevent the development of a sophisticated nuclear weapon by a would-be proliferator. Britain has announced that it will no longer take part in any nuclear tests.

Britain is also committed to the early negotiation of a universally applicable convention banning the production of fissile material for nuclear weapons and other explosive purposes.

Conventional Weapons

The 1990 Conventional Armed Forces in Europe Treaty commits the NATO Allies and members of the former Warsaw Pact to reductions in five major classes of offensive conventional weapons.

The ceilings for both groups of states in the area between the Atlantic and the Ural Mountains are 20,000 tanks, 30,000 armoured combat vehicles, 20,000 artillery pieces, 2,000 attack helicopters and 6,800 combat aircraft. No individual state may hold more than two-thirds of the equipment the Treaty allows its group. Weapons above the agreed ceilings must be destroyed or rendered permanently unfit for further military use. Intrusive arrangements to verify compliance are included in the Treaty. Weapons have been reduced by over 30,000 in accordance with the Treaty's provisions.

Chemical Weapons

Britain took a leading part in the lengthy negotiations on a chemical weapons ban, having abandoned its own chemical weapons in the late 1950s. These negotiations were completed in 1992, and 159 countries, including Britain, have signed a convention which enters into force six months after 65 states have ratified it. By August 1995, 32 had done so.

The Chemical Weapons Convention will prohibit the production, stockpiling and use of chemical weapons. There is a system of declarations and inspections to verify compliance, and provisions for the control and monitoring of the transfer of chemicals which have been identified as potentially usable in making weapons. Britain is active in a preparatory commission which is working out ways of implementing the Convention.

Biological Weapons

The 1972 Biological and Toxin Weapons Convention prohibits the development, production and stockpiling of these weapons but currently lacks methods of verification. A 1991 review conference introduced confidence-building measures providing for exchange of information between the parties to the Convention and set up an expert group to identify and examine potential verification measures. This was followed by a special conference in September 1994 which agreed to establish an *ad hoc* group to take forward work on arrangements for verification. The first meetings of the group took place in Geneva in January and July 1995. Britain is playing a leading role in the important discussions on compliance measures.

Non-Proliferation

Britain aims to:
● prevent the proliferation of nuclear weapons;
● ban the manufacture and possession of chemical and biological weapons;
● control the transfer of ballistic missiles and their components and technology; and
● prevent accumulations of conventional armaments which create regional instability.

Britain has signed a number of agreements designed to control the proliferation of weapons of mass destruction. These include the 1968 Non-Proliferation Treaty on nuclear weapons, the 1972 Biological and Toxin Weapons Convention and the 1993 Chemical Weapons Convention (see p. 127). A review conference was held in New York in April/May 1995 and agreed unanimously to extend the Non-Proliferation Treaty indefinitely.

UN Register of Arms Transfers

Following a British initiative a universal and non-discriminatory register of conventional arms transfers was set up by the UN. The register, covering seven categories of equipment, is designed to introduce greater openness and make it easier for the international community to monitor an excessive arms build-up in any one country. A total of 91 countries submitted data to the register for 1992—its first year of operation—and 88 for 1993.

Confidence-building Measures

Important confidence-building measures regarding military exercises and other activities in Europe are in force.

The Organisation for Security and Co-operation in Europe (OSCE), which was until December 1994 the Conference on Security and Co-operation in Europe (CSCE), provides a forum for dialogue on such matters as arms control. Participants include the republics of the former Soviet Union, the other European states and the United States and Canada.

Under the 1992 Vienna Document, CSCE participating states agreed on a number of further confidence-building measures, including:
● annual exchanges of information on military forces, equipment and budgets;
● prior notification of certain military activities; and
● challenge inspections and evaluation visits to military bases.

At a summit in December 1994 new security measures were agreed, including military contacts and co-operation, arms transfers, global exchange of information, and non-proliferation.

Open Skies Treaty

Britain played an important role in negotiations leading to the signing in March 1992 of the Open Skies Treaty, which will allow flights over the entire territories of its participants by aircraft to monitor military capabilities and activity. The Treaty has been signed by all NATO members, Belarus, Bulgaria, the Czech Republic, Georgia, Hungary, Kyrgyzstan, Poland, Romania, Russia, Slovakia and Ukraine.

When ratified by 20 signatories, the Treaty, which is of unlimited duration, will be phased in over three years; when fully in force, it will promote military openness and enhance security. By March 1995 the Treaty had been ratified by 18 countries.

HUMAN RIGHTS

The protection of human rights is an important part of British foreign policy.

Universal respect for human rights is an obligation under the UN Charter, reinforced by human rights law in the form of UN and regional human rights treaties. The British Government played a key role at the 1993 Vienna UN World Conference on Human Rights, which reaffirmed that human rights are a legitimate concern of the international community. The expressions of concern about human rights do not, therefore, constitute interference in the internal affairs of another state.

The Universal Declaration of Human Rights was adopted by the UN General Assembly in 1948. Since this is not a legally binding document, the General Assembly adopted two international covenants in 1966, placing legal obligations on those states ratifying or acceding to them. The covenants came into force in 1976, Britain ratifying both in the same year. One covenant deals with economic, social and cultural rights and the other with civil and political rights. States which are parties to the covenants undertake to submit periodic reports detailing compliance with their terms. Each covenant has a UN treaty monitoring committee which examines these reports. Britain recognises the competence of these committees to receive and consider state-to-state complaints.

Other international conventions to which Britain is a party include those on:

- the elimination of racial discrimination;

- the elimination of all forms of discrimination against women;

- the rights of the child;

- torture and other cruel, inhuman or degrading treatment or punishment;

- prevention of genocide;

- the abolition of slavery; and

- the status of refugees.

The Council of Europe

Britain is bound by the Council of Europe's Convention for the Protection of Human Rights and Fundamental Freedoms, which covers:
- the right to life, liberty and a fair trial;

- the right to marry and have a family;

- freedom of thought, conscience and religion;

- freedom of expression, including freedom of the press;

- freedom of peaceful assembly and association;

- the right to have a sentence reviewed by a higher tribunal; and

- the prohibition of torture and inhuman or degrading treatment.

Complaints about violations of the Convention are made to the European Commission of Human Rights in Strasbourg. Although one state may lodge a complaint against another, most complaints are brought against states by individuals or groups. The Commission decides whether cases are admissible and, if so, examines the matter with the parties with a view to achieving a friendly settlement. If this fails, the Commission or the state concerned can refer the case to the European Court of Human Rights, which rules on whether the Convention has been breached. Britain accepts the Court's compulsory jurisdiction and the right of individual petition. Britain has signed and ratified the 11th Protocol to the Convention, which concerns the replacement of the existing Commission and Court with a full-time Court.

Organisation for Security and Co-operation in Europe

The OSCE's human rights body, the Office for Democratic Institutions and Human Rights (ODIHR) in Warsaw, is responsible for furthering human rights, democracy and the rule of law. It provides a forum for meetings and expert seminars to discuss the implementation of commitments in the area of human rights. The ODIHR shares and exchanges information on the building of democratic institutions and the holding of elections in participating states. It also co-ordinates the monitoring of elections and provides expertise and training on constitutional and legal matters.

Westminster Foundation for Democracy

The Westminster Foundation for Democracy helps to strengthen pluralistic democratic institutions in other countries.

The three main political parties (see p. 52) are represented on the Board of Governors, who are appointed by the Foreign and Commonwealth Secretary. There is also a representative of the smaller political parties, plus non-party figures drawn from business, trade unions, the academic world and other non-governmental organisations. The Foreign & Commonwealth Office has a non-voting advisory member. The Foundation is independent and the British Government cannot veto projects the Board chooses to support. Advice is given by the Foundation on the development of:

- election systems, administration and monitoring;
- parliaments or other representative institutions;
- political parties;
- free media;
- trade unions; and
- human rights groups.

The Foundation is concentrating its efforts initially on Central and Eastern Europe, the former Soviet Union and on anglophone Africa. It does, however, consider sympathetically applications for projects elsewhere in the world.

INTERNATIONAL CRIME

The British Government attaches importance to action against international terrorism and to international co-operation against drug traffickers and organised crime. Britain and the other members of the European Union have agreed not to export arms or other military equipment to countries clearly implicated in supporting terrorist activity, and to take steps to prevent such material being diverted for terrorist purposes.

It is EU policy that:

- no concessions should be made to terrorists or their sponsors; and

- there should be solidarity among member states in the prevention of terrorism.

Britain participates actively in international forums on co-operation against the illegal drugs trade, maintains a substantial programme of overseas assistance in this field and stations drug liaison officers in a number of countries in order to liaise with the host authorities in the fight against drug trafficking. In recent years Britain has contributed over £20 million to the UN International Drug Control Programme, which has the leading international role against the illegal drugs trade.

EU member states are setting up a central European Police Office (EUROPOL) to provide Union-wide intelligence about serious crime. As a step in this process, a EUROPOL Drugs Unit has already been established. EU member states also belong to the International Criminal Police Organisation (INTERPOL). British liaison with INTERPOL is provided by the National Criminal Intelligence Service (see p. 84).

Under the Maastricht Treaty, work in the areas of justice and home affairs is being intensified through increased intergovernmental co-operation. The first convention agreed under these arrangements, simplifying extradition between member states, was signed in March 1995.

In September 1994 a programme of police and judicial co-operation was agreed between the European Union and the Central and Eastern European states to combat cross-border crime in Europe.

DEVELOPMENT CO-OPERATION

The aim of Britain's overseas aid effort is to improve the quality of life and reduce poverty, suffering and deprivation in developing countries.

British aid, which is delivered through the Foreign & Commonwealth Office's Overseas Development Administration (ODA), was £2,172 million in 1993–94. Included in this was £1,930 million for developing countries, £181 million for countries in transition in

Central and Eastern Europe and the former Soviet Union (see p. 124), and £53 million spent on administration. About 55 per cent was given directly to individual countries and the remainder channelled through international bodies, such as the European Union, the United Nations and the World Bank. In addition, over £240 million was invested in developing countries by the Commonwealth Development Corporation (see below). Some of the aid budget goes to programmes administered by the British Council (see p. 134) and by over 120 non-governmental organisations.

The British aid programme seeks to:

- promote economic growth and reform;
- promote good government;
- finance activities directly benefiting poor people;
- promote better education and health;
- improve the status of women in developing countries; and
- help developing countries to tackle their environmental problems.

Economic Reform

Britain provides bilateral technical assistance, including advice on privatisation and the improvement of essential public services. Much of Britain's aid to help economic reform goes to the World Bank's special programme of assistance for 31 African countries. Zambia, Uganda, Tanzania and Ghana have been among the principal recipients. Aid includes balance-of-payments help to enable countries to import essential goods and meet their other external payments. It also includes the provision of personnel, training and consultancies associated with reforms in areas such as revenue collection, the civil service, public expenditure management and the financial sector.

The Private Sector

The Commonwealth Development Corporation is the Government's main instrument within the aid programme for encouraging private-sector investment in developing countries. It provides loans, equity funds and management services for financially viable investments in agriculture, fisheries, minerals, industry, transport, communications and housing. By the end of 1994 it had investments and commitments worth over £1,700 million in 52 countries, 39 of which are members of the Commonwealth.

In addition, the ODA supports enterprise development through schemes such as:

- initiatives to simplify regulations constraining small firms in Zimbabwe;
- projects supporting various financial and technical services—for example, in Bangladesh and Kenya; and
- new projects to support African business in South Africa.

The ODA has programmes for encouraging all types of enterprise to perform better—for example, in developing exports. In India it is targeting small to medium-sized companies which are starting to export. Spending on projects offering direct support to the private sector was £123 million in 1993–94.

Good Government

Britain believes that progress in economic growth and the reduction of poverty can best be pursued by more open and effective forms of government and the observance of human rights and the rule of law. Britain has supported good government projects, such as assistance for public sector and civil service reform, improving tax and audit administration, reforming legal systems and helping to organise and monitor elections.

Reducing Poverty

About two-thirds of British bilateral aid goes to the poorest countries. In India, Pakistan and Bangladesh projects include rural development, urban slum upgrading and the provision of health, family planning and education services for poor people. Some of the ODA's projects helping the poor are carried out in conjunction with non-governmental organisations. In Africa, for example, such schemes include a clear water sanitation project run by WaterAid, which is helping over 30,000 people in Ethiopia, and a maternal health scheme in Sudan with CARE to improve the health of 100,000 child-bearing women.

Since 1988 Britain has initiated a number of debt-relief schemes, including debt reduction of two-thirds of eligible debt for 20 of the poorest, most indebted countries undertaking economic reform.

Education

ODA-funded education projects cover a range of areas, such as health, political and social life, and the environment. Help is given to education ministries to assist educational planning and to increase the access of disadvantaged groups to teaching facilities. Expenditure on education projects was £117 million in 1993–94.

In 1993–94 over 10,000 students from developing countries, mainly postgraduates, received ODA support to study in Britain and other countries. The ODA also provided more than 2,500 scholarship and fellowship awards; in addition, over 1,250 Foreign & Commonwealth Office awards were made, administered by the British Council. Part of Britain's £60 million aid package to South Africa is a £2 million project that will provide bursaries and loans to 1,200 university and technical students from disadvantaged communities studying science, engineering, commerce and medicine.

The £30 million primary education project in Andhra Pradesh, India, is the largest in the ODA education programme. It has resulted in the training of 165,000 teachers and the construction of 3,000 new classrooms and over 1,000 teacher resource centres. Through another important scheme, which started in 1980, over 5 million primary school children in South Africa have learned to read and write in their own language and in English. Practical education and training is being provided to villagers in Senegal through a scheme run by the British Council and OXFAM and funded by the ODA. The villagers are being shown how to cultivate newly reclaimed dry land.

Health

The ODA invests over £100 million a year on health care and on improving water supplies and sanitation. The main aim is to help bring cheap health care services to the poorest and more vulnerable sections of the community. Assistance is focused on about 20 countries, mostly in Africa and South Asia. Attention is given in particular to:

● helping to establish management systems to ensure the provision of essential health care as efficiently as possible;

● increasing the availability of reproductive health services; and

● improving control of infectious diseases, including tuberculosis, malaria and HIV/AIDS.

Status of Women

Thirteen per cent of Britain's bilateral aid programme in 1993–94 was committed to projects targeted at women in developing countries. The ODA supports activities which help women to gain greater access to education and health services; earn an income; play a greater role in managing public services; gain access to legal training; and learn and develop business skills.

The Environment

Britain helps countries to address their national environmental problems and to take action on global environmental concerns shared by all countries.

Britain has committed about £130 million to the Global Environmental Facility (GEF), which helps developing countries and the countries of Eastern and Central Europe and the former Soviet Union to finance the costs of reducing emissions of greenhouse gases, conserving biological diversity, reducing ozone depletion and tackling international water pollution.

Climate Change

Britain signed the Convention on Climate Change at the 1992 Earth Summit and ratified it in December 1993. The aim of the Convention is to stabilise atmospheric concentrations of greenhouse gases at a level which will prevent dangerous climate change. It commits all parties to prepare national programmes identifying sources of such gases and steps to limit emissions. Britain believes that the best way of assisting developing countries to reduce greenhouse gas emission is through energy efficiency programmes. Between 1991 and 1994 Britain spent over £140 million on projects that promote energy efficiency.

Ozone Depletion

Britain had, by the end of 1994, committed £27 million to the Montreal Protocol's Multilateral Fund, set up to meet the extra costs to developing countries of phasing out ozone-depleting substances.

Biodiversity

The Rio Biodiversity Convention, which Britain signed in June 1992 and ratified a year later, requires countries to take action to halt the loss of animal and plant species and genetic resources, and to produce plans for conserving them.

Britain is helping countries to fulfil their obligations under the Biodiversity Convention through its contributions to the GEF, the British bilateral aid programme and the Darwin Initiative for the Survival of Species, launched at the Earth Summit in 1992.

Saving Forestry

The UN's Food and Agriculture Organisation has estimated that during the 1980s an area of tropical forest nearly the size of England and Wales was destroyed each year. Forests are important for the world's climate since trees absorb CO_2, a gas which contributes to global warming. Forests are also a major habitat for biological diversity.

The ODA has about 200 forestry projects under way or under preparation, costing

£157 million. They are designed to help developing countries use their forests sustainably and to reduce the rate of deforestation.

Britain is providing over £23 million to support a project in the Western Ghats in India which aims to enable local people to provide for their needs from the forests while ensuring that the forests are managed sustainably.

Renewable Natural Resources Research

Nearly £160 million was spent between 1991 and 1994 on research programmes in Britain and overseas for the benefit of developing countries. Programmes have covered agriculture, fisheries and aquatic resources, forestry, livestock, natural resources systems, pest management and post-harvest technology. The ODA introduced a revised renewable natural resources research strategy in April 1995.

Britain is also a founder member of, and substantial contributor to, the institutions of the Consultative Group on International Agricultural Research, which carry out research into the conservation of food and fodder crops.

The Natural Resources Institute, the ODA's scientific executive agency, helps developing countries to improve the productivity and sustainable management of their natural resources through the application of science and technology. Programmes include:

● pest control which relies less on chemical pesticides and minimises the disturbance of wildlife habitats; and

● the use of artificial structures to rehabilitate the graded reefs in the south Pacific and so increase their ability to support the fish population.

Emergency Relief

The ODA's Disaster Unit co-ordinates the British Government's response to natural and man-made disasters overseas and to emergencies involving refugees. The ODA is able to send trained assessors to the disaster area quickly to assist the United Nations in providing vital information on what needs to be done.

Following a British–German initiative, the UN Department for Humanitarian Affairs was established in 1992. The Department is responsible for co-ordinating prompt UN and international reaction to emergencies.

The ODA also funds disaster mitigation projects, such as a 'risk-mapping' programme run by the Save the Children Fund in Malawi, which aims to identify areas most prone to drought.

In 1993–94 Britain spent nearly £180 million on 135 emergencies. In addition, the British public sends substantial sums for emergency relief overseas through non-governmental organisations.

CULTURAL RELATIONS

The British Council is Britain's principal agency for cultural relations overseas, working in 228 towns and cities in 109 countries. The Council:

- helps people to study, train or make professional contacts in Britain;
- enables British specialists to teach, advise or establish joint projects abroad;
- teaches English and promotes its use;
- provides library and information services; and
- makes British arts and literature more widely known.

The Council runs 185 libraries, resource centres and information centres, and 83 English language teaching centres, including 34 in Central and Eastern Europe. In 1993–94 about 8.2 million loans of books and other materials were made to 440,000 library members. About 100,000 people in 40 countries take part in the Council's English courses.

The Council is financed partly by a grant from the Foreign & Commonwealth Office. The training and education programmes organised by the Council as part of the British aid programme are another important source of income. Well over a quarter of the Council's income comes from other earnings.

Educational Exchanges

The British Council recruits teachers for work overseas, organises short overseas visits by British experts, encourages cultural exchange visits and organises academic interchange between British universities and colleges and those in other countries. The Council arranges over 50,000 visits to and from Britain a year.

The ODA helps fund certain Council programmes, such as:

- recruitment of staff for overseas universities;
- secondment of staff from British higher education establishments; and
- organisation of short-term teaching and advisory visits.

The Central Bureau for Educational Visits and Exchanges, which is part of the British Council, promotes partnerships and exchanges between schools, teachers, students and pupils throughout Europe. Opportunities for young people include school and class links and English language summer camps. For the post-16 age group, there are work placements and English language assistants' posts as well as other exchange programmes.

The Arts

The British Council initiates or supports more than 1,400 arts and literature events a year. These activities include tours by British theatre companies, orchestras, choirs, opera and dance companies, and jazz, rock and folk groups, as well as visits by individual actors, musicians and artists. The Council also arranges for directors, designers, choreographers and conductors to work in other countries. In addition, it organises and supports literature, fine arts and other cultural exhibitions and British participation in book fairs and international film festivals.

Further Reading

Britain and Development Aid. Aspects of Britain series, HMSO, 1995.

Britain, NATO and European Security. Aspects of Britain series, HMSO, 1994.

British Council Annual Report.

Departmental Report 1995: The Government's Expenditure Plans 1995–96 to 1997–98. Foreign & Commonwealth Office, including Overseas Development Administration. Cm 2802. HMSO, 1995.

European Union. Aspects of Britain series, HMSO, 1994.

Statement on the Defence Estimates 1995. HMSO, 1995.

10 Defence

Britain's defence policy supports its wider security policy, which is to maintain the country's freedom and territorial integrity and that of its dependent territories as well as its ability to pursue its legitimate interests at home and abroad. As a member of NATO (North Atlantic Treaty Organisation), Britain makes a major contribution to maintaining stability throughout Europe.

INTRODUCTION

With the removal of the strategic threat to Britain as a result of the end of the Cold War, progress is being made in security-building and co-operation with states in central and eastern Europe. However, the end of East–West confrontation has been followed by problems of instability, nationalism and extremism within Europe and beyond. These developments are the major factors shaping defence policy today. Britain and its allies in NATO have responded to these changes by adapting their policies and the structure of their armed forces to meet the defence requirements of the future.

NATO remains the foundation of Britain's defence and security policies. In addition, Britain works to increase security through its membership of the Western European Union (WEU), the European Union (EU), the Organisation for (formerly Conference on) Security and Co-operation in Europe (OSCE—see p. 129) and the United Nations (UN—see p. 112). These organisations have been involved in activities such as negotiating an end to conflicts, peacekeeping deployments and humanitarian missions.

Britain and the other WEU member states are developing the WEU as the defence component of the European Union and as a means of strengthening the European pillar of the Atlantic Alliance. In co-operation with NATO, Britain and the WEU are supporting the implementation of conflict prevention and crisis management measures. At a NATO summit in January 1994 it was decided that NATO assets could be made available for European/WEU operations.

The current fundamental restructuring of Britain's armed forces recognises the need for flexibility in the face of future uncertainty. The armed forces are, therefore, equipped to take part in integrated operations, ranging from small-scale peacekeeping or humanitarian missions to large-scale high–intensity conflict. A new permanent headquarters for joint operations is to be set up at Northwood, London, by April 1996. This will include the core of a deployable headquarters that could be established in a theatre of operations. Britain's nuclear forces (see pp. 141–2) provide the ultimate guarantee for its security.

> By April 1996, the strength of the armed forces will be around 117,000 in the Army, about 66,500 in the Royal Air Force (RAF) and about 48,000 in the Royal Navy. Under plans outlined in the Defence Costs Study, there will be a net reduction of just under 19,000 defence jobs by the year 2000—2,200 in the Army, 7,500 in the RAF, 1,900 in the Royal Navy and 7,100 British-based civil servants.

The highest priority continues to be placed on maximising the cost-effectiveness and military capabilities of the armed forces. Launched in December 1993, the Defence Costs Study—*Front Line First* (see p. 144)— examined all areas of administration and support to the front line to ensure that the money spent contributes directly or indirectly to fighting capability.

NORTH ATLANTIC TREATY ORGANISATION

NATO has provided Britain's main means of defence against a major external threat for the past 45 years. It is the only security organisation with the military means to back up its security guarantees and has consequently undertaken action on behalf of the UN. NATO unites the interests of Europe and North America in the pursuit of peace, stability and well-being in the whole of Europe. All Britain's nuclear forces and most of its conventional forces are committed to NATO.

NATO is continuing the process of adaptation that began with the 1991 Rome Declaration and the resulting new Strategic Concept to allow it to play a wider role in maintaining stability throughout Europe.

January 1994 NATO Summit

The January 1994 NATO Summit marked an important step in the Alliance's post–Cold War evolution. It launched a major initiative called Partnership for Peace, which seeks to deepen political and military ties between NATO and the central and eastern European countries in areas such as peacekeeping and humanitarian operations. By July 1995, 26 states had signed the Partnership for Peace, including Russia, almost all the central and eastern European states, Sweden, Finland, Austria, Malta and most of the central Asian and Trans-Caucasian states of the former Soviet Union.

In addition to its work within NATO on Partnership for Peace, Britain has signed formal Memoranda of Understanding on bilateral defence contacts with Albania, Bulgaria, the Czech Republic, Estonia, Finland, Hungary, Latvia, Lithuania, Poland, Romania, Russia, Slovakia, Slovenia, Sweden and the Ukraine. The Memoranda are designed to promote stability in central and eastern Europe, exchange military information and encourage co-operation on defence equipment. Britain provides advice on civil–military relations, including democratic control and accountability, English language training, defence budgeting and management. These contacts are complementary to those within NATO.

The 1994 NATO Summit also:

- committed the Alliance to continued adaptation of its political and military structures in order to reflect all its roles and the development of the emerging European security and defence identity;
- endorsed the concept of joint task forces which will allow a flexible and effective response to a broad range of missions and for the inclusion of non–NATO forces and operations under WEU auspices;
- reaffirmed that the Alliance remains open to the membership of other European countries; and
- declared NATO's intentions to intensify its efforts against the proliferation of weapons of mass destruction.

NATO Force Structures

The size, availability and deployment of NATO forces continue to reflect the Alliance's defensive nature. Current NATO strategy involves:

- deployment in Europe of smaller and highly mobile forces;
- a move away from the concept of forward presence;
- a reduced reliance on nuclear weapons;
- the scaling back of the state of readiness of allied armed forces; and
- a reduction in training requirements and exercises.

NATO's Strategic Concept recognises that the far-reaching changes in the strategic setting, together with the growth of new risks to international order and stability, require an active response from the Alliance. While the primary role of Alliance military forces remains to guarantee the security and territorial integrity of its members, force levels are being reduced and restructured while missions are being broadened. Force structures comprising reaction, main defence and augmentation forces have been established and are intended to be mutually supporting.

NATO Command Structures

The NATO command structure has been adapted to the changing environment. At the highest level, the number of Commands has been cut back from three to two—Allied Command Europe and Allied Command Atlantic.

There have been considerable modifications in Allied Command Europe. Of importance to Britain is the formation of Allied Forces North West Europe, which incorporates the land mass of Britain and Norway, the United Kingdom air defence region and the North Sea; it is commanded from headquarters at RAF High Wycombe, in Buckinghamshire.

UNITED KINGDOM DEFENCE POLICY

Defence Roles and Military Tasks

British defence policy is defined in terms of overlapping Defence Roles One, Two and Three, which are:

- to ensure the protection and security of Britain and its dependent territories, even when there is no major external threat;
- to insure against any major external threat to Britain and its allies; and
- to contribute to promoting Britain's wider security interests through the maintenance of international peace and stability.

Within these three defence roles are a range of tasks which define the military activities to be undertaken by the Ministry of Defence and the armed forces in order to give effect to defence and security policy.

Britain and Its Dependencies

The armed forces continue to have day-to-day responsibility for safeguarding Britain's territory, airspace and territorial waters. They also provide for the security and reinforcement, as necessary, of the dependent territories and, when required, support for the civil authorities in Britain and the dependent territories.

Maritime Defence

The Royal Navy ensures the integrity of British territorial waters and the protection of British rights and interests in the surrounding seas. The maintenance of a 24-hour-a-day, year-round presence in British waters provides considerable reassurance to merchant ships and other mariners. The Royal Air Force (RAF) also contributes to maritime requirements, including the Nimrod MR2 force, which provides surveillance of surface vessels and submarines.

THE 50TH ANNIVERSARY OF VE DAY

A street party in Oxford Street, London, arranged by the British Red Cross Society, captures the atmosphere of VE Day.

The Queen meets veterans of World War II and their families outside Buckingham Palace, where thousands gathered for a concert held to commemorate the end of the war 50 years earlier.

BRITAIN IN EUROPE

Children at the European School in Culham, Oxfordshire. There are nine such schools within the European Union, providing a multilingual education leading to the European Baccalaureate.

The European Parliament in Strasbourg. Membership increased from 567 to 626 with the accession of Austria, Finland and Sweden in 1995; Britain's allocation of seats is 87.

Britain is a member of CERN, the European Laboratory for Particle Physics, based in Geneva. Shown here is the ALEPH (Apparatus for LEP PHysics) detector, the main component in a high energy physics experiment.

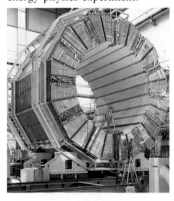

Leighton Moss, Lancashire, is designated as a Special Protection Area for birds under the European Community Birds Directive.

The European Youth Orchestra gives a concert in London's Hyde Park as Britain commemorates the 50th anniversary of the end of the Second World War.

NORTHERN IRELAND PEACE PROCESS

The peace process in Northern Ireland took an important step forward in 1994 with the announcement of a ceasefire by the IRA and the loyalist paramilitary organisations. The process was further enhanced by the publication in February 1995 of *Frameworks for the Future*, which outlines the British and Irish governments' view on where agreement might be found on a political settlement for Northern Ireland.

Pupils at Oakgrove Integrated Primary School, Londonderry, at the site of the city's new Peace Sculpture.

Prime Minister John Major and Irish Premier John Bruton with the *Frameworks for the Future* document.

A bulldozer clears a path through a barrier on the border of Northern Ireland and the Irish Republic, reopening a crossborder road closed for the last 25 years for security reasons.

Land Defence

There are 24 regular infantry battalions committed for activities in Defence Role One. These are augmented by the Territorial Army (see p. 143). Tasks include contributing to national and NATO nuclear forces and maintaining the security of the dependent territories.

Air Defence

Air defence of Britain and the surrounding seas is maintained by a system of layered defences. Continuous radar cover is provided by the Improved United Kingdom Air Defence Ground Environment (IUKADGE), supplemented by the NATO Airborne Early Warning Force, to which the RAF contributes six E–3D aircraft. The RAF also provides six squadrons of all-weather Tornado F3 air defence aircraft, supported by tanker aircraft and, in wartime, an additional F3 squadron and armed Hawk trainer aircraft. Royal Navy air defence destroyers are also linked to the IUKADGE, providing radar and electronic warfare coverage and surface-to-air missiles. Ground-launched Rapier missiles defend the main RAF bases. Naval aircraft also contribute to British air defence.

Overseas Garrisons

Britain maintains garrisons in Hong Kong, Gibraltar, the Sovereign Base Areas of Cyprus and the Falkland Islands. The Hong Kong garrison is being reduced in stages until 1997, when the territory will revert to Chinese sovereignty (see p. 117). Gibraltar provides headquarters and communications facilities for NATO in the western Mediterranean, and Cyprus acts as a base for operations in the Middle East and North Africa.

British forces are stationed in the Falkland Islands to deter possible aggression from Argentina, which maintains its claim to the Islands (see p. 117).

Northern Ireland

The armed forces continue to provide support to the Royal Ulster Constabulary (RUC) in maintaining law and order. There are currently 18 Army infantry units, including six Home Service battalions of the Royal Irish Regiment. The Royal Navy patrols territorial waters around Northern Ireland and its inland waterways in order to deter and intercept the movement of terrorist weapons, although on a much reduced scale following the ceasefire. The Royal Marines provide troops to meet Navy and Army commitments, while RAF helicopters provide support to ground forces.

The absence of large-scale terrorist attacks since the ceasefire announcements by the Provisional IRA (Irish Republican Army) in August 1994 and by loyalist terrorist organisations in the following October (see p. 14) has enabled the RUC to operate with a decreasing level of military support and to make progress towards normal civilian policing. The ceasefire has allowed greater flexibility in the deployment of the armed forces. A number of resident battalions on two-year tours have been released from all routine commitments in support of the RUC, while the armed forces continue to accompany RUC patrols in areas where they may encounter hostility. In addition, two major units have been relocated to their bases in mainland Britain and Germany; they can return to the province at short notice if so required.

Other Tasks

Other Defence Role One tasks include the provision of:

- military support to the machinery of government in war;
- military assistance to government departments, including assistance to maintain the essentials of life in the community and carrying out work of national importance;
- military aid to the civil community, including during emergencies;
- military search and rescue;
- military intelligence and surveillance;
- physical protection and security; and
- state ceremonial and routine public duties.

Britain and Its Allies

This second major defence role is discharged through Britain's membership of NATO.

Maritime Forces

Most Royal Navy ships are committed to NATO. Permanent contributions are made to NATO's standing naval forces in the Atlantic, the English Channel and the Mediterranean. The main components of the Fleet consist of:

- three aircraft carriers operating Sea Harrier aircraft and Sea King anti-submarine warfare helicopters;
- 35 destroyers and frigates;
- 12 nuclear-powered attack submarines; and
- amphibious forces, including two assault ships and a helicopter carrier which is currently under construction.

Land Forces

The multinational Allied Command Europe Rapid Reaction Corps (ARRC) is the key land component of NATO's rapid reaction forces. Britain is the lead nation of the Corps, which became fully operational in 1995.

Britain provides the Corps headquarters and an armoured division based in Germany in peacetime. In addition, it provides a second, more lightly armoured division, based in Britain and comprising two mechanised brigades and an airborne brigade. An airmobile brigade, also based in Britain, will join one of the two multinational divisions in the Corps. Some 55,000 regular British soldiers are assigned to ARRC, together with a substantial number of Territorial Army (see p. 143) and individual reservists.

Air Forces

The RAF makes a major contribution to NATO's Immediate and Rapid Reaction Forces. In all around 100 fixed wing aircraft and 40 helicopters are allocated to support these Reaction Forces. Tornado F3 and Rapier surface-to-air missiles form part of the Supreme Allied Commander Europe's Immediate Reaction Force, while Harrier, Tornado GR1 and GR1a provide offensive support and tactical reconnaissance to the Rapid Reaction Force. Chinook and Puma helicopters provide troop airlift facilities for the ARRC (see above) or other deployed land forces. Tornado F3 and Tornado GR1b aircraft provide air defence or anti-surface attack in support of NATO's maritime reaction forces.

Modified RAF Tornado GR1 aircraft (designated GR1b), equipped with the Sea Eagle missile, have the task of maritime attack. The Tornado GR1b force entered service in 1995. The RAF will continue to provide Nimrod maritime patrol aircraft and search and rescue helicopters.

Since 1991, the number of RAF squadrons in Germany has been reduced to four Tornado GR1 strike/attack squadrons, two Harrier offensive support squadrons and a Puma/Chinook support helicopter squadron at RAF Bruggen and RAF Laarbruch. It is intended that RAF Laarbruch will close in 1999, subject to consultation with the German authorities; the two Harrier squadrons and the support helicopters currently based there will be withdrawn to existing air bases in Britain. The four squadrons of Tornados, however, will remain at RAF Bruggen. These aircraft and personnel, alongside the continuing and significant Army presence in Germany, are a visible sign of Britain's continuing commitment to the defence of Europe.

Other Forces

Britain contributes to NATO's maritime augmentation forces. These are held at the lowest state of readiness and in peacetime comprise ships mainly in routine refit or maintenance. It also contributes special forces to support reaction and main defence force deployments for surveillance, reconnaissance, offensive action and military assistance operations. The United Kingdom Amphibious Force, together with its Dutch counterpart, is assigned to the Supreme Allied Commander Atlantic for the reinforcement of Norway and could be deployed by the Supreme Allied Commander

Europe, for example, with the ARRC. The Force is also a candidate for a range of WEU operations. Assisting these forces are RAF fighter aircraft and a strengthened air transport force.

Wider Security Interests

Military tasks within Defence Role Three are carried out to promote Britain's wider security interests. They may be undertaken unilaterally or multilaterally with support from NATO or directly for UN or OSCE operations.

United Nations Operations

Britain remains a major contributor to UN operations. Contingents are currently deployed in former Yugoslavia (see p. 123), Cyprus, Iraq/Kuwait and Angola; Britain has previously deployed contingents in Cambodia, the Western Sahara and Rwanda. The British manpower contribution to the UN force in Cyprus has been reduced by 50 per cent since 1992, although Britain remains the largest contributor.

Other Operational Deployments

Royal Navy ships of the Armilla Patrol continue to provide reassurance and assistance to entitled merchant shipping in the Gulf area and regularly participate in maritime exercises with navies of Gulf states and coalition allies. The Patrol also conducts interception and boarding operations to ensure that ships do not breach UN sanctions against Iraq (see p. 123).

The number of operations against trafficking in illicit drugs has increased in recent years, especially in the Caribbean, where the West Indies Guardship and other Royal Navy ships work closely with the authorities of the United States, the Dependent Territories and the Regional Security System to combat drug trafficking. Primary responsibility for this work rests with other government departments but the armed forces assist where this can be done without detriment to the performance of other military tasks.

British Garrisons

A British garrison is maintained in Brunei, South-East Asia, at the request of the Brunei Government. The withdrawal of the British garrison in Belize, Central America— originally maintained to deter, and if necessary defend against, possible Guatemalan aggression—was completed at the end of September 1994. This was made possible by Guatemalan recognition of Belize as a sovereign and independent state in 1991 and the establishment of diplomatic relations between the two countries. However, a British military presence is maintained in Belize in the form of a jungle training unit.

Military Assistance

During 1994–95, some 4,100 students from 100 countries attended military training courses in Britain. On 1 January 1995, 395 British Service personnel (53 Royal Navy and Royal Marines, 232 Army and 110 Royal Air Force) were on loan in 24 countries. Their duties include assisting, advising and training the armed forces of the country or territory to which they are loaned.

NUCLEAR FORCES

The Royal Navy's independent nuclear deterrent remains the ultimate guarantee of Britain's security. The current submarine-launched Polaris strategic force is assigned to NATO but remains at all times under the control of the British Government; it enables Britain to provide a second independent centre of decision-making within NATO, thereby enhancing deterrence.

The Polaris force now comprises two nuclear submarines, each capable of carrying 16 Polaris missiles armed with improved British nuclear warheads. The Polaris force is being replaced by four British-built submarines, each of which will carry Trident missiles purchased from the United States. A four-boat force will ensure that one boat is always at sea, invulnerable to pre-emptive attack. Trident's nuclear warheads are British-designed and built. The first Trident submarine, HMS *Vanguard*, began operations in 1995; the second and third, HMS *Victorious* and HMS *Vigilant*, are planned to enter service in 1996 and 1998 respectively.

The Government is committed to maintaining only the minimum deterrent level required for Britain's security. Each Trident submarine will deploy no more than 96 warheads and possibly significantly fewer. On current plans, the explosive power of each submarine will not be much changed from Polaris. When Trident is fully in service, the explosive power of Britain's operational nuclear inventory will be over 25 per cent lower than it was in 1990.

The armed forces also possess sub-strategic nuclear weapons, which provide a link between strategic and conventional forces. Following the end of the Cold War, Britain has made substantial reductions in these weapons, including the elimination of tactical maritime nuclear weapons and a reduction of over 50 per cent in the stockpile of WE177 free-fall nuclear bombs. The remaining WE177s are deployed on dual-capable Tornado aircraft, all of which are available to NATO. In addition, Britain plans to exploit the flexibility and capability of Trident to provide the vehicle for delivery of its sub-strategic deterrent, once the WE177 is withdrawn from service in 1998.

UNITED KINGDOM FORCE STRUCTURES

Defence Equipment Programme

Modern equipment is essential if one of the key aims of Britain's force restructuring programme is to be achieved, namely that of increasing the flexibility and mobility of the armed forces. The successful outcome of the Defence Costs Study (see p. 144) has enabled the British Government to preserve the front line (and its essential operational support) and to make a number of important improvements to its capability.

Current and planned front line improvements for the Royal Navy equipment programme include:

- introduction of Trident submarines to replace Polaris;

- substantial updating of existing nuclear-powered submarines and an invitation to tender for the design and building of a second batch of Trafalgar Class submarines;

- a substantially modernised destroyer and frigate fleet;

- a follow-on batch of 7 Sandown Class single role minehunters;

- introduction of a new helicopter carrier to enhance Britain's amphibious forces;

- 18 new Sea Harrier F/A2 aircraft and the upgrading of the existing Harriers to F/A2 standard; and

- invitations to tender for the design and building of a replacement for the assault ships *Fearless* and *Intrepid*.

The Army front line is being enhanced by:

- Challenger 2 tanks, the first of which entered service in 1995;

- a new attack helicopter to replace the Lynx;

- the Multiple Launch Rocket System and the AS90 self-propelled howitzer, replacing Abbot and M–109 guns;

- improved Rapier and new Starstreak missiles to improve air defence;

- a new medium-range anti-tank missile; and

- a new generation of combat radios.

Improvements for the RAF include:

- the Eurofighter 2000 from the beginning of the next century;

- upgrading of the Tornado GR1 aircraft;

- programmes to enhance the RAF's inventory of air-launched missiles; and

- orders for more EH101 and Chinook support helicopters and/or Hercules C130J aircraft.

THE ARMED FORCES

Commissioned Ranks

Commissions, either by promotion from the ranks or by direct entry based on educational and other qualifications, are granted for short, medium and long terms. All three Services have schemes for school, university and college sponsorships.

Commissioned ranks receive initial training at the Britannia Royal Naval College, Dartmouth; the Royal Military Academy, Sandhurst; or the Royal Air Force College, Cranwell. This is followed by specialist training, which may include degree courses at service establishments or universities.

Higher training for officers is currently provided by the Royal Naval College and Joint Services Defence College, Greenwich; the Army Staff College, Camberley; and the Royal Air Force Staff College, Bracknell. The Defence Costs Study (see p. 144) concluded that courses should be subsumed into a tri-Service course which will reinforce the joint approach to the tactical and operational levels of conflict. As such, the Joint Services Command and Staff College will be established in 1997 at Camberley. The Higher Command and Staff Course, conducted at Camberley, will remain as a focus for the study of the operational level of command, but will be expanded from 24 to 30 officers to increase the joint aspect.

Non-commissioned Ranks

Engagements for non-commissioned ranks in the Army and the RAF range from six months to 22 years; they can be for a maximum of 37 years in the Royal Navy and 32 years in the Royal Marines. There is a wide choice of engagement length and terms of service. Subject to a minimum period of service, entrants may leave at any time, at 18 months' notice (12 months for certain engagements). Discharge may also be granted on compassionate or medical grounds, by purchase or on grounds of conscience.

Throughout their Service careers, non-commissioned personnel receive basic training supplemented by specialist training. Study for educational qualifications is encouraged and Service trade and technical training lead to nationally recognised qualifications.

Reserve Forces

Reserve forces are a central component of Britain's armed forces. They include members who become reservists following a period of regular service (regular reserve); others are volunteers who train in their spare time. Volunteer reserve forces include the Royal Naval Reserve, the Royal Marines Reserve, the Territorial Army, the Royal Auxiliary Air Force and the Royal Air Force Volunteer Reserve. Reserves are available to support regular forces, either as units or as individuals, in time of tension or war. In particular, reserves can provide skills and units not available or required in peacetime. Reserves are also a valuable link between the Services and the civil community. The role of the reserves is likely to increase in importance in the future to include, for example, a role in the range of lesser contingencies in which British forces are liable to be involved.

In April 1995 regular reserves totalled around 262,900 and volunteer reserves and auxiliary forces some 65,800.

ADMINISTRATION

The Defence Budget

The estimated defence budget for 1995–96 is £21,720 million, with expenditure plans for 1996–97 and 1997–98 of £21,920 million and £22,320 million respectively. The Government anticipates a reduction of 14.5 per cent in real terms between 1992–93 and 1997–98. Britain spent 3.8 per cent of Gross Domestic Product on defence in 1992–93; this is expected to fall to 2.8 per cent by 1997–98.

Defence Management

The Ministry of Defence has a dual role as a Department of State and the highest military headquarters of the armed forces. A unified Central Staff made up of military officers and civilians was formed within the Ministry of Defence in 1994 through the abolition of the former Defence Staff and the Office of Management and Budget, continuing a long process of civilian/military integration. It is responsible for defence policy, resource allocation and equipment requirements, direction of operations at the highest level, and management policy for the armed forces and the Ministry of Defence.

Department support services are provided to the Head Office, Commands and budget-holders by, among others, the Procurement Executive, the Defence Intelligence Service, the Defence Estates Organisation, and the Defence Export Services Organisation.

Each Service's Chief of Staff is responsible, through the Chief of the Defence Staff and the Secretary of State for Defence, for the fighting effectiveness, efficiency and morale of his Service. They and the other senior officers and officials at the head of each of the Department's main functions form a single body responsible for all the activities of the Ministry of Defence and the armed forces. This corporate board is chaired by the permanent civilian head of the Department, the Permanent Under-Secretary.

Since 1991, military and civilian managers have been given ever greater authority and responsibility for fulfilling their objectives through the most efficient use of the resources allocated to them. This is aimed at achieving greater value for money and clearer direction and accountability. The recent Defence Costs Study was a radical and comprehensive examination of all aspects of the Ministry of Defence other than the front line itself. Its aim was to identify cost savings that could be made in the support area without reducing front-line effectiveness, and the study teams examined over 30 functional areas. As a result, in July 1994 a coherent package of proposals was announced for savings of over £700 million in 1996–97, rising to £1,000 million a year by the end of the decade, together with a number of enhancements to the equipment programme.

Wherever possible the Study sought to identify and implement changes designed to achieve greater working efficiency rather than financial savings. Major emphasis was placed on a clearer definition of the role of the Head Office, further delegation of responsibility to Commands and budget-holders outside London and the rationalisation of many Commands, training and support activities on a joint-Service basis.

Defence Procurement

About 40 per cent of the defence budget is spent on military equipment, including the procurement of spares and associated costs. The aim is to meet the operational requirements of the armed forces by procuring equipment, works and services from the suppliers offering the best value for money, taking all relevant factors into account. When assessing options, particular consideration is given not just to the initial procurement cost of a project, but also to the costs that could be necessary to support it through its Service life. Competition is fundamental to obtaining value for money and takes place wherever possible. In general, competitions are open to prime and sub-contractors from overseas. Britain also seeks to promote the creation of an open market for defence equipment within Europe.

International Procurement Collaboration

International collaborative projects are becoming increasingly important as equipment development and production costs increase and defence budgets reduce. Britain favours such co-operation wherever it makes economic and military sense by reducing costs and improving standardisation. It therefore plays an active role in NATO's Conference of National Armaments Directors, which promotes equipment collaboration between NATO members. Britain is also a member of the WEU's Western European Armaments Group, which is the main European forum for consultations about armaments.

Current collaborative programmes include:

- the Eurofighter 2000 development (with Germany, Italy and Spain);

- anti-tank guided weapons (with Belgium, France, Germany and the Netherlands);

- a new air defence frigate (with France and Italy);

- the Multiple Launch Rocket System (with the United States, Germany, France and Italy); and

- the EH101 helicopter (with Italy).

Further Reading

Britain, NATO and European Security. Aspects of Britain series, HMSO, 1994.

The Government's Expenditure Plans 1995–96 to 1997–98. Departmental Report by the Ministry of Defence. HMSO, 1995.

Stable Forces in a Strong Britain: Statement on the Defence Estimates 1995. HMSO, 1995.

Front Line First—the Defence Costs Study. HMSO, 1994.

NATO Handbook: Partnership and Co-operation. NATO, 1995.

Further reading

...

Economic
Affairs

11 Economy

Following the recession which began in 1990, the British economy has been growing since 1992, with inflation remaining at historically low levels. Growth has taken place across a broad front with a major contribution coming from exports and more recently investment. The current economic climate is also characterised by a revitalised manufacturing sector, coupled with falling unemployment, low average earnings growth and increased business confidence. The prime objective of government economic policy is to maintain sound public finances by exerting tight control over public expenditure.

National Economy

During the 1980s the British economy expanded faster than those of France and Germany. From 1981 to 1989 it experienced eight years of sustained growth at an annual average rate of over 3 per cent. Subsequently, Britain, in common with other major industrialised nations, was severely affected by recession. In 1990 growth in Britain slowed to 0.6 per cent, and in 1991 gross domestic product (GDP) fell by 2.1 per cent. GDP rose slightly in the second half of 1992 as economic recovery began and has now been growing for three years. Output is presently 9 per cent above the trough of the recession and 5 per cent higher than the previous peak. In the second quarter of 1995 it reached a level 2.9 per cent higher than a year earlier.

ECONOMIC BACKGROUND

The economy is based primarily on private enterprise; the private sector accounts for 79 per cent of output and 85 per cent of employment. Government policy is directed at providing the stability needed by business to plan ahead.

Values for some of the main economic indicators in selected years since 1984 are shown in Table 11.1. For further information see the Statistical Annex on pp. 534-5.

Inflation

During most of the 1950s and the 1960s the inflation rate in Britain rarely rose above 5 per cent. However, in 1971 inflation reached double figures, climbing to 27 per cent in 1975. Contributory factors included oil price rises in 1973 and increases in the

Table 11.1: Economic Indicators

	1984	1989	1994
Gross domestic product[a]	451,131	548,940	570,722
Exports[a]	103,019	126,836	153,679
Imports[a]	103,282	147,615	163,155
Consumers' expenditure[a]	266,486	345,406	358,883
Gross domestic fixed capital formation[a]	78,270	111,470	100,081
Percentage increase in Retail Prices Index	n.a.	7.8	2.4
Workforce in employment (000s)	n.a.	26,929	25,478
Percentage of workforce unemployed	n.a.	6.2	9.4

Sources: *United Kingdom National Accounts 1995 Edition; Economic Trends; Employment Gazette.*
[a]£ million at 1990 market prices.   n.a. = not available.

money supply and public spending. Inflation fell in the early 1980s and stayed low for a number of years. However, it picked up towards the end of the decade and the annual rate rose to 10.9 per cent towards the end of 1990. Inflation has declined substantially since this peak. For the Retail Prices Index (RPI—which records the price of goods and services purchased by households in Britain), the annual rate was 3.6 per cent in August 1995. The RPI excluding mortgage interest payments ('underlying' inflation) was 2.9 per cent in August 1995; it has now been below 3 per cent for almost two years, the longest period since the early 1960s.

Output

The economy grew by 3.9 per cent in 1994. The Government forecasts that GDP growth will slow to a more 'sustainable' rate in 1995 and 1996—coming down to 3.25 per cent in 1995 and 2.75 per cent in 1996, particularly as North Sea oil output increases more slowly.

After the oil price rises of 1973–74, manufacturing output dropped sharply. It later increased, but, in the wake of another oil price rise and stagnation in the world economy, it fell back again in the late 1970s and early 1980s. A period of growth occurred until 1990, but manufacturing output fell significantly during the subsequent recession. Following a rise of 4.2 per cent in 1994, manufacturing output in the three months to July 1995 showed growth of 1.9 per cent, compared with the same period a year earlier.

Oil and gas output passed its peak of the mid-1980s and fell back until 1991, when it

Table 11.2: Output and Employment (Indices: 1990 = 100)

	Output		Employment[a]	
	Index 1993	Index 1994	Index 1993	Index 1994
Agriculture, hunting, forestry and fishing	100.6	103.1	103.4	100.0
Production industries	98.1	103.1	81.7	80.6
of which: Electricity, gas and water	111.8	113.4	} 73.4	65.1
Mining and quarrying	115.2	132.3		
Manufacturing	95.1	99.1	82.4	82.0
Construction	87.2	90.6	75.6	76.3
Services	101.3	104.7	99.1	99.7
GDP	99.6	103.5		
Employees in employment			**94.1**	**94.2**

Sources: *United Kingdom National Accounts 1995 Edition* and *Employment Gazette*
[a]Employment figures relate to Great Britain and cover employees in employment at June on a seasonally adjusted basis.

Table 11.3: Gross Domestic Product by Industry[a]

	1984		1994	
	£ million	per cent	£ million	per cent
Agriculture, hunting, forestry and fishing	6,623	2.4	11,548	2.0
Electricity, gas and water supply	7,258	2.6	15,458	2.7
Mining and quarrying, including oil and gas extraction	21,595	7.7	13,078	2.3
Manufacturing	68,634	24.5	121,272	20.9
Construction	17,287	6.2	31,035	5.4
Wholesale and retail trade, repairs, hotels and restaurants	36,768	13.1	83,472	14.4
Transport, storage and communications	22,204	7.9	49,039	8.5
Financial and business activities, real estate and renting	52,989	18.9	154,550	26.7
Public administration, defence and social security	20,207	7.2	38,797	6.7
Education, health and social work	28,989	10.3	69,116	11.9
Other services	9,617	3.4	22,044	3.8
Total	292,171	104.1	609,409	105.2
Adjustment for financial services	−12,688	−4.5	−29,828	−5.2
Statistical discrepancy	1,170	+0.4	−441	−0.1
GDP at factor cost	280,653	100.0	579,140	100.0

Source: *United Kingdom National Accounts 1995 Edition*
[a]Before provision for depreciation but after deducting stock appreciation.
Note: Differences between totals and the sums of their component parts are due to rounding.

increased by about 2 per cent. In 1993 and 1994 output of oil and gas was exceptionally high, rising by 15 and 27 per cent respectively.

Recent decades have generally seen the fastest growth in the services sector. Services now account for around two-thirds of GDP, compared with about one-half in 1950. Manufacturing contributes less than one-quarter of GDP, compared with over a third in 1950. Table 11.2 compares output and employment in 1993 and 1994, and Table 11.3 compares GDP by industry in 1984 and 1994.

Productivity

Growth in manufacturing output per head in Britain in the 1980s was faster than in all other leading industrialised countries: between 1980 and 1990 it increased by an average of 4.6 per cent a year. In the three months to July 1995, it was up 1.9 per cent on a year earlier, following a 4.8 per cent

increase in 1994. Output per head in the whole economy rose by 3.5 per cent in 1994.

Investment

From 1983 until 1989 fixed investment increased by about 8 per cent a year on average, with particularly rapid growth of over 10 per cent a year between 1986 and 1988. Investment declined between 1990 and 1992, but since 1993 it has recovered, rising by 3.2 per cent in 1994; in the second quarter of 1995 investment grew by 2.6 per cent, compared with a year earlier.

Between 1980 and 1994 the private sector's share of fixed investment grew from 73 to 87 per cent, due in part to privatisation (see p. 200). In the same period, there was a rise in the share of investment undertaken by the services sector and a fall in that carried out by manufacturing. Table 11.4 shows investment by business sector.

Table 11.4: Gross Domestic Fixed Capital Formation (Investment) by Sector 1994

	£ million at market prices	£ million at 1990 prices	Index at 1990 prices (1990 = 100)
Agriculture, hunting, forestry and fishing	943	919	67.2
Mining and quarrying, including oil and gas extraction	3,839	4,310	91.7
Electricity, gas and water	5,372	5,461	115.2
Manufacturing	13,353	11,831	83.2
Construction	727	654	67.8
Services	51,115	52,708	94.3
Dwellings	20,950	20,153	94.0
Transfer costs	3,776	4,045	95.1
Whole economy	**100,075**	**100,081**	**93.0**

Source: *United Kingdom National Accounts 1995 Edition*

An improvement in the quality of investment contributed to a rise in the late 1980s in the net real rate of return on capital employed in non-oil industrial and commercial companies to the highest levels for 20 years. Profitability declined in 1990 and 1991, but since 1992 it has recovered. Non-oil corporate earnings grew strongly in 1994, when net profitability reached 9.5 per cent.

Employment

The workforce in employment fell by around 2 million in the early 1990s following an increase of over 3 million between 1983 and 1990. With economic recovery, employment levels have stabilised at an earlier stage than in previous cycles and are now rising.

Unemployment increased during the early 1990s, and it reached nearly 3 million on a seasonally adjusted basis in late 1992. Since then unemployment has fallen by 680,000 and in August 1995 it was 2.3 million—8.2 per cent of the workforce—the lowest since 1991 (see p. 182).

Overseas Trade

Britain has an open economy in which international trade plays a vital part. The Government welcomed the successful outcome of the Uruguay Round of multilateral trade negotiations held under the auspices of the General Agreement on Tariffs and Trade (see p. 173). The share of GDP accounted for by exports of goods and services has increased from 14 per cent in the early 1960s to 26 per cent. Similar rises have occurred in most other developed countries, reflecting the growing importance of international trade in an increasingly interdependent world economy.

Membership of the European Union (EU) has had a major impact on Britain's pattern of trade. Between 1972 and 1994 the share of Britain's exports of goods going to other EU members rose from a third to over a half. Imports followed a similar trend, growing from about a third to over one-half. The United States accounts for 13 per cent of Britain's exports and 12 per cent of its imports.

For the last 12 years Britain has had a deficit on visible trade. In 1994 it stood at £10,594 million on a seasonally adjusted basis, £2,784 million below the 1993 deficit. Exports continue to perform strongly as a result of improved competitiveness and a sharp recovery in world trade.

The deficit on the balance of payments current account was down from £11,042 million in 1993 to £1,684 million in 1994, its lowest level for nearly a decade. Substantial net earnings on invisible transactions, particularly from financial services, kept the current account in surplus in most years up to 1985, but it has been in deficit since then. The surplus on invisibles was £8,910 million in 1994. In that year exports of services amounted to 29 per cent of exports of goods.

Inward Investment

Britain is recognised as an attractive location for inward direct investment and 13,000 overseas companies are currently operating in Britain, including more than 4,000 from the United States, over 1,000 from Germany and 200 from Japan. This reflects its membership of the EU and proximity to other European markets, its open trading system and 'enterprise culture', stable labour relations and comparatively low personal and corporate taxation. Overseas-owned firms are offered the same incentives as British-owned ones.

In recent years Britain has attracted the greatest share of inward investment into the European Union, including about 40 per cent of Japanese investment and of US investment. It is second only to the United States as a destination for international direct investment.

Energy

With the exploitation of oil and natural gas from the Continental Shelf under the North Sea, Britain is self-sufficient in energy in net terms and expects to remain so for some years. In 1994 it was the world's eighth largest oil producer. The extraction of oil and gas accounted for 2.5 per cent of GDP in 1994, while crude oil and petroleum products made up 6.5 per cent of visible exports.

The benefits to the balance of payments began to appear in the second half of the 1970s and in 1980 Britain had its first surplus on oil trade. Exports, mainly to other EU countries, are equivalent to 65 per cent of domestic oil production. They are partly offset in balance-of-payments terms by imports of other grades of crude oil from the Middle East and elsewhere.

ECONOMIC STRATEGY

The objective of the Government's economic policy is to promote sustained growth and rising prosperity. It seeks to do this by means of structural policies to improve the long-term performance of the economy and by creating a stable macroeconomic environment with low inflation and sound public finances.

Following the suspension in 1992 of sterling's membership of the exchange rate mechanism (ERM) of the European Monetary System, the Government set out a new monetary policy framework for its counter-inflation strategy. This includes a target of keeping underlying inflation within a range of 1 to 4 per cent, bringing it down to the lower half of this range by the end of the present Parliament.

The Government's economic policy is set out in the medium-term financial strategy, which is published each year at the time of the Budget. Within this strategy, the role of monetary policy is to help secure permanently low inflation, while fiscal policy is designed to bring about sound public finances.

Macroeconomic policy is directed towards creating a stable economic environment. Microeconomic policies seek to improve the working of markets and encourage enterprise, efficiency and flexibility through measures such as privatisation, deregulation, cutting out waste and tax reforms (see below).

Monetary Policy

Short-term interest rates remain the key instrument of monetary policy. Monetary policy takes time to influence inflation: hence, interest rate decisions are based on an assessment of the prospects for underlying inflation in one to two years' time. That assessment is based on a wide range of information including monetary and other financial indicators, activity indicators and measures of costs. The main monetary indicators are the growth of 'narrow money', as measured by M0, and 'broad money', M4.[1] Medium-term target ranges have been set at 0 to 4 per cent for M0 and 3 to 9 per cent for M4. Movements in the exchange rate and asset prices, especially house prices, are also taken into account.

Since April 1994 a record has been published of the monthly monetary meeting between the Chancellor of the Exchequer and the Governor of the Bank of England. This,

---

[1] M0 is notes and cash in circulation with the public and banks' holdings of cash and their operational balances at the Bank of England. M4 is notes and cash in circulation with the public together with all sterling deposits held with banks and building societies by the rest of the private sector.

together with the Bank's Quarterly Inflation Report—which is prepared independently of the Treasury—and full explanations whenever interest rates are changed, is designed to make Britain's monetary policy framework one of the most open in the world.

Fiscal Policy

The objective of fiscal policy is to ensure sound public finances, bringing the budget back to balance over the medium term. The Public Sector Borrowing Requirement is projected to return to balance by the end of the decade, with public sector borrowing at a level no higher than is required to finance capital spending from 1997–98. The Government is committed to reducing the share of public expenditure in national income, while value for money is constantly improved.

Within the overall policy of moving towards a balanced budget over the medium term, the Government aims to reduce taxes when possible so as to leave people with more of their own money. The basic rate of income tax has been cut from 33 to 25 per cent, and a lower rate of 20 per cent now applies on the first £3,200 of taxable income (see p. 163).

Supply-side Policies

While macroeconomic policy is directed towards ensuring sustainable growth through low inflation and sound public finances, the Government has sought to improve the supply response, and thus the efficiency, of the economy through microeconomic policies. Action has been taken to expose more of the economy to market forces. Direct controls— for example, on pay, prices, foreign exchange, dividend payments and commercial credit— have been abolished and competition in domestic markets strengthened.

Measures have been implemented to reduce regulatory burdens on business and the number of administrative obstacles facing small firms and self-employed people (see p. 200). Where there is evidence of market failure, and government intervention can be cost-effective and is likely to cause minimal distortion, efforts have been made to increase the flow of investment funds to small firms,

help facilitate innovation in industry and attract industry to the inner cities. Measures have been taken to encourage saving and share ownership; TESSAs (Tax Exempt Special Savings Accounts) and Personal Equity Plans are recent examples (see p. 223).

A White Paper issued in 1994, designed to improve business competitiveness, contains over 60 new measures, many relating to improving education and training and the performance of small businesses (see p. 200). A follow-up White Paper was released in May 1995.

A substantial number of activities have been transferred from the public sector to the private sector by privatisation and contracting out. In addition, the Government is seeking greater efficiency and value for money in the public sector through market testing and competitive tendering, efficiency reviews and scrutinies, and better financial management.

Labour Market

The Government has sought to improve work incentives by reducing personal income tax rates whenever possible, raising tax thresholds and reforming the benefits system. It has also, through the tax system, encouraged the extension of share ownership among employees. A scheme of income tax relief has been introduced to encourage the spread of profit-related pay. The Government has taken steps to achieve a more balanced legal framework for industrial relations. It has expanded training opportunities and put in place a new training framework, with a greater role for employers, so that training better reflects labour market needs. Obstacles to the mobility of labour have also been reduced.

Economic Management

HM Treasury has prime responsibility for the formulation and conduct of economic policy, which it carries out in conjunction with the Bank of England (the central bank—see p. 215) and other government departments—Trade and Industry, Education and Employment, the Environment, Transport, and the Ministry of Agriculture,

Table 11.5: Gross Domestic Product, Gross National Product and National Income

	£ million 1984	£ million 1994
Total final expenditure	418,130	849,471
less imports of goods and services	–92,763	–180,729
Statistical adjustment	485	124
GDP at market prices	325,852	668,866
plus net property income from abroad	4,344	10,519
Gross national product at market prices	330,196	679,385
GDP at factor cost	280,653	579,140
plus net property income from abroad	4,344	10,519
Gross national product at factor cost	284,997	589,659
less capital consumption	–38,758	– 68,150
National income (net national product at factor cost)	246,239	521,509

Source: *United Kingdom National Accounts 1995 Edition*
Note: Differences between totals and the sums of their component parts are due to rounding.

Fisheries and Food. While the Chancellor of the Exchequer makes the decisions about whether to change interest rates, the Governor of the Bank of England is responsible for deciding the precise timing of any interest rate change.

Several other bodies deal with specific aspects of economic policy and the regulation of certain sectors of the economy. These include the Office of Fair Trading and the Monopolies and Mergers Commission (see p. 202).

The Government makes known its economic policies and keeps in touch with developments throughout the economy by means of informal and continuous links with representatives from industrial, financial and commercial sectors as well as other interested parties. Final responsibility for the broad lines of economic policy rests with the Cabinet.

In order to improve economic forecasting, the Government set up a Panel of Independent Forecasters in 1992. The Panel reports to the Chancellor on the current position of, and future prospects for, the economy.

NATIONAL INCOME AND EXPENDITURE

The value of all goods and services produced in the economy is measured by GDP. This may be expressed either in terms of market prices (the prices people pay for the goods and services they buy) or at factor cost (the cost of the goods and services before adding taxes and subtracting subsidies). It can also be expressed in current prices or in constant

Table 11.6: Total Final Expenditure in 1994 at Market Prices

	£ million	per cent
Consumers' expenditure	428,084	50.4
General government final consumption	144,084	17.0
Gross domestic fixed capital formation	100,075	11.8
Value of physical increase in stocks and work in progress	3,303	0.4
Total domestic expenditure	675,546	79.5
Exports of goods and services	173,925	20.5
Total final expenditure	849,471	100.0

Source: *United Kingdom National Accounts 1995 Edition*
Note: Differences between totals and the sums of their component parts are due to rounding.

Table 11.7: Consumers' Expenditure in 1984 and 1994 at Market Prices

	1984	1994	
	per cent	per cent	£ million
Food (household expenditure)	14.7	11.1	47,381
Alcoholic drink	7.2	6.0	25,774
Tobacco	3.3	2.6	11,006
Clothing and footwear	6.6	5.8	24,693
Housing	14.9	15.6	66,618
Fuel and power	4.8	3.5	14,858
Household goods and services	6.5	6.4	27,242
Transport and communications	17.3	17.5	74,796
Recreation, entertainment and education	9.2	9.9	42,548
Other goods and services	14.4	19.4	82,995
Other items [a]	1.1	2.4	10,173
Total	**100.0**	**100.0**	**428,084**

Source: *United Kingdom National Accounts 1995 Edition*
[a] Household expenditure overseas plus final expenditure by private non-profit-making bodies, minus expenditure by foreign tourists in Britain.
Note: Differences between totals and the sums of their component parts are due to rounding.

prices (that is, removing the effects of inflation to measure the volume of growth in the economy). In 1994 GDP at current factor cost totalled £579,140 million. Between 1984 and 1994 the index of GDP at constant factor cost increased by 27 per cent.

Table 11.5 gives figures for GDP, at both current market prices and current factor cost. It also shows the components of two other main aggregates, gross national product and national income.

Table 11.6 shows the categories of total final expenditure in 1994. Consumers' expenditure accounted for 50 per cent of total final expenditure, and exports of goods and services for 20 per cent.

Personal Incomes and Expenditure

Personal disposable income consists of personal incomes after deductions—mainly taxation and social security contributions. This rose fairly steadily from £223,642 million in 1984 to £472,574 million at current prices in 1994. Personal disposable income in 1994 was just under 1 per cent higher in real terms than in 1993. Consumers' expenditure amounted to 91 per cent of post-tax personal income in 1994, compared with 89 per cent in 1993.

Consumers' expenditure rose by 3 per cent in real terms between 1993 and 1994. Table 11.7 shows the changing pattern of consumers' expenditure from 1984 to 1994. Declining proportions are being spent on food and alcoholic drink, tobacco, clothing and footwear, and fuel and power. Over the longer term, as incomes rise, people tend to spend increasing proportions on services. Spending on leisure pursuits and tourism, health and financial services have all shown significant growth in recent years. Housing, food, alcoholic drink, tobacco, clothing and footwear, and fuel and power together accounted for about 32 per cent of the total in 1994.

The ratio of saving to personal disposable income declined substantially during the 1980s. However, in 1992 it increased to 12.2 per cent, falling to 9.4 per cent by 1994.

Sources of Income

The proportion of total personal pre-tax income accounted for by income from employment was 61 per cent in 1994; average gross weekly earnings in April 1995 in Great Britain were £375 for full-time male workers and £270 for full-time female workers. The

Table 11.8: General Government Expenditure

£ thousand million

	1994–95 Provisional outturn	1995–96 Forecast	1996–97 Forecast
Control Total	248.0	255.5	262.8
Cyclical social security	14.1	13.6	13.6
Central government debt interest	17.8	20.7	22.4
Accounting adjustments[a]	8.8	9.7	9.7
General government expenditure (X)[b]	288.7	299.5	308.6
Privatisation proceeds	–6.4	–3.0	–4.0
Lottery-financed spending, and interest and dividend receipts	4.8	5.4	6.4
General government expenditure	287.1	301.9	310.9

Source: HM Treasury

[a] A number of adjustments are needed to relate the Government's forecast for public expenditure to the broader concepts of general government expenditure.

[b] The Government's objective for public expenditure is now expressed in terms of general government expenditure (X)—that is, excluding privatisation proceeds and Lottery-financed spending, and net of interest and dividend receipts.

Note: Differences between totals and the sums of their component parts are due to rounding.

three other main sources of personal income were self-employment (11 per cent), rent, dividends and interest (12 per cent), and social security benefits and other current grants from government (16 per cent).

Public Finance

Public expenditure covers expenditure by both central and local government. Central government expenditure includes money spent on goods and services, and on payments to people, for example, social security and pensions.

General government expenditure (see p. 158) is expected to be around £301,900 million in 1995–96 (see Table 11.8). The Government's policy is to maintain tight control of public spending, so that general government expenditure as a share of GDP declines. Current public expenditure plans provide for 'Control Total' spending (see p. 158) to rise at less than 3 per cent a year in cash terms over the three years to 1997–98.

The diagram on p. 160 shows the main categories of expenditure, together with the main sources of revenue. The government departments with the largest spending programmes are:

- the Department of Social Security (with expenditure estimated at £70,840 million in 1994–95, excluding cyclical social security);
- the Department of the Environment (£39,400 million, of which £29,930 million was on local government);
- the Department of Health (£31,770 million); and
- the Ministry of Defence (£22,170 million).

Tough controls on public expenditure have included cutting waste in government, and reducing spending programmes where possible. Savings have been made in a number of areas, such as defence, housing, roads and social security. Resources are being devoted to priority areas, such as health and education, while additional resources have been made available for science, urban regeneration projects and overseas aid. Private finance (see p. 158) is making a growing contribution, especially in transport.

Education accounts for about 17 per cent of local authority spending; law and order, housing and other environmental services, personal social services, social security, and roads and transport take up most of the remainder.

General government expenditure (excluding privatisation proceeds), as a proportion of GDP, fell from over 47 per cent in 1982–83 to under 40 per cent in 1989–90. The recession in the early 1990s led to a rise in the ratio, to over 44 per cent in 1992–93 and 1993–94, but it is forecast to decline to under 41 per cent by 1997–98 and to 39 per cent by 1999–2000.

Between 1987–88 and 1990–91 the public sector was in surplus, so that the Government repaid debt. The Public Sector Borrowing Requirement (PSBR) rose rapidly during the early 1990s, largely reflecting the impact of the recession, but since then it has fallen and in 1994–95 amounted to £35,300 million, 5.25 per cent of GDP. The PSBR is forecast to continue to fall to £23,600 million in 1995–96 (see Table 11.9), 3.25 per cent of GDP, and to be close to zero by the end of the 1990s.

Private Finance Initiative

The private finance initiative was launched in 1992. Its aim is to utilise private sector efficiency, management expertise and resources in the provision of capital assets and the supply of services traditionally regarded as being exclusively handled by the public sector. The initiative follows on from privatisation, market testing and contracting out. It reflects the shift in the role of the public sector from a provider to a purchaser of services. The Government believes that this will result in projects being better designed and managed, as well as stimulating new investment. Contracts involving capital investment of about £5,000 million are expected to be awarded in 1995 under the initiative. Several transport projects, such as the Channel Tunnel Rail Link (see p. 302), the upgrading of the West Coast main line railway between London and Glasgow (see p. 300) and the extension of the Docklands Light Railway to Lewisham (see p. 303), are being taken forward under the initiative. Other schemes include:

- new prisons in Bridgend and Merseyside (see p. 98);
- over 50 projects, completed or approved, bringing in several hundred million pounds of investment to the National Health Service; and

- about £1,000 million of information technology projects which are in progress or being considered.

The Government has set up the Private Finance Panel (containing high-level representatives from the public and private sectors) to encourage greater participation in the initiative and seek solutions to any problems which might arise. It will not approve capital projects unless private finance options have been explored.

PUBLIC EXPENDITURE TERMS

The three main public expenditure totals are general government expenditure, the 'Control Total' and Supply expenditure.

General Government Expenditure

General government expenditure, excluding privatisation proceeds, is the total spending of central and local government, including central government support for nationalised industries and other public corporations. It is a key public spending aggregate and is used in the medium-term financial strategy (see p. 153), where public spending is set in the context of broader economic policy. As it is usually less affected by institutional differences, it is considered the most appropriate measure for making international comparisons.

Control Total

The Control Total is used by the Government for the purposes of planning and control. The Government seeks to achieve its wider medium-term objective—expressed in terms of general government expenditure excluding privatisation proceeds—by controlling spending within this total. The Control Total, which covers over 80 per cent of government expenditure, includes:

- expenditure for which central government is itself responsible;
- the support it provides or approves for local authority expenditure;
- local authority self-financed expenditure;

Table 11.9: Projected Public Expenditure, Receipts and Borrowing Requirement

£ thousand million

	1994–95	1995–96	1996–97
General government expenditure	287.1	301.9	310.9
of which: public expenditure Control Total	*248.0*	*255.5*	*262.8*
General government receipts	249.4	276.4	293.4
of which: taxes and royalty receipts	*191.0*	*213.4*	*228.6*
social security contributions	*42.1*	*44.3*	*46.7*
Public sector borrowing requirement (PSBR)	35.3	23.6	16.1
PSBR as percentage of GDP	5.25	3.25	2

Source: *Summer Economic Forecast*

- the external financing requirements of public corporations, including nationalised industries; and

- a reserve to cover unanticipated expenditure.

It excludes accounting adjustments and the two main items of expenditure most affected by the economic cycle—debt interest and cyclical social security.

Supply Expenditure

Supply expenditure is financed out of money voted by Parliament in the Supply Estimates (see p. 160). About 69 per cent of all Supply expenditure counts in the Control Total. The main element of the Control Total not funded through Supply Estimates is expenditure financed from the National Insurance Fund.

CONTROL OF PUBLIC EXPENDITURE

The Government's objective is that public expenditure (measured by general government expenditure, excluding privatisation proceeds) should grow by less than the economy as a whole over time, while value for money is constantly improved.

In 1992 it announced a new system of public expenditure control aimed at reducing the share of national income taken by public spending. Annual ceilings are set for the growth of the Control Total, in line with the Government's medium-term objectives.

This 'top-down' approach separates decisions on overall public expenditure levels from the allocation between programmes. Departmental spending decisions are based on allocating available resources within agreed ceilings for aggregate spending; resources are devoted to priority areas, with an emphasis on obtaining maximum value for money. Together with the move to a unified Budget (see below), the new framework represents an important reform of fiscal planning procedures.

Fundamental Expenditure Reviews

The Government announced in 1993 that it would conduct in-depth reviews of all public expenditure by each government department. These reviews examine long-term trends in expenditure, the ways in which services could be delivered more economically and effectively, and areas from which the State could withdraw. Results of the reviews conducted so far, in areas such as social security, health and employment, have identified savings and contributed to some of the increases in efficiency reflected in plans for future spending.

Planning Cycle and the Unified Budget

A new planning cycle took effect with the introduction of the unified Budget arrangements in November 1993, under which the Government presents taxation and spending proposals to Parliament at the same time to allow comparison. The Budget now covers both the Government's taxation plans for the coming financial year and its spending plans for the next three years. The proposals are announced to the House of Commons by the Chancellor of the Exchequer in the Budget statement and are published in the *Financial Statement and Budget Report*. This report also contains a review of recent developments in the economy, together with an economic forecast, and sets out the fiscal and monetary framework within which economic policy operates. This is the medium-term financial strategy.

The Budget statement is followed by the moving of a set of Budget resolutions in which the tax proposals are embodied. These resolutions are the foundation of the Finance Bill, published in January. The Provisional Collection of Taxes Act 1968 allows the tax authorities to collect taxes provisionally, at the levels provided by the Budget proposals, pending enactment of the Finance Bill.

Estimates

The annual Public Expenditure Survey conducted by HM Treasury provides the basis for the Estimates which each government department submits to the Treasury, giving details of its cash requirements for the coming financial year. After Treasury approval, these Supply Estimates are presented to Parliament. Parliamentary authorisation is required for the major part of the new spending plans for the year ahead announced in the unified Budget. Parliament approves them as part of the annual Appropriation Act. Supplementary Estimates may also be presented to Parliament during the course of the year. Individual reports setting out expenditure plans for government departments are published in February or March.

If any Supply Estimate is overspent, the Committee of Public Accounts (see p. 161) may investigate before Parliament is asked to approve any Excess Vote to balance the account. In each parliamentary session, up to three 'Estimates days' are available for debates on the Supply Estimates, following scrutiny by select committees of the House of Commons.

Government Receipts and Expenditure 1994–95

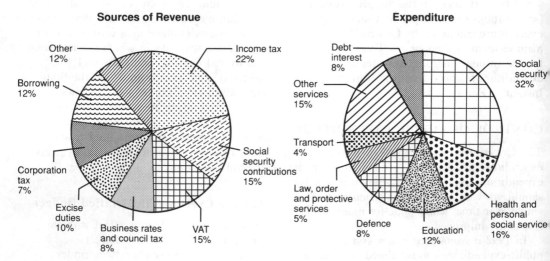

Sources of Revenue

Other 12%
Borrowing 12%
Corporation tax 7%
Excise duties 10%
Business rates and council tax 8%
VAT 15%
Social security contributions 15%
Income tax 22%

Expenditure

Debt interest 8%
Other services 15%
Transport 4%
Law, order and protective services 5%
Defence 8%
Education 12%
Health and personal social service 16%
Social security 32%

Note: As a result of rounding and omission of minor items, percentages do not add up to 100.

Source: HM Treasury.

Cash Limits

The Government sets cash limits on just over 60 per cent of Supply expenditure and is extending the coverage of limits whenever possible. The imposition of cash limits indicates that the Government intends to avoid extra provision for programmes even in the event of unexpected increases in costs. They cover the major part of grants to local authorities, which are financed out of Supply expenditure. Cash limits also apply to some expenditure not voted in the Estimates.

Running cost limits are imposed on the administrative costs of central government, which are identified separately in the Estimates. Any overspending of cash or running cost limits leads to an investigation into the causes and, where appropriate, a reduction in the limits in the following year.

Those Estimates not subject to cash limits mainly finance demand-led services like income support from the Department of Social Security. In such cases, once policy and rates of payment are determined, expenditure depends on factors beyond the direct control of government, such as the number of eligible recipients.

Proposed Changes in Government Accounting Procedures

In July 1994 the Government issued a Green Paper containing proposals to change accounting and budgeting procedures by government departments, which were confirmed in a White Paper published in July 1995. The proposals would involve the replacement of cash-based government accounts by more commercial 'resource accounting' and budgeting methods, a process already adopted in executive agencies and the National Health Service. The new methods are expected to bring improved efficiency and to focus more on departmental objectives and outputs rather than the money available for spending. Departments would have their own balance sheets showing assets and liabilities. Resource accounting is expected to be introduced for most departments in April 1997 and the remainder in April 1998. The first resource-based Public Expenditure Survey is expected to be produced in 2000.

Examination and Audit of Public Expenditure

Examination of public expenditure is carried out by select committees of the House of Commons. These study in detail the activities of particular government departments and require the attendance of ministers and officials for cross-examination. Audit of the Government's spending, which follows up the control inherent in parliamentary approval of the Estimates, is exercised through the functions of the Comptroller and Auditor General, the head of the National Audit Office.

Comptroller and Auditor General

The Comptroller and Auditor General, an officer of the House of Commons appointed by the Crown, has two distinct functions. As Comptroller General, he or she is responsible for ensuring that all revenue and other public money payable to the Consolidated Fund and the National Loans Fund (see p. 162) is duly paid and that all payments from these funds are authorised by statute. As Auditor General, he or she must certify the accounts of all government departments and executive agencies and those of a wide range of other public sector bodies; scrutinise the economy, efficiency and effectiveness of their operations; examine revenue accounts and inventories; and report the results of these examinations to Parliament.

Committee of Public Accounts

The Committee of Public Accounts considers the accounts of government departments, executive agencies and other public sector bodies, and the Comptroller and Auditor General's reports on them and on departments' use of their resources. The Committee takes evidence from heads of departments, agencies and other public sector bodies and submits reports to Parliament. The Government's formal replies to the reports are presented to Parliament in the form of Treasury minutes, and the reports and minutes are usually debated annually in the Commons.

Central Government Funds

The Government's sterling expenditure is largely met out of the Consolidated Fund, an account at the Bank of England into which tax receipts and other revenues are paid. Any excess of expenditure over receipts is met by the National Loans Fund, which is another official sterling account at the Bank of England and is the repository for funds borrowed by the Government. The National Insurance Fund, into which contributions are paid by employers and employed people, is used mainly to pay for social security benefits.

MAIN SOURCES OF REVENUE

The main sources of revenue are:
- taxes on income (including profits), which include personal income tax, corporation tax and petroleum revenue tax;
- taxes on expenditure, which include VAT and customs and excise duties; and
- National Insurance contributions, which give entitlement to a range of benefits.

Other sources are stamp duties, inheritance tax, capital gains tax, and the council tax and business rates.

Taxation Policy

The Government's programme of tax reform has sought to create a climate in which business can thrive and individual initiative is rewarded. Its aims include:
- keeping the overall tax burden as low as possible through firm control over public expenditure;
- reducing marginal tax rates of income and profits to sharpen incentives to work and create wealth;
- maintaining a broad tax base, which helps to keep tax rates low and avoids distorting commercial decisions; and
- shifting the balance of taxation from taxes on income to taxes on expenditure.

The Government also aims to simplify the administration of the tax system and minimise the burdens which compliance places on the taxpayer, and to close tax loopholes.

Tax Measures in the 1994 Budget

The November 1994 Budget contained a number of tax changes designed to maintain the tax base and close tax loopholes, while supporting government policy objectives on health and the environment. Measures included:
- increases in the main personal allowances and income tax thresholds in line with price changes;
- support for environmental and health objectives by raising in real terms road fuel duties by 5 per cent and tobacco duties by 3 per cent, continuing the policy announced in the November 1993 Budget; and
- halting a number of tax avoidance schemes.

In addition, the Budget contained proposals to make it cheaper to employ new staff, encourage investment in small and growing businesses, and help businesses facing higher non-domestic rates bills from 1995–96 (see p. 166).

A new landfill tax was announced in the Budget. The tax, due to be introduced in 1996, is intended to help protect the environment by increasing the cost of disposing of waste in landfill sites and by providing an additional incentive for recycling. To avoid imposing additional costs on business, cuts in employers' National Insurance contributions are planned at the time of the introduction of the new tax.

A package of tax and spending measures to make good the revenue lost as a result of Parliament's subsequent decision to hold the rate of VAT on domestic fuel and power to 8 per cent rather than raising it to 17.5 per cent was announced in December 1994. These included further increases in duties on road fuel and tobacco.

Collection of Taxes and Duties

The Inland Revenue assesses and collects taxes on income, profits and capital, and stamp duty. HM Customs and Excise collects the most important taxes on expenditure (VAT and most duties). Vehicle excise duty is the responsibility of the Department of Transport. National Insurance contributions are the responsibility of the Department of Social Security, although they are mainly collected by the Inland Revenue. The council tax and business rates are collected by local authorities.

Taxes on Income

Income Tax

Taxes on individual incomes are generally progressive in that larger incomes bear a proportionately greater amount of tax. Income tax is imposed for the year of assessment beginning on 6 April. From April 1995 the lower rate of 20 per cent was widened to the first £3,200 of taxable income. The basic rate of 25 per cent applies to the next £21,100 of taxable income. A rate of 40 per cent is levied on taxable income above £24,300. These rates apply to total income, including earned and investment income. Of nearly 26 million income taxpayers, 5 million pay only lower rate tax, about 18 million are basic rate taxpayers and over 2 million are in the higher rate tax band.

A number of allowances and reliefs reduce an individual's income tax liability. All taxpayers, irrespective of sex or marital status, are entitled to a personal allowance against income from all sources. Married women pay their own tax on the basis of their own income. In addition, there is a married couple's allowance, which may be allocated to either partner or they may receive half each. Wives can elect to receive half of the allowance as of right. For 1995–96 the values of the main allowances are £3,525 for the personal allowance and £1,720 for the married couple's allowance. From April 1994 tax relief for some allowances, including the married couple's allowance, was restricted to 20 per cent, and this was reduced to 15 per cent in April 1995.

Among the most important of the reliefs is that for mortgage interest payments on borrowing for house purchase up to the statutory limit of £30,000. From April 1994

relief was reduced from the basic rate to 20 per cent, and this was limited to 15 per cent in April 1995. Relief is usually given 'at source', that is, repayments which the borrower makes to the lender are reduced to take account of tax relief at the appropriate rate and the tax refund is then passed directly by the tax authorities to the building society or bank making the loan rather than to the individual borrower.

Employees' contributions to their pension schemes also qualify for tax relief within limits laid down by Parliament.

Most wage and salary earners pay their income tax under a Pay-As-You-Earn (PAYE) system whereby tax is deducted and accounted for to the Inland Revenue by the employer, in a way which enables most employees to pay the correct amount of tax during the year.

The assessment and collection of personal taxation will be simplified from 1996–97. The option of self-assessment will be extended to all who fill in tax returns (about 9 million people). The changes will allow taxpayers to calculate their own liability to tax, and will introduce a uniform set of dates for the payment of income tax and capital gains tax. They will also replace the 'preceding year' basis of income tax for the self-employed by a simpler 'current year' basis; people becoming self-employed from April 1994 are already being taxed on the latter basis.

In general, income tax is charged on all income which originates in Britain—although some forms of income are exempt, such as certain social security benefits—and on all income arising abroad of people resident in Britain. Interest on certain British government securities belonging to people not ordinarily resident in Britain is exempt. Britain has entered into agreements with many countries to provide relief from double taxation; where such agreements are not in force unilateral relief is often allowed. British residents working abroad for the whole year may benefit from 100 per cent tax relief.

Corporation Tax

The rates of company tax in Britain are lower than in most other industrialised countries. Companies pay corporation tax on their income and capital gains after deduction of certain allowances and reliefs. A company which distributes profits to its shareholders is required to pay advance corporation tax (ACT) on these distributions to the Inland Revenue. This ACT can be set against the company's liability to corporation tax, subject to a limit. If resident in Britain, a shareholder receiving dividends from companies resident in Britain is entitled to a tax credit. This satisfies some or all of the shareholder's liability to income tax on his or her dividend income, or is paid to shareholders not liable to tax.

The main rate of corporation tax is 33 per cent, with a reduced rate of 25 per cent for small companies (those with profits below £300,000 in a year). Marginal relief is allowed for companies with profits between £300,000 and £1.5 million, so that the company's overall rate is between the main rate and the small companies' rate. Capital expenditure on plant and machinery, on scientific research and on industrial buildings qualifies for annual allowances, which are deducted from profits to recognise the depreciation of the items concerned.

Petroleum Revenue Tax

Petroleum revenue tax (PRT), deductible in computing profits for corporation tax, is charged on profits from the production—as opposed, for example, to the refining—of oil and gas in Britain and on its Continental Shelf under licence from the Department of Trade and Industry. Each licensee of an oilfield is charged at a rate of 50 per cent on the profits from that field after deduction of certain allowances and reliefs. New fields given consent for development on or after 16 March 1993 are not liable to PRT.

Inheritance Tax

Inheritance tax is charged on the value of estates at the time of death and is also immediately chargeable on certain lifetime transfers. The majority of business assets are now exempt from inheritance tax, so that most family businesses can be passed on without a tax charge. Tax is charged at a single rate of 40 per cent above the threshold for inheritance tax of £154,000.

There are several important exemptions. Generally, transfers between spouses are exempt, and gifts and bequests to British charities, major political parties and heritage bodies are also normally exempt.

Capital Gains Tax

Capital gains realised on the disposal of assets are liable to capital gains tax or, in the case of companies, to corporation tax. For 1995–96 individuals are exempt from tax in respect of total net gains of up to £6,000 in any one year and most trusts on gains of up to £3,000. Gains are treated as the taxpayer's top slice of income, and are therefore charged at the individual's highest income tax rate or the company's corporation tax rate.

Only gains arising since March 1982 are subject to tax and the effects of inflation are allowed for when measuring gains. Some assets, including the principal private residence, are normally exempt. Gains on government securities and certain corporate bonds are exempt from the tax, as are gains on shares owned under Personal Equity Plans (see p. 223). This last exemption is designed to encourage wider share ownership.

Taxes on Expenditure

Value Added Tax

VAT is a broadly based expenditure tax, chargeable at 17.5 per cent, except on domestic fuel and power, where the rate is 8 per cent. It is collected at each stage in the production and distribution of goods and services by taxable persons. The final tax is borne by the consumer. When a taxable person purchases taxable goods or services, the supplier charges VAT—the taxable person's input tax. When the taxable person supplies goods or services, the customers are then in turn charged VAT, which is the taxable person's output tax. The difference between the output tax and the input tax is paid to, or repaid by, Customs and Excise.

The annual level of turnover above which traders must register for VAT is £46,000. Certain goods and services are relieved from VAT, either by being charged at a zero rate or by being exempt.

- Under zero rating, a taxable person does not charge tax to a customer but reclaims any input tax paid to suppliers. Among the main categories where zero-rating applies are goods exported to other countries, and goods shipped as stores on ships and aircraft; most food; water and sewerage; domestic and international passenger transport; books, newspapers and periodicals; construction of new residential buildings; young children's clothing and footwear; drugs and medicines supplied on prescription; specified aids for handicapped people; and certain supplies by or to charities.

- For exempt goods or services, a taxable person does not charge any output tax but is not entitled to reclaim the input tax. The main categories where exemption applies are many supplies of land and buildings; insurance; postal services; betting; gaming (subject to certain important exceptions); lotteries; finance; much education and training; and health and welfare.

In the November 1994 Budget a number of changes were introduced to reduce the scope for avoiding payment of VAT and to ease burdens on business.

Customs Duties

Customs duties are chargeable on goods from outside the EU in accordance with its Common Customs Tariff. Goods can move freely across internal EU frontiers without making customs entries at importation or stopping for routine fiscal checks. For commercial consignments, excise duty and VAT are charged in the member state of destination, at the rate in force in that state.

Excise Duties

Hydrocarbon oils used as road fuel bear higher rates of duty than those used for other purposes, although the rate of duty on unleaded petrol is lower than that on leaded. Kerosene, most lubricating oils and other oils used for certain industrial processes are free of duty. There are duties on spirits, beer, wine, made-wine (wine with added constituents, such as fruit juice), cider and perry, based on alcoholic strength and volume. Spirits used for scientific, medical, research and industrial processes are generally free of duty. Cigarette duty is charged partly as a cash amount per cigarette and partly as a percentage of retail price. Duty on other tobacco products is based on weight.

Duties are charged on off-course betting, pool betting, gaming in casinos, bingo and gaming machines. Rates vary with the particular form of gambling. Duty is charged either as a percentage of gross or net stakes or, in the case of gaming machines, as a fixed amount per machine according to the cost of playing it and its prize level. A 12 per cent duty on gross stakes is levied on the National Lottery (see p. 460), but there is no tax on winnings.

Vehicle excise duty (VED) on a privately-owned motor car, light van or taxi with fewer than nine seats is £135 a year. The duty on goods vehicles is levied on the basis of gross weight and, if over 12 tonnes, according to the number of axles; the duty is designed to ensure that such vehicles at least cover their share of the full costs of road use through the tax paid (VED and fuel duty). Duty on taxis and buses varies according to seating capacity, and duty on motor cycles according to engine capacity.

Two new duties introduced in 1994 were a 2.5 per cent tax on most general insurance premiums paid from 1 October, and a duty on air passengers, which took effect in November, of £5 for flights to internal and EU destinations and £10 elsewhere.

Stamp Duty

Certain kinds of transfer are subject to stamp duty. These include purchases of houses, at 1 per cent of the total price if this exceeds

£60,000, and instruments such as declarations of trust. Transfers by gift and transfers to charities are exempt.

Taxpayer's Charter

The Taxpayer's Charter sets out the standard of service that people can expect from the Inland Revenue and Customs and Excise. Both departments should be fair, helpful, courteous, efficient and accountable, and keep taxpayers' financial affairs private.

Other Revenue

National Insurance Contributions

There are five classes of National Insurance contribution:

- Class 1—paid by employees and their employers;
- Class 1A—paid by employers on the cash equivalent of the benefit of cars and fuel provided to their employees for private use;
- Class 2—paid by the self-employed;
- Class 3—paid voluntarily for pension purposes; and
- Class 4—paid by self-employed people on their taxable profits between £6,640 and £22,880 a year (in addition to their Class 2 contribution).

Details of the rates of contribution are given in Chapter 25, Social Security, on p. 415.

Local Authority Revenue

Local authorities in Great Britain have four main sources of revenue income: grants from central government; non-domestic rates; council tax; and sales, fees and charges. About 55 per cent of expenditure (excluding sales, fees and charges) is financed by government grants.

Non-domestic rates are a tax on the occupiers of non-domestic property. The rateable value of property is assessed by reference to annual rents and reviewed every five years; the most recent revaluation in Great Britain took place in April 1995. As there are some very large local and sectoral variations in the changes in rateable values, a

transitional scheme has been introduced to limit the maximum real increases and reductions in rates bills which would otherwise arise from revaluation. In England and Wales the non-domestic rate is set nationally by central government and collected by local authorities. It is paid into a national pool and redistributed to local authorities in proportion to their population. In 1995–96 a similar system is being introduced in Scotland involving a unified business rate at the same level as in England. In Northern Ireland rates are not payable on industrial premises or on commercial premises in enterprise zones. Certain other properties in Northern Ireland, such as freight transport and recreational premises, are partially derated.

Domestic property is generally subject to the council tax, which replaced the community charge in April 1993. Each dwelling is allocated to one of eight valuation bands, based on its capital value in April 1991. Capital values are based on the amount each dwelling might have sold for on the open market, subject to certain assumptions, if it had been sold on 1 April 1991. Discounts are available for dwellings with fewer than two resident adults. A council tax payer on a low income may receive council tax benefit of up to 100 per cent of his or her tax bill (see p. 423).

In Northern Ireland, rates—local domestic property taxes based on the value of the property—are collected by local authorities.

PUBLIC SECTOR FINANCIAL OPERATIONS

Debt Management

The Government funds its borrowing requirement by selling debt to the private sector. Public sector borrowing, or debt repayment, each year represents an addition to, or subtraction from, the net debt of the public sector. This debt is the consolidated debt of the public sector less its holdings of liquid assets. Net public sector debt held outside the public sector amounted to £252,000 million at the end of March 1994, representing 38.25 per cent of GDP in 1993–94. This is expected to rise to 42.75 per cent of GDP by the end of March 1996, but thereafter to fall steadily as the PSBR is brought towards balance.

The funding requirement for 1995–96 is forecast to be about £25,600 million, of which National Savings products (see p. 220) are assumed to contribute about £2,500 million, with gilt-edged stock contributing the balance.

Gilt-edged Stock

The major debt instrument is known as gilt-edged stock ('gilts') as there is no risk of default. Gilts are marketable and widely traded. Pension funds and life insurance companies have the largest holdings. The Government publishes an annual debt management report which sets out the framework for issuing gilts in the coming year. Gilts are sold by the Bank of England on the Government's behalf. Issues are primarily by auction (broadly monthly), supplemented by ad hoc 'tap' sales. Gilts include 'conventionals', which pay fixed rates of interest and redemption sums; index-linked stocks, on which principal and interest are linked to the movement in the Retail Prices Index; and floating-rate gilts, with payments linked to short-term interest rates.

The Government has announced that an open sale and repurchase ('repo') market in gilts will be created, and the necessary legislative changes were incorporated in the Finance Act 1995. The new market, which is planned to start in January 1996, is intended to improve the liquidity and efficiency of the gilts market, reducing yields and thus lowering the cost of financing government debt.

Bills

Sterling Treasury bills are sold at a weekly tender; the majority have a maturity of three months. These are used to manage the money markets, rather than to meet the Government's borrowing needs. The Government has also issued bills denominated and payable in European Currency Units (ECUs) since 1988 and longer-dated ECU notes since 1992. The proceeds have been added to the official foreign exchange reserves rather than being used to finance public expenditure.

Other Public Sector Borrowing

The bulk of public corporations' borrowing is funded by central government, although their temporary borrowing needs are met largely from the market, usually under Treasury guarantee. That part of local authority borrowing met by central government is supplied by authorisation of Parliament through the Public Works Loan Board from the National Loans Fund. The Board remains an independent body even though it is merged for administrative purposes with the former National Debt Office, forming the National Investment and Loans Office.

Local authorities may also borrow directly from the market, both short-term and long-term, through a range of instruments. Some public corporations and local authorities borrow on occasion, under special statutory power and with Treasury consent, in foreign currencies.

Further Reading

Better Accounting for the Taxpayers' Money—The Government's Proposals: Resource Accounting and Budgeting in Government. Cm 2929. HMSO, 1995.

Financial Statement and Budget Report, annual report, HMSO.

The Government's Expenditure Plans 1995–96 to 1997–98: HM Treasury, Chancellor of the Exchequer's Smaller Departments. Cm 2817. HMSO, 1995.

Summer Economic Forecast, annual report, HMSO.

United Kingdom National Accounts, annual report, HMSO.

12 Overseas Trade

Overseas trade has been of vital importance to the British economy for hundreds of years. Although small in area and accounting for only about 1 per cent of the world's population, Britain is the fifth largest trading nation in the world. As a member of the European Union (EU), it is part of the world's largest established trading group, responsible for 40 per cent of world exports.

The British Government is a strong supporter of an open multilateral trading system and advocates further trade liberalisation. World trade is set to grow by 5 to 10 per cent a year in the next ten years, due in part to the successful conclusion of the Uruguay Round of negotiations under the General Agreement on Tariffs and Trade (GATT) in 1993. This led to the creation on 1 January 1995 of the World Trade Organisation (WTO), of which Britain is a founder member.

Britain exports more per head than the United States and Japan; its overseas sales of goods and services are equivalent to about a quarter of gross domestic product (GDP). Invisible earnings of British companies place Britain in the top three countries in the international league table of overseas invisibles earners. It is the world's second biggest overseas investor and the leading destination for inward direct investment into the EU.

VISIBLE TRADE

In 1994 Britain's exports of goods were valued at about £134,500 million and its imports of goods at £145,000 million on a balance-of-payments basis (see Table 12.1). Between 1993 and 1994 the volume of exports of goods rose by 10 per cent and their value by 11 per cent. Over the same period, imports grew by 5 per cent by volume and 8 per cent in terms of value. Re-exporting plays a prominent role in trade: a recent Confederation of British Industry/ Lloyds Bank survey found that 45 per cent of British importers export products worth up to £14,000 million a year.

Commodity Composition

Britain has traditionally been an exporter of manufactured goods and an importer of food and basic materials. In 1970 manufactures accounted for 85 per cent of its exports; this fell to around 67 per cent by the mid-1980s as North Sea oil exports increased their share. The proportion of manufactures in exports has since risen, to 83 per cent in 1994 (see Table 12.2). Britain has not, however, had a surplus on manufactures since 1982. Machinery and transport equipment account for about 41 per cent of exports and a similar proportion of imports

Table 12.1: Overseas Trade 1991–93

	1992	1993	1994
Value (£ million)[a]			
EXPORTS			
Goods	107,343	121,409	134,465
Oil	6,652	7,962	8,552
Other goods	100,691	113,477	125,913
Services	34,473	37,978	39,460
Goods and services	**141,816**	**159,387**	**173,925**
IMPORTS			
Goods	120,447	134,787	145,059
Oil	5,104	5,520	4,482
Other goods	115,343	129,267	140,577
Services	29,422	32,293	35,670
Goods and services	**149,869**	**167,080**	**180,729**
Volume indices (1990 = 100)			
EXPORTS			
Goods			
All goods	103.7	107.4	118.1
Non-oil goods	103.5	106.3	116.3
Services	101.7	104.1	106.7
Goods and services	**103.2**	**106.6**	**115.4**
IMPORTS			
Goods			
All goods	100.9	104.8	110.3
Non-oil goods	101.1	104.7	111.3
Services	100.6	99.0	109.0
Goods and services	**100.8**	**103.7**	**110.0**
Unit value indices (1990 = 100)			
EXPORTS			
All goods	103.5	116.1	118.7
Non-oil goods	105.0	118.3	121.6
IMPORTS			
All goods	102.1	112.3	116.1
Non-oil goods	102.9	113.6	117.8
TERMS OF TRADE[b]			
All goods	101.4	103.4	102.2
Non-oil goods	102.0	104.1	103.2

Source: *United Kingdom Balance of Payments 1995 Edition*

[a]Balance-of-payments basis.

[b]Export unit value index as a percentage of import unit value index.

Table 12.2: Sector Analysis of Visible Trade 1994[a]

£ million

	Exports	Imports	Visible balance
Food, beverages and tobacco	10,011	13,831	−3,820
Basic materials	2,561	5,566	−3,005
Oil	8,552	4,482	4,070
Other mineral fuels and lubricants	413	1,215	−802
Semi-manufactured goods	38,426	37,940	486
Finished manufactured goods	73,009	80,865	−7,856
Commodities and transactions not classified according to kind	1,493	1,160	333
Total	**134,465**	**145,059**	**−10,594**

Source: *United Kingdom Balance of Payments 1995 Edition*   [a]Balance-of-payments basis.

(see Table 12.3). Aerospace, chemicals and electronics have become increasingly significant export sectors, while textiles have declined in relative importance.

Since the mid-1970s North Sea oil has made a substantial contribution to Britain's overseas trade both in terms of exports and import substitution. In 1994 exports of fuels in volume terms were about three times their 1975 level; imports were around two-thirds of the 1975 figure. The share of fuels in exports rose from 4 to 22 per cent in the mid-1980s, when North Sea oil and gas production was at its peak, falling back to 7 per cent in 1994. The import share decreased from 18 per cent in 1975 to 13 per cent in the mid-1980s and to 4 per cent by 1994. In 1994 the surplus on trade in oil amounted to more than £4,000 million.

Imported manufactures have taken a

Geographical Distribution of Trade 1994

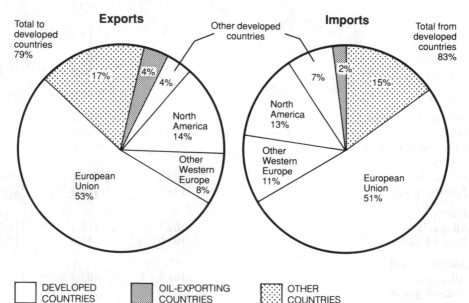

Differences between totals and the sums of their component parts are due to rounding.

Source: *United Kingdom Balance of Payments 1995 Edition*

Table 12.3: Commodity Composition of Visible Trade 1994[a]

£ million

	Exports	Imports
Food and live animals	6,260	12,271
Beverages and tobacco	3,723	2,235
Crude materials	2,379	5,528
of which: Wood, lumber and cork	42	1,400
Pulp and waste paper	43	638
Textile fibres	568	636
Metal ores	659	1,164
Fuels	8,923	5,935
Petroleum and petroleum products	8,515	4,625
Coal, gas and electricity	411	1,307
Animal and vegetable oils and fats	170	541
Chemicals	18,741	14,461
of which: Organic chemicals	4,716	3,510
Inorganic chemicals	1,129	1,090
Plastics	2,794	3,728
Manufactures classified chiefly by material	19,486	24,278
of which: Wood and cork manufactures	169	1,033
Paper and paperboard manufactures	1,991	4,226
Textile manufactures	2,930	4,500
Iron and steel	3,668	2,927
Non-ferrous metals	2,238	3,020
Metal manufactures	2,628	2,874
Machinery and transport equipment	55,351	60,350
Mechanical machinery	16,371	13,223
Electrical machinery	24,904	26,692
Road vehicles	9,404	16,178
Other transport equipment	4,674	4,258
Miscellaneous manufactures	17,323	21,725
of which: Clothing and footwear	3,159	6,314
Scientific and photographic	5,387	4,947
Other commodities and transactions	1,454	988
Total	**133,807**	**148,302**

Source: *Monthly Digest of Statistics*
[a]On an overseas-trade-statistics basis, seasonally adjusted. This differs from a balance-of-payments basis in that, for imports, it includes the cost of insurance and freight, and, for both exports and imports, includes returned goods.

greater share of the domestic market in recent decades. The share of finished manufactures in total imports rose from 25 per cent in 1970 to 56 per cent in 1994, while the share of basic materials fell from 15 to less than 4 per cent between 1970 and 1994. The percentage of food, beverages and tobacco in total imports has been dropping since the 1950s, down to under 10 per cent in 1994, as a result both of the extent to which food demand has been met from domestic agriculture and the decline in the proportion of total expenditure on food.

Geographical Distribution

Britain's overseas trade is mainly—and increasingly—with other developed countries.

Table 12.4: Britain's Main Markets and Suppliers 1994[a]

	Value (£ million)	Share (per cent)
Main markets		
Germany	17,658	13.2
United States	16,807	12.6
France	13,647	10.2
Netherlands	9,750	7.3
Belgium/Luxembourg	7,706	5.8
Italy	6,949	5.2
Irish Republic	6,711	5.0
Spain	5,073	3.8
Sweden	3,347	2.5
Japan	2,991	2.2
Main suppliers		
Germany	22,524	15.2
United States	17,680	11.9
France	15,553	10.5
Netherlands	10,075	6.8
Japan	8,897	6.0
Italy	7,301	4.9
Belgium/Luxembourg	7,272	4.9
Irish Republic	5,817	3.9
Switzerland	4,819	3.2
Sweden	4,159	2.8

Source: *Monthly Digest of Statistics.*
[a] On an overseas-trade-statistics basis, seasonally adjusted.

In 1970 these accounted for 70 per cent of exports and imports; by 1994 the shares were 79 and 83 per cent respectively. The proportion of Britain's trade with non-oil developing nations declined from about 22 per cent in 1970 to 13 per cent in the late 1980s, but has risen since 1992 to 16 per cent of trade in 1994.

In 1972, the year before Britain joined the European Community, 35 per cent of Britain's visible trade was with the other 14 countries which made up the European Union in 1995. The proportion rose to 58 per cent in 1994. Western Europe as a whole took 62 per cent of British exports in 1994.

In 1994 the other 11 countries then making up the EU with Britain accounted for seven of Britain's top ten export markets and six of the ten leading suppliers of goods to Britain (see Table 12.4). In 1990 Germany overtook the United States to become Britain's biggest overseas market; Germany is also Britain's largest single supplier. In 1994

it took 13 per cent of Britain's exports and supplied 15 per cent of its imports.

There have been a number of other changes in the pattern of Britain's overseas trade in recent years. Exports to Japan, which is presently Britain's tenth largest export market, rose by 13 per cent in 1994. Japan has steadily increased its share of Britain's imports and now accounts for 6 per cent. In 1994 there was also a sizeable increase—about 20 per cent—in Britain's exports to other expanding markets in the Asia-Pacific Rim. Hong Kong, Malaysia, Singapore, Korea, Taiwan and Thailand, together with the People's Republic of China and the Philippines, all showed substantial growth in exports from Britain in 1994.

INVISIBLE TRANSACTIONS

Transactions in invisible trade fall into three main groups:
- internationally tradeable services;

- investment income on external assets; and
- non-commercial transfers.

Services range from banking, insurance and stockbroking, tourism, and shipping and aviation to specialist services such as engineering consultancy, computer programming and training. Financial services make a major contribution to overseas earnings: net overseas receipts from services rendered and investment income were £20,400 million in 1994, up from £15,500 million in 1993.

Earnings on external assets and liabilities have rarely been in deficit; transfers, however, have almost always been in deficit. For invisible trade as a whole, the deficit of general government is more than offset by the substantial surplus of the private sector (including public corporations), resulting in an overall surplus. General government transactions are relatively unimportant in either the services or the investment income accounts but they form the greater part of the transfers account. In 1994 the private sector had a surplus of £18,800 million on invisible trade while government had a deficit of £9,900 million (see Table 12.5).

Earnings from private sector services rose in value by 4 per cent in 1994 to £39,000 million; debits, at £33,100 million, were 11 per cent higher than a year previously.

The surplus on private sector investment income was £13,200 million in 1994, up from £3,900 million a year earlier, partly as a result of a large increase in net direct investment earnings. The deficit on private sector transfers was £260 million, while that on government transfers was £5,100 million.

COMMERCIAL POLICY

Britain is an active member of the European Union. It remains committed to the open multilateral trading system and to the further liberalisation of world trade. To this end it has taken a leading part in the activities of such organisations as GATT and its successor the WTO, the International Monetary Fund (IMF) and the Organisation for Economic Co-operation and Development (OECD).

GATT/World Trade Organisation

The eighth and last GATT round—the Uruguay Round—was launched in 1986 and successfully concluded in 1993. It was the largest-ever international trade negotiation and will reduce tariffs on goods and liberalise trade in services and agriculture. Creation of the World Trade Organisation—which now has 125 member states—has put the new

Table 12.5: Britain's Invisible Transactions 1994

£ million

	Credits	Debits	Balance
Private sector and public corporations	117,858	99,094	18,764
Services	38,993	33,147	5,846
of which: Sea transport	4,140	4,539	−399
Civil aviation	5,457	6,081	−624
Travel	10,127	14,501	−4,374
Financial services (net credits)	4,742	− }	11,243
Other business services	14,527	8,026 }	
Investment income	76,745	63,567	13,178
Transfers	2,120	2,380	−260
General government	5,188	15,042	−9,854
Services	467	2,523	−2,056
Investment income	1,438	4,097	−2,659
Transfers	3,283	8,422	−5,139
Total invisible transactions	123,046	114,136	8,910

Source: *United Kingdom Balance of Payments 1995 Edition*

arrangements on a permanent institutional footing. A GATT report has estimated that annual world income will be boosted by at least £330,000 million by 2005, as a result of the Uruguay agreement.

The main features of the new agreement, which is likely to be brought into force in late 1995, are as follows:

- There will be overall tariff reductions across all countries of about 40 per cent (tariff reductions by the EU will average over 33 per cent) and member states have undertaken not to raise tariffs again on 95 per cent of world trade.

- With the formation of the General Agreement on Trade in Services, services are to be brought within the framework of GATT multilateral trade rules. Any remaining restrictions on trade in services will be made transparent and non-discriminatory.

- Agriculture will come fully under the rules of multilateral trade for the first time; there will be a 36 per cent reduction in tariffs as well as substantial cuts in subsidies.

- Agreed multilateral rules will govern trade-related intellectual property rights, providing protection for holders of trademarks, patents, copyrights and design rights.

- Trade in textiles, where restrictions on imports have been allowed under the Multi-Fibre Arrangement (MFA—see p. 248) to balance the interests of exporters and importers, will be reintegrated into the rules of the WTO over ten years.

Britain is now focusing on ensuring that the multilateral trading system of the WTO works properly in practice; it is also seeking to make further progress, through the WTO, in reducing external barriers to trade.

European Union

Austria, Finland and Sweden joined the European Union on 1 January 1995. The single European market 'opened for business' on 1 January 1993, with the essential legislation in place for the free movement of goods, services, people and capital within the EU. Member states are now concentrating on ensuring that the market operates efficiently and completing work in energy and telecommunications liberalisation. Among the changes from January 1993 were:

- the ending of routine customs clearance of commercial goods at national frontiers within the EU;

- the introduction of the right to trade financial services throughout the EU on the basis of a single home authorisation 'passport' (see p. 215); and

- deregulation of airlines, with national flag carriers losing preferential treatment.

Special Trading Arrangements

The EU has association and co-operation agreements with virtually all non-member countries with a Mediterranean coastline, plus Jordan; these give preferential access to EU markets. Non-preferential co-operation agreements have also been made with countries in South Asia and Latin America, as well as with the People's Republic of China, the Association of South East Asian Nations, the Andean Pact and the Central American states. Trade relations with the developing countries of Africa, the Caribbean and the Pacific are governed by the Lomé Convention, which gives these countries tariff-free access, subject to certain safeguards, to the EU for industrial and agricultural products.

Tariff preference is also given to developing countries under the Generalised System of Preferences. This applies to industrial products, including textiles and certain (mainly processed) agricultural products. The scheme concentrates benefits on poorer producers and countries.

Europe Agreements are in place between the EU and Poland, Hungary, the Czech Republic, Slovakia, Bulgaria and Romania; such agreements have also been recently signed with Slovenia and the Baltic states. They are designed to facilitate closer political and economic ties and the eventual creation of a free trade area with a view to those countries becoming full members of the EU. A trade and economic co-operation agreement has also been made with Albania and partnership and co-operation agreements have been concluded with Russia, Ukraine, Belarus, Moldova, Kyrgyzstan and Kazakhstan.

CONTROLS ON TRADE

With the completion of the single European market, all routine internal border controls and requirements were removed for trade in EU goods between the members of the EU. This has substantially cut travel times and costs; for example, freight journey times by road from Britain to Italy have been reduced by up to 24 hours.

Import Controls

Individual national quantitative restrictions are inconsistent with the single European market and following the removal of internal frontiers they have been largely abolished. A system of Union-wide quotas is under discussion between the European Commission and member states. Quantitative restrictions on textiles stem from the MFA, under which there is a series of bilateral agreements. A number of quantitative restrictions are also maintained against non-WTO countries.

Imports of certain other goods are prohibited or restricted in order to protect human, animal or plant life or health. These include firearms and ammunition; nuclear materials; certain drugs; explosives; endangered wildlife and derived products; and certain agricultural, horticultural and food products.

Export Controls

The great majority of British exports to countries outside the EU are not subject to any government control. Controls on certain strategic goods are imposed for a variety of reasons, including foreign policy and non-proliferation concerns, the need to comply with international treaty commitments and the operation of sanctions. The scope of these controls is restricted to what is necessary to meet these requirements. Most controls apply on a worldwide basis. However, certain sanctions and embargoes are applied against specific countries as a result of agreement by members of bodies such as the United Nations.

There are controls relating to the export of conventional military equipment and firearms as well as dual-use industrial goods that can be used for civil and military purposes. Most dual-use industrial goods are allowed to move freely within the EU without an export licence.

Controls on conventional weapons and equipment for manufacture stem from an agreement by members of the Co-ordinating Committee for Multilateral Export Controls (COCOM). Although this body was disbanded in 1994, ex-members are maintaining the controls in their present form. Lists of dual-use related goods are drawn up mainly under agreements of the Australia Group, the Nuclear Suppliers Group and the Missile Technology Control Regime; Britain is a member of all three. The aim is to help prevent the spread of chemical, biological and nuclear weapons and missile systems for their delivery.

GOVERNMENT SERVICES

The Government assists exporters by creating economic conditions favourable to the export trade and by providing practical help, advice and financial support. This includes a wide range of services and assistance to meet the requirements of exporters, especially small and medium-sized enterprises.

Export Promotion Services

Overseas Trade Services (OTS) comprises the leading government departments engaged in export promotion, including the Department of Trade and Industry (DTI), the Foreign & Commonwealth Office (FCO), the Industry Department of the Welsh Office, Scottish Trade International and the Industrial Development Board of Northern Ireland. There are over 2,000 staff worldwide, based at the DTI in London, in regional offices and Business Links (see p. 208) around Britain, and at more than 200 diplomatic posts overseas.

OTS gathers and disseminates export intelligence, helps in researching potential markets, and supports firms participating in trade fairs and missions. In 1994–95 around £190 million was spent on support for exporters.

In England the development of local Business Links is making OTS more accessible to potential users. The DTI is financing up to 70 'export development counsellors' in Business Links to give advice to exporters and outward investors at local business level.

OTS works closely with over 100 'export promoters' seconded from private industry, as well as with the British Overseas Trade Board (BOTB), the BOTB's Area Advisory Groups and with FCO posts abroad. The BOTB's aims are to:

- help guide the Government's export promotion efforts, including the provision of export services; and

- provide advice on policy issues affecting international trade and exports.

The BOTB's Area Advisory Groups, which are made up of business people with expert knowledge of trade with particular world markets, provide advice on the world's main trading areas. The Overseas Projects Board advises on major project business overseas and the Small Firms Committee on matters relating to small businesses. Nearly 200 businessmen and women are involved in the Board's work.

OTS pays special attention to the promotion of exports to its top priority areas in Western Europe, North America, and Japan and the fast-growing countries of the Asia-Pacific Rim. These three areas contain the world's largest and richest markets, and account for around four-fifths of Britain's exports. Emerging markets in other areas, such as Latin America, where some countries have been achieving rapid growth rates, are also being targeted.

The Government has set a target of introducing 30,000 firms to new export markets by the year 2000. It has also announced:

- an improved programme of trade fair and mission support;

- a programme of 'British Excellence' fairs in key markets;

- additional commercial staff abroad and 14 new overseas posts;

- export vouchers for small and medium-sized enterprises to help them buy assistance at Business Links; and

- an 'Export Challenge' for trade associations, to encourage them to improve the international competitiveness of the sectors they represent.

British Invisibles

British Invisibles is an organisation which promotes the international activities of financial institutions and business services. Its role is to suggest and, where possible, implement measures for boosting invisible earnings in Britain and abroad. It also seeks to increase awareness of London as an international financial centre and of the role of the service sector in the British economy.

Export Insurance

ECGD (Export Credits Guarantee Department) is a government department, responsible to the President of the Board of Trade. It helps British firms overcome many of the risks of selling and investing overseas. ECGD supports British exporters of capital goods and services sold on medium- and long-term credit by:

- guaranteeing exporters and financing banks against the risk of non-payment by overseas buyers/borrowers;

- giving interest rate support to British banks, allowing overseas borrowers access to funds at fixed, often favourable, rates of interest; and

- providing reinsurance to British private-sector insurance companies covering exports sold on short-term credit.

In order to encourage investment in less developed countries, ECGD also insures investment earnings against the main political risks, such as war, expropriation and restrictions on repatriation of profits. Particular attention is paid to increasing cover for exports to ECGD's main markets, such as Hong Kong, China, Indonesia, South Africa and Malaysia. The Middle East and East Asia are currently ECGD's largest sources of new business.

In the 1994 Budget the Government announced measures to improve the competitiveness of capital goods exporters by increasing support provided by ECGD. For instance, average premium rates were cut by 10 per cent. ECGD's rates have been reduced by 25 per cent overall since 1992 and cover has been resumed for more than 20 markets worldwide.

BALANCE OF PAYMENTS

The balance-of-payments statistics record transactions between residents of Britain and non-residents. The transactions are classified into two groups: current account, and transactions in Britain's external assets and liabilities, sometimes known as the capital account. The current account records trade in goods (visible trade) and services, including finance, tourism and transport, transactions in investment income, and transfers (invisible trade). Capital transactions include inward and outward investment, overseas transactions by banks in Britain, external borrowing and lending by residents in Britain and drawings on and accruals to the official reserves.

Britain has no exchange controls; residents are free to acquire foreign currency for any purpose, including direct and portfolio investment overseas. There are also no controls on the lending of sterling abroad and non-residents may acquire sterling for any purpose. Gold may be freely bought and sold. Exchange controls were abolished in 1979, and Britain meets in full its obligations on capital movements under an OECD code and under EC directives.

The current account has been in deficit since 1986, although it fell markedly between 1993 and 1994 from £11,000 million to £1,700 million (see Table 12.6). Since 1983 Britain has had a deficit on visible trade; however, it has run a surplus on trade in invisibles in all but five years since 1955. At £10,600 million in 1994, the deficit on visible trade was £2,800 million less than in the previous year. The invisibles surplus increased from £2,300 million to £8,900 million between 1993 and 1994. The surplus on services fell by £1,900 million; that on investment income increased by £8,600 million; and the deficit on transfers was, at £5,400 million, virtually the same as in 1993.

Inward and Outward Investment

The Government welcomes both outward and inward investment.[1] Outward investment helps to develop markets for British exports while providing earnings in the form of investment income. Inward investment is

[1] A distinction needs to be made between capital flows and capital holdings. Flows comprise transactions resulting in a change of ownership of financial assets and liabilities between British residents and non-residents, while holdings are measured by the total values of British external assets and liabilities at the end of the year. Income earned on external assets and liabilities is dealt with in the section on invisibles.

Table 12.6: Britain's Balance of Payments 1990–94

£ million

	1990	1991	1992	1993	1994
Current account					
Visible trade balance	−18,809	−10,284	−13,104	−13,378	−10,594
Invisible transactions balance	−484	1,751	3,636	2,336	8,910
Current balance	−19,293	−8,533	−9,468	−11,042	−1,684
Transactions in assets and liabilities					
British external assets	−80,439	−18,872	−81,385	−155,818	−39,363
British external liabilities	98,560	27,399	86,444	169,330	35,802
Balancing item	1,172	6	4,409	−2,470	5,245

Source: *United Kingdom Balance of Payments 1995 Edition*
Note: Differences between totals and the sums of their component parts are due to rounding.

promoted by DTI's Invest in Britain Bureau (IBB—see p. 212) as a means of introducing new technology, products, management styles and attitudes; creating or safeguarding employment; and increasing exports or substituting imports. In recent years Japanese investment has helped transform the automotive industries in Britain.

The IBB recorded 434 new inward investment decisions in 1994–95 in projects that will create or safeguard almost 90,000 jobs, over 50 per cent of which were expansions to existing investments. Inward investment is playing an increasingly important role in Britain's economy, with overseas firms providing 18 per cent of all manufacturing jobs, 24 per cent of net output, 32 per cent of manufacturing investment and about 40 per cent of manufacturing exports. At present Britain has around 40 per cent of US and Japanese investment in the EU.

At the end of 1994 the stock of inward direct investment (investment in branches, subsidiaries and associated companies which gives the investor an effective role in their management) was £139,700 million, compared with £132,900 million in 1993. The stock of direct investment overseas by British residents was £183,300 million at the end of 1994, compared with £171,000 million in 1993. The inflow of portfolio investment into Britain amounted to £31,800 million in 1994 (£46,800 million in 1993); outward portfolio investment was reduced by £18,600 million in 1994 (compared with a rise of £84,500 million in 1993). An analysis of transactions in Britain's external assets and liabilities for 1992–94 is given in Table 12.7.

Britain's identified external assets at the end of 1994 exceeded liabilities by £17,700 million, compared with £13,200 million a year earlier. Net assets of the private sector and public corporations amounted to £37,300 million and net liabilities of general government to £19,600 million.

At the end of 1993, 84 per cent of outward direct investment was in developed countries, with 35 per cent in the United States and 32 per cent in the EU. Investment from developed countries accounted for 96 per cent of overseas direct investment in Britain: 40 per cent originated in the United States and 31 per cent in the EU.

Table 12.7: Summary of Transactions in External Assets[a] and Liabilities[b] 1992–94

£ million

	1992	1993	1994
Overseas direct investment in Britain	8,513	9,625	6,677
Overseas portfolio investment in Britain	26,714	46,818	31,836
British direct investment overseas	−10,845	−17,135	−16,412
British portfolio investment overseas	−27,337	−84,500	18,552
Borrowing from overseas	52,379	115,955	−3,250
Deposits and lending overseas	−43,928	−52,875	−39,839
Official reserves[a]	1,407	−698	−1,045
Other external liabilities of general government	−1,162	−3,069	541
Other external assets of central government	−682	−610	−619
Total	**5,059**	**13,512**	**−3,561**

Source: *United Kingdom Balance of Payments 1995 Edition.*
[a]Increase −/decrease +
[b]Increase +/decrease −
Note: Differences between totals and the sums of their component parts are due to rounding.

Further Reading

Overseas Trade. Aspects of Britain series, HMSO, 1994.

United Kingdom Balance of Payments 1995 Edition. Central Statistical Office, HMSO.

13 Employment

Britain has a higher proportion of the adult population in work—70 per cent—than any other major EU country. The labour market has changed considerably in recent years as a result of the move away from full-time to part-time employment, the growing proportion of women in the workforce and higher self-employment. Nearly three-quarters of employees now work in the service sector, compared with around one-fifth in manufacturing. Industrial relations have been transformed, and the number of working days lost in 1994 was the lowest on record.

PATTERNS OF EMPLOYMENT

The total workforce in 1995 was around 28 million. The workforce in employment in June 1995 totalled 25.7 million (see Table 13.1), of whom 21.9 million (11 million men and over 10.8 million women) were classed as employees in employment. Employment is recovering following the decline as a result of the recession of the early 1990s. Between

March 1993 (the most recent employment trough) and March 1995 the workforce in employment increased by 360,000.

Nearly two-thirds of women aged 15–64 in Britain are in work, compared with between a third and a half in most other European countries, and only Sweden and Denmark have a higher proportion of women in work. Many employers have developed policies to help women to return

Table 13.1: Workforce in Employment in Britain

Thousands, seasonally adjusted, June

	1985	1990	1993	1994	1995
Employees in employment	21,414	22,909	21,588	21,639	21,889
Self-employed	2,767	3,551	3,178	3,288	3,346
HM Forces	326	303	271	250	230
Work-related government training programmes	176	423	311	302	264
Workforce in employment	24,683	27,186	25,348	25,478	25,729

Source: Central Statistical Office

Full and Part-time Employment in Great Britain, Seasonally Adjusted

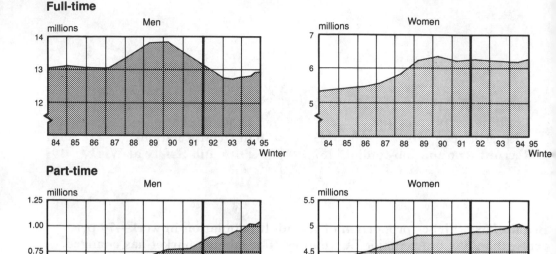

Note: Data are for spring quarters only for 1984–91 and are for every quarter for 1992 onwards. Data from spring 1992 contain unpaid family workers.

Source: *Labour Force Survey Quarterly Bulletin.*

to the labour market. The Government is encouraging voluntary action by employers to increase the employment opportunities for women. It has joined the 'Opportunity 2000' campaign and in 1994 launched a new regional initiative in England, 'Fair Play for Women' (see p. 37).

The long-term trend has been for a fall in full-time employment and a growth in part-time employment (see diagram above). Since 1984 part-time employment in Great Britain has risen by 1.3 million to 6.1 million in spring 1995: 5 million women and 1.1 million men. About 44 per cent of women in employment were working part-time, compared with 8 per cent of men. About 1.3 million people had two or more jobs. 'Teleworking'—people working from home using information technology—is becoming more widespread, especially in journalism, consultancy and computer

programming. About 6 per cent of businesses use teleworking extensively.

Self-employment is increasing again, following a decline during the recession. About 3.3 million people are self-employed in Britain, 19 per cent more than in 1985. The sectors with the highest concentrations of self-employed people are agriculture and construction.

Government Policy

The Government has taken a number of steps to change the labour market, with the aim of creating an economic climate in which business can flourish and create more jobs. These include:

● increasing the flexibility of the labour market, for example, encouraging the adoption of flexible working patterns for more employees;

- removing burdens on employers and workers, including regulatory barriers which hinder recruitment; and
- encouraging better training, especially through employer-led Training and Enterprise Councils and, in Scotland, Local Enterprise Companies (see p. 183).

The Government supports a social dimension to the European Union (see p. 112) which gives priority to the creation and development of jobs and takes into account the different employment patterns and practices in member states.

Employment by Sector

As in other industrialised countries, there has been a marked shift in jobs from manufacturing to service industries (see Table 13.2). Between 1955 and 1995 the proportion of employees in employment engaged in service industries more than doubled, to nearly 76 per cent. In June 1995, 16.1 million people were employed in services in Great Britain, about 2 million more than in 1985 (see Table 13.3). Business activities, education, medical services, distribution, and hotels and catering experienced significant increases. Employment in some services, however, particularly postal services and telecommunications, has fallen.

Most other sectors—manufacturing, construction, agriculture, and mining, energy and water supply—have experienced lower levels of employment, although there are indications that the decline in manufacturing employment may have halted. Nevertheless, by 1995 manufacturing accounted for 18 per cent of employees in employment, compared with 42 per cent in 1955. Traditional manufacturing industries, such as steel and shipbuilding, have recorded particularly large falls in employment. In June 1995 employment in the main manufacturing sectors in Great Britain included:

- 686,000 employees in non-metallic mineral products, metal and metal products;
- 469,000 in paper, pulp, printing, publishing and recording media;
- 445,000 in electrical and optical equipment;
- 429,000 in food products, beverages and tobacco; and
- 381,000 in clothing, textiles, leather and leather products.

Occupational Changes

There has been a gradual move away from manual occupations towards non-manual occupations, which now account for nearly three-fifths of jobs in Great Britain. Self-employment is highest in craft and related occupations (29 per cent of those in this sector in Great Britain in spring 1995), followed by managers and administrators (20 per cent).

Table 13.2: Employees by Main Sector in Britain (at June)

	1990	1993	1994	1995
Thousands				
Service industries	16,308	16,180	16,287	16,547
Manufacturing industries	4,732	3,913	3,894	3,947
Mining, energy and water supply	407	299	266	242
Other industries	1,462	1,195	1,192	1,153
Per cent of employees				
Service industries	71.2	74.9	75.3	75.6
Manufacturing industries	20.7	18.1	18.0	18.0
Mining, energy and water supply	1.8	1.4	1.2	1.1
Other industries	6.4	5.5	5.5	5.3

Source: Central Statistical Office

Table 13.3: Employees in Employment in Services in Great Britain

Thousands: seasonally adjusted, June

	1985	1990	1993	1994	1995
Wholesale and retail trade, and repairs	3,287	3,597	3,500	3,563	3,580
Hotels and restaurants	989	1,216	1,139	1,162	1,238
Transport and storage	868	910	873	873	872
Postal services and telecommunications	442	462	420	410	396
Financial services	858	1,047	959	942	929
Real estate	152	190	237	240	237
Renting, research, computer and other business activities	1,719	2,202	2,209	2,233	2,403
Public administration, defence and compulsory social security	1,424	1,383	1,401	1,374	1,318
Education	1,570	1,805	1,752	1,763	1,770
Health activities	1,296	1,445	1,470	1,457	1,456
Social work activities	654	794	899	927	964
Other community, social and personal activities	831	880	923	936	969
All services	**14,089**	**15,931**	**15,783**	**15,880**	**16,131**

Source: Central Statistical Office

Unemployment

Unemployment in Britain—as measured by the number of people claiming unemployment-related benefits and adjusted for seasonal variation—has fallen by over 600,000 since the end of 1992 and the level of unemployment is below the EU average. The rates of long-term, youth and female unemployment are well below those in most other EU countries. Unemployment began to fall at an earlier stage than in previous economic cycles, reflecting a number of factors, including an improvement in the functioning of the labour market (following measures such as deregulation), more young people staying on in education, and greater efficiency in the placing of unemployed people into work by the Employment Service. In August 1995 claimant unemployment totalled 2.3 million, 8.2 per cent of the workforce. It ranged from 6.4 per cent in East Anglia to 11.6 per cent in Northern Ireland.

The Government has introduced a wide range of measures to help combat unemployment. In 1995–96 about 1.5 million opportunities on employment and training schemes are being offered to help unemployed people. The November 1994 Budget included a major £325 million package of measures targeted on helping the long-term unemployed back to work. Among the measures are:

● the extension to 1998 of the Community Action programme, which provides about 40,000 opportunities a year for people to do voluntary work of benefit to the community on a part-time basis while they actively look for work;

● a doubling to 40,000 of the number of places on the Work Trials scheme, which enables employers to take on unemployed people for up to three weeks on a trial basis;

● the extension throughout Great Britain of the Jobfinder's Grant, available to those out of work for over two years to help fund their costs on returning to work;

- a new national programme, 'Workwise and 1-2-1' providing 133,000 places in 1995–96, designed to provide intensive help with looking for jobs for those aged 18 to 24 who have been unemployed for over a year; and

- further pilot Workstart schemes, under which employers receive a financial incentive for recruiting long-term unemployed people.

A new Jobseeker's Allowance (see p. 422), expected to be introduced in October 1996, will replace unemployment benefit and income support for unemployed people. It is intended to improve the operation of the labour market by helping people in their search for work. To receive the allowance each unemployed person will have to complete a jobseeker's agreement, which will include the steps agreed by the jobseeker to be taken to find work.

TRAINING, EDUCATION AND ENTERPRISE

Employers in Britain spend over £20,000 million a year on employee training and development. The Government funds a number of training, enterprise and vocational education programmes. Its training strategy is designed to increase Britain's prosperity by stimulating enterprise and developing excellence in skills. Individuals are encouraged to train by employers through a number of government initiatives such as Investors in People (see p. 184) and National Vocational Qualifications (NVQs, see p. 442), and by means of tax reliefs and loan schemes. Britain is acknowledged as an innovative world leader in open and flexible learning, for example, through the Open University.

Training and Enterprise Councils

There are 81 Training and Enterprise Councils (TECs) in England and Wales. They are independent companies run by local business leaders. They are accountable to Government through their contracts and are subject to regular monitoring by the Government Offices for the Regions.

The objective of TECs is to develop the skilled workforce necessary for sustaining economic growth and prosperity within their area. Their special focus is to strengthen the skill base and assist local enterprise to expand and compete effectively. As well as managing the provision of training and enterprise programmes previously run by the Government, TECs promote the importance of training as a business strategy—in particular through the Investors in People standard—and foster education–business links.

For 1995–96, £1,434 million is being provided by the Department for Education and Employment to TECs in England to deliver its programmes. TECs also contract with other government departments, in particular the Department of Trade and Industry, to deliver enterprise programmes (see Chapter 14) and can compete for contracts under the Government's Single Regeneration Budget (see p. 345).

Local Enterprise Companies

A separate network of 22 Local Enterprise Companies (LECs) exists in Scotland. These have wider-ranging responsibilities than the TECs, covering economic development and environmental improvement. LECs operate the same major training programmes as TECs, but, unlike them, have no responsibility for work-related further education. They run under the supervision of the two enterprise bodies: Scottish Enterprise and Highlands and Islands Enterprise (see p. 209).

Industry Training Organisations

Industry Training Organisations (ITOs) act as the focal point for training matters in their particular sector of industry, commerce or public service. Their role is to ensure that the skills needs of their sectors are being met and that occupational standards are being established and maintained for key occupations. There are over 120 independent ITOs, covering sectors employing about 85 per cent of the civilian workforce. The National Council of Industry Training Organisations, a voluntary body set up to represent the interests of ITOs, aims to improve their effectiveness, for example, by encouraging good practice.

National Targets for Education and Training

The National Targets for Education and Training were launched by the Confederation of British Industry in 1991 and were supported by over 100 national and local organisations, including all TECs, LECs and ITOs, and other major education, training and employer bodies. The principal aim of the targets is to improve Britain's international competitiveness by raising standards and attainment levels in education and training through ensuring that:

- all employers invest in employee development to achieve business success;
- everyone has access to education and training opportunities, leading to recognised qualifications which meet their needs and aspirations; and
- all education and training develops self-reliance, flexibility and breadth, through fostering competence in core skills.

The Government supports the targets and in 1993 established the independent National Advisory Council for Education and Training Targets (NACETT) to monitor progress towards them; a parallel body, the Advisory Scottish Council for Education and Training Targets, operates in Scotland.

The targets cover both young people and the workforce as a whole. Following a review by NACETT, new, more challenging targets were set in May 1995, relating to the year 2000. The 'Foundation Learning' targets are that:

- by the age of 19, 85 per cent of young people should achieve five GCSEs at grade C or above, an intermediate GNVQ or NVQ level 2;[1]
- 75 per cent of young people should achieve level 2 competence in communication, numeracy and information technology by the age of 19, with 35 per cent reaching level 3 by the age of 21; and

---

[1] For information on General National Vocational Qualifications (GNVQs) and examinations, see Chapter 26.

- by 21, 60 per cent of young people should achieve two GCE A levels, an Advanced GNVQ or NVQ level 3.

The 'Lifetime' targets are that:

- 60 per cent of the workforce should attain NVQ level 3, an Advanced GNVQ or two GCE A levels;
- 30 per cent of the workforce should have a vocational, professional, management or academic qualification at NVQ level 4 or above; and
- 70 per cent of organisations employing 200 or more people and 35 per cent of those employing 50 or more should be recognised as Investors in People.

Separate targets, set within the framework of the national targets, are in force in Scotland.

Training for Work

The Government's Training for Work programme has the objective of helping long-term unemployed adults to find jobs through training and work experience. Training is carried out by training providers under contract with the local TEC or LEC. Each new trainee receives an individually adapted package of training and/or structured work activities. The programme is being reformed during 1995–96 to become more efficient and to improve the proportion of people obtaining a job when leaving the programme, to 50 per cent by 1997–98. About 112,000 places are available in Great Britain in 1995–96, when the programme is expected to help up to 270,000 people.

Investors in People

Investors in People is the main initiative in support of employers' investment in people. It is based on a rigorous national standard which helps companies to improve their performance by linking the training and development of all employees directly to the achievement of business objectives. TECs and LECs provide advice and information to help organisations to work towards the standard. By mid-1995 nearly 2,100 had achieved the Investors in People standard, and over 18,900 had made a formal commitment to work towards it. Over 80 per cent of employers surveyed who had achieved the standard believed that this had improved the quality of their workforce, while three-quarters of employers involved had changed their training practices.

National Training Awards

The National Training Awards are an annual competition designed to promote good training practice by example, rewarding companies which have carried out exceptionally effective training. In 1994 around 80 corporate awards and 20 individual awards were presented to national winners, who were selected from about 250 regional winners.

Career Development Loans

People who live, or intend to undertake vocational training, in Great Britain can apply to one of four major banks for a Career Development Loan. Deferred repayment loans of £200 to £8,000 can help to pay for vocational courses lasting up to two years, or two years of a longer course. More than 67,000 people have borrowed over £192 million through the programme to pay for training.

Small Firms Training Loans

Small Firms Training Loans were introduced in June 1994. The programme helps firms with 50 or fewer employees to meet a range of training-related expenses, including training consultancy. Loans of between £500 and £125,000 are available and repayments can be deferred for up to 13 months.

Skills for Small Businesses

In April 1995 Skills for Small Businesses, a three-year initiative, was introduced. It will help firms with fewer than 50 employees to provide modern skills training. It is designed to help companies by training selected key workers—one per company—who would then pass on their knowledge and expertise to other employees. Under the £63 million programme run by TECs, there will be provision for training of up to

24,000 key employees. A similar programme will be run in Scotland.

Improving the Training Market

The Improving the Training Market programme covers a range of activities funded by the Department for Education and Employment aimed at improving the quality, impact and cost-effectiveness of vocational education and training. Priority is being given to encouraging investment by individuals in learning, supporting the implementation of new qualifications and developing frameworks for the new Modern Apprenticeships (see below).

Training for Young People

The Government is committed to ensuring that high-quality further education or training is available for all young people who can benefit from it. All those aged 16 or 17 who are not in full-time education, a job or a Modern Apprenticeship are guaranteed the offer of a suitable training opportunity.

The objectives of the two main youth programmes—Modern Apprenticeships and Youth Training—are to:

● provide participants with training leading to vocational qualifications at NVQ/SVQ levels 2 and 3 or above (see p. 442) and with broad-based skills necessary to become flexible and self-reliant employees; and

● to meet the skill needs of the national and local economies.

The delivery of training is arranged through TECs and LECs.

Modern Apprenticeships

In 1993 the Government announced its intention to bring in 'Modern Apprenticeships'. Prototype schemes were introduced in September 1994 in 17 sectors such as chemicals, engineering and construction. The number was extended to around 50 when Modern Apprenticeships became fully operational in September 1995. Modern Apprenticeships are designed to build on the best features of existing apprenticeships and to increase significantly the number of young people trained to technician, supervisory and equivalent levels.

Accelerated Modern Apprenticeships have been developed alongside Modern Apprenticeships and started in September 1995. They will provide high-level training for school- and college-leavers.

Youth Credits

Youth Credits are intended to offer young people more individual choice and a greater sense of personal responsibility when buying training. Each credit has a financial value and can be presented to an employer or training provider in exchange for training. In England 16- and 17-year-old school- and college-leavers are eligible to obtain access to Youth Training and Modern Apprenticeships through Youth Credits. Youth Credits will be available to all young people in Wales from April 1996. Under Skillseekers, the equivalent scheme in Scotland, all young people leaving full-time education will be eligible for a Youth Credit by 1996.

Education Initiatives

A major government objective is to raise the motivation and attainment of young people to achieve their full potential and develop the skills needed by the economy. This requires close working relationships between industry and education. Several education initiatives are being implemented, including Education Business Partnerships, Compacts and the National Record of Achievement. Details are given in Chapter 26.

Vocational Qualifications

The proportion of the workforce with qualifications, gained either in school or further education, is growing. Between 1984 and 1994 it rose from 63 per cent to 81 per cent.

The National Council for Vocational Qualifications (NCVQ), established in 1986, has been charged with reforming and rationalising vocational qualifications into a coherent framework. The NCVQ has

developed new National Vocational Qualifications in England, Wales and Northern Ireland (see p. 442). In Scotland the Scottish Vocational Education Council (SCOTVEC) has developed parallel Scottish Vocational Qualifications (SVQs).

NVQs and SVQs are designed for people in the workplace. They are job-specific, based on national standards of competence set by industry and are assessed in the workplace. There are five levels within the NVQ and SVQ framework (see p. 442). NVQs and SVQs at levels 1 to 5 to cover at least 90 per cent of the employed workforce are expected to be in place by the end of 1995. The 1994 White Paper on competitiveness (see p. 200) announced proposals to improve the quality and take-up of NVQs/SVQs. All NVQs/SVQs will be reviewed and updated by March 1998.

Northern Ireland

The Training and Employment Agency, an executive agency within the Department of Economic Development, has primary responsibility for training and employment services. Its overall aim is to assist economic development and help people to find work through training and employment services delivered on the basis of equality of opportunity. The Agency has encouraged each main sector of industry to form a sector representative body to advise on employers' training needs and to develop sectoral training strategies. In addition, the Agency supports company training through its Company Development Programme and encourages management development by providing an extensive range of training programmes and seminars for existing and future managers.

Northern Ireland has its own range of training and employment programmes for people seeking work. The Agency introduced a new Jobskills Programme in April 1995. It is designed to raise the quality of training available to school-leavers and unemployed adults, leading to greater achievement of NVQs. In order to combat the high level of long-term unemployment in Northern Ireland, the Agency is running a pilot Community Work Programme which enables long-term unemployed adults to undertake work of benefit to the community for a period of three years.

RECRUITMENT AND JOB-FINDING

There are a variety of ways in which people can find jobs. In winter 1993–94, according to the Labour Force Survey, the main methods used by people who had found their current job in the previous three months were:

- hearing from someone else who worked there (31 per cent);
- replying to advertisements (25 per cent);
- direct approaches to employers (16 per cent); and
- visiting a Jobcentre (9 per cent).

Government Employment Services

The Government provides a range of services to jobseekers through the Employment Service, an executive agency within the Department for Education and Employment. These include:

- a network of local offices, at which people can find details of job opportunities;
- advice and guidance so that people can find the best route back into employment, for example, by training; and
- a range of special programmes.

The Employment Service has over 1,100 Jobcentres and unemployment benefit offices, and employs about 42,000 staff. Jobcentres are being integrated with the benefit offices to provide a comprehensive service to unemployed people. By mid-1995 about 970 integrated offices had been established. In 1994–95 the Employment Service placed nearly 1.9 million unemployed people into jobs and conducted 8.9 million advisory interviews to help people find appropriate work or places on employment and training programmes. A review of the Employment Service's functions has been carried out to ensure that it is organised as effectively as possible and to see whether any functions could be undertaken in the private sector.

The Jobseeker's Charter contains provisions governing the standard of service to users. These include provisions on the speed of service, and ensuring that vacancies on display boards at offices are up to date and are available, and that those entitled to benefit receive the correct payments promptly.

> The Employment Service is an active participant in the European Employment Services Network (EURES). EURES is a partnership between the employment services in the member states of the European Economic Area. It facilitates the circulation of vacancies in member states through a computer network.

Advisory Services

Through the main Jobcentre services, unemployed people have access to vacancies, employment advice and training opportunities. Advisers provide unemployed people with information on employment and training opportunities available locally. New Client Advisers interview newly unemployed people to check their eligibility for benefit. Together with the unemployed person, they agree a 'Back to Work Plan', which sets out specific courses of action to improve the prospects of finding a job. Thereafter unemployed people are required to attend a Restart advisory interview every six months. Restart interviews are intended to offer help and advice to unemployed people while they are on the unemployment register.

The Service has a wide variety of programmes, including several new ones launched in April 1995. Programmes to help the long-term unemployed include:

- Jobclubs, where participants are given training and advice in job-hunting skills and have access to facilities to help an intensive job search;
- Restart courses, designed to rebuild self-confidence and motivation, and including help with job-hunting skills; and
- Jobplan workshops, which are designed to enable those unemployed for a year to assess their skills, qualities and training needs, and to act as an introduction to future job and training options.

Help for People with Disabilities

Most disabled people assisted by the Employment Service are helped through its 'mainstream' services, and have priority access to most of the main programmes for unemployed people. Services for people with disabilities who need more specialist help to get or keep a job are available through Disability Employment Advisers based in Jobcentres. The advisers are members of local integrated specialist teams—Placing Assessment and Counselling Teams. They are supported by nine regional Ability Development Centres. The teams also work with local employers to encourage them to recruit and retain disabled people.

Access to Work, a programme to help people with disabilities to overcome barriers to employment, was introduced in June 1994, replacing help formerly available under a series of different initiatives. It offers flexible assistance to address a greater range of disabilities and to enable more people to be helped.

Through the Supported Employment Programme, the Employment Service provides employment opportunities for people with severe disabilities who are unable to obtain or retain work in open employment. Around 21,000 opportunities are provided through this programme.

Employment Agencies

There are many private employment agencies, including several large firms with many branches. The total value of the market has been estimated at about £8,000 million a year.

The main trade body for the employment agency industry is the Federation of Recruitment and Employment Services, which regulates the activities of its members by means of a Code of Good Recruitment Practice and by specialist section codes of practice.

The law governing employment agencies is less restrictive than that of most other EU countries. Under the Deregulation and Contracting Out Act 1994 (see p. 202), the licensing of employment agencies was abolished in January 1995. The Act contains powers to prohibit people from operating

agencies when necessary. Agencies have to comply with statutory standards of conduct. This includes a general prohibition on charging fees to jobseekers, although there are conditional exceptions for entertainment and modelling agencies.

TERMS AND CONDITIONS OF EMPLOYMENT

Employment Rights

Employment protection legislation provides a number of safeguards for employees. For example, most employees have a right to a written statement setting out details of the main conditions, including pay, hours of work and holidays.

Employees with the necessary period of continuous employment with their employer (two years) are entitled to lump-sum redundancy payments if their jobs cease to exist (for example, because of technological improvements or a fall in demand) and their employers cannot offer suitable alternative work. Where employers are insolvent, redundancy payments are met directly from the National Insurance fund.

Many employment rights have long applied to part-time workers. In February 1995 the Government introduced new regulations giving part-time employees entitlement to all the same statutory employment rights as full-time employees by removing the distinctions in qualifying conditions between full-time employees and part-time employees (those working between 8 and 16 hours a week).

Minimum periods of notice when employment is to be terminated are laid down for both employers and employees. Most employees who believe they have been unfairly dismissed have the right to complain to an industrial tribunal, provided they have the necessary qualifying period of employment. If the complaint is upheld, the tribunal may make an order for re-employment or award compensation.

New maternity rights were established by
the Trade Union Reform and Employment
Rights Act 1993 and took effect in October
1994. They implemented an EC directive and
coincided with increases in maternity pay. All
pregnant employees, regardless of length of
service, have the right to 14 weeks' statutory
maternity leave with all their non-wage
contractual benefits maintained, and protection
against dismissal because of pregnancy.

Legislation forbids any employment of
children under 13 years of age, and
employment in any industrial undertaking of
children who have not reached the statutory
minimum school-leaving age, with some
exceptions for family undertakings.

Equal Opportunities

The Race Relations Act 1976 makes it
generally unlawful to discriminate on grounds
of colour, race, nationality (including
citizenship) or ethnic or national origin, in
employment, training and related matters. The
Department for Education and Employment
operates a nationwide Race Relations
Employment Advisory Service. Its objective is
to promote those Government policies aimed
at combating racial discrimination in
employment and promoting fair treatment
and equality of opportunity in employment.
Advisers provide employers with advice and
practical help in developing and implementing
effective equal opportunity strategies.

The Sex Discrimination Act 1975, as
amended, makes it generally unlawful in
Great Britain to discriminate on grounds of
sex or marital status when recruiting,
training, promoting, dismissing or retiring
staff. The Equal Pay Act 1970 makes it
generally unlawful to discriminate between
men and women in pay and other terms and
conditions of employment. The Act was
significantly extended in 1984 to meet EU
requirements by providing for equal pay for
work of equal value.

Practical advice to employers and others
on the best arrangements for implementing
equal opportunities policies in Great Britain
is given in codes of practice from the
Commission for Racial Equality and from the
Equal Opportunities Commission (see p. 37),

while the Department for Education and
Employment has also published practical
guidance to employers on how to make
equal opportunities an integral part of
management practice.

New rights for disabled people in
employment in Great Britain are
contained in the Disability
Discrimination Act (see p. 408),
passed in 1995. A new right for
disabled people of non-discrimination
in the labour market is introduced.
Employers with 20 or more employees
will have a duty not to treat a
disabled person less favourably than
other workers unless there are
justifiable reasons, and a duty to
make a reasonable adjustment to the
workplace or working arrangements
where this would help overcome the
practical effects of a disability. A
Code of Practice is planned to give
guidance on the new requirements
and practical advice to employers.

Similar legislation to that in Great Britain
on equal pay and sex discrimination applies
in Northern Ireland; there is at present no
legislation on race relations, but legislation is
to be introduced. Discrimination in
employment on grounds of religious belief or
political opinion is unlawful. The Fair
Employment Commission (see p. 15) has the
task of promoting equality of opportunity and
investigating employment practices, with
powers to issue legally enforceable directions.

Industrial Tribunals

Industrial tribunals have jurisdiction over
complaints on a range of employment rights
including unfair dismissal, redundancy pay,
equal pay, and sex and race discrimination.
They dealt with about 28,000 cases in
1994–95 and the number of cases continues
to grow steadily. In December 1994 the
Government issued a Green Paper containing
proposals to promote the voluntary settlement
of disputes and improve the tribunal system,
so reducing delays and raising the standards
of service.

Earnings

According to the official New Earnings Survey, the average weekly earnings, unaffected by absence and including overtime payments, in Great Britain in April 1995 of full-time employees on adult rates were £336. Earnings were higher for non-manual employees (£372) than for manual employees (£272). Managerial and professional groups are the highest paid. The sectors with the highest average weekly earnings were mining and quarrying (£444) and financial services (£430).

Overtime and other additional payments are particularly important for manual employees, for whom such additional payments represented over one-fifth of earnings. About 50 per cent of manual employees and 18 per cent of non-manual employees received overtime payments.

In the year to July 1995 the underlying average increase in earnings in Great Britain was about 3.25 per cent.

Fringe Benefits

A variety of fringe benefits are used by employers to provide additional rewards to their employees, including schemes to encourage employee financial participation in their companies, pension schemes, private medical insurance, subsidised meals, company cars and childcare schemes.

Many employees are covered by pension schemes provided by their employers. Such benefits are more usual among clerical and professional employees than among manual workers. Nearly 11 million people in Britain are members of occupational schemes.

Company cars are provided for employees in a wide variety of circumstances. It is estimated that around 1.7 million people have a company car and around half of these receive fuel for private motoring in their cars.

The Government has introduced tax reliefs to encourage employers to set up financial participation schemes, and give employees a direct financial stake in the business they work for.

Profit-related pay (PRP) schemes link part of pay to changes in a business's profits. By the end of March 1995 nearly 9,500 PRP schemes were registered with the Inland Revenue, covering about 2.4 million people. Employee share schemes allow employees to receive low-cost or free shares from their employer without paying income tax. By the end of March 1993 about 3.1 million employees had benefited from all-employee profit sharing and Save-As-You-Earn (SAYE) share option schemes.

A committee of inquiry chaired by Sir Richard Greenbury examined executive pay and other benefits, such as share options, and its report, issued in July 1995, contained guidelines for companies. Following the report, the Chancellor of the Exchequer announced changes to the tax treatment of executive share options so that gains from exercising options would be taxable as income rather than as a capital gain.

Hours of Work

Most full-time employees have a basic working week of between 34 and 40 hours, and work a five-day week. When overtime is taken into account, average weekly hours worked in Great Britain in April 1995 were 41.9 for men and 37.6 for women. Average hours worked by full-time and part-time employees and the self-employed were 39.9 for men and 26.9 for women in spring 1995. Hours worked tended to be longest in agriculture, construction and transport and communications, and shortest in most service industries. More men than women work overtime, and those in manual occupations generally work more overtime than employees in non-manual jobs. Flexible working hours were worked by about 15 per cent of female and 10 per cent of male full-time employees in Britain in spring 1994.

In general, there are no limits on hours worked by adults except in a few occupations (such as for drivers of goods and public service vehicles).

The Government is challenging in the European Court a draft EC directive which includes proposals for a maximum 48-hour working week.

Holidays with Pay

There are no general statutory entitlements to holidays, and holiday entitlements are determined by negotiation. Holiday entitlements (excluding public holidays) generally provide for at least four weeks' paid holiday a year. Non-manual workers tend to have longer holidays than manual workers. Holiday entitlements may also be dependent upon length of service.

INDUSTRIAL RELATIONS

The structure of industrial relations in Britain has been established mainly on a voluntary basis. The system is based chiefly on the organisation of employees and employers into trade unions and employers' associations, and on freely conducted negotiations at all levels.

Trends in Bargaining and Pay

There has been a considerable reduction in the proportion of employees and workplaces where pay is determined by collective bargaining. Around 48 per cent of employees in employment in Great Britain work in firms where trade unions negotiate on pay and conditions of employment. Private sector employees are much less likely to be covered by collective bargaining than are public sector employees.

Where agreements in the private sector are industry-wide, they are often supplemented by local agreements in companies or factories (plant bargaining). Where there is no collective bargaining, pay is usually determined by management at local level. Most medium and large employers make some use of performance-related pay systems such as merit pay, financial participation (see p. 190) and individual payment by results. Private sector organisations are more likely to use performance-related pay than public sector bodies.

The Government is committed to the further development of performance-related pay in the public sector as part of its wider objectives for improving the quality of the public services as set out in the Citizen's Charter (see p. 66). Performance-related pay

is being extended in areas such as the Civil Service and education. Greater pay flexibility is also being encouraged in other ways, such as the delegation of pay determination to self-governing trusts in the National Health Service and to grant-maintained schools; from April 1996 all government departments and agencies will have responsibility for their own pay negotiations of staff below senior levels.

'New-style' agreements, often associated with overseas-owned companies, have become more widespread. Features normally include flexibility in working practices, recognition of a single union for all of a company's employees and 'single status', involving the elimination of the traditional distinction between managers, supervisors and other employees.

Employee Involvement

Employers practise a wide variety of methods of informing and consulting their employees, not only through committees but also through direct communication between management and employees. These methods include:

- employee bulletins and reports;
- briefing systems;
- quality circles;
- financial participation schemes; and
- attitude surveys.

The Government is opposed to the EU's proposals for statutory requirements for multinational employers to set up European works councils or other agreements providing for the transnational information and consultation of employees. It believes that companies should be free to develop employee involvement arrangements which are appropriate to their own circumstances and the needs of their employees.

Trade Unions

Trade unions have members in nearly all occupations. They are widely recognised by employers in the public sector and in large firms and establishments. As well as negotiating pay and other terms and conditions of employment with employers, they provide benefits and services such as educational facilities, financial services, legal advice and aid in work-related cases. In recent years many unions have extended considerably the range of services for members.

At the end of 1993 there were 8.7 million trade union members in Britain, the lowest number since 1946. About 60 per cent of union members were male and 40 per cent female. The decline reflects the moves away from manufacturing and public services, both of which have a relatively high level of membership, and the growth in part-time employment. Mergers have resulted in a fall in the number of unions, and several unions are discussing possible mergers.

Unison, with about 1.5 million members, is the biggest union in Britain. It was formed in 1993 from a merger of three unions: the Confederation of Health Service Employees, the National Union of Public Employees and the National and Local Government Officers' Association. Other unions with over 500,000 members are:

- the Transport and General Workers Union (with 949,000 members);

- the Amalgamated Engineering and Electrical Union (835,000);

- GMB (809,000)—a general union with members in a range of public and private sector industries; and

- Manufacturing Science and Finance Union (516,000).

At the end of 1994 there were 267 trade unions on the list maintained by the Certification Officer, who, among other duties, is responsible for certifying the independence of trade unions. To be eligible for entry on the list a trade union must show that it consists wholly or mainly of workers and that its principal purposes include the regulation of relations between workers and employers or between workers and employers' associations.

Trade union organisation varies widely, but there is usually a national executive council or committee. Many unions also have regional and district organisations, while local branches cover one or more workplaces.

Elected workplace representatives are often called 'shop stewards'. Where two or more unions have members in the same workplace, shop stewards' committees may be formed to discuss matters of common concern.

Trades Union Congress

In Britain the national body of the trade union movement is the Trades Union Congress (TUC), founded in 1868. Its affiliated membership comprises 68 trade unions, which together represent some 6.9 million people, or about 80 per cent of all trade unionists in Britain.

The TUC's objectives are to promote the interests of its affiliated organisations and to improve the economic and social conditions of working people. It deals with all general questions which concern trade unions, both nationally and internationally, and provides a forum in which affiliated unions can collectively determine policy. There are six TUC regional councils for England and a Wales Trades Union Council. The annual Congress meets in September to discuss matters of concern to trade unionists. A General Council represents the TUC between annual meetings. In March 1994 the TUC launched a programme of change designed to promote trade unionism and increase its influence on the nation's affairs.

The TUC plays an active part in international trade union activity, through its affiliation to the International Confederation of Free Trade Unions and the European Trade Union Confederation. It also nominates the British workers' delegation to the annual International Labour Conference.

Scotland and Northern Ireland

Trade unions in Scotland also have their own national central body, the Scottish Trades Union Congress, which in many respects is similar in constitution and function to the TUC. Trade unions in Northern Ireland are represented by the Northern Ireland Committee of the Irish Congress of Trade Unions (ICTU). Most trade unionists in Northern Ireland are members of organisations affiliated to the ICTU, while the majority also belong to unions based in Great Britain which are affiliated to the TUC. The Northern Ireland Committee of the ICTU enjoys a high degree of autonomy.

Legal Framework

The Government's reforms of industrial relations and trade union law have helped to change the balance of power between trade unions and employers, and between trade unions and their own members. For example, since 1980 employers have been free to decide whether or not to bargain with a trade union or continue to do so. Legislation for Great Britain is consolidated in the Trade Union and Labour Relations (Consolidation) Act 1992, as amended by the most recent Act, the Trade Union Reform and Employment Rights Act 1993. There is broad parity of provision in respect of industrial relations and trade union law in Northern Ireland.

There were 278,000 working days lost in 205 stoppages of work as a result of industrial action in 1994 (see Table 13.4), the lowest numbers since records began in 1891.

Union Membership and Non-membership Rights

All individuals have the right under the law not to be dismissed or refused employment (or the services of an employment agency) because of membership or non-membership of a trade union. Individuals who believe that they have been dismissed or refused employment on such grounds may complain to an industrial tribunal. All employees who are union members also have the right not to have union membership subscriptions deducted from their pay unless they have authorised this, and renew this at least every three years.

The Conduct of Union Affairs

The law requires a trade union to elect every member of its governing body, its general secretary and its president. Elections must be held at least every five years and be carried out by a secret postal ballot under independent scrutiny. Any union member

who believes that the union has not complied with the statutory requirements may complain to the courts or to the Certification Officer.

A trade union may establish a political fund if it wishes to use its money for what the law defines as 'political objects'. If a union wishes to set up a political fund, its members must first agree in a secret ballot a resolution adopting those political objectives as an aim of the union. The union must also ballot its members every ten years to maintain the fund. Union members have a statutory right to opt out of contributing to a political fund.

The law also gives all union members a statutory remedy if unjustifiably disciplined by their union, for example, for refusing to take part in industrial action or for crossing a picket line. Members also have the right to inspect their union's accounting records and obtain an annual statement from the union about its financial affairs.

Industrial Action

For most of the 20th century trade unions enjoyed wide immunity protecting them from legal proceedings for organising industrial action, so that the organisation of almost any industrial action was protected. Legislative reforms have restricted the scope of these immunities. To have the benefit of statutory immunity (that is, to be 'lawful'), the organisation of industrial action must now be wholly or mainly in contemplation or furtherance of a trade dispute between workers and their own employer, and must not:

- involve workers who have no dispute with their own employer (so-called 'secondary' action);
- involve unlawful forms of picketing;
- be to establish or maintain a union-only labour agreement (the 'closed shop'); or
- be in support of any employee dismissed while taking unofficial industrial action.

Before calling for industrial action, a trade union must first obtain the support of its members in a secret postal ballot and must notify employers of its intention to conduct such a ballot. The union must also provide

Table 13.4: Industrial Disputes 1984–1994

	Working days lost (thousands)	Working days lost per 1,000 employees[a]	Workers involved (thousands)	Number of stoppages
1984	27,135	1,278	1,464	1,221
1989	4,128	182	727	701
1992	528	24	148	253
1993	649	30	385	211
1994	278	13	107	205

Source: Central Statistical Office
[a]Based on the mid-year (June) estimates of employees in employment.

employers, in writing, with at least seven days' notice of official industrial action following a ballot, and with details of the ballot result.

Any trade union member has the right to restrain the union from calling on him or her, and other members, to take action unless a properly conducted secret ballot has supported the action. Anyone deprived of goods or services because of unlawful organisation of industrial action has the right to obtain a court order to stop this happening.

Employers' Organisations

Many employers in Britain are members of employers' organisations, some of which are wholly concerned with labour matters, although others are also trade associations concerned with commercial matters in general. With the move away from national pay bargaining, many employers' associations have moved towards concentrating on areas such as supplying information for bargaining purposes and dealing with specialist issues. As with some of the larger trade unions, a number of employers' associations are increasingly concerned with legislation and other issues relating to Europe.

Employers' organisations are usually established on an industry basis rather than a product basis, for example, the Engineering Employers' Federation. A few are purely local in character or deal with a section of an industry or, for example, with small businesses; most are national and are concerned with the whole of an industry. In some of the main industries there are local or regional organisations combined into national

federations. At the end of 1994, 117 listed and 123 unlisted employers' associations were known to the Certification Officer.

Most national organisations belong to the Confederation of British Industry (see p. 199), which represents directly or indirectly some 250,000 businesses.

Advisory, Conciliation and Arbitration Service

The Advisory, Conciliation and Arbitration Service (ACAS) is an independent statutory body which has a general duty of promoting the improvement of industrial relations. ACAS seeks to discharge its responsibilities through the voluntary co-operation of employers, employees and, where appropriate, their representatives. Its main functions are collective conciliation, provision of arbitration and mediation facilities, advisory mediation services for preventing disputes and improving industrial relations through the joint involvement of employers and employees, and providing an information service. ACAS also conciliates in disputes on individual employment rights.
In 1994 ACAS:

● received 1,313 requests for collective conciliation, with a further 156 requests referred to arbitration or mediation;

● completed nearly 80,000 individual conciliation cases;

● made nearly 3,600 advisory visits;

● assisted with 487 joint working exercises; and

● dealt with almost 526,200 enquiries through its public enquiry points.

In Northern Ireland the Labour Relations Agency, an independent statutory body, provides services similar to those provided by ACAS in Great Britain.

HEALTH AND SAFETY AT WORK

Health and safety standards in Britain are among the best in the world. Recent statistics indicate a reduction in the rate of major and other reported injuries to employees. In 1993–94 the number of deaths from accidents at work fell to 379, the lowest figure recorded. The decline reflects improvements in safety, together with a change in industrial structure away from old heavy industries which tend to have higher risks. About 18 million working days a year are lost as a result of work-related injuries and 13 million from work-related illnesses.

In 1993–94 the Health and Safety Commission (HSC) conducted a review of all health and safety legislation to assess its relevance. It found considerable scope for simplifying legislation without endangering health and safety standards and identified many redundant regulations. The Government has accepted all the HSC's recommendations.

The principal legislation is the Health and Safety at Work etc. Act 1974. It imposes general duties on everyone concerned with work activities, including employers, the self-employed, employees, and manufacturers and suppliers of materials for use at work. Associated Acts and regulations deal with particular hazards and types of work. Employers with five or more staff must prepare a written statement of their health and safety policy and bring it to the attention of their staff.

The Control of Substances Hazardous to Health Regulations 1988 constitute one of the most important sets of regulations made under the 1974 Act. They replaced a range of outdated legislation by a comprehensive and systematic approach to the control of exposure to virtually all substances hazardous to health.

Health and Safety Commission

The HSC has responsibility for developing policy on health and safety at work, including proposals for new or revised regulations and approved codes of practice. It has an obligation to consult those who would be affected and makes recommendations to the appropriate Secretary of State.

The HSC has advisory committees covering subjects such as toxic substances, genetic modification and the safety of nuclear installations. There are also several industry advisory committees, each of which deals with a specific sector of industry.

Health and Safety Executive

The Health and Safety Executive (HSE) is the primary instrument for carrying out the HSC's policies and has day-to-day responsibility for enforcing health and safety law, except where other bodies, such as local authorities, are responsible. Its field services and inspections are carried out by the Field Operations Division. This incorporates the Factory, Agricultural and Quarries inspectorates, together with the regional staff of the Employment Medical Advisory Service and the Field Consulting Groups, which provide technical support to the inspectorates.

In May 1995 the HSE launched a major health management campaign aimed at reducing the number of people—2.2 million a year—who suffer work-related ill health. The campaign, which will run for at least three years, is designed to raise awareness of health risks at work, and to persuade managers to ensure that working conditions do not cause illness among their employees.

The HSE's Technology and Health Services Division provides technical advice on industrial health and safety matters. The Health and Safety Laboratory provides scientific and medical support and testing services, and carries out research.

In premises such as offices, shops,

warehouses, restaurants and hotels, health and safety legislation is enforced by inspectors appointed by local authorities, working under guidance from the HSE. Some other official bodies work under agency agreement with the HSE.

Northern Ireland

The general requirements of the Northern Ireland health and safety legislation are broadly similar to those for Great Britain. They are enforced mainly by the Department of Economic Development and the Department of Agriculture through their health and safety inspectorates, although the district councils have an enforcement role similar to that of local authorities in Great Britain. There is a Health and Safety Agency, roughly corresponding to the HSC but without its policy-making powers, and an Employment Medical Advisory Service.

Further Reading

Employment. Aspects of Britain series, HMSO, 1994.

Employment Gazette. Department for Education and Employment and Central Statistical Office. Monthly.

Essentials of Health and Safety at Work. HSE Books, 1994.

Labour Force Survey Quarterly Bulletin. Central Statistical Office.

14 Industry and Government

The private sector is responsible for over three-quarters of total economic activity. Since 1979 the Government has privatised nearly 50 major businesses and reduced the state owned sector of industry by about two-thirds. It believes that economic decisions are best taken by those competing in the market place, and that its primary role is to encourage enterprise and create the right climate for markets to work better. Government schemes do, however, provide direct assistance or advice, mainly to small and medium-sized businesses without the resources of large companies.

STRUCTURE AND ORGANISATION OF INDUSTRY

In some sectors a small number of large companies and their subsidiaries are responsible for a substantial proportion of total production, for instance in the chemical, motor vehicle, aerospace and transport equipment industries. Private enterprises account for by far the greater part of activity in the agricultural, manufacturing, construction, distributive, financial and miscellaneous service sectors. The private sector contributed 76 per cent of total domestic expenditure in 1994, general government 23 per cent and public corporations 1 per cent.

About 250 British industrial companies each have an annual turnover of over £500 million. The annual turnover of the biggest company, British Petroleum (BP), makes it the 11th largest industrial group in the world and the second largest in Europe. Five British firms are among the top 20 European Union (EU) companies in terms of capital employed.

Small businesses are making an increasing contribution to the economy. Between 1980 and 1993 the number of businesses, the great majority small firms, rose from 2.4 million to 3.6 million. Companies with fewer than 100 employees account for 50 per cent of the private sector workforce and 30 per cent of turnover. About 97 per cent of firms employ fewer than 20 people. Industries with the fastest growth rates in recent years are in the services sector, particularly finance, property, and professional and business services.

Legal Framework

All British companies are registered with the Registrar of Companies in Cardiff, Edinburgh or Belfast, depending on whether a company's registered office is in England or Wales, Scotland or Northern Ireland.

Companies with a place of business or branch in Britain, but which are incorporated overseas, are also required to register.

Legislation deals with capital structure, rights and duties of directors and members, and the preparation and filing of accounts (see p. 207). Most corporate businesses are 'limited liability' companies. The liability of members of a limited company is restricted to contributing an amount related to their shareholding (or to their guarantee where companies are limited by guarantee). In the case of unincorporated businesses, such as sole proprietorships or partnerships, individuals are personally liable for any business debts, except where a member of a partnership is a limited liability company or a limited member of a limited partnership.

Companies may be either public or private. A company must satisfy certain conditions before it can become a public limited company (plc). It must:

- be limited by shares or guarantee and have a share capital;

- state in its memorandum of association that it is to be a public limited company;

- meet specified minimum capital requirements; and

- have as the suffix to its name the words 'public limited company' or 'plc'.

All other British companies are private companies and are generally prohibited from offering their shares to the public.

Industrial Financing

Over half of companies' funds for investment and other purposes are generated internally. Banks are the chief external source of finance, but companies have increasingly turned to equity finance. The main forms of short-term finance in the private sector are bank overdrafts, trade credit and factoring (making cash available to a company in exchange for debts owing to it).

Types of medium- and long-term finance include bank loans, mortgaging of property and the issue of shares and other securities to the public through the London Stock Exchange. The leasing of equipment may also be regarded as a form of finance. Other sources of finance for industry include government, the European Union (EU) and specialist financial institutions, such as financing and leasing, factoring and venture capital companies.

Venture Capital

Venture capital, or private equity capital, provides long-term unsecured capital for companies starting up or expanding as well as those undergoing management buy-outs and buy-ins. Venture capital is available principally from institutions that include independent funds and wholly-owned subsidiaries or divisions of financial institutions, such as banks. The British Venture Capital Association has 107 full members, which represent every major source of venture capital in Britain. Nearly £12,800 million has been invested by venture capital companies in 12,900 businesses since 1984, with £2,074 million being invested in 1,208 businesses in 1994.

The majority of venture capital deals involve investments of over £100,000, averaging in excess of £1 million each in 1994. In that year, 68 per cent of venture capital deals were in expansion stage companies; 67 per cent of the total amount of money was invested in management buy-outs and buy-ins.

Business angels, or private investors, are an increasingly important source of smaller amounts of venture capital. The Enterprise Investment Scheme (EIS) and Venture Capital Trusts (VCTs) seek to encourage private investment in smaller unquoted trading companies by offering individuals tax incentives. The EIS allows business angels to take a position on the boards of the investee company; VCTs are more suited to less active investors. VCTs, which were launched in September 1995, are similar in structure to investment trusts: they invest in unquoted trading companies and are quoted on the Stock Exchange.

Taxation

Rates of corporate taxation have been progressively reduced in recent years (see

p. 164). The main rate of corporation tax is 33 per cent, with a reduced rate of 25 per cent for small firms (those with annual profits of less than £300,000). For companies with profits of between £300,000 and £1.5 million, the overall corporation tax rate is between the main rate and the rate for small firms. Expenditure on business plant and machinery, industrial building, and scientific research qualifies for annual allowances against profit for tax purposes.

Industrial Associations

The Confederation of British Industry (CBI) is the largest employers' organisation in Britain, representing about 250,000 companies from all sectors, which together employ over 50 per cent of Britain's workforce. Membership ranges from the smallest to the largest companies in virtually all business sectors. Most national employers' organisations, trade associations, and some chambers of commerce are also members.

The CBI aims to ensure that the Government, national and international institutions and the public understand the needs, intentions and problems of business, so as to create a climate of opinion in which business can operate efficiently and profitably. It campaigns to lessen the burdens on business, tackle handicaps on competition, and help improve the performance of companies. It offers members a forum, a lobby and a range of advisory services. The CBI also conducts surveys of activity in manufacturing, distribution, financial services, the regions, innovation, and pay and productivity. It has 12 regional offices and an office in Brussels. The CBI is the British member of the Union of Industrial and Employers' Confederations of Europe.

The chambers of commerce represent business views to the Government at national and local levels. They promote local economic development—for example, through regeneration projects, tourism, inward investment promotion and business services, including overseas trade missions, exhibitions and training conferences. Member firms are also supplied with information about overseas buyers and product sourcing. The

Association of British Chambers of Commerce represents more than 214,000 businesses in over 230 chambers of commerce and trade throughout Britain.

The Institute of Directors (IOD) has more than 50,000 members worldwide, including 33,000 members in Britain, many of whom are from small businesses. The IOD provides business advisory services on a range of matters affecting company directors, such as corporate management, insolvency and career counselling, and represents the interests of members to authorities in Britain and the EU. It also offers a full training programme of courses and lectures.

Trade associations represent companies producing or selling a particular product or group of products. They exist to supply common services, regulate trading practices and represent their members to government departments. Department of Trade and Industry (DTI) initiatives encourage trade associations representing companies within the same sector to work more closely together.

GOVERNMENT POLICY

The Department of Trade and Industry is the department mainly responsible for the Government's relations with industry and commerce. Specific responsibilities, which are dealt with in this chapter, include company law, small firms, regional industrial development and inward investment, competition policy and consumer affairs, and intellectual property. The Department of the Environment oversees provision of regional industrial aid through the Government Offices for the Regions. The Scottish, Welsh and Northern Ireland Offices are responsible for industrial policies in their areas. Export promotion is examined in Chapter 12 and technology and innovation in Chapter 20. The DTI's responsibilities for industrial relations are covered in Chapter 13.

The Department of Trade and Industry seeks to help British industry to compete successfully in domestic and overseas markets. It has specified its objectives as:

● identifying business needs through close contact with individual sectors;

- ensuring these needs are taken into account by Government and the EU;
- identifying influences on competitiveness at home and abroad;
- working for global trade liberalisation worldwide and helping businesses take advantage of market opportunities at home and abroad;
- widening choice and stimulating enterprise by promoting competition and privatisation;
- maintaining confidence in markets and protecting consumers by fair regulation;
- reducing unnecessary regulatory and administrative burdens on business;
- promoting innovation and best practice in quality, design and management;
- fostering the creation and development of small and medium-sized businesses;
- responding to the needs of different regions and areas with special difficulties; and
- taking account of environmental issues when developing government policies and stimulating an effective business response to environmental developments.

Competitiveness White Papers

A White Paper on Competitiveness, issued in May 1994, contains a programme of measures to help British business compete effectively in world markets (see p. 154). These were introduced to improve education and training, help small firms to be more innovative and to increase exports, boost regional economies and attract more inward investment. A follow-up White Paper was published in May 1995, detailing progress since 1994 and setting out new policies and initiatives, in particular for smaller companies (see p. 154). Some of the more important measures are covered in this chapter and also in Chapter 13.

Single European Market

The Government believes that the single European market (see p. 120) is beneficial to the economy of each member state: removal of trade barriers should lead to a reduction in business costs and greater competition and efficiency, to the benefit of consumers and job and wealth creation.

Specific advantages of the single market include:

- wider consumer choice;
- removal of barriers to trade through mutual recognition of standards and harmonisation;
- liberalisation of public procurement;
- the right to trade financial services throughout the EU on the basis of a single authorisation 'passport' (see p. 215);
- mutual recognition of professional and vocational qualifications; and
- a reduction in export business bureaucracy.

Privatisation

The Government is of the view that the best way to improve the performance of public sector companies and nationalised industries is to expose them to market forces, through privatisation and the promotion of competition. Privatisation has also provided an opportunity to widen and deepen share ownership by encouraging both employees and the public to take a direct stake in industry. In major flotations, employees in privatised companies are normally given a preferential right to buy shares in the new privatised companies.

Since 1979 the Government has privatised 48 major businesses, with net proceeds to the end of 1994–95 of about £60,000 million. Recent privatisations include British Coal, the electricity industry in Northern Ireland, London's buses and the Government's residual shareholdings in BT (British Telecom), National Power and PowerGen. Legislation has been introduced to enable the private sector to operate rail services (p. 300). Privatisation is also being extended to non-core government activities (including a number of research laboratories—p. 326) and other public sector areas. The Government plans to privatise

Table 14.1: Major Government Sales

	Year of sale	Net equity proceeds (£ million)
BAA	1987	1,182
BT	1984–93	14,247
British Aerospace	1981–85	390
British Airways	1987	853
British Gas	1986–90	5,293
British Petroleum	1979-87	6,084
British Steel	1988	2,425
Britoil	1982-85	962
Cable and Wireless	1981-85	1,021
Rolls-Royce	1987	1,031
Water companies (England and Wales)	1989	3,454
Regional electricity companies (England and Wales)	1990 }	5,756
Electricity generating companies (England and Wales)	1991–94 }	
Scottish electricity companies	1991	2,828[a]
BT secondary share sale	1991	5,128
Northern Ireland Electricity	1992–93	704[a]
BT secondary share sale	1993	5,335[a]
British Coal	1994	963

Source: HM Treasury
[a] Gross proceeds

the modern generating assets of Nuclear Electric and Scottish Nuclear in 1996.

Benefits

The Government believes that the economy has benefited through higher returns on capital in the privatised industries, which now have to compete for funds in the open capital markets. Privatised companies have welcomed the freedom to raise finance in private-sector capital markets.

The consumer has gained from downward pressure on prices and from rising standards of service. The Government has established a system of independent regulation for the privatised utilities. In each of the privatised utility sectors— telecommunications, electricity, gas and so on—a regulatory body has been appointed with a wide range of powers and duties to promote competition and the interests of consumers. These usually include considering all complaints and representations about the company's services. Each privatised utility operates under a pricing policy set by the regulator, which usually limits annual price increases to significantly less than the rate of inflation.

Nationalised Industries

The remaining major nationalised industries are British Rail, Railtrack, the Post Office, London Transport, Nuclear Electric, Civil Aviation Authority, and Scottish Nuclear. Managing boards are appointed by ministers, who have power to give general directions but are not engaged in day-to-day management. Managing boards and staffs of nationalised industries are not civil servants.

The Government considers that nationalised industries should act as commercial enterprises and has set policies to which they are expected to conform. These involve:

● clear government objectives;

● regular corporate plans and performance reviews;

● agreed principles relating to investment appraisal and pricing;

● financial targets and performance aims;

- external financing limits; and
- systematic monitoring.

Deregulation

The Government's aim is to reduce or simplify administrative and legislative burdens on business, particularly small businesses, where the burden of compliance is most demanding. A small firms 'litmus test' is helping to ensure that compliance costs for new regulations are not unduly high. Deregulation helps businesses to contain costs, operate more efficiently and trade more competitively.

Under the Deregulation Initiative, the Government is reducing burdens on business by:

- achieving better regulation, and cutting unnecessary controls and the cost of compliance with essential regulation;

- ensuring that the views of business, and potential costs of compliance, are taken into account in framing new regulations and in negotiating EU proposals;

- increasing official awareness of the needs of business through training and better consultation and communication; and

- improving the quality of service to business generally, whether provided by central or local government.

The existing 3,500 regulations affecting companies are being reviewed by government departments with the help of business people; about 500 provisions were repealed or changed in 1994. The Deregulation and Contracting Out Act enables the Government to amend or repeal primary legislation imposing unnecessary burdens on business.

Regulation of Markets

The aim of Government competition policy is to encourage and enhance the competitive process. It is not the purpose of the policy to protect particular firms that may be adversely affected by competition. When the competitive process itself is frustrated, however, intervention may be justified. The law provides several ways in which market situations can be examined and, if necessary, altered.

Responsibility for competition policy lies with the President of the Board of Trade who enforces the competition law with the Director General of Fair Trading, the Monopolies and Mergers Commission and the Restrictive Practices Court. The main legislation comprises:

- the Fair Trading Act 1973 and the Competition Act 1980, which deal with mergers and monopolies, and anti-competitive practices respectively;

- the Restrictive Trade Practices Act 1976, which regulates agreements between people or companies that could limit their freedom to operate independently; and

- the Resale Prices Act 1976, covering attempts to impose minimum prices at which goods can be sold.

As well as British law, competition policy is also governed by European Community rules. These apply only where an agreement or practice has an effect on trade between member states. Enforcement of these rules is primarily the responsibility of the European Commission, which has powers to investigate and terminate alleged infringements and to impose fines. The Director General assists the European Commission in the application of European Community competition law.

Monopolies

Under the Fair Trading Act 1973, a monopoly is defined first as a situation where a company supplies or purchases 25 per cent or more of a particular product or service in Britain, or a defined part of it; and secondly, as a situation where a group of companies or people together have 25 per cent or more of the market and behave in a way that adversely affects competition (a 'complex monopoly').

The Director General may enquire into possible abuse of a monopoly position and take various measures to remedy the situation. If there is 'prima facie' evidence of a monopoly situation, the matter can be referred for further investigation by the independent Monopolies and Mergers Commission (MMC), whose

CITY LIVERY COMPANIES

City of London livery companies sponsor many creative activities, including embroidery at the Royal School of Needlework at Hampton Court Palace, Surrey.

Former Master of The Mercers' Company Francis Baden-Powell with a portrait of Sir Richard (Dick) Whittington. Dick Whittington travelled to London in 1358 to make his fortune as a 'mercer', dealing in valuable imports such as silks and velvets. His social concern led him to support the poor and needy, and The Mercers' Company received its charter from Richard II during his lifetime; it has been administering charity for nearly 600 years.

THE ELECTRICITY SUPPLY INDUSTRY

Hydro-Electric's Sloy power station, on the banks of Loch Lomond, Scotland. It is the most powerful conventional hydroelectric power station (130-MW capacity) in Britain. The water is carried over 3 km by tunnel through Ben Vorlich, then down the steep side of the mountain in four large pipelines to the power station.

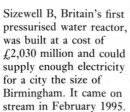

Sizewell B, Britain's first pressurised water reactor, was built at a cost of £2,030 million and could supply enough electricity for a city the size of Birmingham. It came on stream in February 1995.

A 100-kW pilot wood-chip gasification plant at Wellman Process Engineering, West Midlands. Wood chips are gasified to give a flammable gas which can then be used to make electricity. Such biofuels (which include landfill gas, short-rotation coppice and other woods) can make a contribution to the environment and to the agricultural economy.

The main inlet valve gallery at Dinorwig pumped storage station in Gwynedd, Wales. The valves are opened to release water from the high-level reservoir through the system to generate electricity at peak times.

TEXTILES

A technician operates a giant spinning machine at US company Fruit of the Loom's state-of-the-art factory in Londonderry, Northern Ireland.

The wool produced by these rare Wensleydale sheep has recently become prized by some of Britain's leading designers, among them Katherine Hamnett.

members are drawn from a variety of backgrounds and include industrialists, lawyers, economists and trade unionists.

If the MMC finds that a monopoly situation operates, or could be expected to operate, against the public interest, the President of the Board of Trade can either make an order to prevent further detriment or ask the Director General to obtain undertakings from those involved to remedy the situation.

Mergers

In most cases judgment of the advantages and disadvantages of mergers is left to the parties involved, with the market determining the outcome. The great majority of mergers are not considered to pose a threat to competition and are allowed to take place. However, under the Fair Trading Act 1973, the President of the Board of Trade can refer mergers for investigation by the MMC if they could lead to a significant reduction in competition or raise other matters of public concern.

A merger is defined as occurring when two or more enterprises come under common ownership or control. It qualifies for investigation by the MMC where:

- a market share of 25 per cent or more in Britain or a substantial part of it is created or increased; or

- the total value of gross assets to be taken over exceeds £70 million.

After considering advice from the Director General of Fair Trading, the President of the Board of Trade may refer a merger or proposed merger to the MMC. Alternatively, the Director General may be asked to obtain suitable undertakings from the companies involved to remedy the adverse effects identified. If a merger or proposed merger is referred and the MMC finds that it may be expected to operate against the public interest, the President of the Board of Trade can prohibit it or allow it subject to certain conditions being met. Where the merger has already taken place, action can be taken to reverse it. There are special provisions for newspaper and water company mergers.

The Companies Act 1989 and the Deregulation and Contracting Out Act 1994 made changes to merger control procedures. They provide for:

- a voluntary procedure for pre-notification of proposed mergers which offers prompt clearance of straightforward cases; and

- acceptance of enforceable undertakings by the parties concerned to divest assets in order to obviate the need for a full investigation by the Commission.

Certain mergers with an EU dimension, assessed by reference to turnover, come under the exclusive jurisdiction of the European Commission where competition in trade between members of the European Union is affected. The Commission can ban mergers if it concludes that they create or strengthen a dominant position which would significantly impede effective competition within the EU or a substantial part of it; alternatively, it may negotiate undertakings to correct the adverse effect.

Anti-competitive Practices

The Director General of Fair Trading can investigate any course of conduct by a business which appears to be anti-competitive. If a practice is found to be anti-competitive, undertakings may be sought from the business responsible for the conduct. In the event of a suitable undertaking not being given, the matter may be referred to the MMC. In the case of an adverse finding by the MMC, the President of the Board of Trade has powers to take remedial action. Companies are not covered by the legislation if they have a turnover of less than £10 million, or have less than 25 per cent of a relevant market in Britain.

Restrictive Trade Practices

Most commercial agreements containing restrictions on matters such as prices and other conditions of sale and parties or areas to be dealt with have to be submitted to the Director General of Fair Trading for registration. Legal proceedings are normally initiated by the Director General against blatantly anti-competitive agreements which have not been notified.

Once an agreement has been registered, the Director General is under a general duty to refer it to the Restrictive Practices Court. The Court must declare the restrictions in the agreement contrary to the public interest unless the parties can satisfy it that the restrictions fall within set public interest criteria ('gateways'). Restrictions declared contrary to the public interest by the Court are void, and the Court has the power to order the parties not to implement them.

In practice, however, the great majority of agreements are never brought to court because the restrictions they contain are not significant enough to warrant such action. In these circumstances the Director General may be discharged from his duty to bring proceedings.

Resale Price Maintenance

For the most part it is unlawful for suppliers to notify dealers of a minimum resale price for their goods or to make it a condition of supply that their goods be sold at a specified price. It is also unlawful for suppliers to seek to impose minimum resale prices by withholding supplies of goods or by discriminating against price-cutting dealers in other ways. The Director General of Fair Trading, or anyone affected, can take proceedings in the civil courts.

Consumer Protection

Consumer protection is an integral element in the fair operation of markets. The Government believes that consumers' interests are best served by open and competitive markets offering the widest choice of goods and services. There are, however, laws to ensure that consumers are adequately protected.

Legislation covers the sale of goods, the supply of goods and services, and the way that goods and services are described. The marking and accuracy of quantities are regulated by weights and measures legislation Another law provides for the control of medical products, and certain other substances and articles, through a system of licences and certificates. Under EC legislation, it is a criminal offence to supply unsafe consumer products. A range of public safety information for consumers has been made available by the DTI.

The Director General of Fair Trading promotes good trading practices and acts against malpractice. Under the Fair Trading Act 1973, the Director General can make recommendations for legislative or other changes to stop practices adversely affecting consumers' economic interests; encourage trade associations to develop codes of practice promoting consumers' interests; and disseminate consumer information and guidance. The Director General can also take assurances as to future conduct from traders who persistently breach the law to the detriment of consumers. New regulations which came into force in July 1995 empower the Director General to act against traders using unfair contract terms.

The Consumer Credit Act 1974 is intended to protect consumers in their dealings with credit businesses. Businesses connected with the consumer credit or hire industry or which supply ancillary credit services, for example credit brokers, debt collectors, debt counsellors and credit reference agencies, require a consumer credit licence. The Director General is responsible for administering the licensing system, including revoking the licences of those unfit to hold them. Under other regulations he or she also has powers to take court action to prevent the publication of misleading advertisements and powers to prohibit unfit persons from carrying out estate agency work.

The EU's consumer programme covers activities such as health and safety, protection of the consumer's economic interests, promotion of consumer education and strengthening the representation of consumers. The views of British consumer organisations on EU matters are represented by the Consumers in Europe group (UK). British consumer bodies also have a voice on the European consumer 'watchdog' body, the Bureau Européen des Unions de Consommateurs.

Consumer Advice and Information

Advice and information on consumer matters are given by Citizens Advice Bureaux, trading standards or consumer protection departments of local authorities (in Northern Ireland the Department of Economic Development), and, in some areas, by specialist consumer advice centres.

The independent, non-statutory National Consumer Council (and associated councils for Scotland and Wales), which receives government finance, presents the consumer's view to government, industry and others. The General Consumer Council for Northern Ireland has wide-ranging duties in consumer affairs in general.

Consumer bodies for several privatised utilities investigate questions of concern to the consumer. Some trade associations in industry and commerce have established codes of practice. In addition, several private organisations work to further consumer interests. The largest is the Consumers' Association, funded by the subscriptions of its 800,000 members.

Education and Training

A well-educated and well-trained workforce is essential for economic prosperity, especially at a time of intense international competition and rapid technological advance. The Government aims to ensure that education and training are broadly based and that people of all ages can acquire relevant knowledge and skills.

New initiatives on education and training outlined in the competitiveness White Papers include:

- improved careers information, education and guidance for young people;

- a strengthening of academic and vocational qualifications;

- new accelerated modern apprenticeships;

- an initiative to help firms develop and implement training plans;

- making training loans available to smaller firms; and

- a competition open to small firms in England and Wales for the best co-ordinated training projects.

A package of proposed measures for Scotland was announced in April 1995.

Training and Enterprise Councils and Local Enterprise Companies

The Government has set up a network of 81 business-led Training and Enterprise Councils (TECs) in England and Wales; two enterprise bodies run 22 local enterprise companies (LECs) in Scotland. TECs and LECs are independent companies managed by boards of directors, the majority of whom are drawn from private sector business.

They provide training, vocational education and enterprise programmes on behalf of the Government and encourage investment in the development of skills throughout the workforce. In addition, they offer advisory and training services to businesses, including schemes to enhance the expertise of managers. In Scotland the LECs make available the full range of services offered by the Enterprise bodies (see p. 186) —support and advice to businesses, environmental renewal, training programmes for young and long-term unemployed people and encouragement to businesses to invest in management and skills. TECs and LECs also have a key role in regeneration and economic development activities locally and in setting up Business Links and similar operations in Scotland and Wales.

Management Education and Development

The DTI, in conjunction with the Department for Education and Employment (DFEE), works with industry, higher education institutes and business schools to spread awareness about best management practices and to encourage continuous professional development. Performance standards for all levels of management have been devised.

The 'Managing in the 90s' programme aims to improve the competitiveness of business by promoting best management practice. It is concerned with making businesses aware of the need for change and providing them with guidance on how to identify the changes required. Delivered mainly through Business Links and sectoral organisations, the programme offers a range of material and activities which are constantly being developed in response to market needs, such as help with networking and benchmarking between companies.

Management education is on offer at many universities and colleges of higher and further education. Regional management centres have been established in England and Wales by associations of these colleges, and there are several similar organisations in Scotland. Universities run full-time postgraduate programmes at business schools such as those of London, Manchester, Durham, Warwick and Strathclyde universities.

The British Institute of Management encourages excellence in management. Other bodies are concerned with standards and training in specialised branches of management. The employer-led Management Charter Initiative (MCI) is the operating arm of the National Forum for Management Education and Development and the leading industrial body for management standards. More than 1,800 employers, representing a quarter of the total workforce, are members of the MCI, which has 90 local networks working with local employers.

Design, Quality and Standards

Design is a key commercial tool for companies; they aim to become more profitable through the design of products and services which add value and improve performance. The British design consultancy industry has an annual estimated turnover of £1,000 million and employs around 18,000 people, mainly in small consultancies of up to six designers.

The DTI encourages firms to invest in design which can contribute to international competitiveness; it also supports the benefits of good design through the Design Council, an independent body governed by Royal Charter. The Council acts primarily as a provider of analysis and advice on design policy to government, business and education. Design services for industry are supplied through Business Links in England (and

equivalent bodies in Scotland and Wales), with financial support from the DTI (see p. 208).

The Government urges business to consider quality at all stages of design, production, marketing and delivery to customers. Accreditation is a key method of improving quality and competitiveness. Through its support for consultancy projects, the Government helps small and medium-sized firms to learn about and apply quality management techniques based on a national standard—BS EN ISO 9000—meeting international requirements. In order to increase customer confidence, companies are encouraged to obtain assessment and certification to this standard. The competence and performance of organisations undertaking such certification are officially accredited by United Kingdom Accreditation Service (UKAS—see below). Companies certified by accredited bodies are permitted to use the national 'crown and tick' accreditation mark. The DTI's Register of Quality Assessed Companies lists accredited certification bodies and companies assessed by them.

The DTI is responsible for policy relating to the National Measurement System. This provides, through a number of DTI-funded agencies, many of the physical measurement standards and associated calibration facilities necessary so that measurements in Britain are made on a common basis and to the required accuracy. Two of these agencies—the National Physical Laboratory and the Laboratory of the Government Chemist—are to be privatised or contracted out. The National Measurement Accreditation Service (NAMAS), the national accreditation service for calibration and testing laboratories, has merged with the National Accreditation Council for Certification Bodies to form United Kingdom Accreditation Service (UKAS), a private-sector company. The National Weights and Measures Laboratory, which registers weighing and measuring equipment and services equipment manufacturers, is to continue as an executive agency within the DTI.

British Standards Institution

The British Standards Institution (BSI) is Britain's national standards body and is the

British member of the European and international standards organisations. It works with industry, consumers and government to produce standards relevant to the needs of the market and suitable for public purchasing and regulatory purposes.

Government support for the BSI is directed particularly towards European and international standards work. Harmonised standards contribute to the aim of removing technical barriers to trade in the EU. Hence, over 90 per cent of the BSI's work is concentrated on European or international standards. The Kitemark is the BSI's registered product certification trade mark.

Awards

The Queen's Awards for Export, Technological and Environmental Achievement recognise outstanding performance in their respective fields. Awarded annually, they are valid for five years and are granted by the Queen on the advice of the Prime Minister, assisted by an Advisory Committee consisting of senior representatives from business, trade unions and government departments. Any self-contained 'industrial unit' in Britain is eligible to apply, regardless of size, provided it meets the scheme's criteria.

Other awards include the Export Award for Smaller Businesses (for firms employing fewer than 200 people) and the MacRobert Award for engineering in Britain made by the Fellowship of Engineering for successful technological innovation.

Industrial and Intellectual Property

The Government supports innovation by protecting the rights of the originators of inventions, industrial designs and trade marks together with copyright in literary, artistic and musical works. These matters are the responsibility of the DTI's Patent Office, which includes the Design Registry and the Trade Marks Registry. Patent protection is also available under the European Patent Convention and the Patent Co-operation Treaty. Benefits may be claimed in other countries by virtue of separate conventions on industrial property, literary and artistic work,

and music and broadcasting. Recent measures giving greater protection to industrial and intellectual property owners include:

● the adoption of European Community directives on copyright which harmonise rental and lending rights of performers, record producers and broadcasters, and legal protection of computer programs; and

● a new EC regulation on counterfeit and pirated goods.

Company Law

Laws relating to companies are designed to meet the need for proper regulation of business, secure open markets and to create safeguards for those wishing to invest in companies or do business with them. They take account of EC directives on company law, and on company and group accounts and their auditing. The Government's aim is to achieve these objectives while imposing as small a burden as possible on business. Hence, it has removed from certain types of small companies the statutory obligation to have their accounts audited and has introduced a simple procedure for dissolving private companies that are no longer operational. Additionally, it is taking steps to encourage the use of summary financial statements and simplify statutory accounting requirements.

The 1992 Cadbury Committee Report on the management of companies contains a Code of Best Practice for company boards, underpinned by a Stock Exchange requirement for firms to state whether they are complying with the Code and giving reasons for areas of non-compliance. Standards of disclosure have improved since 1992 and they indicate a high level of compliance with the Cadbury recommendations, especially among larger companies. Shareholders, including institutional shareholders, are encouraged by the Government to play a more active role in overseeing management.

Insider dealing in shares is a criminal offence and inspectors may be appointed to investigate possible insider dealing. A licensing procedure ensures the professional competence, integrity and independence of people acting as trustees of bankrupt individuals, or as liquidators, receivers or administrators of insolvent companies.

Business Support Services

To encourage the development of small firms, the DTI is establishing a network of around 200 Business Links in England. This programme is designed to bring together in a single point of access organisations supporting enterprise, such as local companies, Training and Enterprise Councils (TECs), chambers of commerce, local authorities and enterprise agencies. Business Links are local, commercial partnerships, in which larger firms can make contacts and expertise available to smaller firms.

A planned 600 personal business advisers will be able to provide a full range of business consultancy and other services, calling on the services of specialist advisers, such as private-sector export consultants, design advisers, and innovation and technology counsellors. Business Links are also the access point for a new regional supply network designed to promote best practice in supply chain partnerships by including buyers and sellers in both private and public sectors. Every company in England should have easy access to a Business Link by the end of 1995. From April 1996 government office staff providing services to businesses will be seconded to Business Links. Further measures to help small firms, available through Business Links, were outlined in the 1995 competitiveness White Paper:

- an extra £100 million over four years to develop existing management initiatives and make available locally designed business development programmes;
- more advice on innovation and technology, including overseas development; and
- free export help to small firms through export vouchers.

In Scotland, Business Shops, run by local partnerships between Local Enterprise Companies (LECs), local authorities and business support organisations, are being opened, where trained advisers provide information and direct enquiries to the business support services of local partners. Similar arrangements have been set up in

Wales through Business Connect Wales. In Northern Ireland, business services are available from the regional offices of the Local Enterprise Development Unit; in addition, there is a network of local enterprise agencies.

Consultancy

Business Links are the access point for consultancy support for small and medium-sized firms. They are responsible for providing a new flexible consultancy and diagnostic service, which has replaced the Enterprise Initiative Consultancy Scheme. In Scotland, a similar diagnostic and consultancy service is available through Business Shops in lowland Scotland and Business Information Source in the Highland and Islands area. The new services help smaller firms assess their strengths and weaknesses and draw up plans for future development. In addition, a new consultancy brokerage service was introduced in 1995 to assist in selecting consultants. Since 1988, when the Enterprise Initiative Consultancy Scheme was established, over 141,000 businesses have asked for assistance and 70,000 projects have been completed.

Small Firms Schemes

The SPUR scheme offers grants to businesses with up to 250 employees for new product and process development demonstrating a significant technological advance (see p. 325). Since 1991, when the scheme began, grants of £45 million have helped over 500 projects. Under a new SPUR-PLUS scheme, higher maximum grants are available for exceptional projects.

SMART is an annual competition providing grants to individuals and businesses with no more than 50 employees in support of innovative technological projects with commercial potential. Firms which have completed their SMART projects are eligible for enhanced SPUR grants to develop their product. In 1994–95 SMART grants were made to over 180 new projects. The existing SPUR and SMART schemes have been merged and simplified.

Other government assistance to small businesses includes:

- the Small Firms Loan Guarantee Scheme, which helps businesses with viable proposals to obtain finance where conventional loans are unavailable as a result of a lack of financial security or previous performance; the scheme provides banks and other financial institutions with a government guarantee on a certain percentage (70 or 85 per cent) of the loan in return for a premium payment; some £246 million was guaranteed in 1994–95;

- an initiative to encourage informal investment for small firms from a wider range of sources; the Government supports TECs and other organisations in bringing together investors and small firms;

- the Business Start-Up scheme, enabling unemployed people to claim an allowance while establishing a new business; and

- an initiative which allows small firms to develop, in-house, the training skills of key workers.

The Government is also considering a series of measures to help tackle the problem of late payment of commercial debt, including the establishment of a British Standard for prompt payment.

Regional Industrial Development

Industrial policy is designed to encourage enterprise and economic growth in all areas of Britain. However, where additional help is needed, it is focused on the Assisted Areas (Development Areas and Intermediate Areas), which cover around 35 per cent of Britain's working population. The promotion of inward investment is a key element in the Government's regional policy (see p. 212).

The main regional policy instruments are:

- Regional Selective Assistance, available in the Assisted Areas, for investment projects undertaken by firms in manufacturing and some service sectors that will create or safeguard employment;

- Regional Investment Grants, for firms with no more than 25 employees in Development Areas or areas affected by colliery closures;

- Regional Innovation Grants, for firms employing no more than 50 people in Development, Intermediate, Task Force and City Challenge areas or localities affected by colliery closures (see p. 262), as well as some other areas covered by EU schemes; they are also available in certain Scottish urban areas.

Regional Selective Assistance and Regional Investment and Innovation Grants are administered by the Government Offices for the Regions in England, the Scottish Office Industry Department and the Welsh Office Industry and Training Department.

England

Established in 1994, English Partnerships promotes job creation, inward investment and environmental improvement through reclamation and development of vacant, derelict, under-used or contaminated land and buildings. The Rural Development Commission advises the Government on economic and social development in the countryside, assists local enterprises, promotes jobs and supports essential services. The Commission's resources are concentrated in areas of greatest need, known as priority areas (see p. 349), covering about 35 per cent of the area of England.

Scotland

Scottish Enterprise and Highlands and Islands Enterprise provide and manage government and EU support to industry and commerce, in lowland and highland Scotland respectively, operating mainly through the network of LECs (see p. 186). The two bodies have a broad range of powers, including powers to:

- attract inward investment and encourage exports;

- give financial and management support to new businesses and assist existing ones to expand;

- improve the environment by reclaiming derelict and contaminated land; and

- increase job opportunities and skills.

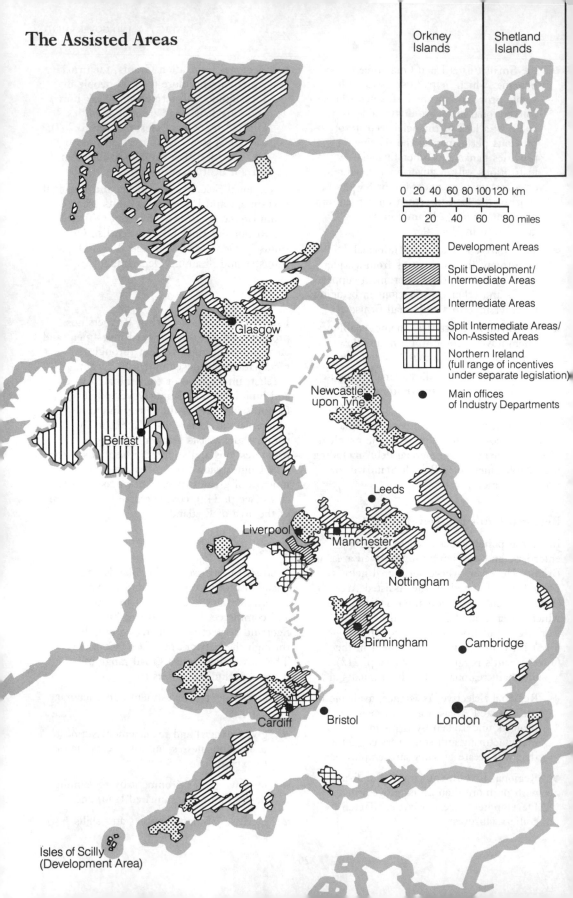

The Assisted Areas

Orkney Islands

Shetland Islands

0 20 40 60 80 100 120 km

0 20 40 60 80 miles

Development Areas

Split Development/
Intermediate Areas

Intermediate Areas

Split Intermediate Areas/
Non-Assisted Areas

Northern Ireland
(full range of incentives
under separate legislation)

● Main offices
of Industry Departments

Glasgow

Belfast

Newcastle
upon Tyne

Leeds

Liverpool

Manchester

Nottingham

Birmingham

Cambridge

Cardiff

Bristol

London

Isles of Scilly
(Development Area)

A major initiative was launched by Scottish Enterprise in 1995 to increase the rate of business start-ups with the objective of creating an additional 25,000 businesses in Scotland by 2000. In 1995–96 the Enterprise networks plan to:

- assist over 15,000 businesses;

- provide 38,000 square metres of commercial and industrial premises; and

- train 37,000 young people and 30,000 unemployed adults.

Wales

The Welsh Development Agency (WDA) was set up in 1976 to promote industrial efficiency and international competitiveness and improve the environment. Providing affordable, high quality sites and premises for existing businesses and inward investors, it has so far spent £822 million on property development. Since 1990 the Agency's property development activities have attracted over £242 million of private-sector investment through Welsh Property Venture.

The WDA seeks to attract investment into Wales and co-ordinates the approach for responding to the need of investors. It has helped to attract over 1,400 projects involving capital investment of £7,200 million and the creation of 84,000 new jobs. Since 1991 the Agency has spent over £90 million on urban regeneration and helped bring in more than £170 million of private-sector investment, including £70 million for urban joint ventures. The WDA's land reclamation programme is the largest and most sustained landscape improvement project in Europe and has the goal of reclaiming all significant derelict sites in Wales by 2000. Its Business Services programme focuses on developing stronger regional clusters (such as supply and service chains), improving standards and efficiency, and helping Welsh companies to exploit new technology.

The Development Board for Rural Wales promotes the economic and social well-being of rural mid-Wales. It is concentrating investment in market towns, especially those in the west, in order to help stimulate business confidence and prosperity. Priority is also being given to activities in smaller communities.

Northern Ireland

Industrial development policy in Northern Ireland is the responsibility of the Department of Economic Development and is delivered through various agencies:

- the Industrial Development Board, which deals with overseas companies considering Northern Ireland as an investment location, as well as the development of local companies with more than 50 employees;

- the Local Enterprise Development Unit, which promotes enterprise and the development of small businesses;

- the Industrial Research and Technology Unit, providing advice and assistance on research and development, innovation and technology transfer; and

- the Training and Employment Agency, which helps with in-company training and management development.

A variety of schemes are on offer to help companies with marketing, exporting, product development and design, improved productivity and quality, training, and research and development. The full range of assistance is made available to those companies able to demonstrate development potential and a prospect of long-term competitive growth. This assistance includes capital grants, loans and share capital investment. The Industrial Development Board also offers stocks of land and industrial premises for purchase or lease. There is exemption from local property taxes for manufacturing premises.

European Union Regional Policy and Aid

The EU seeks to reduce disparities between the different regions of the Union. The principal responsibility for helping poorer areas remains with national authorities, but the EU complements schemes by providing grants and loans from a number of sources, including the European Regional Development Fund (ERDF).

The European Investment Bank (see p. 121) offers loans for public and private capital investment schemes. Assisted projects typically include improvements to and building of infrastructure projects; construction of trans-European transport links (like the Channel Tunnel); support for business and tourism development; and capital investment in industry, such as factory construction.

EU Structural Funds, especially the ERDF, play an important role in regional development. Three areas—Northern Ireland, the Highlands and Islands, and Merseyside—are eligible for assistance; they will receive around £2,000 million of EU funding over the period 1994–99. The ERDF also provides finance for areas of industrial decline and for rural development. Structural Funds are made available to areas suffering from a decline in the coal, steel, textile, fishing and defence industries.

Overall policy and co-ordination of overseas promotion of inward investment are the responsibility of the DTI's Invest in Britain Bureau (IBB), which represents Britain as a whole. It is supported in Britain by several territorial and regional bodies and overseas it operates through British Embassies, High Commissions and Consulates-general.

> Britain's share of US investment into Europe for the period 1950–94 was 41 per cent and its share of Japanese investment into Europe 40 per cent. German government figures for 1982–94 reveal German investment into Britain of 12 per cent, second only to investment into the United States. In 1994–95 the IBB recorded announcements of 434 new projects and 88,000 associated jobs in Britain.

Inward Investment

The Government encourages overseas investment in Britain, recognising the many benefits it brings to the industrial base and the economy as a whole. Some of Britain's new manufacturing techniques and management attitudes were introduced by inward investors, which also create new employment and help boost Britain's balance of payments through higher exports and lower imports. Inward investment also has a positive impact on the performance and competitiveness of British suppliers; product development has also been strengthened.

Many overseas firms are household names in Britain. Overseas companies are responsible for around 18 per cent of British manufacturing employment, 32 per cent of capital investment, 24 per cent of output and 40 per cent of exports.

A growing proportion of inward investment has been through expansion or reinvestment by existing investors. This is likely to continue as firms rationalise their European operations. The IBB and its regional partners give high priority to 'caring for' existing foreign investors, to ensure that they are aware of the advantages of remaining and expanding in Britain.

Similar advice and assistance to that provided in England by regional development organisations is available through:

- Locate in Scotland, operated jointly by the Scottish Office Industry Department and Scottish Enterprise;

- the Welsh Development Agency's International Division; and

- the Industrial Development Board in Northern Ireland.

Further Reading

Competitiveness: Helping Business to Win. Cm 2563, HMSO 1994.

Competitiveness: Forging Ahead. Cm 2867, HMSO 1995.

Department of Trade and Industry 1995: The Government's Expenditure Plans 1995–96 to 1997–98. Cm 2804, HMSO 1995.

Government and Industry. Aspects of Britain series, HMSO, 1995.

15 Finance and Other Service Industries

The service industries, which include finance, retailing, tourism and business services, contribute about 65 per cent of gross domestic product and 75 per cent of employment. Overseas earnings from services amounted to around 30 per cent of the value of exports of manufactures in 1994. The number of employees in services rose from over 13 million in 1983 to 16.5 million by June 1995, much of the rise being accounted for by growth in part-time (principally female) employment. The City of London remains a world leader in the provision of financial services, which make a substantial contribution to Britain's balance of payments.

Average real disposable income per head increased by more than three-quarters between 1971 and 1994 and this was reflected in a rise in consumer spending on financial, personal and leisure services and on the maintenance and repair of consumer durables. Demand for British travel, hotel and catering services rose as real incomes in Britain and other countries increased.

Britain is a major financial centre, housing some of the world's leading banking, insurance, securities, shipping, commodities, futures, and other financial services and markets. Financial services are an important source of employment and overseas earnings. Business services include advertising, market research, management consultancy, exhibition and conference facilities and computing.

By the year 2000, tourism is expected to be the world's biggest industry, and Britain is one of the world's leading tourist destinations. The industry is Britain's second largest, employing about 7 per cent of the workforce. Retailing is also a major employer.

Financial Services

Historically the financial services industry in Britain has been located in the famous 'Square Mile' in the City of London. This remains broadly the case, even though the markets for financial and related services have grown and diversified greatly. Manchester, Cardiff, Liverpool, Leeds, Edinburgh and Glasgow are also financial centres. 'The City', the collection of markets and institutions in and around the Square Mile, is noted for having:

- a larger number of overseas banks than in any other financial centre;

- a banking sector that accounts for about a fifth of total international bank lending;

- one of the world's largest international insurance markets;

- the largest centre in the world for trading overseas equities, accounting for 59 per cent of foreign equities turnover in 1994;

- the world's largest foreign exchange market;

- one of the world's largest financial derivatives markets;

- the greatest concentration of international bond dealers, handling 75 per cent of the secondary market in international bonds in 1994;

- important markets for transactions in commodities; and

- a full range of ancillary and support services—legal, accountancy and management consultancy—which contribute to London's strength as a financial centre.

British financial institutions' net overseas earnings amounted to £20,400 million in 1994, up by nearly a third on 1993.

DEVELOPMENT OF FINANCIAL SERVICES

The growth in international movements of capital in the 1960s and 1970s mainly took the form of increased bank lending and foreign exchange trading. London became the international centre of this activity, particularly in the eurocurrency markets (see p. 225). During the 1980s, with increasing international competition in financial services and developments in technology, London's securities markets grew rapidly. Edinburgh also developed as a centre for fund management.

Some traditional distinctions between financial institutions have been eroded, so that single firms supply a broader range of

services, both in domestic and international markets. There has also been a significant deregulation of Britain's financial services. Major landmarks include:

- the abolition of exchange controls in 1979;

- the abolition in 1981 of the Reserve Asset Ratio requirement, under which banks had to hold 12.5 per cent of their deposits as liquid assets with the Bank of England;

- the Building Societies Act 1986 and subsequent proposals to further ease controls on building societies (see p. 219);

- 'Big Bang', also in 1986 (see p. 224); and

- the Friendly Societies Act 1992 (see p. 220).

The foresight panel for financial services, one of the 15 panels established under the Technology Foresight Programme co-ordinated by the Office of Science and Technology (see p. 318), identified future major changes expected in financial services in its report issued in 1995. These include:

- widespread use of multimedia for delivering retail financial services;

- more sophisticated customer profiling;

- greater choice of financial products; and

- a substantial reduction in the use of cheques.

SUPERVISION

The Government is committed to improving market efficiency by providing a regulatory regime which takes account of developments and provides a proper framework for the sector, in which free and fair competition can take place. HM Treasury is the government department with responsibility for financial services. In particular, it is responsible for legislation covering the supervision of banks, building societies, friendly societies and investment businesses, which are subject to the regulatory system established under the

Banking Act 1987 (see p. 216), the Building Societies Act 1986 (see p. 219) and the Financial Services Act 1986 (see below). The Treasury also oversees the Securities and Investments Board (SIB).

The Department of Trade and Industry (DTI) is responsible for company law and insolvency matters, and for investigations and prosecutions under the Financial Services, Insolvency and Companies Acts. Investigations are carried out with the Serious Fraud Office (see p. 89). The DTI's responsibilities include prudential supervision of insurance undertakings, European Community (EC) insurance directives, and general questions affecting the insurance industry. It also has powers to investigate 'insider dealing'—securities trading carried out on the basis of privileged access to relevant information.

The Treasury negotiates and implements EC directives relating to financial services and is responsible for arrangements with overseas regulators for exchanging information. Various EC directives give or will give banking, insurance and investment services firms the freedom to operate throughout the European Union (EU) on the basis of their home state authorisation.

The Treasury is also charged with encouraging international liberalisation in financial services. Members of the World Trade Organisation reached agreement in July 1995 on a liberalisation package covering banking, insurance and securities trade. Negotiations were conducted under the General Agreement on Trade in Services, which entered into force as part of the GATT Uruguay Round conclusions (see p. 173). International supervisory forums include the Basle Committee on Banking Supervision and the International Organisation of Securities Commissions (IOSCO). IOSCO is the primary international meeting place for regulatory authorities.

Under the Financial Services Act 1986, investment businesses (those dealing in, arranging, managing or giving advice on investments or operating collective investment schemes) require authorisation and are subject to rules on the conduct of business. Most of the Act's powers are delegated to the SIB, which has recognised a number of self-regulating organisations (SROs) and recognised professional bodies (RPBs). It has a duty to assist SROs and RPBs to fulfil their regulatory functions. Most investment businesses are authorised under the Act by virtue of membership of one of these. The SROs are:

- the Investment Management Regulatory Organisation (IMRO), whose members include merchant banks and pension fund managers with mainly corporate clients;

- the Securities and Futures Authority (SFA), whose members include member firms of the London Stock Exchange, as well as futures brokers and dealers, and eurobond dealers; and

- the Personal Investment Authority (PIA), which came into operation in July 1994 and is the main single regulator for retail investment services; these cover the marketing and provision of advice on products like life assurance, pension funds, unit trusts and investment trusts.

Other information relating to supervision and regulation is contained in subsequent sections.

BANK OF ENGLAND

The Bank of England was established in 1694 by Act of Parliament and Royal Charter as a corporate body. Its entire capital stock was acquired by the Government in 1946. The Bank acts as banker to the Government, holding its main accounts, managing Britain's reserves of gold and foreign exchange, arranging new government borrowing and managing the stock of its existing debt. The Bank's main objectives are to:

- ensure the soundness of the financial system through the direct supervision of banks and specialised City institutions;

- promote the efficiency and competitiveness of the financial system, especially in domestic and international payment and settlement systems; and

- provide advice on and implement the Government's monetary policy.

The Banking Act 1987 assigns the Bank of England the overriding objective of protecting depositors. To this end institutions intending to take deposits from the public must gain authorisation from the Bank and submit to its continuing supervision. In order to be and remain authorised, an institution has to satisfy the Bank that it has:

- adequate capital and liquidity;
- a realistic business plan;
- adequate systems and controls;
- adequate provision for bad and doubtful debts; and
- ensured that its business is carried out with integrity and skill, and in a prudent manner.

The Bank's supervision is 'prudential'—it sets minimum standards but offers no guarantee that authorised institutions will not fail or that investors or depositors will be fully compensated. However, if an authorised bank fails, depositors are entitled to limited compensation from the Deposit Protection Fund, financed by contributions levied on the banking system.

Under the deposit protection scheme, customers of banks had been entitled to protection for up to 75 per cent of the first £20,000 deposited in each bank in the event of the bank ceasing to trade. Under a separate scheme, building society depositors had been guaranteed up to 90 per cent.

Both schemes have been brought into line with the EC's Deposit Guarantee Directive, which took effect in Britain in July 1995. As a result, the protection for both schemes is now 90 per cent of the first £20,000, and the schemes cover depositors of banks and building societies at their branches throughout the European Union.

The Bank is the Government's agent for selling marketable debt. It maintains the register of holdings of government securities on behalf of the Treasury, and manages the Exchange Equalisation Account holding the Government's official reserves of gold, foreign exchange, Special Drawing Rights (SDRs—claims on the International Monetary Fund) and European Currency Units (ECUs). The reserves are used to check undue fluctuations in the exchange value of sterling and to enable government departments to meet their foreign currency needs.

The Bank of England provides technical assistance and training to central banks in other countries, especially the Commonwealth. In 1990 it established its Centre for Central Banking Studies to give a more specific focus to these activities and to meet additional demands. Since 1990 the Centre has trained over 2,000 participants from more than 100 countries and co-ordinated technical assistance to over 30 central banks.

The Bank is able to influence money-market conditions through its dealings with the discount houses (see p. 220) which give it powerful influence over short-term interest rates. Discount houses hold mainly Treasury, local authority and commercial bills, and negotiable certificates of deposit financed by short-term loans from the banks. If on a particular day there is a shortage of cash in the banking system as a result, for example, of large tax payments, the Bank relieves the shortage either by buying bills from the discount houses or by lending directly to them. This permits banks to replenish their cash balances at the Bank by recalling some of their short-term loans to the discount houses.

The Bank of England has the sole right in England and Wales to issue banknotes, which are backed by government and other securities. Three Scottish and four Northern Ireland banks also issue notes. These issues, apart from a small amount specified by legislation for each bank, must be fully covered by holdings of Bank of England notes and coinage. Responsibility for the provision of coin lies with the Royal Mint, a government executive agency.

The Bank of England seeks to ensure that

Britain's financial markets are efficient and competitive. To this end it runs two securities settlement systems with in-built payment arrangements—the Central Gilts Office and the Central Moneymarket Office.

The Bank is playing a full part in the work of the European Monetary Institute in Frankfurt, established in 1994 (see p. 119). It is also involved in arranging the implementation of several EC directives. The Bank has developed a framework for the implementation in Britain in 1995 of the EC Capital Adequacy Directive, which sets minimum capital requirements for market risks in the operations of banks and investment firms.

BANKS AND BUILDING SOCIETIES

In addition to banks, the chief institutions offering banking services are the building societies and the Department for National Savings. The 'single passport' system created by the EC's Second Banking Directive allows 'credit institutions' (banks and building societies) to operate throughout the European Economic Area (EEA) on the basis of their home-state authorisation.

A useful distinction can be made between 'retail' and 'wholesale' banking. Retail banking is primarily for personal customers and small businesses. Its main services are cash deposit and withdrawal facilities, and money transmission systems. Competition between banks and building societies in providing services for personal customers has intensified, and there have been a number of mergers or takeovers.

Wholesale business involves taking large deposits at higher rates of interest, deploying funds in money-market instruments (see p. 225) and making large loans and investments. Nearly all banks in Britain engage in some wholesale activities and some, such as the merchant and overseas banks, centre their business on them. Many of the dealings are conducted on the inter-bank market—that is, between banks themselves.

In 1995 there were 379 institutions authorised under the Banking Act 1987, including clearing banks, investment banks, branches of overseas banks from outside the EEA, discount houses and banking subsidiaries of both banking and non-banking institutions from Britain and overseas. A further 102 branches of banks from EEA countries were entitled to take deposits in Britain; such 'European authorised institutions' are authorised by the relevant authority in their home country. Of the total of 481 banks, 307 were members of the British Bankers' Association, the main representative body for British banks.

Retail Banks

The major retail banks have a significant branch network, offering a full range of financial services to both individuals and companies. Services generally available include interest-bearing current accounts, deposit accounts, various kinds of loan arrangements and a full range of money transmission facilities increasingly featuring plastic card technology.

The major banks in England and Wales are HSBC (including its subsidiary Midland), Barclays, Lloyds, National Westminster, the TSB Group and Abbey National; and in Scotland the Bank of Scotland and the Royal Bank of Scotland. Other important retail banks are the Clydesdale Bank, the Co-operative Bank, the Yorkshire Bank and Alliance & Leicester Giro. Northern Ireland is served by branch networks of four major banking groups.

With the growth of financial services and fewer restrictions on competition among financial institutions, the major banks have diversified their services. Most now own finance houses, leasing and factoring companies, merchant banks, securities dealers, insurance companies and unit trust companies.

The banks offer loan facilities to companies and have become important suppliers of finance for small firms. A loan guarantee scheme is supported by the banks, under which 70 per cent (85 per cent in certain cases) of the value of bank loans to small companies is guaranteed by the Government. Some banks have set up special subsidiaries to provide venture capital for companies (see p. 224). Most retail banks maintain overseas subsidiaries and are active in eurocurrency markets (see p. 225).

The total liabilities/assets of the retail banks amounted to over £1,366,000 million in the second quarter of 1995. Liabilities are made up of sterling deposits, foreign currency deposits, items in suspense or transmission, and capital and other funds. The banks' main liquid assets consist of money at call (mainly short-term loans to discount houses), their holdings of Treasury and other bills, short-dated British government securities and balances at the Bank of England. They also hold a proportion of their assets as portfolio investments (mainly longer-dated British government securities) or trade investments.

The main retail banks operate through over 11,000 branches and sub-branches in Britain. National Westminster has the largest number, with 2,410 branches, followed by Barclays (2,090), Lloyds (1,799), Midland (1,706), TSB (1,235), the Royal Bank of Scotland (732), Abbey National (675) and the Bank of Scotland (430). Around three-quarters of adults in Britain have a current account and over one-third a deposit account.

Payment Systems

Apart from credit and debit card arrangements, the main payment systems are run by three separate companies operating under an umbrella organisation, the Association for Payment Clearing Services (APACS), of which 23 banks and building societies are members. One covers bulk paper clearings—cheques and credit transfers. A second deals with high-value clearings for same-day settlement, namely the nationwide electronic transfer service Clearing House Automated Payment System (CHAPS) and the cheque-based Town Clearing (which operates only in the City of London). A third covers bulk electronic clearing for standing orders and direct debits. Membership of each company is open to any bank, building society or other financial institution meeting the criteria for appropriate supervision and volume of transactions.

Plastic Cards

The use of plastic cards has become much more widespread, and around 84 million are in circulation. Among the main types are cheque guarantee cards, debit cards, credit cards, charge cards and cash cards. Often cards combine one or more of these functions. One of the most popular uses is for obtaining cash from automated teller machines (ATMs). All the major retail banks and building societies participate in nationwide networks of ATMs, which give customers access to cash and other services for up to 24 hours a day. About 19,000 ATMs were in operation at the end of 1994.

Cheque guarantee cards entitle holders to cheque-cashing facilities in participating institutions and guarantee retailers that transactions up to the specified guarantee limit—typically £50 or £100—will be honoured. Uniform eurocheques supported by a eurocheque card are available from all major banks. They may be used to obtain cash or make payments in Britain, elsewhere in Europe and in a few other overseas countries. Cheques are made out in the currency of the country in which they are being used.

Credit cards are widely accepted throughout Britain. They are mainly issued by banks. Most cards are affiliated to one of the two major international credit card organisations, Visa and MasterCard. There are a growing number of 'affinity' cards, where the card is linked to an organisation such as a charity or trade union. Credit card users receive a statement each month and must pay off a minimum of the amount owed, interest then becoming chargeable on the remainder. Most users though choose to pay off the full amount owed each month. A charge card, like a credit card, enables the holder to make retail payments, but often has greater facilities than are available from a credit card, such as no credit limit or a very high limit. They are usually available only to those with relatively high income or assets; the credit balance must be settled in full each month. Some of the major retailers issue cards for use within their own outlets.

More people are now paying for goods by debit cards issued by the major retail banks and building societies. Payments can then be deducted directly from the purchaser's current account. There are two debit card schemes in operation: Visa and Switch.

Electronic Banking

Scottish clearing banks have been at the forefront in Britain in introducing information technology, pioneering the use of cash dispensers, satellite payment systems and electronic home, office and corporate banking. The number of home banking services run by the banks and building societies is growing. Customers use a telephone or personal computer to obtain account information, make transfers and pay bills.

> **The National Westminster and Midland banks in conjunction with the telecommunications operator BT launched a £50 million electronic cashless banking experiment, 'Mondex', in Swindon (Wiltshire) in mid-1995. About 40,000 adults in Swindon have been given electronic cards. The cards are 'charged' with money by the user making a call to his or her bank from a new type of telephone, or using a specially adapted cash machine, and the money debited from the user's account. The cards allow a variety of financial transactions without the need for cash, including the payment of bills and the purchase of goods at participating retailers through electronic tills.**

Building Societies

Building societies are mutual institutions, owned by their savers and borrowers, and are the main source of housing finance in Britain. They make long-term loans, mostly at variable rates of interest, against the security of property—usually private dwellings purchased for owner-occupation. Around 60 per cent of adults have building society savings accounts. A variety of savings schemes have been established, and a growing number of societies provide current account facilities such as cheque books and ATMs.

There are 80 registered societies, of which 79 are members of the Building Societies'

Association. Building societies' assets totalled £301,000 million at the end of 1994; about £37,000 million was advanced in new mortgages in 1994. The three largest—the Halifax, Nationwide and Woolwich—account for about one-half of the total assets of all societies. The Council of Mortgage Lenders is a trade body established in 1989 for all mortgage lending institutions, including building societies, insurance companies, finance houses and banks.

The Building Societies Act 1986 enabled societies to diversify into banking and other services and established the Building Societies Commission to carry out the prudential supervision of building societies. Up to 25 per cent of a society's commercial assets may be used for purposes other than loans on first mortgage of owner-occupied houses, including as much as 15 per cent in other types of asset such as unsecured loans. Directly or through subsidiaries, societies may offer services within the general areas of banking, investment, insurance, trusteeship, executorship and estate agency.

Following a review of the 1986 Act, the Government announced its intention to replace the current legislative framework governing building societies' powers by a more permissive regime. At the same time, proposals were put forward to increase the accountability of societies' boards to their members, for example, by improving the information given to members about their rights as shareholders.

As a result of the review, societies will, among other things, be able to make unsecured loans to businesses and wholly own a general insurance company. Measures have also been taken under the Deregulation and Contracting Out Act 1994 (see p. 202) to widen further the powers of building societies and remove or reduce certain statutory burdens. For example, societies will be able to raise up to 50 per cent (up from 40 per cent) of their funds on the wholesale market.

Major changes are taking place in the structure of the industry:

- The Halifax merged with the Leeds Permanent Building Society in August 1995. It plans to ask its members to vote for the conversion of the enlarged Halifax into a public limited company, becoming a retail bank. It would be the second society to convert to a bank under provisions in the 1986 Act, following Abbey National in 1989, and would become Britain's third largest bank.

- The Cheltenham & Gloucester Building Society was taken over by Lloyds Bank in August 1995, and the National and Provincial Building Society is being taken over by Abbey National.

Friendly Societies

Friendly societies have traditionally been unincorporated societies of individuals, offering their members a limited range of financial services, particularly provision for retirement and against loss of income through sickness or unemployment. The Friendly Societies Act 1992 enabled friendly societies to incorporate, take on new powers and offer a broad range of financial services through subsidiaries.

Merchant Banks

Merchant banks have traditionally been concerned primarily with accepting, or guaranteeing, commercial bills and with sponsoring capital issues on behalf of their customers. Today they undertake a diversified range of activities. After the 'Big Bang' some merchant banks acquired securities trading operations. Merchant banks have important roles in equity and debt markets and the provision of advice and financial services to industrial companies, especially where mergers, takeovers and other forms of corporate reorganisation are involved. Management of investment holdings, including trusts, pensions and other funds, is another important function. The sector is split between independent houses and those which are part of larger banking groups.

Overseas Banks

A total of 257 banks incorporated overseas are represented in Britain, including 28 from Japan and 23 from the United States. A total of 102 institutions incorporated in Britain are subsidiaries of overseas companies. They offer a comprehensive banking service in many parts of the world and engage in financing trade not only between Britain and other countries but also between third-party countries.

British-based Overseas Banks

A small number of banks have their head offices in Britain, but operate mainly abroad, often specialising in particular regions. Standard Chartered, which is represented in Asia, Africa and the Middle East, is the major example of this type of bank.

Discount Houses

There are seven discount houses authorised under the Banking Act 1987. They act as financial intermediaries between the Bank of England and the rest of the banking sector, promoting an orderly flow of short-term funds. They guarantee to tender for the whole of the weekly offer of the Government's Treasury bills, which are instruments to raise funds over a period of up to six months. In return for acting as intermediaries, the discount houses have secured borrowing facilities at the Bank of England, acting as 'lender of last resort'. Assets of the discount houses consist mainly of Treasury and commercial bills, negotiable certificates of deposit and short-term loans. Their liabilities are for the most part short-term deposits.

Department for National Savings

The Department for National Savings, a government department, contributes to government borrowing and aims to encourage saving by offering personal savers a range of investments designed to meet various requirements. Certain National Savings products offer tax exempt returns. In March

1995 the total amount invested in National Savings was £51,900 million. Sales of National Savings products totalled £9,200 million in 1994–95. After allowing for repayments, the net contribution to government funding was £3,577 million. The largest single contribution, of £1,485 million, was from Premium Bonds (where interest is in the form of prizes chosen by lottery). Other important products include:

- Savings Certificates, which either pay a fixed rate of interest alone or a lower fixed rate of interest combined with index-linking;

- Income and Capital Bonds;

- Pensioners' Guaranteed Income Bonds, where interest is paid monthly and rates are fixed for five years at a time;

- Children's Bonus Bonds, which are designed to accumulate capital sums for those under 21;

- Ordinary and Investment Accounts, where deposits and withdrawals can be made at post offices throughout Britain; and

- FIRST Option Bonds, which offer a guaranteed rate of interest that is fixed for one year.

INSURANCE

London is the world's leading centre for insurance and for placing international reinsurance; it handles an estimated 20 per cent of the general insurance business placed on the international market. There are two broad categories of insurance: long-term life insurance, where contracts may be for periods of many years; and general insurance, including accident and short-term health insurance, where contracts are for a year or less. Authorised insurance companies are supervised by the Department of Trade and Industry under the Insurance Companies Act 1982.

In addition to the British companies and Lloyd's (see below), a large number of overseas companies are represented, with which many British companies have formed close relationships. Some British companies confine their activities to domestic business but most large companies undertaking general business transact a substantial amount overseas through branches and agencies or affiliated local companies.

Over 800 companies are authorised to carry on one or more classes of insurance business in Britain. The industry employs about 370,000 people. Some companies are mutual institutions, owned by their policy holders. About 440 companies belong to the Association of British Insurers (ABI).

EC directives introducing the 'single-licence' system in insurance came into force in July 1994. Life and non-life direct insurers may operate throughout the EEA on the basis of authorisation in their home state.

Long-term Insurance

As well as providing life cover, life insurance is a vehicle for saving and investment because premiums are invested in securities and other assets. About 30 per cent of adults have life assurance policies. The total long-term insurance assets under management by companies representing about 99 per cent of the British market in 1994 was £406,900 million on behalf of their worldwide operations. Long-term insurance is handled by around 200 companies.

General Insurance

General insurance business is undertaken by insurance companies and by underwriters at Lloyd's. It includes fire, accident, general liability, short-term life, motor, marine, aviation and transport risks. Total ABI member company premium income worldwide in 1993 was £34,000 million, of which £21,000 million was earned in Britain.

Lloyd's

Lloyd's, the origins of which go back to the 17th century, is an incorporated society of private insurers in London. Although its activities were originally confined to marine insurance, a considerable worldwide market for the transaction of other classes of insurance business, such as aviation and motor insurance, has been built up.

Lloyd's is not a company but a market for insurance administered by the Council of

Lloyd's and Lloyd's Regulatory and Market Boards. Business is carried out for individual elected underwriting members, or 'names', trading with unlimited liability in competition with each other and with insurance companies. Since January 1994 corporate members with limited liability have been trading alongside individual members. Both are required to satisfy certain financial requirements and maintain set levels of deposits at Lloyd's.

For the 1995 year of account, there is total market capacity of £10,198 million provided by 14,800 members grouped into 170 syndicates. Each syndicate is managed by an underwriting agent responsible for appointing a professional underwriter to accept insurance risks and settle claims on the syndicate members' behalf. With the exception of motor insurance business, insurance may only be placed through accredited Lloyd's brokers, who negotiate with Lloyd's syndicates on behalf of the insured. Reinsurance constitutes a large part of Lloyd's business.

Lloyd's net premium income in 1992, the most recent year for which figures are available, was £6,331 million. Lloyd's has suffered severe losses, partly as a result of a series of natural disasters, including Hurricane Andrew, which struck Florida and Louisiana in 1992, and also as a result of claims arising from asbestosis and pollution. The Council is taking action to tackle the consequent financial problems through a £2,800 million package of measures, including a levy on 'names' and changes to accounting arrangements which would release profits from 1993 and subsequent accounting years.

Institute of London Underwriters

The Institute of London Underwriters, formed in 1884 as a trade association for marine underwriters, now provides a market where member insurance companies transact marine, energy, commercial transport and aviation business. The Institute issues combined policies in its own name on risks which are underwritten by member companies. The gross premium income processed by the Institute for its member companies in 1994 was nearly £2,100 million. About half of the 65 member companies are branches or subsidiaries of overseas companies.

Insurance Brokers

Insurance brokers acting on behalf of the insured are a valuable part of the company market and play an essential role in the Lloyd's market. Smaller brokers mainly deal with the general public or specialise in a particular type of commercial insurance. Medium to large brokers almost exclusively handle commercial insurance, with the largest dealing with risks worldwide. Some brokers specialise in reinsurance business. The Insurance Brokers (Registration) Act 1977 makes provision for the voluntary registration and regulation of insurance brokers by the Insurance Brokers Registration Council. Only those registered with the Council can use the title 'insurance broker'. In July 1995, 14,600 individuals were registered with the Council, through 1,215 partnerships or sole traderships and over 2,450 limited companies.

Other independent intermediaries may also arrange insurance, but are not allowed to use the title 'insurance broker'. There are about 7,000 independent intermediaries operating under the Association of British Insurers' code of practice.

INVESTMENT

Britain has a great deal of expertise in fund management, which involves managing funds on the investor's behalf, or advising investors on how to invest their funds. The main types of investment fund include pension schemes, life assurance, unit trusts and investment trusts.

Collective investment schemes are becoming more important, particularly in the context of the Government's wish to encourage wider share ownership. Accordingly, regulations are planned to allow a new type of scheme—open ended investment companies (OEICs). They will be similar to unit trusts, but an investor in an OEIC will buy shares rather than units in the company. The new schemes should enable British companies to compete on an equal footing with similar schemes operating elsewhere in the EU.

Pension Funds

Over 13 million people belong to occupational pension schemes and more than 5 million to personal pension schemes. Most occupational pension schemes pay benefits related to final salary, although some are on a 'money purchase' basis where benefits depend on the size of the accrued funds. Benefits are normally funded in advance by employer (and wholly employee) contributions, which are held and invested by trustees on behalf of beneficiaries. Pension funds are major investors in securities markets, holding around 30 per cent of securities listed on the London Stock Exchange. Total British pension fund net assets were worth about £451,000 million at the end of 1994.

The Pensions Act 1995 (see p. 417) includes provisions for several measures designed to increase confidence in the security of occupational pensions, including:

- a statutory minimum solvency requirement;

- the establishment of an Occupational Pensions Regulator with powers to investigate and to impose sanctions; and

- a new compensation scheme to protect members against dishonest removal of assets.

Unit Trusts

Authorised unit trusts are open-ended mutual or pooled investment vehicles which place funds in a wide range of securities markets all over the world. Investors with relatively small amounts to invest are able to benefit from diversified and expertly managed portfolios. The industry has grown rapidly during the last decade, and in 1995 there were nearly 1,600 authorised unit trusts. By September 1995 total assets were £107,800 million, £14,000 million higher than a year earlier. Unit trust management groups are represented by the Association of Unit Trusts and Investment Funds and regulated by IMRO. The trusts themselves are authorised by the SIB.

Investment Trusts

Investment trust companies, which also offer the opportunity to diversify risk on a relatively small lump-sum investment or through regular savings, are listed on the London Stock Exchange and their shares are traded in the usual way. They must invest mostly in securities, and the trusts themselves are exempt from capital gains tax. Assets are purchased mainly out of shareholders' funds, although investment trusts are also allowed to borrow money for investment. There were 314 members of the Association of Investment Trust Companies in October 1995, with £48,800 million worth of assets under management. The largest trust is the venture capital company 3i, which was floated on the London Stock Exchange in 1994.

Growth in Share Ownership

Privatisation (see p. 200) and employee share schemes (see p. 190) have both helped to increase share ownership, in line with the Government's policy of encouraging wider share ownership. About 10 million adults— 22 per cent of the adult population in Great Britain—hold shares.

Another major stimulus to raising share ownership by individuals has been the introduction of Personal Equity Plans (PEPs), which allow investment in shares, unit trusts and investment trusts. Dividends and capital gains on shares held in a PEP are exempt from income tax and capital gains tax, and withdrawals from PEPs are normally tax free. Since their introduction in 1987, over £16,000 million had been invested in some 4.7 million PEPs by April 1994. In 1993–94, 1.4 million general PEPs and 190,000 single company PEPs were opened.

The November 1994 Budget included proposals for PEPs to be extended to cover certain corporate bonds (except those issued by financial services companies), preference shares and 'convertibles' (bonds or preference shares which can eventually be converted into a company's ordinary shares). The first of the new PEPs were offered in July 1995.

SPECIAL FINANCING INSTITUTIONS

Several specialised institutions offer finance and support to personal and corporate sector borrowers. Among public sector agencies are Scottish Enterprise, Highlands and Islands Enterprise, the Welsh Development Agency, the Industrial Development Board for Northern Ireland and ECGD (see p. 176). The main private sector institutions are described below.

Finance and Leasing Companies

The Finance and Leasing Association represents the interests of companies offering motor finance, consumer credit, and business finance and leasing. Its 158 full and associate members undertook new business worth £32,000 million in 1994.

Factoring Companies

Factoring comprises a range of financial services allowing companies to obtain finance in exchange for outstanding invoices due to them. Factoring has developed as a major financial service since the early 1960s. Member companies of the Association of British Factors and Discounters handled business worth £24,400 million in 1994.

Venture Capital Companies

Venture capital companies offer medium- and long-term equity financing for new and developing businesses when such funds are not easily or directly available from traditional sources, such as the stock market or banks. The British Venture Capital Association has 107 full members and makes up virtually all the industry. Many venture capital companies are subsidiaries of other financial institutions, including banks, insurance companies and pension funds. To help encourage the availability of equity and long-term finance for new and growing businesses, the Government facilitated the establishment from April 1995 of new venture capital trusts (see p. 198).

FINANCIAL MARKETS

The City of London's financial markets include the London Stock Exchange, the foreign exchange market, the financial futures and options market, eurobond and eurocurrency markets, Lloyd's insurance market (see p. 221), and bullion and commodity markets. The securities markets are supervised jointly by the Treasury, the Bank of England, SIB and the London Stock Exchange, among others.

London Stock Exchange

The London Stock Exchange plays a vital role in maintaining London's position as one of the world's most important financial centres. Its main administrative centre is in London and there are regional offices in Belfast, Birmingham, Glasgow, Leeds and Manchester. As a result of a set of legal reforms implemented in 1986 and known as 'Big Bang', the Exchange has changed radically over recent years. The most fundamental change has been the move to screen-based trading away from the traditional market floor. CREST, a new computerised settlement system for shares and other securities, is being developed by a project team led by the Bank of England and will replace Talisman, the Exchange's current settlement system.

The Exchange provides a trading platform for domestic equities with its automated price information system, SEAQ, which continuously updates share prices and can be viewed on a wide range of information systems. For trading in foreign equities, London's leading international equity market is supported by the Exchange's electronic price quotation system, SEAQ International.

More than 2,600 British and overseas companies, with a market capitalisation of £4,800,000 million, are listed on the Exchange. In 1994 turnover of British and Irish equities reached £606,000 million, while turnover of foreign equities amounted to £719,000 million.

The gilt-edged market (see p. 167), allows the Government to raise money by issuing loan stock through the Bank of England. The Exchange offers a secondary or trading market where investors can buy or sell gilts. Average daily turnover in the market totalled £6,100 million in 1994.

Recent developments in share trading have included:

- the establishment in June 1995 of the Stock Exchange's new public equity market, the Alternative Investment Market, which caters mainly for small, young or developing companies wishing to raise public finance and to have their shares more widely traded—it operates within a lighter regulatory framework than is applied to shares on the main stock market;

- the opening in September 1995 of Tradepoint, a computer-based, 'order-driven' share dealing system in competition with the Stock Exchange; and

- the introduction in September 1995 of a service run by Electronic Share Information and ShareLink, which allows investors to deal in shares on the Internet.

Money Markets

The London money markets comprise the interbank deposit markets plus a range of other instruments, usually short-term in maturity. Banks are the major participants in these markets, and are supervised by the Bank of England. The Bank also supervises other institutions which operate in the foreign exchange and other wholesale money markets.

Since 1986, large companies have been permitted to issue sterling commercial paper (SCP), which takes the form of negotiable bearer debt securities with a maturity of up to one year. The range of qualifying issuers of SCP has broadened since 1986 to include, for example, banks, building societies and overseas public authorities.

Euromarkets

These are markets in currencies lent or invested outside their domestic marketplace, particularly as a means of financing international trade and investment. Transactions can thus be carried out in eurodollars, eurodeutschemarks, euroyen and so on. London is at the heart of the euromarkets and houses most of the major international banks and securities firms. Distinctions between markets have been breaking down and the euromarkets form a major part of the wider international money and capital markets. Participants in the markets include multinational trading corporations, financial companies, governments and international organisations like the World Bank and the European Investment Bank.

The euro-securities markets have grown considerably in recent years because the instruments traded on them, including eurobonds, euro-medium-term notes (EMTNs) and euro-commercial paper, are seen as flexible alternatives to bank loans. EMTN programmes were introduced in 1986, and EMTN issues rose sevenfold between 1990 and 1993. British building societies are prominent among EMTN issuers. There is a growing private sector market in ECU-denominated deposits, securities and eurobonds.

Foreign Exchange Market

London is the world's biggest centre for foreign exchange trading, accounting for over a quarter of global net daily turnover in foreign exchange. Average daily turnover in London amounts to about US $300,000 million.

The foreign exchange market consists of telephone and electronic links between the participants, which include banks, other financial institutions and several foreign exchange broking firms acting as intermediaries. It provides those engaged in international trade and investment with foreign currencies for their transactions. The banks are in close contact with financial centres abroad and are able to quote buying and selling rates for both immediate ('spot') and forward transactions in a range of currencies and maturities. The forward market enables traders and dealers who, at a given date in the future, wish to receive or make a specific foreign currency payment, to contract in advance to sell or buy the foreign currency involved for sterling at a fixed exchange rate.

Derivatives

Financial derivatives are contracts to buy or sell, at a future date, financial instruments such as equities, bonds or money-market instruments. Their use has grown rapidly, especially among companies and investment institutions, and instruments have become more complex, especially as advances have been made in information technology. Derivatives offer a means of hedging against changes in prices, exchange rates and interest rates. They include:

- futures—agreements to buy or sell financial instruments or physical commodities at a future date;

- options—the right to buy or sell financial instruments or physical commodities for a stated period at a predetermined price; and

- 'over-the-counter' products, including swaps—a foreign exchange swap can convert a money-market instrument in one currency into a money-market instrument in another.

Financial Futures and Options

Banks, other financial institutions, brokers and individual traders are members of the London International Financial Futures and Options Exchange (LIFFE), which trades at the Cannon Bridge development. Futures contracts cover the purchase or sale of a fixed amount of a commodity at a given date in the future at a price agreed at the time of trade. There is also dealing in options on the equity of prominent British companies and in stock index options. LIFFE has the most internationally diverse range of financial futures and options products of any exchange in the world. Turnover on LIFFE totalled 153 million contracts in 1994, 50 per cent more than in 1993.

London Bullion Market

Around 60 banks and other financial trading companies comprise the London gold and silver markets, which, like the foreign exchange market, trade by telephone or other electronic means. Five of the members of the London Bullion Market Association meet twice daily to establish a London fixing price for gold—a reference point for worldwide dealings. The silver fixing is held once a day. Although much interest centres upon the fixings, active dealing takes place throughout the day. London and Zurich are the main world centres for gold dealings.

Commodity, Shipping and Freight Markets

Britain is a major international centre for commodities trading and the home of many of the related international trade organisations. At the London Commodities Exchange, futures in grains and potatoes are traded, as are futures and options on 'soft' commodities (cocoa and coffee). White sugar, raw sugar and dry freight index futures contracts are also traded. The London Metal Exchange is the primary base metals market in the world, trading both spot and forward contracts in aluminium, aluminium alloy, copper, lead, nickel, tin and zinc. The International Petroleum Exchange is Europe's only energy futures exchange. Total turnover of the three exchanges rose by 25 per cent in 1994 to nearly 66 million contracts.

The Baltic Exchange, which finds ships for cargoes and cargoes for ships throughout the world, is the world's leading international shipping market.

Other Services

DISTRIBUTION AND SALES

The distribution of goods, including food and drink, to their point of sale by road, rail, air and sea is a major economic activity. The large retailers and wholesalers of food and drink and clothing operate, either directly or through contractors, extensive distribution networks.

Wholesaling

There were 115,000 businesses, with a turnover of £268,000 million (see Table 15.1), engaged in wholesaling and dealing in Great Britain in 1993. The industry has more than 850,000 employees in Britain.

In the food and drink trade almost all large retailers have their own buying and central distribution operations. Elsewhere in the trade, voluntary 'symbol' groups (for example, Spar and VG) have been formed by wholesalers and small independent retailers. This has helped many smaller retail outlets, including traditional 'corner shops' and village stores, to stay in business, as it has given them the advantages of bulk buying and co-ordinated distribution.

London's wholesale markets play a significant part in the distribution of foodstuffs. New Covent Garden is the main market for fruit and vegetables, Smithfield for meat and Billingsgate for fish.

The Co-operative Movement has its own distribution organisation, the Co-operative Wholesale Society (CWS). Retail co-operative societies buy from the CWS, which is their main supplier. The CWS is also the largest co-operative retailer, with 675 stores located in Scotland, Northern Ireland, the east and south Midlands, and south-east and northern England.

Retailing

In 1993 there were 202,000 retail businesses, with 306,000 outlets, employing 2.3 million people in Great Britain (see Table 15.2). These range from national supermarket chains to corner grocery shops and newsagents, together employing 2.3 million people. During recent years the large multiple retailers have grown considerably, tending to reduce numbers of stores but increase outlet size and diversify product ranges. Some, like Marks and Spencer, J. Sainsbury and Tesco, have acquired retailers or made franchise arrangements abroad. Of the ten largest food retailers in Western Europe, four are British.

Decline has been particularly evident among small independent businesses and retail co-operative societies (see above). Sunday trading laws have been relaxed to allow supermarkets, department stores and other retailers to open for limited periods on Sundays; smaller retailers are permitted to open for longer hours than the larger stores.

The biggest supermarket groups are Tesco, J. Sainsbury, Argyll (principally Safeway) and Asda. These four had a market share of 40 per cent of all food and drink sold in 1994–95. Other important retailers are Marks and Spencer, Somerfield and Kwik Save—the latter is the leading discount food

Table 15.1: Wholesale Trade in Great Britain 1993

	Number of businesses	Turnover[a] (£ million)
Food and drink	14,983	49,494
Petroleum products	896	34,667
Clothing, furs, textiles and footwear	9,815	12,039
Coal and oil merchants	2,733	2,017
Builders' merchants	3,446	8,284
Agricultural supplies and livestock dealing	2,551	8,029
Industrial materials	5,660	23,903
Scrap and waste products	3,294	2,532
Industrial and agricultural machinery	8,583	20,769
Operational leasing	2,090	1,913
Other goods	60,687	103,957
Total wholesaling and dealing	**114,738**	**267,604**

Source: *Business Monitor SDA26. Wholesaling, 1995*
[a]Excludes value added tax.

Table 15.2: Retail Trade in Great Britain 1993

	Number of businesses	Number of outlets	Number of people engaged ('000s)	Turnover[a] (£ million)
Non-specialised stores	23,700	38,175	858	62,707
Specialised stores	178,140	267,653	1,480	85,822
of which:				
Food, drinks or tobacco	47,098	63,183	281	13,293
Pharmaceuticals, cosmetics and toilet articles	7,063	12,333	86	5,533
Businesses having:				
1 outlet	178,744	178,599	750	35,532
2–9 outlets	21,996	59,261	285	16,190
10–99 outlets	968	23,168	278	17,960
100 or more outlets	133	44,800	1,025	78,847
of which:				
All businesses selling food, drinks or tobacco	68,505	95,352	970	65,302
Total retail trade	**201,841**	**305,827**	**2,337**	**148,529**

Source: Business Monitor SDA25. Retailing, 1995.
[a] Includes value added tax.

retailer in Britain. Since the early 1990s several overseas discount food retailers, such as Aldi of Germany and Denmark's Netto, have entered the British market.

Retail co-operative societies are voluntary organisations controlled by their members, membership being open to anyone paying a small deposit on a minimum share. Of the 5,000 retail co-operative outlets, over half sell food and groceries.

Alcoholic drinks are sold mainly in specialist 'off licences' and supermarkets, which have roughly equal sales. The principal off-licence chains are Cellar Five, Oddbins, Threshers and Victoria Wine. The selling of alcohol is closely controlled by law and only permitted between certain hours.

The leading mixed retail businesses include Marks and Spencer, Boots, Woolworth (part of Kingfisher), Storehouse, W. H. Smith, Argos, Littlewoods, Savacentre (J. Sainsbury), John Menzies, Sears, Burton Group and House of Fraser.

About 18 million people regularly buy all kinds of goods and services through mail order catalogues like Freemans, Great Universal Stores, Empire and Littlewoods. In 1993 sales by general mail order totalled more than £4,000 million, 3 per cent of all retail sales. The largest selling items are clothing, footwear, furniture, household textiles and domestic electrical appliances.

Shopping Facilities

Britain has a wide range of complementary shopping facilities inside and outside town and city centres. One of the most significant trends in retailing has been the spread of superstores, many of which have been built away from urban centres in recent years. While the 100 largest retailers account for about three-fifths of retail sales, there continues to be a demand for the products and services provided by small, specialised shops. Encouraged by the Government, the main multiple grocery companies are turning their attention back to town centres, redeveloping existing stores and building smaller outlets, some aimed at the convenience market. Examples include Tesco's 'Metro' format and J. Sainsbury's 'Capital' stores.

Regional out-of-town shopping centres have been established on sites offering good access and parking facilities. One of the first was the Metro Centre at Gateshead, which is the largest of its kind in Europe; Merry Hill at Dudley in the West Midlands attracted 25 million customers in 1994. Other centres include Meadowhall in Sheffield and the Lakeside Centre at Thurrock in Essex, both opened in 1990. About one-half of total food sales are accounted for by superstores away from town centres, compared with a fifth at the beginning of the 1980s. Retailers of non-food goods, such as DIY products, toys, furniture and electrical appliances, sportswear, and office and computer products, have also built outlets away from urban centres. There is a strong trend towards grouping retail warehouses into retail parks, often with food and other facilities.

All new retail development requires planning permission from the local government planning authority. These authorities must consult the appropriate central government department before granting permission for developments of 20,000 sq m (215,000 sq ft) or more. The Government's policy is to encourage the provision of a broad range of shopping facilities to the public. At the same time it seeks to ensure that the effects of major new retail developments, especially those outside urban centres, do not undermine the viability of existing town centres. The Government is intensifying efforts to help revitalise shopping and other facilities in town centres where this is needed.

Rental Services

A broad range of rental services, many franchised, are on offer throughout Britain (see p. 233). These include hire of cars and other vehicles, televisions and video cassette recorders, household appliances such as washing machines and tumble dryers, tools and heavy decorating equipment (ladders, floor sanders and so on) and video films and computer games. Retailing of many types of service is dominated by chains, though independent operators are still to be found in most fields.

Auction Houses

Britain attracts buyers and sellers from around the world and has a long tradition of expertise and innovation in auctioneering. Its chief auction houses are active in the international auction markets for works of art, trading on their acknowledged expertise. The two largest houses, Sotheby's and Christie's, are established worldwide. In 1994 Sotheby's celebrated its 250th anniversary. Sotheby's handled sales valued at £868 million in 1994, while Christie's sales amounted to £820 million. Phillips and Bonhams are also prominent auctioneers.

Other Trends

Many of the large multiple groups sell a much greater number of goods and services than previously. However, in some cases extensive diversification has proved unprofitable and, for example, large food retailers are increasing their range of foods instead. More emphasis is also being placed on selling own-label goods (which now account for up to one-half of goods on sale) and environmentally friendly products, including organic produce. Most superstores and supermarkets offer fresh food, such as meat, fish, vegetables and, in many cases, bread baked on the premises, as well as packaged foods. The major supermarket chains also have their own petrol stations at some of their bigger outlets (see p. 230).

'Stores within stores' are becoming more common; for example, sportswear and sports goods retailers are to be found in many of the big mixed retail stores, while Laura Ashley, the furnishings and fabrics retailer, has opened facilities in Homebase (a DIY chain owned by J. Sainsbury).

Several large retailers have issued their own credit cards for regular customers in an attempt to encourage sales, particularly of high-value goods. Marks and Spencer also offers financial services.

Information Technology

Information technology has become increasingly central to distribution and retailing. Computers monitor stock levels and record sales figures through electronic point-of-sale (EPOS) systems. EPOS systems read a bar-code printed on the retail product that holds price and product information and can be used to generate orders for stock replenishment as well as totalling up bills and providing a receipt for customers.

Techniques such as 'just-in-time' ordering, in which produce arrives at the store at the last possible moment before sale, have become widespread as a result. Most large retailers have set up electronic data interchange (EDI) systems; these enable their computers to communicate with those of their suppliers, and transmit orders and invoices electronically, so reducing errors and saving time.

EFTPOS (electronic funds transfer at point of sale) systems enable customers to pay for purchases using debit cards which automatically transfer funds from their bank account. Several major EFTPOS schemes are well established and the number of terminals is growing rapidly.

'Superscan' technology—which involves customers using an electronic scanning device to work out their own bills, thus avoiding the need to queue at a check-out—is currently undergoing trials in a number of supermarkets. Electronic home shopping, using a television and telephone, and 'online' shopping, where personal computers are linked to databases, are already starting to become established.

Vehicle, Vehicle Parts and Petrol Retailing

In Great Britain 275,000 people were employed in 1995 in retailing motor vehicles and parts, and in petrol stations. Many businesses selling new vehicles are franchised by the motor manufacturers. Drive-in fitting centres sell tyres, exhaust systems, batteries, clutches and other vehicle parts; the largest chains include Kwik-Fit and Associated Tyre Services.

Over one-third of petrol stations are owned by oil companies. The three companies with the largest number of outlets are Shell, Esso and BP. Unleaded petrol accounts for more than half of petrol sold. The majority of petrol stations are self-service.

The number of petrol stations has been reduced by about a half in the last decade as owners focus on larger sites that can accommodate the broad range of retail services, including food, that are now commonly available at petrol stations. Almost one-fifth of petrol sold in Britain comes from supermarket forecourts.

HOTELS, HOLIDAY CENTRES, PUBLIC HOUSES AND CATERING

The hotel and catering trades, which include public houses (pubs) and licensed bars, employ 1.2 million people in Great Britain, including:

- 302,000 in hotels and other residential establishments;
- 336,000 in pubs and bars;
- 304,000 in restaurants, cafés and snack bars; and
- 136,000 in clubs.

Around 161,000 self-employed people also work in these sectors.

There are 52,000 hotels in Great Britain. The largest hotel business is Forte, with 344 hotels in Britain. As well as catering and leisure interests, Forte has substantial overseas interests. At the other end of the scale, numerous guest houses and hotels each have fewer than 20 rooms. Holiday centres, including holiday camps with full board, self-catering centres and caravan parks, are run by Butlins, Holiday Club, Center Parcs, Warner Holidays and Pontin's.

Britain's 100,000 restaurants offer cuisine from virtually every country in the world. Chinese, Indian, Italian and Greek restaurants are among the most popular. 'Fast food' restaurants, an area where franchising plays a significant role, are becoming more widespread. They specialise in hamburgers, chicken, pizza and a variety of other foods to be eaten on the premises or taken away. The most well-known chains, some of which are US-owned, include Wimpy (hamburgers), McDonald's (hamburgers), Burger King (hamburgers), KFC (chicken) and Pizza Hut.

Traditional fish and chip shops are the other main providers of cooked take-away food. Sandwich bars proliferate in towns and cities, typically in areas with high concentrations of office workers.

About 77,000 public houses sell beer, wines, soft drinks and spirits to adults for consumption on the premises, and most also provide hot and cold food; many have separate facilities where children are allowed. Some are owned by the large brewing companies, which either provide managers to run them or offer tenancy agreements; these pubs tend to sell just their own brands of beer, although some also offer 'guest' beers. Others, called 'free houses', are independently owned and managed and frequently serve a variety of beers. Wine bars are normally smaller than pubs and tend to specialise in wine and food; they more closely resemble bars in other parts of Europe.

Permitted opening hours for public houses and bars in England and Wales were extended in 1988; today the more popular pubs and bars open from 11.00 to 23.00 from Monday to Saturday (on Sunday pubs may open between 12.00 and 22.30). The introduction of liquor licences for 'café-style' premises allows children under 14 to accompany their parents to places where alcoholic drinks are served.

TOURISM AND TRAVEL

In the region of 1.5 million people, 25 per cent more than a decade ago, are employed in tourism. The industry contributes £33,000 million annually to the economy—4 per cent of GDP. Britain is the world's sixth leading tourist destination, although its share of world tourism earnings has fallen from 6 to 4.5 per cent in the last ten years. By the year 2000 tourism is expected to be the biggest industry in the world.

Britain's tourist attractions include theatres, museums, art galleries, and historic houses, as well as shopping, sports and business facilities. Domestic and foreign tourists play an ever more important role in supporting Britain's national heritage, creative arts and, to a lesser extent, sport.

Domestic tourism was worth £14,500

million in 1994 (see p. 40). (see p. 40) Of British residents opting to take their main holiday in Britain, around half choose a traditional seaside destination, such as Blackpool (Lancashire), Bournemouth (Dorset) and resorts in Devon and Cornwall. Short holiday breaks (one to three nights), valued at £2,200 million in 1993, make up an increasingly significant part of the market. Shopping accounts for about a quarter of all expenditure on day trips. Scotland has several skiing resorts.

Between 1980 and 1994 the number of overseas visits to Britain grew by two-thirds. In 1994 a record 21 million overseas visitors came to Britain, spending £10,000 million. An estimated 63 per cent were from Europe and 17 per cent from North America, with the United States supplying the largest number of any single country. Business travel accounts for about one-quarter of all overseas tourism revenue.

Most British holiday-makers wishing to go overseas buy 'package holidays' from travel agencies, where the cost covers both transport and accommodation. The most popular package holiday destinations are Spain, France and Greece. Long-haul holidays to places like the United States, the Caribbean and Australia are becoming more popular as air fares come down. Winter skiing holidays to resorts in Austria, France, Italy and Switzerland and other countries inside and outside Europe continue to attract large numbers of Britons.

Britain has around 7,000 travel agencies, nearly all of which belong to the Association of British Travel Agents (ABTA). Although most are small businesses, a few large firms, such as Lunn Poly and Thomas Cook, have hundreds of branches. Some 617 tour operators are members of ABTA; about half are both retail agents and tour operators. ABTA operates financial protection schemes to safeguard its members' customers and maintains codes of conduct drawn up with the Office of Fair Trading. It also offers a free consumer affairs service to help resolve complaints against members and an independent arbitration scheme for tour operators' customers.

Tourist Authorities

The Department of National Heritage is responsible for tourism in England, and the Scottish, Welsh, and Northern Ireland Offices have responsibility for tourism in their respective countries. The government-supported British Tourist Authority (BTA) promotes Britain overseas as a tourist destination and encourages the development of tourist facilities in Britain to meet the needs of overseas visitors. The tourist boards for England, Scotland, Wales and Northern Ireland encourage the development and promotion of domestic tourism and work with the BTA to promote Britain overseas.

> In February 1995 the Government published *Tourism—Competing with the Best*, in which it outlined plans to develop Britain's tourism industry by:
> - raising standards of hotel and other accommodation;
> - improving overseas marketing of Britain as a tourist destination;
> - promoting London more effectively; and
> - making holiday booking arrangements easier.

The BTA and the national tourist boards inform and advise the Government on issues of concern to the industry. They also help businesses and other organisations to plan by researching and publicising trends affecting the industry. The national tourist boards work closely with regional tourist boards, on which local government and business interests are represented. The national tourist boards offer financial assistance to the industry. There are 800 or so Tourist Information Centres in Britain, operating an information service for visitors.

Three accommodation classification and grading schemes are operated by the national tourist boards:

- the Crown scheme for hotels, guest houses, inns, bed and breakfast and farmhouse holiday accommodation. A new Lodge category has been introduced for purpose-built accommodation alongside motorways and major roads;

- the Key (Dragons used in Wales) scheme for self-catering holiday homes; and

- the Quality 'Q' scheme for holiday caravan, chalet and camping parks.

Common standards are applied throughout Britain. All participating establishments are inspected every year.

BUSINESS SERVICES

Exhibition and Conference Centres

Britain is one of the world's three leading countries for international conferences—the others being the United States and France. London and Paris are the two most popular conference cities. A large number of other towns and cities in Britain have facilities for conferences and exhibitions. Total spending in 1993 on conferences and exhibitions amounted to £630 million.

Among the most modern purpose-built conference and exhibition centres are the International Conference Centre in Birmingham; the Queen Elizabeth II and Olympia Conference Centres, both in London; and Cardiff International Arena, a 5,000-seat multi-purpose facility which opened in 1993. Others are located in Brighton (East Sussex), Harrogate (North Yorkshire), Bournemouth, Birmingham, Manchester, Nottingham and Torquay (Devon). In Scotland both Glasgow and Aberdeen have exhibition and conference centres, and a new International Conference Centre has been built in Edinburgh.

Other large exhibition facilities are situated in London at the Barbican, Earls Court, Alexandra Palace and Wembley Arena. A £100 million exhibition and conference facility is planned for London Docklands, to be completed in 1998.

Many of the larger sites belong to a marketing group, the British Conference and Exhibition Centres Export Council.

Franchising

A notable trend in the services sector is the growth of franchising, an operation in which a company owning the rights to a particular form of trading licenses them to franchisees, usually by means of an initial payment with continuing royalties. The main areas include cleaning services, film processing, print shops, hairdressing and cosmetics, fitness centres, courier delivery, car rental, engine tuning and servicing, and fast food retailing.

Advertising and Sponsorship

Britain is a major centre for creative advertising, and multinational corporations often use advertising created in Britain for marketing their products globally. British agencies have strong foreign links through overseas ownership and associate networks.

Spending on advertising in 1994 amounted to £10,200 million, a rise of more than 8 per cent in real terms on the previous year. The press accounted for 55 per cent of the total, television for 28 per cent, direct mail for 10 per cent, and posters, transport, commercial radio and cinema for the rest. The largest advertising expenditure is on food, household durables, cosmetics, office equipment, motor vehicles and financial services. The biggest spenders in 1994 included BT, Ford, Dixons, McDonald's, Tesco and J. Sainsbury. The National Lottery (see p. 460) also quickly established itself as a major spender on advertising. British television advertising receives many international awards.

Campaigns are planned by around 2,000 advertising agencies. In addition to their creative, production and media buying roles, some agencies offer integrated marketing services, such as consumer research and public relations. Leading agencies include Abbott Mead Vickers BBDO, J Walter Thompson, Leo Burnett and Ogilvy and Mather Advertising.

Government advertising campaigns— crime prevention, health promotion, road safety and so on—are organised in the main by the Central Office of Information, an executive agency of the Government (see p. 530), which is able to secure large discounts because of its centralised buying power.

Many advertising agencies have sponsorship departments, which arrange for businesses to sponsor products and events, including artistic, sporting and charitable events. In return for financial or other support, the sponsoring company is associated with a worthy product or event, thereby raising its profile with consumers.

Public Relations

Britain's public relations industry has grown rapidly over the past ten years and is now the most developed in Europe. In 1994 it had an estimated turnover of £1,300 million.

Computing Services

The computing services industry comprises software houses; production of packaged software; consultancy; information technology 'outsourcing'; processing services; and the provision of complete computer systems. It also includes companies providing information technology education and training; independent maintenance; support, contingency planning and recruitment; and contract staff.

The turnover of companies in the Computing Services & Software Association, which represents about 75 per cent of the industry in Britain, totalled over £7,000 million in 1994. Important areas for software development include data and word processing, telecommunications, computer-aided design and manufacturing, defence and consumer electronics.

Management Consultancy

Management consultants provide business solutions by giving advice and technical assistance to business and government clients. Typically, consultants identify and investigate problems and opportunities, recommend appropriate action and help to implement recommendations.

Many British-based consultancies operate internationally; the most recent trend has been for the largest firms to set up offices in

233

Eastern Europe and the Pacific Rim. The 32 member firms of the Management Consultancies Association are among the largest in the industry and account for more than half of management consultancy work; they range from Andersen Consulting and CMG Management, with a strong technical bias, to Coopers & Lybrand and PA Consulting group, which specialise in market/industry sectors. In 1994 member firms earned more than £1,000 million in Britain and £150 million overseas.

Market Research

A wide range of domestic and overseas clients, including government bodies, use Britain's market research facilities. Britain accounts for 9 per cent of worldwide market research spending. The Association of Market Survey Organisations is the main trade organisation, with 35 member companies; in 1994 its members earned £325 million out of an estimated total market research industry turnover of £485 million.

Further Reading

Financial Services. Aspects of Britain series, 1995, HMSO.

16 Manufacturing and Construction Industries

| Introduction | 235 | Construction | 248 |
| Sectors of Manufacturing | 236 | | |

Britain became the world's first industrialised country in the mid 19th century. Wealth was based on manufacturing iron and steel, heavy machinery and cotton textiles, and on coal mining, shipbuilding and trade. Manufacturing still plays an important role and Britain excels in high-technology industries like pharmaceuticals, electronics (including computers), aerospace and offshore equipment, where British companies are among the world's largest and most successful. The British construction industry has made its mark around the world and continues to be involved in some of the most prestigious international building projects.

Introduction

Manufacturing accounted for just over a fifth of gross domestic product (GDP) in 1994 and for about the same proportion of employment. More than four-fifths of visible exports consisted of manufactured or semi-manufactured goods.

Almost all manufacturing is carried out by private-sector businesses.

Following the recent recession, which led to a decline in manufacturing output, output rose by 1.2 per cent in 1993 and by 4.2 per cent in 1994 (see Table 16.2). Employment in

Table 16.1: Manufacturing—Size of Businesses by Turnover and Employment

Annual turnover (£'000)	Number of businesses 1994	Employment size	Number of businesses 1994	Employment 1992[a]
1–36	23,452	1–9	114,293	292,997
37–49	10,621	10–19	16,827	232,428
50–99	26,304	20–49	15,680	481,313
100–249	33,994	50–99	6,100	423,462
250–499	20,249	100–199	3,535	492,422
500–999	15,170	200–499	2,335	720,775
1,000–1,999	10,407	500–999	838	578,031
2,000–4,999	8,120	1,000+	618	2,085,374
5,000–9,999	3,468			
10,000+	4,616			
Total	156,401	Total	160,226	5,306,802

Source: *Size Analysis of United Kingdom Businesses 1994. Business Monitor PA 1003*
[a] Includes secondary non-manufacturing activity.

235

manufacturing in 1994 was 4.2 million compared with 5.4 million in 1984. Total capital investment in manufacturing was £13,400 million in 1994, comprising £11,100 million in plant and machinery, £1,500 million in new building work and £700 million in vehicles.

The most successful manufacturing industry in terms of sales (including exports) to demand in Britain is spirit distilling (mainly whisky). In 1992 the industry's ratio of sales to demand in Britain was 8.8. The next most successful were office machinery, construction equipment, pesticides and tractors.

The construction industry contributed 5 per cent of GDP and about 1.4 million people worked in the industry in 1994, 6 per cent of the total number of employees and self-employed. Between 1993 and 1994 output increased by 4 per cent, following declines in output in 1991, 1992 and 1993 as recession affected the industry. Total domestic fixed capital investment was £700 million in 1994.

Sectors of Manufacturing

Relative sizes of enterprises and the main sectors are shown in Tables 16.1 and 16.2.

Table 16.3 indicates output and investment. A more detailed description of some of the main sectors is given below.

Mineral and Metal Products

British producers delivered 15.7 million tonnes of finished steel in 1994, of which 50 per cent was exported. Over the past ten years annual steel industry exports have increased by 50 per cent, to nearly 8 million tonnes, creating a favourable balance of trade in steel products.

The major areas of steel production are in south Wales and northern England, with substantial further processing in the Midlands. Major restructuring in the steel industry took place during the 1980s and early 1990s. Productivity and efficiency have improved and the industry is now one of the lowest-cost producers in Europe.

British Steel is the fourth largest steel company in the world, employing 41,000 people and producing about three-quarters of Britain's crude steel in 1994. The company's output is based on flat steel products, plate, heavy sections and tubes. These are used principally in the construction, automotive,

Table 16.2: Indices of Manufacturing Output (1990 = 100)				
1992 Standard Industrial Classification Category	Share of output 1990 (weight per 1,000)	1992	1993	1994
Food and beverages	29	99.9	99.9	101.8
Tobacco products	2	107.3	100.4	107.5
Textiles and leather products	14	89.4	89.4	90.4
Wood and wood products	4	87.2	89.3	95.5
Pulp, paper products, printing and publishing	26	95.6	99.0	101.5
Solid and nuclear fuels, oil refining	7	114.9	114.9	115.6
Chemicals and man-made fibres	24	105.0	107.6	112.3
Rubber and plastics products	10	95.6	99.8	109.6
Other non-metallic mineral products	9	86.0	88.9	92.6
Basic metal and metal products	27	86.0	84.8	86.7
Machinery and equipment	21	85.2	85.0	89.2
Electrical and optical equipment	27	96.0	101.2	112.1
Transport equipment	27	90.8	87.8	90.7
Other manufacturing	6	85.9	88.4	89.9
Total	**232**	**94.0**	**95.1**	**99.1**

Source: *United Kingdom National Accounts 1995 Edition*

Table 16.3: Output and Investment in Manufacturing

1992 Standard Industrial Classification category	Gross output (£ million) 1994	Gross domestic fixed capital formation (£ million) 1994
Solid and nuclear fuels, oil refining	2,345	477
Chemicals and man-made fibres	13,697 ⎫	
Other non-metallic mineral products	4,005 ⎬	3,149
Basic metals and metal products	12,483 ⎭	
Machinery and equipment	9,977 ⎫	
Electrical and optical equipment	14,912 ⎬	4,301
Transport equipment	12,707 ⎭	
Food and beverages	16,749 ⎫	
Tobacco products	1,530 ⎪	
Textiles and leather products	6,876 ⎪	
Wood and wood products	1,576 ⎬	5,426
Pulp, paper products, printing and publishing	14,293 ⎪	
Rubber and plastics products	6,467 ⎪	
Other manufacturing	3,646 ⎭	
Total	**121,263**	**13,353**

Source: *United Kingdom National Accounts 1994 Edition*

engineering, transport, metal goods, packaging and energy industries.

Other important steel producers in Britain include Caparo, Allied Steel and Wire, Co-Steel Sheerness, the Glynwed Group and the stainless steel producer Avesta Sheffield. Products manufactured by these companies include reinforcing bars for the construction industry, wire rod, hot rolled and cold finished bars and other special steels for the aerospace and offshore oil and gas industries.

> **In February 1995 British Steel took full ownership of UES Holdings, Europe's biggest producer of engineering steels—these are specialist grades used to make products such as forgings for the automotive and aerospace industries.**

Output of non-ferrous metals and their alloys includes primary and secondary (recycled) aluminium and copper, as well as aluminium and copper and copper alloy semi-manufactures. The production of metal relies mainly on imported ores and recycled material of both domestic and overseas origin.

Britain is a major producer of specialised alloys for high-technology requirements in the aerospace, electronic, petrochemical, and nuclear and other fuel industries. Titanium and titanium alloys, which are light, strong and flexible, are used in aircraft manufacturing, power generation and North Sea oil production. Nickel alloys are utilised in aero-engines for high-temperature environments. In recent years considerable progress has been made in producing 'superplastic' alloys, which are more ductile and elastic than conventional alloys. Aluminium alloys, including aluminium lithium (developed by British Alcan Aluminium), are ideal for use in aircraft, being lighter, stronger and more rigid than normal aluminium. Aluminium alloys typically make up three-quarters of an airframe.

There is also an important sector producing copper and copper alloy semi-manufactures for use in a wide variety of electrical switchgear, wire and cable, tube and fittings for plumbing, and valves and components for the engineering and transport industries.

Ceramics

The ceramics industry manufactures clay products, such as domestic pottery, sanitaryware and tiles, and clay pipes for the building trade. Domestic pottery production includes china, earthenware and stoneware. Tableware is produced in Stoke-on-Trent. Britain is the world's leading manufacturer and exporter of fine bone china; Wedgwood, Spode and Royal Doulton are among the more famous names.

Research is being conducted into ceramics for use in house building and diesel and jet engines. Important industrial ceramics invented in Britain include silicon carbides and sialons, which can withstand ultra-high temperatures.

Glass Products

Flat glass is manufactured through the float glass process, which was developed by Pilkington Brothers and licensed to glassmakers throughout the world. Pilkington has also produced an energy-saving window glass which reflects room heat without impairing visibility and an automotive glass that prevents car interiors overheating and being damaged by heat and sunlight. United Glass is a leading manufacturer of bottles and other glass containers. Glass-reinforced cement composites for the construction industry were invented in Britain in the early 1970s and are made under licence in over 40 countries.

China Clay

Britain is the world's biggest exporter of china clay (kaolin), four-fifths of which is used in paper-making. In 1994, 2.5 million tonnes were sold overseas. The main company is ECC International, part of the English China Clays Group.

Chemicals and Related Products

The products of Britain's chemical industry, the third largest in Europe, underpin almost all other industrial processes and products. It is at the forefront of modern technology, spending more than 7 per cent of total sales on research and development (R & D). The industry provides direct employment for about 280,000 people. Over a half of its output is exported, making it British manufacturing's greatest single export earner. Exports in 1994 were worth £18,700 million,

while imports (mainly consisting of plastics and organic chemicals) were valued at £14,500 million.

Many major chemical companies in Britain are multinationals; several are subsidiaries of overseas companies and others are specialist manufacturers of pharmaceuticals, such as Glaxo Wellcome. Imperial Chemical Industries (ICI), the sixth largest chemical company in the world, manufactures industrial chemicals, paints, materials and explosives. Zeneca produces pharmaceuticals, agrochemicals and seeds, and specialty chemicals. Teesside has been especially successful in attracting investment from some of the largest overseas chemical firms.

Traditionally, Britain has been a major producer of basic industrial chemicals, such as basic organic and inorganic chemicals, plastics and fertilisers, which together comprise around two-fifths of output. The most rapid growth in recent years has been in specialty chemicals, pharmaceuticals and cosmetics.

Sales of basic organic chemicals amounted to £4,100 million and those of other basic industrial chemicals to £7,200 million in 1993. The most important bulk products are ethylene, propylene and benzene. Britain is the world's fourth biggest producer of specialised organic chemicals, with over 7.5 per cent of the world market.

Much inorganic chemical production consists of relatively simple bulk chemicals, such as sulphuric acid and metallic and non-metallic oxides, serving as basic materials for industry. Specialty chemicals include pharmaceutical ingredients, essential oils and flavourings, adhesives and sealants, and explosives, including those used for car safety airbags. Investment in environmentally safe products and processes, for example substitutes for chlorofluorocarbons (CFCs), is increasing.

A sizeable proportion of world R & D in agrochemicals is conducted in Britain. Notable British discoveries include diquat and paraquat herbicides, pyrethroid insecticides, systemic fungicides and aphicides, genetically-engineered microbial pesticides and methods of encouraging natural parasites to eradicate common pests in horticulture.

Exports of soap and detergent preparations in 1994 were valued at £1,400 million. This sector is dominated by Lever Brothers (part of Unilever) and the US-owned Procter and Gamble.

Plastics

Around 200,000 people are employed by nearly 4,000 firms engaged in plastics processing—the conversion of plastics materials into finished or sub-assemblies of final products. Total annual turnover of the plastics processing industry is estimated at £11,300 million; exports reached £2,800 million in 1994. Production includes housewares and components/products for the automotive, electrical/electronic, construction and engineering industries, as well as a broad range of packaging materials.

Paints

Sales of paint, varnishes and painters' fillings were worth £2,200 million in 1993. ICI is the world's largest paint manufacturer. Among its specialised products are new ranges of synthetic resins and pigments, powder coatings, non-drip and quick-drying paints and paints needing only one top coat. Its best-known consumer product is the 'Dulux' paint range. Two of the more significant innovations have been solid emulsion paint and a temporary water-based finish which can be removed easily by chemical treatment, for vehicle bodies and road markings.

Pharmaceuticals

The British pharmaceutical industry is the world's fourth biggest exporter of medicines, accounting for around 12 per cent of the world market. About 300 pharmaceutical manufacturers operate in Britain, including several multinational corporations. The British-owned group Glaxo Wellcome became the largest pharmaceutical company in the world when Glaxo took over Wellcome in 1995. There are also many medium-sized and smaller specialist companies. Total sales in 1994 were around £9,300 million, of which £4,000 million was accounted for by overseas sales. The main overseas markets are Western Europe and North America, with Japan an expanding market.

Some 80,000 people work in the industry, of whom more than a quarter are engaged in R & D. The industry, which is largely based in the South East and East Anglia, invested £2,500 million in R & D in 1994. This sum amounts to one-third of British industry's R & D and represents about a tenth of total world expenditure on pharmaceuticals R & D. Progress in devising vaccines has helped to reduce dramatically the impact of infectious diseases such as whooping cough, mumps and measles.

British firms discovered and developed 13 of the world's 50 best-selling drugs, including Glaxo Wellcome's ulcer treatment Zantac, the best-selling medicine in the world, and Zeneca's beta-blocker Tenormin, for treating high blood pressure. Among Zeneca's newer products are Zestril (for combating high blood pressure), Zoladex (a prostate cancer therapy) and Diprivan (an anaesthetic).

Other major developments pioneered in Britain are semi-synthetic penicillins and cephalosporins, both powerful antibiotics, and new treatments for asthma, arthritis, migraine and coronary heart disease. The world's fifth largest pharmaceutical company, SmithKline Beecham, manufactures four of the world's top-selling antibiotics; it also developed Augmentin, used to treat a range of infections that have become resistant to antibiotics. Glaxo Wellcome's Zofran, an anti-nausea drug for countering the unpleasant side-effects of cancer treatments, is one of the company's most successful new medicines.

British companies lead in the development of molecular graphics. These contribute to the rational design of new and improved medicines through a computer-aided technique for analysing the structures of complicated organic molecules using a visual display unit.

A growing trend is the production of generic drugs. These are versions of branded drugs whose patents have expired. They are mostly unbranded and cheaper than the branded originals. About 50 per cent of doctors' prescriptions in Britain are for generic drugs.

Biotechnology

The British biotechnology industry is second only in pre-eminence to that of the United States. As well as Zeneca, Glaxo Wellcome and SmithKline Beecham, around 30 smaller independent firms, including Celltech, British Biotech, Xenova and Cantab, contribute to the sector.

Biotechnology has improved the specificity of pharmaceuticals through greater understanding of disease at the molecular level. It has enabled companies to manufacture products using genetic modification. Britain has made major advances in the development of drugs such as human insulin and interferons, genetically-engineered vaccines, and in the production of antibiotics by fermentation; alternative bactericidal drugs based on Nisin, a food preservative made in Britain; agricultural products such as infection-resistant crops; and medical diagnostic devices, including the world's best-selling biosensor.

A second generation of vaccines based on recombinant DNA technology includes SmithKline Beecham's Engerix-B vaccine against hepatitis. Therapies based on correcting the function of defective genes are under development. Diseases being targeted include those where a single defective gene needs correcting, such as cystic fibrosis, and those where there are genetic and environmental components, like cardiovascular disease.

Specialist products of Britain's small and medium-sized biotechnology firms comprise, among other items, medical diagnostics and microbial pesticides. Celltech was the first licensed by the United States Government for the large-scale production of monoclonal antibodies, proteins which can seek out a particular substance in the body. They are used to diagnose diseases, identify different blood types and can be employed in the treatment of a range of conditions, including cancer.

Fibres

The main types of synthetic fibre are still those first developed: regenerated cellulosic fibres such as viscose, and the major synthetic fibres like nylon polyamide, polyester and acrylics. Extensive research continues to produce a wide variety of innovative products; antistatic and flame-retardant fibres are examples. More specialist products include the aramids (with very high thermal stability and strength), elastanes (giving very high stretch and recovery) and melded fabrics (produced without the need for knitting or weaving).

Courtaulds, one of Britain's biggest chemical companies, developed Tencel, a solvent-spun, biodegradable fibre. This is twice as strong as cotton while being soft enough to be used by designers of luxury garments.

Mechanical Engineering

The mechanical engineering sector has about 24,000 firms employing over 470,000 people. In 1994 exports totalled £14,200 million, with a trade surplus of £2,600 million. Output includes pressure vessels, heat exchangers and storage tanks for chemical and oil-refining plant, steam-raising boilers (including those for power stations), nuclear reactors, water and sewage treatment plant, and fabricated steelwork for bridges, buildings and industrial installations.

Machine-building is an area where British firms excel, especially in construction and earth-moving equipment, wheeled tractors, internal combustion engines, textile machinery, medical equipment, fork-lift trucks, pumps and compressors. Britain is one of the world's major producers of tractors, which make up around three-quarters of the country's total output of agricultural equipment. Sales of wheeled tractors in 1994 were valued at £1,400 million. Among leading tractor manufacturers are Massey Ferguson, JCB, Case and New Holland.

Widely-used technical innovations include computer-controlled tractors, a highly efficient pesticide sprayer and combined mower/conditioners that reduce the drying time for grass. Much new machinery is designed for use in a variety of conditions to meet the needs of overseas farmers.

Britain is the world's eighth largest producer of machine tools. Almost all are purchased by the engineering, aerospace, automotive, and metal goods industries. The machine tools sector was badly affected by the recent recession, but has started to recover. Total sales of metal-working machine tools were £1,000 million in 1994, 15 per cent up on the 1993 figure. British manufacturers have made technological advances in probes, sensors, co-ordinate measuring devices, laser melting and the installation of flexible manufacturing systems. Computer numerical-controlled machines account for an increasing proportion of output. The 600 Group is the biggest British machine tool company.

Most sales of textile machinery are to export markets. British innovations include computerised colour matching and weave simulation, friction spinning, high-speed computer-controlled knitting machines and electronic jacquard attachments for weaving looms. Bonas Machine Company of Gateshead, producer of electronic jacquards, exports more than 90 per cent of its £46 million annual turnover, to more than 75 countries.

Britain's mining and tunnelling equipment industry leads in the production of coal-cutting and road-heading (shearing) equipment, hydraulic roof supports, conveying equipment, flameproof transformers, switchgear, and subsurface transport equipment and control systems. J.C. Bamford, Britain's biggest construction equipment manufacturer, is the world's leading manufacturer of backhoe loaders and telescopic handlers. Sales of construction equipment, such as excavators and backhoe loaders, rose in 1994 to £2,000 million.

The mechanical lifting and handling equipment industry produces cranes and transporters, lifting devices, escalators, conveyors, powered industrial trucks and air bridges, as well as electronically-controlled and automatic handling systems. In 1994 sales in this sector were worth £3,200 million. Britain is also a major producer of industrial engines, pumps, valves and compressors, and of pneumatic and hydraulic equipment. Companies like Babcock manufacture steam generators and other heavy equipment for power plants. Despite an overall decline in the castings industry,

some foundries have invested in new melting, moulding and quality control equipment.

Electrical, Electronic and Instrument Engineering

Making extensive use of the most advanced technologies, the electrical engineering industry manufactures products for the electricity supply sector: power plant, cable transformers and switchgear, and lighting, plugs and sockets. The domestic electrical appliance sector is dominated by a few large firms. Britain has the fourth largest electronics industry in the world. Products include computers, communications equipment and a large range of components.

> Scotland's 'Silicon Glen' employs 45,000 people in electronics. The electronics industry in Scotland currently produces 11 per cent of European semiconductors, over 35 per cent of all personal computers sold in Europe and over 50 per cent of its automated cash dispensers. Major overseas companies located in the area include IBM, NEC, Compaq and Digital, which are supplied by a strong indigenous electronic components sector.

The major electronic consumer goods produced are television sets and high-fidelity audio and video equipment. Several leading Japanese companies have established manufacturing bases in Britain. British manufacturers have a worldwide reputation for high-quality goods aimed at the upper end of the market.

Computers

This sector produces an extensive range of systems, central processors and peripheral equipment, from large computers for large-scale data-processing and scientific work to mini- and microcomputers for control and automation systems and for home, educational and office use. Between 1993 and 1994 sales of electronic data processing equipment rose from £10,300 million to £13,700 million.

Britain's biggest computer manufacturer is the largely Japanese-owned ICL. Other companies, such as Psion, have concentrated on developing new products for specialised markets. These include hand-held, pocket-sized computers, increasingly used by company sales forces, and notebook and pen computers.

British firms make computer applications software, and are particularly strong in specialist markets such as artificial intelligence, computer-aided design, mathematical software, geographical information systems and data visualisation. The world's first modem (computer telephone link) for portable computers was designed in Britain. Psion is a pioneer of the 'palmtop' computer, which has the equivalent power of a desktop machine. A Scottish firm, Calluna, has designed an extremely small disc drive for use in notebook-sized computers.

British firms and research organisations, with government support, have been involved in the development and application of the family of 'three-five' semiconductor materials, such as gallium arsenide; these are used in a number of microwave devices and in the production of faster-working computers. Major advances are being made by British firms and academic institutions in the field of 'virtual reality', a three-dimensional computer simulation technique with a host of industrial and other applications. It is being used to design buildings and a range of products, including cars, pharmaceuticals and machine tools.

Communications Equipment

Britain's main communications products are switching and transmission equipment, telephones and terminals. As the telecommunications market has become fully liberalised (see p. 310), there has been a growing demand for equipment and services. GPT, formerly GEC Plessey Telecommunications, is Britain's foremost telecommunications manufacturer; its product range includes PBXs (private branch exchanges), transmissions systems and videoconferencing equipment.

Innovative work is being stimulated by the expansion of cable television and the growth in value added network services. There has been rapid expansion in the market for cellular telephones since the second half of the 1980s.

Transmission equipment and cables for telecommunications and information networks include submarine and high-specification data-carrying cables. Supported by a technically advanced cable industry, BT has led in the development of optical fibre communications systems. It has paved the way for simpler and cheaper optical cables by laying the first non-repeatered cable over 100 km (62 miles) long, and by developing the first all-optical repeater.

More than half of the world's undersea communications cables have been made and laid by STC Submarine Systems, which, with its US and French partners, completed the laying of the first transatlantic optical fibre cable in 1988. Now part of Canada's Northern Telecom, STC is building the first fibre-optic cable linking Canada and Europe. The cable, which is being made in Britain and the United States, will carry up to 30,000 telephone calls simultaneously down each of two pairs of optical fibres.

Britain also has a world lead in the transmission of computerised data along telephone lines for reproduction on television screens.

Another sector of the industry manufactures radio communications equipment, radar, radio and sonar navigational aids for ships and aircraft, thermal imaging systems, alarms and signalling equipment, public broadcasting equipment and other capital goods. Radar was invented in Britain and British firms are still in the forefront of technological advances. Racal Avionics' X-band radar for aircraft ground movement control is in use at airports in several overseas countries. Solid-state secondary surveillance radar, manufactured by Cossor Electronics, is being supplied to 50 overseas civil aviation operators. Cable and Wireless's submarine cable-laying robot 'CIRRUS', which can work at depths of up to 1 km (3,280 ft), is controlled entirely by a computer on its mother ship.

Medical and Other Electronic Equipment

A range of electronic measurement and test equipment is made in Britain, as well as analytical instruments, process control equipment, and numerical control and indication equipment for use in machine tools. Companies such as GEC and Oxford Instruments produce electronic medical equipment, including ultrasound scanners, electromyography systems and patient monitoring systems for intensive and coronary care and other uses. Britain pioneered magnetic resonance imaging.

The indigenous electronics components industry is supplemented by subsidiaries of leading overseas companies. An area of rapid change in which Britain is particularly strong is the manufacture of advanced components, such as integrated circuits.

The instrument engineering industry makes measuring, photographic, cinematographic and reprographic equipment; watches, clocks and other timing devices; and medical and surgical instruments. Total sales of this sector amounted to £5,200 million in 1994.

Overseas sales of scientific and photographic equipment were worth £5,400 million in 1994.

Motor Vehicles

Car output is dominated by seven groups, accounting for 99 per cent of the total: Rover (which became a subsidiary of BMW in 1994), Ford (including Jaguar), Vauxhall, Peugeot-Talbot, Honda, Nissan and Toyota. The remainder is in the hands of smaller, specialist producers such as Rolls-Royce, whose cars are renowned for their quality and durability. Rover's production includes the highly successful Land Rover four-wheel drive vehicles and a full range of family cars. Ford has announced that it is to concentrate its world diesel engine production for medium-sized cars and light commercial vehicles at its Dagenham (Essex) plant.

A period of major change has accompanied the arrival of the three major Japanese manufacturers — Nissan, Toyota and Honda — which have invested heavily and introduced new management techniques and production methods. The established motor vehicle manufacturers and components suppliers are restructuring as a result.

> Car production has recovered strongly following the recession: in 1994 nearly 1.5 million cars were manufactured, the highest figure for 20 years, due in large part to a strong export performance. A total of 619,000 passenger cars were exported in 1994, almost three times as many as in 1988.

The motor components industry consists of up to 4,000 companies, including large conglomerates such as Lucas, GKN and Bosch, and is ranked as one of Britain's major industries. Lucas has signed a £1,000 million contract with Volkswagen to supply diesel electronic fuel injection systems.

Shipbuilding and Marine Engineering

Order books of British merchant shipbuilders for new building were estimated to be worth £400 million at the end of 1994; merchant ship repairers had a turnover of £150 million in 1994. The marine equipment industry is a major contributor to the shipbuilding industry, as equipment installed in a ship's hull accounts for about 50 per cent of its total cost. Some 800 firms offer a complete range of products, from diving equipment to sophisticated navigational systems, 75 per cent of which is exported.

More than two decades of oil and gas exploitation in the North Sea have generated a major offshore industry (see p. 256). Shipbuilders and fabricators build floating production units and semi-submersible units for drilling, production and emergency/maintenance support, drill ships, jack-up rigs, modules and offshore loading systems. UIE Scotland, Highlands Fabricators, John Brown and McDermott Scotland are among the larger manufacturers and designers.

Several thousand firms supply other products needed by the offshore industry—such as diving equipment and helicopters—as well as services, including consultancy, design, project management, and R & D to the offshore industry. Their experience of North Sea projects has enabled them to establish themselves in oil and gas markets throughout the world.

Aerospace

Britain's aerospace industry is the third largest in the Western world, after the United States and France. Only nine firms employ 2,500 people or more and two-thirds of the 540 core aerospace companies have fewer than 50 employees. Around 200 companies belong to the Society of British Aerospace Companies, employing over 130,000 people. Total sales of the industry amounted to £12,000 million in 1994 with exports contributing £7,500 million. Aircraft and parts account for around two-fifths of overseas sales, with engines and parts, missiles and aerospace equipment (including satellite equipment) making up the rest.

The impact of recession on the civil aerospace market and reductions in defence orders following the ending of the Cold War, accompanied by fierce international competition in the defence products market, have led to further rationalisation and consolidation in the aerospace industry. Collaborative development of civil and military aircraft and engines, as well as aviation equipment and satellites, is increasing to save on the costs of long-term programmes.

The industry's activities cover designing and constructing airframes, aero-engines, guided weapons, simulators and space satellites, flight controls including 'fly-by-wire' and 'fly-by-light' equipment (see p. 318), avionics and complex components, with their associated services. In order to improve fuel economy, engine and airframe manufacturers use lighter materials such as titanium and carbon-fibre composites (see p. 237), combined with advanced avionics and improved aerodynamic techniques.

Civil Aircraft

As one of the leading British exporters of manufactured goods, British Aerospace (BAe) produces both civil and military

aircraft, as well as guided weapons and aircraft components.

BAe has a 20 per cent share of the European consortium Airbus Industrie, which outsold market leader Boeing in 1994. BAe designs and supplies the wings for the whole family of Airbus airliners, from the short- to medium-haul A320 series (the first civil airliner to use fly-by-wire controls— see p. 318) to the large long-range four-engined A340.

With Aerospatiale of France and Italy's Alenia, BAe has formed a new regional aircraft alliance which jointly markets turboprops and jet aircraft with between 29 and 115 seats; these include BAe's Avro RJ family of regional 'quiet jet' airliners and the 29-seat Jetstream 41 turboprop airliner.

Short Brothers of Belfast (now Canadian-owned) is engaged in the design and production of major civil aircraft sub-assemblies, advanced nacelles (engine casings) and components for aerospace manufacturers as well as in the provision of aviation support services. It designs and builds the wings for the Fokker 100 and 70 jetliners and is a partner in manufacturing the 50-seat Canadair Regional Jet airliner; the Learjet 45, a small business jet aircraft; and the Bombardier Global Express long-range business jet. Pilatus Britten-Norman manufactures the Islander light utility aircraft, which has had sales in over 100 countries.

Military Aircraft and Missiles

British Aerospace is one of the world's top defence companies, with more than four-fifths of its military production having been exported in 1994. The Harrier is a unique vertical/short take-off and landing (V/STOL) military combat aircraft. BAe also produces the Hawk fast-jet trainer and, with McDonnell Douglas, the Goshawk T45 carrier jet trainer. It has a 33 per cent share in the development of the Eurofighter 2000, which had its maiden flight in 1994. This is a European collaborative programme involving companies from Britain, Germany, Italy and Spain.

The Tornado combat aircraft is built by a company set up jointly by BAe, Alenia and Daimler-Benz Aerospace. A £5,000 million order for 48 Tornado bombers for Saudi Arabia was confirmed in 1993, making it one of Britain's biggest ever export deals. Together with Alenia, Daimler-Benz and Aerospatiale, BAe has formed a new company, a military subsidiary of Airbus Industrie, to manage the Future Large Aircraft military transport programme. The United States Air Force has chosen Slingsby Aviation's T67 Firefly training aircraft as its new basic trainer and 113 aircraft are being built. Slingsby also designs and makes composite components for the aviation and other industries.

BAe and Shorts are major suppliers of tactical guided weapon systems for use on land, at sea and in the air.

Helicopters

Westland Helicopters (now part of the GKN group) manufactures the Sea King, Lynx and Apache military helicopters, and, in partnership with Agusta of Italy, the multi-role EH101 medium-lift helicopter. Over 1,000 Westland helicopters are in service in 19 countries. Orders currently being fulfilled include ones for the Royal Navy (for the EH101), Royal Air Force (EH101 and Sea King), and the British Army (Apache) and customers from Brazil (Lynx), Norway (Sea King) and Italy (EH101). Major Sea King upgrading programmes are being undertaken for Australia, Belgium and Norway.

Aero-engines

Rolls-Royce is one of the world's three prime manufacturers of aero-engines, with a turnover in 1994 of nearly £2,000 million for its aerospace division. The company's civil engine group makes engines for airliners and regional, executive and corporate jets. Over 50,000 Rolls-Royce engines are in service with more than 300 airlines in over 100 countries. More than 80 per cent of Boeing 757 operators have selected RB211-535 engines.

The company's latest large engine, the Trent, powers the new generation of wide-body twin-engined airliners, such as Boeing's 777 and the Airbus A330. The Trent 800, which has run at over 100,000 lb thrust, is the most powerful engine ever certificated.

Rolls-Royce is a partner in the five-nation International Aero Engine consortium, which manufactures the low-emission V2500 aero-engine, now in service on the Airbus A320 and A321 as well as the McDonnell Douglas MD90.

The military engine group of Rolls-Royce produces engines for both aircraft and helicopters, and is a partner in the EJ200 engine project for the Eurofighter 2000.

The company also manufactures gas turbines for power generation, for oil and gas pumping and marine propulsion. Turnover of Rolls-Royce's industrial power wing amounted to £1,200 million in 1994, of which 70 per cent came from overseas sales.

Aviation Equipment

Around one-third of the aerospace industry is devoted to designing and manufacturing aviation equipment. British firms have made significant technological advances. Manufacturers like Dowty, GEC-Marconi, Lucas, Smiths Industries, Racal, Normalair-Garrett and BAe provide equipment and systems for engines and aircraft propellers, navigation and landing systems, engine and flight controls, environmental controls and oxygen breathing and regulation systems, electrical generation, mechanical and hydraulic power systems, cabin furnishings, flight-deck controls and information displays. GEC-Marconi is the world's largest manufacturer of head-up displays (HUDs).

British firms have made important advances in developing ejection seats, firefighting equipment and flight simulators, as well as fly-by-wire and fly-by-light technology, where control surfaces are moved by means of automatic electronic signalling and fibre optics respectively, rather than by mechanical means. GEC supplies the fly-by-wire system for the Boeing 777. Britain's aerospace companies provide radar and air traffic control equipment and ground power supplies to airports and airlines worldwide.

Space Equipment and Services

Over 400 companies employing almost 6,500 people are engaged in industrial space activities. Annual turnover in 1993 exceeded £700 million. The industry is strong in the development and manufacture of civil and military communications satellites and associated Earth stations and ground infrastructure equipment. In the field of Earth observation, it plays a leading role in manufacturing platforms, space radar and meteorological satellite hardware, and in the exploitation of space data imaging products. Through its participation in the Intelsat, Inmarsat, Eutelsat and Astra European space projects, Britain has become Europe's biggest user of space. The British Government is the fourth largest contributor to the European Space Agency (ESA); in 1993 its civil and military space budget was in excess of £300 million.

The largest British space company is Matra Marconi Space UK, which, with its French partner, is one of the world's leading space companies. Its current major activities include manufacture of the Skynet 4 military communications satellites, payloads for the Koreasat and Inmarsat 3 communications spacecraft and the European Polar Platform and space radar systems. The company has recently completed work on the SOHO scientific satellite instrumentation.

The National Remote Sensing Centre has a major role in developing the market for Earth observation data, an area in which other British firms—notably Logica, Vega, Science Systems and Cray—have major interests. SERCO is Europe's biggest supplier of technical services in space.

GEC-Marconi produces inertial guidance systems for Ariane 4 as well as electronics components; Pilkington dominates the world market in solar array cover glasses.

Food and Drink

Britain has a large food and drink manufacturing industry, which has accounted for a growing proportion of total domestic food supply in recent decades. In the last few years, it has increased productivity and undergone restructuring, partly in order to take advantage of the single European market. Approximately 500,000 people are employed in the industry.

Frozen and convenience foods, such as ready-prepared meals, salads and pasta, together with yoghurts, dairy desserts and 'instant snacks', have formed some of the fastest-growing sectors of the food market in recent years. Companies have introduced new low-fat and fat-free products such as spreads and ice creams to meet growing consumer demand. There has also been a rise in sales of products for vegetarians (soya-based foods, for instance).

British firms are at the forefront of innovation in the food industry. They support research and development programmes to ensure that products and production methods meet the highest safety standards and the expectations of consumers. New foods, including 'healthy' alternatives, and better packaging are constantly being developed.

Around one-half of liquid milk in Britain is distributed through a doorstep delivery system employing about 26,000 people; the proportion is, however, declining. Household milk consumption per head—1.9 litres (3.4 pints) a week—is among the highest in the world. Consumption of skimmed and semi-skimmed milk continues to rise as people seek to reduce the fat content in their diet.

Milk for manufacturing purposes goes principally into butter, cheese, condensed milk, dried whole and skimmed milk powder, cream and other products like yoghurt. The British dairy industry accounted for 58 per cent of butter supplies to the domestic market in 1994 and 74 per cent of cheese supplies. Butter exports in 1994 were worth £120 million. The other main exports are skimmed milk powder and whole milk powder, valued at £189 million in total and cheese at £124 million.

About 80 per cent of bread is manufactured in large bakeries; the total bread market is valued at £2,900 million a year. A significant increase in the varieties available, greater awareness of the nutritional value of bread and the growth of the sandwich market have helped stabilise consumption in the last few years. Sales of ready-made sandwiches are now worth £1,000 million a year. Exports of biscuits were valued at £240 million in 1994 and those of chocolate and sugar confectionery at £530 million.

Of major significance among the alcoholic drinks produced in Britain is Scotch whisky, which is one of Britain's top export earners. There are 110 distilleries in Scotland, where the best known brands of blended Scotch whisky, such as J & B, Johnnie Walker, Famous Grouse, Bell's and Teacher's, are made from the products of single malt and single grain whisky distilleries. Almost 90 per cent of Scotch whisky production is exported, to over 200 countries. The value of whisky exports was £2,200 million in 1994, Europe taking 35 per cent and the United States 13 per cent by volume.

In 1994 purchases of beer in Britain reached £13,800 million, about 3 per cent of consumers' expenditure. The brewing industry has four major national brewery groups—Scottish & Newcastle, Bass, Whitbread and Carlsberg-Tetley—and about 400 regional and local brewers. British malt, which is made almost entirely from home-grown barley, is used by brewers throughout the world. Demand for traditional cask-conditioned ales ('real ale') continues to rise, while lager now accounts for just over half of all beer sales. In recent years there has been a shift towards stronger bottled beers, a significant proportion of which are imported. Cider is made primarily in south-west England, Gloucester, Hereford and Worcester.

Some 430 vineyards and 150 wineries in Britain (mainly in southern England) produce an average of 1.8 million litres of wine a year.

The soft drinks industry, which has an annual turnover of £6,000 million, produces carbonated drinks, concentrates, fruit juices, and natural mineral and bottled waters. A highly competitive industry, it is the fastest growing sector of the grocery trade, introducing many innovative products.

Tobacco

The British tobacco industry manufactures nearly all cigarettes and tobacco goods sold in Britain. Almost all domestic output is provided by three major manufacturers (Imperial Tobacco, Gallaher and Carreras Rothmans). The industry specialises in the production of high-quality cigarettes made from flue-cured tobacco and achieves

significant exports. Europe, the Middle East and Africa are important markets.

Textiles and Clothing

These products make a substantial contribution to the British economy in terms of employment, exports and turnover. Together with the footwear and leather industries, they employ around 420,000 people, representing 10 per cent of manufacturing employment. For textiles, there is a high degree of regional concentration, particularly in North West England, West Yorkshire (mainly wool), the East Midlands (knitwear), Scotland and Northern Ireland. The clothing industry is scattered throughout Britain, with significant concentrations in Manchester, Leicester and London. The principal products are spun yarns, woven and knitted fabrics, apparel, industrial and household textiles, and carpets based chiefly on wool, cotton and synthetic fibres. Exports of textiles, clothing and footwear totalled more than £6,000 million in 1994.

The textile and clothing industry has around 13,000 firms, comprising a few large multi-process companies and two of the world's largest firms—Coats Viyella and Courtaulds Textiles—as well as a large number of small and medium-sized firms.

The international Multi-Fibre Arrangement (MFA—see p. 174) has allowed a measure of restraint on imports into the European Union from low-cost countries; however, the MFA is being phased out over ten years to the year 2005. Increased investment in new machinery and greater attention to design, training and marketing have helped the industry to raise competitiveness. New technologies, largely designed to improve response times and give greater flexibility in production, are being used throughout the industry.

Britain's wool textile industry is one of the most important in the world. West Yorkshire is the main producing area, but Scotland is also famous as a specialist producer of high-quality yarns and tweeds. Raw wool is scoured and cleaned in Britain in preparation for woollen and worsted spinning and weaving (worsted is fine wool fabric often used for making suits). British mills also process rare fibres such as cashmere and angora. Sales of the wool textile industry amounted to £1,300 million in 1994.

Low-cost competition has cut progressively into British markets for cotton and allied products. Production includes yarn and fabrics of cotton, synthetic fibres and cotton-synthetic mixes, with large-scale dyeing and printing of cotton and synthetic fibre fabric. The linen industry is centred in Northern Ireland.

The high quality and variety of design make Britain one of the world's leading producers of woven carpets. Over half the value of carpet and rug output is made up of tufted carpets. Woven carpets, mainly Axminster, account for most of the remaining sales. There is a higher wool content in woven types, although in these, too, considerable use is being made of synthetic fibres.

Industrial textiles account for an increasing proportion of textile industry output, covering products such as conveyor belting and geotextiles used in civil engineering. Many of these are non-woven. Synthetic polypropylene yarn is used in the manufacture of carpet backing and ropes, and woven into fabrics for a wide range of applications in the packaging, upholstery, building and motor vehicle industries.

The clothing industry is more labour intensive than textiles, with about 7,700 companies. While a broad range of clothing is imported from Europe and Asia, British industry supplies about one-half of domestic demand. Exports have risen since the British fashion designer industry regained prominence during the 1980s and traditional British tailoring enables branded clothing companies such as Burberry's to compete overseas. The hosiery and knitwear industry comprises about 1,500 companies, mainly in the east Midlands and Scotland.

Paper, Printing and Publishing

There are 99 paper and board mills employing 25,000 people. Among the largest British groups are Shotton, St Regis and Bridgewater. Production has been concentrated in large-scale units to enable the industry to compete more effectively within the single European market. Between 1985 and 1994 output increased by 57 per cent. Over half the industry is made up of forestry product companies from Scandinavia, North America, Australia and elsewhere. There has been a significant trend towards waste-based packaging grades. Usage of recycled waste paper is increasing and research is helping to extend it. In 1994 the total amount of waste paper used in British newspapers accounted for four-fifths of newsprint produced. Waste paper provides over half of the industry's fibre needs.

Employment in the paper products, printing and publishing industries is 450,000. Much printing and publishing employment and output is in firms based in south-east England. Mergers have led to the formation of large groups in newspaper, magazine and book publishing. Reed Elsevier, one of the world's biggest publishing businesses, resulted from a merger between Reed International and the Dutch company Elsevier in 1993. More than £2,800 million worth of books were sold in Britain in 1994. The book-publishing industry is a major exporter, selling one-third of production in overseas markets. Security printers (of, for example, banknotes and postage stamps) are also important exporters, the major company being De La Rue.

Construction

Annual output of the construction industry is around £50,000 million. Most construction work is done by private firms, 98 per cent of which employ fewer than 25 people. While only 86 out of a total of 195,000 firms employ more than 600 people directly, these companies undertake about 20 per cent of all construction in Britain. Some larger firms own quarries and factories for materials manufacture, and sophisticated plant. Some undertake responsibility for all stages of projects from initial design to final construction.

Efficiency and productivity in construction have benefited from greater off-site fabrication of standardised components and from computerised techniques such as electronic load safety measures for cranes, distance measuring equipment, computerised stock ordering and job costing, and computer-aided design.

The Department of the Environment assists British construction and building products and materials firms to secure overseas contracts by, for instance, arranging inward and outward trade missions.

Building Materials and Products

A vast range of products is used in the construction process, from glass and bricks to tiles and bathroom fittings. These materials are estimated to make up around 40 per cent of the value of construction output. In 1994 sales of construction materials were worth about £30,000 million, with exports amounting to £3,000 million.

Most crushed rock, sand and gravel that is quarried by the aggregates industry is used in construction. The brick industry, one of Britain's oldest, is regarded as the world's most technically advanced: in the late 1980s over £300 million was invested in improving production. Portland cement, a 19th-century British innovation, is the most widely used chemical compound in the world.

Britain is also a world leader in the manufacture of glass used in windows, doors and cladding. Pilkington developed the float process for manufacturing distortion-free flat glass (see p. 238), which is licensed throughout the world. Substantially more energy efficient, flat glass is used to allow more light into buildings and to provide insulation against heat loss in winter. The manufacture and supply of windows and doors is carried out by a large number of companies operating in one of three distinct product sectors—timber, metal (aluminium and steel) and UPVC.

Project Procurement, Management and Financing

The common basis of procurement is a lump-sum contract with provision for variation. The largest projects are often carried out under the direction of construction managers or management contractors. Clients generally employ architects, project managers or civil engineers to advise on the feasibility of projects, draw up plans, and inspect and supervise the construction work.

Private and public sector projects are managed in a variety of ways. Most clients invite construction firms to bid for work by competitive tender, having used the design services of a consultant. The successful contractor will then undertake on-site work with a number of specialist sub-contractors. Alternative methods of contracting are becoming more common: for example, contracts might include subsequent provision of building maintenance or a comprehensive 'design-and-build' service, where a single company accepts responsibility for every stage of a project.

Under the Government's Private Finance Initiative announced in 1992 (see p. 158), private sector companies are becoming involved in large-scale public infrastructure projects, including building the Ashford International Passenger Station and the Heathrow Express line. In January 1995 the Government issued invitations to tender for four 'DBFO' ('Design, Build, Finance and Operate') road contracts.

The Government provides substantial work for the construction industry. Recently, several projects have been built and paid for by private consortia, which then charge the public for their use for a fixed period of time before transferring ownership back to the public sector; these are known as 'BOOT' ('Build, Own, Operate and Transfer') schemes. Two examples are the toll bridge over the River Thames at Dartford, Kent (see p. 295) and the second River Severn bridge under construction (see p. 295).

Major Construction Projects in Britain

The most important recent construction project is the Channel Tunnel, the largest single civil engineering project ever undertaken in Europe (see p. 302).

Completed in 1993, its estimated cost was £10,000 million. Building work was carried out by a consortium of ten French and British contractors working together as Transmanche Link (TML). The tunnel is nearly 50 km (31 miles) long and is 70 m (230ft) below sea level at its deepest. Associated projects included a new international station at Waterloo in London and an international terminal at Folkestone. A new international passenger station is being built at Ashford in Kent (see p. 302).

Other major building projects in hand or recently completed are the M25 motorway widening scheme, the M74 in Scotland, the Severn Estuary crossing, the extensive development in London's Docklands, and the Sizewell B nuclear power station in Suffolk. Both Stansted and Manchester airports have been substantially redeveloped. There has also been large-scale redevelopment of sports stadiums, including Twickenham and Murrayfield (in Edinburgh) rugby grounds, and Manchester United and Arsenal football grounds. A new £16 million football stadium has been built to house Middlesbrough football club. Major redevelopment work has begun at the Wimbledon lawn tennis complex, which will lead to the construction of new courts.

Housing

During 1994 construction of 200,000 dwellings was started in Great Britain, 8 per cent more than in 1993. Starts by private enterprise were 157,000, by housing associations 41,000 and in the public sector 1,400. Around 181,000 dwellings were completed: 144,000 by the private sector, 34,000 by housing associations and 1,900 by the public sector. The total value of new housing orders was £7,100 million.

Building Regulations

The Department of the Environment's building regulations prescribe minimum standards of construction in England and Wales. Administered and enforced by local government, the regulations apply to new building, the installation or replacement of fittings, alterations and extensions to existing buildings and to certain changes of use of existing buildings. Similar controls apply in Scotland and Northern Ireland. An alternative to local authority building control was introduced in 1984, involving private certification of compliance with building regulations. The British Standards Institution is making Britain's contribution to the drafting of European standards, which are increasingly replacing national construction standards.

Research and Advisory Services

The Building Research Establishment, an executive agency of the Government, provides advice and research services to the Government on the design, construction and performance of buildings, together with the health and safety of people in and around buildings. Its areas of expertise include prevention and control of fires and protection of the environment. It has a key role in developing European codes and standards, and has strong links with a variety of international organisations. Major construction and materials firms, universities, colleges and research associations, as well as the British Board of Agrément, carry out research and provide advisory services. The Building Centre supplies exhibition and information services on materials, products, techniques and building services.

Overseas Contracting and Consultancy

British companies are engaged in many major projects throughout the world and have been in the forefront of innovative methods of management contracting and construction management. They are increasingly engaged in developing privately-financed projects. Contractors and consultants undertake the supervision and all or part of the construction of a project. Consultants are involved in the planning, design and supervision of construction projects. British contractors and consultants have a reputation for integrity and independence.

British contractors are currently undertaking, or have recently completed, work in 134 overseas countries and have a permanent presence in 97 of them. In 1994 they won new international business valued at £3,800 million, 14 per cent more than in 1993, with the main increases reported in the European Union, the Middle East and Hong Kong; about 30 per cent of all new contracts came from North America. Important international contracts won in 1994–95 included:

- various joint ventures connected with the new Hong Kong airport—terminal buildings, runways and roads as well as track work for the airport railway;

- a power station in Indonesia;

- city development contracts in Leipzig and Halle; and

- a power project in Oman.

British engineering consultants are engaged in projects in 130 countries, having offices in most of those countries. In 1994 members of the Association of Consulting Engineers were engaged in new work overseas valued at £20,000 million. The capital value of projects under way at the end of 1994 was £64,000 million. British consulting engineers had estimated gross earnings in 1994 of £630 million from overseas commissions. The three largest categories of work covered roads, bridges and tunnels; thermal power stations; and water supply. The largest markets were the Far East, Africa, India and the Middle East. Major international projects include:

- a gas plant in Norway;

- hydroelectric works in Pakistan;

- roads and bridges in China;

- a thermal power station in Saudi Arabia; and

- housing and infrastructure works in Russia.

Further Reading

Aerospace Industry. Aspects of Britain series, HMSO, 1993.
Overseas Trade. Aspects of Britain series, HMSO, 1994.

17 Energy and Natural Resources

Energy production is a vital part of Britain's economy. It directly employs about 300,000 people—5.5 per cent of industrial employees. Offshore oil and gas also provide employment for 250,000 in support industries. The energy sector accounts for 5 per cent of gross domestic product (GDP), 10 per cent of total investment, 42 per cent of industrial investment, and 10 per cent of annual business expenditure on research and development. It also includes three of Britain's ten largest companies—Shell, BP and British Gas. Privatisation and liberalisation have increased the number of firms operating in the energy market. Cumulative production of oil (1,800 million tonnes since 1975) is about one-fifth of maximum estimated recoverable reserves. The value of non-fuel minerals output approached £2,000 million in 1993.

Energy Resources

Britain has the largest energy resources of any country in the European Union (EU) and is a major world producer of oil and natural gas—known as primary sources. The other main primary sources are coal, nuclear power and some water power; secondary sources (derived from primary sources) are electricity, coke and smokeless fuels, and petroleum products.

In 1994 Britain was a net exporter of fuels—39 million tonnes of oil equivalent—representing a surplus of £3,300 million, more than £1,900 million higher than in 1993.

Coal still supplies a significant, but declining, proportion of the country's primary energy needs—23.9 per cent of total home consumption in 1994. Nuclear power provided about 26 per cent of electricity supplied by the British electricity companies in 1994.

Ownership and Extraction

With the major exceptions of gold, silver, oil and natural gas (owned by the Crown), and most coal, minerals in Great Britain are mainly privately owned. In Northern Ireland gold and silver are owned by the Crown, while rights to exploit petroleum and other minerals (except 'common substances', ncluding sand and gravel, and crushed ock) are vested in the Department of conomic Development.

On the United Kingdom Continental Shelf UKCS; see map, p. 257) the right to work ll minerals except coal is vested in the rown. Following the privatisation of British oal, the exclusive right to extract coal, or icense others to do so, both on land in Great 3ritain and under the sea, is now vested in he Coal Authority. Normally, ownership of ninerals belongs to the owner of the land surface, but in some areas, particularly those with a long history of mining, these rights ave become separated. Mining and quarrying are usually carried out by privately wned companies.

ENERGY POLICY

The President of the Board of Trade, who heads the Department of Trade and Industry (DTI), is responsible for most energy matters in Great Britain. However, the Secretary of State for the Environment is responsible for energy conservation and efficiency matters. Electricity in Scotland is under the Secretary of State for Scotland, who also has a direct interest in a wide range of energy concerns. The Secretary of State for Northern Ireland is responsible for all energy matters there.

The aim of the Government's energy policy is to ensure secure, diverse and sustainable supplies of energy in the forms that people and businesses want, and at competitive prices. Health, safety and environmental policies, as well as EU and other international commitments, have also to be borne in mind.

Key elements are to:

- encourage competition among producers and choice for consumers, and maintain a legal and regulatory framework to enable markets to work well;

- ensure service in a commercial environment, with customers paying the full cost of energy resources they consume;

- ensure that the discipline of the capital markets is applied to state-owned industries by privatising them where possible;

- have regard to the impact of the energy sector on the environment, including taking measures to meet international commitments;

- promote energy efficiency; and

- promote wider share ownership.

The independent regulators' main role is to encourage the development of competition and to protect the interests of consumers by administering price controls and enforcing standards of service in remaining areas of monopoly.

Privatisation

British Gas, Britoil, Enterprise Oil, and the non-nuclear electricity supply industry in Britain are in the private sector. The Coal Industry Act 1994 has enabled privatisation of the coal industry to take place. The Government proposes to privatise Britain's two nuclear generating companies, though leaving the older reactors in public ownership (see p. 266).

Liberalisation

Liberalisation—the introduction of competition into markets—increases incentives to minimise costs, to produce the quality and range of services customers demand, to innovate, and to price in line with costs. The Government believes that competition will give consumers the freedom to choose which company will supply them. Liberalisation of the gas and electricity markets, and suppliers' commitment to the principles of the Citizen's Charter, open the way to significant improvements in the services offered. Customers are to be compensated when standards set by the regulators are not met.

International Commitments

Britain is actively engaged in international collaboration on energy questions, notably through its membership of the EU and of the International Energy Agency (IEA: an autonomous part of the Organisation for Economic Co-operation and Development,

Table 17.1: Inland Energy Consumption (in terms of primary sources)[a]

million tonnes oil equivalent

	1984	1990	1991	1992	1993	1994
Oil	85.5	78.3	77.8	78.3	78.9	77.9
Coal	48.7	67.4	67.6	63.6	55.6	52.2
Natural gas	48.2	50.6	54.1	55.0	62.6	65.2
Nuclear energy	14.5	16.3	17.4	18.5	21.5	21.2
Hydro-electric power	0.4	0.4	0.4	0.5	0.4	0.5
Net imports of electricity	–	1.0	1.4	1.4	1.4	1.5
Total	197.2	214.1	218.7	217.2	220.4	218.5

Source: Department of Trade and Industry

[a]Adjustments in the figures for recent years are the result of methodological review.

Note: Differences between totals and the sums of their component parts are due to rounding.

with 23 member countries). The European Energy Charter Treaty, signed in 1994, is the first major economic agreement between the former Soviet Union, as well as central and Eastern Europe, and the West, and the first international agreement enshrining trade in energy products in international law.

Britain supports the continuing development of the single market in energy in the EU, particularly through trans-European networks and the removal of obstacles to trade in the EU's gas and electricity markets.

Energy Report

The purpose of the Government's second annual energy report, published in April 1995 and with a range of information about markets, prices, regulation and the environment, is to help competitive markets to develop by setting out the key elements of energy policy.

An independent energy panel advises on the preparation of the report. Energy suppliers and users serve on the panel.

ENERGY CONSUMPTION

During 1983–94, when Britain's GDP rose by about 29 per cent, final energy consumption on an 'energy supplied' basis increased by only 12 per cent. Energy consumption by final users in 1994 amounted to 152.1 million tonnes of oil equivalent[1] on an 'energy supplied' basis, of which transport consumed 33 per cent, industrial users 25 per cent,

domestic users 29 per cent, and commerce, agriculture and public services 13 per cent.

ENERGY EFFICIENCY

Britain's consumers spend about £53,000 million a year on energy. The Energy Efficiency Office (EEO), part of the Department of the Environment, estimates that 20 per cent—or £10,600 million—could be saved cost effectively, both through improved management and through energy efficiency investment, usually on plant replacement. Energy efficiency improvements offer a fast, cost-effective means of reducing carbon dioxide (CO_2) emissions. The EEO encourages investment in energy efficiency improvements through various programmes (see below). Its budget for 1995–96 has been increased to £135 million.

Combined Heat and Power

Combined Heat and Power (CHP) is an energy-efficient technology which puts heat which would otherwise be wasted to use. CHP can increase overall efficiency to as much as 70–90 per cent, compared with 30–50 per cent for conventional electricity generation. Apart from saving money, this benefits the environment by reducing emissions of greenhouse gases, including CO_2. In spring 1995 total installed capacity of CHP in Britain was approximately 3,200 megawatts (MW) on 1,200 sites.[2]

[1]1 tonne of oil equivalent = 41.868 gigajoules.

[2]1 MW = 1,000 Kilowatts (kW).

Energy Efficiency Schemes

The Home Energy Efficiency Scheme gives advice and grants to householders on low incomes or over the age of 60 for draught-proofing and loft and water tank insulation. Government spending on the programme, £77 million in 1994–95, is to grow to about £100 million during 1995–96. The Small Company Environmental and Energy Management Assistance Scheme (SCEEMAS) has been devised primarily to support the EU eco management and audit scheme (see p. 369) in Britain. SCEEMAS provides grants to help small manufacturing and industrial organisations, with up to 250 employees worldwide, obtain consultancy advice in establishing an environmental management system. Grants of up to 50 per cent will be paid towards the cost of consultancy fees.

The Energy Design Advice Scheme (EDAS), funded by the DTI, aims to improve the energy and environmental performance of the building stock. The EDAS makes low-energy building design expertise more accessible for the energy efficiency and restoration of buildings.

The EEO's initiative for business and the public sector, the Making a Corporate Commitment campaign, underlines the need for senior management to commit itself to raise the profile of energy efficiency within its organisation and provides a focus for action. Over 1,800 organisations have joined the campaign to date.

Publicity campaigns (the latest being 'Wasting Energy Costs the Earth'), which include extensive media coverage, tell householders how they can combat global warming by improving the energy efficiency of their homes.

The Standard Assessment Procedure (SAP) for home energy rating has been incorporated into the revised building regulations for England and Wales. From July 1995, all new dwellings, including conversions, submitted for building control will be required to have a SAP rating.

The Energy Saving Trust is an independent organisation set up by the Government, British Gas and the electricity companies to develop new programmes to promote the efficient use of energy. It is currently preparing proposals for the Government's consideration.

OIL AND GAS

Britain has substantial oil and gas reserves offshore on the UKCS. Recent trends have been the exploitation of smaller reservoirs and an increase in production, with significant discoveries, especially west of Shetland, still to be developed.

In 1994, 40 companies were supplying gas to industrial and commercial consumers. There was record gas production for the fifth year in a row, the highest rate of oil production for nearly ten years and record numbers of development wells being drilled on the UKCS.

All plans for the development of oil and gas fields must be approved by the Government. It has granted exploration and production licences as a result of 15 offshore licensing rounds since 1964. By the end of 1994, 5,506 wells had been or were being drilled in the UKCS: 2,595 development wells, 1,818 exploration wells and 1,093 appraisal wells.

Oil and Gas Licensing

The 15th round, which closed in July 1994, requested applications for 81 blocks in the established areas of the central and southern North Sea. Awards for 29 of the blocks were quickly made. For the 16th round nominations for inclusion were received from 29 companies for a total of 328 blocks; 164 were offered. A number are in environmentally sensitive areas. If awarded, there will be strict licence conditions to ensure that there are no adverse effects on wildlife or habitat. In March 1995, 691 blocks were nominated for inclusion in the 17th round.

Offshore Supplies

The role of the Oil and Gas Projects and Supplies Office (OSO) of the DTI is to assist

Britain's oil and gas supplies industry to win an increasing share of a world market worth over £140,000 million. It provides market information, encourages increased competitiveness, promotes Britain's capabilities and supports British bids. The OSO focuses on markets where British companies have the best opportunities and where government action can increase these opportunities.

All oil companies, their suppliers and the DTI are partners in the Cost Reduction in the New Era Initiative, which has led to a fall of 30 per cent in capital costs since 1992.

Research

The Offshore Energy Technology Board advises the OSO on its offshore technology programme. A number of universities, research institutes and private-sector companies carry out oil-related research. Funding comes from private-sector oil and supplies companies, the OSO, the Marine Technology Directorate Ltd and the Petroleum Science and Technology Institute. The Offshore Technology Park in Aberdeen comprises several research facilities.

Since 1965 the industry has generated trading profits of some £165,000 million, of which £60,000 million have been reinvested in the industry, £77,000 million paid to the Exchequer, and £28,000 million left for disposal by the oil companies. High levels of investment in 1991–93 have produced strong rises in output.

Proceeds from the sale of oil in 1994–95 were up 9.5 per cent on 1993–94; those from the sale of gas were up 7 per cent. Total value of oil and gas produced onshore is estimated at £385 million in 1994, compared with £300 million in 1993.

Economic and Industrial Aspects

In 1994 UKCS oil and gas production accounted for nearly 2 per cent of Britain's gross national product. Total revenue from the sale of oil and gas produced from the UKCS in 1994 is estimated at £9,500 million

and £3,800 million respectively. Taxes and royalty receipts attributable to UKCS oil and gas are estimated at £1,600 million in 1994–95.

Gross capital investment from British sources in the oil and gas extraction industry amounted to some £3,600 million in 1994, compared with £4,700 million in 1993. This was about 16 per cent of British industrial investment and 4 per cent of gross domestic fixed capital formation. Some 27,300 people were employed offshore in September 1994.

Offshore Safety

Offshore health and safety are the responsibility of the Health and Safety Executive (HSE; see p. 195). Government funding for the HSE's Offshore Safety Division reached £35 million in 1994–95.

OIL

For centuries small quantities of oil have been produced in mainland Britain. The first onshore production well was at Hardstoft (Derbyshire) after the First World War. Some 250 onshore wells came into operation in 1939–40, though by the early 1960s they were producing only 150,000 tonnes a year— about 0.3 per cent of refinery output. Britain was almost wholly dependent for its oil supplies on imports. However, the first notable offshore discovery of oil in the UKCS was made in 1969 and the first oil brought ashore in 1975. Output of crude oil and natural gas liquids (NGLs) in Britain in 1994 averaged 2.72 million barrels (about 360,000 tonnes) a day, making Britain the world's eighth largest producer.

North Sea Fields

There were 62 offshore fields producing crude oil at the end of February 1995, and 24 new offshore development projects (nine of them for oil) were approved during 1994.

The fields with the largest cumulative production totals are Forties and Brent. Ninian, Piper, Beryl, Fulmar, Magnus, Statfjord (UK) and Claymore are other high producers. Remaining recoverable reserves of

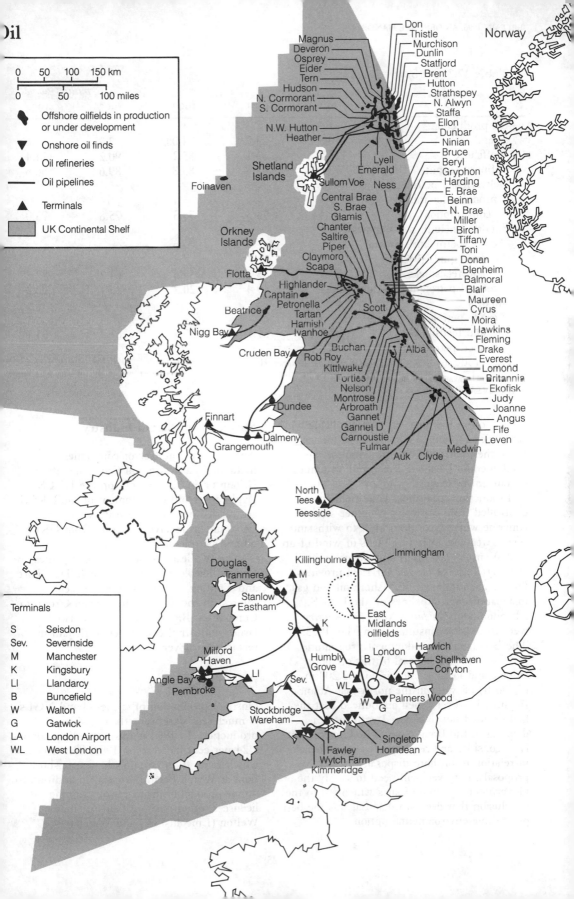

Table 17.2: Oil Statistics

million tonnes

	1984	1991	1992	1993	1994
Oil production:[a]					
land	0.3	3.7	4.0	3.7	4.6
offshore	125.7	83.1	85.2	90.2	114.4
Refinery output	73.2	85.5	85.8	89.6	86.6
Deliveries of petroleum products for inland consumption	81.4	74.5	75.5	75.8	75.0
Exports (including re-exports): crude petroleum, natural gas liquids (NGLs) and feedstocks	75.9	55.1	57.6	64.2	82.2
refined petroleum products	16.4	19.4	20.2	23.1	22.2
Imports: crude petroleum, NGLs and feedstocks	32.3	57.1	57.7	61.7	53.1
refined petroleum products	23.1	10.1	10.6	10.1	10.4

Source: Department of Trade and Industry

[a] Crude oil plus condensates.

UKCS oil in the 'proven' plus 'probable' categories amount to 2,865 million tonnes, while the total remaining potential of the UKCS could be about 7,000 million tonnes on current estimates.

Production from most large fields is controlled from platforms of either steel or concrete which have been built to withstand severe weather, including gusts of wind of up to 260 km/h (160 mph) and waves of 30 m (100 ft). The Petroleum Act 1987 provides for the abandonment of offshore oil and gas installations and pipelines on the UKCS. Abandonment *Guidance Notes for Industry* were issued for consultation in May 1995. The Brent Spar abandonment programme provided for the disposal of this offshore storage and loading buoy in over 2,200 m (7,300 ft) of water in the north-east Atlantic. In June, however, Shell announced that they had decided not to proceed with the sea disposal of the Brent Spar. The Government is to consider any requests its owners make in relation to onshore disposal. Further proposals, however, will need to satisfy the Government on those issues which led to the conclusion that deep sea disposal was the best practicable environmental option.

Structure of the Oil Industry

About 250 private sector companies, including many large oil firms, operate in Britain or engage in work on the UKCS. Exploration and development of the UKCS are carried out by the private sector. The Government receives royalties from UKCS oil and petroleum revenue tax.

The two leading British oil companies are British Petroleum (BP) and Shell Transport and Trading, which has a 40 per cent interest in the Royal Dutch/Shell Group of Companies. BP and Shell are the two largest industrial companies in Britain in terms of turnover.

Land-based Fields

Onshore production of crude oil and NGLs is much less significant than offshore production. In 1994 it was 4.6 million tonnes, a 24 per cent increase on 1993, 89 per cent of which came from Britain's largest onshore field at Wytch Farm (Dorset). In addition to minor production from various mining licensees, other onshore fields include Welton (Lincolnshire) and Wareham

(Dorset). Small independent companies play an increasingly prominent role in onshore exploration. At the end of 1994, 158 landward petroleum licences were in force, covering an area of 20,858 sq km (8,050 sq miles).

Refineries

Britain's refinery industry (14 refineries) is one of the most modern and efficient in Europe. In 1994 the refinery sector processed 93.1 million tonnes of crude and process oils (3 per cent down on 1993). About 80 per cent of output (by weight) is in the form of lighter, higher-value products such as gasoline, DERV and jet kerosene. By comparison, the proportion of Western European refinery output accounted for by these higher-value products is about 70 per cent.

Consumption

Deliveries of petroleum products for inland consumption (excluding refinery consumption) in 1994 included 22.8 million tonnes of motor spirit, 12.9 million tonnes of DERV fuel, 7.3 million tonnes of aviation turbine fuel, 7.8 million tonnes of gas oil and 10.8 million tonnes of fuel oils.

Trade

Britain's refinery sector has set new records for exports in each of the three years 1992–94. In 1994, it exported nearly 30 million tonnes of refined petroleum products and NGLs (separated at North Sea terminals), 32 per cent of its output (worth £1,100 million to the balance of payments). Virtually all exports went to Britain's partners in the EU and the IEA, the largest markets being France, the Irish Republic, Italy, the Netherlands and Germany, and, outside the EU, the United States.

Oil Pipelines

Oil pipelines brought ashore about 80 per cent of offshore oil in 1994. Some 2,500 km (1,560 miles) of major submarine pipeline brings oil ashore from the North Sea oilfields. Major crude oil onshore pipelines (from harbours, land terminals or offshore moorings to refineries) include those connecting Grangemouth to Finnart, Cruden Bay to Grangemouth, and Purbeck to Southampton. Onshore pipelines also carry refined products to major marketing areas; for example, a 423-km (263-mile) pipeline runs from Milford Haven to the Midlands and Manchester, while similar pipelines run from Fawley to Wolverhampton and from Lindsey to north London. Chemical pipelines include one from Mossmorran to Grangemouth and another (405 km; 252 miles) from Grangemouth to Stanlow.

GAS

Public supply of manufactured gas in Britain began in the early 19th century in central London. For many years gas was produced from coal, but during the 1960s growing imports of oil brought about production of town gas from oil-based feedstocks. Following the first commercial natural gas discovery in the UKCS in 1965 and the start of offshore gas production in 1967, supplies of offshore natural gas grew rapidly and by 1977 natural gas had replaced town gas in the public supply system in Great Britain.

> Up to the end of 1994 some £15,000 million had been spent on developing natural gas resources on the UKCS and 1,031,876 million cubic metres had been produced. Britain is the world's fifth largest gas producer— after Russia, the United States, Canada, and the Netherlands.

Structure

When it was privatised in 1986, British Gas plc was given a monopoly of supplies to premises taking less than 25,000 therms a year. Contract customers taking more than this were able, in theory, to buy their gas from other suppliers. Since 1988 various steps have been taken to develop competition in gas supply. In 1993 the Government required

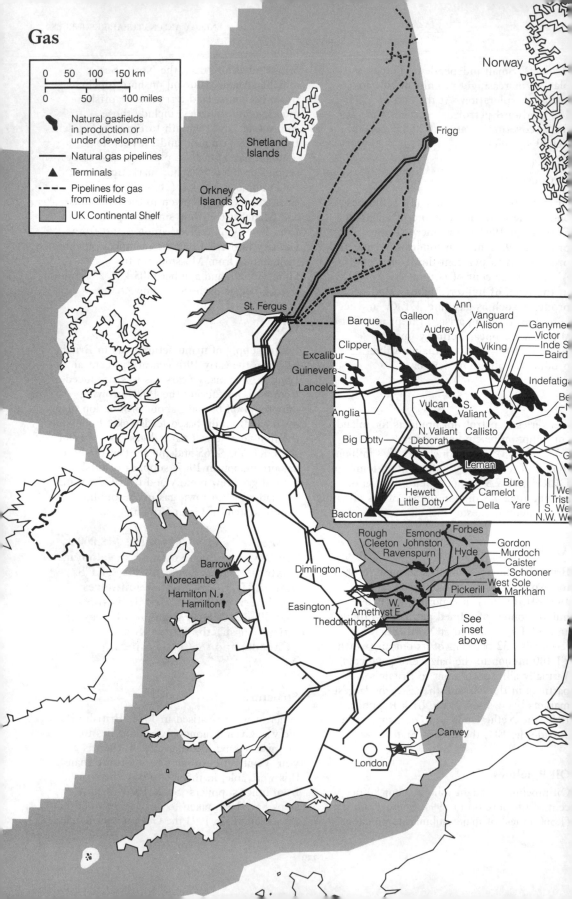

Gas

Natural gasfields in production or under development

Natural gas pipelines

Terminals

Pipelines for gas from oilfields

UK Continental Shelf

0 50 100 150 km
0 50 100 miles

Norway

Shetland Islands

Orkney Islands

St. Fergus

Frigg

Inset labels:
Barque
Galleon
Ann
Vanguard
Alison
Ganyme[de]
Victor
Clipper
Audrey
Viking
Inde S
Baird
Excalibur
Guinevere
Lancelot
Indefatig[able]
Be
Anglia
Vulcan
S. Valiant
Big Dotty
N. Valiant
Callisto
Deborah
Leman
G
Bure
We
Hewett
Camelot
Tris[t]
Little Dotty
Della
Yare
S. We
Bacton
N.W. W

Rough
Cleeton
Esmond
Johnston
Ravenspurn
Forbes
Hyde
Gordon
Murdoch
Caister
Schooner
West Sole
Markham
Pickerill

Barrow
Morecambe
Hamilton N.
Hamilton

Dimlington

Easington
W.
Amethyst E
Theddlethorpe

See inset above

Canvey

London

British Gas to separate its supply and transportation activities and to bring forward removal of its tariff monopoly to March 1996, with a phased opening of the domestic market (18.4 million customers) in 1996–98.

The Gas Bill, now before Parliament, would reform the gas industry, so as to bring consumers the benefits of competition. In particular, it would provide for a new licensing framework for:

- gas suppliers, who sell piped gas to consumers;

- public gas transporters, who operate the pipeline system through which such gas will normally be delivered; and

- gas shippers, who are to arrange with transporters for appropriate amounts of gas to be moved through the pipeline system.

The regulatory regime for the private gas sector charges the Office of Gas Supply (Ofgas) with ensuring that British Gas is operating within the terms of its authorisation. The Gas Consumers' Council, independent of both British Gas and Ofgas, is responsible for investigating consumer complaints.

Production

In 1994 indigenous production of natural gas amounted to 69,960 million cubic metres. This included 4,694 million cubic metres of gas used for drilling, production and piping operations on North Sea production platforms and at terminals. Total availability of UKCS gas amounted to 71,400 million cubic metres—7.7 per cent higher than in 1993. In addition, about 3,275 million cubic metres of gas were imported from Norway. Some 1,092 million cubic metres were exported. Natural gas accounts for 65.7 per cent of total inland primary fuel consumption in Britain. Natural gas from the three most prolific of the 50 or so offshore gasfields— Leman, Indefatigable (South) and the Hewett area—accounted for over half the cumulative total gas produced in the UKCS. In addition to supplies from gasfields, associated gas,[3]

delivered to land via the Far North Liquids and Associated Gas System (FLAGS) and from Alwyn North, made further significant contributions. Gas from the South Morecambe field in the Irish Sea and from the twin North Sean and South Sean fields is used to augment supplies to meet peak demand in winter.

There are various methods of natural gas storage, including salt cavities and storage facilities for liquefied natural gas. The partially depleted Rough field is used as a major gas store. Gas is drawn from the national transmission system in summer and injected into the Rough reservoir for rapid recovery during periods of peak winter demand.

Reserves

Remaining recoverable gas reserves in present discoveries are estimated at between 660,000 million and 1.92 million million cubic metres. If possible gas from existing discoveries and potential future discoveries are added, the remaining total reserves are estimated to be in the range of 1.226 million million to 3.8 million million cubic metres. Indigenous offshore natural gas reserves are likely to meet most of the British demand well into the next century.

Transmission

The British Gas national and regional high-pressure pipeline system of some 267,300 km (167,060 miles) transports natural gas around Great Britain. It is largely supplied from five North Sea shore terminals, and one in Barrow-in-Furness (Cumbria). The high pressure transmission system is inspected regularly.

Newly built natural gas pipelines, run by independent operators, run from Horndean to Barking and from Theddlethorpe to Killingholme.

Consumption

Sales of natural gas in Britain totalled 706 terawatt[4] hours (TWh) in 1994. About 53 per cent of this is for industrial and commercial

---

[3]Mainly methane, produced and used on oil production platforms.

[4]1 TW = 1,000 gigawatts. 1 GW = 1,000 MW.

purposes, the remainder being for domestic use. Gas is used extensively in industries requiring the control of temperatures to a fine degree of accuracy, such as the pottery and glass industries, and in certain processes for making iron and steel products.

Some 281 TWh of this gas were sold to industry in Britain, and 95 TWh to commercial (including other non-domestic) users. Industrial gas prices have fallen by about 39 per cent in real terms since privatisation, and domestic prices by 15.5 per cent. An increasingly large part of domestic demand is for gas for central heating. In 1994, 330 TWh were sold to domestic users.

Development

British Gas has a worldwide reputation for gas technology, with a research and development programme totalling £79.7 million in 1994. It is one of nine companies to join in building an interconnector linking the British and European gas grids, to come into operation by late 1998, for a total investment of £170 million. Among its overseas activities, the company is drilling to add to reserves in the Gulf of Thailand and developing a gas field in Trinidad.

COAL

The size of the British coal industry has reduced drastically since the 1960s. Yet coal mining in Britain can be traced back to Roman times. Taxes raised on its sale helped pay for rebuilding London, and St Paul's Cathedral, after the Great Fire of 1666. Coal played a crucial part in the industrial revolution of the 18th and 19th centuries. In its peak year, 1913, the industry produced 292 million tonnes of coal, exported 74 million tonnes and employed over a million workers. In 1947 (when 200 million tonnes were produced) the coal mines passed into public ownership, and the National Coal Board (now British Coal) was set up.[5] In 1955 there were 850 British Coal collieries in operation; by 1994 the number had dwindled to 15 (excluding Asfordby in Leicestershire,

still under development), with a labour force of 7,400 and some 3,000 contractors. Despite this, the year also saw growth in the private sector, as nine mines which British Coal had previously closed were transferred under licence to private-sector owners. Coal production, reflecting a fourfold increase in labour productivity since 1986, was 48 million tonnes.

Privatisation

The Coal Industry Act 1994 enabled privatisation of the industry to take place. Five regional coal companies and seven care-and-maintenance collieries (23 collieries and 32 opencast sites in all) were offered for sale. The three English regions were bought by RJB Mining plc; the South Wales company went to Celtic Group Holdings Ltd; and the Scottish company to Mining (Scotland) Ltd. Four care-and-maintenance[6] collieries were also sold. Total proceeds from the sales came to about £960 million.

Coal Authority

Set up under the Coal Industry Act 1994, the Coal Authority took over ownership of coal reserves from British Coal. Its role is to:

- make these reserves available for coal mining and coal bed methane operations;
- license coal mining;
- take responsibility for the physical legacy of past mining, to the extent that this arises out of the ownership of the coal reserves and is not taken over by the private sector; and
- make available mining records and geological information.

Market for Coal

In 1994 inland consumption of coal was 81.7 million tonnes, of which about 77 per cent was by power stations, 11 per

---

[5]British Coal will continue to have residual functions beyond 1995.

[6]Collieries had been kept open on a care-and-maintenance basis, but not producing, to enable British Coal to offer them for sale to the private sector.

cent by coke ovens and 5 per cent by domestic users. Exports were 1.2 million tonnes, while imports amounted to 15 million tonnes.

Production

In 1994 total output of 48 million tonnes included 31.1 million tonnes of deep-mined coal and 16.6 million tonnes from opencast mines.

Research

Work on the £44 million coal liquefaction plant project at Point of Ayr (Clwyd) ended in late 1994.

It successfully demonstrated technology to produce high grade petrol and diesel fuels from a range of coals. The Government has encouraged the formation of an industry-led consortium, Clean Coal Power Generation Group, to pursue coal gasification. Its initial objective was to develop the air blown gasification cycle, a power generation technology. There are about 40 projects in progress within this and related initiatives, to a total project value of £74 million, including £14 million from the DTI.

ELECTRICITY

England and Wales

The privatised electricity supply industry in England and Wales consists of two main generating companies, the National Grid Company (NGC) and 12 regional electricity companies (RECs). The two main non-nuclear generators, National Power and PowerGen, the publicly owned nuclear generator, Nuclear Electric plc, and other generators and importers sell electricity to suppliers through a market known as the pool. The NGC operates the transmission system, which transfers electricity in bulk across the national grid. The NGC is owned by the RECs through a holding company.

Distribution—the transfer of electricity from the national grid to consumers via local networks—is carried out by the RECs. Supply is the purchase of electricity from generators and its sale to customers. RECs have a monopoly of all franchise sales (to consumers taking less than 100 kW) in their regions. These RECs are known as first-tier suppliers. Above 100 kW the market is already open to competition, and consumers may have contracts with a second-tier supplier, who could be one of the generators, a REC from a different region, or an independent supplier.

The Government sold its remaining 40 per cent shareholding in each of National Power and PowerGen in March 1995.

Scotland

Scottish Power plc and Scottish Hydro-Electric plc generate, transmit, distribute and supply electricity. They are also contracted to buy all the output from Scottish Nuclear Ltd, a government-owned company which operates the nuclear power stations at Hunterston (Strathclyde) and Torness (Lothian). ScottishPower and Scottish Hydro-Electric have access, under contract, to a stated capacity in each other's generating stations. This gives each company access to a good range of generating fuels.

Associated Functions

Certain service and co-ordinating functions for the industry are undertaken by the Electricity Association, jointly owned by the electricity companies of Great Britain. Regulation of the industry is the responsibility of the Office of Electricity Regulation, headed by the Director General of Electricity Supply (DGES), whose duties include the promotion of competition and the protection of consumer interests. In 1994–95 the DGES asked National Power and PowerGen to sell 4,000 MW and 2,000 MW respectively of oil- and coal-fired capacity. The aim is to increase the number of independent generators and thus competition.

Northern Ireland

Responsibility for transmission, distribution and supply of electricity lies with Northern Ireland Electricity (NIE) plc, privatised in

Electricity

Orkney Islands

Shetland Islands

	km	miles
0 20 40 60 80 100 120 km		
0 20 40 60 80 miles		

■ Conventional power stations (250 MW and over)

□ Conventional power stations (250 MW and over) under construction

● Nuclear power stations

○ Under construction

◆ Power-producing reactors of the UKAEA or BNFL

★ Hydro-electric power stations (over 45 MW capacity)

▲ Pumped storage schemes

Dounreay

Fasnakyle

Peterhead

Foyers

Rannoch   Errochty

Cruachan   Clunie

Lochay

Sloy   Longannet

Cockenzie   Torness

Inverkip

Hunterston B

Coolkeeragh   Chapelcross   Blyth A
Blyth B

Ballylumford   Galloway

Kilroot   Hartlepool

Calder Hall   Wilton

Roosecote

Heysham II

Heysham I   Drax   Eggborough   Killingholm
PowerGen

Ferrybridge C   Brigg

Deeside   Fiddler's   Thorpe Marsh   Killingholme A

Wylfa   Ferry   Keadby   West Burton

Dinorwig   Ince   Humber

Connah's   Ratcliffe-   Cottam

Quay   Staythorpe   on-Soar   High Marnham

Ffestiniog   Castle Donington

Corby   King's Lynn

Rugeley   Peterborough

Rheidol   A and B   Willington

Drakelow   A and B   Sizewell

B and C   Little Barford

Ironbridge   Rye House   Sizewell

Barking

Pembroke   Tilbury   Bradwell

W. Thurrock   Medway

Aberthaw B   Didcot   Grain

Oldbury   Didcot B

Seabank   Littlebrook   Richboroug

Kingsnorth

Hinkley Pt. A   Hinkley Pt. B   Dungeness B

Fawley   Dungeness A

1993. Three private companies generate electricity from four power stations. The largest power station, Ballylumford, is being converted from oil to gas firing and accounts for almost half Northern Ireland's generating capacity. Regulation of the industry is the responsibility of the Office of Electricity Regulation (NI), headed by the Director General of Electricity Supply (NI).

Consumption

In 1994 sales of electricity through the distribution system in Britain amounted to 284,439 GWh. Domestic users took 35 per cent of the total, industry 32 per cent, and commercial and other users the remainder.

Generation

National Power owns 28 operational fossil-fuelled power stations, which, together with their hydro schemes, generate about 35 per cent of the electricity supplied to the transmission and distribution networks in England and Wales. PowerGen's 19 operational fossil-fuelled power stations and other hydro schemes together generate about 26 per cent. The nuclear stations in Great Britain generate almost 27 per cent.

In 1994–95, 54 per cent of electricity used in Scotland was produced by Scottish Nuclear's two stations. In addition to nuclear generation, Scotland's electricity needs are met from hydro, coal, and gas—a total output capacity of 9,900 MW. Scottish Nuclear sells 74.9 per cent of its output to ScottishPower and the rest to Hydro-Electric.

Non-nuclear power stations owned by Britain's major power producers consumed 50.6 million tonnes of oil equivalent in 1994, of which coal accounted for 71 per cent and oil 7 per cent.

The growing number of independent generators and 'autogenerators' (who produce power for their own use) have equal access with the major generators to the grid transmission and local distribution systems.

To control acid emissions National Power and PowerGen expect to complete their programme of fitting flue gas desulphurisation (FGD) equipment to 6 GW of their generating capacity by the end of 1996. ScottishPower is evaluating FGD equipment with a view to fitting this at its main coal station, Longannet. In addition, a ten-year programme to control emissions of oxides of nitrogen (NO_x) through the installation of low-NO_x burners at 12 major power stations in England and Wales is in progress. ScottishPower is fitting low-NO_x

Table 17.3: Generation by and Capacity of Power Stations owned by the Major Generating Companies in Britain

	Electricity generated (GWh)			Per cent	Output
	1984	1989	1994[a]	1994	capacity (MW)
Nuclear plant	49,498	66,740	83,944	27.7	11,649
Other steam plant	209,121	219,712	175,362	57.9	38,513
Gas turbines and oil engines	1,947	529	244	0.1	1,605
Pumped storage plant	2,055	1,910	1,463	0.5	2,788
Natural flow hydro-electric plant	3,368	4,002	4,317	1.4	1,350
CCGTs	–	–	36,971	12.2	8,387
Renewables other than hydro	–	4	506	0.2	85
Total	265,990	292,896	302,807	100	64,377
Electricity supplied (net)[a]	246,367	271,714	284,835		

Source: Department of Trade and Industry
[a] Electricity generated less electricity used at power stations (both electricity used on works and that used for pumping at pumped-storage stations).
Note: Differences between totals and the sums of their component parts are due to rounding.

burners, and refurbishing electrostatic precipitators, at Longannet.

The increase in the number of combined cycle gas turbines (CCGTs) has been a significant development in electricity generation. CCGTs are quicker and cheaper to build than conventional plant. They use natural gas, are low in sulphur emissions, and help reduce CO_2 emissions. In England and Wales, 17 such stations (total declared net capacity 9.2 GW) are generating electricity; 4 (total registered capacity 4.4 GW) are under construction; and 8 (total registered capacity 4.8 GW) have consents and are likely to go ahead. Some 13 per cent of electricity in Britain was derived from gas in 1994.

The NGC, together with Electricité de France, runs a 2,000-MW cross-Channel cable link, providing the capacity for the transmission of electricity between the two countries. The link has generally been used to supply baseload electricity—electricity that needs to be generated and available round the clock—from France to England. Imports of electricity met about 5 per cent of Britain's electricity needs in 1994.

Transmission lines linking the Scottish and English grid systems enable cross-border trading. This interconnector is run jointly by the NGC and ScottishPower. The capacity of the interconnector has been increased from 850 MW to 1,600 MW, and there are plans for further enhancement of the line's capacity. NIE plc and ScottishPower plan to construct a 250-MW interconnector between Scotland and Northern Ireland. Reports on two public inquiries are awaited.

Nuclear Power

In 1956 the world's first industrial-scale nuclear power station, at Calder Hall (Cumbria), began to supply electricity to the national grid. It, together with the Magnox station at Chapelcross (Dumfries and Galloway), is still operated by British Nuclear Fuels plc (BNFL). The electricity generated at Chapelcross is sold to England. There are also 14 commercial nuclear power stations operated by Nuclear Electric and Scottish Nuclear. The former has 6 Magnox stations (with capacities ranging from 245 to 950 MW) and 5 Advanced Gas-cooled Reactor stations (AGRs; ranging from 1,110 MW to 1,250 MW). Scottish Nuclear operates two 1,320-MW AGR stations. Nuclear Electric has also built Britain's first pressurised water reactor (PWR; 1,188 MW) at Sizewell (Suffolk). Three Magnox stations (one each in England, Wales and Scotland) have reached the end of their commercial life and have been shut down, before being decommissioned.

Nuclear power generation increases diversity of energy supply and helps maintain its security, and nuclear stations produce no sulphur dioxide (SO_2) or CO_2. A non-fossil fuel obligation (NFFO), placed on the RECs in England and Wales, requires them to contract for specified amounts of electricity from non-fossil sources. They contract for this non-fossil capacity at prices above the market rate and the difference is returned to them through the fossil fuel levy (10 per cent) on electricity sales. Although most NFFO electricity comes from nuclear sources, a small but increasing amount comes from renewables.

Under its NFFO contract, Nuclear Electric obtains a premium price on output up to a certain limit in each year until the contract ends in 1998. For output above this level, Nuclear Electric gets the same price as other generators. It expects these prices to enable the full cost of nuclear generation to be met, including the decommissioning of its two closed Magnox stations at Berkeley (1989) and Trawsfynydd (1993).

Nuclear Energy Agreement

The NFFO does not apply in Scotland where, under the Nuclear Energy Agreement (NEA), ScottishPower and Scottish Hydro-Electric are required to take all of the electricity generated by Scottish Nuclear. From 1990 to 1994 the price which Scottish Nuclear received for its output was fixed above the market rate for electricity. The price is now set to taper until 1998 to one based on the market rate for electricity in England and Wales. Therefore Scottish Nuclear's income under the NEA will depend on the market rate. The NEA is due to run until 2005.

CONSTRUCTION

Giant tunnel boring machines at work on the Jubilee Line Extension, Britain's newest underground railway, which will connect London's West End with the east and south-east of the city and is due to be completed in March 1998.

Britain's first 'stealth' building is designed to be invisible to radar. Using technology originally developed to make military aircraft deflect enemy radar, the design of British Airways' new operations centre overcomes the danger that buildings near the airport's runways could confuse radar signals between traffic control and aircraft.

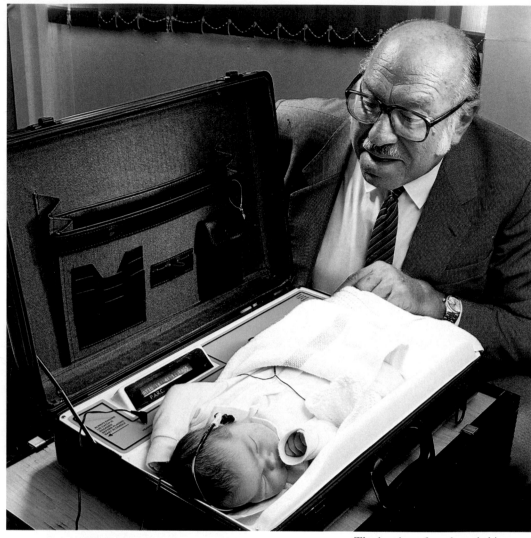

The hearing of newborn babies can now be tested quickly and simply using the Auditory Response Cradle developed jointly by Hillingdon Hospital, Middlesex, and Brunel University, London.

Dorman Diesels (now Perkins Engines) has gained a Queen's Award for the Environment for the development of the SE Minnox range of engines, which greatly reduce pollutant emissions.

The Engineering and Physical Sciences Research Council supports research into optical solitons—light waves that do not disperse and distort, and which, when used in an optical fibre of the kind shown here, vastly increase the distance and speed of communication. The optical fibre itself has the capacity, in theory, to carry at one time all the conversations going on in the world twice over.

Cassava is the staple food for a quarter of the world's population. Researchers at Silsoe College, Cranfield University, Bedfordshire, have developed a low-cost extruder—a machine which dries the cassava, extending its use as a food in developing countries.

Dummies are used in a variety of crash impact tests, designed to help evaluate the safety of seats fitted in cars, trains, aircraft and helicopters, at Millbrook Proving Ground in Bedfordshire.

"Strive for Perfection in everything you do."

Putting the finishing touch on a Rolls-Royce: the famous vertical radiator grille.

CONSTRUCTION

Giant tunnel boring machines at work on the Jubilee Line Extension, Britain's newest underground railway, which will connect London's West End with the east and south-east of the city and is due to be completed in March 1998.

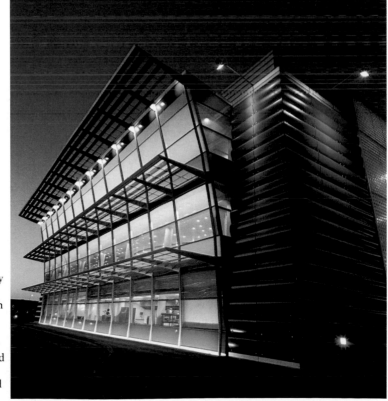

Britain's first 'stealth' building is designed to be invisible to radar. Using technology originally developed to make military aircraft deflect enemy radar, the design of British Airways' new operations centre overcomes the danger that buildings near the airport's runways could confuse radar signals between traffic control and aircraft.

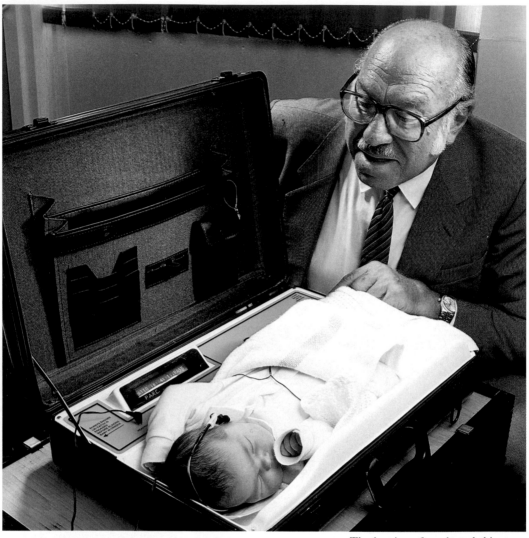

The hearing of newborn babies can now be tested quickly and simply using the Auditory Response Cradle developed jointly by Hillingdon Hospital, Middlesex, and Brunel University, London.

Dorman Diesels (now Perkins Engines) has gained a Queen's Award for the Environment for the development of the SE Minnox range of engines, which greatly reduce pollutant emissions.

The Engineering and Physical Sciences Research Council supports research into optical solitons—light waves that do not disperse and distort, and which, when used in an optical fibre of the kind shown here, vastly increase the distance and speed of communication. The optical fibre itself has the capacity, in theory, to carry at one time all the conversations going on in the world twice over.

Cassava is the staple food for a quarter of the world's population. Researchers at Silsoe College, Cranfield University, Bedfordshire, have developed a low-cost extruder—a machine which dries the cassava, extending its use as a food in developing countries.

TRANSPORT DESIGN AND SAFETY

Dummies are used in a variety of crash impact tests, designed to help evaluate the safety of seats fitted in cars, trains, aircraft and helicopters, at Millbrook Proving Ground in Bedfordshire.

"Strive for Perfection in everything you do."

Putting the finishing touch on a Rolls-Royce: the famous vertical radiator grille.

Technologies supported under recent NFFO and renewables obligations in Britain[1]

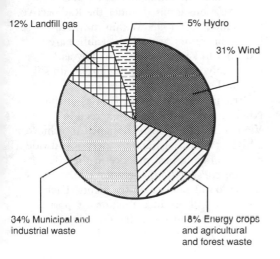

12% Landfill gas

5% Hydro

31% Wind

34% Municipal and industrial waste

18% Energy crops and agricultural and forest waste

[1] Contracted capacity (MW DNC) under the Third Order for England and Wales and First Orders for Scotland and Northern Ireland.

Source: Department of Trade and Industry.

Nuclear Review

The main conclusions of this review, undertaken by the Government and published in May 1995, are that:

- Britain's AGRs and PWRs should be transferred to the private sector;

- the parts of Nuclear Electric and Scottish Nuclear to be privatised will be subsidiaries of a single holding company with headquarters in Scotland;

- Magnox stations and their liabilities will be kept in the public sector;

- the Government sees no case at present for providing public funds for building new nuclear power stations;

- the nuclear element of the fossil fuel levy, and the premium element of the NEA, will cease on privatisation; and

- renewable energy (see below) will continue to be supported through the fossil fuel levy on electricity bills.

In the Government's opinion, the review confirms the importance of nuclear power to the country's energy needs, and suggests that nuclear power will continue to have an important role, as long as it is competitive and able to maintain high standards of safety and environmental protection.

British Nuclear Fuels

BNFL provides services covering the whole of the nuclear fuel cycle. The company is wholly owned by the Government.

BNFL's thermal oxide reprocessing plant (THORP) at Sellafield (Cumbria) began operations in 1994. Built at a cost of £2,800 million, including its share of associated facilities, THORP reprocesses spent fuel from British and overseas nuclear reactors. Environmental protection plant costing £600 million was brought on stream at the same time. BNFL already supplies fuel for the PWR at Sizewell and for all Magnox and AGR stations in Britain. The Sellafield Mixed Oxide Fuel plant, currently under construction and due to become operational in late 1997, will blend plutonium recovered from reprocessing with uranium, to make mixed oxide fuel for use in reactors worldwide. BNFL contributes waste management and decommissioning expertise to international joint ventures. A subsidiary company, BNFL Inc, has won environmental restoration contracts with the United States Department of Energy.

AEA Technology

AEA Technology is the commercial business of the United Kingdom Atomic Energy Authority, which provides science and engineering services to the nuclear industry worldwide and to other industrial sectors.

UKAEA Government Division

UKAEA Government Division is responsible for the safe management and decommissioning of UKAEA's nuclear facilities and the safe management of its radioactive waste. It is also responsible for Britain's fusion programme (see below).

Nuclear Research

Most of the DTI's nuclear expenditure is on the decommissioning of redundant nuclear research and development facilities. These include research and demonstration power reactors, such as the Steam Generating Heavy Water Reactor at Winfrith in Dorset, and Windscale AGR (Cumbria), and the Dounreay Fast Reactor and the Prototype Fast Reactor in the Highland region. The radioactive wastes arising from this programme are stored safely until their final disposal in authorised purpose-built facilities.

The Government plans to spend £15.7 million in 1995–96 on fusion research. About half of this is Britain's contribution to the EU Joint European Torus nuclear project at Culham (Oxfordshire). The remaining half goes to fund a national programme of fusion research carried out by the UKAEA as part of the EU fusion programme.

The DTI also funds assessments of advanced reactor safety and of international safety standards, and the transfer of technology to help improve nuclear safety in the former Soviet Union, and in central and eastern Europe. In 1995 it contributed £5 million to the nuclear safety account at the European Bank for Reconstruction and Development, which finances safety improvements at the higher-risk nuclear plants in those countries.

Nuclear Safety

Both public and private nuclear operators will be subject to the same rigorous safety regime that applied before privatisation of the relevant parts of Scottish Nuclear and Nuclear Electric. This regime is enforced by the HSE's Nuclear Installations Inspectorate (NII), which ensures that high standards of safety are incorporated into the design, construction, operation, maintenance and decommissioning of all nuclear plant, and eventual disposal of resulting wastes. While the safety of such plant in Britain is the ultimate responsibility of the nuclear operator, the NII has the power to shut down a plant if it thinks it unsafe and may also require improvements to an installation if it believes the appropriate standards of safety are not being met.

Discharges of radioactive waste have to be kept within the limits and conditions set by authorisations granted under the Radioactive Substances Act 1993. Within maximum dose limits, operators of nuclear facilities are required to keep discharges as low as reasonably achievable and failure to do so makes them liable to prosecution.

Britain is one of 58 signatories of the Nuclear Safety Convention agreed in Vienna in 1994. This is designed to achieve a high standard of nuclear safety worldwide, by encouraging best practice in the safe design, construction, operation and regulation of nuclear power plants. Each signatory will produce a national report stating how it meets or intends to meet a range of nuclear safety obligations set out in the Convention.

Emergency Plans

The precautions taken in the design and construction of nuclear installations in Britain, and the care taken in their operation and maintenance, reduce the chance of accidents which might affect the public to an extremely low level. However, all operators are required, as a condition of their site licences, to prepare emergency plans, including those for dealing with an accidental release of radioactivity. These are regularly tested in exercises under the supervision of the NII.

International conventions have been established on the early notification of a nuclear accident which may have possible transboundary effects, and on the mutual provision of assistance in the event of a nuclear accident or radiological emergency.

NEW AND RENEWABLE SOURCES OF ENERGY

The Government encourages development of new and renewable energy sources wherever they have prospects of being economically attractive and environmentally acceptable. It is working towards 1,500 MW (3 per cent of Britain's current capacity) of new electricity generating capacity from renewable energy sources, for Britain as a whole, by 2000. Achieving this capacity could produce annual savings of 2 million tonnes of CO_2, 100,000 tonnes of SO_2 and about 30,000 tonnes of NO_x. Looking further ahead, renewables might be able to supply up to 20 per cent of Britain's 1991 electricity needs by 2025, under severe pressures of need and economics. Making NFFO orders is the Government's main instrument for helping to develop the new capacity. Through the NFFO the Government aims to create an initial market for electricity-producing technologies close to commercial competitiveness, so that the most promising renewables can compete without financial support.

Three renewables Orders have been made for England and Wales and one each (in 1994) for Scotland and Northern Ireland. At the end of 1994, 144 projects contracted in England and Wales under the first two orders were operating, with a declared net capacity of 325 MW. The first Scottish Renewables Obligation was for 76 MW capacity.

The main renewable technologies identified as relevant to Britain are:

● biofuels (landfill gas, energy from wastes, and energy crops);

● solar energy (active, passive and photovoltaics);

● wind; and

● hydro.

Among new sources under investigation are advanced fuel cells.

International collaboration is undertaken through multilateral and bilateral arrangements within the IEA and the EU. These include:

● JOULE, which supports research into economically viable and environmentally sound energy technologies;

● THERMIE, which aims to promote innovative energy technologies in energy efficiency, renewable energy and clean coal and hydrocarbons; and

● ALTENER, which is designed to foster development of renewable sources in the EU, and increase trade in products, equipment and services.

Non-energy Minerals

Although much of Britain's requirements for industrial raw materials is met by imports, the non-energy minerals it produces make an important contribution to the economy. Output of non-energy minerals in 1993 totalled 325 million tonnes, valued at £1,832 million. Construction raw materials, in particular aggregates, form the bulk of the value of non-energy minerals production. The total number of employees in the extractive industry was some 32,000 in 1993.

Exploration

The Government is seeking to restrict the growth in England of quarries supplying rock, and sand and gravel for construction. It also expects the construction industry to double the amount of recycled and secondary material it uses, and to reduce its dependence on primary aggregates extracted on land from 83 to 68 per cent by 2006. Coastal superquarries from outside England may make an increased contribution to aggregates requirements in the future. Scottish Office guidelines on minerals working in Scotland include a policy that there should be no more than four superquarries in Scotland over the period to 2009.

The British Geological Survey continues a long-term programme for the DTI aimed at identifying areas with mineral potential. Gold exploration by the private sector has decreased but continues, especially in Scotland, Northern Ireland and south-west England. In Wales small-scale production of gold takes place at the Gwynfynydd mine. Planning permission for a small underground gold mine at Cononish, near Tyndrum (Perthshire), and for a small opencast gold mine at Cavancaw in Northern Ireland has recently been granted.

Production

In terms of value, production of limestone and dolomite was estimated at £514 million in 1993, sand and gravel £440 million, clays £302 million (with china clay valued at £230 million), igneous rock £250 million, sandstone £74 million, potash £71 million, salt £51 million, chalk £38 million, silica

Table 17.4: Production of Some of the Main Non-energy Minerals

million tonnes

	1984	1988	1994
Sand and gravel	100.6	136.4	100.0
Silica sand	4.3	4.3	3.6
Igneous rock	36.9	52.0	57.8
Limestone and dolomite	93.5	125.7	111.7
Chalk[a]	12.0	14.5	9.1
Sandstone	15.1	18.9	16.1
Gypsum	3.1	3.7	2.5
Salt, including salt in brine	7.3	6.3	6.6
Common clay and shale[a]	17.8	18.9	10.9
China clay	3.3	3.3	2.6[b]
Ball clay	0.6	0.7	0.7
Fireclay	0.8[a]	1.1	0.5
Iron ore	0.4	0.2	0.0
Potash	0.5	0.8	0.9
Fluorspar	0.1	0.1	0.1
Fuller's earth	0.3	0.2	0.2

Source: *British Geological Survey, United Kingdom Minerals Yearbook*
[a] Great Britain only.
[b] Moisture-free basis.

sands £36 million, gypsum and anhydrite £18 million, fluorspar £9 million and tin £7 million. In 1993 the production of metals in non-ferrous ores totalled 3,000 tonnes, mainly tin from Cornwall. In 1994 South Crofty, the one remaining Cornish tin mine and one of the very few sources of tin in the EU, produced 1,919 tonnes of tin-in-concentrate, a 14 per cent decrease on 1993 and equivalent to about 18.5 per cent of Britain's demand. Some lead and a little zinc are produced as by-products of fluorspar.

Water

Britain's water supplies are obtained mostly (about 75 per cent) from surface sources such as mountain lakes, reservoirs and river intakes, and partly (about 25 per cent) from groundwater. The 22-month wet period from July 1992 brought about a rapid recovery in water resources, especially in eastern, southern and central England. In August 1995, during an exceptionally dry spell, the Government set out the measures it is taking to achieve a more sustainable pattern of use of water resources. About 99 per cent of the

population in Great Britain and 97 per cent in Northern Ireland are served by the public water supply system. Water put into the public supply system (including industrial and other uses) in England and Wales amounted to 16,433 megalitres (Ml) a day in 1994, of which average domestic daily consumption per household was 380 litres. An average of 2,272 Ml a day was supplied in Scotland in 1993–94.

Some 51,658 Ml a day were abstracted in England and Wales in 1993, of which public water supplies accounted for 16,651 Ml a day. The electricity generating companies and other industry took 30,474 Ml a day. Fish farming, cress growing and amenity ponds took 3,817 Ml a day. Agriculture took 140 Ml a day.

England and Wales

The Secretaries of State for the Environment and for Wales, the Director General of Water Services and the National Rivers Authority (NRA) are the principal regulators. The Drinking Water Inspectorate regulates drinking water quality. The Minister of Agriculture, Fisheries and Food and the Secretary of State for Wales are responsible

Some Minerals Produced in Britain

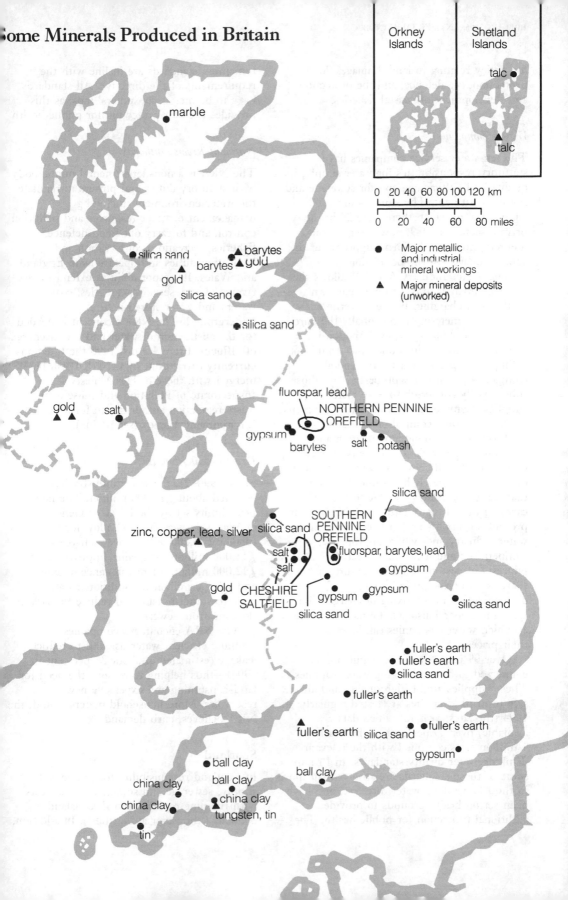

Orkney Islands

Shetland Islands

talc

talc

0 20 40 60 80 100 120 km

0 20 40 60 80 miles

● Major metallic and industrial mineral workings

▲ Major mineral deposits (unworked)

marble

silica sand

barytes

barytes gold

gold

silica sand

silica sand

gold ▲ ▲ salt

fluorspar, lead

NORTHERN PENNINE OREFIELD

gypsum

barytes salt potash

silica sand

zinc, copper, lead, silver silica sand

SOUTHERN PENNINE OREFIELD

salt

fluorspar, barytes, lead

salt

gypsum

gold CHESHIRE SALTFIELD

gypsum gypsum

silica sand

silica sand

fuller's earth

fuller's earth

silica sand

fuller's earth

fuller's earth ▲ fuller's earth silica sand

gypsum

ball clay

china clay ball clay ball clay

china clay china clay

tungsten, tin

tin

for policy relating to land drainage, flood protection, sea defence, and the protection and development of coastal fisheries.

Water Companies

The ten water service companies have statutory responsibilities for water supply, its quality and sufficiency, and for sewerage and sewage treatment. The supply-only companies, of which there were 29 in the private sector in 1989, now, after various mergers, number 21. They supply water to about a quarter of the population.

The Water Industry Act 1991 allows the water companies to determine their own methods of charging. In the Government's view, water metering is potentially the fairest way of paying for water, even though it would take time to introduce and would not be appropriate everywhere. In general, companies require new properties and those substantially converted to have metered supplies. Commercial and industrial concerns are metered on a compulsory basis.

A system of economic regulation and guaranteed standards of service is overseen by OFWAT, the office of the Director General of Water Services. It has a duty to ensure that water companies are able to finance the carrying-out of their statutory obligations; it promotes economy and efficiency within the water industry and, where appropriate, competition; and it has to protect the interests of customers and to ensure that there is no undue preference or discrimination in the fixing of charges. The Director General also sets limits to the rate at which water companies can increase their prices.

Over 99 per cent of the population is connected to mains drinking water supplies. These supplies are of high quality and all are safe to drink. Supplies are tested regularly; in 1994 (the latest year for which data are available) over 99 per cent of the nearly 4 million tests complied with the relevant drinking water quality standards. In Britain some of these standards are stricter than those in the EC drinking water directive, and have been set on health grounds to provide additional protection for public health. The

remaining standards are in line with the requirements of the directive. All standards have to be met at consumers' taps, as this provides the best protection for public health.

National Rivers Authority

The NRA is a non-departmental public body with statutory duties and powers to regulate the water environment, including management of water resources and pollution control, and to carry out flood defence, fisheries, recreation, conservation and navigation duties and operations in England and Wales. Its responsibilities extend to all rivers, lakes, reservoirs, estuaries, coastal waters and water stored naturally underground. The NRA's consent is needed for the abstraction of water and the discharge of effluent. From 1 April 1996 the functions currently carried out by the NRA will be merged with those of Her Majesty's Inspectorate of Pollution and those of the waste regulation authorities to form the Environment Agency (see p. 368).

Development Projects

Since 1990–91, the water industry has invested about £15,000 million. The new price limits set by the Director General of Water Services in 1994 allow for a further £24,000 million over ten years: £11,000 million for quality improvements, £12,000 million for maintenance of assets and £1,000 million for additional water resources and measures to reduce the risk of flooding from sewers.

The NRA encourages companies to promote efficient water use and to reduce leakage (estimated at about 25 per cent in 1994)—thus helping to remove the need for land-consuming and expensive new reservoirs. More household meters would, the NRA believes, curb demand.

Scotland

In Scotland responsibility for public water supply, sewerage and sewage disposal rests with the nine regional and three island councils ('the water authorities'). In addition, the Central Scotland Water Development Board (CSWDB) is responsible for providing water in bulk to five regional councils in central Scotland. In 1994–95 the CSWDB supplied authorities with an average 261 Ml a day. From April 1996 three new public water authorities, North, West and East, will be responsible for water and sewerage services in Scotland. The independent Scottish Water and Sewerage Customers Council, a representative body for consumers, will also be established.

The Secretary of State for Scotland is responsible for promoting conservation of water resources and provision of adequate water supplies. He has a duty to promote the cleanliness of rivers and other inland waters, and the tidal waters of Scotland. River purification authorities have a statutory responsibility for water pollution control, which will be taken over by the new Scottish Environment Protection Agency, to be set up in April 1996.

Water is charged for according to type of consumer: domestic consumers pay council water charges or metered charges; non-domestic consumers pay non-domestic water rates, or metered charges. For sewerage services, domestic consumers pay through the council tax, and non-domestic consumers pay non-domestic sewerage rates and, where appropriate, trade effluent charges. Charges and rates are decided by each authority. From April 1996 charging will become the responsibility of the three new water authorities.

Scotland has a relative abundance of unpolluted water from upland sources.

Northern Ireland

The Department of the Environment for Northern Ireland is responsible for public water supply and sewerage throughout Northern Ireland. It is also responsible for the conservation and cleanliness of water resources and, with the Department of Agriculture, may prepare a water management programme with respect to water resources in any area. There is a domestic water charge which is contained in the regional rate, while agriculture, commerce and industry pay metered charges. There are abundant potential supplies of water for both domestic and industrial use. An average of 670 Ml of water a day was supplied in 1993–94.

Research

Several organisations and centres of expertise provide water research services to government, the NRA, water companies and the Scottish river purification authorities.

The Water Research Centre, a private company, has a large programme of research into, for example, environmental issues and drinking water safety.

Research carried out by institutes of the Natural Environment Research Council (see p. 323) embraces river modelling, water quality, climate change, effects on resources and the impact of pollution on freshwater.

Among its various roles the Institute of Hydrology studies the statistics of floods and droughts.

Further Reading

The Energy Report 1: Competition, Competitiveness, and Sustainability [1995]. Department of Trade and Industry. HMSO.

The Energy Report 2: Oil and Gas Resources of the United Kingdom 1994. Department of Trade and Industry. HMSO.

Digest of United Kingdom Energy Statistics 1995. Department of Trade and Industry. HMSO.

United Kingdom Minerals Yearbook 1994. British Geological Survey. HMSO.

Digest of Environmental Statistics. No 17, 1995. Department of the Environment. HMSO.

Energy and Natural Resources. Aspects of Britain series. HMSO, 1992.

18 Agriculture, the Fishing Industry and Forestry

Major recent developments in British agriculture have been the ending of the milk marketing schemes, and the conclusion of the Uruguay Round agreement on agriculture signed by the European Union in April 1994. In that year the aggregate income of the agricultural sector increased in real terms for the third year in succession. Environmental schemes underline Britain's commitment to environmentally sensitive agriculture.

Agreement has been reached on a new fisheries access regime for Spain and Portugal in the EU's western waters and on stricter enforcement of catch limits in international fisheries off the coast of Canada.

Agriculture

In 1994 British agriculture, forestry and fishing employed 2.1 per cent of the total workforce. Food, feed and beverages accounted for about 10 per cent of Britain's imports by value, compared with about a quarter in the 1960s. The agricultural contribution to gross domestic product (GDP) was £7,800 million in 1994, 1.4 per cent of the total. Britain is a major exporter of agricultural produce and food products, agrochemicals and agricultural machinery.

The Government has three main objectives for the farming, fisheries and food industries:

● to improve the economic performance of the agriculture, fisheries and food industries by creating the conditions in which they can flourish efficiently and sustainably;

● to promote the provision of safe, high-quality food; and

● to protect and enhance the rural environment, and to protect farm animals by encouraging welfare standards.

The Ministry of Agriculture, Fisheries and Food (MAFF) has published a range of customer service standards or codes of practice in accordance with the principles of the Citizen's Charter. MAFF's regional service centres, which deal directly with farmers over matters such as grants and licences, were first set performance targets in December 1992; these were revised and the number of targets increased in January 1995. All 12 of the Ministry's specialised Inspectorates, which enforce quality and fish or animal health standards, published comparable documents in 1994. Six MAFF executive agencies now have service standards. The Scottish Office Agriculture and Fisheries Department sets out its standards of service and performance targets in a charter standard statement called *Serving Scottish Farmers*.

Land Use

The area of agricultural land has been declining, although there has been a reduction in the net rate of loss in recent years. In 1994 there were 11.3 million hectares (27.9 million acres) under crops and grass. A further 5.8 million hectares (14.3 million acres) were used for rough grazing, most of it in hilly areas. Soils vary from the thin poor ones of highland Britain to the rich fertile soils of low-lying areas such as the fenlands of eastern England. The climate is generally temperate, though rainfall distribution over Britain is uneven. The South East receives only about 600 mm (2 ft) a year, compared with over 1,500 mm (5 ft) in parts of west Scotland, Cumbria and Wales. Autumn 1994 saw rather mild weather over much of Britain, helping to extend the grazing season and enabling late cuts of silage to boost fodder stocks.

Land Use in Britain

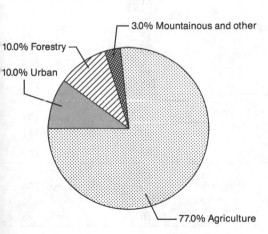

3.0% Mountainous and other
10.0% Forestry
10.0% Urban
77.0% Agriculture

Farming

In 1994 there were some 244,300 farm holdings in Britain (excluding minor holdings

too small to be surveyed on a regular basis), with an average size of 70.1 hectares (173.2 acres)—again excluding minor holdings. About two-thirds of all agricultural land is owner-occupied. Some 44.6 per cent of holdings are smaller than 8 European size units (ESU).[1]

Agricultural Land Use 1994

TOTAL AREA ON AGRICULTURAL HOLDINGS

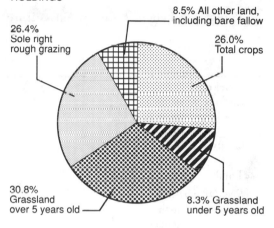

8.5% All other land, including bare fallow
26.4% Sole right rough grazing
26.0% Total crops
30.8% Grassland over 5 years old
8.3% Grassland under 5 years old

CROPS

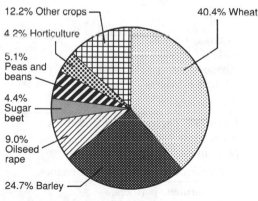

12.2% Other crops
4.2% Horticulture
5.1% Peas and beans
4.4% Sugar beet
9.0% Oilseed rape
24.7% Barley
40.4% Wheat

Labour productivity increased by 28 per cent during 1984–94. Total income from farming (that of farmers, partners, directors

---

[1]ESUs measure the financial potential of the holding in terms of the margins which might be expected from crops and stock. 8 ESU is judged the minimum for full-time holdings.

and their spouses, and family workers—see Table 18.1) was estimated at £4,212 million in 1994, 6.9 per cent more than in 1993. In real terms this measure of income is about 25 per cent higher than a decade ago.

At the end of 1993 the industry's gross capital stock, valued at 1990 prices, amounted to some £30,470 million, of which buildings and works made up over two-thirds. The level of capital stock is now estimated to be some 6.2 per cent below the 1983–85 average. This decline reflects a reduction in the stock

of plant and machinery, and, to a lesser extent, in vehicles. Since 1989, however, the stock of buildings and works has changed little and still remains greater than it was in 1985.

PRODUCTION

Home production of the principal foods is shown in Table 18.2 as a percentage by weight of total supplies (that is, production plus imports minus exports).

Table 18.1: Labour Force in Agriculture

	'000 persons 1983–85 average	'000 persons 1994
Workers		
Regular whole time		
hired: male	116	72
female	10	10
family: male	30	21
female	5	3
Total	162	107
Regular part-time		
hired: male	19	19
female	22	18
family: male	13	13
female	6	7
Total	61	56
Seasonal or casual		
male	58	54
female	39	28
salaried managers[a]	8	8
Total workers	328	253
Farmers, partners and directors		
whole-time	202	173
part-time	90	111
Total farmers, partners and directors	292	283
Total farmers, partners, directors and workers	620	536
Spouses of farmers, partners and directors (engaged in farm work)	76	78
Total labour force (including farmers and their spouses)[b]	695	614

Source: *Agriculture in the United Kingdom 1994*
[a]This figure relates to Great Britain only.
[b]Figures exclude schoolchildren and most trainees.
Note: Differences between totals and the sums of their component parts are due to rounding.

Table 18.2: British Production as a Percentage of Total New Supplies

Food Product	1983–85 average	1994 (provisional)
Beef and veal	99	100
Eggs	97	96
Milk for human consumption (as liquid)	100	99
Cheese	69	71
Butter	63	60
Sugar (as refined)	55	60
Wheat	104	121
Potatoes	92	88

Source: MAFF

Livestock

Over half of full-time farms are devoted mainly to dairy farming or to beef cattle and sheep. The majority of sheep and cattle are reared in the hill and moorland areas of Scotland, Wales, Northern Ireland and northern and south-western England. Beef fattening occurs partly in better grassland areas, as does dairying, and partly on arable farms. British livestock breeders have developed many of the cattle, sheep and pig breeds with worldwide reputations, for example, the Hereford and Aberdeen Angus beef breeds, the Jersey, Guernsey and Ayrshire dairy breeds, Large White pigs and a number of sheep breeds. Developments in artificial insemination and embryo transfer have enabled Britain to export semen and embryos from high-quality donor animals. Livestock totals are given in Table 18.3.

Cattle and Sheep

Cattle and sheep constitute about 45 per cent of the value of Britain's gross agricultural output. Dairy production is the largest part of the sector, followed by cattle and calves, and then fat sheep and lambs. Most dairy cattle in Britain are bred by artificial insemination. In 1994 the average size of dairy herds was 67 (excluding minor holdings), while the average yield of milk for each dairy cow was 5,372 litres (1,182 gallons). Average household consumption of liquid (including low-fat) milk per head in 1994 was 1.95 litres (3.4 pints) a week.

More than half of home-fed beef

Table 18.3: Livestock and Livestock Products

	1983–85 average	1992	1993	1994 (provisional)
Cattle and calves ('000 head)	13,153	11,804	11,729	11,834
Sheep and lambs ('000 head)	34,842	43,998	43,901	43,295
Pigs ('000 head)	7,910	7,609	7,754	7,797
Poultry ('000 head)[a]	80,139	91,671	97,179	93,813
Milk (million litres)	15,870	14,011	14,095	14,425
Hen eggs (million dozen)	937	806	803	811
Beef and veal ('000 tonnes)	1,105	968	879	945
Mutton and lamb ('000 tonnes)	303	392	397	391
Pork ('000 tonnes)	740	809	821	856
Bacon and ham ('000 tonnes)	208	168	181	182
Poultry meat ('000 tonnes)	842	1,077	1,076	1,079

Source: MAFF

[a]Includes ducks, geese and turkeys. Figures for the latter are for England and Wales only.

Note: With the exception of milk and hen eggs, from 1992 figures have been adjusted from a 53-week to a 52-week basis.

production originates from the national dairy herd, in which the Holstein Friesian breed is predominant. The remainder is derived from suckler herds producing high-quality beef calves, mostly in the hills and uplands. The traditional British beef breeds, such as Hereford and Aberdeen Angus, and increasingly imported breeds, such as Charolais, Limousin, Simmental and Belgian Blue, are used for beef production. In 1994 the size of the beef-breeding herd continued to expand. The dairy herd decreased slightly.

Britain has a long tradition of sheep production, with more than 60 native breeds and many cross-bred varieties. Sheepmeat production is the main source of income for sheep farmers, and wool provides additional return.

Grass (including silage) covers most British agricultural land and supplies 60–80 per cent of the feed for cattle and sheep. Grass production has been enhanced by the increased use of fertilisers, methods of grazing control, and improved herbage conservation for winter feed. Certain sheep and cattle feed extensively on rough grazings, producing young animals for fattening elsewhere.

A harmonised identification system throughout the EU enables animals to be traced to their farm of origin, for disease control purposes and for checking payments made under the Common Agricultural Policy (CAP).

Pigs

Pig production occurs in most areas but is particularly important in East Anglia and Yorkshire. There is an increasing concentration into larger breeding units—about 20 per cent of holdings with breeding sows account for 80 per cent of the national breeding herd.

Poultry

High husbandry standards and the use of improved genetic stock have helped to increase efficiency in poultry meat production. Larger companies have bought up smaller concerns and a more efficient industry has resulted. The increase in demand is partly satisfied by imports. Poultry production in 1994 was 1.08 million tonnes—a small increase on 1993—dominated by broilers. Broiler production, at 830,000 tonnes, was 4,000 tonnes below the level for 1993. Broilers from the 8 per cent of holdings with over 100,000 table birds account for well over a half of the total flock. Production of hen eggs went up from 803 million dozen in 1993 to 811 million dozen in 1994. Britain remains broadly self-sufficient in poultry meat and eggs (see p. 277).

Animal Welfare

The welfare of farm animals is protected by legislation and it is an offence to cause unnecessary pain or distress to livestock on agricultural land. More detailed requirements are laid down in regulations and welfare codes. There are further controls to safeguard the welfare of animals in markets, during transport and at slaughter. The Farm Animal Welfare Council, an independent body set up by the Government, advises on legislative or other changes relating to farm animal welfare.

EC rules on the protection of animals at slaughter, adopted in 1993, came into force in 1995. These rules require all member states to apply the high standards which already exist under British legislation.

From late 1994 the trade in live animals was disrupted by the refusal of the major passenger ferry companies to carry live animals, accompanied by public protest against the trade, particularly at the south coast ports. Negotiations on Community-wide rules governing the transport of live animals had been continuous since earlier that year, and in June 1995 agreement was finally reached between the EU member states. The new rules agreed are a significant step forward in that they introduce, for the first time, maximum limits on journeys for livestock being transported in the EU. They also incorporate feeding and watering intervals which have to be observed on the way, and tough new measures for enforcing the rules right across the Community. During 1995 the Government took action to:

- bring forward from 1997 the review of production systems for calves across the EU;

- urge an EU ban on the veal crate system, already illegal in Britain, when the review is in progress;

- bring into immediate effect a revised order for the welfare of animals during transport in Great Britain, which enables prosecution of an exporter who has not complied with the required journey plan without good reason—with penalties of up to £1,000 an animal in the event of conviction in court; and

- take further steps to promote production of beef and veal by humane methods.

Crops

The farms devoted primarily to arable crops are found mainly in eastern and central-southern England and eastern Scotland. The main crops are shown in Table 18.4. In Britain in 1994 cereals were again grown on about 3 million hectares (7.5 million acres), an area 13 per cent down on 1992 as a direct result of the introduction of compulsory set-aside. Production of wheat and oats was up on 1993, but that of barley was down.

About 30 per cent of barley production is normally used for brewing, malting and distilling (there were plentiful supplies of good-quality malting barley from the 1994 harvest), and virtually all the remainder for animal feed.

Large-scale potato and vegetable cultivation can be found on the fertile soils throughout Britain, often with irrigation. Principal areas are the peat and silt fens of Cambridgeshire, Lincolnshire and Norfolk; the sandy loams of Norfolk, Suffolk, West Midlands, Nottinghamshire, South Yorkshire and Lincolnshire; the peat soils of South Lancashire; and the alluvial silts of parts of the Thames and Humber valleys. Early

Table 18.4: Main Crops

	1983–85 average	1992	1993	1994 (provisional)
Wheat				
Area ('000 hectares)	1,845	2,067	1,759	1,811
Production ('000 tonnes)	12,606	14,095	12,890	13,164
Yield (tonnes per hectare)	6.83	6.82	7.33	7.27
Barley				
Area ('000 hectares)	2,029	1,297	1,164	1,106
Production ('000 tonnes)	10,624	7,365	6,038	5,862
Yield (tonnes per hectare)	5.06	5.68	5.19	5.30
Oats				
Area ('000 hectares)	116	100	92	109
Production ('000 tonnes)	532	502	479	606
Yield (tonnes per hectare)	4.60	5.01	5.23	5.59
Potatoes				
Area ('000 hectares)	195	180	170	164
Production ('000 tonnes)	6,700	7,802	7,065	6,445
Yield (tonnes per hectare)	34.35	43.34	41.56	39.30
Oilseed rape				
Area ('000 hectares)	262	421	418	496
Production ('000 tonnes)	792	1,166	1,136	1,265
Yield (tonnes per hectare)	3.02	2.76	2.72	2.55
Sugar beet				
Area ('000 hectares)	198	197	197	195
Production ('000 tonnes)	8,076	9,300	8,988	8,016
Yield (tonnes per hectare)	40.80	47.21	45.62	41.11

Sources: *Agriculture in the United Kingdom 1994*, and *Agricultural Census, June 1994*

potatoes are produced in Shropshire, Pembrokeshire, Cornwall, Devon, Essex, Kent and Cheshire. Production of high-grade seed potatoes is confined to Scotland, Northern Ireland and the Welsh borders.

Sugar from home-grown sugar beet provides just over 60 per cent of home needs, most of the remainder being refined from raw cane sugar imported under the Lomé Convention (see p. 174).

Horticulture

In 1994 the land utilised for horticulture (excluding potatoes, peas for harvesting dry and mushrooms) was about 189,000 hectares (467,000 acres). Vegetables grown in the open accounted for 67 per cent of this, orchards for 17 per cent, and soft fruit and ornamentals (including hardy nursery stock, bulbs and flowers grown in the open) for 7 per cent each. More than one vegetable crop is, in some cases, taken from the same area of land in a year, so that the estimated area actually cropped in 1994 was 240,400 hectares (593,000 acres).

Mushrooms and lettuces are the single most valuable horticultural crops, with farm gate values of £179 million and £105 million respectively in 1994. Apples are also a significant crop. Output of dessert and cooking apples reached 324,000 tonnes, compared with 30,000 tonnes for pears.

Field vegetables account for 55 per cent of the value of horticultural output and are widely grown throughout the country. Most horticultural enterprises are increasing productivity with the help of improved planting material, new techniques and the widespread use of machinery. Some field vegetables, for example, are raised in blocks of compressed peat or loose-filled cells, a technique which reduces root damage and allows plants to establish themselves more reliably and evenly.

Glasshouses are used for growing tomatoes, cucumbers, sweet peppers, lettuces, flowers, pot plants and nursery stock. Widespread use is made of automatic control of heating and ventilation, and semi-automatic control of watering. Low-cost plastic tunnels extend the season for certain crops previously grown in the open.

Alternative Crops

The Government is contributing £1.3 million in 1995–96 towards research into oils for industry uses, fibres and energy crops. Oilseeds, for instance, can be used in lubricants, paints, varnishes and pharmaceuticals; flax, hemp and straw in paper, textiles and brake linings. Set-aside (see p. 284) can provide an opportunity to grow crops for non-food uses.

Organic Farming

The Government launched a voluntary Organic Aid Scheme in England in 1994, with a budget of about £1.5 million in 1995–96. It offers payments to farmers over a five-year period to help with the costs of converting land to organic production. Parallel schemes, worth about £500,000 a year, run in Scotland, Wales and Northern Ireland. Other government help for the organic sector covers the development of regulatory standards and a research programme (worth about £1 million a year).

The organic production and processing standards are implemented by the United Kingdom Register of Organic Food Standards, which has a board of independent experts appointed by ministers.

FOOD SAFETY

EU food law harmonisation covers food safety, fair trading and informative labelling. The Government's system for identifying food safety risks involves food surveys, investigations and research. Results of government action are always published. Food law enforcement falls mainly to local authorities.

In particular, MAFF has programmes to promote food safety and against diseases affecting food supply. Its expenditure on food safety research in 1994–95 was about £10 million. The link between diet, nutrition and health is one of the main subjects studied.

Among the groups assisting MAFF on food safety, the Steering Group on Chemical Aspects of Food Surveillance monitors through surveillance the need for action to ensure the chemical safety, nutritional adequacy and authenticity of food. The Advisory Committee on the Microbiological Safety of Food provides agriculture and health ministers with independent advice on the risk to humans from foodborne micro-organisms.

EXPORTS

Provisional data for 1994 suggest that the value of exports related to agriculture (food, feed and drink), at some £9,000 million, was about 11 per cent greater than 1993. The main markets are Western Europe, North America and the Middle East.

Exports include speciality products such as fresh salmon, whisky (exports to the EU alone were worth £816 million, worldwide £2,185 million), biscuits, jams and conserves, and tea, as well as beef and lamb carcasses, and cheese.

Export promotion for food and drink is headed by Food From Britain, an organisation funded by MAFF (£5.25 million in 1994–95) and industry. For agricultural products and machinery, and food processing equipment, MAFF co-ordinates export promotion and organises trade fairs and ministerial visits to special markets in other countries.

One of the world's largest agricultural events, the annual Royal Agricultural Show, held at Stoneleigh in Warwickshire, enables visitors to see the latest techniques and improvements in British agriculture. Some 180,000 visitors attended in 1995, of whom 4,000 were from overseas. Other major agricultural displays include the Royal Smithfield Show, held every other year in London, which exhibits agricultural machinery, livestock and carcasses; the Royal Highland Show; the Royal Welsh Show; and the Royal Ulster Agricultural Show.

MARKETING

The Marketing Development Scheme, introduced in 1994, makes available about £10 million to Britain's agriculture and food industries over three years. The scheme,

which is directed at non-capital expenditure, aims to help industry develop the management skills necessary to improve its marketing performance. By June 1995 some 140 projects had been awarded funding, representing grant of over £5.5 million.

Agricultural goods are sold by individuals, private traders, and producers' co-operatives and special boards. The four statutory milk marketing schemes in Great Britain came to an end in November 1994 and the scheme in Northern Ireland came to an end in March 1995. Producers are now free to sell their milk to whomever they wish. Dairy companies are now free to buy direct from producers. The Milk Marketing Boards (MMBs) no longer buy and sell milk, but exist in residuary form in order to deal with outstanding liabilities and dispose of retained assets.

Milk Marque, the England and Wales MMB's successor co-operative, has responsibility for certain of the milk marketing assets of the MMB. Scottish Milk, Aberdeen Milk Co. and the North of Scotland Milk Co-operative Society are the successor co-operatives in Scotland. United Dairy Farmers is the Northern Ireland MMB's successor co-operative.

The Government also participates in the EU's Processing and Marketing Grant. This scheme is directed at capital expenditure on the processing and marketing of primary agricultural products; the first two groups of awards, announced in February and June 1995, involved a commitment of over £16 million.

A Milk Development Council has been established to continue some of the activities which were carried out by the MMBs in Great Britain, such as on-farm research and development, genetic evaluation and livestock improvement work, human nutritional guidance, industry statistics and the provision of market information. The Potato Marketing Scheme in Great Britain will come to an end after the 1996–97 crop season. Arrangements for wool continue to be administered by the British Wool Marketing Board.

Much agricultural and horticultural produce, such as grain, fruit and vegetables, is handled by marketing co-operatives and other farmers' businesses; these had a turnover of some £3,720 million in 1994.

ROLE OF THE GOVERNMENT

Four government departments have joint responsibility for agriculture and fisheries matters—MAFF; The Scottish Office Agriculture and Fisheries Department; the Welsh Office; and the Department of Agriculture for Northern Ireland.

Common Agricultural Policy

The original aims of the CAP were to increase agricultural production through the promotion of technical progress, rational development and efficiency, thus providing a fair standard of living for producers, to stabilise markets and to ensure the availability of supplies to consumers at reasonable prices. For many commodities support prices are set annually; there are also levies on imports to maintain internal market prices. Surpluses are bought by intervention boards (the Intervention Board executive agency in Britain) to be stored and sold when appropriate. Intervention stocks can be disposed of within the EU where this can be done without disrupting internal markets. Intervention stocks have decreased significantly over the last three years, partly as a result of the 1992 reforms (see p. 283).

Exports, from the market and intervention stocks, are facilitated by the provision of export refunds to bridge any gap between EU prices and world prices. In some cases there are also direct payments to producers—for example, the Arable Area Payments Scheme (see p. 285), the Suckler Cow Premium, the Beef Special Premium and the Sheep Annual Premium (see p. 283). The support prices, as well as rates of levy, export refunds and other aids, are set in European Currency Units and are converted into the currencies of the member states at fixed rates of exchange—so-called 'green rates'. These green rates are kept broadly in line with market rates in accordance with agreed rules.

Nearly all the EU's agricultural expenditure (£25,400 million in 1994) is channelled through the European Agricultural Guidance and Guarantee Fund. The Fund's guarantee section finances market support arrangements, including direct payments made under the CAP, while the guidance section provides funds for structural reform—for example, farm modernisation and investment—and payments to assist certain farmers to change to alternative enterprises.

Public Expenditure under the CAP by the Intervention Board and the Agricultural Departments

FORECAST 1994/95

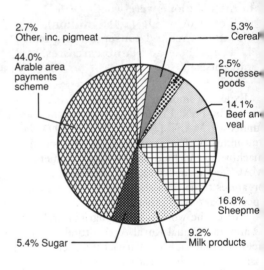

2.7% Other, inc. pigmeat

44.0% Arable area payments scheme

5.4% Sugar

5.3% Cereal

2.5% Processed goods

14.1% Beef and veal

16.8% Sheepmeat

9.2% Milk products

The Government believes that the CAP should be further reformed so as to achieve progressive reductions in product-linked support and protection. This, it is hoped, would lead to the eventual removal of artificial restrictions on production and the creation of a competitive and market-oriented farming industry. Any remaining support could then be better aimed at environmental and other specific objectives.

Pressures arising from the prospect of EU enlargement to the East would be a factor in such change, requiring other member states to focus on the need for further reform—because extending the present CAP to

Central and Eastern Europe would lead to an unacceptable increase in its cost and would prevent the EU from meeting its General Agreement on Tariffs and Trade (GATT—see p. 173) commitments.

Reforms

Those reforms agreed in 1992 have been implemented for arable crops (see p. 285), beef and sheep. Commitment to environmental protection, which Britain secured as part of the CAP, has been followed in a number of areas.

Beef. In 1994–95 the beef market was affected by new trade rules on bovine spongiform encephalopathy (BSE—see p. 286), and ferry company restrictions on live calf exports. The Government makes payments to beef farmers through the EU beef premium schemes. Under the Beef Special Premium, a payment (of up to £86 in 1995) is made not more than twice in the life of male beef animals. The cost of 1995 payments is estimated at £228 million. The Suckler Cow Premium Scheme provides a payment, worth £114.43 in 1995, for cows suckling beef calves, at a total cost of £235 million. There is also support for beef prices through EU beef intervention and export subsidy schemes. Export subsidies are estimated at some £79 million in 1994–95; and intervention storage and other costs some £7 million. Receipts from the sale of intervention beef in 1994–95 are estimated at about £95 million. The Government minimises the use of intervention. By July 1995, British beef intervention stocks were less than 10,000 tonnes.

Sheepmeat. The Sheep Annual Premium Scheme comprises a headage payment on eligible ewes paid to producers—£16.96 a ewe in 1994. A supplement of £5.24 a ewe was paid in Less Favoured Areas (LFAs). Claims for ewe premium are subject to individual producer quotas on the number of animals eligible. Total sheep premium quota for Britain is some 19.6 million.

Environment. Member states are obliged to reduce pollution and nuisance from agriculture and to protect agriculture from the effects of pollution.

The CAP reform measures adopted in 1992 meant significant changes in the support arrangements for the main arable and livestock schemes. The Integrated Administration and Control System, introduced in 1993 and fully operational by January 1996, aims to improve control of CAP expenditure and to reduce the scope for fraud. It requires farmers to submit an annual application with details of all land farmed on a field-by-field basis. The details are held on a computerised database, from which a co-ordinated series of administrative checks on subsidy claims and farm inspections can be made. Late or inaccurate applications are subject to stringent and automatic penalties.

GATT Uruguay Round

The Final Act of the GATT Uruguay Round of multilateral trade negotiations was signed in April 1994 (see p. 173). One of the aims of the Uruguay Round agreements is to introduce, for the first time, disciplines on the use of agricultural subsidies. The agricultural commitments made by the EU and other major exporters include cuts in the volume of subsidised exports, in expenditure on export subsidies, in domestic support and in tariffs and tariff equivalents. The Government expects the reformed CAP to meet the new GATT requirements without substantial further change.

Price Guarantees, Grants and Subsidies

Expenditure in Britain in 1994–95 on CAP market regulation and on price guarantees, grants and subsidies was estimated at £268 million and £2,436 million respectively.

Farmers are eligible for grants aimed at environmental enhancement of their farms.

In LFAs, where land quality is poor, farmers benefit from enhanced rates of grant and special payments on livestock (hill livestock compensatory allowances—HLCAs). There are headage payments on breeding cattle and sheep, and their purpose is to support the continuation of livestock farming in hills and uplands, thus conserving the countryside and maintaining a viable population in the LFAs.

Producers in the LFA (United Kingdom)[2] are estimated to receive direct livestock subsidy payments of over £600 million in 1995, of which over £100 million comes from HLCAs.

Smallholdings and Crofts

In England and Wales county councils let smallholdings to experienced people who want to farm on their own account. Councils may lend working capital to them. At 31 March 1994 there were 33,362 smallholdings in England and 6,125 in Wales. Land settlement in Scotland has been carried out by the Government, which, while now seeking to dispose of holdings to its sitting tenants, still owns and maintains 109,000 hectares (269,230 acres) of land settlement estates, comprising 1,416 crofts and holdings.

In the crofting areas of Scotland—the former counties of Argyll, Inverness, Ross and Cromarty, Sutherland, Caithness, Orkney and Shetland—much of the land is tenanted by crofters (smallholders). They enjoy the statutory protection provided by crofting legislation and can benefit from government schemes which exist to support and help crofting communities, such as agriculture and livestock improvement schemes. Most crofters are part-time or spare-time agriculturalists, using croft income to supplement income from activities such as weaving, fishing, tourism and other occupations. The Crofters Commission has a statutory duty to promote the interests of crofters and to keep all crofting matters under review.

Agricultural Landlords and Tenants

About one-third of agricultural land in England and Wales is rented. To encourage landowners to offer more land for rent and to increase the number of opportunities for new entrants to become established, the Agricultural Tenancies Act 1995 has been introduced. It gives landlords and tenants in England and Wales greater freedom to decide the terms of new tenancy agreements which are taken up from September 1995. Full relief

from inheritance tax on new tenancies from that date will also encourage landowners to offer tenancies.

In Scotland, just under 50 per cent of farmland is rented, partly because of the relatively large areas of common grazings tenanted by crofters.

Most farms in Northern Ireland are owner-occupied, but, under a practice known as 'conacre', occupiers not wishing to farm all their land let it annually to others. Land let under this practice—about one-fifth of agricultural land—is used mainly for grazing.

Agriculture and Protection of the Countryside

During 1993 Britain secured EU agreement that member states should be able to attach appropriate environmental conditions to the payment of livestock subsidies. Further progress was made in improving the environmental potential of set-aside— arable land deliberately not used for agricultural purposes.

Environmentally Sensitive Areas

The ESA scheme (see Table 18.5) encourages farmers to maintain or adopt environmentally beneficial agricultural practices in parts of the country where the landscape, wildlife or historical features are of national importance. ESAs are regularly reviewed and information on their economic and environmental impact is published. The newest, designated in 1994, include Dartmoor and the Cotswold Hills in England, the Argyll Islands and Shetland Islands of Scotland, and the Sperrins and Slieve Gullion in Northern Ireland.

Participation in the ESA scheme is voluntary. Farmers enter into ten-year agreements with the relevant agriculture department. An agreement specifies the agricultural management practices to be carried out. Each ESA has varying tiers of such practices, from basic care and maintenance to more extensive forms of management and environmental restoration. Details also vary, but participants may not convert grassland to arable and are subject to restrictions on fertiliser and chemical usage.

---

[2]Designation of LFA status is decided by the EU. The case for LFAs in Britain was submitted to the EU as covering all of Britain.

Table 18.5: ESAs as at 31 March 1994

	Number of ESAs	Farmers with agreements	Land designated '000 hectares ('000 acres)	Areas covered by agreements	Payments to farmers in 1994–95 (£ '000)
England	22	6,141	1,149 (2,839)	396 (978)	20,083
Wales	6	883	520 (1,284)	87 (212)	1,536
Scotland	10	899	1,439 (3,556)	221 (546)	1,044
Northern Ireland	5	1,400	220 (543)	38 (94)	600

Sources: MAFF; Welsh Office; The Scottish Office; Northern Ireland Office

Most ESAs also restrict or control the numbers of stock on the land as well as operations such as the timing of cultivation. The annual payments (between £8 and £400 a hectare, depending on the needs of each tier) are designed to compensate for reduced profitability through the adoption of these less intensive production methods, and for the further work some management practices require. Additional payments are made for specific items, such as hedgerows and stone wall renewal, set out in conservation plans, and for allowing public access to suitable farmland.

Other Schemes

The Farm Woodland Premium Scheme offers incentives to farmers to plant woodlands on agricultural land. Trees planted on arable or improved grassland qualify for annual payments of up to £250 a hectare for either ten or 15 years, depending on the type of woodland created. Between April 1992 and March 1995, applications to plant nearly 23,500 hectares (58,750 acres) of woodland in Britain were approved. Three-quarters of this area will be planted with broadleaved trees.

Under the Arable Area Payments Scheme, growers can claim area-based payments on cereals, oilseeds, protein and linseed crops. For the main scheme, growers must set aside part of the area on which they claim payment; for the simplified scheme, no set-aside is required, but the claim must not exceed 15.6 hectares (39.7 acres). In 1994 some 47,000 applications were received in Britain for some 4.3 million hectares (10.5 million acres).

The Habitat Scheme offers annual payments, ranging from £125 to £525 a hectare, to farmers to promote nature conservation on their farms by taking carefully selected areas of land out of production for ten or 20 years and managing them in environmentally beneficial ways. In 1994 the Government expanded the Nitrate Sensitive Areas (NSA) Scheme in England by introducing 22 new NSAs to bring the total to 32. NSAs help protect selected groundwater sources used to supply drinking water. The Organic Aid Scheme helps farmers wishing to convert to organic production.

Two further schemes have been introduced:

● in 1994 the Countryside Access Scheme, to increase opportunities for public access on set-aside land; and

● in 1995 the Moorland Scheme, to protect and improve the upland moorland environment by encouraging LFA farmers outside ESAs to graze fewer sheep where this would improve the condition of heather and other moorland vegetation.

Programmes of schemes along broadly similar lines are being introduced in Scotland, Wales and Northern Ireland. By the time all the schemes are fully operational, annual expenditure on these new measures in Britain will exceed £100 million.

Rural Economy

A special programme, agreed with the EU and administered locally, supports development of rural areas by helping farmers to adapt to changing conditions and to make best use of the resources available to them. Eleven areas (for example, Lincolnshire, Gwynedd, and Dumfries and Galloway) in

Great Britain have been designated to receive funds under Objective 5b of the EC Structural Funds. Such a designation depends on an area being rural, having a low GDP and population density, and being substantially dependent on agriculture. Costs over the period 1994–99 (in England) to support the agriculture sector from the European Agriculture Guidance and Guarantee Fund are estimated at £56 million, plus £56 million from national public expenditure.

A study published in late 1994 estimated that farmers in Britain earned about £675 million a year from activities such as bed and breakfast, riding and game shoots—nearly 4 per cent of what they receive from agricultural activities. The study indicates that some 10 per cent of farmers earn more than £300 million between them from diversification—some more than £50,000 a year each.

Rural White Paper

MAFF and the Department of the Environment are to publish a White Paper on the future of the rural areas of England. Other government departments whose policies impinge on the countryside are also involved. Its purpose is to examine the many economic, social and environmental changes taking place in rural society. A rural development strategy is in progress in Scotland. A similar five-year initiative is in progress for Northern Ireland.

Agricultural Training

ATB-Landbase, an independent company, currently acts as the Industry Training Organisation (see p. 183) for agriculture and commercial horticulture. ATB-Landbase oversees the industry's training needs and arranges training through its network of providers and instructors. It currently operates under contracts with the Government, which allots the funding. Training and Enterprise Councils and Local Enterprise Companies (see p. 183), as well as the expanding network of Business Links (see p. 208), help develop business skills. ATB-Landbase also arranges training in wider rural skills, business management and the management of shows and similar events.

The agricultural colleges and independent instructors also help to provide training in the agricultural and horticultural businesses.

Professional, Scientific and Technical Services

In England and Wales ADAS (Food, Farms, Land and Leisure), an executive agency of MAFF and the Welsh Office, provides professional, scientific and technical services for agriculture and its ancillary industries. Most types of advice and servicing are on a fee-paying basis, although initial advice to farmers on conservation, use of land for woodlands and animal welfare is available free. The Government also contributes towards the funding of the Farming and Wildlife Advisory Group to provide free initial conservation advice. Similar services in Scotland come from The Scottish Office Agriculture and Fisheries Department through the Scottish Agricultural College. In Northern Ireland they are available from the Department of Agriculture's agriculture and science services.

CONTROL OF DISEASES AND PESTS

Farm Animals

Britain maintains its high animal health status by enforcement of controls on imports of live animals and genetic material, including frequent checks on imported consignments at destination points. There are safeguards to prevent the importation of diseased animals and genetic material from regions or countries affected by disease. Veterinary checks include 24-hour periods of import and export surveillance at all south and east coast ports, as well as checks on all individual consignments originating from outside the EU. The number of consignments failing to meet animal health requirements in 1994 was low.

The number of new cases of the cattle disease BSE continues to decline as predicted as a result of measures in place to control the disease. EC rules continue to apply to trade in beef with Britain. In July 1995, these rules were amended slightly. Meat may now be exported without any further restriction from any animals aged less than 30 months at slaughter. (The previous requirement was that they should be born after 1 January 1992.) Any other beef on the bone must be certified as coming from animals who have resided only on holdings which have been free of BSE for the past six years.

Professional advice and action on the statutory control of animal disease and the welfare of farm livestock are the responsibility of the State Veterinary Service. It is supported by the laboratories of the Veterinary Investigation Service in England and Wales, which charge for their diagnostic service to private veterinary practitioners and have an important role in animal disease surveillance. A similar service is provided in Scotland by the Scottish Agricultural College.

Rabies

Special measures apply to prevent rabies entering Britain. Dogs, cats and certain other mammals are subject to import licence and six months' quarantine. From July 1994 commercially traded dogs and cats from other EU states which satisfy strict conditions have been allowed entry without quarantine. There are severe penalties for breaking the law. No cases of rabies outside quarantine have occurred in Britain since 1970.

Fish

The fisheries departments operate statutory controls to prevent the introduction and spread of serious diseases of fish and shellfish. These controls include the licensing of live fish imports, the licensing of deposits of shellfish on the seabed, and movement restrictions on sites where outbreaks of notifiable diseases have been confirmed.

Plants

The agriculture departments are responsible for limiting the spread of plant pests and diseases and for preventing the introduction of new ones. They issue the health certificates required by other countries to accompany plant material exported from Britain, and authorise growers who wish to sell on the EU's single internal market. Certification schemes encourage the development of healthy and true-to-type planting stocks.

Pesticides

All pesticides must be approved for their safety and efficacy. There are strict controls on the supply, storage and use of pesticides, and their maximum residue levels in food. Controls on pesticides are the joint responsibility of six government departments on the basis of advice from the independent Advisory Committee on Pesticides. Progress has been made in establishing an effective European system.

Veterinary Medicinal Products

The authorisation and manufacture of veterinary medicinal products are controlled by legislation. Licences are issued by the Veterinary Medicines Directorate on behalf of the agriculture and health ministers for products that have been approved on the basis of safety, quality and efficacy. Independent expert advice on these criteria and on suspected adverse reactions is provided by the Veterinary Products Committee. Approval of veterinary medicines was harmonised under an EU-wide system from January 1995.

The Fishing Industry

The fishing industry provides 59 per cent by quantity of British fish supplies, and is an important source of employment and income in a number of ports. Cod, haddock, whiting, herring, plaice and sole are caught in the North Sea off the east coasts of Scotland and England; mackerel, together with cod and other demersal fish (those caught on or near the bottom of the sea), are found off the west coast of Scotland; sole, plaice, cod, herring and whiting in the Irish Sea; and mackerel, sole and plaice off the south-west coast of England. Nephrops, crabs, lobsters and other shellfish are taken from the inshore waters all around the coast. A fleet also operates in distant waters—around Greenland and north Norway, for example.

Fish Caught

In 1994 demersal fish accounted for 43 per cent by weight of total landings by British fishing vessels, pelagic fish (those caught near the surface) for 44 per cent and shellfish for 13 per cent. Landings of all types of fish (excluding salmon and trout) by British fishing vessels totalled 874,900 tonnes compared with 857,600 tonnes in 1993. Cod and haddock represented 16 and 15 per cent respectively of the total value of demersal and pelagic fish landed, while anglerfish (10 per cent), plaice and mackerel (each with 9 per cent), and hake and whiting (each with 5 per cent) were the other most important sources of earnings to the industry. The quayside value of landings of all sea fish, including shellfish, by British vessels in 1994 was £561 million.

The Fishing Fleet

At the end of 1994 the British fleet consisted of 10,295 registered vessels, including 450 deep-sea vessels longer than 24.4 m (80 ft). Under an EU commitment to reduce fishing, Britain operates a decommissioning scheme to bring the fleet size into line with fishing opportunities. In 1993–94 135 vessels were scrapped at a cost of £7.8 million; in 1994–95 162 vessels went, at a cost of £8.9 million. Total government financial commitment to decommissioning in the period 1993–98 is some £53 million.

Among the main ports from which the fishing fleet operates are Aberdeen, Peterhead, Fraserburgh (Grampian), Lerwick (Shetland), Kinlochbervie, Ullapool (Highland), North Shields (Tyne and Wear), Hull, Grimsby (Humberside), Lowestoft (Suffolk), Brixham (Devon), Newlyn (Cornwall), and Kilkeel, Ardglass and Portavogie (Northern Ireland).

In its effort to conserve fish stocks, the Government takes account of biological and environmental considerations and of marine ecology. Its primary purpose is to create a safe, efficient industry, its capacity tuned to what stocks will bear.

Fish Farming

Fish farming is centred on Atlantic salmon and rainbow trout, which are particularly suited to Britain's climate and waters. Production of salmon and trout has grown from less than 1,000 tonnes in the early 1970s to 64,066 tonnes of salmon (all in Scotland) and 15,088 tonnes of trout in 1994. Scotland produces the largest amount of farmed salmon (with a first-sale value in excess of £200 million) in the EU. Shellfish farming concentrates on molluscs such as oysters, mussels, clams and scallops, producing an estimated 4,160 tonnes a year.

The fish and shellfish farming industries make an important contribution to the rural economy, especially in remote areas such as the Highlands and Islands of Scotland. In

Table 18.6: Imports and Exports of Fish

	1992	1993	1994 (provisional)
Imports			
Salt-water and shellfish	432,045	398,094	419,202
Freshwater fish	52,973	44,172	38,439
Fish meals	237,256	261,211	247,721
Fish oils	121,156	127,211	138,368
Exports and re-exports			
Salt-water fish and fish products	389,532	350,607	338,788
Freshwater fish	22,665	25,385	33,374
Fish meals	5,687	8,703	17,039
Fish oils	8,824	8,289	12,121

tonnes

Sources: MAFF; The Scottish Office; Northern Ireland Office

1994 the industries were estimated to have a combined wholesale turnover of some £246.5 million. Production is based on 974 businesses operating from 1,638 sites and employing more than 3,000 people.

Administration

The fisheries departments are responsible for the administration of legislation concerning the fishing industry, including fish and shellfish farming, and for fisheries research. The safety and welfare of crews of fishing vessels and other shipping matters are provided for under legislation administered by the Department of Transport.

The Sea Fish Industry Authority is concerned with all aspects of the sea fish industry, including consumer interests. It undertakes research and development, provides training, and encourages quality awareness. It also acts as an agent to pay government grants (£2.5 million in 1994–95) towards the cost of work necessary to obtain a Department of Transport vessel safety certificate.

Fishery Limits

British fishery limits extend to 200 miles or the median line (broadly halfway between the British coast and the opposing coastline of another coastal state), measured from baselines on or near the coast of Britain. Only British vessels may fish within six miles of the coast. Certain other EU member states have fishing rights between six and 12 miles in certain areas and for named species, as British vessels have in other member states' coastal waters. Outside 12 miles EU vessels may fish against agreed EU quotas in named areas. The only non-EU countries whose vessels may fish in EU waters are those with which the EU has reciprocal fisheries agreements (Norway and the Faroes) which define areas and quantities (by species) of permitted catch.

Common Fisheries Policy

Britain plays an active role in the implementation and development of the EU's Common Fisheries Policy (CFP). The CFP's system for the conservation and management of the EU's fishing resources means that total allowable catches are set each year in order to conserve stocks. Decisions are based on independent scientific advice. These catch levels are then allocated between member states on a fixed percentage basis, taking account of traditional fishing patterns. Activity is also regulated by a number of technical conservation measures, including minimum mesh sizes for towed nets and net configuration restrictions, minimum landing sizes and closed areas designed mainly to protect young fish. All commercial fishing vessels in Britain have to be licensed. However, implementation of restrictions on days at sea has been suspended pending a ruling from the European Court of Justice. Each member state is responsible for enforcement of the rules on its own fishermen and those of other member states in its own waters. Compliance is monitored by EU inspectors.

North Atlantic Fisheries

Outline agreement has been reached on the arrangements to integrate Spain and Portugal fully into the CFP from 1 January 1996. Spanish access will be limited to 40 vessels at one time in the Irish Box—the area immediately north, west and south of Ireland; Spanish boats will be excluded from the Irish Sea and the Bristol Channel; and arrangements will be introduced to ensure that fishing in western waters does not increase.

An agreement reached in 1995 between the EU and Canada over fisheries in the north-west Atlantic has four main features:

- neutral observers on board all vessels fishing in the area, to monitor compliance with all internationally agreed conservation measures;
- new conservation measures for Greenland halibut;
- an agreed share-out of the total allowable catch of 27,000 tonnes of Greenland halibut between Canada and the EU; and
- Canada to repeal legislation authorising the seizure of Spanish and Portuguese boats in international waters.

Fisheries Agreements

The CFP also covers the common organisation of the market in fishery and aquaculture products and policies on the size and structure of the EU fleet.

CFP provisions are supplemented by a number of fisheries agreements between the EU and third countries, the most important for Britain being the agreements with Norway, Greenland and the Faroe Islands. EU catch quotas have also been established around Spitzbergen (Svalbard).

Fish and Shellfish Hygiene

Community legislation sets minimum hygiene standards for the production and marketing of fish and shellfish. Live bivalve molluscs (oysters, mussels and cockles) can be marketed only if they come from areas classified by the Government according to strict microbiological standards.

Salmon and Freshwater Fisheries

Salmon and sea-trout are fished commercially in inshore waters around the British coast. Eels and elvers are also taken commercially in both estuaries and fresh water. Angling for salmon and sea-trout (game fishing) and for other freshwater species (coarse fishing) is popular throughout Britain. There is no public right to fish in freshwater lakes and rivers in Great Britain. In England and Wales those wishing to fish such waters must first obtain permission from the owner of the fishing rights and a licence from the National Rivers Authority. In Scotland salmon fishing is administered by district salmon fishery boards. In Northern Ireland fishing is licensed by the Fisheries Conservancy Board for Northern Ireland and the Foyle Fisheries Commission in their respective areas, and 65 public angling waters, including salmon, trout and coarse fisheries, are accessible to Department of Agriculture permit holders.

Research

Departmental funding of research and development in agriculture, fisheries and food

in 1995–96 amounts to about £184 million. This includes funding by MAFF, the Scottish Office Agriculture and Fisheries Department, and the Department of Agriculture for Northern Ireland. The Government funds research:

- to support the improvement of the economic performance of the agriculture, fishing and food industries;
- to protect the public by ensuring food safety, controlling animal diseases with implications for human health, and providing flood protection;
- to enhance the rural and marine environment; and
- to promote animal welfare.

It looks to industry to fund those areas of research where individual firms or ventures gain direct benefit. Research is carried out in government research establishments, research institutes, specialist laboratories and universities.

Agriculture and Food

The Biotechnology and Biological Sciences Research Council (BBSRC; see p. 323) is responsible for research in biological sciences that underpin food and agriculture. The Natural Environment Research Council (NERC; see p. 323) is responsible for research on the environment, including agricultural aspects. These research councils receive funds from the science budget through the Office of Science and Technology, and income from work commissioned by MAFF, by industry and by other bodies. They carry out research at their institutes and in higher education institutions through their grant schemes.

ADAS carries out research and development under commission from MAFF and under contract for other bodies. Work is carried out at research farms across England and Wales, through regional centres and on clients' premises.

MAFF also commissions research at its other agencies—the Central Veterinary Laboratory and the Central Science Laboratory—and increasingly through open competition. The five Scottish Agricultural and Biological Research Institutes, funded by the Scottish Office Agriculture and Fisheries Department, cover areas of research complementary to those of the BBSRC institutes, while including work relevant to the conditions of northern Britain. Development work in Scotland is carried out by the Scottish Agricultural College, which operates from three centres. In Northern Ireland the Department of Agriculture does basic and applied research in its specialist research divisions and at its three agricultural colleges. It also has links with the Queen's University of Belfast and the Agricultural Research Institute of Northern Ireland.

Fisheries and Aquatic Environment

MAFF laboratories deal with marine and freshwater fisheries, shellfish, marine pollution, fish farming and disease. MAFF also commissions research work from the Natural Environment Research Council, the Sea Fish Industry Authority and a number of universities. It has two seagoing research vessels. In Scotland, the Scottish Office Agriculture and Fisheries Department undertakes a similar, and complementary, range of research and also has two seagoing vessels. The Department of Agriculture laboratories in Northern Ireland undertake research on marine and freshwater fisheries, and also have a seagoing research vessel.

Forestry

Woodland covers an estimated 2.4 million hectares (5.9 million acres) in Britain: about 7 per cent of England, 15 per cent of Scotland, 12 per cent of Wales and 5 per cent of Northern Ireland. This is about 10 per cent of the total land area and well below the 25 per cent average for the whole of Europe.

Britain's forestry programme protects forest resources and conserves woodland as a home for wildlife and for public recreation. It also promotes the market for home-grown timber.

The area of productive forest in Great Britain is 2.17 million hectares (5.36 million acres), 38 per cent of which is managed by the Forestry Commission. The rate of new planting in 1994–95 was 8,765 hectares

(21,649 acres) by the Commission and 18,128 hectares (44,776 acres) by other woodland owners, with the help of grants from the Commission, mainly in Scotland. In 1994–95, 9,986 hectares (24,665 acres) of broadleaved trees were planted, a practice encouraged on suitable sites. Much new planting is by private owners.

> The forest area has doubled since 1919. Since the mid–1980s nearly 220,000 hectares (545,000 acres) of new woodland have been created. Forestry employs more than 40,000 people. Britain's woodlands produce about 7 million cubic metres (250 million cubic feet) of wood a year—about 15 per cent of total consumption. The Government is spending £242 million to support the management of state and private forests and their expansion in the three years 1994–95 to 1996–97.

The volume of timber harvested on Commission lands in 1994–95 totalled 4.3 million cubic metres (150 million cubic feet).

The Commission's Woodland Grant Scheme pays grants to help create new woodlands and forests and regenerate existing ones. Approval was given for 24,263 hectares (59,930 acres) of new planting in 1994–95, including 5,633 hectares (13,914 acres) of new natural regeneration. Annual management grant is available under the scheme as a contribution towards the cost of management operations needed to safeguard or enhance the special environmental value of a woodland, improve woods which are below environmental standards or create, maintain or enhance public access.

The Forestry Commission and Forestry Policy

The Forestry Commission, established in 1919, is the government department responsible for forestry in Great Britain. The Commissioners advise on forestry matters and are responsible to the Secretary of State for Scotland, the Minister of Agriculture, Fisheries and Food, and the Secretary of State for Wales.

Within the Commission, the Forestry Authority controls tree felling, provides grants and advice to private woodland owners, and sets standards for the forestry industry as a whole. Forest Enterprise, an executive agency of the Commission, develops and manages the Commission's forests and forestry estate, supplying timber and opportunities for recreation, and enhancing nature conservation and the forest environment. The Policy and Resources Group sees to parliamentary business, policy development, and European and international liaison.

The Commission has sold 115,313 hectares (284,823 acres) of forest land since 1981 and, at the Government's request, has to dispose of 100,000 hectares (247,000 acres) during the 1990s. The Commission is financed partly by the Government and partly by receipts from sales of timber and other produce, and from rents.

Forestry Initiatives

Plans for 12 Community Forests[3] in England—for example, Thames Chase (east of London), Mercia (Staffordshire), Great North (Tyne and Wear), Mersey (close to Liverpool) and Bristol/Avon—have been approved. A new national forest in the English Midlands (500 sq km; 200 sq miles) is being established. In Wales, the Valleys Forest Initiative encourages local communities to participate in the development of 350 sq km (135 sq miles) of existing forest in the

---

[3] The Forestry and Countryside Commissions and local authorities plan to create Community Forests near certain towns as recreational and productive woodlands in areas that at present do not have them.

valleys of south Wales—about 20 per cent of the land area—which is owned by the Forestry Commission. Community forests are also being promoted and developed in Scotland and Northern Ireland.

Forestry Research

The Forestry Commission maintains two principal research stations, at Alice Holt Lodge, near Farnham (Surrey), and at Bush Estate, near Edinburgh, for basic and applied research into all aspects of forestry. Aid is also given for research work in universities and other institutions. There is an increasing number of co-operative research projects with international partners, and Commission specialists are undertaking overseas consultancies. A database on forestry and tree-related research in Great Britain has been compiled by the Forestry Research Co-ordination Committee and is updated annually.

The Forestry Authority conducts an annual survey of forest condition to monitor the effects of climatic environmental stress factors on broadleaves and conifers.

Forestry in Northern Ireland

The Department of Agriculture may acquire land for afforestation and give financial and technical assistance for private planting. The state forest area has grown steadily since 1945. By 1994, 75,500 hectares (186,500 acres) of plantable land had been acquired, of which 60,800 hectares (150,000 acres) were planted. There were 17,000 hectares (42,000 acres) of privately owned forest. Some 470 staff are employed by the forestry service.

Further Reading

Agriculture, Fisheries and Forestry, Aspects of Britain series, HMSO, 1993.
Agriculture in the United Kingdom 1994. HMSO.
Forestry Commission. Annual report. HMSO.

19 Transport and Communications

Britain's transport and communications infrastructure is developing rapidly. The Channel Tunnel (see p. 302) has linked the rail transport system of Great Britain to that of the European mainland. Britain's road network is being improved, with the emphasis on upgrading existing routes rather than building new motorways. Investment at seaports and airports and in air traffic control equipment continues to expand capacity and ease the international movement of people and goods. Britain's telecommunications infrastructure continues to develop, with several new entrants to the market since 1991.

Transport

There has been a considerable increase in passenger travel in recent years—in Great Britain it rose by 29 per cent between 1984 and 1994. Travel by car and van rose by 38 per cent and air travel was up by roughly two-thirds. However, travel by motor cycle, pedal cycle and by bus and coach has been declining. In all, car and van travel accounts for 87 per cent of passenger mileage within Great Britain, buses and coaches for about 6 per cent, rail for 5 per cent and air 1 per cent. The amount of freight moved by road increased by 21 per cent between 1984 and 1994. Total motor traffic for 1994 is estimated at 421,900 million vehicle-km.

Car ownership has also risen substantially. In all, 68 per cent of households in Great Britain had the regular use of one or more cars in 1993; 23 per cent had the use of two or more cars. At the end of 1994 there were 25.2 million vehicles licensed for use on the roads of Great Britain, of which 21.2 million were cars (including 2.2 million company cars); 2.0 million light goods vehicles; 580,000 other goods vehicles; 720,000 motor cycles, scooters and mopeds; and 150,000 buses and coaches.

Research on transport issues is undertaken by a number of public sector bodies and by industry, especially the motor, aviation, marine and oil industries. Research is also commissioned by the Department of Transport, the Civil Aviation Authority (CAA—see p. 308), British Rail (BR—see p. 300) and London Transport (LT—see p. 298). In addition to the Transport Research Laboratory, which was due to be privatised in 1995, the Department of Transport uses a wide range of contractors, including consulting engineers, universities, and institutes and laboratories of the research councils (see pp. 321–5).

ROADS

The total road network in Britain in 1994 was 389,200 km (243,200 miles). Trunk motorways accounted for 3,200 km (2,000 miles) of this, less than 1 per cent, and other trunk roads for 14,400 km (9,000 miles), or 3.7 per cent. However, motorways carry 16 per cent of all traffic and trunk roads another 16 per cent. Combined, they carry over half of all goods vehicle traffic in Great Britain.

A Road User's Charter was published in April 1994, setting out the standards expected of the Highways Agency (see below) on motorways and trunk roads. These cover matters such as safety and security on the road network, maintenance and improvement of the network, and answering queries and complaints.

Management

Responsibility for trunk roads, including most motorways, rests in England with the Secretary of State for Transport, in Scotland with the Secretary of State for Scotland and in Wales with the Secretary of State for Wales. Central government meets the majority of the costs of construction and maintenance. The Highways Agency, an executive agency of the Department of Transport, is responsible for building, improving and maintaining motorways and trunk roads in England. Its total budget is £1,864 million in 1995–96. In Northern Ireland the Department of the Environment for Northern Ireland is responsible for the construction, improvement and maintenance of all public roads.

The main highway authorities for non-trunk roads in England are at present the county councils, the metropolitan district councils and the London borough councils. In Wales, the highway authorities are the county councils until April 1996, when the new unitary authorities (see p. 72) take over. Likewise in Scotland, the new unitary councils will take over these responsibilities from the regional councils in April 1996. The islands councils will retain their highway responsibilities.

Road Programme

In a 1994 review of the motorway and trunk road programme in England, schemes in the programme were assessed for priority. The most important projects are to be implemented more quickly. By contrast, 49 schemes that were no longer environmentally acceptable or not needed in the foreseeable future were withdrawn, and preparation work was suspended on 67 others. In particular, the number of proposals for building new publicly-funded trunk routes was sharply reduced. Increased emphasis is being placed on smaller schemes to reduce accident and congestion blackspots, with a 40 per cent rise in funding being announced in December 1994 for smaller schemes.

In spring 1995, 53 motorway and trunk

Table 19.1: Road Length (as at April 1994)

kilometres

	Public roads	All-purpose trunk roads and trunk motorways	Trunk motorways[a]
England	279,073	10,412	2,700
Scotland	52,226	3,133	274
Wales	33,709	1,700	123
Northern Ireland	24,184	2,337[b]	111
Britain	389,192	17,582	3,208

Source: Department of Transport

[a] In addition, there were 44 km (28 miles) of local authority motorway in England and 31 km (20 miles) in Scotland.
[b] Class A road.

road schemes were under construction in England and 271 further schemes were in preparation. Expenditure of £1,090 million on new trunk road construction is planned for 1995–96, with eight new schemes due to start. The trunk road maintenance programme is £500 million. Surveys have shown that the condition of trunk roads has improved since the mid-1980s. Support for local authority road schemes is now approved on a package basis, with local authorities being encouraged to submit bids for a package of measures covering both roads and public transport. For 1995–96, the Department of Transport has approved 37 package bids totalling £79 million. A total of £346 million of government grant is available to support local authority spending on transport in England in 1995–96.

Road communications in Wales will benefit from the second Severn crossing, the recent completion of the M4 motorway and improvements to the A55 and A465 roads. The A55 is now dual carriageway across the mainland. The Welsh Office's trunk road and transport programme for 1995–96 will cost £187 million. A total of £109 million is also being made available in 1995–96 for local authority capital expenditure on transport. This includes about £80 million for specific major road improvements.

A scheme for a 10,400-km (6,500-mile) national cycle network was among the first proposals to be approved for funding by the Millennium Commission. The project, towards which the Commission is providing £43 million, will see 4,000 km (2,500 miles) completed by the year 2000. The Government is providing £3 million in 1995–96 for a cycle network in London.

The Government has committed £538 million between 1995–96 and 1997–98 to trunk road construction and improvement in Scotland. The main priorities within the trunk road programme are the upgrading to motorway of the Glasgow to Carlisle route, some 60 per cent of which was ready by January 1995, and the completion of the motorway network in central Scotland. These routes provide important links for commerce and industry to the south and to mainland Europe. The Government's strategy also includes a series of 'route action plans' designed to make significant improvements to safety and journey times on specific major routes. A total of £172 million is being made available in 1995–96 for local authority capital expenditure on roads and transport schemes in Scotland.

In Northern Ireland the emphasis is on improving arterial routes, constructing more bypasses, and improving roads in the Belfast area.

Private Finance

The Government is encouraging greater private sector involvement in the design, construction, operation and funding of roads. Privately funded schemes completed in recent years, being built or undergoing planning procedures include:

- a crossing of the River Thames at Dartford, which opened to traffic in 1991 and links into the M25 London orbital motorway;

- a bridge between the mainland of Scotland and Skye, which opened in October 1995;

- a second crossing of the River Severn, scheduled for completion in summer 1996; and

- a relief road north of Birmingham, which would be the first overland toll route in Britain, and which is the subject of a public inquiry that opened in summer 1994.

The Government is assessing the feasibility of introducing electronic tolls on the motorway network, which at present has no tolls. The Government is stimulating the private sector road operating industry and harnessing private sector capital through a number of projects whereby the private sector will design, build, finance and operate new roads in return for payments from the Government principally related to traffic volumes.

Licensing and Standards

The Driver and Vehicle Licensing Agency (DVLA) maintains official records of drivers and vehicles in Great Britain. At the end of 1994 it held records on 35.2 million drivers and 25.5 million licensed vehicles. New drivers of motor vehicles must pass a driving test before getting a full licence to drive.

In May 1995 the Government announced proposals for introducing a separate test of driving theory for learner drivers. The test, which will have to be passed before taking the present on-road practical test, will last about half an hour and consist of about 35 multiple-choice questions on matters such as traffic signs, safety aspects of vehicles and driver attitude. These arrangements will be in force from July 1996.

The Driving Standards Agency is the national driver testing authority in Great Britain. It also supervises professional driving instructors and the compulsory basic training scheme for learner motor cyclists. Minimum ages are:

- 16 for riders of mopeds, drivers of small tractors, and disabled people receiving a mobility allowance;

- 17 for drivers of cars and other passenger vehicles with nine or fewer seats (including that of the driver), motor cycles and goods vehicles not over 3.5 tonnes permissible maximum weight;

- 18 for goods vehicles weighing over 3.5, but not over 7.5, tonnes; and

- 21 for passenger vehicles with more than nine seats and goods vehicles over 7.5 tonnes.

Before most new cars and goods vehicles are allowed on the roads, they must meet certain safety and environmental requirements, based primarily on standards drawn up by the EU. This form of control, known as type approval, is operated by the Vehicle Certification Agency.

The Vehicle Inspectorate is responsible for ensuring the roadworthiness of vehicles. It does this through the annual testing of vehicles, including heavy goods vehicles, light goods vehicles, public service vehicles, cars and motor cycles. It also ensures the compliance of drivers and vehicle operators with legislation through roadside and other enforcement checks.

In Northern Ireland the Driver and Vehicle Testing Agency (DVTA) is responsible for testing drivers and vehicles under statutory schemes broadly similar to those in Great Britain. Private cars four or more years old are tested at DVTA centres.

Road Safety

Although Great Britain has one of the highest densities of road traffic in the world, it has a good record on road safety, with the lowest road accident death rate in the EU. Figures for 1994 show that 3,650 people were killed on the roads (down 4 per cent on 1993 and the lowest since records began), 46,500 seriously injured and 265,000 slightly injured. This compares with nearly 8,000 deaths a year in the mid-1960s. Several factors, such as developments in vehicle safety standards, improvements in roads, and the introduction of legislation on seat-belt wearing and drinking and driving, have contributed to the long-term decline in deaths and serious casualties.

In March 1995 the Government announced that seat belts would have to be fitted to every coach and minibus used specifically for transporting children.

The Government's aim is to reduce road casualties by one-third by the end of the century, compared with the 1981–85 average. Priority is given to reducing casualties among vulnerable road-users (children, pedestrians, cyclists, motor cyclists and elderly people), particularly in urban areas, where about 75 per cent of road accidents occur. Other strategies for reducing casualties focus on improvements in highway design, better protection for vehicle occupants, encouraging the use of cycle helmets and measures to combat drinking and driving.

Deaths on Britain's Roads 1926–1994

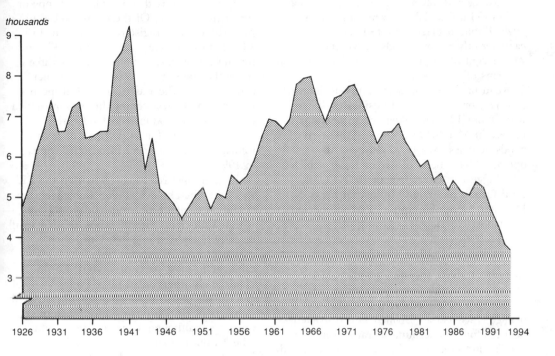

thousands

Source: Department of Transport

Spending on local road safety schemes will increase to £60 million by 1997–98, up 20 per cent on 1995–96 levels.

Traffic in Towns

Traffic management schemes are used in many urban areas to reduce congestion, create a better environment and improve road safety. They include bus lanes, facilities for pedestrians and cyclists, and traffic-calming measures such as road humps to constrain traffic speeds in residential areas. Local authorities can introduce 20 mph (32 km/h) zones, subject to central government consent. About 170 have been set up.

Many towns have shopping precincts designed for the convenience of pedestrians, from which motor vehicles are excluded for all or part of the day. Controls over on-street parking are enforced through excess charges and fixed penalty fines, supported where appropriate by powers to clamp or remove vehicles.

The first part of a 505-km (315-mile) network of priority 'red routes' in London came into operation in March 1995. Marked by red lining and special signs, these routes are subject to special stopping controls and other traffic management measures, strictly enforced with higher penalties. The Traffic Director for London is co-ordinating the introduction and operation of red routes throughout London. A pilot scheme in north and east London, introduced in 1991, led to significant falls in bus journey times and a more dependable service, with a consequent rise in passenger numbers.

ROAD HAULAGE

Road haulage traffic by heavy goods vehicles amounted to 137,800 million tonne-km[1] in 1994, 7 per cent more than in 1993. There has been a move towards larger and more efficient vehicles carrying heavier loads— about 80 per cent of the traffic, measured in tonne-km, is now carried by vehicles of over 25 tonnes laden weight. Journey lengths are

[1] A tonne-km is equivalent to 1 tonne transported for 1 km.

increasing, with the average haul now being 86 km (53 miles), 23 per cent longer than in 1979. Public haulage (private road hauliers carrying other firms' goods) accounts for 73 per cent of freight carried in Great Britain in terms of tonne-km.

Road haulage is predominantly an industry of small, privately owned businesses. There were about 121,000 holders of an operator's licence in March 1995, with 403,000 heavy goods vehicles. Nearly 90 per cent of operators have fleets of five or fewer vehicles. The biggest in Great Britain are NFC plc, LEP Group plc, P & O Industrial Services Division, Ocean Group plc, Parcelforce and Transport Development Group plc.

Licensing and Other Controls

In general, those operating goods vehicles or trailer combinations over 3.5 tonnes gross weight require a goods vehicle operator's licence. Licences are divided into restricted licences for own-account operators carrying goods connected with their own business, and standard licences for hauliers operating for hire or reward. Proof of professional competence, financial standing and good repute is needed to obtain a standard licence. In Northern Ireland own-account operators do not require a licence, although this is under consideration.

EC regulations prescribe maximum limits on driving times and minimum requirements for breaks and rest periods for most drivers of heavy goods vehicles over 35 tonnes. Drivers' activities are recorded by means of a tachograph. Drivers of goods vehicles which are exempt from EC rules are subject to separate British drivers' hours rules, which normally require drivers to keep a written record of their activities when driving vehicles of over 3.5 tonnes. Speed limiters must also be fitted to heavy lorries. Originally these had to be set to limit speed to 60 mph (97 km/h). However, in January 1994 a programme began to reduce this gradually to 56 mph (90 km/h).

International Road Haulage

International road haulage has grown rapidly and in 1994 about 1.7 million road goods vehicles were ferried to mainland Europe or the Irish Republic. Of these, 469,000 were powered vehicles registered in Britain. In 1994 British vehicles carried almost 13 million tonnes internationally, about three times the amount for 1984. About 95 per cent of this traffic was with the European Union. The largest commodity group carried is agricultural produce and foodstuffs, which accounted for 34 per cent of inward tonnage and 25 per cent of outward tonnage in 1993.

International road haulage within the EU was fully liberalised in 1993. 'Cabotage' (the operation of domestic road haulage services within a member state by a non-resident) will be fully liberalised in 1998. Until then, quotas of permits are available which allow cabotage in most parts of western Europe. Haulage elsewhere takes place under bilateral agreements, most of which allow unrestricted numbers of British lorries into the country concerned, although some require permits. The European Conference of Transport Ministers issues a limited but increasing number of permits giving free access to, and transit across, a number of countries in central and eastern Europe.

PASSENGER SERVICES

Buses

Almost all bus services in Great Britain are provided by companies in the private sector, ranging from major groups with over 5,000 buses to small operators with fewer than five. The largest operator is Stagecoach Holdings. Outside London, operators may provide services without restriction, although controls may be imposed on the number of vehicles operating if this would otherwise cause congestion or danger to other road users. Although most local bus services are provided commercially, local authorities may subsidise the provision of services which are not commercially viable but which are considered to be socially necessary, after competitive tender. Local bus mileage outside London in 1993–94 was up 24 per cent on its 1985–86 pre-deregulation level.

London Transport (LT) is a statutory

corporation responsible for providing public transport in London. It no longer has its own buses, but organises about 650 bus routes through private sector companies operating under contract. A London Bus Passenger's Charter sets service standards. LT completed the privatisation of its bus operating subsidiaries by the end of 1994. In the longer term deregulation of bus services in London is proposed. Provision would be made for operating socially necessary but uneconomic services and the continuation of a London-wide concessionary travel scheme.

Bus priority measures, such as bus lanes and traffic light priority signalling, form an important element in many local authorities' package bids to the Department of Transport (see p. 295). A further £8 million has been allocated in 1995–96 to continue development of a London bus priority network. Also, new information systems are being provided to assist passengers. For example, in Southampton a bus passenger information system known as Stopwatch provides information to passengers at 30 stops.

In Northern Ireland subsidiaries of the publicly owned Northern Ireland Transport Holding Company supply almost all road passenger services. Citybus Ltd operates services in Belfast, and Ulsterbus Ltd runs most of the services in the rest of Northern Ireland. These companies have about 285 and 1,200 vehicles respectively. As well as the two major operators, there are about 75 small privately owned undertakings, often operating fewer than five vehicles.

Coaches

In Britain long-distance coach services are provided by companies in the private sector. There are no restrictions on routes served or the number of vehicles operated. A national network of routes is maintained by the National Express company, largely through franchised operations. Passenger comfort in coaches has improved in recent years, for example through the provision of refreshment facilities on some services.

While all regular, and some shuttle, overseas coach services still require authorisation or permission from the authorities of the

countries to or through which they travel, most tourist services within the EU have been liberalised. Operators no longer need prior permission to run either holiday shuttle services, where accommodation is included as part of the package, or occasional coach tours to, from or within another member state. Since 1993 passenger cabotage has been allowed for tours where a single vehicle carries the same group of passengers throughout a journey. From January 1996, this will extend to all non-regular services.

Taxis

There are about 58,000 licensed taxis in Great Britain, mainly in urban areas; London has about 18,000. In London and several other major cities taxis must be purpose-built to conform to very strict requirements and new ones have to provide for people in wheelchairs. In many urban districts drivers must have passed a test of their knowledge of the area. At present, a local authority can only limit the number of licensed taxis if it is satisfied that there is no unfulfilled demand for taxis in its area. Private hire vehicles with drivers ('minicabs') may be booked only through the operator and not hired on the street. In most areas outside London private hire vehicles are licensed; there are about 52,000 in England and Wales outside London. It is estimated that at least 40,000 minicabs operate in London.

Having reviewed the taxi licensing regime in England and Wales, in February 1995 the Government announced that it intends to maintain the distinction between taxis and minicabs, and will introduce a licensing system for minicabs in London when legislation permits. The power of local authorities to control numbers of taxis would be phased out.

There are about 4,000 licensed taxis in Northern Ireland. Licences are issued by the Department of the Environment for Northern Ireland on a broadly similar basis to that in Great Britain.

RAILWAYS

Railways were pioneered in Britain: the Stockton and Darlington Railway, opened in

1825, was the first public passenger railway in the world to be worked by steam power. The main railway companies in Great Britain were nationalised in 1948, coming under the control of the British Railways Board. This rail network is now being privatised.

Privatisation

The Government's approach, enshrined in the Railways Act 1993, includes:

- the franchising of all BR's existing passenger services to the private sector;
- the transfer of BR's freight and parcels operations to the private sector;
- the creation of a new right of access to the rail network for private operators of both passenger and freight services;
- the separation of track from train operations, under which Railtrack—at present a government-owned company—is responsible for operating all track and infrastructure, with passenger services being run by BR until they are franchised;
- the appointment of a Rail Regulator to oversee the fair application of arrangements for track access and charging, and a Franchising Director responsible for negotiating, awarding and monitoring franchises;
- opportunities for the private sector to lease stations; and
- improved grant arrangements for individual rail services or groups of services.

Railtrack is seeking private sector finance to improve the network—for example, it is working with a private sector consortium to implement proposals to modernise the West Coast Main Line, for which contracts are expected to be let in 1995–96. The Government intends to float Railtrack on the Stock Exchange during the present Parliament.

BR has restructured its passenger services into 25 train operating units as a basis for the privatised railway network. The Government has set the Franchising Director targets of awarding the first six franchises by the end of 1995 and over half of BR's current passenger services by April 1996. Invitations to tender for the first three franchises—South West Trains, Great Western and London Tilbury Southend—were issued in May 1995. Also in May 1995 the Franchising Director announced that overall fare levels would not be allowed to rise above the rate of inflation for three years from January 1996. For the following four years, they would be limited to the rate of inflation less 1 per cent.

Three rolling stock leasing companies have taken over virtually all of BR's passenger rolling stock, leasing it to the operators, including BR pending franchising. The three companies are expected to be sold to the private sector during 1995.

Three new, competing, bulk commodity rail freight companies, each with a geographic heartland, were set up in 1994 and are due to be privatised by the end of 1995. They are:

- Transrail Freight, covering the west, including Scotland and Wales;
- Loadhaul, in the north-east; and
- Mainline Freight, in the south-east.

The parcels business was also being sold in 1995. In June 1995 the Government invited private sector bids for Rail Express Systems, the BR business which operates trains for the Royal Mail, including 22 Travelling Post Offices on which mail is sorted overnight by Post Office staff. Freightliner, which carries containers between major ports and inland terminals, is also being privatised.

New regulations require rail operators to prepare a 'safety case' to demonstrate that safe practices will be followed at all times; these cases are validated by Railtrack. Railway employees who undertake work with safety implications are required to be fit and competent. The Railway Inspectorate, part of the Health and Safety Executive (see p. 195), is responsible for validating Railtrack's own safety case.

Operations

In 1994–95 BR's turnover, including financial support and income from other activities, was £6,236 million. It received grants of £2,054 million from the

Table 19.2: Railway Operations

	1990–91	1991–92	1992–93	1993–94	1994–95
Passenger journeys (million)	763	740	745	713	702
Passenger-km (million)	33,191	32,057	31,693	30,362	28,655
Freight traffic (million tonnes)	138	136	122	103	97
Trainload and wagonload traffic (million net-tonne km)	15,986	15,347	15,509	13,764	12,979
Assets at end of period:					
Locomotives	2,030	1,896	1,794	1,688	1,680
High Speed Train power units	197	197	197	197	197
Other coaching units	13,631	12,925	12,309	11,802	11,483
Freight vehicles[a]	20,763	19,877	15,912	13,871	13,379
Stations (including freight and parcels)	2,615	2,556	2,543	2,553	2,562
Route open for traffic (km)	16,584	16,558	16,528	16,536	16,542[b]

Source: British Railways Board, Railtrack
[a] In addition, a number of privately owned wagons and locomotives are operated on the railway network for customers of British Rail.
[b] Provisional

Government as support for railway operations and to cover the cost of restructuring.

As part of the Citizen's Charter initiative, BR has published a Passenger's Charter. Compensation is payable to passengers if performance falls by more than a small margin below the standards set in the Charter. Under the privatisation arrangements, franchisees will be required to produce their own charters, which will include targets at least as demanding as BR's existing ones.

Investment

There has been substantial investment in Britain's railways in recent years. BR's programme totalled £300 million in 1994–95, while Railtrack invested £500 million. Major areas of expenditure included rolling stock and facilities for Channel Tunnel traffic (see p. 302).

Passenger Services

The passenger network (see map facing inside back cover) comprises a fast inter-city network, linking the main centres of Great Britain; local stopping services; and commuter services in and around the large conurbations, especially London and south-east England. InterCity 125 trains, travelling at maximum sustained speeds of 125 mph (201 km/h), are the world's fastest diesel trains. Following the introduction of electric InterCity 225 trains, Britain has more services running at over 100 mph (160 km/h) than any other country in Europe.

About 30 per cent of route-mileage is electrified, including the East Coast Main Line linking London and Edinburgh. A new generation of diesel multiple-unit trains has been introduced on regional services. The first of a new generation of electric trains entered service in Kent in 1992, with the first 674 coaches for suburban traffic in service by 1995, and 164 for main line use both in Kent and between London and Peterborough being delivered.

Freight

Nearly 90 per cent of rail freight traffic by volume is of bulk commodities, mainly coal, coke, iron and steel, building materials and petroleum. The opening of the Channel Tunnel has presented an important opportunity for non-bulk freight movement.

The Government makes grants available to encourage companies to move goods by rail rather than road; more than 200 schemes have been helped since 1975 at a cost of over £80 million. The Department of Transport budget for freight grants in 1995–96 is £14.4 million. New freight operators have had rights of open access to the rail network since April 1994, allowing services to be set up in competition with existing hauliers.

Northern Ireland

In Northern Ireland, the Northern Ireland Railways Company Ltd, a subsidiary of the Northern Ireland Transport Holding Company, operates the railway service on about 336 km (210 miles) of track. It published a revised passenger charter in 1992 which includes a compensation scheme that operates if targets for punctuality and reliability are not met.

Channel Tunnel

The Channel Tunnel, the largest civil engineering project in Europe to be financed by the private sector, was opened to traffic in 1994. The project, which is estimated to have cost about £10,000 million, was undertaken by Eurotunnel, a British–French group which has a 65-year operating concession from the British and French governments. Construction was carried out for Eurotunnel by Transmanche Link, a consortium of ten British and French construction companies.

Eurotunnel Services

Eurotunnel operates shuttle trains through twin one-way rail tunnels between the terminals near Folkestone and Calais, with the journey taking about 35 minutes from platform to platform. These trains provide a drive-on, drive-off service, with separate shuttle trains for passenger and freight vehicles. Car and coach passengers stay with their vehicles during the journey. Lorry drivers travel separately from their vehicles, in a carriage at the front of the shuttle. Eurotunnel runs passenger shuttle services every 15 minutes and freight shuttle services every 20 minutes at peak periods.

Railway Services

About £1,400 million has been invested in new passenger and freight rolling stock and infrastructure improvements for Channel Tunnel services. About 30 Eurostar high-speed trains will run each day between the London terminal at Waterloo and Paris or Brussels. Daytime passenger services from the Midlands, northern England and Scotland to Paris and Brussels should begin operating in 1996. Overnight services from London, south Wales, Scotland, the Midlands, the North West and the South West to continental Europe will also start in 1996. A part-privately funded international station is being built at Ashford in Kent, scheduled for completion by the end of 1995.

Freight services through the Channel Tunnel are operating from a network of regional terminals to major industrial centres on the Continent. Four terminals—in London, Glasgow, Manchester and Birmingham—started operations when the tunnel opened. Because of infrastructure improvements and advanced wagon designs, over 90 per cent of standard continental 'swap-bodies' are able to travel over the lines between the tunnel and the British terminal network, even though the British loading gauge is smaller than the continental gauge. The terminal facilities allow freight to be transferred between road and rail easily.

A new private sector rail link between London and the Channel Tunnel is proposed to meet the forecast growth in demand for through rail services. The route for the rail link will pass through Kent, crossing the River Thames near Dartford. It will then run through the east of London to a second London terminal at St Pancras. A Bill has been introduced in Parliament, using the hybrid Bill procedure (see p. 57), for the construction of the rail link. By the end of 1995, the Government is expected to have chosen from among several bids the private sector consortium that will carry forward the scheme.

Other Railways in London

London Underground Ltd (LUL), a subsidiary of LT, operates services on 392 km (245 miles) of railway, of which about 170 km (106 miles) are underground. The system has 245 stations, with 466 trains running in the peak period. About 764 million passenger journeys were made on London Underground trains in 1994–95. LUL has a charter that commits it to provide a certain level of service to passengers. It includes a compensation scheme that applies when delays of 15 minutes or more occur within LUL's control. The most recent version was introduced in 1995. LUL has also been set more demanding performance targets for 1995–96.

Major investment in the Underground is under way or planned. Work started in 1993 on an extension of the Jubilee Line to Stratford (east London) via Docklands and the north Greenwich peninsula. The extension is scheduled to open in 1998. Routes being considered include CrossRail, which would link Paddington with Liverpool Street, and a line from Chelsea to Hackney. Total LUL investment in new lines will be well over £500 million in 1995–96, of which most will be spent on the Jubilee Line. LUL has also applied for the parliamentary Order necessary to build a northern extension to the East London Line to Dalston, where it would link with BR's North London Line.

The Docklands Light Railway (DLR), a 22-km (14-mile) route with 27 stations, connects the City of London with Docklands, Beckton and Stratford. An extension under the River Thames is planned to Greenwich and Lewisham, to be built by one of four private sector consortia shortlisted in February 1995. The DLR's operations will be franchised to the private sector in 1996, the eventual aim being to transfer the railway as a whole into the private sector.

The Government has set aside funding for the Croydon Tramlink, which would connect Croydon with Wimbledon, Beckenham and New Addington. This project would be a joint venture between LT and the private sector. Government financial support would be subject to satisfactory private sector bids.

Other Urban Railways

The Glasgow Underground, a heavy rapid transit system, operates on a 10-km (6-mile) loop in central Glasgow. The Tyne and Wear Metro is a 59-km (37-mile) light rail system connecting Newcastle upon Tyne with Gateshead, North and South Shields, Heworth and Jarrow. An extension to Sunderland is currently being planned. Two light railway systems have been constructed in recent years:

- the Greater Manchester Metrolink, which connects Altrincham and Bury with Manchester city centre on a 31-km (19-mile) route, to which further extensions are planned; and
- the South Yorkshire Supertram, which is a 29-km (18-mile) system connecting Meadowhall, Hillsborough and Halfway to Sheffield City Centre.

The Government has announced that it will provide the major proportion of the funding for the Midlands Metro Line 1, a 21-km (13-mile) system between Birmingham and Wolverhampton. Construction is due to begin before the end of 1995. Other schemes with parliamentary approval include the Leeds Supertram and the Greater Nottingham Light Rapid Transit. There are also plans for a privately financed and run light railway between Caernarfon and Porthmadog in north Wales.

Traditional tramcars still operate in Blackpool, the Isle of Man and Llandudno.

Private Railways

There are over 100 small, privately owned passenger-carrying railways in Great Britain, mostly operated on a voluntary basis and providing limited services for tourists and railway enthusiasts. The main aim of most of these railways is the preservation of steam locomotives. They generally run on old BR branch lines, but there are also several narrow-gauge lines, mainly in north Wales.

INLAND WATERWAYS

Inland waterways are popular for recreation, make a valuable contribution to the quality of Britain's environment, play an important part in land drainage and water supply, and are used to a limited extent for freight-carrying. The greatest amounts of freight are carried on the rivers Thames, Forth, Humber and Mersey and the Manchester Ship Canal. The majority of waterways are primarily for leisure use, but about 620 km (385 miles) are maintained as commercial waterways.

> The first new stretch of canal in Britain since 1905 was opened in April 1995 near Leeds (West Yorkshire). The £20 million scheme enhances the Aire and Calder Navigation's freight-carrying potential and provides new facilities for leisure craft.

The publicly owned British Waterways is responsible for 3,200 km (2,000 miles) of waterways in Great Britain. It is developing its historical heritage for recreational and commercial use, often in conjunction with the private sector. In 1994–95 British Waterways' turnover amounted to £86.8 million, including a government grant of £48.9 million to maintain its waterways to statutory standards.

SHIPPING AND PORTS

In December 1994 British companies owned 678 trading vessels of 100 gross tonnes or more, totalling 13.0 million deadweight tonnes. Among the ships owned by them were 176 vessels totalling 7.7 million deadweight tonnes used as oil, chemical or gas carriers and 473 vessels totalling 5.2 million deadweight tonnes employed as dry-bulk carriers, container ships or other types of cargo ship. In all, 73 per cent of British-owned vessels are registered in Britain or British dependent territories such as Bermuda.

The tonnage of the British-registered trading fleet has been declining. In recognition of this, measures to encourage British shipowners to register their vessels in Britain have been introduced. These include the relaxation of officer nationality rules, announced in June 1995. Except on 'strategic'

ships, this will open positions to officers of any nation provided they hold British certificates of competency or equivalents. Fiscal changes announced in 1994 enable shipowners to carry forward tax charges resulting from ship sales to set against further investment within a six-year period.

Cargo Services

About 94 per cent by weight (76 per cent by value) of Britain's foreign trade is carried by sea. In 1992 British seaborne trade amounted to 311 million tonnes (valued at £178,000 million). British-registered ships carried 19 per cent by weight and 36 per cent by value. Tanker cargo accounted for 44 per cent of this trade by weight, but only 7 per cent by value.

Virtually all scheduled cargo-liner services from Britain are containerised. The British tonnage serving these trades is dominated by a relatively small number of private sector companies which, in deep-sea trades, usually operate in conjunction with other companies on the same routes in organisations known as 'conferences'. The object of these groupings is to ensure regular and efficient services with stable freight rates, to the benefit of both shipper and shipowner. In addition to the carriage of freight by liner and bulk services between Britain and the rest of Europe, there are many roll-on/roll-off services to carry cars, passengers and commercial vehicles.

Passenger Services

In 1994 37 million international sea passenger movements took place between Britain and the rest of the world, compared with about 96 million international air passenger movements. Almost all passengers who arrived at or departed from British ports travelled to or from the continent of Europe or the Irish Republic. In 1994 about 236,000 people embarked on pleasure cruises from British ports. Traffic from the southern and south-eastern ports accounts for a substantial proportion of traffic to the continent of Europe. The main British operators are Stena Sealink Line, P & O European Ferries and Hoverspeed, although not all their vessels are under the British flag. Services are provided by roll-on/roll-off ferries, hovercraft, hydrofoils and high-speed catamarans. There has been a trend towards usage of larger vessels in recent years as the ferry companies prepared for competition from the Channel Tunnel.

Domestic passenger and freight ferry services also run to many of the offshore islands, such as the Isle of Wight, the Orkney and Shetland islands, and the islands off the west coast of Scotland. It is estimated that in 1992 there were about 36 million passengers on such internal services.

Merchant Shipping Legislation and Policy

The Government's policy is to promote open and competitive shipping markets. Regulations administered by agencies of the Department of Transport provide for marine safety and welfare, investigation of accidents and prevention and cleaning up of pollution from ships.

Britain plays a significant role in the formulation of shipping policy within the EU. All international services and most cabotage services within the EU have been liberalised. Full cabotage liberalisation will be achieved over the next ten years. Work is progressing well to introduce the measures in a European programme to improve maritime safety and prevent pollution.

Ports

The Government's policy has been to:

● remove constraints on the ability of ports to operate efficiently;

● enable them to compete more fully on an equal footing; and

● expose the ports industry as a whole to the marketplace.

There are about 80 ports of commercial significance in Great Britain, and in addition several hundred small harbours cater for local cargo, fishing vessels, island ferries or recreation. There are three broad types of port—trust ports owned and run by a board constituted as a trust, those owned by local authorities and company-owned ports. Most operate with statutory powers under private

Acts of Parliament. Major ports controlled by trusts include Aberdeen, Dover, Ipswich, Milford Haven and Tyne. Local authorities own many small ports and a few much larger ports, including Portsmouth and the oil ports in Orkney and Shetland. The Ports Act 1991 facilitates the transfer of trust ports fully to the private sector; Clyde, Forth, Medway, Tees and Hartlepool and the Port of London Authority dock at Tilbury have already moved to the private sector. The port of Dundee is seeking to do likewise.

Associated British Ports Holdings PLC, Britain's largest port owner and operator, operates 22 ports, including Cardiff, Grimsby and Immingham, Hull, Newport, Southampton and Swansea. Together its ports handled 110 million tonnes of cargo in 1994. Other major ports owned by companies include Felixstowe, Liverpool, Manchester and a group of ferry ports, including Harwich (Parkeston Quay) and Stranraer.

Port Traffic

In 1994 traffic through British ports amounted to 538 million tonnes, comprising 179 million tonnes of exports (its highest ever level), 190 million tonnes of imports and 169 million tonnes of domestic traffic (which included offshore traffic and landings of sea-dredged aggregates). About 55 per cent of the traffic was in fuels, chiefly petroleum and petroleum products.

Britain's main ports, in terms of total tonnage handled, are given in Table 19.3. Forth, Milford Haven and Sullom Voe (Shetland) mostly handle oil, while the main ports for non-fuel traffic are Dover, Felixstowe, Grimsby and Immingham, Liverpool, London, and Tees and Hartlepool.

Container and roll-on/roll-off traffic in Britain has increased sixfold since 1970 to 108 million tonnes in 1994 and now accounts for 78 per cent of non-bulk traffic. The leading ports for container traffic are Felixstowe, London and Southampton. Those for roll-on/roll-off traffic are Dover (Britain's leading seaport in terms of the value of trade handled), Felixstowe, Grimsby and Immingham, Portsmouth and Ramsgate.

Northern Ireland has four fully-equipped

Table 19.3: Traffic Through the Principal Ports of Great Britain

million tonnes

	1979	1989	1990	1991	1992	1993	1994
London	52.1	54.0	58.1	52.8	48.9	50.9	51.8
Forth	29.1	22.9	25.4	22.9	23.3	26.4	44.4
Tees and Hartlepool	40.2	39.3	40.2	42.9	43.4	42.7	43.0
Grimsby and Immingham	26.3	38.1	39.4	40.2	40.8	41.3	42.9
Sullom Voe	20.0	40.7	36.0	35.9	41.4	39.4	38.6
Milford Haven	41.5	33.0	32.2	35.7	35.6	35.7	34.3
Southampton	25.2	26.1	28.8	31.5	29.8	30.9	31.5
Liverpool	15.3	20.2	23.2	24.8	27.8	30.5	29.5
Felixstowe	5.3	16.5	16.4	16.1	18.0	20.3	22.1
Medway	18.9	14.0	13.6	16.1	14.3	13.6	14.7
Dover	6.4	13.5	13.0	12.0	13.1	13.8	14.1
Orkneys	17.8	4.5	8.6	9.2	8.5	11.9	14.1
Port Talbot	6.3	8.7	8.9	9.4	9.4	10.1	11.1

Source: Department of Transport

ports, at Belfast, Larne, Londonderry and Warrenpoint, which handle worldwide trade. Belfast is the principal freight port, handling over half of all cargo through its modern roll-on/roll-off facilities. It handled 9.3 million tonnes in 1993.

Development

Most recent major port developments have been at east- and south-coast ports. For example, at Felixstowe a £50 million extension to the terminal was completed in 1990; a new £100 million terminal on the River Medway caters for deep-sea container traffic; and Dover has started on a £100 million programme to develop its western docks to meet competition from the Channel Tunnel. A new cool store has been opened at Tees and Hartlepool, and there are plans for a new grain terminal. A 16-hectare (40-acre) car terminal has been built at Tyne. Recent investment by Associated British Ports includes:

● an £18 million third berth at the Immingham oil terminal, opened in 1994;

● a £13 million roll-on/roll-off terminal at Immingham, opened in June 1995;

● an £11 million roll-on/roll-off facility at Hull;

● a £3.5 million vehicle handling terminal at Grimsby; and

● two new terminals costing £3 million at Newport, specially designed for handling animal feedstuffs.

Purpose-built terminals for oil from the British sector of the North Sea have been built at Hound Point on the Forth, on the Tees, at Flotta and at Sullom Voe (one of the largest oil terminals in the world). Supply bases for offshore oil and gas installations have been constructed at several ports, notably Aberdeen, Great Yarmouth and Heysham.

Safety at Sea

The Department of Transport has two executive agencies concerned with safety at sea—the Coastguard Agency and the Marine Safety Agency (MSA). The former is responsible for HM Coastguard and the Marine Pollution Control Unit (see p. 371). The latter has taken over the former Surveyor General's Organisation and the Register of Shipping and Seamen. The MSA carries out inspections on British and foreign ships using British ports to ensure that they comply with international safety, pollution prevention and operational standards. It sets the standards and monitors the training, examination and certification of British seafarers.

HM Coastguard is responsible for co-ordinating civil maritime search and rescue operations around the coastline of Britain. In a maritime emergency the coastguard calls on and co-ordinates facilities such as:

- coastguard helicopters and cliff rescue companies;
- lifeboats of the Royal National Lifeboat Institution (a voluntary body);
- Ministry of Defence aeroplanes, helicopters and ships; and
- merchant shipping and commercial aircraft.

In 1994 HM Coastguard co-ordinated action in 5,891 incidents (including cliff rescues), in which 11,560 people were helped.

Some locations around Britain are hazardous for shipping. Measures are taken to reduce the risk of collision, including the separation of ships in internationally agreed shipping lanes. The traffic separation scheme in the Dover Strait, one of the busiest seaways in the world, is one such scheme. It is monitored by radar from the Channel Navigation Information Service near Dover. Ships are encouraged to report their movements and these are tracked. Those found to be contravening the regulations are identified and action is taken.

Following the grounding of the MV *Braer* off the Shetlands in 1993, the Government set up an inquiry to advise on further measures to prevent pollution from merchant shipping. The Government accepted 86 of the report's 103 recommendations, which it is in the process of implementing. One recommendation concerned the poor standard of foreign fish factory ships ('klondykers') in British waters. The Government has introduced a tightening of the licence regime for fish factory ships—the number of licences is now limited, applications for licences must be submitted 28 days in advance and unlicensed vessels will be asked to leave British waters.

The lighthouse authorities, which control about 370 lighthouses and other lights and buoys, are:

- the Corporation of Trinity House, which covers England, Wales and the Channel Islands;
- the Northern Lighthouse Board, for Scotland and the Isle of Man; and
- the Commissioners of Irish Lights for Northern Ireland and the Irish Republic.

They are funded mainly by light dues levied on shipping in Britain and Ireland. The Ports Act 1991 provided for the transfer of certain lights and buoys to harbour authorities where these are used mainly for local rather than general navigation. Responsibility for pilotage within harbours rests with harbour authorities under the Pilotage Act 1987.

CIVIL AVIATION

Airlines are seeking opportunities for modernisation, and the aviation authorities are negotiating new international rights and improving facilities such as air traffic control. British airlines are entirely in the private sector, as are a number of the major airports.

Air Traffic

Total capacity offered on all services by British airlines amounted to 27,700 million tonne-km in 1994: 20,400 million tonne-km on scheduled services and 7,400 million tonne-km on non-scheduled services. British airlines carried 43.9 million passengers on scheduled services and 27.1 million on charter flights; 96 million passengers travelled by air (international terminal passengers) to or from Britain, a 10 per cent increase on 1993.

The value of Britain's overseas trade carried by air in 1992 was about £44,000 million—10 per cent of exports by value and also 10 per cent of imports. Air freight is important for the carriage of goods with a high value-to-weight ratio, especially where speed is essential.

British Airways

British Airways plc is one of the world's leading airlines. In terms of international scheduled services it is the largest in the world. During 1994–95 its turnover from airline operations was £7,100 million. The British Airways group carried 27.6 million passengers on scheduled and charter flights both within Britain and internationally.

The British Airways scheduled route network serves 153 destinations in 72 countries. Its main operating base is London's Heathrow airport, but services from

Gatwick and regional centres such as Birmingham, Glasgow and Manchester have been expanding. Scheduled Concorde supersonic services operate from London Heathrow to New York and, in summer, Toronto, crossing the Atlantic in about half the time taken by subsonic aircraft. In March 1995 British Airways had a fleet of 283 aircraft, the largest in Western Europe, including seven Concordes and 62 Boeing 747s. Its first services with the new Boeing 777s were due to start in the autumn of 1995.

Other Airlines

Other major British airlines include:

- Britannia Airways, the world's largest charter airline, which carried 7.9 million passengers in 1994 and has 29 aircraft;
- British Midland, which operates a large network of scheduled services, and has 32 aircraft; and
- Virgin Atlantic, which operates scheduled services between Britain, seven North American destinations, Athens, Dublin, Hong Kong and Tokyo, with 16 aircraft.

Helicopters and Other Aerial Work

Helicopters are engaged on a variety of work, especially operations connected with Britain's offshore oil and gas industry. The main offshore operators in Britain are Bond Helicopters, British International Helicopters and Bristow Helicopters, with 43, 25 and 56 helicopters respectively in 1993. Light aircraft and helicopters are also used in other important commercial activities, such as charters, search and rescue services, load-lifting, aerial surveying and photography, and police and air ambulance operations. In March 1995 the Government published a study into the potential for a new heliport to serve central London.

Aviation Policy

The Government's civil aviation policy aims to maintain high standards of safety and security and to achieve environmental improvements by reducing noise and

emissions from aircraft. It seeks to promote the interests of travellers by encouraging a competitive British industry, and is committed to encouraging more international services to and from regional airports. The Government has taken the lead in the EU and with bilateral partners in negotiating freer arrangements within which airline competition can flourish; arrangements within the European Economic Area (see p. 120) are now almost fully liberalised. New arrangements with an increasing number of countries are resulting in better provision of services at more competitive fares.

Civil Aviation Authority

The CAA is an independent statutory body responsible for the economic and safety regulation of the industry and, jointly with the Ministry of Defence, for the provision of air navigation services. Its board members are appointed by the Secretary of State for Transport. The CAA's primary objectives are to ensure that British airlines provide air services to satisfy all substantial categories of public demand at the lowest charges consistent with a high standard of safety, and to further the reasonable interests of air transport users.

Air Safety

British airlines have a good safety record. In all but two of the 12 years to 1994, there were no passenger fatalities in accidents involving large commercially registered British aircraft in British airspace. In this period no crew or passenger fatalities associated with British-registered aircraft occurred in foreign airspace.

Every company operating aircraft used for commercial air transport purposes must possess an Air Operator's Certificate, which the CAA grants when it is satisfied that the operator is competent to operate its aircraft safely. The CAA's flight operations inspectors, who are experienced civilian pilots, together with airworthiness surveyors, check that satisfactory standards are maintained. All aircraft registered in Britain must be granted a Certificate of Airworthiness by the CAA before being flown. In this and many other aspects of its work, the CAA is increasingly working to standards developed with its European partners in the Joint Airworthiness Authorities.

Each member of the flight crew of a British-registered aircraft, every ground engineer who certifies an aircraft fit to fly, and every air traffic controller must hold the appropriate official licence issued by the CAA. To qualify for a first professional licence, a pilot must undertake a full-time course of instruction approved by the CAA— or have acceptable military or civilian flying experience—and pass ground examinations and flight tests.

Air Traffic Control and Navigation Services

Civil and military air traffic control over Britain and the surrounding seas, including a large part of the North Atlantic, is carried out by the National Air Traffic Services (NATS), jointly operated by the CAA and the Ministry of Defence. NATS also provides air traffic control at most major British airports.

Britain plays a major role in European air traffic control developments through participation in a number of international forums. It has put forward several European initiatives, including the centralised management of traffic flows throughout

Europe, which is being progressively implemented over the period 1991–96. Within Britain, NATS has an investment programme running at around £75 million a year, which includes the construction of a new air traffic control centre for England and Wales, due to become operational in 1996. The Government has also approved a new air traffic control centre for Scotland to be designed, financed, built and maintained by the private sector.

Airports

Of the 142 licensed civil aerodromes in Britain, about one-fifth handle more than 100,000 passengers a year each. Of these, 14 handle over 1 million passengers a year each (see Table 19.4). In 1994 Britain's civil airports handled a total of 123.9 million passengers (122.4 million terminal passengers and 1.6 million in transit), and 1.6 million tonnes of freight.

Proposals have been put forward for a fifth terminal at Heathrow, which could eventually handle 30 million passengers a year. A public inquiry on the planning application opened in May 1995.

Heathrow is the world's busiest airport for international passengers and is Britain's most important airport for passengers and air freight,

Table 19.4: Passenger Traffic at Britain's Main Airports

million passengers

	1990	1991	1992	1993	1994
London Heathrow	42.6	40.2	45.2	47.9	51.7
London Gatwick	21.0	18.7	20.0	20.2	21.2
Manchester	10.1	10.1	12.0	13.1	14.6
Glasgow	4.3	4.2	4.8	5.2	5.6
Birmingham	3.5	3.2	3.8	4.2	4.9
London Stansted	1.2	1.7	2.4	2.7	3.3
Edinburgh	2.5	2.3	2.7	2.9	3.1
Newcastle	1.6	1.5	2.0	2.1	2.5
Aberdeen	1.9	2.0	2.2	2.3	2.2
Belfast International	2.3	2.2	2.3	2.2	2.1
Luton	2.7	2.0	2.0	1.9	1.8
East Midlands	1.3	1.1	1.3	1.4	1.6
Bristol	0.8	0.8	1.0	1.1	1.3
Cardiff Wales	0.6	0.5	0.7	0.8	1.0

Source: Department of Transport

handling 52 million passengers (including transit passengers) and 967,000 tonnes of freight in 1994. Gatwick is also one of the world's busiest international airports. The Government accepts that there is a strong case for further runway capacity in the south-east, but options for new runways at Heathrow or Gatwick will not be considered further.

Ownership and Control

Seven airports—Heathrow, Gatwick, Stansted and Southampton in south-east England, and Glasgow, Edinburgh and Aberdeen in Scotland—are owned and operated by BAA plc. Together they handle about 72 per cent of air passengers and 82 per cent of air cargo traffic in Britain.

Many of the other airports are controlled by local authorities, including Manchester, which is the third largest airport in Britain. A total of 12 major local authority airports now operate as companies. The Government is encouraging their privatisation. For example, East Midlands International Airport was sold by its local authority shareholders in 1993 and Cardiff Wales Airport was sold in April 1995. Councils which sell shareholdings in airports before April 1997 will be able to spend three-quarters of the proceeds on other capital projects.

The CAA has responsibility for the economic regulation of the larger airports. It has powers to take action to remedy practices considered to be unreasonable or unfair, in particular any abuse of an airport's monopoly position, and also to limit increases in charges to airlines at certain airports. All airports used for public transport and training flights must also be licensed by the CAA for reasons of safety. Stringent requirements, such as the provision of adequate fire-fighting, medical and rescue services, must be satisfied before a licence is granted. Following a review, the Government announced in March 1995 that the regulatory system would be streamlined and improved, including the provision of better information to airlines about proposals for airport charges.

Strict security measures are in force at Britain's airports; these were tightened in 1994 with the introduction of regulations requiring airlines to account for and authorise for carriage every item of hold baggage placed on board international flights originating in Britain. This has not only improved security but should also cut down on misrouted baggage.

Communications

The telecommunications industry is one of the most rapidly growing sectors of the British economy. Despite the growth in electronic means of communication in recent years, postal services continue to be important. The volume of mail in Britain is increasing rather than declining, partly as a result of the growth in direct mail marketing.

TELECOMMUNICATIONS

Major changes have occurred since 1981, with the progressive introduction of competition into the markets for telecommunications equipment and services. British Telecommunications plc (BT), which was privatised in 1984, faces increasing competition in the provision of services over fixed links. The principal feature of the regulatory regime is an independent industry regulator, the Director General of Telecommunications.

Duopoly Review

In 1991 a major review of government telecommunications policy resulted in the publication of a White Paper, *Competition and Choice: Telecommunications Policy for the 1990s*. This stated that the Government would end the 'duopoly policy', under which only two companies, BT and Mercury Communications, were permitted to run nationwide fixed-link telecommunications systems. Other important points contained in the review were:

● greater freedom for existing mobile telecommunications operators and permission for cable television operators to provide telephone services in their own right;

- the introduction of 'access deficit contributions' payable to BT by operators interconnecting with BT's network whose customers use BT's local network when making calls;

- the introduction of 'international simple resale'[2] to destinations with equivalent freedom to Britain; and

- the establishment of a new regime for national numbering, taken over by the Office of Communications (OFTEL—see below), and the modification of operators' licences to allow for the introduction of number portability.

Office of Telecommunications

OFTEL, a non-ministerial government department, is the independent regulatory body for the telecommunications industry. It is headed by the Director General of Telecommunications, whose functions include:

- ensuring that licensees comply with the conditions of their licences;

- initiating the modification of licence conditions by agreement or a referral to the Monopolies and Mergers Commission (see p. 202);

- promoting effective competition in the telecommunications industry;

- providing advice to the President of the Board of Trade on telecommunications matters; and

- investigating complaints.

The Director General also has a duty to promote the interests of consumers in respect of prices, quality and variety in telecommunications services. A key area of regulatory activity relates to 'interconnection', where one operator charges another for the right to route calls over its network. OFTEL is making progress on seeking a fair and transparent regime for this, including changes to BT's licence which were agreed by BT in March 1995. OFTEL launched a wide-ranging review of the regulatory regime in December

1994. This put forward options for changing the interconnection regime and looked at issues such as capacity charging for interconnection and providing and funding universal service.

OFTEL has taken over responsibility for

In May 1995 OFTEL published the results of a large consumer survey. Among other things, this showed that 53 per cent of people thought that telephone services had got better over the previous five years, while only 5 per cent thought they had got worse; 40 per cent thought that value for money had got better, and 19 per cent that it was worse.

About one in five people with a telephone also had an answerphone.

administering the national telephone numbering scheme. A major change took place in April 1995 when an extra digit, 1, was introduced after the initial 0 to all area dialling codes in Britain. Thus, for example, the 071 code for inner London became 0171 and the 0232 code for Belfast became 01232. Five cities with greater need for additional capacity—Bristol, Leeds, Leicester, Nottingham and Sheffield—were given entirely new codes. These changes open up the opportunity to use 8,000 million extra numbers to provide customers with new services. OFTEL is hoping to see a 'number portability' scheme, enabling someone who wishes to change service-provider at the same address to retain their existing number, rather than having to change it as at present, become widely available by the end of 1995.

BT

BT runs one of the world's largest public telecommunications networks, including:

- 20.6 million residential lines;
- 6.4 million business lines;
- telex connections to about 30,000 British companies;
- more than 130,000 public payphones; and
- a wide range of specialised voice, data, text and visual services.

The inland telephone and telex networks

---

[2]The use of international leased circuits connected with the public switched network at both ends.

are fully automatic. International direct dialling is available from Britain to 200 countries, representing 99 per cent of the world's telephones. Following the sale of its shares in three tranches between 1984 and 1993, the Government has only a residual stake in BT to enable it to meet outstanding commitments under the bonus scheme which accompanied the privatisation.

Network Modernisation

BT has invested £20,000 million since 1985 in the modernisation and expansion of its network to meet increasing demand for basic telephone services and for more specialised services. The company has more than 2.6 million km (1.6 million miles) of optical fibre laid in its network in Britain, a higher proportion than any other world operator. There are more than 7,000 digital and modern electronic exchanges serving about 98 per cent of telephone lines. The combination of digital exchange switching and digital transmission techniques, using optical-fibre cable and microwave radio links, is substantially improving the quality of telephone services. It also makes possible the provision of a wider range of services through the company's main network.

General Services

BT's services include:
- a free facility for emergency calls to the police, fire, ambulance, coastguard, lifeboat and air-sea rescue services;
- directory enquiries;
- various chargeable operator-connected services, such as reversed-charge calls;
- an operator-handled 'Freefone' service and automatic Freefone and 'Lo-call' facilities that enable callers to contact organisations anywhere in Britain, either free or at local call rates;
- premium-rate services which allow callers to obtain information from independent providers; and
- select network services such as caller display, reminder calls, three-way calling, call waiting and call diversion, which are available to customers on digital exchanges.

Public payphone modernisation has included additional provision on sites convenient for travellers, such as train carriages, London Underground platforms and motorway service areas. A number of cashless call services are available, including the Phonecard service using prepaid cards, BT chargecards, and phones that accept credit cards. More than 40,000 payphones accept BT phonecards and 30,000 accept credit or charge cards. There are about 200,000 private rented payphones on premises to which the public has access.

BT Electronic Information Services (an electronic mail and information service) forms part of the company's portfolio of global network services. Through links with other databases, a wide range of other services, such as company accounting and market research information, banking services, holiday booking and reservation facilities, insurance and financial markets information, and BT's telephone directories, are available.

International Services

BT is the second largest shareholder in the International Telecommunications Satellite Organisation (INTELSAT), of which 125 countries are members, and in the European Telecommunications Satellite Organisation (EUTELSAT). It is also a leading shareholder in the International Maritime Satellite Organisation (INMARSAT), with interests in a number of other consortia.

BT operates satellite earth stations in the London Docklands and at Goonhilly Downs (Cornwall), Madley (near Hereford), Aberdeen, and Mormond Hill (Grampian). Its range of digital transmission services includes a number available overseas, including 'Satstream' private-circuit digital links covering North America and Western Europe, using small-dish aerials. Extensive direct-dial maritime satellite services are available for vessels worldwide. In-flight operator-controlled telephone call facilities are provided via Portishead radio station near Bristol. Digital transmission techniques have been introduced for services to the United States, Japan, Hong Kong and Australia via the Madley and Goonhilly stations.

To increase its presence in the world market, BT has entered into several joint ventures with overseas firms: MCI in the United States, for example; the German industrial group VIAG; and Grupo Santander in Spain.

Mercury Communications

Mercury Communications Ltd, which is part of the Cable & Wireless group and is 20 per cent owned by Bell Canada Enterprises, has constructed its own long-distance all-digital network. The network runs from the north of Scotland to the south coast, linking over 100 cities and towns across Britain. Mercury now offers a service to all the population, including both business and residential customers.

Major customers can have a direct digital link between their premises and the Mercury network. Routeing devices have also been developed to enable customers to use Mercury indirectly via their existing exchange lines. Businesses can take advantage of savings plans and automatic discounts as well. There are Mercury-compatible phones which connect the caller to the network at the push of a button. In addition, many customers are now able to use the Mercury network by dialling an access code.

International services are provided by satellite communications centres in London's Docklands, in Oxfordshire and at Brechin in Scotland, as well as by submarine cable links to Europe and the United States.

Other Operators

Other operators include Kingston Communications, which is the long-established network operator for the Kingston upon Hull area of Britain. The duopoly review (see p. 310) allowed other would-be operators to apply for licences to provide telecommunications services over fixed links. In the first seven months of 1995, the Government granted six new licences. Earlier licensees included:

- COLT, which is focusing on business customers in the Greater London area;

- Energis, one of the first electricity companies to expand its interests into telecommunications, which is using its infrastructure as a platform for installing new optical fibre networks;

- Ionica, which is installing a new national network using radio to provide the final connection to customers;

- Sprint, the third-largest long-distance telephone company in the United States, which is seeking to expand its domestic and international services in Britain; and

- Vodafone, the well-established mobile operator, which was granted a licence for fixed services in 1993.

Mobile Communications

The Government has encouraged the expansion of mobile telecommunications services. It has licensed Vodafone and Telecom Securicor Cellular Radio to run competing national cellular radio systems. Considerable investment has been made in establishing their networks to provide increased capacity for the growing numbers of mobile phone users (4.5 million by September 1995). The two companies also run the pan-European mobile system, known as GSM, in Britain.

Britain was the first country to offer personal communications network (PCN) services, which are intended to allow the same telephone to be used at home, at work and as a portable wherever there is network coverage. PCNs operate in the frequency range around 1.8 gigahertz. The Mercury One-2-One service started in 1993, and Hutchison Microtel's Orange service was launched in 1994.

National Band Three Ltd is licensed to offer a nationwide trunked radio service, while 32 licences have been awarded for London and regional services. Five licences to operate mobile data networks and another six to run nationwide paging networks have also been granted. A government consultation paper on increasing the availability of the radio spectrum was published in May 1995. This would allow new radio-based services for small and medium-sized businesses.

Cable Television Franchises

The Government concluded in the duopoly review that cable operators should be able to offer voice telephony in their own right, which they could previously make available only in conjunction with BT or Mercury. In all, 63 of the 80 local cable television franchises in operation by the beginning of 1995 also offered voice telephony services. By then, the cable operators had installed 718,000 telephone lines in Britain, compared with 2,200 lines in January 1991. The OFTEL consumer survey (see p. 311) showed that 12 per cent of people for whom such services were available had taken them up.

Cable & Wireless

Cable and Wireless plc provides a wide range of telecommunications services in over 50 countries worldwide. Its main business is the provision and operation, through the companies of the Cable & Wireless federation, of public telecommunications services in over 30 countries and territories, including Hong Kong, the United States and Japan, under franchises and licences granted by the governments concerned. It also supplies and manages telecommunications services and facilities for public and private sector customers, and undertakes consultancy work worldwide. It operates a fleet of 15 ships and 18 submersible vehicle systems for laying and maintaining submarine telecommunications cables. Its strategy is to build on its regional hubs in Asia, Western Europe and the Caribbean. It links these hubs through its worldwide network of cable and satellite communications.

POSTAL SERVICES

The Post Office, founded in 1635, pioneered postal services and was the first to issue adhesive postage stamps as proof of advance payment for mail.

The Royal Mail provides deliveries to 25 million addresses and handles over 67 million letters and parcels each working day, which comes to over 16,700 million items a year. About 500,000 parcels a day are handled. Mail is collected from over 100,000 posting boxes, as well as from post offices and large postal users.

The Royal Mail has invested substantially in the latest mail-sorting technology, and mechanisation has been introduced at all stages of the sorting process. Automatic sorting utilises the information contained in the postcode; the British postcode system is one of the most sophisticated in the world, allowing mechanised sorting down to part of a street on a postman's round and, in some cases, to an individual address.

Britain has good international postal services, with prices among the cheapest. Royal Mail International dispatches 717 million items a year, including over 600 million by air. It has its own mail-handling centre at Heathrow, which handles about four-fifths of outward airmail. It uses 1,400 flights a week to send mail direct to over 300 destinations worldwide.

Post Office Counters Ltd handles a wide range of transactions; it acts as an agent for the letters and parcels businesses, government departments, local authorities and Alliance & Leicester Giro—formerly Girobank, which was transferred to the private sector in 1990. There are just under 20,000 post offices, of which 700 are operated directly by the Post Office. The remainder are franchise offices or are operated on an agency basis by sub-postmasters.

Post Office Specialist Services

The Post Office offers a range of specialist services. Parcelforce 'Datapost', a door-to-door delivery service, provides overnight delivery throughout Britain and an international service to over 160 countries. 'Datapost Sameday' provides a rapid delivery within or between major cities in Britain. The Philatelic Bureau in Edinburgh is an important outlet for the Post Office's philatelic business, including sales to overseas collectors or dealers. The British Postal Consultancy Service offers advice and assistance on all aspects of postal business to overseas postal administrations, and over 50 countries have used its services since 1965.

Competition in Postal Services

The Post Office has a monopoly on the conveyance of letters within Britain, but the President of the Board of Trade has the power to suspend the monopoly in certain areas or for certain categories of mail and to license others to provide competing services. He has suspended the monopoly on letters subject to a minimum fee of £1.

The Government has been considering options for the future of the Post Office. In May 1995 it announced a new business regime for the Post Office, which will involve:
- removing existing capital financing limits;
- turning the main operating units into separate subsidiary limited companies; and
- making full use of the Private Finance Initiative (see p. 158) to support moves into new markets.

Private Courier and Express Service Operators

Private-sector couriers and express operators are allowed to handle time-sensitive door-to-door deliveries, subject to a minimum fee of £1. The courier/express service industry has grown rapidly and the revenue created by the carriage of these items is estimated at over £3,000 million a year. Britain is one of the main providers of monitored express deliveries in Europe, with London an important centre for air courier/express traffic.

Further Reading

Competition and Choice: Telecommunications Policy for the 1990s. Cm 1461. HMSO, 1991.

New Opportunities for the Railways. Cm 2012. HMSO, 1992.

Telecommunications. Aspects of Britain series, HMSO, 1994.

Transport and Communications. Aspects of Britain series, HMSO, 1992.

Transport Statistics Great Britain, annual report. HMSO.

20 Science and Technology

Britain has a long tradition of research and innovation in science, technology and engineering in universities, research institutes and industry. Science and technology are critical elements in the innovation process, which is essential for competing successfully in domestic and international markets.

INTRODUCTION

British achievements in science and technology in the 20th century include fundamental contributions to modern molecular genetics through the discovery of the three-dimensional molecular structure of DNA (deoxyribonucleic acid) by Francis Crick, Maurice Wilkins, James Watson and Rosalind Franklin in 1953 and of cholesterol, vitamin D, penicillin and insulin by Dorothy Hodgkin.

Notable contributions in other areas over the past 25 years have been made by Stephen Hawking in improving the understanding of the nature and origin of the universe; Brian Josephson in superconductivity (abnormally high electrical conductivity at low temperatures); Martin Ryle and Antony Hewish in radio astrophysics; and Godfrey Hounsfield in computer assisted tomography (a form of radiography) for medical diagnosis.

Other pioneering work included the discovery in 1985 by British Antarctic Survey scientists of the hole in the ozone layer over the Antarctic. Also in 1985 Alec Jeffreys invented DNA fingerprinting, a forensic technique which can identify an individual from a small tissue sample. More recently there have been several British breakthroughs in genetics research, including the identification of the gene in the Y chromosome responsible for determining sex, and the identification of other genes linked to diseases, including cystic fibrosis and a type of inherited heart disease. Gene therapy has begun in the treatment of cystic fibrosis. The world's first pig with a genetically modified heart has been bred by scientists at Cambridge University, an important milestone in breeding animals as organ donors for people.

Nobel Prizes for Science have been won by over 70 British citizens, more than any other country except the United States.

Research and Development Expenditure

Total expenditure in Britain on scientific research and development (R & D) in 1993 was £13,752 million, 2.2 per cent of gross domestic product. About 50 per cent of the funding was provided by industry and around 33 per cent by government. Significant contributions were also made by private endowments, trusts and charities. Industry also funds university research and finances

Table 20.1: Company Investment on R & D

	R & D annual investment (£ million)	R & D as % of sales
Glaxo	858	15.2
SmithKline Beecham	638	9.8
Unilever	543	1.8
Zeneca	518	11.6
Shell Transport and Trading	437	0.7
GEC	406	7.0
Wellcome[a]	346	17.5
BT	265	1.9
Rolls-Royce	218	6.9
ICI	184	2.0

Source: *The 1995 UK R & D Scoreboard*, DTI.
[a] Merged with Glaxo in March 1995.
Note: R & D expenditure includes expenditure overseas

contract research at government establishments. Some charities have their own laboratories and offer grants for outside research. Contract research organisations carry out R & D for companies and are playing an increasingly important role in the transfer of technology to British industry.

Total spending on R & D in industry amounted to £9,069 million in 1993. Of this total, British industry's own contribution was 72 per cent, with 12 per cent from government and the rest from overseas. Since the ending of the Cold War, there has been a marked shift in the balance between civil and defence-related R & D, reflected, for example, in a reduction in real terms in aerospace R & D.

According to reports by listed British companies, there was a rise of 4 per cent in investment in R & D in 1994–95, continuing a five-year upward trend. The chemistry and biotechnology-based sectors—chemicals, pharmaceuticals and health care—continue to grow in importance, accounting for 40 per cent of R & D spending by listed companies. Three of the four companies with the largest investment in R & D—Glaxo Wellcome, SmithKline Beecham and Zeneca—are in these sectors (see Table 20.1). Electronics and aerospace are also areas of R & D strength. Some examples of recent notable R & D projects in these areas are given below.

Chemicals

Research carried out by the chemicals industry over the past few years has led to significant technological and commercial breakthroughs. ICI (now Zeneca) pioneered the microbial production of a biodegradable plastic, Biopol, and is at the forefront of global efforts to develop substitutes for chlorofluorocarbons (CFCs—see p. 373).

Pharmaceuticals is the most research intensive sector of the chemicals industry. British firms have been responsible for discovering and developing 13 of the world's 50 best-selling drugs (see p. 239). Research conducted by ICI, Glaxo Wellcome, SmithKline Beecham and Fisons led to the development of the first successful beta blockers, drugs used in the treatment of cardiovascular conditions; semi-synthetic penicillins; vaccines; and treatments for cancer, asthma, migraine and arthritis. Glaxo Wellcome is the world's biggest pharmaceutical company. Its new £700 million research centre at Stevenage (Hertfordshire) was officially opened in April 1995.

Among a host of other research projects are the application of biotechnology to pharmaceuticals, disease resistant crops, new forms of food, plant science, and the development of advanced materials such as engineering plastics. The biotechnology sector continues to grow, with an increasing number of companies engaged in the development and manufacture of products using genetic modification techniques.

Electronics

British firms and research organisations, with government support, are leading in the development and application of the family of 'three-five' semiconductor materials (such as gallium arsenide). These materials have a wide variety of uses including lasers for optical fibre communications, microwave devices for satellite communications, and high efficiency solar cells.

BT (British Telecom) is in the forefront of the development of optical fibre cable and developed the first all-optical repeater. Britain also has a world lead in the transmission of computerised data along telephone lines for reproduction on television screens. Up to 800 R & D projects are carried out by BT at any one time; a recent example is the development of a video handset with an optical telephone link. Around two-thirds of its research is in software engineering.

Aerospace

Britain has led the world in many aspects of aerospace R & D over the past 80 years. Pioneering achievements include radar, jet engines, Concorde, automatic landing, vertical take-off and landing, flight simulators and ejector seats. British Aerospace, with Marconi and Dowty Boulton Paul, developed a system known as 'fly-by-wire', in which flying control surfaces are moved by electronic rather than mechanical means. GEC developed the world's first optically signalled ('fly-by-light') system. The concept of head-up display (HUD) was pioneered and developed in Britain. This system electronically projects symbols into the pilot's view, avoiding the need to look down at instruments. GEC has also developed a holographic HUD, which enables pilots to fly at high speeds at very low altitude in darkness.

GOVERNMENT ROLE

Science and technology issues are the responsibility of a Cabinet Minister, the President of the Board of Trade, acting on behalf of the Prime Minister. The Minister is supported by the Office of Science and Technology (OST)—which became part of the Department of Trade and Industry (DTI) in 1995; the OST is headed by the Government's Chief Scientific Adviser. The OST provides a central focus for the development of government policy on science and technology, both nationally and internationally, including strengthening the science base and maximising its contribution to economic performance and the quality of life. It co-ordinates science and technology policy across government departments.

The term 'science and engineering base' is used to describe the research and postgraduate training capacity based in the universities and colleges of higher education and in establishments operated by the research councils, together with the national and international central facilities (such as CERN—see p. 333) supported by the councils and available for use by British scientists and engineers. There are also important contributions from some private institutions, mainly those funded by charities. Universities and other institutions of the science and engineering base are the main providers of basic research and much of the strategic research (research likely to become applicable) carried out in Britain. They also increasingly collaborate with the private sector in the conduct of specific applied research. Nearly two-thirds of the Government's spending on civil R & D supports basic and strategic research carried out in the science and engineering base.

The OST has specific responsibility for the Science Budget and seven government-financed research councils (see pp. 321–5): the Engineering and Physical Sciences Research Council (EPSRC), the Medical Research Council (MRC), the Particle Physics and Astronomy Research Council (PPARC), the Natural Environment Research Council (NERC), the Biotechnology and Biological Sciences Research Council (BBSRC), the Economic and Social Research Council (ESRC) and the Council for the Central Laboratory of the Research Councils (CCLRC). OST funding provides assistance for research, through the research councils, in the following ways:

- awarding grants and contracts to universities and other higher education establishments and to research units;

- funding research council establishments;

- supporting postgraduate study; and

- subscribing to international scientific organisations.

The OST also supports universities (whose main source of funding is the appropriate higher education funding council) through programmes administered through the Royal Society and the Royal Academy of Engineering (see p. 331).

Table 20.2: Science Budget 1995–96

	£ million	%
BBSRC	161.6	12.6
EPSRC	365.7	28.5
ESRC	61.2	4.8
MRC	277.8	21.7
NERC	155.5	12.1
PPARC	196.4	15.3
Royal Society	25.7	2.0
Royal Academy of Engineering, OST initiatives, CCLRC and other payments	37.8	2.9

Source: OST

Finance

Government finance for R & D goes to research establishments, higher education institutions and private industry, as well as collaborative research programmes. Total net government R & D expenditure (both civil and defence) in 1994–95 was £5,853 million, of which £3,068 million was devoted to civil science. The Science Budget (see Table 20.2) totals £1,281.7 million for 1995–96; £67 million, or about 5 per cent of the total, is allocated to priority initiatives designed to advance the Government's policy on science, engineering and technology. Government funding through the Science Budget has increased by over 30 per cent in real terms since 1979–80.

Among government departments, the Ministry of Defence (MoD—see p. 326) has the largest research budget. The main civil departments involved are the Department of Trade and Industry (see p. 325), the Ministry of Agriculture, Fisheries and Food (MAFF—see p. 327) and the Department of the Environment (see p. 327).

Strategy

A number of changes in the funding and organisation of British science and technology are being implemented. They are based on the principles set out in the White Paper, *Realising Our Potential: A Strategy for Science, Engineering and Technology*, published in 1993 and the first major review of science for over 20 years.

The White Paper aimed to create a closer partnership between government, industry and the scientific community in developing strengths in areas of importance to the future economic well-being of Britain. In particular, it established the Technology Foresight Programme to identify opportunities for the public and private sectors to work together in R & D projects with commercial potential over the next 15 to 20 years.

The programme is co-ordinated by a joint industry/academic steering group under the chairmanship of the Government's Chief Scientific Adviser. Following consultation with over 10,000 organisations and individuals, reports by 15 independent Technology Foresight panels on different business sectors were published in March and April 1995. Each report contains recommendations which are being pursued as the programme moves forward.

The steering group also identified six cross-sectoral themes or priority areas, including:

- communications and computing power (with applications in all economic sectors);

- new organisms, products and processes from genetics (with applications in health, agriculture, food and environmental protection);

- materials science, engineering and technology;

- production processes and services;

- pollution monitoring and control technologies, and technologies for conserving energy and other resources; and

- social trends (improving understanding of human factors involved in markets and scientific advance).

The findings of the Foresight reports and the steering group report are being disseminated widely to achieve the following aims:

- ensuring that scientific excellence is sustained;

- increasing collaboration between industry and academic institutions in areas of economic importance by building on the links generated in the initial consultation;

- influencing government priorities in science, engineering and technology programmes and in government regulation and training responsibilities;

- guiding future priorities where support from academic institutions would be most helpful; and

- helping industry to develop more informed business and investment strategies.

Government departments, the universities and higher education funding councils, and the research councils will be expected to reflect Foresight priorities in their research spending allocations. The private sector will be encouraged to take account of the priorities both in participating in collaborative research programmes and in strategic planning.

The Government is providing £40 million for a competitive Foresight Challenge, with industry and academics invited to propose collaborative R & D projects in areas identified by the Foresight reports. The awards will be matched by equivalent funding from industry. Other measures intended to encourage research and training in economically significant disciplines were announced during 1995. These included an expansion of the Realising Our Potential Award (ROPA) scheme, which focuses on researchers already working closely with industry and provides funding for separate 'curiosity-driven' research. Further sums were also made available to research councils to expand the Co–operative Awards in Science and Engineering (CASE) scheme, which funds students carrying out work relevant to the needs of industry. A pilot industry-led CASE scheme involving 120 student awards was launched in 1994 and will be extended in future years.

LINK

The LINK scheme provides a government-wide framework for collaborative research in support of wealth creation and improvement of the quality of life. LINK aims to promote partnerships in high quality, commercially relevant research projects between industry and higher education institutions and other research base organisations. Under the scheme, government departments and research councils fund up to 50 per cent of the cost of research projects, with industry providing the balance. LINK is now operating through 43 programmes. More than 570 projects worth over £300 million have been started, involving over 800 companies and 130 research base institutions. The Government relaunched LINK in March 1995, following a review which recommended improvements to make the scheme more flexible and effective in responding to the needs of industry and the research base. LINK will be an important mechanism for implementing collaborative research programmes arising from the Technology Foresight Programme.

Forward Look

The second Forward Look of government-financed science, engineering and technology was published in May 1995. The purpose of the Forward Look is to set out the Government's strategy for science, engineering and technology, taking into account the activities of the private sector and European and other international developments. It also reports on progress in implementing the 1993 White Paper's objectives.

Public Awareness Campaign

A major policy initiative in the White Paper was the announcement of a campaign to promote the public awareness of science, engineering and technology. This seeks to:

- increase public awareness and appreciation of the contribution that science, engineering and technology make to Britain's economic wealth and quality of life; and

- raise levels of understanding of scientific terms, concepts and issues, so that public debate on controversial scientific and technological issues becomes better informed.

In implementing the campaign, the Government supports a number of programmes and events, such as the British Association's annual science festival and the

National Science, Engineering and Technology Week. The second of these weeks, held in March 1995, consisted of over 1,100 events in all parts of Britain attended by more than 600,000 people.

Women in Science, Engineering and Technology

A Development Unit was established in the OST in 1994 to promote the role of women in science, engineering and technology. It was set up in response to an independent report which found that women were under-represented in these sectors, and that there were too few women at senior levels; many women drop out of a science career after completing a PhD. OST funding of 12 Royal Society Dorothy Hodgkin fellowships is designed to help retain some of the best women in science.

RESEARCH COUNCILS

Each research council is an autonomous body established under Royal Charter, with members of its governing council drawn from the universities, professions, industry and government. Councils support research, study and training in universities and other higher education institutions, through their own institutes, and international research centres. In addition to funding from the OST, the research councils receive income for research commissioned by government departments and from the private sector. Income from commissioned research is particularly important for the BBSRC and NERC.

Engineering and Physical Sciences Research Council

The EPSRC, the research council with the largest R & D budget—over £341 million in 1995–96—has responsibility both for sustaining particular disciplines (chemistry, mathematics, physics and all branches of engineering) and for developing close links with the industries underpinned by these disciplines. The physical sciences and engineering are a vital foundation for wealth creation.

The work of the EPSRC is divided into 14 programmes supporting research into core disciplines in the physical sciences and engineering, and in 'generic technologies'. These generic technologies and various sector-based initiatives are relevant to a wide range of industrial activities. Many of the generic technologies were a key concern of the Technology Foresight panels. The work includes projects on information technology and computing science, engineering materials and design, and integrated production.

The EPSRC has the major responsibility for a programme aimed at encouraging innovative business processes and technology in manufacturing industry. Working in collaboration with the ESRC, BBSRC, government departments and industry, the Innovative Manufacturing Initiative focuses on specific sectors of industry. The first four sector targets are aerospace, construction, land transport and process industries.

The Council's environmental interests include its clean technology programme, in co-operation with the DTI, the Department of the Environment, the BBSRC and ESRC. The programme aims to find ways of forestalling pollution in industrial processes rather than removing it at the 'end of the pipe'. Priority areas include cleaner synthesis, recycling and recovery, and sustainable cities.

The EPSRC is also engaged in:

- supporting training in core disciplines at higher education institutions (involving some 8,000 students) and in encouraging technology transfer through collaboration with universities and industrial companies (for example, through the Teaching Company Scheme—see p. 326);

- providing access for British researchers to high quality national and international facilities; and

- managing high performance computer facilities for use by all the research councils.

Medical Research Council

The MRC, with an R & D budget of £277 million in 1995–96, is the main government agency supporting medical research. It promotes and supports research and training aimed at maintaining and improving human health, advancing knowledge and technology, and providing well-trained staff to meet the needs of user communities, including the providers of health care and the biotechnology, food, health care, medical instrumentation, pharmaceutical and other biomedical-related industries.

> Immunology is one of the fastest growing areas of the biomedical sciences. Fundamental studies on the body's response to infection will provide a better basis for future prevention and treatment of a range of diseases. A new centre to carry out this work is being set up as a joint venture between the MRC, BBSRC, the Department of Health and Glaxo Wellcome. Based at the Institute of Animal Health, Compton (Berkshire), it will be named the Edward Jenner Institute for Vaccine Research, after the physician who pioneered vaccination in the 18th century.

About half the MRC's expenditure is made through its own institutes and units, which have close links with universities and medical schools, the rest going mainly on grant support of research in universities. The Council has three large institutes—the National Institute for Medical Research at Mill Hill in London, the Laboratory of Molecular Biology at Cambridge and the Clinical Sciences Centre at the Royal Postgraduate Medical School, London. It has 40 research units and a number of smaller teams, and funds about 1,500 research grants.

Areas in which the MRC is conducting research include:

- Molecules and cells, and inheritance and development—work which will help in identifying novel pharmaceuticals and in the detection, prevention and treatment of genetic diseases.

- Infections and immunity—these areas include work on developing new vaccines and identifying novel targets for antiviral chemotherapy. The Council has a major research programme on HIV infection and AIDS.

- Environmental health—to determine the health impact of particular environmental hazards.

- Cancer—to increase understanding of tumour biology, develop methods of detecting cancer, identify preventive strategies, and develop and evaluate better methods of early detection and treatment. The MRC's work complements that of the medical research charities and involves important international collaboration.

- Neurosciences and mental health—research aimed at improving understanding of the central nervous system. A wide range of mental diseases, including psychoses, dementia and addiction, are studied, and the work should lead to better methods for their diagnosis, prevention and treatment.

- Systems-oriented research—this concerns main body systems, particularly cardiovascular studies, haematology, respiratory disease, reproduction, calcium metabolism and bone disorders, rheumatology, dental research, nutrition and metabolism.

- Health services and public health research—the Council works with the government health departments, the National Health Service (NHS) and ESRC on research to examine and improve the effectiveness of medical practice and health care.

Particle Physics and Astronomy Research Council

The main task of the PPARC, with an R & D budget of £196 million in 1995–96, is to sustain and develop Britain's long tradition of excellence in research into fundamental physical processes. The PPARC maintains four research establishments: the Royal Greenwich Observatory at Cambridge, the Royal Observatory at Edinburgh and overseas observatories on La Palma in the Canary Islands and on Hawaii. The PPARC is a major source of funding for many leading university physics departments in Britain.

The PPARC supports research in three main areas:

- particle physics—theoretical and experimental research into elementary particles and the fundamental forces of nature;

- astronomy (including astrophysics and cosmology)—studying the origin, structure and evolution of the universe, and the life cycle and properties of stars; and

- planetary science (including solar terrestrial physics)—studying the origin and evolution of the solar system and the influence of the Sun on planetary bodies, particularly Earth.

The Council's work is in fields where international co-operation is particularly important: substantial contributions are made by it to the European Space Agency (ESA) and the European Laboratory for Particle Physics (CERN—see p. 333), where the proposed Large Hadron Collider (LHC) will become a major research interest. Approval to go ahead with the project was reached in 1994 and the facility will be completed by 2008.

Current theories on the forces controlling the universe do not adequately explain how matter gets its mass. Following the decision to build the Large Hadron Collider, this and other outstanding questions may be answered. The facility will enable elemental particles to be smashed together at greater energies than have been achieved before. Physicists will look for evidence of the existence of a theoretical particle which they believe gives other particles their mass—the Higgs boson, named after Professor Peter Higgs of Edinburgh University.

Biotechnology and Biological Sciences Research Council

The BBSRC, with an R & D budget of £161 million in 1995–96, sustains a broad base of interdisciplinary research and training to underpin the biology-based industries including agriculture, pharmaceuticals, chemicals and food.

Research at the Babraham Institute near Cambridge has led to the production of the world's first calves of predetermined sex. The technique for separating sperm into fractions which produce male and female calves was developed in collaboration with scientists in the United States and the British biotechnology company, Animal Biotechnology Cambridge. It uses a process known as flow cytometry and exploits the fact that 'female' sperm carrying the X chromosome contain 4 per cent more DNA than 'male' sperm carrying the Y chromosome. The method has important implications for the economics of the beef and dairy industries.

The Council operates programmes in both fundamental and strategic research. The scientific themes are biomolecular sciences, in conjunction with the EPSRC; genes and developmental biology; biochemistry and cell biology; plant and microbial sciences; animal sciences and psychology; and engineering and physical sciences. The Council funds directed programmes on agricultural systems, on chemicals and pharmaceuticals, and on food. Research is supported in eight institutes sponsored by the BBSRC, in four interdisciplinary research centres and in universities.

BBSRC has an important role in training scientists and engineers; it has over 2,000 research studentships, including 600 funded through the CASE and industry-led CASE schemes (see p. 320), as well as an expanding postdoctoral fellowship scheme.

Natural Environment Research Council

In 1995–96 NERC will spend £196 million on R & D in the following areas:

- management of land, water and the coastal zone, and the identification and sustainable exploitation of land, freshwater and marine-based resources;

- understanding and protecting biodiversity;
- waste management, biological treatment of pollution, and land restoration;
- pollution of air, land, sea and freshwater in relation to environmental and human health;
- environmental risks and hazards, including the release of genetically-modified organisms and improved prediction of future events; and
- global change, including prediction on a range of time and space scales.

The Council supports research in its own establishments as well as research and training in universities. It also provides a range of facilities for use by the environmental science community, including a marine research fleet. NERC establishments include the British Geological Survey, the British Antarctic Survey, the Centre for Coastal Marine Sciences and the Centre for Ecology and Hydrology, together with university-based units.

A new national centre for oceanographic science and technology, the Southampton Oceanography Centre, was opened in 1995. It is a national focus for research, training and support in oceanography, geology and aspects of marine technology and engineering. The Centre is a joint venture with Southampton University and incorporates the former NERC Institute of Oceanographic Sciences Deacon Laboratory, as well as some departments of the university.

NERC has a substantial income from commissioned research—about £40 million a year—and its staff provide a range of expert services. Many NERC programmes have important implications for environmental conservation.

A comprehensive geological survey of Britain's inner continental shelf, undertaken by the British Geological Survey, has yielded a detailed picture of the area and associated natural resources. Britain is the first country to have completely mapped its offshore area in this way.

Economic and Social Research Council

ESRC, with an R & D provision of

£63 million for 1995–96, supports research to increase understanding of social and economic change in order to enhance economic competitiveness and the quality of life, and to contribute to the effectiveness of public services and policy. All research funded by ESRC is conducted in higher education institutions or independent research institutes. The main areas for the Council's research are economic performance, environmental change, social cohesion, government and public service, health and welfare, and human development and learning.

The Council devotes a substantial part of its expenditure to training that will develop and maintain a first-class research base in the social sciences. Over 1,000 postgraduate students are supported through research training awards, advanced course awards and fellowships. Through its participation in the Teaching Company Scheme, ESRC promotes partnerships between social scientists and business by placing graduates in companies for short-term projects.

Council for the Central Laboratory of the Research Councils

The CCLRC was established as an independent body with effect from April 1995. It promotes scientific and engineering research by providing facilities and technical expertise to meet the needs of the other research councils and their user communities.

Among its facilities, the Rutherford Appleton Laboratory has the most powerful laser devoted to civil research in Europe—Vulcan—which is capable of simulating conditions inside stars. Its ISIS facility is the world's most powerful pulsed source of neutrons and muons, and is used by about 2,000 scientists from over 20 countries to investigate the microscopic properties of materials. The Daresbury Laboratory's facilities include the Synchrotron Radiation Source, which generates intense beams of electromagnetic radiation for the study of materials.

The CCLRC is responsible for two research establishments which were formerly part of the EPSRC: the Rutherford Appleton Laboratory at Chilton in Oxfordshire and the Daresbury Laboratory near Warrington in Cheshire. These centres provide facilities too large or complex to be housed by individual academic institutions. They also undertake contract and collaborative research with industry and other research organisations, both in Britain and overseas.

GOVERNMENT DEPARTMENTS

Department of Trade and Industry Activities

Although most industrial research and development is financed by industry, the DTI gives assistance where there is a sound case for doing so. In 1994–95 its net expenditure on R & D was estimated at £248 million, covering general industrial innovation, aeronautics, space (see p. 328), nuclear and non–nuclear energy, and support for statutory, regulatory and policy responsibilities. A further £104 million was allocated to technology transfer and related activities, in particular:

- supporting technological opportunities and potential partners, both in Britain and overseas;

- continuing direct single-company support to smaller firms under the SMART competition and the SPUR scheme (see p. 208) for the development of new products and processes; and

- concentrating support from the DTI's innovation budget for collaborative industry R & D on those projects that will result in exceptional economic benefits.

The DTI spent £27 million on non-nuclear energy research for the offshore oil and gas industry, coal technology and renewable energy sources in 1994–95.

Innovation

Innovation—the successful exploitation of new ideas—is vital in maintaining an economy based on competitive wealth creation. Through its Innovation Unit, which includes 20 seconded industrialists, the DTI seeks to influence the thinking of business, education, the media and government, as well as the public, in various ways such as:

- strengthening the partnership between government and industry;

- improving commercial exploitation of Britain's science and technology base;

- facilitating exchange of technology between business sectors;

- improving communications between investors and business regarding innovation; and

- encouraging a more positive public attitude to innovation, as well as to science and technology.

In Northern Ireland the Industrial Research and Technology Unit has a similar role to that of the DTI's Innovation Unit.

The DTI's industrial innovation programmes have shifted away from supporting technology generation towards concentrating on the exploitation and transfer of technology and the promotion of innovation. In particular, the DTI is:

- improving companies' access to local innovation services through Business Links (see p. 208);

- encouraging industry to collaborate with the science base in R & D projects under the LINK scheme (see p. 320);

- putting more effort into helping firms of all sizes work together to undertake R & D projects, including those under the EUREKA initiative (see p. 333); and

- facilitating companies' access to best practice and technology from overseas and helping companies, especially small and medium-sized concerns, to identify technological opportunities and potential partners, both in Britain and overseas.

Technology Transfer

The DTI is significantly improving companies' access to science and technology by making innovation services available locally, for example through Business Links.

Many local innovation networks already exist which bring together expertise in higher education institutions, technical colleges, industrial research organisations and other bodies. The DTI intends to build on these networks and improve access to them for small and medium-sized establishments.

Academic–Business Partnerships

The Government supports the transfer of knowledge, skills and technology through partnerships between universities and business.

The Teaching Company Scheme (TCS) enables young graduates to work in industry for two years on technology transfer projects under the joint supervision of academic and company staff. There are currently over 500 TCS programmes. In addition, new Teaching Company Scheme Centres for Small Firms have been opened at selected universities to help smaller businesses obtain easier access to universities.

The Postgraduate Training Partnership scheme enables postgraduates to undertake practical research in research and technology organisations under the joint guidance of academics and industrialists. The aim is to increase the number of people with PhDs possessing the skills and experience needed by industry.

The DTI partly funds another partnership scheme, the Shell Technology Enterprise Programme for undergraduates, which aims to encourage smaller firms to employ graduates while persuading undergraduates to consider careers in small firms. In 1996 about 1,200 undergraduates will spend eight weeks during their final summer holiday working on a technology-based project identified by their host company.

Aeronautics

The DTI's Civil Aircraft Research and Demonstration Programme (CARAD) supports research and technology demonstration in the aircraft and aero-engine industry, helping it to compete effectively in world markets. The programme is part of a national aeronautics research effort, with over half of the research work supported being conducted in industry

and the universities, and the remainder at the Defence Evaluation and Research Agency (see p. 327). Priority areas are aircraft exhaust emissions, advanced materials, and safety problems such as explosion hazards. In 1995–96 the provision for aeronautics is £19.7 million.

Launch Aid is a means of providing government assistance for specific development projects in the aerospace industry. Projects supported have included British Aerospace's contribution to three types of Airbus aircraft, the Rolls-Royce RB-211 and International Aero Engine V2500 engines and the civil version of the EH101 helicopter.

Industrial Research Establishments

The DTI acts as the main customer, on behalf of industry, for the development of new measurement standards under the National Measurement System (NMS—see p. 206) and materials metrology programmes. Most of the work of the National Physical Laboratory (NPL) is in support of these programmes; part of the work of the Laboratory of the Government Chemist (LGC) and the National Engineering Laboratory (NEL) also supports the NMS.

In common with other departments, the DTI has reviewed the future of its laboratories, having previously established them as executive agencies. In 1994 the Government decided that their future would be in the private sector. In July 1995 a private sector contractor was appointed to run the NPL for five years; the NEL was sold to a private sector firm in October 1995; and the LGC is to be established as an independent non-profit-making private sector company by the end of 1995–96.

Ministry of Defence

Ministry of Defence provision for R & D in 1995–96 is £2,460 million. About £663 million of this is for medium- and long-term applied research relevant to military needs. With the ending of the Cold War, the Government is committed to achieving a gradual reduction in real terms in spending on defence R & D.

In April 1995 the MoD's Defence Research Agency was enlarged with the addition of most of the Ministry's other non-nuclear science and technology establishments to form the Defence Evaluation and Research Agency (DERA), the largest single scientific employer in Britain. Its role is to supply scientific and technical services primarily to the Ministry but also to other government departments.

The DERA subcontracts research to industry and universities, ensuring that their know-how is harnessed to meeting military requirements. It also works closely with industry in order to see that scientific and technological advances are taken forward at an early stage into development and production. This technology transfer is not just confined to the defence industry but has also led to important 'spin offs' into civil markets, in fields ranging from new materials and electronic devices to advanced aerodynamics. The latter in particular has been instrumental in giving Britain a leading role in civil aircraft design.

Recent innovations include the development of an advanced composite rotor for the Lynx helicopter; and the invention of a special form of highly porous silicon, which can be made to emit light when irradiated with ultra-violet light, opening up the technology of silicon opto-microelectronics.

Ministry of Agriculture, Fisheries and Food

MAFF co-ordinates its research programme with The Scottish Office Agriculture and Fisheries Department, the Department of Agriculture for Northern Ireland and the research councils, particularly the BBSRC (see p. 323). It also covers the research interests of the Welsh Office Agriculture Department.

The research programme reflects the Ministry's wide-ranging responsibilities for protecting and enhancing the rural and marine environment; protecting the public, especially in food safety and quality, flooding and coastal defence, and animal health and welfare; and improving the economic performance of the agriculture, fishing and food industries.

The budget for research expenditure in 1995–96 is £140 million, including support for the Royal Botanic Gardens, Kew (see p. 332). Research is contracted increasingly through open competition with research councils, the Ministry's agencies, non–departmental public bodies, higher education institutions and other organisations.

> The need to avoid overproduction of food crops and put the land set aside to good use has led MAFF to initiate a major research programme in non-food areas. Research in the use of crops to generate energy and industrial raw materials is under way and new work is planned on novel fibres, pharmaceuticals and oils.

Department of the Environment

The Department of the Environment funds research in several policy areas: environmental protection, including radioactive substances; water; the countryside; planning and inner cities; local government; housing; building and construction; and energy efficiency. The three largest programmes are those on pollution-related climate change, regional and urban air quality, and the safe disposal of radioactive waste. Total research expenditure in 1995–96 is estimated at £97 million.

Department of Health

The Department of Health has developed an R & D programme for the National Health Service (NHS) which will provide a scientific basis for health promotion and health care. A key aim is to increase the effectiveness of the NHS by creating a sound base from which strategies in health care, operational policy and management can be defined and practice improved. The Department also manages a Health and Personal Social Service research programme concerned with the needs of ministers and policy-makers, with emphasis on improved efficiency. Total research expenditure in 1995–96 is estimated at £74 million, with a further £413 million likely to be spent by the NHS.

New arrangements to identify and distribute funds for R & D carried out in the Department, in NHS hospitals and by non-departmental public bodies are due to be introduced from April 1996. The funds will be allocated through a single R & D budget, administered by a central R & D committee.

Overseas Development Administration

The Overseas Development Administration (ODA) commissions and sponsors research on topics relevant to those geographical regions designated as the primary targets of the aid programme and of benefit to the poorest people in those countries. Provision for R & D in 1995–96 is £83 million.

The ODA's support for R & D is organised into five main programmes, covering renewable natural resources; engineering-related sectors (water and sanitation, energy efficiency and geoscience, urbanisation and transport); health and population; economic and social development; and education.

R & D is also carried out as part of Britain's bilateral aid to particular countries. It draws upon a range of professional expertise in agencies such as the Transport Research Laboratory, the British Geological Survey and the Institute of Hydrology. The ODA contributes towards international centres and programmes undertaking R & D aimed at solving problems faced by developing countries. It also contributes to science and technology through the European Union. The EU's Science and Technology for Development programme seeks to stimulate simultaneous study in various parts of the world of specific scientific issues in health, nutrition and agriculture, which can then contribute to progress in all developing countries.

The Scottish Office

The Scottish Office both contracts and itself undertakes a wide range of R & D commissions. Total R & D planned expenditure in 1995–96 is £77 million in support of its policy responsibilities, especially agriculture, fisheries, health, the environment, education and home affairs. In some areas—medicine, agriculture and biological sciences, fisheries and marine science—research in Scotland has an international reputation.

Space Activities

Britain's support for civil space research is co-ordinated by the British National Space Centre (BNSC), a partnership between government departments and research councils. BNSC encourages the competitiveness of the space industry and the exploitation of opportunities in space, based on appraisal of project costs and potential technological and commercial benefits. Through BNSC, Britain spent around £194 million on space activities in 1994–95, with funding mainly from the DTI, the research councils, the Department of the Environment and the Meteorological Office. Around two-thirds of Britain's space expenditure was devoted to programmes shared with the European Space Agency (ESA). The remainder supported a programme of R & D in higher education institutions, government establishments and industry; over 400 companies and other organisations are engaged in the space industry (see p. 244).

Around half of Britain's space programme is concerned with satellite-based Earth observation (remote sensing) for commercial and environmental applications. Britain has committed around £115 million to ESA's ERS-1 and ERS-2 satellites, which were launched in 1991 and April 1995 respectively. It provided two of the instruments on both satellites: a synthetic aperture radar and an along track scanning radiometer (ATSR). The radar is capable of supplying high resolution images of the Earth with 24-hour coverage, irrespective of cloud cover conditions. The ATSR measures global sea surface temperature to a very high degree of accuracy. British remote sensing instruments are also at work on a number of other satellites.

The Earth Observation Data Centre at Farnborough (Hampshire), operated by the National Remote Sensing Centre, is one of the ESA's four main processing and archiving facilities for storing and distributing ERS data for both scientific and commercial purposes.

Britain is also contributing £284 million to an important new Earth observation mission due to be launched in 1998 and known as ENVISAT-1. ENVISAT, carrying a new generation of ESA environmental instruments, including a new radar, will fly on the British-led Polar Platform. Britain is leading the development of ENVISAT's advanced radar, and an advanced version of the precision instrument that measures infra-red emissions over land and sea.

Britain has a world class reputation for its space science, and has to date participated in all ESA's science missions. A quarter of Britain's space budget is devoted to science, including astronomy, planetary science and geophysics. Science contributions have been made to missions ranging from the Hubble Space Telescope, for which British Aerospace built the solar panels, to the Ulysses solar space probe, which was the first spacecraft to overfly the poles of the sun (the south solar pole in 1994 and the north late in 1995). Britain is contributing substantially to the joint ESA-National Aeronautics and Space Administration (NASA) Cluster and SOHO missions to study the Sun, the Earth's magnetosphere and the solar wind, and to the Infrared Space Observatory, all due to be launched in 1996. It is also participating in the ESA's X-ray spectroscopy mission, due to be launched in 1999.

British-built instruments will play a important role in a project designed to help explain how life started on Earth. They will be aboard the Cassini-Huygens mission to be launched by the ESA and NASA in 1997. The mission will land a probe on Titan, Saturn's largest moon and the only satellite with an atmosphere. It is thought that conditions on Titan resemble those which existed on Earth before life began.

There are bilateral agreements for scientific research between Britain and other countries, such as the United States through NASA, Russia through the Russian Space Agency, and Japan. British groups have been engaged in developing, for example, the widefield camera for ROSAT (the German, British and US X-ray satellite), a spectrometer for the Japanese-built Yohkoh satellite, and an X-ray telescope for the Russian Spectrum-X mission.

Britain actively supports and provides international co-ordination for research into space debris.

A major area of British space expertise is satellite communications. In Europe, Britain is both a leading producer and user of satellite communications technology (see p. 242). It is contributing to preparations for future ESA satellite communications missions, including ARTEMIS, which will provide important communications links for the ENVISAT programme.

RESEARCH IN HIGHER EDUCATION INSTITUTIONS

The higher education funding councils in England, Scotland and Wales (see p. 444) are the largest single source of finance for universities and other higher education institutions in Great Britain. About 40 per cent of research carried out in higher education institutions is financed from resources allocated by these bodies. These funds pay for the salaries of permanent academic staff, who usually teach as well as undertake research, and contribute to the infrastructure for research. In Northern Ireland academic institutions are funded by the Department of Education for Northern Ireland. The quality of research performance of departments is a key element in the allocation of funding. Every four years the funding councils carry out a research assessment exercise to measure the quality of research in each subject across all higher education institutions in Britain. The next assessment will take place in 1996.

The research councils also support R & D in higher education institutions in two main ways. First, they provide awards to about 15,000 postgraduate students in science, social sciences, engineering and technology. Secondly, they give grants and contracts to institutions for projects, particularly in new or developing areas of research, and support units and facilities for research. The research councils have become responsible for meeting all the costs of the projects they support in higher education institutions, except for the costs associated with the salaries of permanent academic staff and the costs of premises and central computing.

The other main channels of support for scientific research in higher education institutions are charities, government departments, industry and the European Union. Institutions are expected to recover the full cost of short-term commissioned research from the Government and industry. The high quality of research in higher education institutions, and their marketing skills, have enabled them to attract more funding from a larger range of external sources, especially in contract income from industry.

Institutions undertaking research with the support of research council grants have the rights over the commercial exploitation of their research, subject to the prior agreement of the sponsoring research council. They may make use of technology transfer experts and other specialists such as BTG (see below) to help to exploit and license commercially the results of their research.

Science Parks

Science parks are partnerships between higher education and industry to promote commercially focused research and advanced technology. At the end of 1994 there were 46 such parks in operation, generally at or near universities. They are host to more than 1,200 companies and some of the larger parks have in excess of 70 companies on site. Most firms are engaged in work on computing, robotics, electrical engineering, chemicals and biotechnology. Research, development and training are their most common activities, rather than large-scale manufacturing. The newest science park is the Staffordshire Technology Park at Stafford, which opened in May 1995. Another is planned at Dartford, attached to the University of Greenwich.

A growing number of universities offer industry interdisciplinary research centres with exploitable resources. These include access to analytical equipment, library facilities and worldwide databases as well as academic expertise.

OTHER ORGANISATIONS

Industrial Research and Technology Organisations

Research and Technology Organisations (RTOs) are independent organisations carrying out commercially relevant research and other services on behalf of industry, often relating to a specific industrial sector. Britain has the largest RTO sector in Europe, consisting of around 70 organisations, which together employ over 10,000 people.

Charitable Organisations

Medical research charities are a major source of funds for biomedical research in Britain. Their combined contribution in 1994–95 was about £400 million. The three largest contributors were the Wellcome Trust—the world's largest medical charity—with a contribution of £149 million, the Imperial Cancer Research Fund (£56.7 million) and the Cancer Research Campaign (£45 million). The Cancer Research Campaign opened Britain's largest multidisciplinary centre for evaluating potential cancer treatments in May 1995 at the Institute of Cancer Research at Sutton (Surrey).

BTG

The British Technology Group, privatised in 1992, has changed its name to BTG and was floated on the London Stock Exchange in July 1995. BTG is among the world's leading technology transfer companies. It identifies commercially promising technology from universities, research institutions and companies worldwide; protects these technologies through patents; negotiates licences with industrial partners on a worldwide basis; and shares the net revenues with the sources of the inventions.

BTG holds over 9,000 patents and patent applications, covering 1,300 inventions with 470 current licence agreements. Its areas of activity include pharmaceuticals, agribusiness,

HORTICULTURE

Students at Wye College, in Ashford, Kent, examine the effect of nitrogen concentrations on onions. The College is London University's international centre of excellence for studies in agriculture, horticulture, and the rural environment and economy.

Wye College directs the research and development of the National Fruit Collections; here scientists are using computer-based image analysis to help develop techniques for the identification of apple varieties and clones.

Competitors at the UK Giant Vegetable Championship, held in Spalding, Lincolnshire.

Major conservation and recreation areas

Orkney Islands

Shetland Islands

National Parks (Regional Parks in Scotland)

Forest Parks

Areas of Outstanding Natural Beauty (National Scenic Areas in Scotland)

Heritage Coast (Coastal Conservation Zones in Scotland)

National Trails

World Heritage Sites

SCOTLAND

Speyside Way

West Highland Way

Southern Upland Way

NORTHERN IRELAND

Northumberland

North York Moors

Cleveland Way

Wolds Way

Lake District

Yorkshire Dales

Pennine Way

Peak District

Snowdonia

Offa's Dyke Path

Peddars Way and Norfolk Coast Path

The Broads

(Special protected area)

WALES

ENGLAND

Pembrokeshire Coast

Brecon Beacons

Pembrokeshire Coast Path

Ridgeway

Thames Path

North Downs Way

South Downs Way

Exmoor

Dartmoor

South West Coast Path

South West Coast Path

0 20 40 60 80 100 km

0 20 40 60 miles

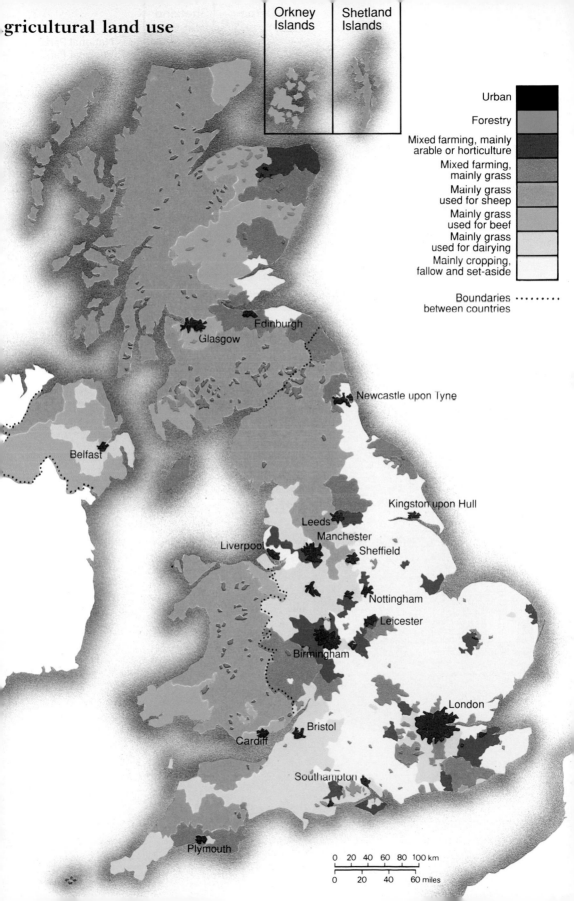

gricultural land use

Orkney Islands
Shetland Islands

Urban
Forestry
Mixed farming, mainly arable or horticulture
Mixed farming, mainly grass
Mainly grass used for sheep
Mainly grass used for beef
Mainly grass used for dairying
Mainly cropping, fallow and set-aside

Boundaries ·········· between countries

Glasgow
Edinburgh
Newcastle upon Tyne
Belfast
Kingston upon Hull
Leeds
Manchester
Liverpool
Sheffield
Nottingham
Leicester
Birmingham
London
Bristol
Cardiff
Southampton
Plymouth

0 20 40 60 80 100 km
0 20 40 60 miles

BRITISH NEWSPAPER LIBRARY

The British Newspaper Library in London is comprehensive from the 1840s onwards, containing full sets of the main London editions of all national daily and Sunday newspapers from the start of publication until the present day. The collections also contain many items dating from well before this period, as well as many regional and overseas newspapers.

A journal dated 1846 is hand-sewn by a skilled craftswoman in the Library's bindery and conservation workshop.

automotive engineering, medical technology, electronics and telecommunications.

Professional Institutions and Learned Societies

There are numerous technical institutions and professional associations in Britain, many of which promote their own disciplines or the education and professional well-being of their members.

The Council of Science and Technology Institutes has seven member institutes representing biology, chemical engineering, chemistry, food science and technology, geology, hospital physics and physics.

The Engineering Council promotes the study of all types of engineering in schools and other organisations, in co-operation with its 210 industry affiliates, which include large private sector companies and government departments. Together with 39 professional engineering institutions, the Council accredits courses in higher education institutions. It also advises the Government on academic, industrial and professional issues.

More than 300 learned societies play an important role in advancing science and technology through meetings, publications and sponsorship.

Royal Society

The most prestigious learned society is the Royal Society, founded in 1660. It has over 1,100 Fellows and more than 100 Foreign Members. Many of its Fellows serve on governmental advisory councils and committees concerned with research. The Society's estimated net expenditure on science and technology in 1995–96 is £27 million. Almost 80 per cent of the money which it distributes is derived from the Government, the remainder coming from private sources.

The Society encourages scientific research and its application through a programme of meetings and lectures, publications, and by awarding grants, fellowships and other funding. It recognises scientific and technological achievements through election to the Fellowship and the award of medals

and endowed lectureships. As the national academy of sciences, it represents Britain in international non-governmental organisations and participates in a variety of international scientific programmes. It also facilitates collaborative projects and the exchange of scientists through bilateral agreements with academies and research councils throughout the world. It gives independent advice on scientific matters, notably to government, and represents and supports the scientific community as a whole.

The Royal Society is increasingly active in promoting scientific understanding and awareness among the general public, as well as science education. It also supports research into the history of science.

Royal Academy of Engineering

The national academy of engineering in Britain is the Royal Academy of Engineering, founded in 1976. The Academy has 1,010 Fellows, 62 Foreign Members and 14 Honorary Fellows. It promotes excellence in engineering for the benefit of society. In 1995–96 it is receiving a grant of £2.6 million from the OST and plans to raise over £6 million from other sources.

The Academy's programmes are aimed at attracting first-class students into engineering, raising awareness of the importance of engineering design among undergraduates, developing links between industry and higher education, and increasing industrial investment in engineering research in higher education institutions.

Other Societies

In Scotland the Royal Society of Edinburgh, established in 1783, promotes science by awarding scholarships, organising meetings and symposia, publishing journals and awarding prizes. It also administers fellowship schemes for postdoctoral research workers.

Three other major institutions publicise scientific developments by means of lectures and publications for specialists and schoolchildren. Of these, the British Association for the Advancement of Science (BAAS), founded in 1831, is mainly concerned with science, while the Royal Society of Arts, dating from 1754, deals with the arts and commerce as well as science. The Royal Institution, which was founded in 1799, also performs these functions and runs its own research laboratories.

The Committee on the Public Understanding of Science (COPUS), set up in 1986 by the Royal Society, the BAAS and the Royal Institution, acts as a focus for a wide-ranging programme to improve public awareness of science and technology.

Zoological Gardens

The Zoological Society of London, an independent scientific body founded in 1826, runs London Zoo, which occupies about 15 hectares (36 acres) of Regent's Park, London. The Society is responsible for the Institute of Zoology, which carries out research in support of conservation. The Institute's work covers a broad range of topics, including ecology, behaviour, reproductive biology and conservation genetics. The Society also operates the Conservation and Consultancy Division, which is concerned with practical field conservation, primarily in East and Southern Africa, the Middle East and parts of Asia.

Whipsnade Wild Animal Park near Dunstable (Bedfordshire) is also managed by the Society. Other well-known zoos include those in Edinburgh, Bristol, Chester, Dudley and Marwell (near Winchester).

Botanic Gardens

The Royal Botanic Gardens, founded in 1759, covers 121 hectares (300 acres) at Kew in west London and a 187-hectare (462-acre) estate at Wakehurst Place, Ardingly, in West Sussex. They contain the largest collections of living and dried plants in the world. Research is conducted into all aspects of plant life, including physiology, biochemistry, genetics, economic botany and the conservation of habitats and species. Kew has the world's most comprehensive seed bank for wild species and is active in programmes to return endangered plant species to the wild. It participates in joint research programmes in more than 50 countries.

The Royal Botanic Garden in Edinburgh, founded in 1670, is a centre for research into taxonomy (classification of species), for the conservation and study of living plants and for horticultural education.

Scientific Museums

The Natural History Museum has 67 million specimens, ranging from a blue whale skeleton to minute insects. It is one of the world's principal centres for research into natural history, offering an advisory service to institutions all over the world.

The Science Museum promotes understanding of the history of science, technology, industry and medicine. Its extensive collection of scientific instruments and machinery is complemented by interactive computer games and audio-visual equipment for visitors to use. In this way, the museum explains scientific principles to the general public and documents the history of science, from early discoveries to space age technology. These two museums are in South Kensington, London. Other important collections include those at the Museum of Science and Industry in Birmingham, the Museum of Science and Industry in Manchester, the Museum of the History of Science in Oxford, and the Royal Scottish Museum, Edinburgh.

Science Festivals

Science festivals are a growing feature of local co-operative efforts to further understanding of the contribution made by science to everyday life. Schools, museums, laboratories, higher education institutions and industry contribute to a large range of special events.

The oldest and most widely publicised science festival is the British Association Annual Festival of Science, held at a British university. The BAAS is also involved in organising the National Science, Engineering and Technology Week (see p. 321). The largest science festival in one place is the annual Edinburgh international science festival; in 1995 it included 350 events and attracted about 180,000 visitors.

INTERNATIONAL COLLABORATION

Britain has a key role in a wide variety of major international scientific facilities and research programmes.

European Union

Since 1984 the EU has run a series of R & D framework programmes in several strategic sectors, with the aim of strengthening the scientific and technological basis of European industry and improving its international competitiveness.

The Fourth Framework Programme runs from 1994 to 1998. It has a budget of 12,000 million ECUs (about £10,200 million) and provides funds for international collaborative research in fields such as biotechnology, industrial materials and information technology. Britain played a significant role in shaping its structure and priorities. It also helped secure agreement that the EU should develop 'generic' technologies with a broad range of industrial applications, rather than just funding research projects to meet the needs of specific industrial sectors. The EU has also agreed that more resources should be devoted to disseminating technology from research projects to small and medium-sized enterprises.

Examples of the many EU research activities involving British organisations include the following programmes:

- Britain contributes to the EU Nuclear Fusion Programme, part of the Fourth Framework Programme, in particular by supporting the British programme of research into fusion undertaken at Culham, Oxfordshire, and by hosting the EU's Joint European Torus (JET) project, also based at Culham.

- The EU's Information Technology Programme, also part of the Fourth Framework Programme, is a shared cost collaborative programme, designed to help build the services and technologies that underpin the information society. The programme is open to companies, academic institutions and research bodies. Britain is currently participating in 369 projects in the programme.

Other International Activities

Over 600 British organisations have taken part in EUREKA, an industry-led scheme to encourage European co-operation in developing and producing advanced technology products with worldwide sales potential. Britain is currently involved in 282 projects, including research into a high-quality digital audio broadcasting system and a sub-programme for helping the projection of ideas with an environmental theme. There are 25 members of EUREKA, including the 15 EU countries and the European Commission.

The COST (European Co-operation in the field of Science and Technical research) programme encourages co-operation in national research activities across Europe, with participants from industry, academia and research laboratories. Transport, telecommunications and materials have traditionally been the largest areas supported. New areas include physics, neuroscience and forestry and forest products. There are currently 25 member states and Britain takes part in almost all of about 120 current COST actions.

Other examples of international collaboration include the European Space Agency (see p. 328) and CERN, the European Laboratory for Particle Physics, based in Geneva. Scientific programmes at CERN aim to test, verify and develop the 'standard model' of the origins and structure of the universe. There are 19 member states. Britain's programme is co-ordinated through the CCLRC and the subscription is paid by the PPARC.

Contributions to the high-flux neutron source at the Institut Laue-Langevin and the European Synchrotron Radiation Facility, both in Grenoble, are paid by the EPSRC. The PPARC is a partner in the European Incoherent Scatter Radar Facility within the Arctic Circle, which conducts research on the ionosphere.

Through the MRC, Britain participates in the European Molecular Biology Laboratory (EMBL), based in Heidelberg, Germany. Britain was chosen as the location for the European Bioinformatics Institute, an outstation of the EMBL. The Institute, based in Cambridge, provides up-to-date information on molecular biology and genome sequencing for researchers throughout Europe. It became fully operational in 1995.

The MRC pays Britain's contribution to the Human Frontier Science programme, which supports international collaborative research into brain function and biological function through molecular level approaches. It also pays Britain's subscription to the International Agency for Cancer Research.

NERC has a major involvement in international programmes of research into global change organised through the World Climate Research Programme and the International Geosphere-Biosphere Programme. NERC also supports Britain's subscription to the Ocean Drilling Program and is involved in a wide range of other international activities.

Britain is a member of the science and technology committees of international organisations such as the OECD and NATO, and of various specialised agencies of the United Nations. Among non-governmental organisations, the research councils, the Royal Society and the British Academy are members of the European Science Foundation, and a number of British scientists are involved in its initiatives.

Staff in British Embassies and High Commissions promote contacts in science, engineering and technology between Britain and overseas countries and help to inform a large number of organisations in Britain about science, engineering and technology developments overseas. There are science and technology sections in Paris, Bonn, Washington, Tokyo and Moscow.

The British Council (see p. 134) promotes better understanding and knowledge of Britain and its scientific and technological achievements. It encourages exchange of specialists, supplies specialised information, and fosters co-operation in research, training and education. The Council also identifies and manages technological, scientific and educational projects in developing countries. The research councils maintain, with the British Council, a joint office in Brussels to promote European co-operation in research.

Further Reading

Competitiveness: Forging Ahead. Cm 2867. HMSO, 1995.

Forward Look of Government-funded Science, Engineering and Technology 1995. HMSO, 1995.

Progress through Partnership: Report from the Steering Group of the Technology Foresight Programme 1995. HMSO, 1995.

Realising Our Potential: A Strategy for Science, Engineering and Technology. Cm 2250. HMSO, 1993.

Science and Technology. Aspects of Britain series, HMSO, 1995.

The
Environment

21 Housing and Regeneration

Home ownership, choice in renting and the effective use of resources to provide help where it is needed are key themes in the Government's housing policies. Strategies to enhance the urban and rural environments include improvements to housing and diversification of tenure, along with measures such as land preparation and development, job creation and training. A Single Regeneration Budget funds regeneration programmes in England. A total of £1,329 million will be spent from this in 1995–96, in addition to funding for schemes outside this budget and regeneration programmes in Wales, Scotland and Northern Ireland.

Housing

In all, 200,000 dwellings were completed in Britain in 1994, a rise of 8 per cent on 1993. Growth in owner-occupation has been particularly marked, increasing from 50 per cent in 1971 to 67 per cent at the start of 1995. Both public and private sectors build housing, but most dwellings are built by the private sector for sale to owner-occupiers. Local authorities are encouraged to see their housing role as more of an enabling one, working with housing associations and the private sector to increase the supply of low-cost housing for sale or rent without necessarily providing it themselves. Housing associations are now the main providers of new 'social housing'. This allows local authorities to concentrate their resources on improving the management of their own stock. To stimulate the private rented sector, which has been declining for most of this century, rents on new private sector lettings in Great Britain were deregulated in 1988. Since then, the sector has grown to about 10 per cent of households.

Administration

The Secretary of State for the Environment in England and the Secretaries of State for Wales, Scotland and Northern Ireland are responsible for formulating housing policy and supervising the housing programme.

The construction or structural alteration of housing is subject to building regulations laid down by the Government. In addition, warranty arrangements provided by the National House-Building Council cover many new houses. It sets standards and enforces them by inspection, and provides cover against major structural defects for at least ten years.

White Paper

In June 1995 the Government set out its housing policies in a White Paper *Our Future Homes.* Key features of the White Paper include commitments to:

- a sustainable expansion in home ownership, based on low interest rates, economic stability and stable house prices, with a new grant scheme to help housing association tenants to buy their own homes;

- a sustained revival in private renting, based on a deregulated private rented sector and the establishment of housing investment trusts to encourage financial institutions to invest;

- the creation of a new framework for social rented housing with rents remaining affordable to tenants in low-paid work, a greater diversity of social landlords, more transfers of local authority housing to new landlords outside the public sector and commercial providers allowed to compete alongside housing associations for grants to provide social housing;

- a fairer system for allocating social housing, with the retention of a safety net for families and vulnerable people who lose their homes through no fault of their own and further funding to ensure there is no necessity for people to sleep rough; and

- a target to build half of all new homes on re-used sites.

Home Ownership

The number of owner-occupied dwellings in Great Britain amounted to 15.8 million at the end of 1994, compared with 4.1 million in 1950.

Mortgage Loans

Most people buy their homes with a mortgage loan, using the property as security. Building societies are the largest source of such loans, although banks and other financial institutions also take a significant share of the mortgage market, while some companies make loans for house purchase available to their employees. The amount that lenders are prepared to advance to a would-be house purchaser is generally calculated as a multiple of his or her annual income, typically up to two-and-a-half or three times earnings, and the term of the loan is commonly 25 years. Owner-occupiers get tax relief on interest payments on mortgages of up to £30,000 on their main home; from April 1995 this has been assessed at 15 per cent rather than at the basic 25 per cent rate of income tax.

The recent recession and difficulties in the housing market have meant that some homeowners have experienced problems, seeing a fall in the value of their homes or having trouble keeping up with mortgage payments. The Government's policies to overcome these problems are based on maintaining a healthy economy, low interest rates and stable house prices which help keep home ownership affordable. Numbers of

Tenure in Great Britain, 1994

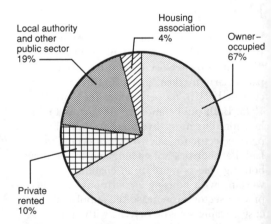

Source: *Department of the Environment*

repossessions in the first half of 1995 were down 35 per cent from their 1991 peak.

Right to Buy and Low Cost Ownership

With a few exceptions, secure public tenants in England and Wales of at least two years standing are entitled to buy their house or flat at a discount dependent upon the length of the tenancy. Similar provisions apply in Scotland and Northern Ireland. A total of 2.0 million council, housing association and New Town houses were sold in Great Britain between 1979–80 and 1994–95. Sales are continuing at a rate of about 60,000 a year.

Other schemes to encourage low-cost home ownership include cash grants to help tenants of social housing become home owners, shared ownership schemes and discounted sales of empty properties owned by local authorities. Scottish Homes has a scheme to encourage private developers to build for owner-occupation or market rents in

areas they would not normally consider. In 1995–96 planned investment in the scheme is about £34 million. A shared ownership scheme in Northern Ireland is administered by the Northern Ireland Co-ownership Housing Association. Detailed guidance for local authorities and housing associations on the range of low-cost home ownership initiatives available was issued in Wales in 1993.

Privately Rented Housing

The proportion of households renting from private landlords declined to a low point of 8.6 per cent in the late 1980s, but has now increased to 10.0 per cent. The Government's policy is to increase the availability of privately rented accommodation by removing disincentives to letting. To accomplish this, from January 1989 new private sector lettings were deregulated, and two new forms of tenancy were introduced:

House prices 1983–1994

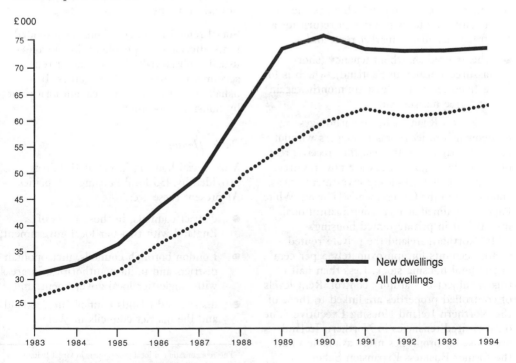

Source: *Housing and Construction Statistics*

Type of Accommodation Occupied

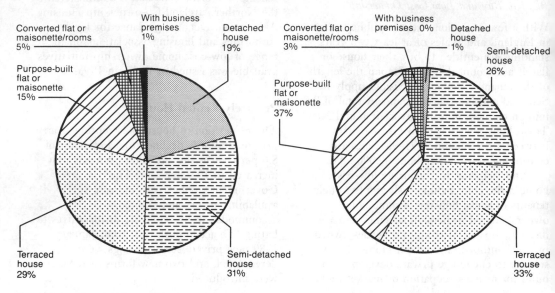

All households

Converted flat or maisonette/rooms 5%

With business premises 1%

Detached house 19%

Purpose-built flat or maisonette 15%

Terraced house 29%

Semi-detached house 31%

Local authority tenants

Converted flat or maisonette/rooms 3%

With business premises 0%

Detached house 1%

Semi-detached house 26%

Purpose-built flat or maisonette 37%

Terraced house 33%

Source: *General Household Survey 1993*

- the assured tenancy, which gives the tenant long-term security in return for a freely negotiated market rent; and

- the assured shorthold tenancy (short assured tenancy in Scotland), which is for a fixed term of at least six months, again at a free market rent.

A 'Rent a Room' scheme encourages homeowners to let rooms to lodgers without having to pay tax on the rent they receive; rents of up to about £62 a week are now tax-free. New proposals for housing investment trusts, announced in the Government's Housing White Paper, are aimed at increasing institutional investment in private rented housing.

In Northern Ireland the private rented sector accounts for approximately 5 per cent of the total housing stock. Less than half of this is subject to statutory control. Rent levels of controlled properties are linked to those of the Northern Ireland Housing Executive. The only assured tenancies in Northern Ireland are those on properties made available under the former Business Expansion Scheme; shorthold tenancies are available.

Social Housing

Social rented housing is housing provided at rents affordable to people on low incomes, usually substantially below market rents. It accounts for over a fifth of homes. It is usually either owned by local authorities or by housing associations.

Public Housing

Most social housing in Great Britain is provided by 455 local housing authorities.[1] At present these are:

- district councils, in those parts of England with two-tier local government;

- London borough councils, metropolitan districts and unitary authorities, in areas with single-tier local government; and

- district and islands councils in Scotland and the district councils in Wales.

[1] The reorganisation of local government in Great Britain (see p. 72) will change these arrangements as new local authorities take over in places.

Public housing is also provided by Scottish Homes (which has a stock of about 53,000 houses) and the Development Board for Rural Wales, although the latter is to transfer all its 1,200 houses to other social landlords by April 1996. The Northern Ireland Housing Executive is responsible for the provision and management of public housing in Northern Ireland. Public housing authorities in Great Britain own about 4.6 million houses and flats; the Northern Ireland Housing Executive owns over 152,000 homes.

Since 1988, 41 local authorities have transferred all their housing stock to housing associations—involving approximately 185,000 properties—and others are considering doing so. The transfer of local authority housing stock has raised £2,800 million of private-sector finance for social housing.

Local authorities meet the capital costs of modernising their stock by:

- borrowing from the Public Works Loan Board (an independent statutory body set up to make loans to local authorities) or on the open market;

- using part[2] of the proceeds from the sale of local authority houses and other assets; or

- drawing on their revenue accounts.

Councils must maintain housing revenue accounts on a 'ring-fenced' basis to keep them separate from other council funds. The Government grants local authorities in England and Wales Housing Revenue Account Subsidy, mainly to cover the cost of rent rebates. This is worth £4,118 million in England and £227 million in Wales in 1995–96. In Scotland, Housing Support Grant of £22 million is available in 1995–96 for those authorities which are in deficit on their housing revenue accounts.

Local authority housing investment programmes allocations, which control the amount that local authorities can borrow for council housing and other general purposes, total £994 million in England for 1995–96, and £299 million in Wales. In Scotland, local authorities have received capital allocations amounting to £424 million for investment in

council homes. In Northern Ireland, the Housing Executive's capital programme is financed mainly by borrowing from government and receipts from house sales. In 1995–96 borrowing will total £81 million. Revenue expenditure is funded from rental income and by a government grant, which in 1995–96 is about £123 million.

Housing Associations

Housing associations, which are non-profit-making, are now the main providers of new low-cost housing for rent and for sale to those on low incomes and in the greatest housing need. Many associations specialise in providing supported housing to meet the special needs of those with learning difficulties (mental handicap), drug and alcohol problems, young people at risk and the frail elderly. The housing association sector is expanding rapidly. Associations own, manage and maintain over 950,000 homes and about 65,000 hostel and special-needs bed-spaces in Great Britain, providing homes for well over 1 million people.

In Great Britain new housing schemes carried out by associations qualify for Housing Association Grant if the association concerned is one of about 2,800 registered with the Housing Corporation (in England), Scottish Homes or Housing for Wales. These three organisations are statutory bodies which supervise and pay grant to housing associations in their respective parts of Great Britain. Broadly similar assistance is available to associations in Northern Ireland.

The Housing Corporation's approved development programme provides for about £1,200 million in grants in 1995–96. The Government encourages housing associations to increase the amount of private finance they draw in. This allows more homes to be built with the available public resources. In 1995–96, Housing Corporation funding will provide an additional 58,000 lettings for rent or shared ownership. Local authority resources might provide a further 12,000.

In 1995–96 Scottish Homes' development programme expenditure is £320 million,

---

[2] In Scotland, all these proceeds can be used.

while the 1994–95 target for private finance attracted was £175 million. Housing for Wales is managing a net capital programme of £93 million in 1995–96, with a target of making available at least 3,400 new homes. Government provision to the housing association movement in Wales was almost £500 million between 1991–92 and 1994–95. Private sector finance generated over the same period is forecast to reach almost £264 million. Northern Ireland's registered housing associations started 1,000 units of accommodation in 1994–95, and now have a stock of about 15,000 units for rent. They have a budget for building for rent of £40.5 million in 1995–96, which, with an additional £10 million of private finance, will provide a further 1,200 units of rented accommodation. Government plans allow for total funding of £243 million over the period 1992–93 to 1996–97.

Other Voluntary Sector Bodies

As well as housing associations, other voluntary sector bodies have a role to play in housing matters. Such groups undertake a number of roles, for example advising people about their rights under housing law or encouraging energy efficiency in the home. The Government allocates grants to assist the work of such bodies. In England in 1995–96 about £382,000 is being made available to 13 housing groups; in Scotland aid of over £900,000 in 1995–96 is being given to about 20 voluntary bodies for work on homelessness and other housing matters.

Tenants' Rights

Local authority tenants in England, Scotland and Wales have security of tenure and other statutory rights, which are set out in a *Council Tenant's Charter*. In addition to the right to buy (see p. 339), these include the right to get certain urgent repairs done quickly at no cost to themselves and the right to be paid when they move home for certain improvements they have made. Tenants also have the right to take over the running of their estates through tenant management organisations (TMOs). Over 100 TMOs are

operational and about 100 more are under development. Compulsory competitive tendering is being introduced for council house management; tenants must be kept closely involved in the process.

In England and Wales the rights of housing association tenants are protected under Tenants' Guarantees, which are issued by the Housing Corporation and Housing for Wales. They cover matters such as tenancy terms, principles for setting rent levels and the allocation of tenancies. Under these guarantees, tenants receive contractual rights in addition to their basic statutory rights, and associations are required to set and maintain rents at levels affordable by those in low-paid employment. Similar non-statutory guidance based on joint proposals from Scottish Homes and the Scottish Federation of Housing Associations, has been implemented in Scotland. In Northern Ireland, the Department of the Environment for Northern Ireland has issued a Tenants' Guarantee, similar to the English and Welsh versions, for tenants of registered housing associations.

Following a Citizen's Charter commitment, the Government launched a Housing Association Tenants' Ombudsman Service in 1993 under the auspices of the Housing Corporation. The scheme, which covers England, allows independent investigation of tenants' complaints against their housing association, giving them a right similar to that for council tenants through the local government ombudsman. The Government announced in the housing White Paper that it intends to make the service statutorily independent. Similar schemes have been launched in Scotland and Northern Ireland.

Housing for Older People

Sheltered housing, which comprises accommodation with an alarm system and the services of a resident warden, may be provided for elderly people who need support. Increasing emphasis is being placed on schemes to help them to continue to live in their own homes by, for example, adapting their present homes to meet their needs. In

England, home improvement agencies can help elderly people, people with disabilities and those on low incomes to carry out repairs and improvements to their properties. Corresponding provision is made for Scotland under the Care and Repair scheme co-ordinated by Scottish Homes.

> Continuing government support for home improvement agencies over a further five-year period was announced in 1994. In England alone, £4.2 million of government help will go to support 125 home improvement agencies and Care and Repair Ltd., a national co-ordinating body, in 1995-96.

Rural Housing

Where there is an identified need for low-cost housing in rural areas, local authorities can exceptionally allow housing in areas where development would not normally be allowed, so long as the new housing can be reserved to meet those needs. The Housing Corporation also funds a special rural programme to build houses in small villages; between 1989-90 and 1994-95 it approved funding for the building of about 10,800 such homes.

Housing for Wales has a major role in rural housing provision, with at least a quarter of its programme devoted to rural areas. The Welsh Office also supports low-cost schemes for rural housing. In February 1995 it announced nearly £1.5 million of help for 13 schemes. In Scotland, considerable progress is being made through a range of initiatives launched in 1990 as part of the Scottish Homes Rural Strategy. Scottish Homes has invested over £325 million in rural areas since 1989-90, providing 9,000 homes. In 1995-96 it will spend more than £60 million in rural areas making available 1,720 homes. The Northern Ireland Housing Executive operates a rural strategy which directs special action both in public housing and also on the house renovation grant scheme for private housing, which it administers.

Improving Existing Housing

In urban areas of Britain, slum clearance and redevelopment used to be major features of housing policy, but there has been a trend in recent years towards the modernisation and conversion of sub-standard homes in order to retain existing communities. Housing conditions have improved considerably, but problems remain in some areas where there are concentrations of dwellings requiring substantial repairs.

Social Housing

Under the Estate Action programme, central government helped local authorities improve run-down estates, investing in greater security, transforming poorly-designed blocks and introducing greater variety and choice and more responsive management. Over £2,000 million of public funds had been spent through this programme by the end of 1994-95 and 540,000 homes had been improved in around 170 authorities. The Government is building on this approach through the Single Regeneration Budget (SRB—see p. 345), which encourages local authorities in England to tackle social and economic problems alongside housing improvements. In the first bidding round for the SRB, about 40 per cent of successful projects included improvements to housing.

On some of the worst estates, tenants have voted for housing action trusts to take over their housing from the local authority; the aim is to provide radical new solutions promoting the physical, social, economic and environmental regeneration of the areas. Six trusts have now been established.

Over the next ten years, the Government plans to tackle the problems of the most deprived estates by:

- improving the physical quality of the estates;
- encouraging diversity of tenure, increasing home ownership and renting from private social landlords; and
- improving economic and social conditions.

It will use a combination of public

investment and the transfer of estates to new social landlords to bring in private finance.

In Wales, Estate Partnership funding is available to tackle the problems of selected estates; £10.6 million of central government support has been allocated for this in 1995–96 to supplement local authority and private sector contributions.

Private Housing

The Government also offers help through house renovation grants to owners of private housing who are on low incomes and unable to afford necessary repairs and improvements. Specific help is available to disabled people who need adaptations to their home. Since 1990, house renovation grants, disabled facilities grants, and minor works assistance grants have provided up to 100 per cent support for essential repairs and improvements to the poorest home owners. Over 350,000 grants were given in England alone between 1990 and 1995, totalling more than £1,000 million.

The Government has announced its intention to legislate to reform the renovation grant system to give local authorities increased discretion in deciding claims for renovation grant. The aim is to strengthen the ability of local authorities to target resources at:

- renewal areas declared by the local authority;
- improving the housing conditions of vulnerable people; and
- supporting community care policies and enabling elderly, ill or disabled people to continue to live independently.

In Scotland, local authorities award grants for improvement and repair. Scottish Homes also has the power to provide grants to complement the role of local authorities in private house renewal. In Northern Ireland, grants are allocated on a similar basis to that in England and Wales through the House Renovation Grants scheme, administered by the Northern Ireland Housing Executive. In isolated rural areas, a grant to replace dwellings which cannot be restored is also available through this scheme.

Homelessness

By law, local authorities have a duty to secure permanent accommodation for households which they accept as unintentionally homeless and in priority need. The latter category includes pregnant women, people with dependent children, and those who are vulnerable because of old age, mental or physical handicap or other special reasons. The number of households in England accepted as homeless has been falling since 1991 (see Table 21.1).

> Grants totalling £6.9 million in 1995–96 are being made available to voluntary organisations which provide direct assistance to single people in need of accommodation.

The Government intends to reform the homelessness legislation. The aim will be to give fairer access to long-term social housing, while ensuring a safety net for families and vulnerable people who lose their home. In Scotland, where the number of homeless households continued to rise until 1993–94, the position is under review following consultations in 1994.

Most people accepted as homeless have some form of accommodation, even though this may be temporary, overcrowded or otherwise unsatisfactory, and those entitled to rehousing are found accommodation by local authorities. Only a small proportion of the homeless are 'roofless'—that is, literally without accommodation and therefore forced to sleep rough. In 1990 the Government established the Rough Sleepers Initiative to

Table 21.1: Households in England Accepted as Homeless

1989[a]	122,180
1990[a]	140,350
1991[a]	144,780
1992	142,890
1993	132,380
1994	122,660

Source: Department of the Environment
[a]1989, 1990 and first quarter 1991 figures are based on estimates in line with a new definition introduced in the second quarter of 1991.

Table 21.2: Rough Sleepers Counted in Central London

Month and Year	Number
March 1992	440
November 1992	419
June 1993	358
November 1993	287
May 1994	268
November 1994	288
May 1995	270

Source: Department of the Environment

tackle the problem in central London, with resources of £96 million. This provided about 950 new places in short-term hostels and about 1,800 permanent and 700 leased places in accommodation for hostel dwellers to move on into. A further £86 million has been made available to continue the Initiative until 1996 to provide at least 1,500 more permanent homes, together with the professional help necessary to assist people to settle into a new life. In the housing White Paper, the Government announced that the Initiative would be continued beyond March 1996 in central London and that it would consider assisting similar developments in areas outside central London where rough sleeping is a major problem.

Since 1990 more than £20 million has been spent by the Department of Health on the Homeless Mentally Ill Initiative, a programme to provide accommodation and psychiatric care for mentally-ill people who have been sleeping rough in central London. The Department has a long-term commitment to help with the running costs of the accommodation. It also funds, or has recently funded, 34 health care projects designed to ensure that homeless people have access to health services. Some £3 million has been made available over the three years to March 1996 to enable doctors and other health workers to visit hostels, day centres and other places where homeless people congregate.

A voluntary sector count, held in May 1995, found that 270 people were sleeping rough in central London, compared with estimates of over 1,000 before the Rough Sleepers Initiative began (see Table 21.2).

During the period 1991–94, extra capital allocations of around £29 million were given to housing authorities in Scotland for homelessness projects. In January 1994 the Government announced £4 million of additional funding to tackle homelessness in Wales. Local authorities were invited to present bids.

Regeneration

Economic trends in recent decades have altered traditional locations and patterns of employment and brought profound changes to local economies. Many inner city areas have suffered from long-established industries moving out or closing, leaving problems of dereliction and unemployment. A report commissioned by the Government, *Assessing the Impact of Urban Policy*, was published in 1994. It concluded that the gap between 57 urban priority areas and other places in England had narrowed in the period 1979–80 to 1990–91. Nevertheless, areas of deprivation still exist. Likewise, rural areas have had to adapt to the need in recent years to diversify away from farm production.

The Government is tackling urban problems in England with the Single Regeneration Budget (SRB), which brought together 20 previous programmes from five government departments. Urban problems in Scotland, Wales and Northern Ireland are being tackled by Partnerships, the Programme for the Valleys and Belfast Action Teams respectively, as well as by many other government programmes. Other programmes and policies are addressing the needs of rural areas.

Single Regeneration Budget

The Secretary of State for the Environment has overall responsibility for the SRB. It is intended to promote more flexible and locally responsive forms of regeneration, building on the approach pioneered with the City Challenge initiative (see below). It came into operation in April 1994, with a total expenditure of about £1,440 million in the first year. Its 1995–96 allocation is £1,330 million. Existing commitments from the constituent programmes are being met, but as these commitments expire the money released is being allocated through a bidding procedure.

> More than 200 bids for SRB funding were approved in December 1994, with funding of £125 million in 1995–96, rising to £225 million in each of the two following years. These projects are expected to attract £4 of private or other public money for every £1 of SRB money awarded to them. Benefits will include support for over 7,500 voluntary groups and the completion or improvement of more than 50,000 homes. A new bidding round is being held in 1995 for projects starting in April 1996.

Integrated Government Offices for the Regions (GORs) combine the former regional offices of the Departments of the Environment, Employment, Trade and Industry, and Transport. There are also senior headquarters representatives in each office. The main programmes funded by the SRB are administered by the GORs.

City Challenge

Under the City Challenge initiative, launched in 1991, local authorities were invited, in partnership with the private and voluntary sectors, local communities and government agencies, to submit imaginative and comprehensive plans for regenerating key neighbourhoods by tackling the problems of physical decay, lack of opportunity and poor quality of life. The best of these proposals are receiving government funding of £37.5 million over five years, subject to satisfactory progress being made towards achieving agreed targets and objectives.

There have been two rounds of the City Challenge competition. In the first pilot round, 11 local authorities in England were selected to draw up detailed plans for action, which commenced in 1992. The 20 authorities successful in the second round competition began work on their five-year programmes in 1993.

In the five-year period to 1997–98,

£1,163 million of City Challenge money is expected to attract over £3,500 million of private sector investment. A national evaluation of City Challenge is under way to measure the effectiveness of the initiative.

Urban Development Corporations

Twelve urban development corporations (UDCs) were set up in England by the Government to reverse large-scale urban decline, the first two, London Docklands and Merseyside, in 1981. Ten others were subsequently set up: Birmingham Heartlands, Black Country (West Midlands), Bristol, Leeds, Central Manchester, Plymouth, Sheffield, Trafford Park (Greater Manchester), Teesside, and Tyne and Wear. These UDCs covered about 16,000 hectares (about 40,000 acres), and public expenditure on the programme will be £243 million in 1995–96, including spending on the Docklands Light Railway (see p. 303). Leeds was wound up in March 1995, with Bristol scheduled to be wound up in December 1995 and Central Manchester in March 1996. All the other UDCs are to be wound up by March 1998.

Task Forces

Task Forces were first set up in 1986. These are small teams of five or six people drawn from government departments, local authorities and the private and voluntary sectors, which operate in the most deprived urban areas in England. Task Forces concentrate on the economic regeneration of designated inner city areas, by:

- improving local people's employment prospects;

- supporting training and education initiatives; and

- identifying and removing barriers to employment.

They also aim to stimulate enterprise development and strengthen the capacity of communities to meet local needs. Task Forces have a limited life; an important part of their work is to build up local organisations to which they can hand over as they withdraw. Since 1986 Task Forces have spent over £148 million, which has helped to provide over 37,000 jobs, more than 17,000 training places, and supported over 44,000 businesses.

English Partnerships

English Partnerships, a government regeneration agency, promotes the development of vacant, derelict and contaminated land throughout England. Its key objectives are to:

- stimulate local enterprise;

- create job opportunities; and

- improve the environment.

These objectives are expected to be achieved in partnership with the public, private and voluntary sectors. In 1994–95, its first full year of operation, more than 250 new projects were approved, creating 13,200 jobs, reclaiming over 1,600 hectares (4,000 acres) and attracting £300 million in private finance. For 1995–96 English Partnerships has a total programme of about £270 million. It is also eligible for assistance from the European Regional Development Fund (see p. 121).

Safer Cities

Higher than average crime rates, and the fear of crime, are particular problems in inner city areas. Safer Cities projects bring together all sections of the local community to tackle crime and the fear of crime. Since the programme's launch in 1988 3,600 crime prevention and community safety measures have been initiated, with funding of £22 million. Nine new projects in England commenced in 1993, and a further 20 projects in 1994. Examples of help include providing activities for young people who might be tempted to commit crime, and fitting good quality locks to houses on estates with a high burglary rate. Successes include a 40 per cent reduction in burglaries on a Wolverhampton estate and a 60 per cent reduction in car crime in a Bradford car park.

Compacts

A large number of schools/industry 'Compacts' have been introduced since 1988 in urban areas in England. Employers work with schools to guarantee a job with training for all school-leavers aged 16 to 18 who meet agreed targets for motivation and achievement. In 1995–96 50 inner-city Compacts are in operation in England, involving 180,000 young people, 10,000 employers and 800 schools. Since 1992, Compacts have been extended beyond inner-city areas; there are now 53 compacts in other areas.

Regional Enterprise Grants

The Regional Enterprise Grant programme (see p. 209) has also been brought within the SRB. This supports investment and innovation projects in small firms in designated areas. A total of £11.8 million was paid out in 1994–95.

Other Measures

The first of a network of City Technology Colleges was opened near Birmingham in 1988; 15 are currently operating. Intended to raise educational standards, the colleges are established jointly by government and industry. While teaching the full National Curriculum (see p. 435), they emphasise science, technology and business understanding.

Training programmes such as Youth Training (see p. 185) and Training for Work (see p. 184) are helping many people in the inner cities. About one-third of young people participating in Youth Training are from inner cities. There are over 100 Employment Service 'outreach' staff based in or visiting inner city areas, helping unemployed people look for jobs and encouraging them to participate in employment and training programmes. These supplement normal jobcentre services. In 1992–93 there were about 500 inner city Jobclubs, many catering for people with literacy and numeracy or language difficulties. In addition, funds are available for innovative projects to help unemployed people in inner cities and other deprived areas back into work or training. Many of the independent Training and Enterprise Councils (see p. 183) are working in Task Force areas, City Challenge areas or other pockets of deprivation; they often play an important part in partnership approaches to regeneration.

The Government encourages tourism as a force for improving inner city areas. Several major projects which create a cultural and artistic focus for inner city regeneration have been undertaken. Examples include the development of the Royal Armouries Museum at Clarence Dock in Leeds, due to open in spring 1996 at a cost of £42 million, and the International Convention Centre in Birmingham. The English Tourist Board and regional tourist boards encourage promotional activities in inner city areas through local initiatives bringing together tourist boards, local authorities, the private sector and other agencies.

In March 1994 the Government launched the Urban Forum, a new national body that brings together voluntary organisations engaged in urban policy and regeneration. Its aims are to:

- act as a communication channel between the voluntary sector and the Government;

- develop new ideas; and

- encourage local communities and voluntary groups to engage in regeneration partnerships.

The Department of the Environment is making grants totalling £810,000 to 15 voluntary organisations for regeneration projects in 1995–96 under its Special Grants Programme.

City Pride

The Government announced its City Pride initiative in 1993. Civic and business leaders in three pilot cities—Manchester, London and Birmingham—were invited to come forward with proposals for building on the strength of their areas. These were published in September 1994, January 1995 and June 1995 respectively. The GORs will work closely with representatives of these cities.

European Union Programmes

Run-down areas in Britain benefit from the EU Structural Funds (see p. 121). These mainly come from the European Regional Development Fund (ERDF), which finances infrastructure projects and support for industry, among other things. Objectives for the Funds include regenerating areas affected by industrial decline and combating long-term unemployment, both problems common in inner city areas. The Department of the Environment is responsible for the co-ordination of ERDF programmes in the English regions. About £1,195 million has been allocated to declining industrial regions in England during the period 1994 to 1996.

Following a review of the Structural Funds, the recommendations of which took effect in January 1994, Merseyside qualified for 'Objective 1' support—to promote economic development in underdeveloped regions. This justifies the highest level of Structural Funds support. Merseyside stands to receive about £633 million from the Funds between 1994 and 1999.

In March 1995 it was announced that six non-Objective 1 urban areas in England were to receive funding worth £37 million under the URBAN Community Initiative, an EU-wide scheme to promote urban regeneration complementing domestic programmes. This is in addition to £13 million of URBAN funding previously announced for the Objective 1 area, Merseyside.

Coalfield Areas Fund

The Coalfield Areas Fund was set up with the aim of alleviating the economic effects of colliery closures on local communities. A total of £5 million was made available through the Fund in 1993–94 and 1994–95. This supported 35 projects put forward by 17 local authorities. It is estimated that about 1,700 jobs were created in 1993–94 and that 19,000 sq m (205,000 sq ft) of new or improved business and commercial floorspace were provided.

Groundwork Trusts

Groundwork trusts seek to tackle

environmental problems arising from dereliction and vandalism and to increase public awareness of opportunities to change and improve local environments. They work in partnership with public bodies, the private sector, voluntary organisations and individuals. Traditionally, such trusts have tended to concentrate on fringe urban or suburban areas, but increasingly they are also becoming involved in inner city areas. For example, a trust has recently been set up in the Hackney area of inner London. The Groundwork Foundation is a national body providing the trusts with advice and support.

Government funding for Groundwork in 1995–95 is £6.2 million in England. There were 40 trusts in England and Wales by March 1995, compared with 22 in 1990–91.

Enterprise and Simplified Planning Zones

Since 1981 the Government has set up 28 enterprise zones, including four extensions. Each zone runs for a period of ten years from designation; most have therefore already reached the end of their lives. Benefits in the zones include:

- exemption from the national non-domestic rate (the local property tax payable by non-domestic property owners);

- 100 per cent allowances for corporation and income tax purposes for capital expenditure on industrial and commercial buildings; and

- a much simplified planning system.

It is expected that there will be seven zones operating in January 1996, including one extension. At present it is not intended to extend the enterprise zone scheme by designating any further sites. However, the Government has retained the option of establishing further zones in exceptional circumstances.

Simplified planning zones (SPZs) can help local authorities to secure development in parts of their areas. An SPZ scheme, which also lasts for ten years, provides full planning permission for specified types of development. Like enterprise zones, from which the concept was derived, SPZs are useful as part of an overall package to generate private sector interest in an area. The procedures for establishing an SPZ have been streamlined to encourage their use. By March 1995 12 were in operation.

Rural Development

The economy of the countryside has come under great pressure in recent years. Limited job opportunities for school leavers and young adults have caused a drift to urban areas, mirrored by an influx into rural areas of town-dwellers. However, this consists mainly of commuters and retired people, and so the opportunity to create new jobs is low. A forthcoming rural White Paper, announced by the Government in 1994, will examine the economic, social and environmental changes taking place in the countryside. It will also set out the Government's strategy for rural areas.

The first Rural Challenge competition took place in 1994. This is an annual competition, aimed at encouraging public and private bodies and the voluntary sector to form partnerships to tackle local economic and social problems. Up to £1 million in funding can be obtained. Winning projects in 1994 included the renovation of an old pumping station in Nottinghamshire. The second round of Rural Challenge was launched in March 1995.

The Rural Development Commission (RDC) is the main government agency for diversifying rural enterprise in England while at the same time protecting the countryside. The RDC gives financial support and business and marketing advice to help develop the rural economy, as well as providing sites and work spaces. Its main economic programmes are concentrated in priority rural development areas, which cover about 35 per cent of the area of England and take in over 2.7 million people. The RDC spent £35.4 million in 1992–93; this is forecast to rise to £43.8 million in 1995–96.

Some rural areas are also eligible for help

from the ERDF. Objective 5b is concerned with promoting regeneration in rural areas by speeding up agricultural adjustment and assisting development. About £381 million has been allocated to promote the development of rural areas between 1994 and 1996.

Public Sector Land

The Department of the Environment promotes the sale and development of vacant and under-used public sector land. Information is being assembled on key sites with development potential, and where there are no firm plans to market or develop land, action will be taken to encourage and promote the sale of sites. Since 1989, registers of unused or under-used public sector land have been maintained by the owners. Under the 'Public Request to Order Disposal' scheme, members of the public are encouraged to request the Secretary of State to order public bodies to dispose of such land on the open market.

In 1994 the rules governing the way local authorities can spend the proceeds of asset sales were altered to encourage the sale of surplus land. This has the effect of increasing the proportion of the proceeds that councils can spend on new capital projects in those cases where they have had to spend money preparing the land for sale.

Wales, Scotland and Northern Ireland

Wales

A new Strategic Development Scheme was launched in Wales in 1994, into which the previous Urban Programme was subsumed. Schemes worth £57 million were approved for 1995–96, with economic and environmental projects receiving priority. In addition, Urban Investment Grant encourages private sector developments on derelict and run-down sites in urban areas; the 1995–96 budget is £8 million.

The Government aims to remove all significant dereliction in Wales by the end of the 1990s. The Welsh Development Agency (see p. 25) may acquire and reclaim derelict land or make grants to local authorities, other

public bodies and the private sector for this purpose. It also undertakes substantial urban and rural development and environmental programmes; their combined budgets in 1995–96 are almost £40 million. Land use is also encouraged by the Land Authority for Wales, a statutory body with powers to make land available for development in circumstances where the private sector would find this difficult or impossible.

The first Programme for the Valleys, which ran from 1988 to 1993, was an extensive scheme of economic and urban regeneration, covering an area of about 2,200 sq km (860 sq miles) in the south Wales valleys. In 1993 the Secretary of State for Wales launched a new five-year Programme. It builds on the success of the first Programme by continuing many of its measures, and also introducing new initiatives for the social, economic and environmental regeneration of the Valleys. The five aims of the new Programme are to:

- create more, better-quality jobs;

- improve training, education and transport, so that local people can benefit;

- improve the quality of the environment;

- improve the quality and choice of housing; and

- improve the health of local people.

The Cardiff Bay Development Corporation was set up in 1987 to bring forward redevelopment in an area of south Cardiff, once its commercial centre. Government support for the Corporation in 1995–96 will be £51 million. The Corporation's regeneration strategy includes the construction of a £147 million barrage across Cardiff harbour mouth, which will create a large freshwater lake and 12 km (7 miles) of waterside frontage. Work commenced on the barrage in 1994 and is scheduled to be completed in 1998. It is expected that with the barrage more than 23,000 new jobs will be created in the Cardiff Bay area, 4,400 new homes will be built and over £1,200 million of private investment be attracted.

Scotland

In 1988 the Government set out in the White Paper *New Life for Urban Scotland* its strategy for improving the quality of life for people living on peripheral estates in Scotland. The strategy builds on the experience gained from inner city regeneration schemes such as the Glasgow Eastern Area Renewal. Its main aim was to encourage residents to take more responsibility for the improvement of their own communities.

The focus of regeneration effort is four Partnerships in areas of Dundee, Edinburgh, Glasgow and Paisley. These are led by The Scottish Office and involve other bodies and groups, including Scottish Enterprise (see p. 209), Scottish Homes (see p. 339), local authorities, the private sector and local communities. Their objectives include plans to:

- improve the quality and tenure mix of housing available to local people;

- improve employment prospects by providing increased avenues for training and further education; and

- tackle social and environmental problems on the estates.

Over 2,000 new homes have been or are being built, and 7,000 improved.

Other peripheral estates and inner-city areas continue to receive substantial support through such sources as the Urban Programme, Scottish Homes and Scottish Enterprise. Scottish Homes is leading 15 Smaller Urban Renewal Initiatives, in which it is investing £32 million in 1995–96. This will provide 850 new or improved homes.

Five Safer Cities programmes have been launched in Scotland, including schemes in Aberdeen, Edinburgh, Glasgow and Dundee. Four are still in existence, and £253,000 will be spent on them by central government in 1995–96.

The Local Enterprise Companies (LECs—see p. 183), working under contract to Scottish Enterprise, have substantial budgets and a flexible range of powers and functions to improve the environment and encourage business and employment in their areas. In particular, Scottish Enterprise operates a Local Enterprise Grants for Urban Projects scheme, which aims to foster private sector investment for projects in deprived areas. The areas of need in which the scheme operates include the four Partnership areas, and other areas showing similar characteristics of deprivation. LECs can also support projects in their areas. Responsibility for derelict land reclamation rests with Scottish Enterprise, LECs and Highlands and Islands Enterprise. They may acquire and reclaim land either by agreement or compulsorily; increasingly they seek to work with the private sector to bring land back into use.

A review of urban regeneration policy in Scotland, launched in 1993 and completed by January 1995, concluded that in future about two-thirds of Urban Programme money would be allocated to new 'priority partnership areas', to be designated by The Scottish Office following discussions with city and district partnerships. The remaining one-third would be available to support regeneration initiatives in other eligible disadvantaged areas.

The Compact scheme (see p. 347) has been introduced in Scotland, with 12 Compacts in operation. In all, 7,400 young people participate in Compacts, as do many of the 10,500 employers and business organisations in Education Business Partnerships in Scotland. The Training and Employment Grants scheme is designed to increase access to employment opportunities for young and long-term unemployed people.

Northern Ireland

Urban Development Grant is the principal urban regeneration measure in Northern Ireland, with projected expenditure of £5.4 million in 1995–96. It is targeted at the most run-down parts of Belfast and Londonderry. Grants may also be paid to landowners who restore or improve derelict sites in Northern Ireland.

A comprehensive development programme aims to revitalise the commercial areas of Belfast. In 1995–96 regeneration programmes have a combined allocation of £7.3 million. The Making Belfast Work initiative, which now includes the former Belfast Action Teams, launched in 1988, is designed to reinforce efforts to alleviate economic, educational, social and environmental problems in the most disadvantaged areas of Belfast. In addition to extensive funding already allocated to mainstream departmental programmes, Making Belfast Work has provided a further £169 million approximately for the period 1988–89 to 1995–96. The Laganside Corporation was established in 1989 to regenerate Belfast's riverside area. Its government grant in 1995–96 is £7.6 million.

The Community Regeneration and Improvement Special Programme aims to regenerate disadvantaged smaller towns. It is jointly funded by the Department of the Environment for Northern Ireland and the International Fund for Ireland. A total of 35 small towns have been assisted since the programme was started in 1990.

Further Reading

Assessing the Impact of Urban Policy. HMSO, 1994.

Housing. Aspects of Britain series. HMSO, 1993.

New Life for Urban Scotland. HMSO, 1988.

Our Future Homes. HMSO, 1995.

Urban Regeneration. Aspects of Britain series. HMSO, 1995.

Annual Reports

Building Societies Commission. HMSO.

Housing and Construction Statistics. HMSO.

The Housing Corporation. Housing Corporation.

The Rural Development Commission. RDC.

22 Planning and Conservation

Britain seeks to balance the demands for land from business, housing, transport, farming and leisure, and to protect the environment by means of a statutory system of land-use planning and development control. Government agencies and voluntary bodies work to conserve Britain's natural heritage and historic monuments; over 500,000 important buildings and 6,700 sites of special scientific interest receive statutory protection.

PLANNING

Direct responsibility for land-use planning in Great Britain lies with local authorities. The Secretaries of State for the Environment, Wales and Scotland have overall responsibility for the operation of the system. The Department of the Environment brings together the major responsibilities in England for land-use planning, housing and construction, countryside policy and environmental protection. The Welsh Office and The Scottish Office have broadly equivalent responsibilities, which also extend to transport. In Northern Ireland the Department of the Environment for Northern Ireland is responsible for planning matters; its six divisional planning offices work closely with the district councils.

In England the Department of the Environment provides national and regional guidance on planning, while strategic planning at the county level is the responsibility of the county councils. At present, district councils are responsible for local plans and development control, except for minerals and waste, which are 'county matters'. In London and the former metropolitan counties, there is a unitary planning system. The boroughs and metropolitan districts prepare unitary development plans and are responsible for development control. The local government reorganisation (see p. 72) will alter these arrangements.

In Wales, planning responsibilities are at present split in the same way as in non-metropolitan parts of England, but from April 1996 responsibility will rest with the new unitary authorities (see p. 74). In Scotland, The Scottish Office provides national planning guidance. Regional and district councils undertake planning functions at present, dividing responsibilities on a basis broadly similar to that in England and Wales. In the more rural regions and the islands, the regional and islands councils respectively have responsibility for all planning functions. After April 1996, the new unitary councils will take over responsibility.

Development Plans

Development plans have a central role in shaping development patterns in an area, as planning decisions must be made in accordance with the development plan unless material considerations indicate otherwise. The preparation of a district-wide development plan is mandatory.

The present development plan system in England and Wales involves structure, local and unitary development plans:

- structure plans, setting out broad policies for the development and use of land, are adopted by county councils, which also draw up local plans for minerals and, in England, waste;

- local plans, prepared in general conformity with the adopted structure plan, and providing detailed guidance for development, are adopted by district councils and National Park authorities; and

- unitary development plans, setting out both strategic and detailed land use and development policies, are adopted by metropolitan districts or London boroughs.

Following local government reorganisation (see p. 72), some district councils in England will acquire unitary status. Unless these are given a unitary development plan function, they will become the structure plan authority for their area. In most cases the Secretary of State for the Environment has asked that these unitary authorities work with the surrounding county council or with neighbouring unitary authorities on a joint structure plan corresponding to the original county area.

In Scotland regional or islands authorities prepare structure plans. Local plans are drawn up by those districts with planning responsibilities, islands authorities, and in some rural areas by regional planning authorities. However, from April 1996, the new councils will undertake plan preparation. In some cases this may be done by a joint committee of more than one council. Under Northern Ireland's single-tier system, plans are prepared by the Department of the Environment for Northern Ireland.

Members of the public are encouraged to become involved in the formulation of plan policies and proposals. They can formally object and make their case in public to an independent inspector. When formulating their plans, planning authorities must take account of any strategic or regional guidance issued by the Secretary of State and any statements of government planning policy.

An important element of the Government's strategy for sustainable development is for full use—having regard to the quality of the urban environment—to be made of urban land in existing towns and cities, so avoiding the need to develop 'green field' sites and reducing transport demands.

Green Belts

'Green Belts' are areas intended to be left open and free from inappropriate development. Their purposes are to:

- restrict the sprawl of large built-up areas;

- safeguard the surrounding countryside;

- prevent neighbouring towns merging;

- preserve the special character of historic towns; and

- assist in urban regeneration.

They also have a recreational role. Green Belts have been established around major cities, including London, Aberdeen, Edinburgh, Glasgow, Merseyside, Greater Manchester and the West Midlands, as well as several smaller towns. Some 1.5 million hectares (3.8 million acres) are designated as Green Belt in England and 155,000 hectares (380,000 acres) in Scotland. The Government attaches great importance to the protection of Green Belts and expects local planning authorities to do likewise when considering planning applications.

In January 1995 the Government published strengthened planning guidance on Green Belts in England. This removed a former concession allowing new institutional building there, and brought in a new policy on the re-use of buildings which includes specific safeguards for the Green Belt.

Development Control

Most development requires specific planning permission. Applications are dealt with in the light of development plans and other material planning considerations, including national and regional guidance. In 1994 about 482,000 applications for planning permission were received by district councils in England alone; in total, about 380,000 applications were granted in this period. The Government has set local authorities in England a target of deciding 80 per cent of applications within eight weeks. In recent years there has been good progress towards this target (see Table 22.1). As part of the Citizen's Charter initiative (see p. 66), the Government publishes planning performance checklists twice yearly, showing how well each of these local planning authorities are meeting this target.

Local planning authorities in England and Wales are required to publicise planning applications locally. Methods commonly used include site notices, newspaper advertising and notifying neighbours. In Scotland the applicant is required to notify the owners, occupiers and, in some cases, lessees of neighbouring land and buildings when the application is submitted to the planning authority. Newspaper advertisement is required for certain types of development.

The applicant has a right of appeal to the Secretary of State if the local authority refuses planning permission, grants it with conditions attached, or fails to decide an application within eight weeks (or whatever longer period is agreed with the applicant). The majority of appeals are decided on the basis of written submissions. However, either party has the right to be heard by an inspector (or 'reporter' in Scotland) at a public local inquiry or, where a less formal arrangement is appropriate, at a hearing. A local inquiry is usually held for more complicated or controversial applications. Similar provision is made in Northern Ireland for the hearing of representations at public inquiries; for planning applications which do not give rise to public inquiries, the applicant has a right of appeal to the independent Planning Appeals Commission.

The Secretaries of State can direct that a planning application be referred to them for decision. They generally only use this power to 'call in' proposals which raise planning issues of national or regional importance. The applicant and the local planning authority have the right to be heard by a person appointed by the Secretary of State, and a public inquiry will normally be held. In Northern Ireland, major planning applications are dealt with under the Planning (NI) Order 1991, which allows for a public inquiry in certain circumstances.

Table 22.1: Planning Applications and Decisions by District Councils, England

	Total applications determined (thousands)	Percentage within eight weeks
1988–89	618	51
1989–90	597	46
1990–91	518	53
1991–92	482	60
1992–93	439	63
1993–94	446	65
1994–95	452	65

Source: Department of the Environment

Environmental Impact Assessment

Planning applications for certain types of development must be accompanied by an environmental impact assessment. This should describe the likely environmental effects and measures to minimise them. These statements are available to the public and to statutory bodies such as the Countryside Commission and English Nature (see p. 359). The planning authority must consider the environmental statement, and any representations received on it, before granting planning permission.

Architectural Standards

The Government encourages high standards in new building, although it advises local planning authorities not to impose their architectural tastes on developers. The Department of the Environment, in collaboration with the independent Royal Institute of British Architects (RIBA) and the National House-Building Council, sponsors the biennial Housing Design Awards Scheme for England and Northern Ireland, with categories for renovation and new building. Scotland and Wales have similar award schemes. Royal Fine Art Commissions for England and Wales and for Scotland advise government departments, planning authorities and other public bodies on questions of public amenity or artistic importance.

The RIBA, the principal professional body for architects, together with the Architects Registration Council of the United Kingdom, exercises control over standards in architectural education and encourages high architectural standards in the profession. The Royal Incorporation of Architects in Scotland is allied to it, as is the Royal Society of Ulster Architects.

CONSERVATION

Britain has a long tradition of conservation, and for many years has had policies and laws designed to protect both its natural environment and built heritage. A wide variety of designations are used to protect areas, sites and monuments that are of special interest to conservationists, and various organisations work towards the conservation of different aspects of Britain's national heritage.

Britain participated fully in the United Nations Conference on Environment and Development (UNCED), popularly known as the 'Earth Summit', held in Rio de Janeiro in June 1992, and is committed to carrying the process forward. Among the agreements reached was a framework convention on climate change (see p. 133), a convention on biodiversity (see p. 133), 'Agenda 21' (an action framework for the 21st century), a declaration setting out clear principles for sustainable development, and a declaration for the management of forests.

In January 1994, Britain published its national strategies for sustainable development, climate change (see p. 373), biodiversity (see p. 365) and forestry. The sustainable development strategy describes the likely state of the British environment over the next 20 years, the pressures on it and the ways in which various sectors of the economy might develop more sustainably. Britain's impact on the world environment is also described. The strategy included the establishment of three bodies to assist policy on sustainable development:

- an independent panel, which advises on issues of major strategic importance to sustainable development and produced its first report in January 1995;

- a 'round table', which brings together interests such as business, local government and academics to discuss these matters with ministers; and

- 'Going for Green', an independent committee which will seek to persuade individuals and groups to commit themselves to sustainable development.

A steering group for the biodiversity action plan (see p. 365) has members drawn from central and local government, the nature conservation agencies, business, farming and land management, and the voluntary sector. The Department of the Environment is responsible for countryside policy and environmental protection in England; the Department of National Heritage has responsibility for the listing of buildings and for scheduled ancient monuments. The Welsh Office, The Scottish Office and the Department of the Environment for Northern Ireland have broadly equivalent responsibilities. Agencies such as English Nature, English Heritage, the Countryside Commission and their equivalents carry out many functions on behalf of the Government. In addition, the local authorities and a wide range of voluntary organisations are actively involved in environmental conservation and protection.

This Common Inheritance

The environment White Paper *This Common Inheritance*, published in September 1990, was the first comprehensive statement by the Government of its policy on issues affecting the environment. It summarised more than 350 proposals for tackling such diverse issues as global warming, pollution control, the regulation of land use and planning, the rural economy, the countryside and wildlife. Four progress reports have been published. The most recent, published in March 1995, sets out about 600 commitments, including 20 new ones. For the first time, it also sets out the Government's priorities for the year ahead, and lists existing targets for air, water and land.

Buildings and Monuments

Lists of buildings of special architectural or historical interest are compiled by the Government, in England with the advice of English Heritage. In Scotland and Wales, buildings are listed by Historic Scotland and Cadw: Welsh Historic Monuments, executive agencies of the Scottish and Welsh Offices respectively. It is against the law to demolish, extend or alter the character of any 'listed' building without prior consent from the local planning authority or the appropriate Secretary of State. The local planning authority can issue 'building preservation notices' to protect unlisted buildings that are at risk for six months while the Government considers whether they should be listed. The Department of the Environment for Northern Ireland is directly responsible for the listing of buildings there.

Ancient monuments are similarly protected through a system of scheduling. English Heritage, the government agency responsible for the conservation of historic remains in England, has embarked upon a programme to evaluate all known archaeological remains in England. This is expected to result in a significant increase in the number of scheduled monuments. A similar effort is being made to increase the number of listed buildings and scheduled monuments in Wales.

The Government announced in March 1995 that in future owners and the public would be asked for their views on those proposals for listing that result from a current English Heritage study. A Green Paper, to be published later in 1995, will look at the question of consultation for other listing proposals.

Many of the royal palaces and parks are open to the public; their maintenance is the responsibility of the Secretaries of State for National Heritage and for Scotland. English Heritage cares for over 400 properties on behalf of the Secretary of State for National Heritage, advises her or the Secretary of State for the Environment on certain categories of applications for consent to alter or demolish scheduled monuments and listed buildings, and gives grants for the repair of ancient monuments and historic buildings in England. Many of the properties in its care are now being managed locally; 120 agreements for this are expected to have been made by the end of 1995–96. Most of its monuments are open to the public. Core government funding for English Heritage is £105 million in 1995–96.

In Scotland and Wales Historic Scotland, which cares for 330 monuments, and Cadw, which manages 129, perform similar functions, with advice from an Ancient Monuments Board and Historic Buildings Council for each country. The Department of the Environment for Northern Ireland has 181 historic monuments in its care, and is advised by a Historic Buildings Council and a Historic Monuments Council.

Table 22.2: Scheduled Monuments and Listed Buildings

	Listed buildings	Scheduled monuments
England	447,400	15,300[a]
Wales	17,200	2,800
Scotland	41,500	6,200
Northern Ireland	8,600	1,100

Source: Department of the Environment

[a]This is the number of register entries, some of which cover more than one site. There are approximately 22,000 individual sites in England.

Local planning authorities have designated more than 8,000 'conservation areas' of special architectural or historic interest in England; there are over 400 in Wales, 674 in Scotland and 40 in Northern Ireland. These areas receive additional protection through the planning system, particularly over the proposed demolition of unlisted buildings. Grants and loans are sometimes available from the appropriate historic buildings and monuments body for works which make a significant contribution towards the preservation or enhancement of a conservation area.

In June 1995 the Government strengthened the ability of local planning authorities in England and Wales to protect conservation areas. New powers allow them to withdraw 'permitted development' rights for certain types of development, giving them greater influence over changes that would affect the external appearance of houses.

The National Heritage Memorial Fund helps towards the cost of acquiring, maintaining or preserving land, buildings, works of art and other items of outstanding interest which are also of importance to the national heritage. Government funding totals £8.8 million in 1995–96. It also acts as the distributing body for the heritage share of the proceeds from the National Lottery (see p. 460).

Industrial, Transport and Maritime Heritage

Britain was the first country in the world to industrialise on a large scale, and many advances in manufacturing and transport were pioneered in Britain. This has resulted in a large industrial heritage, the importance of which is being increasingly recognised. Key sites are scheduled or listed; one of the most important, the Ironbridge Gorge, where Abraham Darby (1677–1717) first smelted iron using coke instead of charcoal, has been designated a World Heritage Site (see p. 366). Other museums devoted to the preservation of industrial buildings and equipment have also been set up.

Britain, which pioneered railways, has a fine heritage of railway buildings and structures, and there is an active movement to preserve it, with many volunteers. A large number of disused railway lines have been bought by railway preservation societies and returned to operation, often using preserved steam locomotives, and several railway museums have been established. British Rail formed a railway heritage committee in February 1995 to oversee transfers of historic railway artefacts and records to museums and record offices.

In March 1995 the Government announced a £50,000 grant to support the compilation of a database listing all ship preservation projects in Britain. The database will help inform future decisions on funding, ensuring that available support is directed to the most important projects.

Reminders of Britain's maritime past are also preserved. At Portsmouth are preserved HMS *Victory*, Nelson's flagship, HMS *Warrior*, the world's first iron battleship, and the remains of *Mary Rose*, an early 16th-century warship, raised from the seabed in 1982. The Imperial War Museum has opened the cruiser HMS *Belfast* to the public in the Pool of London. Isambard Kingdom Brunel's SS *Great Britain*, the world's first large screw-driven ship, is preserved in Bristol.

A voluntary body, the Maritime Trust, has been established to preserve vessels and other maritime items of historic or technical interest. The Trust's vessels include the clipper *Cutty Sark* at Greenwich. In all, it is estimated that some 400 historic ships are preserved in Britain, mostly in private hands.

Voluntary Sector

Among the organisations which campaign for the preservation and appreciation of buildings are:

- the Society for the Protection of Ancient Buildings;
- the Ancient Monuments Society;
- the Georgian Group;
- the Victorian Society;
- the Twentieth Century Society;
- the Architectural Heritage Society of Scotland;
- the Ulster Architectural Heritage Society;
- the Architectural Heritage Fund; and
- the Council for British Archaeology.

While funded largely by private donations, the national amenity societies have paid professional staff and statutory responsibilities, in recognition of which they receive government support.

The National Trust (for Places of Historic Interest or Natural Beauty), a charity with over 2 million members, owns and protects 243 historic houses open to the public, in addition to over 243,000 hectares (600,000 acres) of land in England, Wales and Northern Ireland. Scotland has its own National Trust.

The Civic Trust makes awards for development and restoration work which enhances its surroundings. It undertakes urban regeneration projects and acts as an umbrella organisation for nearly 1,000 civic societies. There are associate trusts in Scotland, Wales and north-east England.

The Countryside and Nature Conservation

Four government agencies are responsible for countryside policy and nature conservation in Great Britain:

- the Countryside Commission and English Nature, which both act in England;
- the Countryside Council for Wales (CCW); and
- Scottish Natural Heritage (SNH).

The Joint Nature Conservation Committee (JNCC) is the mechanism through which the three nature conservation agencies in England, Wales and Scotland fulfil their responsibilities for international nature conservation matters and those affecting Great Britain as a whole. The JNCC also undertakes research in connection with these responsibilities and sets standards for data, monitoring and other matters connected with nature conservation. Important work in 1994–95 included the development of targets under the biodiversity action plan. It includes representatives from Northern Ireland and independent members, and has a supporting specialist staff. Its 1995–96 budget is about £5 million.

Countryside Agencies

The Countryside Commission, the CCW and SNH are responsible for promoting the enhancement of the natural beauty and amenity of the countryside and encouraging the provision of facilities for open-air recreation. They are expected to respect the needs of those who live and work in the countryside. Activities undertaken by these bodies include:

- advising the Government on countryside matters;

- assisting the provision by local authorities and others of facilities for recreation in the countryside, often within easy reach of towns;

- providing and improving recreational paths; and

- undertaking research projects.

Total funding for the countryside agencies in 1995–96 is £42 million for the Countryside Commission, £18 million for the CCW and £40 million for SNH.

The Countryside Commission runs the Countryside Stewardship scheme, launched in 1991, which offers incentives to farmers and other land managers to enhance valuable landscapes and habitats and improve access to the countryside. The scheme is to transfer to the Ministry of Agriculture, Fisheries and Food in April 1996. In Wales the CCW is running a pilot scheme. Called Tir Cymen, it adopts a slightly different approach in that it applies to entire farms.

The Countryside Commission recognises over 210 country parks and over 230 picnic sites in England. A further 35 country parks and about 30 picnic sites in Wales are recognised by the CCW. In Scotland there are 36 country parks, and many local authority and private sector schemes for a variety of countryside facilities have been approved for grant aid by SNH.

Nature Conservation Agencies

English Nature, the CCW and SNH are the Government's statutory advisers on nature conservation in their areas. Their work includes:

- establishing and managing national nature reserves and encouraging the establishment of local nature reserves;

- advising the Government;

- identifying, notifying and monitoring Sites of Special Scientific Interest (SSSIs);

- providing general nature conservation information and advice;

- giving grants; and

- supporting and conducting research.

English Nature's funding for 1995–96 is £40.4 million.

There are over 300 national nature reserves covering some 190,000 hectares (468,000 acres) in Great Britain, and two statutory marine nature reserves, surrounding the islands of Lundy, off the Devon coast, and Skomer, off the coast of Dyfed. About 6,700 SSSIs have been notified in Great Britain for their plant, animal, geological or physiographical features. Some are of international importance and have been designated for protection under the EC Birds Directive or the Ramsar Convention (see p. 365). Local authorities have declared about 395 local nature reserves in England, 17 in Scotland and 21 in Wales.

In England, to assist those who have an interest or involvement in environmental planning and conservation action, English Nature has mapped and is describing 'Natural Areas'. These have a distinctive character that derives from the underlying geology, land forms, flora and fauna, and the land uses and settlement patterns of the area. The Natural Areas framework, which has been subject to public consultation, will underpin all of English Nature's work in future. This is being run in parallel with the Countryside Commission's Countryside Character Programme.

English Nature enters into land management agreements with owners and occupiers of SSSI land, increasingly to support management that is beneficial for its wildlife and natural features. Payments made under these agreements total £7 million a year. Overall, English Nature's grant schemes provide more than £2 million a year to assist local action to sustain biodiversity and geodiversity. SNH and the CCW also enter into land management agreements.

The Department of the Environment for Northern Ireland has responsibility for both nature and countryside conservation. In 1995–96 funding for its conservation measures is £6.6 million. The Council for Nature Conservation and the Countryside advises the Department on nature conservation matters, including the establishment and management of land and marine nature reserves and the declaration of

Areas of Special Scientific Interest. In all, 72 Areas of Special Scientific Interest had been declared by March 1995, covering 75,000 hectares (185,000 acres), and 47 statutory nature reserves have been established.

County wildlife trusts, urban wildlife trusts and the Royal Society for the Protection of Birds (RSPB) play an important part in protecting wildlife, having established between them over 2,000 reserves. The county and urban trusts are affiliated to a parent organisation, RSNC The Wildlife Trusts. The RSPB is the largest voluntary wildlife conservation body in Europe.

Wildlife Protection

The principal piece of legislation protecting wildlife in Great Britain is the Wildlife and Countryside Act 1981. This has:

- extended the list of protected species;

- restricted the introduction into the countryside of animals not normally found in the wild in Britain; and

- afforded greater protection for SSSIs than previously and made provision for marine nature reserves.

There is also provision for reviews of the list of protected species to be conducted by the three official nature conservation agencies, acting jointly through the JNCC, every five years, and for recommended changes to be submitted to the Secretary of State for the Environment. In Northern Ireland separate legislation on species and habitat protection is in line with the rest of Britain.

Species Recovery and Reintroduction

Extensive research and management are carried out to encourage the recovery of populations of species threatened with extinction. The three nature conservation agencies have also set up recovery programmes for a number of threatened species of plants and animals. English Nature's programme covers 32 species, including the dormouse, the Plymouth

pear and the fen raft spider. The aim is to ensure the survival of self-sustaining populations of these threatened species in the wild. SNH has a programme covering 17 species.

Schemes have been devised to reintroduce species into areas in which they used to be found. For example, the red kite had died out in England and Scotland, although it was still found in Wales and mainland Europe. An international project was co-ordinated by the JNCC and the RSPB to bring adult birds from Sweden and Spain and release them into the wild in areas which the species no longer inhabited. Other species reintroduced in recent years include the white-tailed sea eagle and the large blue butterfly. The Royal Botanic Gardens at Kew holds seeds from about 3,000 plant species which are extinct or under severe threat in the wild, and has had some success with reintroduction projects. The Royal Botanic Gardens in Edinburgh also plays a significant role.

Tree Preservation and Planting

Tree preservation orders enable local authorities to protect trees and woodlands in the interests of amenity. Once a tree is protected, it is in general an offence to cut down, reshape or generally wilfully destroy it without permission. The courts can impose substantial fines for breaches of such orders.

Government approval for the last two community forests in a programme of 12 was given in March 1995. One will be near Bristol, the other in south Hertfordshire. The other ten forests are near Bedford, in Greater Manchester, east of London, near Middlesbrough, in Nottinghamshire, in Tyne and Wear and north-east Durham, near Sheffield, in south Staffordshire, near Swindon, and near Warrington. The programme is run by the Countryside Commission and the Forestry Commission in partnership with local authorities.

Broadleaved Tree-planting 1970-71 to 1993-94

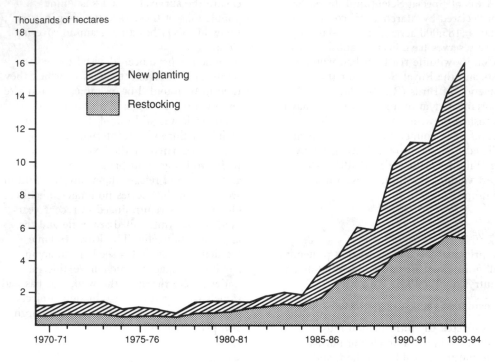

Thousands of hectares

New planting
Restocking

1970-71   1975-76   1980-81   1985-86   1990-91   1993-94

Source: Forestry Commission

Where protected trees are felled in contravention of an order or are removed because they are dying, dead or dangerous, replacement trees must be planted. Local authorities have powers to enforce this.

Tree planting is encouraged through various grant schemes. The planting of broadleaved trees has increased tenfold since 1985. Major afforestation projects include the creation of a new national forest in the Midlands.

The Coast

Local planning authorities are responsible for planning land use at the coast; they also aim to safeguard and enhance the coast's natural attractions and preserve areas of scientific interest. The protection of the coastline against erosion and flooding is administered centrally by the Ministry of Agriculture, Fisheries and Food, the Welsh Office and The Scottish Office. Operational responsibility lies with local authorities and the National Rivers Authority (see p. 368). New measures to protect the coast of England were announced by the Government in July 1994. These include the establishment of a standing forum on coastal management and a review of by-laws relating to coastal management. Certain stretches of undeveloped coast of particular beauty in England and Wales are designated as heritage coast; jointly with local authorities, the countryside agencies have designated 45 heritage coasts, protecting 1,525 km (948 miles).

English Nature, through its Campaign for a Living Coast, provides funds for groups setting up voluntary marine nature reserves or producing management plans for England's estuaries. So far, seven reserves have been grant-aided and 21 estuary management plans produced, covering 70 per cent of England's total estuarine area. There are 29 marine consultation areas in Scotland. Statutory bodies taking decisions that affect these areas are asked to consult SNH.

The National Trust, through its Enterprise Neptune campaign, raises funds to acquire stretches of coastline of great natural beauty and recreational value. About £21 million has been raised so far and the Trust now protects 884 km (550 miles) of coastline in England, Wales and Northern Ireland. The National Trust for Scotland also owns large parts of the Scottish coastline and protects others through conservation agreements.

National Parks, Areas of Outstanding Natural Beauty and National Scenic Areas

The Countryside Commission and the CCW can designate National Parks and areas of outstanding natural beauty (AONBs), subject to confirmation by the Secretaries of State for the Environment and for Wales respectively.

Ten National Parks have been established in England and Wales. Their aim is first to provide protection for the outstanding countryside they contain and secondly to provide opportunities for access and outdoor recreation. They are 'national' in the sense that they are of value to the nation as a whole. However, most of the land remains in private hands. Special National Park authorities have been set up, one for each park. Among other things, they:

- act as the development control authority for their areas;
- negotiate land management agreements and encourage farmers to manage their land in the traditional way;
- look after footpaths and negotiate agreements for public access; and
- set up information centres and employ rangers.

At present, most of these authorities are committees of county councils for the relevant areas. However, under the Environment Act 1995 the Government is establishing new independent authorities to run all the parks from April 1997. This will allow better protection and management of the park areas. The Norfolk and Suffolk Broads have their own independent authority and enjoy protection equivalent to that of a National Park. It is intended that the New Forest in Hampshire should enjoy similar protection, and in July 1994 the Government announced that the planning policies that apply to a National Park would also apply to the New Forest.

A total of 40 AONBs have been designated, covering around 20,200 sq km (7,900 sq miles) in England and 830 sq km (320 sq miles) in Wales. They comprise parts of the countryside which lack extensive areas of open country suitable for recreation and hence National Park status, but which nevertheless have an important landscape quality. Local authorities are encouraged to give special attention to AONBs in their planning and countryside conservation work.

In Scotland there are four regional parks and 40 National Scenic Areas, covering more than 11,000 sq km (4,300 sq miles), where certain kinds of development are subject to consultation with SNH and, in the event of a disagreement, with the Secretary of State for Scotland. Working parties have made recommendations for the management of the

Table 22.3: National Parks and Other Designated Areas, December 1994

	National Parks area (sq km)	Percentage of total area	Areas of Outstanding Natural Beauty[a] (sq km)	Percentage of total area
England	9,631	7	20,198	16
Wales[b]	4,098	20	833	4
Scotland	–	–	10,018	13
Northern Ireland	–	–	2,849	20

Sources: Countryside Commission, Countryside Council for Wales, Scottish Natural Heritage, Department of the Environment for Northern Ireland
[a]National Scenic Areas in Scotland.
[b]December 1993.

Cairngorms and for Loch Lomond and the Trossachs, two areas of outstanding natural importance in Scotland. For the former, the Government has announced a Cairngorms Partnership, as recommended by the working party. In the latter case, it is proposed that the new local authorities will establish a joint committee for the area. In the wider countryside SNH provides grants for a range of countryside projects.

In Northern Ireland the Council for Nature Conservation and the Countryside advises the Department of the Environment for Northern Ireland on the preservation of amenities and the designation of areas of outstanding natural beauty. In all, nine such areas have been designated, covering over 2,800 sq km (1,100 sq miles); seven areas are being managed as country parks and one as a regional park.

There are 11 forest parks in Great Britain, covering some 2,400 sq km (950 sq miles) and administered by the Forestry Commission. There are nine in Northern Ireland, where they are administered by the Forest Service of the Department of Agriculture.

Public Rights of Way and Open Country

County and metropolitan district councils in England and Wales are responsible for keeping public rights of way signposted and free from obstruction. Public paths are usually maintained by these highway authorities, which also supervise landowners' duties to repair stiles and gates. In Scotland, planning authorities are responsible for asserting and protecting rights of way. Local authorities in Great Britain can create paths, close paths no longer needed for public use and divert paths to meet the needs of either the public or landowners. Farmers in England and Wales are required by law rapidly to restore public paths damaged by agricultural operations. In England and Wales there are some 225,000 km (140,000 miles) of rights of way.

There are 17 approved national trails in England and Wales, covering about 3,500 km (2,200 miles), and three approved long-distance routes in Scotland, covering about 580 km (360 miles).

Approval for a new national trail along the line of Hadrian's Wall was announced in October 1994, and formal consultations are under way into the designation of the Cotswold Way as a national trail. In Scotland, a new Great Glen Way is at an advanced stage of planning.

The Countryside Commission intends to help authorities bring all rights of way in England into good order by the end of the century, and a Parish Path Partnership scheme has been introduced, which is designed to stimulate local involvement and improvement. By early 1995, 28 local authorities had joined the scheme, which is receiving £3.8 million of government funding. The CCW is also establishing a network of public rights of way, and a Public Paths Campaign has been introduced. In Scotland a major new 'Paths for All' initiative is planned by SNH to promote better access to countryside close to towns and cities.

> **Approval for England's first national trail planned specifically for horse riders and mountain bikers, the Pennine Bridleway, was announced by the Government in January 1995. The cross-Pennine route will cover 333 km (208 miles) from Cumbria to Derbyshire.**

There is no automatic right of public access to open country, although many landowners allow it more or less freely. A scheme to encourage farmers to open 'set-aside' land (see p. 284) to the public was launched in September 1994. Local planning authorities in England and Wales can secure access by means of agreements with landowners. If agreements cannot be reached, authorities may acquire land or make orders for public access. Similar powers cover Scotland and Northern Ireland; in Northern Ireland the primary responsibility lies with district councils. In Scotland there is a tradition of freedom to roam, based on tolerance between landowners and those seeking reasonable recreational access to the hills.

Common land totals an estimated 600,000 hectares (1.5 million acres) in England and

Wales, but a legal right of public access exists for only one-fifth of this area. Common land is usually privately owned, but people other than the owner may have various rights over it, for example, as pasture land. Commons are protected by law and cannot be built on or enclosed without the consent of the Secretaries of State for the Environment or Wales. There is no common land in Scotland or Northern Ireland.

Voluntary Sector

Many voluntary organisations are concerned to preserve the amenities of the countryside, including the Council for the Protection of Rural England, the Campaign for the Protection of Rural Wales, the Association for the Protection of Rural Scotland and the Ulster Society for the Preservation of the Countryside.

International Action

Britain plays a full part in international action to conserve wildlife. Its international obligations include the Berne Convention on the conservation of European wildlife and natural habitats, and EC directives on the conservation of wild birds (the Birds Directive) and of natural habitats and wild fauna and flora. The implementation of the latter directive, which came into force in October 1994, entails the designation of Special Areas of Conservation (SACs). Together with Special Protection Areas (SPAs) designated under the Birds Directive, the SACs will contribute to a EU-wide network of protected sites to be known as 'Natura 2000'. In March 1995, the Government published a draft list of over 280 areas for consultation. By August 1995, 107 SPAs had been designated.

Britain is also party to the Ramsar Convention on wetlands of international importance. By August 1995 a total of 90 sites in Britain had been designated under this convention, together with a further site in one of Britain's dependent territories. Britain is a party to the Convention on International Trade in Endangered Species of Wild Fauna and Flora, which prohibits commercial trade in highly endangered species and regulates trade in less threatened species by means of a permit system. Britain is supporting measures to improve the enforcement of the Convention.

The Convention on Biological Diversity was signed by over 150 countries, including Britain, at the June 1992 'Earth Summit'. It requires countries to develop national strategies for the conservation and sustainable use of biological diversity. Britain's action plan for implementing this was published in January 1994. Drawn up after extensive consultation, it provides a strategy for the protection of biodiversity in Britain in the next 10–20 years. The key objectives of this are to conserve and, where practicable, enhance:

- the overall population and natural ranges of native species, and the quality and range of wildlife habitats and ecosystems;

- internationally important and threatened species, habitats and ecosystems;

- species, habitats and natural and managed ecosystems that are characteristic of local areas; and

- the biodiversity of natural and semi-natural habitats where this has been diminished over recent decades.

The plan commits the Government to increasing public awareness of the conservation of biodiversity and to contributing to biodiversity conservation on a European and global scale. A steering group which is taking forward these commitments will be responsible for developing a range of targets for key species and habitats for 2000 and 2010; these will be published later in 1995.

The Darwin Initiative forms part of the measures announced by Britain at the UNCED meeting. It is intended to make British experience available to developing countries with important biological resources. Some £9 million will be made available over the first four years of the Initiative. By March 1995, 53 projects, totalling £5.6 million, had been approved.

Environmental Improvement

The Government assists local voluntary organisations to promote projects such as creating parks, footpaths and other areas of greenery in cities; conserving the industrial heritage and the natural environment; and recycling waste. The Department of the Environment makes grants through the Environmental Action Fund, worth almost £4 million in 1995–96, to support projects which actively assist in tackling environmental problems. The Civic Trust manages a Local Projects Fund for the Department, from which £260,000 will be available in 1995–96.

The Scottish Office Environment Department is making £430,000 available in 1995–96 to 46 environmental organisations under its Special Grants (Environmental) Programme to help them carry out environmental conservation, improvement and education work. Scottish Enterprise and Highlands and Islands Enterprise (see p. 205) are responsible for environmental improvement and land reclamation in Scotland. The Government's programme of Environmentally Sensitive Areas (see p. 284) supports environmentally sensitive practices that protect and enhance the countryside.

World Heritage Sites

Britain is well represented in the World Heritage List, which was established under the World Heritage Convention to identify and secure lasting protection for those parts of the world heritage of outstanding universal value. So far 13 sites in Britain have been listed. These are:

- Canterbury Cathedral, with St Augustine's Abbey and St Martin's Church, in Kent;
- Durham Cathedral and Castle;
- Studley Royal Gardens and Fountains Abbey, in North Yorkshire;
- Ironbridge Gorge, with the world's first iron bridge and other early industrial sites, in Shropshire;
- the prehistoric stone circles at Stonehenge and Avebury, in Wiltshire;
- Blenheim Palace, in Oxfordshire;
- the city of Bath, in Avon;
- Hadrian's Wall;
- the Tower of London;
- the Palace of Westminster, Westminster Abbey and St Margaret's, Westminster, also in London;
- the islands of St Kilda, in Scotland;
- the castles and town walls of King Edward I, in north Wales; and
- the Giant's Causeway and Causeway Coast, in Northern Ireland.

Support for these sites under various programmes can be considerable. For example, Durham Cathedral received £95,000 in government repair grant in 1994–95.

Further Reading

Conservation. Aspects of Britain series, HMSO, 1993.

Digest of Environmental Protection and Water Statistics. Annual report. HMSO.

Environmental Appraisal of Development Plans: a Good Practice Guide. HMSO, 1993.

Planning. Aspects of Britain series, HMSO, 1992.

This Common Inheritance: UK Annual Report 1995. HMSO, 1995.

23 Control of Pollution

For more than a century Britain has been developing policies to protect the environment against pollution from industry and other sources. Laws were introduced at an early stage to control air and water pollution—for example, the Alkali Act 1863 and, more recently, the Clean Air Acts 1956 and 1968. Legislation, revised regularly to meet changing circumstances, sets out a wide range of powers and duties for central and local government, covering all types of pollution, from greenhouse gases to litter. Successes include a 60 per cent reduction in lead inputs to coastal waters between 1985 and 1993, and a fall of over 50 per cent in sulphur dioxide emissions since 1970.

Introduction

Britain supports international co-operation on matters of environmental protection. It develops much of its legislation on pollution control in collaboration with its partners in the European Union and organisations such as the Organisation for Economic Co-operation and Development and the United Nations. With increasing scientific understanding of global pollution problems, the Government is considering how the principle of 'sustainable development', the theme of a major United Nations conference in June 1992 (see p. 356), can further guide its policies and actions. Assistance is also given to developing countries for environmental projects, while an Environmental Know How Fund was set up in 1992 to help central and eastern Europe and the former Soviet Union.

Administration

Executive responsibility for pollution control is divided between local authorities and central government agencies. Central government makes policy, exercises general budgetary control, promotes legislation and advises pollution control authorities on policy implementation. The Secretary of State for the Environment has general responsibility for co-ordinating the work of the Government on environmental protection. In Scotland and Wales the respective Secretaries of State are responsible for co-ordinating pollution control within their countries. In Northern Ireland, this responsibility rests with the Department of the Environment for Northern Ireland. Local authorities also have important duties and powers. They are responsible for matters such as:

- collection and disposal of domestic wastes;
- keeping the streets clean from litter;
- control of air pollution from domestic and from many industrial premises; and
- noise and general nuisance abatement.

The National Rivers Authority (NRA) is responsible for monitoring water quality and the control of water pollution in England and Wales. It spent £89.9 million on pollution control in 1994–95. In Scotland, the river purification authorities have statutory responsibility for water pollution control; the aggregate annual expenditure of the seven mainland authorities is more than £13 million. In Northern Ireland, water quality is monitored by the Environment Service of the Department of the Environment for Northern Ireland.

In England and Wales Her Majesty's Inspectorate of Pollution (HMIP) has an important role in the control of emissions to land, air and water from certain industrial processes through the mechanism of 'integrated pollution control' (see p. 369). Her Majesty's Industrial Pollution Inspectorate (HMIPI) is the Scottish equivalent of HMIP.

> The Environment Act 1995 includes provisions to bring together the functions of HMIP and the NRA, together with those presently exercised by waste regulation authorities, into a single Environment Agency. A Scottish Environment Protection Agency will be set up to combine the functions of HMIPI, the river purification authorities and the waste regulation and some of the air pollution functions of the district and islands councils. It is expected that the environment agencies will come into being in April 1996.

An independent standing Royal Commission on Environmental Pollution advises the Government on national and international matters concerning the pollution of the environment, on the adequacy of research and on the future possibilities of danger to the environment. So far it has produced 18 reports on a variety of topics, for example the use of incineration in refuse disposal.

Business and Consumer Involvement

The Government has launched a number of initiatives to help business improve its environmental performance, ensure business concerns are taken into account when policy is made, and help consumers assess firms' environmental credentials. For example, the Environmental Technology Best Practice Programme provides information to business about the cost-effective reduction of pollution and waste. Priority areas for the programme are chosen in consultation with industry. In February 1995 the Government announced the Small Company Environmental and Energy Management Assistance Scheme, which will make grants to small companies to improve their environmental performance.

Advisory Committee on Business and the Environment

The Advisory Committee on Business and the Environment comprises 26 business leaders, appointed by the Government and serving in a personal capacity. Its roles are:
- advising the Government on environmental issues of concern to business;
- providing a link with international business initiatives on the environment; and
- helping to mobilise the business community through demonstrating good environmental practice.

Much of the Committee's work is carried on through working groups which concentrate on a particular area.

British Standard on Environmental Management

In 1994 the British Standards Institution (see p. 206) published BS7750, the world's first standard for environmental management systems. Having been tested in a wide range of businesses and other bodies, the standard can be used by any organisation. BS7750 shares many features of the widely-used BS EN ISO 9000—formerly BS5750—quality management standard. The first BS7750 certificates were awarded to 20 companies in March 1995.

Eco-Management and Audit

In 1993 the European Union adopted a regulation setting up a voluntary eco-management and audit scheme, which became operational throughout the EU in April 1995. Although it is intended primarily for the manufacturing, power and waste disposal sectors, its use can be extended to other sectors on an experimental basis. The first such adaptation was the British scheme for local government. Registration covers individual sites[1] rather than companies' entire operations. An essential component is an environmental management scheme such as BS7750, which has been designed to be fully compatible with the scheme. Those seeking registration must first prepare and publish an environmental statement which, together with the management system, needs to be verified by an accredited independent body. A full cycle of review and verification must be conducted at least once every three years.

> In August 1995 five British companies became the first in Europe to register their sites for the eco-management and audit scheme. This entitles them to use a special statement and graphic incorporating the European gold stars on a blue background, so that members of the public can identify which sites are participating in the scheme.

Integrated Pollution Control

Under the Environmental Protection Act 1990, a system of 'integrated pollution control' (IPC) is being phased in to control certain categories of industrial pollution. The potentially most harmful processes are specified for IPC, and require authorisation from HMIP. The NRA is responsible for monitoring waters receiving discharges authorised under IPC. Emissions to air from more minor processes are controlled under a parallel system of local authority air pollution control. In granting authorisation for releases under IPC, HMIP requires the use of the best available techniques not entailing excessive cost to prevent or minimise polluting emissions and to ensure that any releases are made harmless. The staff of the Inspectorate has been increased considerably to allow the full implementation of IPC, and its performance report shows that the number of regulatory visits is well above target.

In Scotland, IPC is administered by HMIPI jointly with the river purification authorities. In Northern Ireland broadly similar controls are exercised by the Environment Service, and proposals are being formulated for the introduction of a system of air pollution control similar to IPC. The Government has secured agreement to the introduction of IPC on the British model within the EC, where a directive on integrated pollution prevention and control is expected to be adopted shortly.

Land

Certain local authorities are designated as waste collection, waste disposal or waste regulation authorities, responsible for different parts of the process of dealing with controlled wastes. Legislation has also established a licensing system for waste disposal sites, treatment plants and storage facilities receiving controlled wastes. 'special'—that is, hazardous—wastes are subject to additional controls. Responsibility for proper handling of waste falls on everyone who has control of it from production to final disposal or reclamation. Operators now remain responsible for their sites until the waste regulation authority is satisfied that no future hazard is likely to arise. In England and Wales local authorities' waste disposal operations are being transferred to 'arm's length' companies or private contractors so as to separate them

---

[1]Or operational units in the case of local authorities.

from the authorities' other jobs of setting policies and standards, and enforcement. The new Environment Agency will take over local authority waste regulation functions.

In Scotland, the district and islands councils are responsible for the collection and disposal of refuse. They are currently also the waste regulation authorities, but the new Scottish Environment Protection Agency will take over that function. In Northern Ireland, responsibility for the collection, disposal and regulation of waste currently rests with the district councils. However, the separation and centralisation of waste regulation is proposed.

HMIP, the NRA and the Hazardous Waste Inspectorate for Scotland may advise local authorities on how to improve their control of waste management and on how to work towards environmentally acceptable standards for dealing with hazardous wastes. In Northern Ireland, similar advice is offered to district councils by the Environment Service.

The Government has introduced a landfill tax (see p. 162), which will provide a fiscal incentive for waste minimisation and recycling.

Litter

It is a criminal offence to leave litter in any public place in the open air or to dump rubbish except in designated places. The maximum penalty was raised in 1992 to £2,500. Local authorities have a duty to keep their public land as free of litter and refuse (including dog faeces) as practicable. Members of the public have powers to take action against those who fail to comply with their responsibilities.

To help counteract the problem of litter, financial support—totalling £3 million in 1995–96—is given to the Tidy Britain Group, which is recognised as the national agency for tackling litter. It provides a comprehensive programme in collaboration with local authorities and the private sector. The Group secures sponsorship from industry to undertake anti-litter programmes such as its Neighbourhood Care Scheme.

Recycling and Materials Reclamation

The Government encourages the reclamation

and recycling of waste materials whenever this is the best practicable environmental option; its target is for half of all recyclable household waste to be recycled by 2000. Local authorities have to make plans for the recycling of waste. Waste disposal authorities in England must pay 'recycling credits' to waste collection authorities to pass on the full equivalent in disposal costs where waste is recycled. In Wales and Scotland, the same authorities handle waste collection and disposal, so that the need for payments does not arise. The Environment Act 1995 gives the Government reserve powers to place an obligation on businesses to re-use, recover or recycle products and materials.

Britain's first recycled products guide was published in March 1995 by Waste Watch, a national body promoting waste reduction and recycling. The guide lists over 400 products which contain recycled materials.

The Government has supported pilot recycling initiatives in Sheffield, Cardiff, Dundee and the county of Devon, which have tested a variety of collection and sorting methods. Members of the public can deposit used glass containers for recycling in bottle banks. There are over 15,000 such sites in Britain, and about 4,500 can banks. There are also nearly 6,000 paper banks and, in some places, plastics or textiles banks. In addition, voluntary organisations arrange collections of waste material, and the local authority can pay them a recycling credit for doing so.

Water

All discharges to water in Britain require the consent of the regulatory authority. In England and Wales the NRA's principal method of controlling water pollution is through the regulation of all effluent discharges into groundwaters, inland and coastal waters (except those releases subject to IPC, which are controlled by HMIP). The NRA maintains public registers containing information about water quality, discharge consents and authorisations from HMIP.

HMIP maintains registers of authorisations and associated monitoring. The new Environment Agency will take over these functions from April 1996. Similar arrangements apply in Scotland, where control is exercised by the river purification authorities. In Northern Ireland the Environment Service is responsible for controlling water pollution.

The Government introduced regulations for a new system of classifying water quality in England and Wales in 1994. This system will provide the basis for setting statutory water quality objectives (SWQOs). It is intended that, following a pilot phase, these will be phased in gradually, specifying for each individual stretch of water the standards that should be reached and the target date for achieving them. The system of SWQOs will provide the framework for the NRA to set discharge consents. Once objectives are set, the NRA will be under a duty to use its powers to ensure that they are met. In February 1995 the Government announced consultations on a small batch of pilot SWQOs. The experience gained from these will be valuable in determining whether to proceed in other water catchment areas and, if so, what targets for implementation would be realistic.

More than 95 per cent of the population in Britain live in properties connected to a sewer, and sewage treatment works serve over 80 per cent of the population. In England and Wales the water industry is committed to an investment programme of some £11,000 million over ten years for improvements to water quality. Progressively higher treatment standards for industrial waste effluents and new measures to combat pollution from agriculture are expected to bring further improvements in water quality. In Scotland, sewage treatment and disposal come within the water and sewerage programme, which will total more than £728 million in the three years to 1995–96.

Over the past 30 years, notable progress has been made in cleaning up the previously heavily polluted major estuaries of the east coast of Britain, including the Forth, Tees, Thames and Tyne. Results from the monitoring of inland waters in England and Wales indicate good progress, with over 90 per cent of rivers and canals now of good or fair quality.

Bathing Waters and Coastal Sewage Discharges

The water industry is investing roughly £2,000 million to provide treatment of coastal sewage discharges and improve the quality of Britain's bathing waters. In the 1994 tests of bathing water quality, 82 per cent of identified bathing waters (376 out of 457) in Britain met the mandatory coliform bacteria standards of the EC bathing water directive, compared with 66 per cent of beaches in 1988. The bulk of the improvement programme should be complete by about the end of 1995. Sea dumping of sewage sludge will cease by the end of 1998.

Marine Environment

In 1992 a new Convention for the Protection of the Marine Environment of the North East Atlantic was agreed in Paris. It covers both land and sea, sets targets for the introduction of additional safeguards for the area, and requires contracting parties to take all possible steps to prevent or eliminate pollution through an action plan subject to annual review. Britain is also a leading participant in the series of North Sea Conferences, an international forum of countries bordering the North Sea. Good progress is being made in meeting North Sea Conference targets for reducing the input of dangerous substances into the sea. For example, direct and riverine inputs of cadmium, lead and mercury to coastal waters were more than halved between 1985 and 1993.

International action on the prevention of pollution from ships is taken through the International Maritime Organization (IMO). Britain applies international requirements to all ships in British waters and to British ships wherever they are. Enforcement is undertaken by the Department of Transport.

The Marine Pollution Control Unit (MPCU), part of the Coastguard Agency, is responsible for dealing with spillages of oil or other hazardous substances from ships at sea. The Government's national contingency plan, which is developed and maintained by the MPCU, sets out arrangements for dealing with pollution. The Unit has at its disposal various counter-pollution facilities, including:

- remote sensing surveillance aircraft;
- aerial and seaborne spraying equipment;
- stocks of oil dispersants;
- mechanical recovery and cargo transfer equipment; and
- specialised beach cleaning equipment.

Licences for oil and gas exploration include special conditions designed to protect the environment. These conditions are set in consultation with a number of bodies with environmental interests, including the relevant government departments and the Joint Nature Conservation Committee (see p. 359). Applicants for licences in sensitive areas must demonstrate that they have addressed the environmental concerns when developing their work programme. Before commencing offshore operations, the operators are required to have oil spill contingency plans. In addition, all discharges that contain oil are controlled under the Prevention of Oil Pollution Act 1971, and limits are set for the permissible level of oil discharged. In response to requests from the North Sea Conference, progressively tighter limits on oil discharged with drill cuttings have been set. This has resulted in the quantity of oil discharges from this source from installations in British waters falling from 18,500 tonnes in 1988 to 3,820 tonnes in 1994.

Britain ended the dumping of industrial waste at sea in 1992. Waste has not been licensed for incineration at sea since 1990. Under the North East Atlantic Convention, and the earlier convention it replaces, the dumping at sea of most types of waste will be phased out over the next few years. In February 1994 Britain announced that it was accepting an internationally-agreed indefinite ban on the sea dumping of low and intermediate level radioactive waste.

Air

Air quality in Britain has improved considerably in the last 30 years. Total emissions of smoke in the air have fallen by over 85 per cent since 1960. London and other major cities no longer have the dense smoke-laden 'smogs' of the 1950s and in central London winter sunshine has increased by about 70 per cent since 1958. However, new concerns have arisen, especially over the emissions from the growing number of motor vehicles and the possible impact on health. Measures have consequently been adopted to reduce substantially emissions from new vehicles (see p. 374).

Responsibility for clean air rests primarily with local authorities. They may declare 'smoke control areas' within which the emission of smoke from chimneys is an offence. About two-thirds of the dwellings in conurbations are covered by smoke control orders—around 6,340 are in force. Those industrial processes with the greatest potential for harmful emissions are controlled under the Environmental Protection Act 1990, enforced in England and Wales by HMIP, and are becoming subject to IPC. Processes with a significant but lesser potential for air pollution require approval from local authorities. Local authorities also control emissions of dark smoke from trade and industrial premises.

In October 1994 the Government announced funding of £5 million for a co-ordinated programme of research on air pollution and respiratory disease. Ten key areas will be addressed, including the short- and long-term effects of exposure to air pollutants, and the development of methods for measuring personal exposure to air pollutants.

Britain's automatic air quality monitoring network is being extended and upgraded at a cost of over £4 million a year. Since 1990, the Department of the Environment's Air Quality Bulletins have made daily air pollution data from the monitoring network available to the public. These give the concentrations of three main pollutants—ozone, nitrogen dioxide and sulphur dioxide (SO_2), together with an air pollution forecast—and grade air quality on a scale between 'very poor' and 'very good'. The information features in television and radio weather reports, and appears in many national and local newspapers. The data are also available on a special free telephone number, on videotext systems and on the Internet.

The Environment Act 1995 provides a new framework for air quality management, including the publication by the Government of a national strategy which will set air quality standards and targets for the pollutants causing the most concern. It also places new duties on local authorities to assess air quality in their boundaries and to prepare action plans where standards are not met or are unlikely to be met in future.

Climate Change

The greenhouse effect is a natural phenomenon keeping the earth at a temperature which can sustain life. But increasing man-made emissions of 'greenhouse gases', such as carbon dioxide (CO_2), methane and nitrous oxide (N_2O), are leading to greater concentrations of these gases in the atmosphere, which could affect climates worldwide. In 1988 the United Nations Environment Programme and the World Meteorological Organisation established the Intergovernmental Panel on Climate Change (IPCC) to consider climate change and possible responses to it. Britain chairs the working group which assesses the scientific evidence on climate change. In its 1990 report, last updated in 1994, the IPCC concluded that man-made emissions would lead to additional warming of the earth, and that, without any change in emissions, global average temperature would increase by about 0.3°C a decade, which would be faster than at any time over the past 10,000 years. Such changes could have major effects on the world. The IPCC is currently preparing an update of this assessment.

Britain is on target to exceed its commitments under the United Nations framework convention on climate change signed at the 'earth summit' (see p. 356). Chief among these is a pledge to return CO_2 emissions to 1990 levels by 2000. It is now estimated that by 2000 these will be between 6 and 13 million tonnes lower than in 1990.

Britain's national programme for combating the threat of global climate change includes:

- the introduction of VAT on domestic fuel and higher duties on road vehicle fuel;

- the creation of an Energy Saving Trust, which aims to promote the efficient use of energy, particularly in the home;

- tighter building regulations to promote the energy efficiency of new houses and business premises;

- government publicity on energy conservation in homes and businesses; and

- targets for energy saving in central and local government offices.

The UN framework convention was reviewed in Berlin in March April 1995, at which Britain called for reductions in total greenhouse gas emissions of 5 to 10 per cent on 1990 levels by 2010. A deadline of 1997 was set for agreeing further reductions in emissions. The meeting also agreed the principle of joint implementation, under which developed countries may sponsor reduction measures in developing countries and have the resultant saving credited against their own quota.

Britain is conducting extensive research into climate change. The research programme includes the work of the Hadley Centre for Climate Prediction and Research, which was opened in 1990 to build on the Meteorological Office climate modelling programme, and the construction of an advanced climate change detection instrument for launch on a satellite towards the end of the 1990s.

Ozone Layer

The Government is committed to the earliest possible phasing out of all ozone-depleting substances. Britain was one of the first 25 signatories to the Montreal Protocol, which deals with the protection of the ozone layer. The protocol was last strengthened in 1992, and now requires chlorofluorocarbons (CFCs), 1,1,1 trichloroethane and carbon tetrachloride to be phased out by the end of 1995. The supply of halons was phased out by the end of 1993. There is provision for

Emissions of Sulphur Dioxide and Nitrogen Oxides

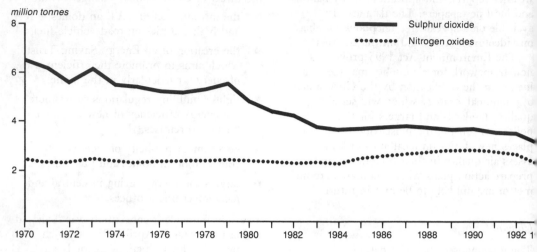

Source: Department of the Environment.

exemptions for any essential uses. Controls were also introduced on methyl bromide and on hydrochlorofluorocarbons (HCFCs—transitional substances with less ozone-depleting capacity than CFCs), which are needed in a number of areas if industry is to move away from CFCs quickly but which will themselves be phased out by 2030. European Community regulations required CFCs and carbon tetrachloride to be phased out by the end of 1994 (again with exemptions for essential uses), have brought forward the phase-out of HCFCs by 15 years and have capped the supply of methyl bromide.

Emissions of Sulphur Dioxide and Oxides of Nitrogen

SO_2 and oxides of nitrogen (NO_x) are the main gases that lead to acid rain. The principal sources are combustion plants that burn fossil fuels, such as coal-fired power stations, and, for NO_x, road transport. National SO_2 emissions have fallen by over 40 per cent since 1970 and a substantial programme seeks to ensure that this fall continues. For example, under the EC directive on the control of emissions from large combustion plants, the Government has published a national plan setting out phased reductions in emissions from existing plants

of NO_x up to 1998 and of SO_2 up to 2003. A new United Nations agreement on SO_2 was reached in 1994, with Britain accepting an 80 per cent reduction on 1980 levels by 2010, with intermediate targets of 50 per cent reductions by 2000 and 70 per cent by 2005. The Government will consult on a draft strategy to implement this during 1995.

The damaging effect of acid depositions from combustion processes on freshwaters and soils has been demonstrated by scientific research. The Government is spending about £10 million a year on an extensive research programme into the causes and effects of acid rain, and the likely results of possible abatement technologies. Lower emissions of SO_2 over the past 20 years (see graph) have led to the first signs of a decrease in acidification in some lochs in south-west Scotland.

Vehicle Emissions

Stringent emission standards for passenger cars were introduced at the end of 1992, which effectively require petrol-engined cars to be fitted with catalytic converters. These typically reduce emissions by over 75 per cent. Diesel cars are also subject to strict controls on particulate emissions. Since 1994, vans have had to meet the same limit as cars. Stricter controls for heavy diesel vehicles, including lorries and buses, were introduced in 1993. Further cuts will be introduced in 1997.

Compulsory tests of emissions from vehicles in use are a key element in Britain's strategy for improving air quality. Britain has introduced metered emission tests and smoke checks into the annual test for cars and vans and into the annual roadworthiness test for lorries and buses. In September 1995, in-service limits were further tightened, with special tests to be applied to catalyst vehicles from January 1996. Enforcement checks carried out at the roadside or in operators' premises also include at least a visual check for excessive smoke. Wherever possible, a smoke meter is used for borderline cases. The Vehicle Inspectorate (see p. 296) carried out more than 248,000 enforcement checks in 1993–94. In October 1994 the Secretary of State for Transport announced that the Vehicle Inspectorate would—in addition to its normal roadside enforcement activities—be making special efforts to crack down on polluting vehicles in a series of special campaigns. This is set to continue for the foreseeable future.

As a result of these measures, a marked and progressive decline in regulated pollutants is expected, which will continue until well into the first decade of the 21st century.

Sales of unleaded petrol have risen from virtually nothing in the mid-1980s to over 60 per cent of all petrol sold. This is due mainly to:

● a gradual increase in the differential in duty between leaded and unleaded petrol;

● the requirement for all new cars from October 1990 onwards to be capable of running on unleaded petrol; and

● the necessity for cars fitted with catalytic convertors to use unleaded petrol.

These measures have contributed to a 70 per cent reduction of lead in the air.

> The Government Car Service, which among other things provides official transport to ministers, took delivery of an environmentally-friendly gas-powered car in October 1994. Following trials of this car, an assessment will be made of how far to go in converting the rest of the car fleet.

Regulations were introduced in 1994 which for the first time set compulsory limits to the volatility of petrol. The expected benefits include a reduction in volatile organic compounds. The regulations also introduce a new EC standard for low sulphur diesel fuel,

Emissions of Carbon Dioxide

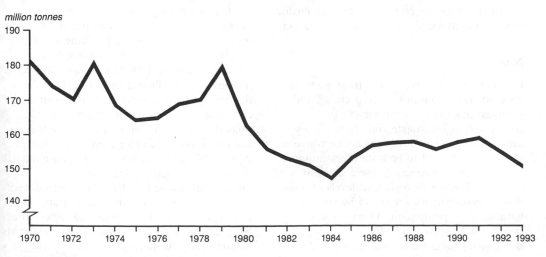

million tonnes

Source: Department of the Environment.

which will further reduce particulate emissions from the whole diesel fleet.

In February 1995 the Government announced a programme to cut vehicle pollution in city streets. This included:

- new resources for a crackdown on polluting vehicles in 23 cities and towns;

- the more rapid introduction of tighter emission standards in the annual 'MOT' test of vehicle roadworthiness;

- a prosecutions crackdown, with fines of up to £2,500;

- automatic prosecution for motorists and vehicle operators who exceed limits by ignoring vehicle maintenance; and

- an urgent study into the possibility of roadside checks for vehicles burning too much oil.

To tackle CO_2 emissions, in the November 1993 Budget the Chancellor of the Exchequer announced a long-term strategy of annual increases in road fuel duties averaging at least 5 per cent in real terms. This is expected to save about 2.5 million tonnes of carbon in the year 2000, representing a quarter of the reduction in total CO_2 emissions that Britain is required to make under the framework climate change convention.

Internationally developed standards have also been implemented in Britain to control the emission of smoke, vented fuel and unburned hydrocarbons from civil aircraft. International standards to control NO_x and carbon monoxide will be incorporated into domestic legislation.

Noise

Local authorities have a duty to inspect their areas for noise nuisance from premises and vehicles, machinery or equipment in the street, and to investigate complaints. They must serve a noise abatement notice where the noise is judged to be a statutory nuisance. They can also designate 'noise abatement zones' within which registered levels of noise from certain premises may not be increased without their permission. There are also specific provisions in law to:

- control noise from construction and demolition sites;

- control the use of loudspeakers in the streets; and

- enable individuals to take independent action through the courts against noise nuisance.

The Government believes that wherever possible attempts should be made to resolve problems informally. However, this may not always be possible, and in March 1995 it issued a consultation paper which included a recommendation that consideration be given to the creation of a criminal offence of night-time noise disturbance. This would involve an objective standard, based on World Health Organisation guidelines, on the levels of noise likely to cause sleep disturbance.

Regulations set out the permissible noise levels for various classes of new vehicle, and a new EC noise directive is due to be implemented by October 1996. Compensation may be payable for loss in property values caused by physical factors, including noise from new or improved public works such as roads, railways and airports. Regulations also require highway authorities to make grants available for insulation of homes that would be subject to specified levels of increased noise caused by new or improved roads. Noise insulation may also be provided where construction work for new roads will seriously affect nearby homes for a substantial period of time. Equivalent regulations for new railways are being introduced.

Britain has played a leading role in negotiations aimed at phasing out older, noisier subsonic jet aircraft. Flying non-noise certificated aircraft has been banned in Britain, and since 1990 British operators have no longer been allowed to add to their fleets further 'Chapter 2' aircraft (noisier planes, as classified by international agreement). The phased implementation of a complete ban on the operation of Chapter 2 aircraft began in April 1995, and it is intended to phase out all these types by April 2002. Various operational restrictions have been introduced to reduce noise disturbance further at Heathrow, Gatwick and Stansted, where the Secretary of State for Transport has assumed responsibility for noise abatement. These measures include:

- restrictions on the type and number of aircraft operating at night;

- the routeing of departing aircraft on routes chosen to minimise noise nuisance; and

- quieter take-off and landing procedures.

The Government has introduced a control system for night flights combining a noise quota with a ceiling on the total number of movements. The population disturbed by aircraft noise[2] at Heathrow fell from 591,000 in 1988 to 429,000 in 1991, even though the number of air transport movements increased. This was largely because of the phasing out of older, noisier aircraft. Under government proposals announced in 1993, airfield authorities would be given powers to enforce noise amelioration schemes. The Secretary of State would have powers to compel airfield authorities to prepare such a scheme.

Radioactivity

Man-made radiation represents only a small fraction of that to which the population is exposed; most is naturally occurring. A large proportion of the man-made radioactivity to which the public is exposed comes from medical treatments, such as X-rays. Nevertheless, the man-made fraction is subject to stringent control. Users of radioactive materials must be registered by HMIP in England and Wales or their equivalents in Scotland and Northern Ireland; authorisation is also required for the accumulation and disposal of radioactive waste. The Health and Safety Executive (see p. 195), through its Nuclear Installations Inspectorate, is responsible for granting nuclear site licences for major nuclear installations. No installation may be constructed or operated without a licence granted by the Executive.

The National Radiological Protection Board (NRPB) provides an authoritative point of reference on radiological protection. Following the accident at the Chernobyl nuclear power station in the then Soviet Union in 1986, the Government set up a national radiation monitoring network and overseas nuclear accident response system (RIMNET). An interim version began operating in 1988. A larger and more fully automated system, with 92 monitoring stations across Britain, became operational in 1993.

In 1987 the Government announced measures to deal with the problem of radon, a naturally occurring radioactive gas which can accumulate in houses. These included a free survey by the NRPB for householders living in radon-affected areas. The NRPB has designated several 'radon-affected areas', for example, Cornwall, Devon, Northamptonshire and parts of Derbyshire and Somerset. Householders in these areas are eligible for free radon tests.

Radioactive Waste Disposal

Radioactive wastes vary widely in nature and level of activity, and the methods of disposal reflect this. Some wastes can be disposed of safely in the same way as other industrial and household wastes. UK Nirex is responsible for developing a deep disposal facility for solid low-level and intermediate-level radioactive waste. It is concentrating detailed geological investigations on an area near the British Nuclear Fuels site at Sellafield, in Cumbria. As part of these studies, Nirex has applied for planning permission for an experimental underground rock laboratory, known as a 'rock characterisation facility'.

The Department of the Environment is sponsoring research, in collaboration with other countries, into disposal of high-level or heat-generating waste. This waste will first be stored in vitrified form for at least 50 years to allow the heat and radioactivity to decay.

All contracts for reprocessing spent nuclear fuel from overseas entered into since 1976 include provisions for the resulting waste to be returned to the country of origin.

Genetically Modified Organisms

Genetically modified organisms (GMOs) have many potential beneficial uses, for example, improving crops or clearing up contaminated

---

[2] That is, living within the 57 Leq noise contour, which is regarded as the onset of disturbance. Using the older, broadly comparable, 35 NNI measure, about 1.6 million people were affected in 1979.

land. However, their release into the environment could have harmful effects unless precautions are taken. The Environmental Protection Act 1990 and regulations which came into force in 1993 contain powers to ensure that any risks to the environment, including mankind, from the release of GMOs are prevented or minimised. The new legislation sets up a consent system for experimental releases of GMOs and for the EU-wide approval of GMO products. The Government has announced, in the light of experience and developing knowledge, 'fast track' procedures for the approval of low-risk GMOs so that their benefits may be enjoyed as soon as possible with the least burden on industry consistent with safety. The Government published an advice booklet on genetic modification and food in February 1995.

Environmental Research

Research into environmental protection is essential to the Government's environmental policies. Total spending on environmental research and development in 1994–95 was very substantial, running into hundreds of millions of pounds. The Department of the Environment spent an estimated £113 million on science and technology in 1994–45, researching into subjects including:

- climate change;

- atmospheric pollution and its monitoring;

- toxic chemicals and GMOs;

- waste disposal; and
- water quality and health.

Other departments have substantial programmes, notably the Ministry of Agriculture, Fisheries and Food, The Scottish Office Agriculture and Fisheries Department and other official bodies such as the NRA and the Meteorological Office.

Research Councils

Basic and strategic research is carried out by government-funded research councils (see pp. 321–5). Most have a role in environmental protection research, but particularly important is the Natural Environment Research Council (NERC), which has a Science Budget allocation of £157 million in 1995–96. NERC undertakes and supports research in the environmental sciences and funds postgraduate training. Its programmes encompass the marine, earth, terrestrial, freshwater, polar and atmospheric sciences. NERC stresses international collaborative work on global environmental issues. For example, it is helping to develop global atmospheric climate models and strengthening atmospheric research in the Arctic. A major research programme, the Terrestrial Initiative in Global Environmental Research, aims to assess the likely impact of climate change on Britain and elsewhere. NERC also co-ordinates the development and operation of the Environmental Change Network.

Further Reading

Pollution Control. Aspects of Britain series, HMSO, 1993.
Digest of Environmental Statistics. Annual report. HMSO.
The UK Environment. HMSO, 1992.
This Common Inheritance: UK Annual Report 1995. HMSO, 1995.

Social and
Cultural Affairs

24 Health and Social Services

Total spending on health and social services in 1995–96 is expected to be £39,876 million: £39,414 million on health and £462 million on social services. National Health Service spending in Britain was equivalent to 5.8 per cent of the gross domestic product in 1994–95, compared with 4.7 per cent in 1978–79. Key elements of the Government's spending plans include: continued expansion of primary care (family health services); improvements in the mental health services and development of maternity care and services for cancer patients; and a significant improvement in the standards of services that patients can expect to receive under the Patient's Charter.

The National Health Service (NHS) provides a full range of medical services which are available to all residents, regardless of their income. Local authority personal social services and voluntary organisations provide help and advice to the most vulnerable members of the community. These include elderly, physically disabled and mentally ill people, those with learning disabilities (mental handicap) and children in need of care.

Central government is directly responsible for the NHS, which is administered by a range of local health authorities and health boards throughout Britain, and for the social security system. Personal social services are administered by local authorities but central government is responsible for establishing national policies, issuing guidance and overseeing standards. Joint finance and planning between health and local authorities aims to prevent overlapping of services and to encourage the development of community services.

Spending on the health service has increased substantially in real terms since 1980, and is planned to grow further over the next two years. More patients are being treated than ever before. Spending on the personal social services is determined by local authorities. Central government has restricted the total expenditure of individual local authorities, but spending has risen substantially in real terms since the late 1970s, reflecting the priority given to this sector.

The NHS health programme consists of:

- Hospital and Community Health Services (HCHS), providing all hospital care and a range of community health services;

- Family Health Services (FHS), providing general medical, dental, pharmaceutical and some ophthalmic services, and covering the cost of medicines prescribed by general practitioners (GPs);

- Central Health and Miscellaneous Services (CHMS), providing services most effectively administered centrally, such as welfare food (which includes free milk and vitamins to families with children under five, and expectant mothers, on Income Support) and support to the voluntary sector; and

- the administrative costs of the health departments.

Major Policy Developments

Reforms in Management

The NHS and Community Care Act 1990 introduced wide-ranging reform in management and patient care in the health and social care services. The NHS reforms, which came into effect in 1991, aim to give patients, wherever they live in Britain, better health care and greater choice of service:

1. Health authorities and health boards have been given a new role as purchasers of health care on behalf of their local residents, and are responsible for assessing local health care needs and ensuring the availability of a full range of services to meet identified health needs. They ensure that those needs are met within existing resources.

2. Each health authority is funded to buy health care for its local residents through arranging contracts with hospitals and other health service units in either the public or the private sector. For the first time hospitals are directly funded for the number of patients they treat, making it easier for GPs to refer patients outside their area if treatment elsewhere is faster and better. However, powers exist for allocating resources where the urgent need for treatment does not allow NHS contracts to be arranged in advance.

3. The contracts agreed between health authorities and hospitals set out the quality, quantity and cost of the services to be

delivered during the year. The contracts secured by each health authority are based on wide consultation with all local GPs.

4. Hospitals may apply to become self-governing NHS trusts (see p. 392), independent of local health authority control but remaining within the NHS. They are accountable to the relevant health department, treating NHS patients, and are funded largely through general taxation, under contracts with health authorities.

5. GPs from larger medical practices may apply to join the general practitioner fundholding scheme (see p. 390), under which they receive an annual budget directly from the health authority, enabling them to buy certain hospital services for their patients.

The reforms in community care provision, which came into force between 1991 and 1993, establish a new financial and managerial framework which aims to secure the delivery of good quality services in line with national objectives. They are intended to enable vulnerable groups in the community to live as independently as possible in their own homes for as long as they are able and wish to do so, and to give them a greater say in how they live and how the services they need should be provided. (For fuller details see p. 406.)

Broadly similar changes have been introduced under separate legislation in Northern Ireland, where health and personal social services are provided on an integrated basis by health and social services boards.

Patient's Charters

Patient's Charters are part of the health departments' response to the Citizen's Charter (see p. 66). The Charters support the objectives of the NHS reforms: to improve standards of health care and sensitivity to patients in the NHS. They set out for the first time the rights of patients and the standards of care they can expect to receive from the NHS. The responsibility for implementing the Patient's Charters rests with all parts of the NHS, English regional offices, purchasers and providers of services (see above), and is carried out mainly through contract arrangements.

As well as restating the existing rights that patients have under the NHS, the original Patient's Charter in England, which came into force in 1992, introduced three new rights. These are that patients must:

- be given detailed information on local health services, including quality standards and maximum waiting times;

- be guaranteed admission for treatment no later than two years from the date of being placed on a waiting list; and

- have any complaint about NHS services investigated, and receive a full reply as soon as possible.

In England the Patient's Charter also sets national charter standards, which are not legal rights but specific standards of service that the NHS aims to provide. These cover respect for the individual patient; waiting times for ambulances, clinical assessment in accident and emergency departments and appointments in out-patient clinics; and cancellation of operations. Also included are local charter standards of service which health authorities aim to provide (see below).

Separate Patient's Charters have been developed for Scotland, Wales and Northern Ireland.

In England a new maternity services charter, describing key standards and rights, was published in 1994. This leaflet is the first of a series of special documents based on the Patient's Charter. Others in preparation deal with long-term NHS care services and health services for children.

In England an updated and expanded Patient's Charter was issued in January 1995. This has been extended to cover dental, optical and pharmaceutical services and the hospital environment, including cleanliness and security. It sets out new rights and standards, including:

- a guarantee that all patients will be treated within 18 months of going on a waiting list;

- a guarantee of no more than one year's waiting time for coronary artery by-pass grafts; and

- a right to receive advance notification if being admitted to a mixed sex ward.

All family health services authorities in England have produced local charters, which include statements of the standards of service patients can expect to receive from the authorities. Staff in GP practices are being encouraged to produce their own practice charters, setting out the standards of service they offer their patients. By June 1995 nearly three-quarters of GP surgeries in England had their own practice charter.

Openness in the NHS

The Code of Practice on Openness in the NHS came into force in June 1995. Designed to make NHS organisations more accountable and provide greater public access to information, the Code will apply to NHS Trusts, district and family health services authorities and local health practitioners such as GPs, dentists and pharmacists. It sets out the information that NHS Trusts and health authorities should publish or otherwise make available.

These include, among other things:

- information about what services are provided, the targets and standards set and results achieved, and the costs and effectiveness of the service;

- details of important proposals on health policies or proposed changes in the way the services are delivered; and

- information about how people can have access to their own personal health records.

A Code of Practice on Openness in the Health and Personal Social Services is being developed for Northern Ireland.

Developing Health Strategies

The Government emphasises the importance of promoting health as well as treating illness. Preventive health services such as health education, and the responsibility that individuals have for their own health, play a major part in this. While great progress has been made in eliminating infectious diseases such as poliomyelitis and tuberculosis, there is still scope for greater success in controlling the major causes of early death and disability.

The White Paper *The Health of the Nation*, published in 1992, sets out a strategy for improving health in England; its long-term aim is to enable people to live longer, healthier lives. It set targets for improvements in the following areas:

- coronary heart disease and stroke (the major cause of premature death in England);
- cancers (now the biggest cause of death across all ages);
- accidents (the commonest cause of death in those under 30);
- mental illness (a leading cause of ill-health and also a cause of many suicides); and
- HIV/AIDS and sexual health (HIV/AIDS is perhaps the greatest new public health threat this century—see p. 400—and there is much scope for reducing sexually transmitted diseases and unwanted pregnancies, especially among teenagers).

Targets were set for:

- reducing death rates (for example, from coronary heart disease and stroke in those under 65 by at least 40 per cent by the year 2000);
- reducing ill-health (such as the incidence of invasive cervical cancer by at least 20 per cent by 2000); and
- reducing risk behaviour (for example, the percentage of smokers to no more than 20 per cent of the population by 2000).

The strategy is now well into full implementation. In most areas there has been steady progress towards the targets but in a few cases, such as teenage smoking and obesity, figures are either on the increase or remain static. While the NHS has a central role in working towards the targets, the strategy also emphasises that there is a role for everyone in improving the nation's health.

Strategies have also been developed for Scotland, Wales and Northern Ireland which reflect the health variations in the different parts of Britain. In Wales, where the first of Britain's four national health strategies was published in 1990, areas for improvement include, among others: cancers, cardiovascular disease, maternal and early child health, physical disability, mental handicap and mental health, and injuries. Scotland's national strategy, *Scotland's Health: A Challenge to Us All*, published in 1992, places special emphasis on coronary heart disease, cancer, HIV/AIDS, accidents, dental and oral health, smoking, alcohol and drug misuse. Northern Ireland's strategy, published in 1991, sets targets for improvements in eight key areas, which include circulatory diseases, cancers, respiratory diseases, child and maternal health, and mental health.

National activity in England includes, for example, interdepartmental taskforces on accident prevention, nutrition, smoking, the workplace and physical activity, work with professional and voluntary bodies, and the provision of guidance setting out a range of possible actions for each tier of the NHS. At local level, the NHS is being encouraged to form 'healthy alliances' with agencies ranging from the voluntary sector through to industry and the media. Progress towards the targets is monitored regularly and formally reviewed, and periodic progress reports are published. Similar initiatives are being taken in Scotland, Wales and Northern Ireland.

The Government is working closely with the World Health Organisation (WHO) in presenting *The Health of the Nation* as one possible approach for other countries wishing to develop a strategic approach to improving health.

Improving London's Health Services

The Government's strategy to improve health services in the London area was launched in February 1993. It proposed to:

- develop better, local and accessible primary and community health services;
- provide a better-balanced hospital service, on fewer sites;
- streamline specialist services; and
- consolidate medical education and research, chiefly through mergers of free-standing undergraduate medical colleges with the multifaculty colleges of London University.

As a result:

- a London Initiative Zone was established as a focus for new investment and new approaches in primary health care and community-based services. Since 1993–94 an extra £210 million has been invested in developing primary care, and capital funding of £170 million over six years is being made available for improving GP surgeries, health centres and other premises;

- regional health authorities are continuing to implement proposals for restructuring the acute hospital service in London;

- plans to strengthen specialist services by concentrating them in fewer, high-quality centres of excellence were announced in April 1995.

The Health Survey for England

The 1993 Health Survey for England was published in March 1995. This was the third annual survey designed to monitor trends in the nation's health. Some of its main findings show:

- 44 per cent of men and 32 per cent of women aged 16 and over were overweight and a further 13 per cent of men and 16 per cent of women were found to be obese.

- Only one in ten adults (12 per cent of men and 9 per cent of women) were free from all of the four main modifiable risk factors of cardiovascular disease— smoking, raised blood pressure, raised cholesterol, and lack of physical activity.

- among people who drank alcohol, 20 per cent of men and 14 per cent of women said that they felt that they ought to cut down their drinking.

- Men were twice as likely as women to have had a heart attack (4 per cent and 2 per cent respectively), but a quarter of both men and women said that they had a cardiovascular disorder diagnosed by a doctor at some time in their lives.

- Among men participation in physical activity decreased steadily with age but among women there was little difference in activity between the ages of 16 and 54. Relatively low levels of activity among young women (16–24) reflected the fact that they were less likely to have taken part in sports activities than men of the same age and less likely to have done housework, gardening or DIY than women in older age-groups.

The National Health Service

The NHS is based upon the principle that there should be a full range of publicly provided services designed to help the individual stay healthy. The services are intended to provide effective and appropriate treatment and care where necessary while making the best use of available resources. All taxpayers, employers and employees contribute to its cost so that those members of the community who do not require health care help to pay for those who do. Some forms of treatment, such as hospital care, are provided free; others (see p. 387) may be charged for.

Growth in real spending on the health service is being used to meet the needs of increasing numbers of elderly people and to take full advantage of advances in medical technology. It is also used to provide more appropriate types of care, often in the community rather than in hospital, for priority groups such as elderly and mentally ill people and those with learning disabilities. Increased spending has, in addition, been allocated to combat the growing problems arising from alcohol and drug misuse; and to remedy disparities in provision between the regions of Britain.

In June 1995 the Government announced six national priorities for the NHS in England over the next three to six years. These are:

- further developing a primary-care-led NHS;

- securing a comprehensive range of secure, residential, in–patient and community services for people with mental illness;

- improved cost-effectiveness;

- giving greater voice to the users of services, and their carers;

- securing better services to meet the continuing health care needs of elderly, disabled or vulnerable people; and

- developing NHS organisations as good employers.

Similar priorities have been identified in Scotland, Wales and Northern Ireland.

The Voluntary Sector

Government grant aid to voluntary organisations working in health and personal social services in England exceeded £19.5 million in 1994–95. The grants go primarily to national organisations dealing with children, elderly people, carers and people from ethnic minorities, as well as those looking after people with mental illness, physical or learning disabilities, or suffering from the effects of HIV/AIDS or the misuse of alcohol or drugs. In Scotland grants to voluntary organisations in social welfare increased by 18 per cent in 1994–95, with grants to a wide range of bodies. Health authorities and local authorities have similar powers to make grants to local organisations.

In Northern Ireland the Department of Health and Social Services plans to spend £17.7 million in support of the voluntary sector in the period 1995–96 to 1997–98.

Market Testing

The Government stresses the need for collaboration between the public and private health sectors and for improving efficiency in order to secure the best value for money in the provision of health care services.

Since 1983 the market testing of catering, laundry and domestic services has produced cumulative savings of over £1,000 million, which has been reinvested into direct personal care. NHS managers have already market-tested most non-clinical services, including administrative and financial services as well as various aspects of information technology and communications. They are now beginning to test clinical support services such as pathology and pharmacy.

ADMINISTRATION

The Secretary of State for Health in England and the Secretaries of State for Scotland, Wales and Northern Ireland are responsible for all aspects of the health services in their respective territories. The Department of Health is responsible for national strategic planning in England. Within the Department

---

Table 24.1: Clients of selected advisory and counselling services, Britain

	1971	1981	1991	Thousands 1993
Citizens Advice Bureaux	1,500	4,515	8,278	8,253
Samaritans	–	1,700	2,500	2,400
Law Centres Federation	1	155	452	525
Youth Access	–	30	113	250
Disablement Information and Advice Lines	–	40	75	184
Childline	–	—	69	81
Relate (marriage guidance)	22	38	70	76
Alcoholics Anonymous	6	30	45	47
Cruse Bereavement Care	5	9	23	29
Turning Point (for people suffering from the misuse of drugs or alcohol and for those with mental illness)	–	–	–	22
Catholic Marriage Advisory Council	3		17	20
Al-Anon Family Groups	1	7	13	12

Source: *Social Trends*

of Health the NHS Executive is responsible for developing and implementing policies for the provision of high quality health services. The Scottish Office Home and Health Department, the Welsh Office and the Department of Health and Social Services in Northern Ireland have similar responsibilities.

District health authorities in England and Wales and health boards in Scotland are responsible for securing hospital and community health services in their areas. At present England also has regional authorities responsible for planning, resource allocation, major capital building work and certain specialised hospital services. The health authorities and boards co-operate closely with local authorities responsible for social work, environmental health, education and other services. Family health services authorities (health boards in Scotland)—one for each district—arrange for the provision of services by doctors, dentists, pharmacists and opticians, as well as administering their contracts. There are community health councils (local health councils in Scotland) for each district, representing local opinion on the health services provided.

In Northern Ireland health and social services boards are responsible as agents of the Department of Health and Social Services for assessing the health and social care needs of their resident populations. The representation of public opinion on these services is provided for by area health and social services councils.

Legislation passed in 1995 aims to continue streamlining of the administrative structure of the NHS in England and Wales. The measures will be fully in force from April 1996 and will:

- abolish the regional health authorities in England, and replace them with eight regional offices of the NHS Executive, employing a maximum of 1,100 staff and operating with a lighter touch; and

- replace district health authorities and family health services authorities with single all-purpose health authorities.

The abolition of regional health authorities and merger of district health authorities and family health services authorities will result in savings approaching £60 million in 1996–97. By 1997–98, when the new structure is fully implemented, these savings will rise to nearly £150 million a year, and will be retained by the NHS and reinvested in patient care.

Finance

Almost 83 per cent of the cost of the health service in Great Britain is paid for through general taxation. The rest is met from:

- the NHS element of National Insurance contributions, paid by employed people, their employers, and self-employed people (13 per cent);

- charges towards the cost of certain items such as drugs prescribed by family doctors, and general dental treatment (3.5 per cent); and

- other receipts, including land sales and the proceeds of income generation schemes (0.8 per cent).

Health authorities may raise funds from voluntary sources. Certain hospitals increase revenue by taking private patients, who pay the full cost of their accommodation and treatment.

Almost 80 per cent of medical prescription items are supplied free. Prescription charges do not apply to the following:

- children under 16 years (or young people under 19 and still in full-time education);

- expectant mothers and women who have had a baby in the past year;

- women aged 60 and over and men aged 65 and over;

- patients suffering from certain specified medical conditions;

- war and armed forces disablement pensioners (for prescriptions which relate to the disability for which they receive a war pension); and

- people in families who are receiving Income Support, Family Credit or Disability Working Allowance (and had savings of £8,000 or less when Disability Working Allowance was claimed—see p. 421); and people or families with low incomes.

Health Service Expenditure in England

NHS Gross Expenditure 1994–95 (estimate)

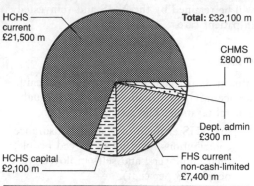

HCHS current £21,500 m

Total: £32,100 m

CHMS £800 m

Dept. admin £300 m

FHS current non-cash-limited £7,400 m

HCHS capital £2,100 m

Hospital and Community Health Services Gross Current Expenditure by Sector 1992–93

Total: £20,331 m

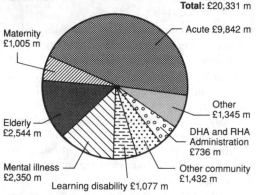

Maternity £1,005 m

Acute £9,842 m

Other £1,345 m

DHA and RHA Administration £736 m

Elderly £2,544 m

Mental illness £2,350 m

Other community £1,432 m

Learning disability £1,077 m

1. Other community services include health visiting, immunisation, screening, health promotion and community dental services.

2. Other services include ambulances, the blood transfusion service, mass radiography and the Service Increment for Teaching and Research (SIFTR).

Non-cash-limited Family Health Services Gross Expenditure 1993–94

Total: £6,909 m

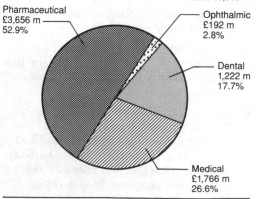

Pharmaceutical £3,656 m 52.9%

Ophthalmic £192 m 2.8%

Dental 1,222 m 17.7%

Medical £1,766 m 26.6%

Source: *Department of Health. The Government's Expenditure Plans 1995–96 to 1997–98.*

There are proportional charges for most types of NHS dental treatment, including examinations. However, women who were pregnant when the dentist accepted them for treatment or who have had a baby in the past year, anyone under the age of 18 (or 19 if in full-time education), people in families receiving Income Support or Family Credit, and people in families assessed as having a low income, do not have to pay.

Sight tests are free to children, full time students under the age of 19, people in families receiving Income Support, Family Credit or Disability Working Allowance and those with specified medical needs. A voucher to help with the cost of spectacles is also available for children, full-time students under the age of 19, people receiving the above benefits and those requiring certain complex lenses. Other people on low incomes may apply for help under the NHS Low Income Scheme.

Hospital staff are salaried and may be employed full time or part time. Family practitioners (doctors, dentists, optometrists and community pharmacists) are self-employed or, in the case of pharmacists, employed by a pharmacy company, and have contracts with the NHS. GPs are paid by a system of fees and allowances designed to reflect responsibilities, workload and practice expenses. Dentists providing treatment in their own surgeries are paid by a combination of capitation fees for treating children, continuing care payments for adults registered with the practice, and a prescribed scale of fees for individual treatments. Community pharmacists who dispense from their own or their company's premises are refunded the cost of the items supplied, together with professional fees. Ophthalmic medical practitioners and ophthalmic opticians taking part in the general ophthalmic service receive approved fees for each sight test carried out.

Staffing

The NHS is one of the largest employers in the world, with a workforce of nearly 1 million people. Staff costs account for two-thirds of total NHS expenditure and 70 per cent of current expenditure on hospitals and community health services. The sharp fall in the numbers of directly employed ancillary staff and of maintenance and works staff reflects the continuing effect of competitive tendering (see p. 76). Between 1983–84 and 1993–94:

- The number of NHS medical and dental staff in England rose by 21 per cent to 51,000, while in Scotland the increase was 9 per cent to 7,000. In England on average the number of hospital medical consultants grew by 2.5 per cent a year and the number of junior doctors by 1.8 per cent. In Scotland on average the number of hospital medical consultants grew by 1.7 per cent a year and the number of junior doctors by 1.1 per cent.

- The number of scientific, professional and technical staff in England rose by 33 per cent.

- The number of nursing and midwifery staff, who make up 47 per cent of the NHS workforce, decreased by 8 per cent. The drop in their numbers in 1993 reflects the growth in bursaried students under the Project 2000 nurse training scheme—see p. 405. (Project 2000 trainees have full student status and are not NHS employees.) The change masks an underlying trend of an increase of 8 per cent in the number of qualified nursing and midwifery staff since 1983.

- The number of general and senior managers has risen in recent years, which reflects the progressive introduction of management posts in a series of phased stages since 1986.

The Government's aim throughout the service is progressively to introduce greater pay flexibility to allow managers to relate pay to local markets and reward individual performance. A number of measures are being taken to provide a more effective workforce through better management development, education and training (see p. 404).

Health Service Commissioners

Health Service Commissioners (one each for England, Scotland and Wales) are responsible for dealing with complaints from members of the public about health service bodies. The three posts are at present held by one person (with a staff of 80), who is also Parliamentary Commissioner for Administration (Ombudsman—see p. 60). As Health Service Commissioner, he reports annually to Parliament. In Northern Ireland the Commissioner for Complaints has a similar role.

The Health Service Commissioner can investigate complaints that a person has suffered injustice or hardship as a result of:

- a failure in a service provided by a health service body;

- a failure to provide a service which the patient was entitled to receive; or

- maladministration by an NHS authority—that is, something that the NHS authority failed to do or did in the wrong way.

Complaints must be sent to the Ombudsman in writing, and the health service body concerned should first have been given a reasonable opportunity to respond.

At present the Health Service Ombudsman's jurisdiction does not extend to complaints about clinical judgment, family practitioners, personnel matters and the use of a health authority's discretionary powers. The Government proposes to introduce legislation to extend the Commissioner's powers to cover cases involving clinical judgments and those about family health services.

New NHS Complaints System

Following an independent review of all aspects of NHS complaints procedures published in 1994, the Government is to introduce a new complaints system from April 1996. Under this, complaints to hospitals, and to community health and primary care services, will be dealt with in a similar fashion at two distinct levels. The new procedures aim to resolve complaints speedily at a local level; independent panels will be an option for dealing with complaints that cannot be resolved simply and quickly.

FAMILY HEALTH SERVICES

The family health services are those given to patients by doctors (GPs), dentists, opticians and pharmacists of their own choice. They remain the first point of contact most people have with the NHS. Every year there are about 250 million consultations with GPs and about 6 million people visit a pharmacy every day. Many of those who visit their GP or dentist need no clinical treatment but instead healthy lifestyle counselling and preventive health care advice. The Government's longstanding policy has been to build up and extend these services in order to improve health and relieve pressure on the far more costly secondary care sector (that is, hospital and specialist services).

GPs provide the first diagnosis in the case of illness, give advice and may prescribe a suitable course of treatment or refer a patient to the more specialised services and hospital consultants. About four-fifths of GPs in Britain work in partnerships or group practices. Primary health-care teams also include health visitors and district nurses, midwives, and sometimes social workers and other professional staff employed by the health authorities. About a quarter of GPs in Great Britain and about half in Northern Ireland work in health centres. As well as providing medical and nursing services, health centres may also have facilities for health education, family planning, speech therapy, chiropody, assessment of hearing, physiotherapy and remedial exercises. Dental, pharmaceutical and ophthalmic services, hospital out-patient and supporting social work services, may also be provided.

There have been substantial increases in primary health care staff in recent years. For example, between 1984–85 and 1994–95 the number of GPs in England increased by 11 per cent (to over 28,700); average patient list size fell by 10 per cent (to just under 1,900); and the number of family dentists increased by 15.4 per cent (to nearly 15,800). The wholetime equivalent number of GP practice nurses increased by almost fivefold—to 9,600—and the number of opticians increased by over 16 per cent (to 6,000).

Special funds have been earmarked by the Government for improving the quality of primary health care in inner city areas. Efforts have also been made to improve health services for ethnic minority groups. The NHS Ethnic Health Unit, set up in 1993, works with health authorities, NHS Trusts and GPs to ensure that people from different ethnic backgrounds derive full benefit from the *Health of the Nation* strategy (see p. 384), local health purchasing policies, the Patient's Charter (see p. 382), the Care in the Community initiatives and the developing role of primary care. The Unit achieves this through a number of initiatives and project funding, which aim to promote the voice of minority ethnic groups in NHS decision-making at local level. Funding of over £1 million in 1995 was committed to projects, which included: a Muslim health initiative in south London; assessment of the needs of the Chinese community for acute hospital services in Birmingham; and monitoring experiences of cancer patients from Asian communities in north west England.

The Government has funded a number of initiatives aimed at raising standards within pharmacies and making fuller use of pharmacists' skills. At the local level a large number of family health services authorities have involved pharmacists in health promotion campaigns and in working closely with GPs in managing the drugs bill.

Recent Developments

GP Fundholders

In England and Wales GP practices with 7,000 patients or more (5,000 or more from April 1996) may apply for fundholding status. The corresponding figures in Scotland are 6,000 and in Northern Ireland 5,000. This is a voluntary scheme which gives larger medical practices the opportunity to manage NHS money for the benefit of their patients. It aims to improve services for patients and enable GPs to explore more innovative methods of providing health care. GP fundholders are responsible for part of their own NHS budgets, enabling them to buy certain non-urgent hospital services. NHS costs of prescription charges and part of the cost of running the practice are also covered. Fundholders may negotiate for services directly with hospitals from both public and private sectors in any health authority or health board in Britain. GP fundholders may buy NHS community nursing services for their patients, including district nursing and health visiting services and (except in Northern Ireland) community psychiatric and community mental handicap nursing. In 1993–94 GP fundholders in England made efficiency savings of £64 million, to be used to benefit patients, for example, by buying new equipment or more hospital care, or improving premises.

A new option—community fundholding—has been introduced for small practices with at least 3,000 patients, or as a stepping stone for larger ones who are not yet ready to become standard fundholders.

By April 1995 some 10,400 GPs in over 2,600 practices in England had become fundholders, and over 41 per cent of the population are now registered with a fundholding GP.

Contracts

The performance-related contract for GPs, introduced in 1990, is designed to raise standards of care, extend the range of services available to patients and improve patient choice. The changes are intended to make it easier for patients to see their GP at times convenient to them; or to change doctors; and to encourage doctors to practise more preventive medicine.

The new contract for dentists, introduced in 1990, aims at improving care and providing more information to patients about general dental services. As a result NHS dental care now includes preventive care as well as restorative treatment. All adult patients are now offered 'continuing care', and dentists are encouraged to practise more preventive dentistry for children. There are also incentives for dentists to undertake further training.

Plans to improve NHS dentistry were announced in April 1995. Immediate improvements to the existing system include:

- reinforcing the priority given to children's oral health by relating payments to dentists to disease levels in children most in need; and
- developing the community dental service to meet the needs of patients in areas where there may be difficulty in obtaining NHS treatment under the general dental service.

In the longer term the Government aims to introduce a system of local contracts between health authorities and dental practices similar to that operating in other parts of the health service.

GP/FHSA Links

Electronic links between GPs and family health services authorities are being developed; these aim to replace a paper-based system with the interchange of electronic data. The main benefits will be: speedier processing of claims; faster transfer of patient medical records; reduced clerical effort; and the elimination of the risk of losing paperwork in transit.

Clinical Audit

Clinical audit is a programme that requires all healthcare professionals to look systematically at the procedures used for diagnosis, care and treatment, examining how associated resources are used and investigating the effect care has on the outcome and quality of life for the patient.

The Government has so far allocated £280 million for clinical audit; by March 1994 over 20,000 clinical audits had been established.

Midwives, Health Visitors and District Nurses

Midwives provide care and support to women throughout pregnancy, birth and the post-natal period (up to 28 days after the baby is born). Midwives work in both hospital and community settings.

Since October 1994 district nurses and health visitors in eight pilot schemes in England have been able to prescribe from a limited list of drugs and medical appliances. These schemes are based in GP fundholding practices and are intended to reduce significantly the time patients have to wait for relief of their symptoms.

Health visitors are responsible for the preventive care and health promotion of families, particularly those with young children. They have a public health role, identifying local health needs and working closely with GPs, district nurses and other professions. District nurses give skilled nursing care to people at home or elsewhere outside hospital; they also play an important role in health promotion and education.

HOSPITAL AND SPECIALIST SERVICES

A full range of hospital services is provided by district general hospitals. These include treatment and diagnostic facilities for in-patients, day-patients and out-patients; maternity departments; infectious diseases units; psychiatric and geriatric facilities; emergency units; rehabilitation facilities; and other forms of specialised treatment. There are also specialist hospitals or units for children, people suffering from mental illness, those with learning disabilities, and elderly people, and for the treatment of specific diseases. Examples of these include the world-famous Hospital for Sick Children (Great Ormond Street) and the Moorfields Eye Hospital, both in London. Hospitals designated as teaching hospitals combine treatment facilities with training medical and other students, and research work.

Many of the hospitals in the NHS were built in the 19th century; some trace their origins to much earlier charitable foundations.

Much has been done to improve and extend existing hospital buildings and many new hospitals have been or are being opened.

- In England 85 major building schemes, each costing over £1 million, were due for completion in 1994–95. An additional 238 schemes, costing over £2,000 million in the next three years, are planned.

- In Scotland in 1994–95 £183 million was spent on hospital improvements; this is increasing to £204 million for 1995–96.

Recent policy in England and Wales has

been to provide a balanced hospital service centred around a district general hospital, complemented as necessary by smaller, locally based hospitals and facilities.

The hospital service is now treating more patients a year than ever before. In England between 1992–93 and 1993–94 the total number of operations rose by 6 per cent to 5.4 million, with heart operations up by 14 per cent to 132,000. Over the same period, the number of hip operations rose by 2 per cent to over 58,000, and eye lens operations went up a tenth to 131,000.

Waiting Times

Over the last few years there have been substantial reductions in the number of patients waiting more than 12 months for in-patient or day case treatment.

- In England in March 1995 fewer than 32,000 patients had been waiting over a year for hospital treatment, compared with more than 200,000 in 1987. Since March 1988 the average waiting time for in-patient and day case treatment has fallen from over nine months to four.

- In Scotland in 1994–95 the number of patients waiting over a year for hospital treatment fell from 4,193 to 1,588, while the number waiting for over 18 months fell from 1,838 to 99.

- In Wales in March 1995 the number of patients waiting over a year for hospital treatment was 4,100 compared with 10,100 in 1990. There were no patients waiting longer than two years.

The expanded Patient's Charter guarantees for hospital patients, effective from April 1995, are shown on p. 383.

NHS Trusts

Under the NHS and Community Care Act 1990 hospitals and other health service units (for example, ambulance services and community health services) may apply to become independent of direct local health authority control and establish themselves as self-governing NHS Trusts. Parallel legislation was introduced in Northern

Ireland to create Health and Social Services Trusts, which are broadly similar to NHS Trusts. The Trusts remain within the NHS, accountable to the appropriate Secretary of State and finally to Parliament. NHS Trusts are required to publish their business plans and annual reports and accounts, and to hold at least one public meeting a year. From September 1995 all annual reports must contain information about management costs.

Each NHS Trust is run by a board of directors. Trusts are free to employ their own staff and set their own rates of pay, although staff transferring to Trust employment retain their existing terms and conditions of service. Trusts are also free to carry out research and provide facilities for medical education and other forms of training. They derive their income mainly from NHS contracts to provide services to health authorities and GP fundholders. They may treat private patients and generate income provided this does not interfere with NHS obligations. By April 1995, 433 NHS Trusts were running in England, delivering nearly 100 per cent of NHS hospital and community health services. At the same date in Northern Ireland, 14 trusts were delivering over 70 per cent of the health and personal social services for the population.

Organ Transplantation

The United Kingdom Transplant Support Service Authority provides a centralised organ matching and allocation service. During 1994, 1,744 kidney transplants were performed. A similar service exists for corneas and, in 1994, 2,536 were transplanted.

Heart transplant operations have been conducted at Papworth Hospital in Cambridgeshire and Harefield Hospital in London since 1979. There are six other designated heart transplant centres in England, while Scotland's first unit opened in Glasgow in 1991. Programmes for combined heart and lung and lung transplantation are in progress and in 1994, 328 heart, 117 lung, and 52 heart/lung transplants were performed. The world's first combined heart, lungs and liver transplant operation was carried out at Papworth in 1987.

There are six designated liver transplant units in England and Scotland's first liver transplant centre opened in Edinburgh in 1992. In 1994 635 liver transplants were performed.

A voluntary organ donor card system enables people to indicate their willingness to become organ donors in the event of their death. The NHS Organ Donor Register, a computer database, was launched in October 1994. By October 1995 it contained over 2 million names.

Commercial dealing in organs for transplantation is illegal.

Blood Transfusion Services

Blood transfusion services are run by the National Blood Authority in England, the Scottish National Blood Transfusion Service, the Welsh Health Common Services Agency in Wales and the Northern Ireland Blood Transfusion Agency.

In England alone around 2.4 million donations are given each year by voluntary unpaid donors and separated into many different life-saving products for patients. Red cells, platelets and other products with a limited 'shelf life' are prepared at blood centres, and the more complex processing of plasma products is undertaken at the Bio Products Laboratory in Elstree (Hertfordshire) and the Protein Fractionation Centre in Edinburgh.

Each of the four national bodies co-ordinates programmes for donor recruitment, retention and education, and donor sessions are organised regionally, in towns, villages and workplaces. Donors are normally aged between 18 (17 in Scotland) and 65. Blood centres are responsible for blood collection, screening, processing and supplying hospital blood banks. They also provide wide-ranging laboratory, clinical, research, teaching and advisory services and facilities. These are subject to nationally co-ordinated quality audit programmes.

Britain is completely self-sufficient in 'fresh' blood products and the National Blood Authority aims to meet fully the demand for plasma products in England. Scotland is already self-sufficient in all blood products.

Ambulance and Patient Transport Services

NHS emergency ambulances are available free of charge for cases of sudden illness or collapse, for accidents and for doctors' urgent calls. Rapid response services, in which paramedics use cars and motor cycles to reach emergency cases, have been introduced in a number of areas, particularly London and other major cities with areas of high traffic density. Helicopter ambulances serve many parts of England and an integrated air ambulance service is available throughout Scotland.

Non-emergency patient transport services are available free of charge to NHS patients considered by their doctor (or dentist or midwife) to be medically unfit to travel by other means. The principle applied is that each patient should be able to reach hospital in a reasonable time and in reasonable comfort, without detriment to his or her medical condition. In many areas the ambulance service organises volunteer drivers to provide a hospital car service for non-urgent patients.

Patients on Income Support, Family Credit or with low incomes may have their travelling expenses reimbursed.

Rehabilitation

Rehabilitation services are available for elderly, young, and mentally ill people, and for those with physical or learning disabilities who need such help to resume life in the community. These services are offered in hospitals, centres in the community and in people's own homes through co-ordinated work by a range of professionals.

Medical services may provide free artificial limbs and eyes, hearing aids, surgical supports, wheelchairs, and other appliances. Following assessment, very severely physically disabled patients may be provided with environmental control equipment which enables them to operate devices such as alarm bells, radios and televisions, telephones, and heating appliances. Nursing equipment may be provided on loan for use in the home.

Local authorities may provide a range of facilities to help patients in the transition from hospital to their own homes. These include the provision of equipment; help with cleaning, shopping and cooking; care from domestic help workers; and professional help from occupational therapists and social workers. Voluntary organisations also provide services, complementing the work of the statutory agencies and widening the range of services.

Hospices

A number of hospices provide care for terminally ill people (including children), either directly in-patient or day-care units or through nursing and other assistance in the patient's own home. Control of symptoms and psychological support for patients and their families form central features of the modern hospice movement, which started in Britain and is now worldwide. Some hospices are administered entirely by the NHS; the rest are run by independent charities, some receiving support from public funds. The number of voluntary hospices has more than doubled in the past ten years. There are over 176 hospices in England and Wales, providing over 2,682 beds; in Scotland 13 independent voluntary hospices provide almost 236 beds; and in Northern Ireland there are 4 independent hospices providing 64 beds.

From 1995–96 the funding allocated to health authorities to support hospices and similar organisations has been built into authorities' general allocations and is no longer separately identified, except for the £6.8 million allocated to health authorities in England to enable them to arrange for drugs to be supplied to hospices without charge. The National Council for Hospice and Specialist Palliative Care Services covers England, Wales and Northern Ireland; its Scottish counterpart is the Scottish Partnership Agency for Palliative and Cancer Care.

Private Medical Treatment

The Government's policy is to welcome cost-effective co-operation between the NHS and

DEVELOPMENTS IN SPORT

Wheelchairs used for sports such as road/track racing, basketball, tennis and rugby are built to clients' specifications by Bromakin Wheelchairs of Loughborough, Leicestershire.

The Skikart, a new British-designed racing toboggan, has two skis linked to a saddle and is steered by leaning the body and using foot stirrups at the end of each ski.

SOCIAL SERVICES

Many local authorities provide free or subsidised travel, such as this specially adapted bus in Aberdeen, for elderly people within their areas.

There is a long tradition in Britain of voluntary service to the community, including the provision of a range of personal social services.

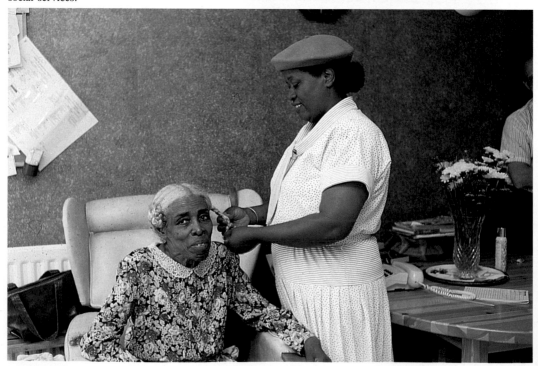

Community Service Volunteers
help organise summer play
schemes for children with
special needs.

A local authority day nursery in
Bradford. In allocating places in their
day nurseries and other facilities, local
authorities give priority to children with
special social, learning or health needs.

The proceeds from Britain's National Lottery, which started in November 1994, are used to help charities, sport, the arts, heritage and the Millenium Fund. Here presenter Noel Edmonds is seen with the winner of the competition to start the first prize draw.

Harayir, ridden by Richard Hills, wins the 1,000 Guineas at Newmarket in May 1995, during the first race meeting to take place on a Sunday with on- and off-course betting.

the independent sector in meeting the nation's health needs. It believes that this will benefit the NHS by adding to the resources devoted to health care and offering flexibility to health authorities in the delivery of services. Some health authorities share expensive facilities and equipment with private hospitals, and NHS patients are sometimes treated (at public expense) in the private sector to reduce waiting lists. The scale of private practice in relation to the NHS is, however, very small.

It is estimated that about three-quarters of those receiving acute treatment in private hospitals or NHS hospital pay-beds are covered by health insurance schemes, which make provision for private health care in return for annual subscriptions. Over 3 million people subscribe to such schemes, half of them within group schemes, some arranged by firms on behalf of employees. Subscriptions often cover more than one person (for example, members of a family); about 12 per cent of the population in Britain are covered by private medical insurance. Tax relief on private health insurance premiums paid by people aged 60 and over is designed to encourage the increased use of private health facilities. Figures for 1994–95 show that approximately 550,000 people aged over 60 received this tax relief at the cost of £95 million.

Many overseas patients come to Britain for treatment in private hospitals and clinics, and Harley Street in London is an internationally recognised centre for medical consultancy.

Parents and Children

Special preventive services are provided under the NHS to safeguard the health of expectant mothers and of mothers with young children. Services include free dental treatment, dried milk and vitamins; health education; and vaccination and immunisation of children against certain infectious diseases (see p. 401).

Since 1994 government policy has been to offer women more choice in maternity care provision and to move towards greater community-based care. Following comprehensive reviews of maternity care provision, the NHS is working towards implementing recommendations that the woman and her baby should be at the centre of all planning and provision in decisions on the care they receive.

A woman is entitled to care throughout her pregnancy, the birth and the postnatal period. Care may be provided by a midwife, a community-based GP, a hospital-based obstetrician, or a combination of these. The birth may take place in a hospital maternity unit, a midwife/GP-led unit, or at home. Most babies are born in hospital. On return home, a midwife will visit until the baby is at least ten days old and after that a health visitor's services are available. Throughout her pregnancy and for the first year of her baby's life, a women is entitled to free prescriptions and dental care.

A comprehensive programme of health surveillance is provided for pre-school children in clinics run by the community health authorities, and increasingly by GPs. This enables doctors, dentists and health visitors to oversee the physical and mental health and development of pre-school children. Information on preventive services is given and welfare foods are distributed. The school health service offers health care and advice for schoolchildren, including medical and dental inspection and treatment where necessary.

Child guidance and child psychiatric services provide help and advice to families and children with psychological or emotional problems.

In recent years special efforts have been made to improve co-operation between the community-based child health services and local authority social services for children. This is particularly important in the prevention of child abuse and for the health and welfare of children in care (see p. 411).

Human Fertilisation and Embryology

The world's first 'test-tube baby' was born in Britain in 1978, as a result of the technique of *in vitro* fertilisation. This opened up new horizons for helping with problems of infertility and for the science of embryology.

The social, ethical and legal implications were examined by a committee of inquiry under Baroness Warnock (1984) and led eventually to the passage of the Human Fertilisation and Embryology Act 1990, one of the most comprehensive pieces of legislation on assisted reproduction and embryo research in the world.

This Act set up the Human Fertilisation and Embryology Authority (HFEA) to license and control centres providing certain infertility treatments, undertaking human embryo research or storing gametes or embryos. The HFEA maintains a code of practice giving guidance about licensed centres, and reports annually to Parliament.

Commercial surrogacy agencies and advertising of, or for, surrogacy services are prohibited; legislation to ban the use of fetal ovarian tissue in fertility treatment was passed in 1994.

Family Planning

Free family planning advice and treatment is available from GPs or from family planning clinics. Clinics are also able to provide condoms free of charge. The *Health of the Nation* White Paper contains the objective of ensuring the provision of effective family planning services for those who want them.

Abortion

Under the Abortion Act 1967, as amended, a time limit of 24 weeks applies to the largest category of abortion—risk to the physical or mental health of the pregnant woman—and also abortion for similar risk to any existing children of her family. There are three categories in which no time limit applies: to prevent grave permanent injury to the physical or mental health of the woman; where there is a substantial risk of serious fetal handicap; or where continuing the pregnancy would involve a risk to the life of the pregnant woman greater than if the pregnancy were terminated. The Act does not apply in Northern Ireland.

Based on provisional figures, in 1994:

- 149,640 legal abortions were performed on women resident in England, a decrease of 1 per cent compared with 1993;
- 29 per cent of abortions in England were carried out on women in their early 20s, while only 13 per cent were on those aged 35 and over; and
- 18 per cent of abortions in England were on women aged under 20; of these, 11 per cent were on girls aged under 16.

Drug Misuse

Government Strategy

The misuse of drugs, such as heroin, cocaine and amphetamines, is a serious social and health problem, and the Government has made the fight against such misuse a major priority. In December 1993 the Central Drugs Co-ordination Unit was set up to look at existing government strategy in England and to propose changes where appropriate. After consultation, these changes were issued in the White Paper, *Tackling Drugs Together*, issued in May 1995. This contains a new drugs strategy for England for 1995–98. The strategy aims to take action by vigorous law enforcement, accessible treatment and a new emphasis on education and prevention to:

- increase the safety of communities from drug-related crime;
- reduce the acceptability and availability of drugs to young people; and
- reduce the health risks and other damage related to drug misuse.

The Government considers that a multi-agency co-ordinated approach at both national and local levels will be needed to achieve these aims. The Department of Health will be responsible for co-ordinating publicity campaigns and developing a range of materials aimed at increasing public awareness of the risk of drug taking.

At a local level the strategy proposes setting up new Drug Action Teams. Largely based on district health authority boundaries, the teams will consist of senior representatives of the police, probation, health and local authorities, and the prison service where relevant. Their role will be to ensure that action to implement the strategy is taken locally and that progress is monitored and evaluated.

Similarly in Scotland the report of the Ministerial Drugs Task Force—*Drugs in Scotland: Meeting the Challenge*—sets out the framework for tackling drug misuse in a coherent and co-ordinated way. Work on a Northern Ireland policy statement began in 1994. Research on various aspects of drug misuse is funded by several government departments. The Government is advised on a wide range of matters relating to drug misuse and connected social problems by the Advisory Council on the Misuse of Drugs.

Drug Statistics

Recent drug statistics show that between 1993 and 1994:

- the number of drug addicts in Britain notified to the Home Office increased by 21 per cent (to 34,000);

- the proportion of those notified who are addicted to heroin, the most frequently reported drug, fell to below 66 per cent, but this is balanced by an increase in notifications of addiction to methadone, which now accounts for over 46 per cent of notifications (an addict can be reported as addicted to more than one notifiable drug);

- there was no change to the proportion of those who were reported to be addicted to cocaine, at just over 9 per cent of the total;

- in general the highest numbers of all categories of notified addicts are to be found in London, the north west of England and some other conurbations; and

- the proportion of addicts injecting drugs fell slightly from 56 per cent to 54 per cent.

Prevention

The Government has run national mass media publicity campaigns since 1985 to persuade young people not to take drugs, and to advise parents, teachers and other professionals on how to recognise and combat the problem. They have included warnings of the dangers of heroin misuse and of the risks of transmitting HIV, the virus which causes AIDS (see p. 400), through the sharing of injecting equipment. Since 1991–92 the focus has changed to give greater emphasis to locally-based campaigns and includes work on solvent misuse. A national television and press campaign, aimed at raising parental awareness, was launched in 1994, at a cost of £2.6 million.

The Home Office Drugs Prevention Initiative provides funding for local drugs prevention teams in 12 areas in England. The teams aim to strengthen community resistance to drug misuse by supporting a wide range of drugs prevention activities. Since the Initiative began in 1990 over 1,500 projects have been supported. The 1995–96 budget for the initiative is approximately £5.5 million and funding will continue until March 1999. The Initiative's main objective until 1999 will be to assess the outcomes of the various community-based approaches to drugs prevention

The Government makes funds available through local education authorities in England and Wales to provide in-service training for teachers involved in drug-prevention work in schools. As part of the National Curriculum in England and Wales (see p. 435), children in primary and secondary schools receive education on the dangers of drug misuse. A circular on drug prevention and schools, containing guidance to help schools provide effective drug education programmes, was launched in May 1995.

Separate measures have been introduced in Scotland to discourage drug misuse through publicity campaigns and action in the education service and the community.

National Drugs Helpline

A national drugs and solvents telephone helpline, set up in April 1995, provides a

24-hour free confidential advice, counselling and information service throughout Britain to drug misusers, their families and friends, and those wishing to know more about drugs and solvent misuse.

Treatment and Rehabilitation

Treatment for drug dependence includes: residential detoxification and rehabilitation; community drug dependency services; needle and syringe exchange schemes to combat the spread of HIV/AIDS and other blood-borne infections; advice and counselling; and after-care and support services. Facilities are provided by both statutory and independent agencies. A task force has been set up to review the effectiveness of treatment services for drug misusers in England. Its report is expected in January 1996.

The total amount available to health authorities in England in 1995–96 is over £26.7 million. An additional £1 million is being made available to develop a range of intervention services for young people at significant risk, or at an early stage of drug misuse. In addition, a specific grant is payable each year to local authorities to enable them to support voluntary organisations providing services to drug and alcohol misusers.

In Scotland, £8 million is being made available in 1995–96 for the support of drug misuse services.

An increasing number of GPs also treat drug misusers, but only a limited number of doctors are licensed to prescribe certain controlled drugs such as heroin and cocaine to drug misusers. (However, any doctor may prescribe these drugs for the treatment of organic injury or disease, and any doctor can prescribe methadone as a substitute drug for drug misusers.) All doctors must notify the authorities of any patient they consider to be addicted to certain controlled drugs, and guidelines on good medical practice in the treatment of drug misuse have been issued to doctors.

Other Services

A number of non-statutory agencies work with and complement health service provision. Advice and rehabilitation services, including residential facilities, for example, are provided by many voluntary organisations. Support in the community is provided by the probation service and local social services departments (and in Scotland by social work departments).

Solvent Misuse

Government policy aims to prevent solvent misuse through educating young people, parents and professionals and, where practicable, restricting the sales of solvent-based liquefied gas and aerosol products to young people. National television and press publicity campaigns, targeted at parents, were run in 1992 and 1994.

In England, Wales and Northern Ireland it is an offence to supply such substances to children under 18 if the supplier knows or has reason to believe they are to be used to cause intoxication. In Scotland proceedings can be taken under the common law.

The Department of Health funds a hospital-based unit in London to collect and publish annually the mortality statistics associated with solvent misuse. The statistics for 1993 show the number of deaths having fallen to 73, the lowest figure for ten years.

Alcohol Misuse

Alcohol is consumed by over 90 per cent of the adult population. It is estimated that about 7.8 million people over 16 in England and Wales (26 per cent of men and 11 per cent of women) drink more than the currently recommended sensible levels and that 1.5 million people drink at a dangerous level. An estimated 9 million working days each year are lost through alcohol-related absence. The costs of alcohol misuse to the NHS have been estimated (at 1990 prices) at £149 million a year, and the total cost to society at £2,500 million.

The Government recognises the harm that results from the misuse of alcohol; its approach is to encourage people who wish to drink to confine their drinking to sensible levels and to appropriate occasions. It considers that education about sensible drinking helps individuals to make informed choices about their drinking. It seeks to tackle alcohol-related problems through a co-ordinated programme of action across government departments, and involving health and local authorities, the independent sector, employers and the alcohol industry.

In reports published in 1986 and 1987 the British medical profession advised that sustained drinking above 21 units of alcohol a week by men and 14 units a week by women progressively increased the risk to health, and that drinking over 50 units a week by men and over 35 units by women was definitely dangerous. (A unit is 8 grammes of pure alcohol: roughly equivalent to half a pint of ordinary strength beer or lager; or a glass of wine; or—in England, Scotland and Wales—a pub measure of spirits.)[1] The Government incorporated this advice in the *Health of the Nation* targets relating to alcohol. The sensible drinking message is currently under review in the light of recent scientific and medical research.

Part of the funds of the Health Education Authority (see p. 402) are for promoting the sensible drinking message in England, and equivalent bodies are similarly funded in other parts of Britain. At a local level this requires co-ordinated action by a wide range of organisations with an interest in the use or misuse of alcohol.

Treatment and rehabilitation within the NHS include in-patient and out-patient services in general and psychiatric hospitals and specialised alcoholism treatment units. Primary care teams (GPs, community psychiatric nurses and social workers) and voluntary organisations providing treatment and rehabilitation in hostels, day centres and advisory services also play an important role.

The development of services to help problem drinkers and their families is being taken forward within the framework of community care. Local authorities are required to identify the need for alcohol misuse services in their area, and to list the services provided in their community care plans (see p. 406). They are then responsible for arranging for the needs of individuals with alcohol problems to be assessed, and for buying an appropriate course of care.

There is close co-operation between statutory and voluntary organisations. In England the voluntary agency Alcohol Concern, which is receiving a government grant of about £366,800 in 1995–96, plays a prominent role in improving services for problem drinkers and their families; increasing public awareness of alcohol misuse and harm-free drinking; and improving training for professional and voluntary workers.

Between 1990–91 and 1997–98 a total government contribution of £9 million is being allocated to Alcohol Concern for improving and extending the network of care, advisory and counselling services. In addition, a grant of £2.5 million is being paid to local authorities during 1995–96 to help voluntary agencies improve and extend provision for alcohol and drug misusers. The Scottish Council on Alcohol undertakes similar work in Scotland, with the help of a government grant (£200,000 in 1995–96). Research and surveys on various aspects of alcohol misuse are funded by several government departments.

Smoking

Cigarette smoking is the greatest preventable cause of illness and death in Britain. It is associated with around 110,000 premature deaths and an estimated 50 million lost working days each year, and costs the NHS an estimated £610 million a year for the treatment of related diseases (for example, heart disease, lung cancer and bronchitis). In addition, smoking by pregnant women is associated with low birth weight in infants. The Government is following an active health education policy supported by voluntary agreements with the tobacco industry (see below) aimed at reducing the level of smoking.

The Government aims to reduce smoking in England from the present 30 per cent of adults to 20 per cent by the year 2000. Smoking is also being tackled as a priority in Wales, Scotland and Northern Ireland and similar targets have been set for the year 2000.

---

[1] In Northern Ireland a pub measure of spirits is bigger than in the rest of Britain and is measured as one and a half units.

A three-year national campaign in England, costing a total of £13.5 million a year, started in 1994. Aimed at adult smokers, particularly parents, the campaign is being backed up by local activities to help people to stop smoking. Education on the harmful effects of smoking is included in the National Curriculum for all pupils in publicly maintained schools in England and Wales. In Scotland the Health Education Board for Scotland (see p. 402) operates a free telephone helpline, 'Smokeline', which has received over 280,000 calls since 1992 and has been successful in helping a large number of people to stop smoking. The Board will spend some £712,000 on smoking initiatives in 1995–96.

The Government also supports the work of the voluntary organisation Action on Smoking and Health (ASH), whose services include a workplace services consultancy, offering advice and help to employers in formulating anti-smoking policies. The Government is committed to creating a smoke-free environment, with facilities where appropriate for those who wish to smoke, and has published a code of practice on smoking in public places. Health authorities have been asked to promote non-smoking as the normal practice in health service buildings and to give help and advice to people who want to give up smoking. It is estimated that passive smoking may cause a number of deaths through lung cancer every year.

The Tobacco Control Alliance, founded in 1994 and supported by over 40 organisations, calls for a concerted effort to eliminate tobacco use in Britain, to create an environment where children are relieved of the pressure to start smoking, and to encourage and help current smokers to quit.

Tobacco Advertising and Promotion Controls

All tobacco advertising is banned on television, and cigarette advertisements are banned on radio. Other forms of advertising and promotion of tobacco products are regulated by two voluntary agreements between the Government and the tobacco industry.

- The first agreement bans tobacco advertising in cinemas and in young women's magazines. It also prohibits outdoor poster advertising within 200 metres outside schools; places an upper limit on poster advertising expenditure; and requires the tobacco industry to remove all permanent shopfront advertising by the end of 1996. It also requires that government health warnings appear on all tobacco advertising, alerting the consumer to the risks associated with smoking.

- The voluntary agreement on sports sponsorship covers levels of spending, restrictions on sponsorship of events chiefly for spectators under 18 years, and controls over the siting of advertising at televised events.

The health warnings which appear on packets of tobacco products are governed by law and not by voluntary agreement. Packets of cigarettes and rolling tobacco must carry one of the following warnings:

- Smoking kills.

- Smoking causes heart disease.

- Smoking causes fatal diseases.

- Smoking causes cancer.

- Smoking when pregnant harms your baby.

- Protect children: don't make them breathe your smoke.

All tobacco products must also carry the warning 'tobacco seriously damages health'.

AIDS

Up to the end of June 1995 a total of 11,051 cases of AIDS had been reported in Britain, of whom 7,571 (69 per cent) had died; the total number of recognised HIV infections was 24,502. The latest medium-term projection (published in June 1993) shows that new cases of AIDS among homosexual men will level out and that HIV infection is declining among injecting drug misusers, but there will be a steady increase in AIDS cases through heterosexual contact.

Government Strategy

Key elements of the Government's strategy for dealing with the disease include:

- encouraging appropriate behaviour change by increased targeting of sections of the population at particular risk, including homosexual and bisexual men and drug misusers;

- sustaining and improving general public awareness;

- continuing to make HIV testing facilities more widely known, and encouraging health authorities to commission additional accessible HIV testing sites; and

- continued funding for the voluntary sector.

The Government's commitment to policies in this area is demonstrated by its inclusion of HIV/AIDS with sexual health as one of the five key areas in the *Health of the Nation* White Paper. HIV/AIDS has also been identified as a health priority in Scotland. A concerted approach is being maintained, spanning government, the NHS, local authorities and the voluntary sector (including women's groups, Britain's religious communities and organisations working with ethnic minorities).

In England NHS funding for HIV/AIDS increased from £211 million in 1994–95 to £245 million in 1995–96, and local authority funding increased from £12.9 million to £13.4 million. In Scotland a record £24 million has been made available to health boards for HIV/AIDS and drug misuse in 1995–96, in addition to their general allocations for HIV/AIDS-related purposes, and within local authority grant-aided expenditure around £3 million has been identified for AIDS-related work. Details of Britain's contribution to international co-operation on AIDS are given in Chapter 9.

Voluntary Organisations

Voluntary agencies concerned with HIV/AIDS include the Terrence Higgins Trust, London Lighthouse, Body Positive, National AIDS Trust, and Scottish AIDS Monitor, which promote knowledge about the disease and help people with AIDS and HIV. Both London Lighthouse and the Mildmay Mission Hospital, in London, provide hospice care and community support. The Government will continue distributing grants on a yearly basis, taking into account developing health priorities and the ability of voluntary bodies to raise funds from other sources for HIV/AIDS work.

Infectious Diseases

District health authorities (health boards in Scotland and Northern Ireland) carry out programmes of immunisation against diphtheria, measles, mumps, rubella, poliomyelitis, tetanus, tuberculosis and whooping cough.

A £20 million nationwide campaign to immunise all children between 5–16 (5–18 in Scotland) with measles and rubella vaccine was launched in November 1994—the largest immunisation campaign yet mounted in Britain.

A new immunisation, 'Hib', was introduced in 1992, offering protection against invasive haemophilus disease, a major cause of meningitis in children under five years. As a result, notifications of Hib infections in England and Wales fell by 87 per cent between October–December 1992 and October–December 1993.

Immunisation is voluntary, but parents are encouraged to protect their children. The proportion of children being vaccinated has been increasing since the end of 1978. GPs who achieve targets of 70 and 90 per cent uptake of child immunisation receive special payments.

The Public Health Laboratory Service provides a network of bacteriological and virological laboratories throughout England and Wales which conduct research and assist in the diagnosis, prevention and control of communicable diseases. Similar facilities are provided in Scotland by the Scottish Centre for Infection and Environmental Health and, as in Northern Ireland, by some hospital laboratories.

Cancer Care

Controlling cancer forms an enormous part of the NHS's work, consuming nearly 10 per cent of its total budget. In April 1995 the Government outlined proposals for reorganising the provision of cancer services in Britain. It proposes care at three levels:

- *primary care*, with detailed discussions between GPs and the hospital service to clarify patterns of referral and follow-up;

- *designated cancer units*, which will be created in many district hospitals and will be large enough to support multi-disciplinary clinical teams, with sufficient expertise and facilities to manage the more common cancers; and

- *designated cancer centres*, which will treat less common cancers, as well as providing more specialised treatments that are too technically demanding, or require too much specialised equipment to be provided for the cancer units.

The reduction of deaths and illness from cancer is a key area in the Government's *Health of the Nation* White Paper. The targets set are:

- to reduce breast cancer deaths among women invited for screening by at least 25 per cent by the year 2000;

- to reduce the incidence of invasive cervical cancer by at least 20 per cent by the year 2000;

- to halt the year-on-year increase in the incidence of skin cancer by 2005; and

- to reduce the death rate for lung cancer under the age of 75 by at least 30 per cent in men and by at least 15 per cent in women by 2010.

Cancer Screening

Breast cancer is recognised as a major health problem in Britain. In England and Wales some 13,000 women die from it each year and 1 in 14 women in England will develop it. Britain was the first country in the European Union to introduce a nationwide breast screening programme, under which women aged between 50 and 64 are invited for mammography (breast X-ray) every three years by computerised call and recall systems.

Some 1,600 women die each year in England and Wales from cancer of the cervix. The nationwide cervical screening programme aims to reduce death from cancer of the cervix by inviting women aged between 20 and 64 (20 and 60 in Scotland) to take a free smear test at least every five years. Health authorities must ensure that the results of a smear test are returned from the laboratory to the patient within a month.

Special payments are made to GPs who achieve targets of 50 and 80 per cent for the uptake of smear tests. The Government estimates that over 98 per cent of GPs now earn bonus payments for meeting cervical screening targets.

Deaths from cervical cancer in England and Wales have fallen since the programme began, dropping from 1,942 in 1988 to 1,647 in 1992.

Health Education

Responsibility for health education in Britain lies with four separate health education authorities, which work alongside the national health departments. All four authorities form part of the NHS. They are the Health Education Authority; Health Promotion Wales; The Health Education Board for Scotland; and the Health Promotion Agency for Northern Ireland. All have broadly similar responsibilities. Their aims are:

- to provide information and advice about health directly to members of the public;

- to support other organisations and health professionals who provide health education to members of the public; and

- to advise the Government on health education.

In addition, the Health Education Authority has the major executive responsibility for public education in Britain about AIDS. It also assists in the provision of training for HIV/AIDS workers, and provides a national centre of information and advice on health education. Major campaigns carried out by the Authority include those focusing on coronary heart disease, smoking and alcohol misuse.

Almost all health authorities have their own health education service, which works closely with health professionals, health visitors, community groups, local employers and others to determine the most suitable local programmes. Increased resources in the health service are being directed towards health education and preventive measures. GPs receive special annual payments for health promotion programmes.

Healthier Eating

There has been growing public awareness in recent years of the importance of a healthy diet. Medical research has shown that a diet which is low in fats, especially saturates, and rich in fruits, vegetables and starchy foods contributes to good health and can reduce the risk of certain serious illnesses, such as coronary heart disease and stroke.

The *Health of the Nation* White Paper followed the recommendations of the Committee on Medical Aspects of Food Policy (COMA) that people should reduce their average intakes of total fat and saturated fatty acids in order to reduce cardiovascular disease. It contained a number of dietary targets, and the Nutrition Task Force was established to devise a programme to achieve them. Launched in March 1994, the programme is being implemented through a number of project teams in information and education, catering, the NHS and the food chain.

In Scotland the Scottish Action Diet Group is preparing an action plan designed to deliver the changes recommended in a 1993 working party report on the improvements required in the Scottish diet.

Nutritional labelling indicating the energy, fat, protein and carbohydrate content of food is being encouraged on a voluntary basis. The major supermarket chains and most food manufacturers have already introduced voluntary labelling schemes. Nutrition labelling is compulsory on products for which a nutritional claim is made.

COMA's recent reports have covered the nutritional needs of elderly people (1992) and weaning (1994).

ENVIRONMENTAL HEALTH

In Britain there is no single government department responsible for the whole environmental health function. The role of central government departments includes the formulation of policy, drafting and processing of legislation on environmental health services, provision of guidance on the legislation, and, in some areas, enforcement. Environmental health services are mainly operated at local level through regional and district local government units.

Central government departments require environmental health services to provide data on housing conditions, inspection of food premises, samples of food taken for analysis, accidents at work and in the home, morbidity and mortality; these are used in assessing which services are meeting present needs and in setting targets for future requirements.

Professionally trained environmental health officers are mainly employed by district councils. They are concerned with: inspection, health education and regulation.

In Northern Ireland district councils are responsible for noise control; collection and disposal of refuse; clean air; and food composition, labelling and hygiene.

The Institute for Environment and Health, a public body established by the Medical Research Council (see below) in 1993, is concerned mainly with the chemical hazards to which people may be exposed through the environment. In Scotland the Scottish Centre for Infection and Environmental Health provides surveillance and advisory services on environmental health matters.

Safety of Food

It is illegal to supply food unfit for human consumption or to apply any treatment or process to food which makes it harmful to health. Places where food or drink is prepared, handled, stored or sold must comply with certain hygiene provisions. Environmental health officers may take away for examination samples of any food intended for sale or human consumption. Specific regulations control the safety of milk, meat, ice-cream and shellfish. The Food Safety and

Science Group within the Ministry of Agriculture, Fisheries and Food and the appropriate divisions in the Scottish and Northern Ireland health departments help ensure the safety and quality of Britain's food. The Departments work closely with the food industry, local authorities, environmental health departments and consumer bodies to help ensure the provision of safe food in order to protect public health. (For further details on food safety, see Chapter 18.)

SAFETY OF MEDICINES

Only medicines which have been granted a product licence may be sold or supplied to the public. Licences are issued following scientific assessment by the Medicines Control Agency of the Department of Health. (The Veterinary Medicines Directorate of the Ministry of Agriculture, Fisheries and Food is similarly responsible for animal medicines.)

A number of committees provide independent advice to Ministers. The Medicines Commission advises on matters connected with the safety of human and veterinary medicines; its duties also include hearing appeals from companies against advice that a product licence should not be granted. The Committee on Safety of Medicines advises on the safety, quality and efficacy of medicinal products for human use.

In 1994, for example, a new homoeopathic registration scheme was set up, covering homoeopathic products for oral and/or external use. Registered products have to satisfy high standards of quality and safety although no evidence of efficacy is required. The Advisory Board on Homoeopathic Products was also established in 1994.

RESEARCH

The Department of Health in England manages a programme of health and personal social services research. Priority areas include population studies of health and social well-being and research into lifestyle issues, prevention of illness, social care for adults and children, and health services organisation.

Wales also participates in the Department of Health's programme of centrally commissioned research. A research and development strategy for the NHS in Scotland was published in 1993.

It is intended that up to 1.5 per cent of NHS expenditure will be used for research and development by 1997.

A national centre for primary health care research and development was opened in June 1995. Based at Manchester University, the centre is being supported by a Department of Health grant of up to £1.5 million a year over ten years.

The Department of Health is involved in international research and development, and takes part in the European Union's medical and public health research programme.

For further details of the NHS research and development strategy, as well as information on the work of the Medical Research Council (the main government agency for the support of biomedical and clinical research) see Chapter 20.

THE HEALTH PROFESSIONS

Doctors and Dentists

Only people on the medical or dentists' registers may practise as doctors or dentists in the NHS. University medical and dental schools are responsible for teaching; the NHS provides hospital facilities for training. Full registration as a doctor requires five or six years' training in a medical school and hospital, with a further year's experience in a hospital. For a dentist, five years' training at a dental school is required.

An extensive review of specialist medical training was carried out in 1992–93 and plans for implementing its recommendations are in progress. These are expected to have a major impact on the organisation of NHS services and on the role and responsibilities of hospital doctors. They will include shorter, more intensive and better structured training programmes which, together with the reduction from three to two training grades, will shorten the minimum training time for hospital specialists. The changes are expected to increase the amount of service provided to NHS patients by consultants rather than those still in training.

404

The regulating body for the medical profession is the General Medical Council and, for dentists, the General Dental Council. The main professional associations are the British Medical Association and the British Dental Association.

Nurse, Midwives and Health Visitors

There are two routes to registration as a nurse or midwife: either through a higher education diploma or a degree course.

Most students undertake the pre-registration Diploma in Higher Education (Project 2000) programme, which emphasises health promotion as well care of the sick and enables students to work either in hospitals or in the community. The course lasts three years and consists of periods of college study combined with practical experience in hospitals or in the community. The first half of the course comprises a common foundation programme; the second half comprises one of the following specialist branches: adult nursing, mental health nursing, learning disability nursing, and children's nursing.

Midwifery training for registered general nurses or registered general nurses (adult) takes 18 months, but for others, including direct entrants, the training lasts three years.

Health visitors are registered general nurses or registered nurses (adult) who have completed a course in health visiting. In September 1995 new standards were introduced and by 1988 all courses will be at degree rather than at diploma level.

District nurses are registered general nurses or registered nurses (adult) who provide care for clients in the community. As with health visitors, new standards were introduced in September 1995. By 1998 all courses will be at degree rather than at diploma level. In Northern Ireland health visitors, district nurses and schools', community psychiatric, community mental handicap and occupational health nurses undertake a one-year diploma course.

The United Kingdom Central Council for Nursing, Midwifery and Health Visiting is responsible for regulating and registering these professions.

Pharmacists

Only people on the register of pharmaceutical chemists may practise as pharmacists. Registration requires three or four years' training in a school of pharmacy, followed by one year's practical experience in a community or hospital pharmacy approved for training by the Royal Pharmaceutical Society of Great Britain or the Pharmaceutical Society of Northern Ireland (regulatory bodies for the profession).

Opticians

The General Optical Council regulates the professions of ophthalmic optician and dispensing optician. Only registered ophthalmic opticians (or registered ophthalmic medical practitioners) may test sight. Training of ophthalmic opticians takes four years, including a year of practical experience under supervision. Dispensing opticians take a two-year full-time course with a year's practical experience, or follow a part-time day-release course while employed with an optician.

Other Health Professions

Chiropodists, dietitians, medical laboratory scientific officers, occupational therapists, physiotherapists and radiographers may, on qualification, apply for state registration. Each profession has its own board under the general supervision of the Council for Professions Supplementary to Medicine. Applications for a further two boards have been made from art, drama and music therapists, and from orthotists and prosthetists. State registration is mandatory for employment in the NHS and local authorities and is highly recommended in other public services and the private sector.

Dental therapists and dental hygienists are almost exclusively recruited from certified dental nurses who have taken at least one year's training. Dental therapists then take a two-year training course and dental hygienists a one-year course; both carry out some simple dental work under the supervision of a registered dentist.

National and Scottish Vocational Qualifications (NVQs and SVQs—see p. 184) have been developed for health care support workers, ambulance personnel, operating department practitioners, physiological measurement technicians and administrative and clerical staff.

HEALTH ARRANGEMENTS WITH OTHER COUNTRIES

The member states of the European Economic Area (see p. 120) have special health arrangements under which EEA nationals resident in a member state are entitled to receive emergency treatment, either free or at a reduced cost, during visits to other EEA countries. There are also arrangements for referral for specific treatment in certain circumstances and to cover people who go to work or live in other EEA countries. In addition, there are reciprocal arrangements with some other countries under which medical treatment is available to visitors to Britain if required immediately. Visitors are generally expected to pay if the purpose of their visit is to seek medical treatment. Visitors who are not covered by reciprocal arrangements must pay for any medical treatment they receive.

Personal Social Services

Personal social services help elderly people, disabled people and their carers, children and young people, people with mental illness or learning disabilities, and families. Major services include skilled residential and day care, help for people confined to their homes, and the various forms of social work. The statutory services are provided by local government social services authorities in England and Wales, social work departments in Scotland, and health and social services boards in Northern Ireland. Alongside these providers are the many and varied contributions made by independent private and voluntary services. Much of the care given to elderly and disabled people is provided by families and self-help groups.

There are an estimated 7 million informal carers in Britain, at least 1.8 million of whom provide over 20 hours of care a week. Legislation passed in 1995 gives carers the right to have their own needs assessed by local authorities and gives those local authorities the power to provide support and services.

Demand for personal social services is rising because of the increasing number of elderly people, who, along with disabled and mentally ill people, or those with learning disabilities, can lead more normal lives in the community, given suitable support and facilities.

Recent figures for services provided or bought by local authorities show a marked growth in the numbers of people being cared for at home. For example, in England between 1993 and 1994:

- the number of hours of home help and home care provided increased by 24 per cent (to 2.2 million), and the number of households receiving care increased by 5 per cent (to 537,000);

- places provided at day centres increased by 7 per cent (to 56,200), while attendances increased by 6 per cent (to 446,000);

- the number of meals provided at home and in luncheon clubs increased by 3 per cent (to 794,000), while the number receiving meals increased by 5 per cent (to 300,000).

Almost all the growth in home help and home care was in the independent sector, where provision in 1994 amounted to 19 per cent of the total compared with less than 5 per cent in 1993.

Management Reforms

New policies on community care in England, Wales and Scotland have been implemented in stages under the NHS and Community Care Act 1990. In Northern Ireland similar arrangements were introduced in April 1993 under equivalent legislation. Many of the procedures which local authorities are implementing correspond to similar procedures being introduced in the NHS (see p. 382). Local authorities increasingly act as enablers and commissioners of services after assessing their populations' needs for social care.

They are now responsible for funding and arranging social care in the community for people who require public support. This includes the provision of home helps or home care assistants to support people in their own homes, and making arrangements for residential and nursing home care for those no longer able to remain in their own homes. Previously, residents of these homes who obtained public funding received help principally through special higher levels of Income Support (see p. 422). In 1994–95 a central government grant of over £1,000 million has been made available to local authorities for community care in England. This includes an extra £20 million for developing respite and domiciliary care.

Local authorities are expected to have community care charters in place by April 1996. These will give local people more information about the services and standards they can expect under the community care reforms. In Scotland the timetable for introduction will be longer because of the reorganisation of local government, with new councils coming into force in April 1996 (see p. 72).

Elderly People

Between 1981 and 1991 the number of people over 60 in Great Britain increased by about 500,000; little change is expected over the period 1991 to 1996. The number of people aged 75 and over in Britain is projected to rise from 3.9 million in mid-1993 to 4.5 million in mid-2003—an increase of 14 per cent. About 5 per cent of those aged 65 or over live in residential homes.

Services for elderly people are designed to help them live at home whenever possible. These services may include advice and help given by social workers, domestic help, the provision of meals in the home, sitters-in, night attendants and laundry services as well as day centres, lunch clubs and recreational facilities. Adaptations to the home can overcome a person's difficulties in moving about, and a wide range of equipment is available for people with difficulties affecting their hearing or eyesight. Alarm systems have been developed to help elderly people obtain assistance in an emergency. In some areas 'good neighbour' and visiting services are arranged by the local authority or a voluntary organisation. Elderly people who live in residential care homes or nursing homes are subject to charging with a means test. Those who cannot afford to pay have their costs met by the State. Local authorities may also levy charges for domiciliary services.

Many local authorities provide free or subsidised travel for elderly people within their areas. Local authorities also provide residential care for elderly people and those in poor health.

As part of their responsibility for public housing, local authorities provide homes designed for elderly people; some of these developments have resident wardens. Housing associations and private builders also build such accommodation.

Table 24.2: Local authority net current expenditure in real terms* on personal social services

England and Scotland			£ million
	1989–90	1990–91	1991–92	1992–93
Elderly	2,225	2,292	2,234	2,248
Children	1,624	1,719	1,718	1,784
People with learning difficulties	600	658	721	776
Young physically disabled	259	267	316	363
Mentally ill	107	114	177	218
Other	216	223	257	248
Total expenditure	**5,030**	**5,270**	**5,424**	**5,638**

Source: *Social Trends*
*At 1992–93 prices.

Disabled People

Britain has an estimated 6 million adults with one or more disabilities, of whom around 400,000 (7 per cent) live in communal establishments. Over the past ten years there has been increasing emphasis on rehabilitation and on the provision of day, domiciliary and respite support services to enable disabled people to live independently in the community wherever possible.

Local social services authorities help with social rehabilitation and adjustment to disability. They are required to identify the number of disabled people in their area and to publicise services. These may include advice on personal and social problems arising from disability, as well as on occupational, educational, social and recreational facilities, either at day centres or elsewhere. Other services provided may include adaptations to homes (such as ramps for wheelchairs, and ground-floor toilets), the delivery of cooked meals, and help in the home. In cases of special need, help may be given with installing a telephone or a television. Local authorities and voluntary organisations may provide severely disabled people with residential accommodation or temporary facilities to allow their carers relief from their duties. Specially designed housing may be available for those able to look after themselves.

The Independent Living (1993) Fund is an independent and discretionary trust which provides financial help to very severely disabled people of working age to enable them to live independently in the community. The Fund works in partnership with local authorities, which are expected to make a contribution in the form of services equivalent to what they would have spent on residential or nursing care.

Some authorities provide free or subsidised travel for disabled people on public transport, and they are encouraged to provide special means of access to public buildings. Special government regulations cover the provision of access for disabled people in the construction of new buildings.

The Disability Discrimination Act, passed in 1995, is designed to tackle discrimination against disabled people in Britain by providing them with a more accessible environment. The Act:

- provides a right for disabled people in employment and places a duty on employers with 20 or more staff to consider reasonable adjustments to the terms on which they offer employment where these would help to overcome the practical effects of a disability;

- provides a right of access to goods and services which will make it unlawful to refuse to serve a disabled person and may require service providers to make reasonable adjustments to their services to make them more accessible; and

- establishes a National Disability Council to advise the Government on its strategy for eliminating discrimination against disabled people. The Council will be responsible for producing codes of practice in the areas of goods and services based on what is required by the legislation.

People with Learning Disabilities (Mental Handicap)

The Government's policy is to encourage the development of local services for people with learning disabilities and their families through co-operation between health and local authorities, and voluntary and other organisations.

Local authority social services departments are the leading statutory agency for planning and arranging services for people with learning disabilities. They provide short-term care, support for families in their own homes, residential accommodation and support for various types of activities outside the home. The main aims are to ensure that as far as possible people with learning disabilities can lead full lives in their communities and that no one is admitted to hospital unless it is necessary on health grounds.

The NHS provides specialist services where the general health needs of people with learning disabilities cannot be met by ordinary NHS services, and residential care or those with severe disabilities or whose needs can only effectively be met by the NHS.

Mentally Ill People

Government policy aims to ensure that people with mental illnesses should have access to all the services they need as locally as possible. The cornerstone of community care policy for mentally ill people is the Care Programme Approach. Under this, each patient in contact with the specialist services should receive an assessment and a care plan, be appointed a key worker to keep in touch with him or her, and be given regular reviews. Implementation of this approach is being closely monitored by the NHS Executive.

While the total number of places for mentally ill people in the large hospitals has continued to fall, this has been matched by increasing provision of alternative places in smaller NHS hospitals, local authority accommodation and private and voluntary sector homes.

Arrangements made by social services authorities for providing preventive care and after care for mentally ill people in the community include day centres, social centres and residential care. Social workers help patients and their families with problems caused by mental illness. In some cases they can apply for a mentally disordered person to be compulsorily admitted to and detained in hospital under the Mental Health Act 1993. The Mental Health Act Commission provides important safeguards for these patients to ensure that the Act is used appropriately. Different arrangements apply in Scotland and Northern Ireland.

A specific grant of £47.3 million for 1995–96 to local authorities in England is designed to encourage them to increase the level of social care available to mentally ill patients, including those with dementia who need specialist psychiatric care in the community.

Legislation before Parliament aims to provide a new power of 'supervised discharge' for severely mentally ill patients in England and Wales who need special support after they leave hospital. Under this patients who do not receive the services they need or comply with any requirements placed on

them must have their care plans reviewed, and where appropriate their readmission to hospital under the Mental Health Act 1983 may be considered. In addition supervision registers for discharged patients most at risk were introduced in April 1994. These are to be maintained by the providers of services for mentally ill people and will allow hospital staff to keep track of discharged patients. Similar arrangements, called community care orders, have been introduced in Scotland under the same legislation. For details of the Government's homeless mentally ill initiative, see p. 345.

The first government-backed national survey of mental illness began in April 1993. The survey, which covers adults aged 16 to 64 living in communal establishments as well as those living in private households, aims to provide up-to-date information on mental illness among adults, as well as associated social disabilities. It is also examining the varying use of health, social and voluntary care services, and the risk factors associated with mental illness. Its first report was published in May 1995.

A three-year public information campaign began in spring 1993 to increase people's awareness and understanding about mental illness and suicide.

There are many voluntary organisations concerned with those suffering from mental illness or learning disabilities, and they play an important role in providing services for both groups of people.

Help to Families

Social services authorities, through their own social workers and others in the voluntary sector, give help to families facing special problems. This help takes the form of services for families with children in need or at risk of harm or neglect, including some who may need care away from their own families; and support for family carers who look after elderly and other family members, in order to give them relief from their duties. There is also help for single parents. Local authorities or voluntary organisations now run many refuges for women, often with young children, whose home conditions have become intolerable. The refuges provide short-term accommodation and support while attempts are made to relieve the women's problems. Many authorities also contribute to the cost of support and counselling for families (such as marriage guidance) carried out by voluntary organisations.

The Government's Parenting Initiative, announced in 1994, provides funding to organisations which help families seeking practical help with parenting problems. Projects for which grants have been awarded include the provision of:

- an information pack on parenting for schools (The Gulbenkian Foundation);

- advice and support to step- and grandparents (Stepfathering Association); and

- advice and information for separated parents (National Family Mediation).

Day Care for Children

Day care facilities for children under five are provided by local authorities, voluntary agencies and privately. In allocating places in their day nurseries and other facilities, local authorities give priority to children with special social, learning or health needs. Local authorities also register and inspect childminders, private day nurseries and playgroups in their areas and provide support and advice services. Day care figures for 1994 show that the number of places for children in day nurseries and with childminders has continued to grow.

In 1993 the Government launched a £45 million scheme to help create childcare facilities in Great Britain for children over five after school hours and during the holidays. The scheme is operated through Training and Enterprise Councils and Local Enterprise Companies (see p. 183). These organisations are developing local partnerships with employers, schools, parents, local authorities and voluntary organisations. As a result of this initiative over 26,000 new out-of-school child care places have been created.

Child Protection

Cases of child abuse are the joint concern of a number of different agencies and professions. Area child protection committees provide forums for discussion and co-ordination and draw up policies and procedures for handling these cases. The Government's central training initiative on child abuse, established in England and Wales in 1986, consists of a variety of projects, including training for health visitors, school nurses, and local authority social services staff. Guidelines and training packs have been developed for those implementing the Children Act 1989 (see below). The training initiative is now combined with a treatment initiative which began in 1990 to provide grant funding for a range of child abuse treatment projects. In Scotland the Government provides support for child abuse training at the University of Dundee and through a specific grant scheme for local authorities.

The results of a wide-ranging research programme into child abuse in Great Britain were published in June 1995.[2] Among its findings researchers found that:

- about 160,000 children a year were being referred into the protection system. A third came from lone parent families, and two-thirds were living in a household that lacked a wage earner. Domestic violence and mental illness were features in 15 per cent of cases. One in seven of the parents had themselves been abused as children.

- about 40,000 enquiries ended without any action being taken after professionals had made informal checks. In a further 80,000 cases matters were quickly allowed to rest after parents had been interviewed; and

- in the small number of cases where abuse was established, 96 per cent of children involved in such cases stayed at home, and where they were removed, 70 per cent returned home within six months.

[2] Child Protection: Messages From Research. HMSO, £14.

Children in Care

Local government authorities must provide accommodation for children who have no parent or guardian, have been abandoned, or whose parents are unable to provide for them.

The Children Act 1989, which came into effect in England and Wales in 1991, recasts the legislative framework for children's services, care and protection into a single coherent structure. It lays new duties on local authorities to safeguard and promote the welfare of children. Under the Act parents of children in care retain their parental responsibilities but act as far as possible as partners with the authority. There is a new requirement to prepare a child for leaving the local authority's responsibility and to continue to advise him or her up to the age of 21. Local authorities are required to have a complaints procedure with an independent element to cover children in their care.

The figures confirm that the number of children looked after by local authorities continues to decline as local authorities respond to the requirement of the Children Act that wherever possible children should remain at home with their families.

In March 1993:

- there were 51,000 children looked after by local authorities in England and Wales, 7 per cent fewer than in the previous year;

- most of the children were in foster placements. Although the total number of children in foster placements decreased from 31,700 in 1992 to 30,700 in 1993, numbers in other types of accommodation, such as residential homes, fell more sharply. As a result there was a small increase in the proportion of foster children; and

- during the same period the number of children on child protection registers increased by 7 per cent to 34,900.

In England and Wales a child may be brought before a family proceedings court if he or she is neglected or ill-treated, exposed to moral danger, beyond the control of parents, or not attending school. The court can commit the child to the care of a local authority under a care order. Under the Children Act 1989 certain preconditions have to be satisfied to justify an order. These are that the child is suffering or is likely to suffer significant harm because of a lack of reasonable parental care or because he or she is beyond parental control. However, an order is made only if the court is also satisfied that this will positively contribute to the child's well-being and be in his or her best interests. In court proceedings the child is entitled to separate legal representation and the right to have a guardian to protect his or her interests.

All courts have to treat the welfare of the child as the paramount consideration when reaching any decision about his or her upbringing. The family proceedings court consists of specially trained magistrates with power to hear care cases as well as all other family and children's cases.

Recent concerns over standards of care in certain local authority children's homes have prompted a number of official inquiries whose recommendations are now being implemented. They include:

- Norman Warner's inquiry into the selection of staff in children's homes and the support and guidance available to them after appointment (1992);

- the Howe inquiry into staff conditions, and management and training for all residential care staff in adult and children's homes (1992);

- the Skinner review of residential child care in Scotland (1992); and

- a report by the Social Services Inspectorate on children's homes in England (1993). This was the first national report to come from a team of both SSI Inspectors and young people who had themselves been in care.

The Support Force for Children's Residential Care, set up in response to the Warner Report, gives practical advice and assistance to purchasers and providers of residential care for children in England and Wales. In June 1995 it published a code of employment practice for people involved in appointing staff in children's residential care.

In Scotland children who have committed offences or are in need of care and protection may be brought before a children's hearing, which can impose a supervision requirement on a child if it thinks that compulsory measures are appropriate. Under these requirements most children are allowed to remain at home under the supervision of a social worker but some may live with foster parents or in a residential establishment while under supervision. Supervision requirements are reviewed at least once a year until ended by a children's hearing. The Children (Scotland) Act 1995, which will come into force within the next two years, implements proposals in the White Paper *Scotland's Children: Proposals for Child Care Policy and Law*. In addition to the major legislative changes, a number of improvements in child care services, policy and practice have already been made through administrative means, increased funding has been devoted to the training of social work staff.

In Northern Ireland the juvenile court may place children who are in need of care, protection or control into the care of a fit person (including a health and social services board or trust), or may make them subject to a supervision order. Children in trouble may be required to attend an attendance centre, be committed to a training school, or may be detained in a remand home. The Children (Northern Ireland) Order 1995 provides Northern Ireland with legislation broadly equivalent to the Children Act 1989 in England and Wales and creates a separation between the treatment of children in need of care and young offenders. The legislation is expected to come into force in October 1996.

Fostering and Children's Homes

When appropriate, children in care are placed with foster parents, who receive payments to cover living costs. Alternatively, the child may be placed in a local authority, voluntary or private children's home or other suitable residential accommodation, including boarding school. In Scotland local authorities are responsible for placing children in their care in foster homes, in local authority or voluntary homes, or in residential schools.

Similar provisions apply in Northern Ireland. Regulations concerning residential care and the foster placement of children in care are made by central government.

Adoption

Local authorities are required by law to provide an adoption service, either directly or by arrangement with a voluntary organisation. Agencies may offer adoptive parents an allowance in certain circumstances if this would help to find a family for a child. Adoption is strictly regulated by law, and voluntary adoption societies must be approved by the appropriate Secretary of State. The Registrars-General keep confidential registers of adopted children. Adopted people may be given details of their original birth record on reaching the age of 18, and counselling is provided to help them understand the circumstances of their adoption. An Adoption Contact Register enables adopted adults and their birth parents to be given a safe and confidential way of making contact if that is the wish of both parties. A person's details are entered only if they wish to be contacted.

A government White Paper on adoption in England and Wales was published in 1993. It includes proposals to allow children aged 12 or over to agree to the making of their adoption order and to have the right to take part in their own adoption proceedings; simpler alternatives to adoption for step-parents, relatives or long-term foster parents; and streamlined arrangements for adopting from overseas.

In Scotland a review of adoption law published in 1993 led to a number of changes which were introduced in the Children (Scotland) Act 1995.

Social Services Staff

The effective working of the social services depends largely on professionally qualified social workers. Training programmes in social work are provided by universities and colleges of higher and further education. The Central Council for Education and Training in Social Work is the statutory body responsible for promoting and regulating social work training. A programme to introduce two-year courses leading to a new professional qualification, the Diploma in Social Work (DipSW), has been implemented. National Vocational Qualifications are being developed for other staff, including those in residential day and domiciliary care services.

In England and Wales professional social workers (including those in the NHS) are employed mainly by the social services departments of local authorities. In Northern Ireland social work services are provided by social workers employed by health and social services boards and trusts. Others work in the probation service, the education welfare service, and in voluntary and private organisations. In Scotland local authority social work departments provide most services, including those to the NHS and in criminal justice. There is also a growing voluntary sector.

The Government is committed to improving social work training and each of the four countries of Britain has a personal social services training strategy whose objectives include increasing the supply of qualified social workers, improving the quality of qualifying training and the training of the existing workforce.

Further Reading

One Year On...: A Report on the Progress of the Health of the Nation. Department of Health, 1993.

On the State of the Public Health 1994. The Annual Report of the Chief Medical Officer of the Department of Health, HMSO, 1995.

Health in Scotland 1994. HMSO, 1995.

Scotland's Children: Proposals for Child Care Policy and Law, Cm 2286, HMSO, 1993.

Social Welfare. Aspects of Britain series, HMSO, 1995.

Tackling Drugs Together: A Strategy for England 1995–1998. HMSO, £7.

25 Social Security

Social security is the Government's largest expenditure programme. Planned spending in 1995–96 is £86,300 million—almost one-third of public expenditure. Developments during the last year include the reform of benefits for unemployed people, measures to improve work incentives, changes in the provision for incapacity, proposals to improve the system for assessing child support, and measures to curb the growth in benefit payments for housing costs.

As part of its long-term review of public spending (see p. 159), the Government is examining the social security programme and reforming the structure of the present system to ensure it involves:

- better targeting of those in need;

- encouraging more self-provision; and

- providing more incentives to work.

The social security system is designed to secure a basic standard of living for people in financial need by providing income during periods of inability to earn (including periods of unemployment), help for families and assistance with costs arising from disablement. Nearly a third of government expenditure is devoted to the social security programme, which provides financial help for people who are elderly, sick, disabled, unemployed, widowed, bringing up children or on very low incomes.

Some benefits depend on the payment of contributions by employers, employees and self-employed people to the National Insurance Fund, from which benefits are paid. The Government also contributes to the Fund. Other social security benefits are non-contributory and are financed from general taxation; some of these are income-related, being available to people whose income falls below a certain level (see p. 422). Appeals about claims for benefits are decided by independent tribunals.

ADMINISTRATION

Administration in Great Britain is handled by six separate executive agencies of the Department of Social Security, together employing a total of some 88,000 staff:

- the Benefits Agency, responsible for paying the majority of social security benefits;

- the Child Support Agency, responsible for collecting and enforcing maintenance payments for children (see p. 419);

- the Contributions Agency, responsible for handling National Insurance contributions;

- the Information Technology Services Agency, responsible for computerising the administration of social security;
- the Resettlement Agency, responsible for hostels for single homeless people; and
- the War Pensions Agency, set up in April 1994, responsible for delivering services to war pensioners.

The Employment Services Agency of the Department for Education and Employment pays unemployment benefits and income support to unemployed people on behalf of the Benefits Agency. The housing and council tax benefit schemes are administered by local authorities, which recover most of the cost from the Government.

In Northern Ireland contributions as well as social security benefits are administered by the Social Security Agency. The qualifying conditions for receipt of the various benefits are the same as those for Great Britain. The housing benefit scheme is administered by the Northern Ireland Housing Executive and the Rate Collection Agency; council tax does not apply in Northern Ireland.

A major programme to improve quality and customer service is in progress. The Benefits Agency, for example, is moving towards one-stop service delivery (a single contact point to handle each customer's business with the Agency where appropriate).

The Benefits, Contributions, Resettlement and War Pensions Agencies publish customer charters.

Anti-fraud Measures

Further measures are being introduced to improve the prevention and detection of social security fraud. These include:

- greater financial incentives to local authorities to prevent and detect fraud in the benefits they administer;
- better use of information technology; and
- better targeting of resources, and additional resources where necessary.

In 1993–94 a record £654 million of fraud was identified and stopped. In the three years since its formation, the Benefits Agency has saved over £1,500 million through anti-fraud work.

Advice about Benefits

The demand for advice about benefits is partly met by the Freeline Social Security Service, which handles over 1 million calls each year. The Ethnic Freeline Service provides information on social security in Urdu, Punjabi and Chinese. There is also a freeline service in Welsh.

The Department of Social Security produces a wide range of leaflets and posters providing general information on entitlement and liability. These are available in English and a number of other languages.

CONTRIBUTIONS

Entitlement to National Insurance benefits such as retirement pension, incapacity benefit, unemployment benefit, maternity allowance and widow's benefit, is dependent upon the payment of contributions. There are five classes of contributions. **The rates given below are effective from April 1995 to April 1996:**

- Class 1—paid by employees and their employers. Employees with earnings below £58 a week do not pay Class 1 contributions. Contributions on earnings of £58 a week and over are at the rate of 2 per cent of the first £58 of total earnings and 10 per cent of the balance, up to the upper earnings limit of £440 a week. Employers' contributions are subject to the same threshold. On earnings above the threshold, contributions rise in stages from 3 per cent of total earnings up to a maximum of 10.2 per cent when earnings are £205 or more a week; there is no upper earnings limit. The contribution is lower if the employer operates a 'contracted-out' occupational pension scheme (see p. 418).
- Class 1A—paid by employers who provide their employees with fuel and/or a car for private use. A Class 1A contribution is payable on the cash equivalent of the benefit provided.

- Class 2—paid by self-employed people. Class 2 contributions are at a flat rate of £5.75 a week. The self-employed may claim exemption from payment of Class 2 contributions if their profits are expected to be below £3,260 for the tax year. Self-employed people are not eligible for unemployment and industrial injuries benefits.

- Class 3—paid voluntarily to safeguard rights to some benefits. Class 3 contributions are at a flat rate of £5.65 a week.

- Class 4—paid by the self-employed on their taxable profits over a set lower limit (£6,640 a year), and up to a set upper limit (£22,880 a year) in addition to their Class 2 contribution. Class 4 contributions are payable at the rate of 7.3 per cent.

Employees who work after pensionable age (60 for women and 65 for men) do not pay contributions but the employer continues to be liable. Self-employed people over pensionable age do not pay contributions.

BENEFITS

For most contributory benefits there are two conditions. First, before benefit can be paid at all, a certain number of contributions have to be paid. Second, the full rate of benefit cannot be paid unless contributions have been paid or credited to a specific level over a set period. A reduced rate of benefit is payable dependent on the level of contributions paid or credited. For example, a great many of those receiving retirement pensions and widows' benefits receive a percentage-based rate of benefit. Benefits are increased annually in line with percentage increases in retail prices. The main benefits (payable weekly) are summarised on pp. 417–23. **The rates given are those effective from April 1995 until April 1996.**

Social Security Expenditure: Great Britain 1994–95

Analysis of planned expenditure 1994–95

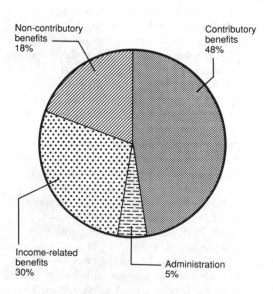

Non-contributory benefits 18%

Contributory benefits 48%

Income-related benefits 30%

Administration 5%

Percentage of expenditure by broad groups of beneficiaries 1994–95

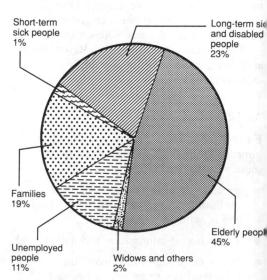

Short-term sick people 1%

Long-term sic and disabled people 23%

Families 19%

Unemployed people 11%

Widows and others 2%

Elderly peopl 45%

Source: *Social Security Departmental Report: The Government's Expenditure Plans 1995–96 to 1997–98.*

Retirement Pension

A state retirement pension is payable, if the contribution conditions have been met, to women at the age of 60 and men at the age of 65. The Sex Discrimination Act 1986 protects employees of different sexes in a particular occupation from being required to retire at different ages. This, however, has not affected the payment of the state retirement pension at different ages for men and women.

Legislation was introduced in 1995 to equalise the state pension age for men and women at 65. The change will be phased in over ten years, starting from April 2010. Women born before 6 April 1950 will not be affected; their pension age will remain at 60. The new pension age of 65 will apply to women born on or after 6 March 1955. Pension age for women born between these dates will move up gradually from 60 to 65.

The state pension scheme consists of a basic weekly pension of £58.85 for a single person and £94.10 for a married couple, together with an additional earnings-related pension. Pensioners may have unlimited earnings without affecting their pensions. Those who have put off their retirement during the five years after state pension age may earn extra pension. A non-contributory retirement pension of £35.25 a week is payable to people over the age of 80 who meet certain residence conditions, and who

Table 25.1: Estimated Numbers Receiving Benefits[a] in Great Britain 1994–5 (forecast)

Benefit	Contributory (C) or non-contributory (NC)	Thousands
Retirement pension	C	10,087
Widows' benefits	C	313
Unemployment benefit	C	445
Sickness benefit[b]	C	141
Invalidity benefit[b]	C	1,857
Maternity allowance	C	15
Non-contributory retirement pension	NC	29
War pension	NC	312
Attendance allowance	NC	1,084
Disability living allowance	NC	1,420
Disability working allowance	NC	5
Invalid care allowance	NC	279
Severe disablement allowance	NC	342
Industrial injuries disablement benefit[c]	NC	000[d]
Industrial death benefit	NC	20
Income support	NC	5,899
Child Benefit	NC	
number of children		12,685
number of families		6,950
One parent benefit	NC	938
Family credit	NC	591
Housing benefit	NC	
rent rebate		2,981
rent allowance		1,776
Council tax benefit	NC	5,641

Source: *Social Security Departmental Report: The Government's Expenditure Plans 1995–96 to 1997–98.*

[a] Figures are for beneficiaries at any one time.
[b] Incapacity Benefit from April 1995.
[c] Refers to the numbers of pensions in payment and not beneficiaries.
[d] Figures not available at time of going to print.

have not qualified for a contributory pension. People whose pensions do not give them enough to live on may be entitled to income support (see p. 422). Over 10 million people in Great Britain received a basic state pension in 1994.

Rights to basic pensions are safeguarded for people whose opportunities to work are limited while they are looking after a child or a sick or disabled person. Men and women may receive the same basic pension, provided they have paid full-rate National Insurance contributions when working. From April 1999 the earnings-related pension scheme will be based on a lifetime's revalued earnings instead of on the best 20 years. It will be calculated as 20 per cent rather than 25 per cent of earnings, to be phased in over ten years from 1999. The pensions of people retiring this century will be unaffected.

Occupational and Personal Pensions

Employers may 'contract out' their employees from the state scheme for the additional earnings-related pension and provide their own occupational pension instead. Their pension must be at least as good as the state additional pension. Joining an employer's contracted-out scheme is voluntary: employers are not free to contract out employees from the earnings-related pension scheme without the employees' consent. The State remains responsible for the basic pension.

Occupational pension schemes cover about half the working population and have nearly 11 million members. The occupational pension rights of those who change jobs before pensionable age, who are unable or who do not want to transfer their pension rights, are now offered some protection against inflation. Workers leaving a scheme have the right to a fair transfer value. The trustees or managers of pension schemes have to provide full information about their schemes.

Increasing numbers of pensioners receive income from occupational pensions and investment income. Around two-thirds of all pensioners now receive an occupational pension worth, on average, over £70 a week,

while more than three-quarters of pensioners have some form of income from their investments, receiving an average of over £43 a week.

As an alternative to their employers' scheme or the state additional earnings-related pension scheme, people are entitled to choose a personal pension available from a bank, building society, insurance company or other financial institution. Five million people have contracted out of the state earnings-related pension scheme and taken out personal pensions. Legislation passed in 1995 requires occupational schemes to provide equal treatment between men and women and to make personal pensions more flexible and attractive to a broader age range.

A Pensions Ombudsman deals with complaints about maladministration of pension schemes and adjudicates on disputes of fact or law. A pensions registry helps people trace lost benefits.

Parents and Children

Most pregnant working women receive **statutory maternity pay** directly from their employer. It is paid for a maximum of 18 weeks to any woman who has been working for the same employer for 26 weeks and who earns on average at least £58 a week. She will receive 90 per cent of her average weekly earnings for the first six weeks and a lower rate of £52.50 a week for the remaining 12 weeks. Women who are not eligible for statutory maternity pay because, for example, they are self-employed, have recently changed jobs or given up their job, may qualify for a weekly maternity allowance, which is payable for up to 18 weeks. This amounts to £52 a week for working women and £45.55 a week for those not in work.

All pregnant employees have the right to take 14 weeks' maternity leave.

A payment of £100 from the Social Fund (see p. 418) may be available if the mother or her partner are receiving income support, family credit or disability working allowance (see p. 421). It is also available if a woman adopts a baby.

Non-contributory **child benefit** of £10.40 a week for the eldest qualifying child and

£8.45 for each other child is the main social security benefit for children. Tax-free and normally paid to the mother, child benefit is payable for children up to the age of 16 and for those up to 19 if they continue in full-time non-advanced education. In addition, **one-parent benefit** of £6.30 a week is generally payable to certain people bringing up one child or more on their own, whether as their parents or not. A **non-contributory guardian's allowance** of £11.05 a week for an orphaned child is payable to a person who is entitled to child benefit for that child. This is reduced to £9.85 if the higher rate of child benefit is payable for the child. In exceptional circumstances a guardian's allowance may be paid on the death of only one parent.

At the end of 1994 child benefit was paid for 12,600,600 children, an increase on the previous year of 35,400.

Child Support Agency

An estimated 1.4 million lone parents bring up over 2 million children in Britain. The Child Support Agency (CSA), which started work in April 1993, is gradually replacing the court system for obtaining basic child maintenance. The CSA is responsible for assessing, collecting and enforcing child maintenance payments and for tracing absent parents. Assessments are made using a formula which takes into account each parent's income and essential outgoings.

Changes to the child support arrangements were introduced in February 1994 to take account of concerns raised by members of the public and MPs. The Government believes that the formula approach to assessment of maintenance is appropriate for most separated parents. However, a case has been made for further changes.

Legislation passed in 1995 introduces a system of departures from the formula assessment of child support to allow the amount of maintenance payable to be varied in a small proportion of cases from 1996–97. Other measures are designed to improve the review process in child support and to introduce a child maintenance bonus worth up to £1,000 when the parent with care of the child returns to work.

In its first two years the CSA has cleared over 900,000 cases, including over 450,000 maintenance assessments.

In Northern Ireland the child support maintenance scheme is operated by the Northern Ireland Child Support Agency, which was established at the same time as the CSA. Although the two agencies operate under separate legislation, reciprocal arrangements are in place to ensure that they can deliver an integrated service throughout Britain.

Childcare Changes

From October 1994 families claiming family credit (see p. 423), disability working allowance (see p. 421), housing benefit and council tax benefit (see p. 423) and who pay for childcare for children aged under 11, can have up to £40 a week in childcare charges offset against their earnings when their benefit entitlement is worked out. This help is for families who use formal childcare through registered childminders and day nurseries. In the long term it is estimated that around 150,000 families will gain from this initiative, including about 50,000 who are expected to take up work as a direct result of the change.

Widows

Widows under the age of 60, or those over 60 whose husbands were not entitled to a state retirement pension when they died, receive a tax-free single payment of £1,000 following the death of their husbands, provided that their husbands had paid a minimum number of National Insurance contributions. Women whose husbands have died of an industrial injury or prescribed disease may also qualify, regardless of whether their husbands had paid National Insurance contributions.

A widowed mother with a young family receives a **widowed mother's allowance** of £58.85 a week, with a further £9.85 for a child for whom the higher rate of child benefit is payable and £11.05 for each subsequent child. A widow's basic pension of £58.85 a week is payable to a widow who is 55 years or over when her husband dies or when her entitlement to widowed mother's allowance ends. A percentage of the full rate is payable to widows who are aged between 45 and 54 when their husbands die or when their entitlement to widowed mother's allowance ends. Special rules apply for widows whose husbands died before 11 April 1988. Entitlement continues until the widow remarries or begins drawing retirement pension. Payment ends if she lives with a man as his wife. Widows also benefit under the industrial injuries scheme.

A man whose wife dies when both are over pension age inherits his wife's pension rights just as a widow inherits her husband's rights.

Sick and Disabled People

Statutory Sick Pay and Incapacity Benefit

A large variety of benefits is available for people unable to work because of sickness or disablement. Employers are responsible for paying **statutory sick pay** to employees from the fourth day of sickness for up to a maximum of 28 weeks. Since April 1995 there has been a single rate of statutory sick pay for all qualifying employees provided their average weekly earnings are at least equivalent to the lower earnings limit for the payment of National Insurance contribution. The weekly rate is £52.50.

A new benefit—**incapacity benefit**—replaced the former sickness and invalidity benefits from 13 April 1995. The aim is to focus incapacity provision on people who have a medical condition which makes it unreasonable to expect them to seek or to be available for work. Entitlement to incapacity benefit begins when entitlement to statutory sick pay ends or, for those who do not qualify for statutory sick pay, from the first day of sickness.

The new benefit has three rates:

- a lower rate of £44.40 a week for the first 28 weeks;
- a higher rate of £52.50 a week between the 29th and 52nd week; and
- a long-term rate of £58.85 a week from the 53rd week of incapacity.

It comprises certain age additions and increases for adult and child dependants. It is taxable from the 29th week of incapacity.

A new, more objective medical test of incapacity for work has been introduced for incapacity benefit as well as for other social security benefits paid on the basis of incapacity for work. The new test usually applies after 28 weeks' incapacity for work and assesses ability to perform a range of work-related activities rather than the ability to perform a specific job. Separate arrangements exist for people who are mentally ill or disabled.

Existing recipients of invalidity benefit moved to the new incapacity benefit and will receive transitional protection to prevent any loss in income. Transitional protection may be lost if there is a change in the claimant's circumstances. New and existing cases will be subject to the new incapacity test except for a number of specified exemptions. The changes are expected to reduce public expenditure by some £3,000 million in the first three years.

Severe Disablement Allowance

A severe disablement allowance of £35.55, plus an age-related addition of up to £12.40 a week, may be payable to people who have not been able to work for at least 28 weeks because of illness or disability and who cannot get incapacity benefit because they have not paid enough National Insurance contributions. Claims may be made by people aged between 16 and 65. Once a person has qualified for the allowance, there is no upper limit for receipt. Additions for adult dependants and for children may also be paid. From April 1995 new claimants must satisfy the same incapacity test as used in incapacity benefit (see above).

People who become incapable of work after their 20th birthday must also be medically assessed as at least 80 per cent disabled for a minimum of 28 weeks. People already in receipt of certain benefits, such as the middle or higher rate of disability living allowance, will automatically be accepted as 80 per cent disabled.

Other Benefits

Disability living allowance is a tax-free benefit with two components for people disabled before the age of 65 who need help with personal care or with mobility. The care component has three weekly rates—£46.70, £31.20 and £12.40. The mobility component has two rates—£32.65 and £12.40.

Motability, an independent charitable organisation, helps disabled drivers to obtain vehicles or powered wheelchairs on favourable terms by using the higher rate mobility component of disability living allowance or the war pension mobility supplement. Applications for vehicles increased by over 10 per cent in 1993–94 compared with the previous year. Almost 5 per cent of all new cars registered in Britain in 1994 were bought under the Motability scheme, which currently has more than 200,000 customers.

A non-contributory, tax-free **attendance allowance** of £31.20 or £46.70 a week may be payable to people severely disabled at or after age 65, who have personal care needs, depending upon the amount of attention they require. The higher rate of attendance allowance and/or disability living allowance is paid to people who are terminally ill.

A non-contributory **invalid care allowance** of £35.25 weekly may be payable to people between 16 and pensionable age who cannot take up a paid job because they are caring for a person receiving either attendance allowance or the higher or middle care component of disability living allowance. An additional carer's premium may be paid if the recipient is also receiving income support, housing benefit or council tax benefit. It is estimated that some 1.5 million adults in Great Britain care for a disabled person for at least 20 hours a week.

Disability working allowance is an income-related tax-free benefit which helps some disabled people aged 16 or over who work an average of 16 hours a week or more and have an illness or disability which puts them at a disadvantage in getting a job. Awards are for fixed periods of six months. To qualify a person must either:

- be getting disability living allowance, or an analogous benefit, such as constant attendance allowance under the war pensions or industrial injuries disablement scheme; or

- have an invalid three-wheeler or other vehicle under the NHS Act 1977; or

- have been entitled to one of the following in at least one of the 56 days before the date of claim: higher rate short-term incapacity benefit; long-term incapacity benefit; severe disablement allowance; or the disability premium or higher pensioner premium with income support, housing benefit or council tax benefit.

The allowance is available to single people, lone parents and couples. The rate depends on the person's income and size of family, and the ages of any children. The allowance is not payable if capital or savings exceed £16,000.

Industrial Injuries Disablement Benefits

Various benefits are payable for disablement caused by an accident at work or a prescribed disease. The main benefit is industrial injuries disablement benefit; disablement benefit of up to £95.30 a week is usually paid after a qualifying period of 15 weeks if a person is 14 per cent or more physically or mentally disabled as a result of an industrial accident or a prescribed disease.

Basic disablement benefit can be paid in addition to other National Insurance benefits, such as incapacity benefit. It can be paid whether or not the person returns to work and does not depend on earnings. The degree of disablement is assessed by an independent adjudicating medical authority and the amount paid depends on the extent of the disablement and on how long it is expected to last. Except for certain progressive respiratory diseases, disablement of less than 14 per cent does not attract disablement benefit. In certain circumstances additional allowances, such as constant attendance allowance and exceptionally severe disablement allowance, may be payable. In some cases reduced earnings allowance may be payable.

Unemployment Benefit

Unemployment benefit of £46.45 a week for a single person or £75.10 for a couple is payable for up to a year in any one period of unemployment. Periods covered by unemployment or incapacity benefit, maternity allowance or some training allowances which are eight weeks or less apart, are linked for unemployment benefit to form a single period of interruption of work. Everyone claiming unemployment benefit has to be available for work, but unemployed people wishing to do voluntary work in the community may do so in some cases without losing entitlement to benefit. People seeking unemployment benefit must not have become unemployed voluntarily or have lost their job through misconduct. They are expected to look actively for work and must have good reasons for rejecting any job that is offered.

Income Support

Income support is payable to people who are not in work, or who work fewer than 16 hours a week, and whose financial resources are below certain set levels. It consists of a personal allowance ranging from £28 weekly for a single person or lone parent aged under 18 to £73 for a couple, at least one of whom is aged over 18. Additional sums, known as premiums, are available to families, lone parents, pensioners, long-term sick and disabled people, and those caring for them who qualify for the invalid care allowance.

The income support scheme sets a limit to the amount of capital a person may have and still remain entitled. People with savings or capital worth more than £8,000 are ineligible; savings between £3,000 and £8,000 will reduce the amount received.

Although only about one-fifth of claims from unemployed people result in payment of unemployment benefit (see p. 421), a large proportion of those signing on as unemployed at any one time rely partly or wholly on income support. This is either because they are disqualified from unemployment benefit or have not paid sufficient contributions to qualify for it, or because their entitlement to it has run out, or because they are entitled to income support as well.

Planned Changes

Legislation passed in 1995 will replace unemployment benefit and income support

for unemployed people with a **jobseeker's allowance** from October 1996. The new benefit will be more clearly focused on helping unemployed people into work. All unemployed people will be required to enter into a jobseeker's agreement, setting out a plan of action to seek work. Most recipients will qualify through a means test, and the benefit will be paid at rates determined by family circumstances on a similar basis to income support.

Those with a sufficient contribution record will have a personal jobseeker's allowance for up to six months. To enhance incentives to take up or keep part-time work, both jobseeker's allowance and income support will incorporate a Back to Work Bonus scheme. People who have been unemployed for three months or more and work part time will keep the first £5 of their earnings (£10 for couples, £15 for lone parents, disabled people and some people in special occupations) in any week in which they work while receiving benefit. An amount equal to half of any earnings above that level will count towards the build-up of a bonus amount. This will be paid as a tax-free lump sum, up to a maximum of £1,000, when the unemployed person moves into employment which removes entitlement to jobseeker's allowance or income support. The part-time earnings of a partner will also count towards the build-up of the bonus amount, and a bonus payment may be made when it is the partner who moves into work which removes entitlement to benefit.

The introduction of jobseeker's allowance will change the role of income support, which will no longer offer a general safety net, but rather provide support for certain groups in defined circumstances. It will help those not required to be available for work, such as pensioners, disabled people, lone parents and those who are longer-term sick.

The introduction of jobseeker's allowance is expected to reduce expenditure on benefits by around £270 million in a full year of operation.

Housing Benefit

The housing benefit scheme assists people who need help to pay their rent (rent and/or domestic rates in Northern Ireland), using general assessment rules and benefit levels similar to those for the income support scheme. At present people whose net income is below certain specified levels qualify for housing benefit of up to 100 per cent of their rent. Unlike income support (see p. 422), the housing benefit scheme sets a limit of £16,000 on the amount of capital a person may have and still remain entitled.

Proposed Changes

From October 1995 housing benefit will be calculated by reference to the general level of rents for similar properties in the same area. The new measures are designed to ensure that private sector tenants receiving benefit have an incentive to choose better value for money accommodation at the outset of a tenancy. The changes will apply to new claims to benefit from October 1995 and to existing claimants when they change address.

Council Tax Benefit

Council tax benefit helps people to meet their council tax payments. The scheme offers help to those claiming income support and others with low incomes. Subject to rules broadly similar to those governing the provision of income support and housing benefit (see above), people may receive rebates of up to 100 per cent of their council tax. At present over 5 million households receive such help. A person who is solely liable for the council tax may also claim benefit (called 'second adult rebate') for a second adult who is not liable to pay the council tax and who is living in the home on a non-commercial basis.

Residence Test

In August 1994 a new residence test came into force, requiring claimants to establish that they are habitually resident in Britain before a claim for income support, housing benefit or council tax benefit can be paid. The test brings Britain into line with most other European countries, which already limit access to their benefit systems to those who have lived in the country for some time.

Family Credit

Family credit is payable to low-paid employed and self-employed working families with children. It is payable to couples or lone parents. At least one parent must work for a minimum of 16 hours a week. The amount payable depends on a family's net income (excluding child benefit) and the number and ages of the children in the family. A maximum award, consisting of an adult rate of £45.10 weekly, plus a rate for each child varying with age, is payable if the family's net income does not exceed £73 a week. The award is reduced by 70 pence for each pound by which net income exceeds this amount. In certain cases where children under 11 have formal childcare arrangements, up to £40 a week can be deducted from net income before family credit is assessed. Family credit is not payable if a family's capital or savings exceed £8,000.

Social Fund

The Social Fund consists of regulated payments, which do not have limited resources, and discretionary payments, which are paid out of an annual budget (£140 million in 1995–96).

The regulated payments are:

- maternity payment—£100 for each baby born or adopted. Payable to those on income support, family credit or disability working allowance;

- funeral payment—includes up to £500 for specified funeral directors' services, plus the reasonable costs of all burial or cremation expenses. Available to those on income support, family credit, housing benefit, council tax benefit or disability working allowance; and

- cold weather payment—£7 a week (£8.50 from November 1995) towards the extra cost of heating in very cold weather from October to March. Payable to those on income support who are elderly, disabled or have children under five years.

The discretionary payments are:

- community care grants to help, for example, people resettle into the community from care, or to remain in the community, and to ease exceptional pressure on families. Available to those on income support;

- budgeting loans for difficult intermittent expenses after 26 weeks on income support; and

- crisis loans to help people facing an emergency or disaster where there is a serious risk to health or safety. There is no qualifying benefit for this loan.

War Pensions and Related Services

Pensions are payable for disablement or death as a result of service in the armed forces or for certain injuries received in the merchant navy or civil defence during wartime, or to civilians injured by enemy action. The amount paid depends on the degree of disablement: the pension for 100 per cent disablement is £101.10 a week.

There are a number of extra allowances. The main ones are for unemployability, restricted mobility, the need for care and attendance, the provision of extra comforts, and as maintenance for a lowered standard of occupation. An age allowance of between £6.75 and £20.80 is payable weekly to war pensioners aged 65 or over whose disablement is assessed at 40 per cent or more.

Pensions are also paid to war widows and other dependants. (The standard rate of pension for a private's widow is £76.35 a week.) At present the war widow's pension is withdrawn on re-marriage and a lump sum worth one year's pension is awarded. Legislation passed in 1995 restores the pension should the former war widow remarry and become widowed again, divorced or legally separated.

The War Pensions Agency maintains a welfare service for war pensioners, war widows and other dependants. It works closely with ex-Service organisations and other voluntary bodies which give financial aid and personal support to those disabled or bereaved as a result of war.

Table 25.2: Tax Liability of Social Security Benefits

Not Taxable	Taxable
Attendance allowance	Incapacity benefit
Child benefit	(long term or short term higher rate)
Child's special allowance	Income support paid to unemployed people
Council tax benefit	Industrial death benefit pensions
Disability living allowance	Invalid care allowance
Disability working allowance	Jobseeker's allowance (from October 1996)[a]
Family credit	Retirement pension
Guardian's allowance	Statutory maternity pay
Housing benefit	Statutory sick pay
Incapacity benefit (short term lower rate)	Unemployment benefit
Income support[b]	Widowed mother's allowance
Industrial disablement benefit	Widow's pension
Invalidity benefit	
Maternity allowance	
One-parent benefit	
Severe disablement allowance	
Sickness benefit	
War disablement pension	
War widow's pension	

Source: *Social Security Departmental Report: The Government's Expenditure Plans 1995–96 to 1997–98.*

[a] That part of the jobseeker's allowance equivalent to the individual or couple rate of personal allowance, as appropriate.

[b] That part of income support payable in place of unemployment benefit is taxable when paid to unemployed people who have to sign on, or to strikers or those directly interested in a trade dispute.

Concessions

Other benefits for which unemployed people and those on low incomes may be eligible include exemption from health service charges (see p. 387), grants towards the cost of spectacles, free school meals and free legal aid.

Since April 1994 people on low incomes, as well as all pensioners, widows and long-term sick people on invalidity benefit, have received extra help to meet the cost of VAT on their fuel bills. In 1994–95 some 15 million people will benefit, at a cost of £381 million.

Reduced charges are often made to unemployed people, for example, for adult education and exhibitions, and pensioners are usually entitled to reduced transport fares.

Taxation

The general rule is that benefits which replace lost earnings are subject to tax, while those intended to meet a specific need are not (see Table 25.2). Various income tax reliefs and exemptions are allowed on account of age or a need to support dependants.

ARRANGEMENTS WITH OTHER COUNTRIES

As part of the European Union's efforts to promote the free movement of labour, regulations provide for equality of treatment and the protection of benefit rights for employed and self-employed people who move between member states. The regulations also cover retirement pensioners and other beneficiaries who have been employed, or self-employed, as well as dependants. Benefits covered include child benefit and those for sickness and maternity, unemployment, retirement, invalidity, accidents at work and occupational diseases.

Britain also has reciprocal social security agreements with a number of other countries which also provide cover for some National Insurance benefits and family benefits.

In 1994 675,000 British National Insurance pensions were paid overseas, at a cost of some £900 million.

Further Reading

Security, Equality, Choice: The Future for Pensions. Cm 2594-1. HMSO, 1994.

Social Welfare. Aspects of Britain series, HMSO, 1995.

The Government's Expenditure Plans 1994–95 to 1996–97. Department of Social Security. Cm 2813. HMSO, 1995.

Which Benefit? Leaflet FB2, issued by the Benefits Agency. Available free from social security offices, post offices or Employment Service Jobcentres.

26 Education

Over half a million teachers are employed in Britain's 29,900 state,[1] 1,800 special and 2,500 fee-paying independent schools, which are attended by over 9 million pupils. About 67 per cent of pupils continue studying after the age of 16. The proportion of young people entering universities and colleges has risen from one in eight in 1980 to almost one in three. Continuing education for adults is provided by a variety of colleges and institutions, including universities, which have seen a 140 per cent increase in older students since 1979. Expenditure on education in Britain was £31,500 million in 1992–93.

HISTORY

England and Wales

Although government grants for education were first made in 1833, it was the 1870 Education Act in England and Wales which enshrined the idea of compulsory elementary education with government aid. There were two types of elementary school— church voluntary schools and state schools provided by school boards. Attendance at school became compulsory in 1880 for children aged between five and ten, and the school leaving age was progressively raised to 14 by 1918.

A co-ordinated national system of education was introduced for the first time by the 1902 Education Act, under which local government became responsible for state education and for helping to finance the voluntary schools. The system was supervised by the Board of Education.

In 1944 a new Education Act raised the school leaving age to 15, and schools were divided into primary and secondary. All children were given a secondary education, and the newly created Ministry of Education was empowered to develop a national education policy. Local government remained responsible for administering the system.

Children were allocated to different secondary schools—grammar, secondary technical or secondary modern—on the basis of selection tests taken at the age of 11. The local education authorities were required to prepare and submit to the Minister of Education development plans covering the whole process of primary and secondary education and at the same time to proceed with the planned development of technical and adult education through schemes of further education.

In the 1960s and 1970s the selective system was gradually replaced by comprehensive schools, which take pupils of all abilities. The school leaving age was raised to 16 in 1972–73.

---

[1]For ease of reference the term 'state school' is used to cover schools maintained from public funds.

Scotland

In Scotland an Act passed in 1872 transferred responsibility for education from the churches to elected school boards, which provided compulsory education for children between the ages of five and 13, and evening schools for young people over 13. The boards were also responsible for enforcing the code of the then Scotch Education Department (now The Scottish Office Education Department), which was set up at about this time to supervise the working of the new system and to administer the distribution of the parliamentary grant.

In 1901 the school leaving age was raised to 14. An Act passed in 1918 replaced the boards by local government authorities and made the provision of secondary education mandatory for all children wanting it. Church schools were transferred to education authorities, while preserving their denominational character. The school leaving age was raised to 15 in 1947 and to 16 in 1972–73.

Northern Ireland

Education in Northern Ireland was brought into a single system by legislation passed in 1923, under which local government took over responsibility for its administration, supervised by the Ministry of Education. Children were required to receive 'elementary' education between the ages of six and 14. Secondary education remained largely in the hands of voluntary bodies, with assistance provided from public funds. Technical education was provided almost entirely by the local education authorities. The school leaving age was raised to 15 in 1947 and to 16 in 1972–73.

Reform

During the 1970s concern arose about the quality of education provided by Britain's schools and the lack of a formal national school curriculum. As a result, the three education systems have undergone the most far-reaching reforms since 1945.

ADMINISTRATION

The Secretary of State for Education and Employment has overall responsibility for school and post-school education in England. The Secretaries of State for Scotland, Wales and Northern Ireland exercise similar responsibilities in those countries.

The government education departments are the Department for Education and Employment in England, the Welsh Office Education Department, The Scottish Office Education Department and the Department of Education for Northern Ireland. They formulate education policies and are also responsible for the supply and training of teachers.

Most state school education is the responsibility of education authorities, which are part of the local government system; the rest is provided by self-governing grant-maintained (GM) schools (see p. 428). In Northern Ireland the education service is administered locally by five education and library boards.

Education authorities pay teachers and other staff, provide and maintain buildings, and supply equipment and materials. Governing bodies in GM schools are responsible for these functions.

SCHOOLS

Finance

LEA-maintained Schools

Local education authorities (LEAs) in England and Wales are responsible for most of the public expenditure on schools; a large amount of this, however, is indirectly funded by the Government through the Revenue Support Grant, which is made to local government councils. Councils are free to decide how much of this grant should be distributed to education and the other services for which they have responsibility. There are also central government grants supporting expenditure made by LEAs on items such as the National Curriculum (see p. 435), local management of schools, teacher recruitment, support for information technology and health education in schools. Finance also goes to inner city schools facing particularly severe problems.

Additional government grants are made for capital expenditure at voluntary-aided schools (see below).

The rest of LEA expenditure on education is met by local taxes and by the non-domestic rates paid by business and commerce.

Grant-maintained Schools

State grant-maintained (GM) self-governing schools are not financed by LEAs, as they have chosen to opt out of LEA control (see below). Instead, the Funding Agency for Schools in England calculates and pays grants to GM schools from public funds and is responsible for financial monitoring. The Agency is responsible to the Secretary of State for Education and Employment, who appoints its members. Grant-maintained schools in Wales are funded by the Welsh Office.

Scotland and Northern Ireland

In Scotland most state schools are provided by local government authorities, which are also education authorities; self-governing schools are funded directly by the Government. The education authorities are financed in a similar way to those in England and Wales.

The costs of the education and library boards in Northern Ireland are met by the Department of Education.

School Management

England and Wales

There are four kinds of state school that are wholly or mainly supported from public funds:

- county schools, which are owned and funded by LEAs;
- voluntary schools, mostly established by religious denominations; the governors of some types of voluntary school contribute to capital costs;
- special schools; and
- self-governing GM schools (see below).

LEA-financed Schools

Each LEA-maintained county, voluntary and special school has a governing body which includes governors appointed by the LEA, elected teacher and parent governors, and people co-opted from the local community. Voluntary schools also have governors from the church associated with the school.

All LEA county and voluntary schools manage their own budgets. LEAs allocate funds to the schools, largely on the basis of pupil numbers. The school governing body is responsible for overseeing spending and for most aspects of staffing, including appointments and dismissals. LEAs also fund special schools for pupils with special educational needs (see p. 432); all these schools will have full control over their budgets by April 1996.

Each LEA is responsible for deciding whether funds should be provided for nursery education.

Grant-maintained Status

Some 15 per cent of secondary schools in England are grant-maintained (GM) self-governing schools. In Wales the proportion is approximately 5 per cent. GM status is achieved if the school's parents support the idea in a ballot and if the Secretary of State approves the school's proposals for GM status. Under the 1993 Education Act the governing bodies of non-GM state schools must consider each year whether or not to hold a ballot on GM status. If they decide not to hold a ballot, they must give reasons to parents for this decision.

The governing body for GM schools consists of parents, teachers and people from the community served by the school. Governors take all decisions about school management, employ and pay staff, are responsible for school premises, and may acquire or dispose of land.

City Technology Colleges

City technology colleges are non-fee-paying independent schools created by a partnership of government and private sector sponsors.

The promoters own or lease the schools, employ teachers and other staff, and make substantial contributions towards the costs of building and equipment. There is no LEA involvement. The colleges teach the National Curriculum but with an emphasis on mathematics, technology and science. There are 15 city technology colleges in England, with over 11,000 pupils.

Specialist Schools

The specialist schools programme was launched in 1993 with the creation of technology colleges. These are state secondary schools which teach the National Curriculum but with a special emphasis on technology, science and mathematics. The programme was extended in March 1995, when a scheme for a national network of language colleges was launched. These colleges concentrate on teaching modern foreign languages while continuing to deliver the full National Curriculum.

To become a technology or language college, a school must have the backing of a private-sector sponsor. Capital and annual grants are available from public funds to complement business sponsorship. There are currently 101 technology colleges and six language colleges in England.

Scotland

In Scotland most schools have school boards consisting of elected parent and staff members as well as co-opted members. They are required to promote contact between parents, the school and the community, and are involved in the appointment of senior staff and the community use of school premises.

Devolved management is to be in place in primary and secondary schools by April 1996, and in special schools by April 1997. Devolved management does not have to be in place until April 1998 for primary schools with full-time teaching headteachers.

Parents of children at state schools can opt for self-governing status following approval by a ballot; the school then receives funding directly from central government instead of the education authority. The first self-governing school came into existence in April 1994.

Northern Ireland

The main categories of school supported by public funds are:

- controlled schools, which are owned by the education and library boards and financed 100 per cent from public funds;

- voluntary maintained schools, most of which are owned by the Roman Catholic Church and are largely financed from public funds;

- voluntary grammar schools, which may be owned by denominational or non-denominational bodies and are largely financed from public funds; and

- grant-maintained or controlled integrated schools, taking both Protestant and Roman Catholic pupils.

All publicly financed schools are managed by boards of governors, which include elected parents and teachers among their members.

Although all schools must be open to pupils of all religions, most Roman Catholic pupils attend Catholic maintained schools or Catholic voluntary grammar schools, and most Protestant children are enrolled at controlled schools or non-denominational voluntary grammar schools.

The Government has a statutory duty to encourage integrated education as a way of breaking down sectarian barriers. There are 28 integrated schools and it is expected that pupil numbers will rise from the current level of some 5,000 (about 2 per cent of the school population) to over 6,300 by 1997. Integrated schools are financed by the Government. Existing controlled, maintained and voluntary grammar schools can apply to become integrated following a majority vote by parents.

All nursery, primary and secondary schools are financed on the basis of a formula which relates a major part of each school's resources to the number of pupils it can attract. All secondary schools have delegated budgets under which the Board of Governors decides spending priorities. Nursery and primary schools have partially delegated budgets with responsibility for the non-staff elements of their budgets. In 1995–96 most primary schools had full delegation of budgets on a voluntary basis.

School Places

Education authorities are responsible for providing school places, with the exception of GM schools in England and Wales, where governing bodies are responsible.

Under the 1993 Education Act the Funding Agency for Schools in England may take on some responsibility for securing enough school places in individual LEA areas. In areas where between 10 and 75 per cent of pupils are being educated in GM primary or secondary schools, the LEA and the Agency may be jointly responsible. Once 75 per cent of primary or secondary pupils are in GM schools, the Agency may be solely responsible for the provision of school places. The Agency can only be involved in the provision of school places if the Secretary of State makes an order to that effect.

Pupils

Parents are required by law to see that their children receive efficient full-time education, at school or elsewhere, between the ages of five and 16 in Great Britain and four and 16 in Northern Ireland. About 93 per cent of pupils receive free education financed from public funds, while the others attend independent schools paid for by fees from parents.

Boys and girls are taught together in most primary schools. More than 80 per cent of pupils in state secondary schools in England and Wales and about 64 per cent in Northern Ireland attend mixed schools. In Scotland all state secondary schools are mixed. Most independent schools (see p. 433) for younger children are mixed; the majority providing secondary education are single-sex, although the number of mixed secondary schools is growing.

Nursery and Primary Schools

Although there is no statutory requirement to educate under-fives, nearly 55 per cent of three- and four-year-olds in Britain attend nursery schools or classes. In addition, many children attend pre-school playgroups, most of which are organised by parents and incorporated in the Pre-School Learning Alliance.

In July 1995 the Government launched a voucher scheme to provide a pre-school place for every four-year-old in Britain whose parents wish to take it up. Every parent with a child in this age group will be given a voucher worth £1,100, which they can exchange for:

- a part-time place in a nursery class in an independent, voluntary or state school; or
- a full-time place in a reception class in a state school; or
- up to a full-time place in any other private or voluntary institution, such as a playgroup or private nursery.

The first places under the scheme will be available from April 1996, and the scheme will become fully operational one year later. Different voucher arrangements are to be made in Northern Ireland, where children start school at an earlier age than in the rest of Britain.

Compulsory education begins at five in Great Britain and four in Northern Ireland, when children go to infant schools or departments; at seven many go on to junior schools or departments. The usual age for transfer from primary to secondary schools is 11 in England, Wales and Northern Ireland, but some local authorities in England have established first schools for pupils aged five to eight, nine or ten, and middle schools for age-ranges between eight and 14. In Scotland primary schools take children from five to 12, when they transfer to secondary schools. For information on independent schools, see p. 433.

Secondary Schools

Around nine-tenths of the state secondary school population in Great Britain attend comprehensive schools. These take pupils without reference to ability or aptitude and provide a wide-ranging secondary education for all or most of the children in a district.

Schools in England and Wales can be organised in a number of ways. They include:

- those that take the age-range from 11 to 18;
- middle schools (see p. 430); and
- schools with an age-range of 11 or 12 to 16, combined with a sixth-form college or a further education college for pupils over 16.

Most other children attend grammar or secondary modern schools, to which they are allocated after selection procedures at the age of 11.

Scottish secondary education is almost completely non-selective; the majority of schools are comprehensives covering the age-range 12 to 18.

In Northern Ireland secondary education is organised largely along selective lines, the 71 grammar schools admitting some 59,000 pupils on the basis of tests in English, maths and science. Over 89,000 pupils attend non-grammar secondary schools. Some secondary schools are run on a non-selective basis.

Table 26.1: School Pupils by Type of School in Britain	
	1992–93
Nursery schools	109,000
Primary schools	5,077,000
Secondary schools	3,606,000
All public sector[a]	8,791,000
Independent schools	607,000
Special schools[b]	115,000
Total pupils	**9,513,000**

Sources: Department for Education and Employment, Welsh Office, The Scottish Office Education Department and Department of Education, Northern Ireland
Note: Differences between totals and the sums of their component parts are due to rounding.
[a]Excludes public sector special schools.
[b]Includes state and independent schools.

Rights of Parents

Parents must be given general information about a school through a prospectus and the school's annual report or, in Scotland, the school's handbook. They also have a statutory right to express a preference for a particular school for their child, and there is an appeal system if their choice is not met.

In England and Wales parents choosing among local secondary schools have the right to see:

- national performance tables showing the latest public examination results, vocational qualification results and rates of absence on a school-by-school basis; and
- information in each school's prospectus on public examination results, vocational qualification results, attendance rates and the destinations of school leavers.

National tables are published on the performance of all secondary schools throughout Britain, including information on the 16 to 18 age group. Summaries of school inspection reports (see p. 439) are given to parents.

All state schools in England and Wales have to give parents a written annual report on their child's achievements, containing details about:

- the child's progress in all subjects and activities;
- the child's general progress and attendance record;
- the results of National Curriculum assessments and of public examinations taken by the child;
- comparative results of pupils of the same age in the school and nationally; and
- information about the arrangements for discussing pupils' school reports with teachers.

All parents are invited to an annual meeting in order to discuss the governors' annual report.

In Scotland national guidelines to schools on reporting to parents advise that they should provide information about their child's attainment in the various subjects, teachers' comments on his or her progress and details about steps to build on success or overcome difficulties. One main school report each year is advised, together with one brief update report.

The Northern Ireland system for reporting to parents is broadly similar to that in England and Wales.

Parents' Charters

The Government has published parents' charters for England, Wales, Scotland and Northern Ireland which explain the rights of parents in the education of their children. Updated parents' charters for England and Wales were published in June 1994, and a revised charter for Scotland was published in January 1995.

Failing Schools

If school inspectors in England and Wales identify a school failing to give its pupils an acceptable standard of education, the LEA can appoint new governors and withdraw delegated management from the school. As an alternative, central government can put the school under new management until its performance reaches a satisfactory level. The new management is financed from central government. After further advice from the schools inspectorate (see p. 439), the Secretary of State decides whether to end the new management's period of care for the school; if this is done, the school becomes grant maintained.

Ethnic Minority Children

Most school-aged children from ethnic minorities were born in Britain and tend to share the interests and aspirations of children in the population at large. Nevertheless, a substantial number still have particular needs arising from cultural differences, including those of language, religion and custom.

The education authorities have done much to meet these needs. English language teaching continues to receive priority, with a growing awareness of the value of bilingual support in the early primary years. Schools may teach the main ethnic minority community languages at secondary level in England and Wales as part of the National Curriculum. Schools have to take account of the ethnic and cultural backgrounds of pupils, and curricula should reflect ethnic and cultural diversity. Measures have been taken to improve the achievement of ethnic minority pupils, and to prepare all children, not just those of ethnic minority origin, for living in a multi-ethnic society.

Special Educational Needs

Special educational needs comprise learning difficulties of all kinds, including mental and physical disabilities which hinder or prevent learning. LEAs are required to identify children whose learning difficulties are very severe or complex and to assess and meet their needs. They should also enable parents to be involved in decisions about their child's special education in partnership with the school.

If the LEA believes that it should determine the education for the child, it must draw up a formal statement of the child's special educational needs and the action it intends to take to meet them.

In England and Wales parents have a right of appeal to the Special Educational Needs Tribunal if they disagree with the LEA decisions about their child's special educational needs. The Tribunal's verdict is final and binding on all parties.

Under the 1993 Education Act there are statutory time limits within which LEAs in England and Wales must carry out procedures for making assessments and statements. Similar timetables for Scotland are operated through guidance from The Scottish Office Education Department. A state school named in a statement of special educational needs is required to admit the child.

Wherever possible, children with special educational needs are educated in ordinary schools. Placement in an ordinary school must be compatible with the needs of the child and with the provision of efficient education for the other children in the school. The LEA is required to comply with parents' choice of school unless this is inappropriate for the child, involves an inefficient use of resources or is incompatible with the efficient education of other children.

A Code of Practice has been issued by the Government offering practical guidance to all LEAs and state schools in England and Wales on how to identify, assess and monitor all pupils with special educational needs. A series of measures to monitor the implementation of the Code has also been set up.

Each school in England and Wales must formulate a policy on pupils with special educational needs and must publish information about that policy. Annual reports to parents must report on the success of these policies.

In Scotland the choice of school is a matter for agreement between education authorities and parents. In January 1995 HM Inspectors of Schools published a report which reviewed practice in pre-school provision, schools and further education colleges in Scotland. The report sets out clear, basic principles which emphasise the importance of partnership between all involved in meeting special educational needs.

In Northern Ireland steps are being taken to introduce changes similar to those in England and Wales.

There are nearly 1,800 special schools (both day and boarding) in Britain for pupils with special educational needs. Some of these are run by voluntary organisations and some are established in hospitals. They cater for some 115,000 pupils. The pupil/teacher ratio in special schools is 5.8 to 1 compared with 10.5 to 1 in 1970–71.

The Government has published guidance for parents of children with special needs in England, Wales and Scotland which sets out the rights and responsibilities of parents in their child's education.

Health and Welfare of Schoolchildren

Physical education, including organised games, is part of the curriculum of all maintained schools, and in England and Wales playing fields must be available for pupils over the age of eight. Most secondary schools have a gymnasium.

Government health departments are responsible for the medical inspection of schoolchildren and for advice on, and treatment of, medical and dental problems. The education service seeks to help prevent and deal with juvenile drug misuse and to help prevent the spread of AIDS. In England government funds support the training of teachers with responsibility for drug education.

Guidance on drug prevention in England's schools was issued by the Government in May 1995. The document outlines how to teach pupils about the dangers of drug misuse and advises schools on developing policies in drug education and prevention. Additional guidance is provided in a government White Paper—*Tackling Drugs Together*—also published in May 1995.

LEAs and GM schools are responsible for providing school meals for pupils. They are free to decide the nature of the meals service, taking account of local circumstances. In Northern Ireland school meals must be provided for primary, special and grant-aided nursery school pupils.

Free meals must be provided for children whose parents receive a social security benefit called income support, but all other pupils have to be charged for meals. Although LEAs do not have to provide milk to any pupil, they must, if they choose to do so, provide free milk to pupils of parents in receipt of income support and can offer subsidised milk to other pupils.

LEAs must provide or arrange free of charge the transport they consider necessary to enable pupils living in their area to attend school. The most common grounds for this are distance, safety or pupils' special educational needs. LEAs must publish details each year about their school transport policies.

Corporal punishment is prohibited by law in state schools in Britain, and for pupils in independent schools whose fees are met wholly or partly from public funds.

Independent Schools

Fee-paying independent schools must register with the appropriate central government education department and are open to inspection. They can be required to remedy serious shortcomings in their accommodation or teaching and to exclude anyone regarded as unsuitable to teach in or own a school. About 7 per cent of schoolchildren attend independent schools.

There are nearly 2,500 independent schools in Britain educating over 600,000 pupils of all ages. They charge fees varying from around £300 a term for day pupils at nursery age to over £4,000 a term for senior boarding pupils. Many offer bursaries to help pupils from less well-off families. Such pupils may also be helped by LEAs—particularly if the authorities' own schools cannot meet the needs of individual children—or by the Government's Assisted Places Scheme, under which financial assistance is given according to parental income. Over 38,000 places are offered in England, Wales and Scotland under the scheme. The Government also gives income-related help with fees to about 550 pupils at five music schools and the Royal Ballet School; there are also a limited number of similar scholarships at cathedral choir schools.

Independent schools range from small kindergartens to large day and boarding schools, and from new and, in some cases, experimental schools to ancient foundations. The 600 boys', girls' and mixed preparatory schools prepare children for entry to senior schools. The normal age-range for these preparatory schools is from seven-plus to 11, 12 or 13, but many have pre-preparatory departments for younger children. A number of independent schools have been established by religious orders and ethnic minorities.

Independent schools for older pupils— from 11, 12 or 13 to 18 or 19—include about 550 which are often referred to as 'public schools'. These belong to the Headmasters' Conference, the Governing Bodies Association, the Society of Headmasters and Headmistresses of Independent Schools, the Girls' Schools Association and the Governing Bodies of Girls' Schools Association.

In Northern Ireland there are 20 independent schools educating nearly 1,000 pupils. These schools are subject to inspection by the Department of Education.

Teachers

England and Wales

Teachers in state schools in England and Wales are appointed by LEAs or school governing bodies. They must hold qualifications approved by the Department for Education and Employment.

Almost all entrants to teaching in state schools in England and Wales complete an approved course of teacher training. These courses are offered by university departments of education as well as other higher education establishments (see p. 443). One of the two main qualifications is the four-year Bachelor of Education (BEd) honours degree. The other is the successful completion of a three-year degree course, topped up by a one-year Postgraduate Certificate in Education (PGCE) course.

Formal teacher appraisal is being introduced in English and Welsh schools. By September 1995 all teachers had entered the first year of their two-year appraisal cycle, which is intended to assist professional development, strengthen the management of schools and improve the quality of education provided to pupils. Consideration is being given to ways of ensuring that teachers' pay is more closely related to performance.

Reform of Initial Teacher Training

Under new government reforms in England and Wales, schools can play a much larger part in initial teacher training by taking on more responsibility for planning and managing courses and for the selection, training and assessment of students, usually in partnership with institutions. The reforms enable schools to train students to teach their specialist subjects, assess pupils and manage classes. The first courses following the new criteria began in 1994.

The reforms allow consortia of schools to run courses for postgraduate students if they wish to do so. Other courses, including all undergraduate courses, are run by universities and colleges in partnership with schools.

In September 1995 the new Teacher Training Agency became responsible for financing initial teacher training courses, ensuring that national standards are met and promoting teaching as a career.

In Wales, responsibility for the funding of initial teacher training remains with the Higher Education Funding Council for Wales, which will also be able to fund such training in schools. The Funding Council will also assume responsibility for accrediting institutions and schools providing courses.

Other Training

Under the Licensed Teacher Scheme, a trainee teacher is appointed to the school, which provides training and pays a salary; on successful completion of a two-year period of in-service training, qualified teacher status is granted. Qualified teachers from other European Union countries are usually granted qualified teacher status.

Scotland

All teachers in education authority schools must be registered with the General Teaching Council (GTC) for Scotland. The GTC is responsible for disciplinary procedures under which teachers guilty of professional misconduct may be removed permanently or temporarily from the register. Advice is given by the GTC to the Secretary of State on teacher supply and the professional suitability of teacher-training courses.

All entrants to the teaching profession are graduates. New primary teachers qualify either through a four-year BEd course or a one-year postgraduate course at a higher education teacher-training institution. In addition, the University of Stirling offers courses which combine academic and professional training for future primary and secondary teachers. Teachers of academic subjects at secondary schools must hold a degree containing two passes in the subjects which they wish to teach. Secondary school teachers must undertake a one-year postgraduate training course.

Under new guidelines on initial teacher-training courses, students on the one-year postgraduate course for secondary teachers spend 22 weeks in school during their courses. The overall school placement for the undergraduate BEd degree for primary school teachers is 30 weeks over the four-year period of the course. On the one-year postgraduate course for primary school teachers, students spend 18 weeks in school and 18 weeks in college-based study.

All new pre-service and major in-service courses provided by teacher training institutions must be approved by The Scottish Office Education Department and a validating body.

Education authorities have developed schemes to implement national guidelines for staff development and appraisal. Schemes must ensure that all teachers have been appraised at least once by the end of the 1995–96 school session.

Northern Ireland

Teacher training is provided by Queen's University, in Belfast, the University of Ulster, two colleges of education and the Open University (OU—see p. 445). The principal courses are BEd Honours (four years) and the one-year Postgraduate Certificate of Education. The OU course is part time and lasts 18 months. Education and library boards have a statutory duty to ensure that teachers are equipped with the necessary skills to implement education reforms and the Northern Ireland school curriculum.

School Curriculum

England and Wales

The National Curriculum consists of core subjects, which are compulsory for five- to 16-year-olds, and foundation subjects, which must be studied to the age of 14 at least. In England the core subjects of the curriculum are English, mathematics and science, and the foundation subjects are technology (design and technology, and information technology), history, geography, music, art, physical education and, for secondary school pupils, a modern foreign language.

This is also the case in Wales but, in addition, Welsh is a core subject in Welsh-speaking schools and a foundation subject in non-Welsh speaking schools. Nearly all primary schools in Wales teach Welsh as a first or second language and about a quarter use Welsh as the sole or main medium of instruction. In secondary schools, Welsh is compulsory for pupils aged 11 to 16 in Welsh-speaking schools and for pupils aged

11 to 14 in other schools. By August 1999 Welsh will be compulsory for almost all 11- to 16-year-old pupils.

There is more choice in the curriculum for pupils aged 14 to 16. History, geography, art and music are all optional subjects, as are technology and a modern foreign language in Wales. In England a modern foreign language and technology are currently optional subjects for 14- to 16-year-olds, but will become compulsory in September 1996.

Religious education is required for all pupils as part of the basic curriculum and all secondary schools must provide sex education. Parents have a right to withdraw their children from these subjects.

Following a thorough review in 1994, a revised National Curriculum is being introduced for five- to 14-year-olds in September 1995 and for 14- to 16-year-olds from September 1996. The new streamlined requirements are designed to release more time for schools to use outside the statutory curriculum and give teachers more scope to use their professional discretion.

The National Curriculum now gives greater emphasis to information technology (IT), with the publication of separate programmes of study and attainment targets. Schools are also required to provide pupils with the opportunity to develop IT skills in all other National Curriculum subjects.

National testing and assessment of pupils' performance at the ages of seven, 11 and 14 is confined to the core subjects. All 11- and 14-year-olds are tested in English, mathematics and science, whereas seven-year-olds are tested in mathematics and English only. In Wales the three age groups are also tested in Welsh.

The General Certificate of Secondary Education (GCSE) is the major qualification taken by pupils at the end of compulsory schooling at the age of 16. The proportion of pupils with five or more GCSEs at grades A to C has risen significantly in recent years. In England the proportion rose from nearly 33 per cent in 1988–89 to over 43 per cent in 1993–94.

General oversight of examination standards rests jointly with the School Curriculum and Assessment Authority in England and the Assessment Authority for Wales.

The Independent Appeals Authority for School Examinations hears appeals against grades awarded in GCSE and GCE A level and AS examinations (see p. 440) when the appeals procedures of the examining body concerned have been exhausted.

A new vocational course for pupils aged 14 to 16 was announced in November 1994. The new Part One General National Vocational Qualification (GNVQ) is broadly equivalent to two GCSE courses and is being piloted in 115 secondary schools in England and Wales from September 1995. It covers three subject areas—business, health and social care, and manufacturing. Three new subject areas will be introduced in 1996: art and design, information technology, and leisure and tourism.

New GCSE (Short Course) qualifications are to be introduced from September 1996. These will take half the time typically allotted to a GCSE and will be available in modern foreign languages, religious education, design and technology, and information technology. Further courses are being developed in art, geography, history, music and physical education. For schools in Wales a GCSE (Short Course) qualification in Welsh will be introduced.

Scotland

The content and management of the curriculum are not prescribed by statute and responsibility rests with education authorities and headteachers, though guidance is provided by the Secretary of State and the Scottish Consultative Council on the Curriculum. The Council has recommended that secondary level pupils should follow a broad and balanced curriculum consisting of English, mathematics, science, a modern European language, social studies, technological activities, art, music or drama, religious and moral education, and physical education.

A major programme of curricular review and development has been carried out for the five to 14 age-range. The Government has issued guidance on English language, mathematics, expressive arts, Latin, Gaelic, modern languages, environmental studies and religious and moral education. Under new arrangements, standardised tests in English and mathematics are given to pupils in the five to 14 age group whenever they complete one of five levels. A major programme to extend modern language teaching to primary schools is in progress.

Provision is made for teaching in Gaelic in Gaelic-speaking areas and in some other areas where education authorities have identified this as a priority.

Pupils take the Scottish Certificate of Education (SCE) at Standard Grade at the end of their fourth year of secondary education, normally around the age of 16. The proportion of pupils leaving school with no SCE qualification has fallen significantly from one pupil in four in 1983–84 to fewer than one in ten in 1993–94.

The Higher Grade can be taken in the fifth and/or sixth year of secondary education. Some pupils also sit examinations for the Certificate of Sixth Year Studies or take vocational National Certificate units (see p. 441).

Northern Ireland

The common curriculum in all publicly financed schools is made up of religious education and six broad areas of study: English, mathematics, science and technology, the environment and society, creative and expressive studies, and, for secondary schools, language studies.

The school curriculum also includes four compulsory cross-curricular themes: cultural heritage, education for mutual understanding, health education and information technology. Secondary schools have two additional themes—economic awareness and careers education.

Following reviews of the curriculum, new arrangements are to take effect from September 1996. These are broadly similar to those taking place in England and Wales and will allow schools and pupils more flexibility in the choice of subjects in the curriculum as a whole. Teaching of the statutory curriculum in primary schools will

take up about 85 per cent of teaching time. Programmes of study for pupils aged 12 to 14 are being reviewed to take account of the changes proposed for primary school children.

Arrangements to assess pupils' progress at the ages of eight, 11 and 14 were piloted again in 1994–95. Statutory pupil assessment will be introduced in the 1996–97 school year. As in England and Wales, the GCSE examination is used to assess 16-year-old pupils.

Religious Education and Collective Worship in Schools

In England and Wales state schools must provide religious education and a daily act of collective worship for all registered pupils. Every LEA has to produce an agreed religious education syllabus, which must be reviewed every five years. Syllabuses must reflect Christianity while taking account of the other main religions practised in Britain.

In July 1994 model syllabuses for religious education in England were published. These were developed by the School Curriculum and Assessment Authority along with representatives of Christian denominations, other faith communities and teachers. The syllabuses are intended to help promote the quality and standing of religious education and to assist LEAs to prepare syllabuses. LEAs may adopt one of the models in full or draw on them when preparing the local syllabus. Parents have the right to withdraw their children from religious education classes and from collective worship. Voluntary-aided schools provide the opportunity for denominational religious education.

Scottish education authorities are required to see that schools practise religious observance and give pupils religious instruction; parents may withdraw their children if they wish. Certain schools provide for Roman Catholic children, but in all schools there are safeguards for individual conscience.

In Northern Ireland, schools must provide religious education and collective worship, although parents have the right to withdraw their children from both. A core syllabus has been approved by the four main churches in Northern Ireland and this must be taught in all grant-aided schools.

Sex Education

Under the 1993 Education Act all state secondary schools in England and Wales are required to provide sex education for all pupils registered at the school. This must include education about HIV and AIDS and sexually transmitted diseases. In state primary schools the governors must consider whether sex education should be offered beyond the requirements of the National Curriculum Science Order.

Sex education in state schools must encourage young people to have regard to moral considerations and the value of family life. Parents are entitled to withdraw their children from sex education classes other than those required by the National Curriculum Science Order. All state schools must publish in their prospectus a summary of the content and organisation of any sex education provided.

In Scotland, government guidance on sex education is provided to education authorities and headteachers, who are responsible for its content.

Curriculum Development and Assessment

The School Curriculum and Assessment Authority in England and the Curriculum and Assessment Authority for Wales are responsible for:

- keeping all aspects of the school curriculum and of school examinations under review;
- advising the Government on the curriculum, and assessment and examination arrangements; and
- publishing information about the curriculum.

All GCSE and other qualifications offered to pupils of compulsory school age in state schools in England and Wales must be approved by the Government. Associated syllabuses and assessment procedures must comply with national guidelines and be approved by the relevant curriculum and assessment authority.

In Scotland curriculum development is undertaken by the Scottish Consultative Council on the Curriculum in close consultation with The Scottish Office Education Department. The Scottish Examination Board liaises with the Council on links between the curriculum and assessment.

The Northern Ireland Council for the Curriculum, Examinations and Assessment is responsible for the curriculum and its assessment as well as the conduct of examinations in Northern Ireland.

Information Technology

The National Curriculum places a strong emphasis on the use of information technology (IT) to ensure that all children are appropriately versed in the new technologies. In England the average number of pupils per microcomputer in primary schools in 1993–94 was 18 compared with 25 in 1991–92 and 107 in 1984–85. In secondary schools the average number of pupils per microcomputer was ten in 1993–94 compared with 13 in 1991–92 and 60 in 1984–85.

In 1995–96 the Department for Education and Employment (DFEE) is continuing to support the provision of microcomputers, software and training in IT in schools through the Grants for Education and Support Training (GEST) programme.

Other DFEE programmes include funding for:

- development and use of CD-ROM technology in schools;
- investigating the potential of interactive multimedia technology as a teaching aid and assessing its full use for curriculum development in schools; and
- consultation on the use of information superhighways in education.

In Wales the Welsh Office also has a grant programme to support microcomputers in schools and has financed the installation of satellite television equipment in all secondary schools. This is used to teach modern foreign languages and other subjects such as geography and science. There is also a scheme to supply all primary schools in Wales with CD-ROM equipment.

The Government also finances the National Council for Educational Technology, which promotes the development and effective use of new technologies throughout the education system. The corresponding body in Scotland is the Scottish Council for Educational Technology.

In Scotland computing studies are included in the five to 14 national guidelines on environmental studies. In most secondary schools, first and second year pupils take a short course in computing; third and fourth year pupils choose between a Standard Grade course or a National Certificate module. Similarly, fifth and sixth year pupils are able to choose between Higher Grade and a number of National Certificate modules.

In Northern Ireland, IT is one of the four compulsory educational cross-curricular themes forming part of the curriculum for primary and secondary pupils in publicly financed schools.

Other Educational Aids

The BBC (British Broadcasting Corporation) and the independent broadcasting companies transmit radio and television programmes designed for schools. Teachers' notes, pupils' pamphlets and computer software accompany many broadcast series.

School Inspections

Various inspectorates report to the Government on the quality of education provided by schools.

England

In England the independent Office for Standards in Education (OFSTED) advises the Secretary of State on quality, standards and efficiency, and regulates a system of school inspections. The inspection cycle began in September 1993 for secondary schools and in September 1994 for primary and other schools.

Every school has to be inspected every

four years by a team of independent inspectors—headed by a registered inspector—containing educationists and lay people. Inspections take place according to agreed national standards monitored by OFSTED. Parents are sent a summary of the inspection report, which is published. School governing bodies have to prepare action plans to follow it up and then report back to parents on their progress. OFSTED is headed by Her Majesty's Chief Inspector of Schools.

Wales

Her Majesty's Chief Inspector of Schools for Wales has similar functions to those of OFSTED. All schools are inspected every five years in the first instance.

Scotland

In Scotland HM Inspectors of Schools are responsible for independent evaluation of education standards and for advising the Secretary of State. Full reports on inspections are published and a short summary given to parents. The Inspectorate's Audit Unit collects, analyses and publishes evidence about the performance of schools and education authorities. Evidence is published on a comparative basis, and recommendations are made for action and improvement.

Northern Ireland

The Education and Training Inspectorate advises on quality and standards in schools. Each school has to be inspected every five years, and reports of inspections are published. From 1996 general inspection teams will include lay people. Boards of Governors respond to inspectors' findings by indicating any action planned and submitting details to the Department of Education.

Schools, Careers and Business

One of the Government's key objectives is to help young people develop the skills the economy needs.

Education Business Partnerships, consisting of representatives from industry, education and the wider community, aim to bring about closer links between education and industry in Great Britain and ensure that young people develop the skills to help them succeed in the labour market. They are supported by Training and Enterprise Councils, Local Enterprise Companies and LEAs.

One of the main schemes managed by the Partnerships is the Teacher Placement Service (TPS), funded by the Government. The TPS organises placements in business for teachers and lecturers to extend their professional and personal development, improve learning opportunities for young people, and provide better careers education services. Since 1989 some 100,000 teachers have been on placements.

Compacts bring together employers, young people, schools, colleges and other bodies involved in training in order to help young people achieve more at school, and to continue education and training after the age of 16. Under Compact schemes, young people work towards agreed goals; in return for achieving them, employers provide a number of incentives.

Careers

Most schools have a written policy statement on careers education and guidance, a careers co-ordinator and an agreement with their local careers guidance service about the co-ordinated contribution they will make to student development. LEAs are active participants in the majority of careers service organisations.

Careers services in schools and colleges are supported by materials produced by the Careers and Occupational Information Centre.

In Northern Ireland careers education is one of the six compulsory education themes forming part of the secondary school curriculum (see p. 437). The Careers Service is part of the Training and Employment Agency.

All state secondary schools in England and Wales have to provide leavers with a National Record of Achievement setting out their school attainments, including public examination and National Curriculum assessment results. In Scotland the Record is not compulsory.

In Northern Ireland all pupils in secondary education are issued with a record of achievement on leaving school, and from 1997–98 this will apply to primary schools.

EDUCATION AFTER 16

About 67 per cent of pupils choose to continue in education after 16. This takes place in school sixth forms, sixth-form colleges, further education colleges, universities and other higher education institutions.

Broadly speaking, education after 16 is divided into further and higher education. Further and adult education is largely vocational and covers courses up to and including GCE A level and AS qualifications, GNVQ Advanced level or their equivalents (see p. 441). Higher education covers advanced courses at levels higher than GCE A level or equivalent.

Almost 4 million people were enrolled on further education courses in 1992–93. By 1995–96 every 16- and 17-year-old leaving full-time education in Great Britain will be encouraged to undertake vocational education or training by the offer of a Youth Credit, enabling them to buy training from the establishment of their choice (see p. 186).

In 1992–93 there were 1.4 million home and overseas students in higher education, of whom 47 per cent were women.

In 1993 the Government published charters for the users of further and higher education in England, Wales and Scotland, setting out the standards of service which users should expect. Further education colleges also have individual charters. Similar charters are to be published in Northern Ireland.

Credit accumulation and transfer schemes are in use in many English and Welsh post-school establishments. In Scotland a credit accumulation scheme covers courses in all further and higher education. Similar schemes in higher education in Northern Ireland are compatible with those of institutions in the rest of Britain.

The national computer-based Educational Counselling and Credit Transfer Information Service (ECCTIS) provides prospective students and their advisers with quick and easy access without charge to information about 100,000 course opportunities at over 700 universities and colleges of higher and further education throughout Britain. ECCTIS, which is available to subscribing institutions on CD-ROM, can be found at over 4,500 locations in over two-thirds of secondary schools with sixth forms, as well as the majority of further education colleges, higher education institutions, careers offices and training and enterprise councils; ECCTIS is also available at British Council offices throughout the world.

Schools and Sixth-form Colleges

Having taken the GCSE examination (see p. 436), students in England, Wales and Northern Ireland can stay on at school or be educated in a further education college. Students in England and Wales can also study at sixth-form colleges. They study for examinations which are the main standard for entry to higher education or professional training. These include the academic General Certificate of Education (GCE) Advanced (A) level, the Advanced Supplementary (AS) examination, Advanced General National Vocational Qualifications (GNVQs) and National Vocational Qualifications (NVQs). The GCE A level is taken at the age of 18 or 19 after two years' study; part of the qualification is based on course work and the rest on written test papers. AS levels enable sixth-form pupils to study a wider range of subjects. Students specialising in the arts, for example, can continue to study technological subjects at this level. Requiring the same standard of work as A levels, an AS level occupies half the teaching and study time of an A level.

Equality of status for academic and vocational qualifications is being promoted in England, Wales and Northern Ireland. The new GNVQs for young people in full-time education between the ages of 16 and 18 provide a broad-based preparation for a range of occupations and higher education, and are designed to have parity of esteem with GCE A levels. There are three GNVQ levels—Advanced, Intermediate and Foundation. An Advanced GNVQ—called the vocational A level—requires a level of

achievement broadly equal to two GCE A levels. GNVQs may also be taken in combination with other qualifications, such as GCE A levels or GCSEs.

A study of GCE A level and GCSE examination standards is to be carried out by the School Curriculum and Assessment Authority and the Office for Standards in Education, following the eighth successive annual increase in 1995 in the pass rate for A levels.

Scotland

Pupils staying on at school after the end of compulsory education study for the Higher Grade Scottish Certificate of Education exam at the age of 16–18; passes at this grade are the basis for entry to higher education or professional training. The Certificate of Sixth Year Studies (CSYS) is for pupils who have completed their Higher Grade main studies and who wish to continue studies in particular subjects.

A flexible system of vocational courses for 16- to 18-year-olds has been introduced in schools and colleges in disciplines such as business and administration, engineering and industrial production. These courses are also intended to meet the needs of many adults entering training or returning to education. The courses lead to the award of the non-advanced National Certificate, intended for students over 16 who have successfully completed a programme of vocational courses based on short study units. Similar unit-based courses are also available at advanced levels.

General Scottish Vocational Qualifications (General SVQs) are designed to meet the needs of 16- to 19-year-olds at school or in further education colleges. Broadly compatible with the GNVQs in the rest of Britain, General SVQs are a stepping-stone to higher education or further training. They are accredited and awarded by the Scottish Vocational Education Council (SCOTVEC).

A new system of courses and awards for fifth- and sixth-year pupils will take effect in the late 1990s. Under this, Highers will remain but courses will be based on units called modules. The recommended study time for each Higher will be extended from

120 hours to 160 hours. Existing courses validated by the Scottish Examinations Board and SCOTVEC will be drawn into a unified system of curriculum and assessment. Advanced Higher courses will be developed, incorporating the current Certificate of Sixth Year Studies and building on Highers to provide a two-year 320-hour course.

Further Education Colleges

People over the age of 16 can also take courses in further education colleges. Much further education is work-related and vocational. Further education institutions supply much of the education element in government-sponsored training programmes, such as Jobskills.

Table 26.2: Students Enrolled in Further Education in Britain

	1982–83	1992–93
Further education enrolments:[a]		
Full-time	422,000	586,000
Part-time	2,885,000	3,201,000
All further education	**3,307,000**	**3,787,000**

Source: Department for Education and Employment
[a]Includes enrolments on Youth Training in public sector colleges and adult education centres.

Many students on further education courses attend part time, either by day release or block release from employment or during the evenings. The system has strong ties with commerce and industry, and co-operation with business is encouraged by the Government and its agencies. Employers are normally involved in designing courses.

Courses are run by nearly 580 institutions of further education, many of which also offer higher education courses (see p. 443). In England and Wales each is controlled by an autonomous further education corporation and governing body with substantial representation from business. Scottish colleges are controlled by an autonomous board of management.

Funds are allocated to institutions by further education funding councils in England and Wales; part of the funding is not cash limited and is directly related to student numbers. The Scottish Office Education Department distributes funds to colleges in Scotland. In Northern Ireland further education colleges are financed via the education and library boards by the Department of Education.

Institutions in England, Wales and Scotland are obliged to publish information about the use of their financial and other resources. Expenditure plans provide for a record 25 per cent rise in full-time equivalent student numbers in England and a 28 per cent rise in Wales over the three-year period from 1993. The number of full-time equivalent students in Scotland is projected to rise by more than 25 per cent between 1991 and 1996.

Funding councils in England and Wales send out independent inspectors to assess the quality of the education provided by colleges. Inspectors publish reports containing quality assessments, and colleges are obliged to explain how they will put things right if there are major criticisms. Each college has to publish information about its examination results annually. Colleges in Scotland are inspected by the Schools Inspectorate and in Northern Ireland by the Education and Training Inspectorate.

Vocational Qualifications

The National Council for Vocational Qualifications (NCVQ) is establishing a new framework of National Vocational Qualifications (NVQs) in England, Wales and Northern Ireland. These are based on national standards that define the competence, knowledge and understanding that employers need. Awarding bodies have been reforming their qualifications for accreditation by the National Council.

The following five levels of NVQs have been established:

Level 1—Foundation
Level 2—Basic craft
Level 3—Technician, advanced craft, supervisor
Level 4—Higher technician, middle management
Level 5—Middle to higher management.

NVQs consist of units setting out the standards which the individual must reach in a range of job-related tasks. Performance of candidates is assessed by observation in the workplace. This assessment consists of practical work, oral questioning, course work and tests. NVQs are designed mainly for people in work, although they can also be studied in colleges and some schools. NVQs at levels 1 to 4 are available in most occupations. In Scotland there is a similar system of Scottish Vocational Qualifications (SVQs).

NVQs and SVQs have equal recognition throughout Britain. The GNVQ and General SVQ system for students in full-time education is described on p. 441.

Examining Bodies

About 90 per cent of vocational qualifications in England, Wales and Northern Ireland are assessed by three examining bodies and accredited by the NCVQ:

- The Business and Technology Education Council (BTEC) plans and administers a unified national system of courses at all levels; the most popular subjects are business, engineering and construction.

- The City and Guilds of London Institute provides mostly part-time qualifications in areas such as engineering, construction, catering, hairdressing and community care.

- The RSA Examinations Board is the largest provider of information technology qualifications throughout Britain and offers qualifications in areas ranging from management/customer service to retailing and wholesaling.

These three main vocational awarding bodies offer GNVQs and a wide range of NVQs, which will eventually replace most of their existing awards. Other vocational qualifications are awarded by a large number of professional bodies. The Scottish Vocational Education Council (SCOTVEC) is the main accreditation and awarding body in Scotland.

National Targets for Education and Training

The Government has endorsed new national targets for education and training announced in 1995 by the National Advisory Council for Education and Training Targets. The main targets, which have been set for the year 2000, are that:

- by age 19, 85 per cent of young people should achieve five GCSEs at Grade C or above, an Intermediate GNVQ or an NVQ Level 2; and

- by age 21, 60 per cent of young people should achieve two GCE A levels, an Advanced GNVQ or an NVQ Level 3.

Higher Education

Higher education, which consists of degree and equivalent courses, has experienced a dramatic expansion since the 1980s. The total number of higher education students in Britain almost doubled between 1979 and 1993 to some 1.5 million. The proportion of young people entering full-time higher education in Britain rose from 12 per cent in 1979 to some 30 per cent in 1993.

In order to maintain British expertise in technology, recent government schemes have sought to expand higher education and research in electronics, engineering and computer science by making available extra student places, offering bursaries to able young students to study for engineering degrees and providing additional staff and research fellowships.

Higher education institutions are responsible for providing high-quality education. The Higher Education Quality Council, financed by subscriptions from institutions, ensures that satisfactory quality control arrangements are in place. The higher education funding councils for England, Scotland and Wales (see p. 444) carry out assessments of the education provided by institutions, publish regular reports on their findings and aim to ensure that any serious problems are put right by the university or college concerned. Acting on behalf of the

Department of Education for Northern Ireland, the Higher Education Funding Council for England publishes reports on the quality of education in the two Northern Ireland universities.

Table 26.3: Students Enrolled in Higher Education in Britain

	1982–83	1993–94
Higher education enrolments:[a]		
Full-time	553,000	1,038,000
Part-time[b]	297,000	503,000
All higher education	**850,000**	**1,541,000**

Source: Department for Education and Employment
[a]Excludes nursing and paramedic enrolments.
[c]Includes the Open University.

Finance

Higher education is largely financed by public funds, tuition fees for students paid through the student awards system and income received by institutions from research contracts and other sources.

Government finance for higher education institutions in England, Scotland and Wales is distributed by higher education funding councils responsible to their respective Secretary of State. In Northern Ireland grant is paid direct to the two universities by the Department of Education, following advice from the Northern Ireland Higher Education Council. The private University of Buckingham does not receive any public grants.

Finance from the funding councils helps meet the costs of teaching, research and related activities in all publicly funded universities and higher education colleges. In addition to teaching students, institutions undertake paid training, research or consultancy for commercial firms (see p. 326). Many establishments have endowments or receive grants from foundations and benefactors.

Student Grants and Loans

Over 95 per cent of full-time students resident in England and Wales on first degree and other comparable higher education courses receive mandatory awards covering tuition fees and a maintenance grant. The level of the grant depends on the income of the student and of the student's parents or spouse. Awards are made by LEAs in England and Wales. The Government reimburses in full the amount spent by education authorities on mandatory awards. Similar schemes are administered by the Student Awards Agency for Scotland and the Northern Ireland education and library boards. LEA grants for other courses can be given at their discretion.

Most students on courses of full-time, non-postgraduate higher education can also take out a loan to help pay their maintenance costs. Loans are not means tested and repayments are indexed to inflation. The scheme is designed to share the cost of student maintenance more equitably between students, parents and the taxpayer. In 1993–94 loans worth £317 million were made to 430,000 students in Britain, representing 47 per cent of those eligible. Loans are administered by the Student Loans Company in Glasgow.

Limited access funds administered by universities and colleges are available to people in cases where access to higher and further education might be inhibited by financial considerations or where students face real financial difficulties. In 1995–96, there is provision of £27.7 million in England and £4.1 million in Scotland for this purpose.

Grants for postgraduate study are offered by the government education departments and by the research councils. Increasing numbers of scholarships are available from research charities, endowments and particular industries or companies.

Access Courses

Access and foundation courses provide a preparation and an appropriate test before enrolment on a course of higher education for prospective students who do not possess the standard entry qualifications (GCE A levels and equivalent qualifications). Many are from the ethnic minority communities. The growth of access courses has been very rapid in recent years; about 1,200 are now available nationwide.

The Scottish Wider Access Programme (SWAP) is designed to promote greater participation in higher education by mature students and those without the normal entry requirements. Successful completion of a SWAP course guarantees a higher education place.

Universities

There are some 90 universities, including the Open University. They are governed by royal charters or by Act of Parliament and enjoy academic freedom. They appoint their own staff, decide which students to admit, provide their own courses and award their own degrees. The universities of Oxford and Cambridge date from the 12th and 13th centuries, and the Scottish universities of St Andrews, Glasgow, Aberdeen and Edinburgh from the 14th and 15th centuries. All the other universities in Britain were founded in the 19th and 20th centuries. The 1960s saw considerable expansion in the number of new universities. The number of universities also jumped considerably in 1992, when polytechnics and some other higher education establishments were given the freedom to become universities and chose to exercise it.

Applications for first degree courses are usually made through the Universities and Colleges Admission Service (UCAS), in Cheltenham.

First degree courses are mainly full time and usually last three years in England, Wales and Northern Ireland. However, there are some four-year courses, and medical and veterinary courses normally require five years. All traditional first degree courses in Scotland require a minimum of three years' study. The ratio of staff to full-time students in Britain is about 1 to 13.2.

Universities offer courses in a wide range of subjects, including traditional arts subjects and science and technology. Some courses lead to the examinations of the chief professional bodies, and to qualifications such as those of the BTEC.

Many universities have close links with commerce and industry, with some students having a job and attending on a part-time basis.

Degree titles vary according to the practice of each university. In England, Wales and Northern Ireland the most common titles for a first degree are Bachelor of Arts (BA) or Bachelor of Science (BSc) and for a second degree Master of Arts (MA), Master of Science (MSc), and Doctor of Philosophy (PhD). In the older Scottish universities Master is used for a first degree in arts subjects. Uniformity of standards between universities is promoted by employing external examiners for all university examinations.

The Open University and other universities are responsible for validating degrees at higher education institutions without degree-awarding powers.

Many staff combine research with teaching duties. The number of postgraduates has increased by over 60 per cent in the last decade; two-thirds are on taught courses. The Government is encouraging universities to co-operate closely with industry on research. Around 50 science parks have been set up by higher education institutions in conjunction with industrial scientists and technologists to promote the development and commercial application of advanced technology.

The Open University

The Open University is a non-residential university offering degree and other courses for adult students of all ages in Britain and the other member countries of the European Union.

The University uses a combination of specially produced printed texts, correspondence tuition, television and radio broadcasts, audio/video cassettes and computing. For some courses, there are residential schools. There is a network of study centres for contact with part-time tutors and counsellors, and with fellow students. Formal academic qualifications are not required to register for most courses, but the standards of the University's degrees are the same as those of other universities. Its first degrees are the BA (Open) or the BSc (Open), which are general degrees awarded on a system of credits for each course completed. In 1995 there were some 92,000 registered undergraduates, and in all some 157,000 first degrees have been awarded since the University started its courses in 1970.

The University also has a programme of higher degrees. About 9,000 students were registered on higher degree courses in 1995. There are also programmes for professionals in a variety of fields.

The University has advised many other countries on setting up similar institutions, and has contributed to projects such as the European Distance Education Network. It is financed by the Higher Education Funding Council for England.

Further Education for Adults

Further education for adults is provided by further education institutions, adult centres and colleges run by LEAs, and voluntary bodies such as the Workers' Educational Association. The duty to secure it is shared by the further education funding councils, The Scottish Office Education Department (SOED) and LEAs.

The councils and the SOED fund formal academic and vocational courses, courses providing access to higher education and courses in basic literacy and numeracy, including English for speakers of other languages. LEAs are responsible for the less formal leisure and recreational courses. The councils, the SOED and the LEAs must take account of adult students with special educational needs.

University departments of continuing education also provide courses for adults.

Basic Skills Agency

The Basic Skills Agency (BSA) is concerned with adult literacy, numeracy and related basic skills in England and Wales. It provides consultancy and advisory services; funds local development projects, including research; publishes materials for teachers and students; and organises and sponsors staff training. Government funding of the BSA is worth about £4 million in 1995–96.

Following a recent government review, the BSA has become a more general basic skills unit. Its responsibilities now cover basic skills

training in the workplace for the unemployed and for young people as well as its traditional work with adults.

National Organisation of Adult Learning

The National Organisation of Adult Learning—formerly the National Institute of Adult Continuing Education and still known as NIACE—is the national body representing adult learners in England and Wales. It convenes conferences, seminars and meetings, collects and disseminates information, conducts enquiries and research, undertakes special projects and works with other organisations.

Open and Distance Learning

The terms 'open' and 'distance' learning broadly mean learning undertaken without the direct supervision of a tutor through use of various media, such as television. More and more further education colleges are incorporating many distance learning materials and methods in their mainstream courses.

Scottish Community Education Council

The Scottish Community Education Council advises the Government and promotes all community education matters, including adult literacy and basic education, and youth work.

Educational Research

Educational research is supported financially by government departments, the Economic and Social Research Council, philanthropic organisations, higher education institutions, teachers' associations and other agencies.

The major research institutions outside the universities are the autonomous National Foundation for Educational Research in England and Wales and the Scottish Council for Research in Education.

LINKS WITH OTHER COUNTRIES

Large numbers of people come to Britain from other countries to study, and British people work and train overseas. The British aid programme encourages links between educational institutions in Britain and developing countries.

There has been an expansion of interest in European studies and languages, with exchanges of teachers, schoolchildren and students taking place.

European Union Schemes

Exchange of students is promoted by the EU scheme ERASMUS. Under the scheme, grants are provided to enable EU students and those from other countries belonging to the European Economic Area (see p. 120) to study in other states. The programme covers all academic subjects, and the period of study normally lasts between three and 12 months. In 1992–93 over 8,000 British students studied in Europe under the scheme.

LINGUA is an EU programme which aims to promote competence in foreign languages. LINGUA offers funding which contributes towards in-service training for teachers, student exchanges based on project work, and the development of new teaching methods.

A new EU education programme—SOCRATES—was adopted by the Council of Ministers in March 1995. The programme is the first major EU initiative to encourage practical co-operation across all levels of education throughout the European Union. Under the scheme, schools in different European countries will be able to develop partnerships with one another so that pupils will be able to participate in a variety of educational projects throughout the European Union.

The ERASMUS and LINGUA programmes have been incorporated into SOCRATES, which has a budget of £689 million over five years.

Youth for Europe III aims to bring together young people from different cultural and social backgrounds in the European Union through a wide range of exchanges. The five-year programme started in 1995 and has an EU budget of £102 million.

A new EU vocational training programme —LEONARDO DA VINCI—came into force in January 1995 and replaces a number of previous programmes, including COMETT (university/industry co-operation) and PETRA (training of young people).

EU member states have created nine European schools, including one at Culham, Oxfordshire, for pupils aged between four and 19 to provide a multilingual education for the children of staff employed in EU institutions.

Overseas Students in Britain

British universities and other further and higher education establishments have built up a strong reputation overseas by offering tuition of the highest standards and maintaining low student-to-staff ratios.

In 1992–93 there were nearly 105,000 overseas students at publicly funded higher and further education institutions in Britain. Their numbers have increased by 76 per cent since 1982–83.

In general, overseas students following courses of higher or further education in Britain pay fees covering the full cost of their courses.

Nationals of other member countries of the European Union generally pay the lower level of fees applicable to British students; if their courses are designated for mandatory awards, they may be eligible for fees-only awards from LEAs. Students attending Scottish institutions apply either to the Student Awards Agency for Scotland or the regional or island councils.

Government Scholarship Schemes

The Government makes considerable provision for foreign students and trainees under its overseas aid programme and through other award and scholarship schemes. In 1993–94 some 21,000 overseas students were supported, at a cost of £147 million.

The Foreign & Commonwealth Office (FCO) finances the British Chevening Scholarships, a worldwide programme offering outstanding graduate students and young professionals the opportunity to spend time studying at British universities and other academic institutions. In 1994–95 the FCO spent some £30 million on about 5,000 scholarships for students from 146 countries. These included jointly funded scholarships for overseas students co-sponsored by the FCO, business and industry, grant-giving foundations, the Churches and universities; nearly 800 scholarships were provided under these arrangements in 1994–95.

Outside the aid programme, the Overseas Research Students Awards Scheme, funded by the Department for Education and Employment, provides assistance for overseas full-time postgraduate students with outstanding research potential.

Other Schemes

Many public and private scholarships and fellowships are available to students from overseas and to British students who want to study overseas. Among the best known are the British Council Fellowships, the Commonwealth Scholarship and Fellowship Plan, the Fulbright Scholarship Scheme, the British Marshall Scholarships, the Rhodes Scholarships, the Churchill Scholarships and the Confederation of British Industry Scholarships. Most British universities and colleges also offer bursaries and scholarships for which graduates of any nationality are eligible.

THE YOUTH SERVICE

The youth service—a partnership between local government and voluntary organisations —is concerned with the informal personal and social education of young people aged 11 to 25 (five to 25 in Northern Ireland).

Many of the voluntary organisations were established at the end of the 19th century and in the first decade of the 20th. In 1944 the Education Act provided for the development of a youth service in England and Wales by LEAs in partnership with the voluntary organisations.

Local authorities maintain their own youth centres and clubs and provide most of the public support for local and regional voluntary organisations. The service is said to reach around 5 million young people, the voluntary organisations contributing a

significant proportion of overall provision.

The Department for Education and Employment's Youth Service Unit gives grants to the national voluntary youth organisations to meet 50 per cent of the cost of programmes designed to promote access to the youth service, support training for voluntary youth workers and help improve the efficiency and effectiveness of the organisations.

Funded primarily by central government, England's National Youth Agency provides:

- support for those working with young people;
- information and publishing services; and
- support for curriculum development.

It is also responsible for the accreditation of training and staff development for youth workers.

The Welsh Office provides grant aid to national youth service bodies with headquarters in Wales and has established a Wales Youth Agency.

In Scotland the youth service forms part of the community education provision made by local authorities. It is also promoted by the Scottish Community Education Council. The Scottish Office gives grants to voluntary youth organisations to assist them with their headquarters expenditure and staff training and development.

In Northern Ireland the education and library boards provide and fund youth clubs and outdoor activity centres, help pay the running costs of registered voluntary youth units, advise and support youth groups and assist young people visiting the rest of Britain, Ireland and overseas in connection with annual camps and award schemes. The Youth Council for Northern Ireland advises the education system on the development of the youth service, promotes provision of facilities and encourages cross-community activity among young people.

Voluntary Youth Organisations

National voluntary youth organisations undertake a significant share of youth activities through local groups, which raise most of their day-to-day expenses by their own efforts. Many receive financial and other help from LEAs, which also make available facilities in many areas. The voluntary organisations vary greatly in character and include the uniformed organisations, such as the Scouts and Girl Guides. Some organisations are church-based. Some also represent Jews and Muslims. Sport and the arts are catered for by various bodies. In Wales, Urdd Gobaith Cymru (the Welsh League of Youth) provides cultural, sporting and language-based activities for young Welsh speakers and learners.

Thousands of youth clubs encourage their members to participate in sport, cultural and other creative activities. Some youth clubs provide information, counselling and advice.

Many local authorities and voluntary youth organisations make provision for the young unemployed, young people from the ethnic minorities, young people in inner cities or rural areas and those in trouble or especially vulnerable. Other areas of concern are homelessness and provision for handicapped young people.

Many authorities have youth committees on which official and voluntary bodies are represented. They employ youth officers to co-ordinate youth work and to arrange in-service training.

Youth Workers

In England and Wales a two-year training course at certain universities and higher education colleges produces qualified youth and community workers; several undergraduate part-time and postgraduate courses are also available. In Scotland one-, two- and three-year courses are provided at colleges of education. Students from Northern Ireland attend courses run in universities and colleges in Britain and the Irish Republic.

Other Organisations Concerned with Young People

Finance is provided by many grant-giving foundations and trusts for activities involving young people. The Prince's Trust and the Royal Jubilee Trust provide grants and practical help to individuals and organisations; areas of concern include urban deprivation, unemployment, homelessness, and young offenders. Efforts are also made to assist ethnic minorities.

The Duke of Edinburgh's Award Scheme challenges young people from Britain and other Commonwealth countries to meet certain standards in activities such as community service, expeditions, social and practical skills and physical recreation.

Voluntary Service by Young People

Thousands of young people voluntarily undertake community service designed to help those in need, including elderly and disabled people. Many schools also organise community service work as part of the curriculum.

Further Reading

Education after 16. Aspects of Britain series, HMSO, 1994.
Education Reforms in Schools. Aspects of Britain series, HMSO, 1994.

27 Religion

Everyone in Britain has the right to religious freedom without interference from the community or the State. Religious organisations and groups may own property, conduct ceremonies such as weddings and funerals, run schools, and promote their beliefs in speech and writing. There is no religious bar to the holding of public office.

INTRODUCTION

Most of the world's religions are represented in Britain. There are large Hindu, Jewish, Muslim and Sikh communities, and also smaller communities of Baha'is, Buddhists, Jains and Zorastrians, but Britain is predominantly Christian. Non-religious alternatives for humanists and atheists are offered by organisations such as the British Humanist Association and the National Secular Society, although most humanists and atheists do not belong to organised groups.

Religious Freedom

Britain has a long tradition of religious tolerance. Freedom of conscience in religious matters was achieved gradually from the 17th century onwards. The laws discriminating against minority religious groups were gradually enforced less harshly and then finally repealed. Heresy ceased to be a legal offence with the passage of the Ecclesiastical Jurisdiction Act 1677, and the Toleration Act 1688 granted freedom of worship to Protestant minority groups.

In 1828 the repeal of the Test and Corporation Acts gave nonconformists full political rights, making it possible for them to be appointed to public office. Roman Catholics gained political rights under the Roman Catholic Relief Act 1829, and the Jewish Relief Act 1858 enabled Jews to become Members of Parliament. The religious tests imposed on prospective students and academic staff of the universities of Oxford, Cambridge and Durham were successively abolished by Acts of 1854, 1856 and 1871. Similar restrictions on the staff of Scottish universities were formally removed in 1932.

The past 30 years have seen an increasingly diverse pattern of religious belief and affiliation in Britain. This has been linked both to patterns of immigration and to new religious directions among some of the indigenous population. Social structures have been gradually changing to accommodate this. For example, arrangements are made at many places of work to allow the members of the various faiths to follow their religious observances.

Relations with the State

There are two established churches in Britain, that is, churches legally recognised as official churches of the State: in England the Church of England, and in Scotland the (Presbyterian) Church of Scotland. Ministers of the established churches, as well as clergy belonging to other religious groups, work in services run by the State, such as the armed forces, national hospitals and prisons, and are paid a salary for such services by the State. Voluntary schools provided by religious denominations may be wholly or partly maintained from public funds. Religious education in publicly maintained schools is required by law throughout Britain, as is a daily act of collective worship (see p. 437). Religious broadcasting is subject to some legislative controls (see p. 487).

The State does not contribute to the general expenses of church maintenance, although some state aid does help repair historic churches. In 1994–95, for instance, English Heritage grants to churches totalled £12 million as compared to the £120 million spent on the buildings by parishes. Assistance is also given to meet some of the costs of repairing cathedrals and comparable buildings; some £4 million is being made available in 1995–96. This funding is not restricted to Church of England buildings.

The Government shares with the Church of England the upkeep of nearly 300 churches of special architectural or historic importance which are no longer required for regular parish use and for which no alternative use can be found. The contribution for the period 1994 to 1997 will be about £7.2 million. In 1993 the Historic Chapels Trust was launched, with the aim of preserving the redundant chapels and places of worship of other denominations and faiths.

Involvement in Social Issues

Religious involvement in broader social issues was highlighted in the Church of England report *Faith in the City: A Call for Action by Church and Nation*, published in 1985. This led to the establishment in 1988 of the Church of England's Church Urban Fund, which aims to raise money for the Church's work in inner cities and other priority areas. By June 1994 it had raised over £20.7 million and given grants to 1,176 inner city projects. Organisations belonging to other churches and religious groups are also closely involved with a wide range of social issues.

The Inner Cities Religious Council is a consultative body created by the Department of the Environment in 1992 to advise it on issues relating to Britain's inner cities. The Council aims to provide religious groups with a new way of working together in the inner cities and deprived urban areas. It is chaired by a government minister at the Department of the Environment and its members are drawn from the Christian, Hindu, Jewish, Muslim and Sikh faiths.

Statistics on Religious Affiliation

There is no standard information about the number of members of religious groups since questions are not normally asked about religious beliefs in censuses or for other official purposes, except in Northern Ireland. Each group adopts its own way of counting its members, and the membership figures in this chapter—often supplied by the religious groups themselves—are therefore approximate.

There has been a fall in recent years in the number of full-time ministers and the number of adults recorded as members of most of the larger Christian churches. At the same time there has been significant growth in a range of independent churches, and in new religious movements. Surveys have also revealed that many people who do not belong to religious groups claim to be religious and say they believe in God.

ESTABLISHED CHURCHES

Church of England

The Church of England, founded by St Augustine of Canterbury in AD 597, became the established church during the Reformation in the 16th century. Its form of worship was set out in successive versions of the Book of Common Prayer from 1549 onwards. The Church of England's relationship with the State is one of mutual obligation, since the Church's privileges are balanced by certain duties it must fulfil. People who are not members of the Church of England are entitled to a Church of England wedding or funeral.

The Monarch is the 'Supreme Governor' of the Church of England and must always be a member of the Church, and promise to uphold it. Church of England archbishops, bishops and deans of cathedrals are appointed by the Monarch on the advice of the Prime Minister, although the Crown Appointments Commission, which includes lay and clergy representatives, plays a decisive part in the selection of archbishops and diocesan bishops. All clergy swear allegiance to the Crown. The Church can regulate its own worship. The two archbishops (of Canterbury and York), the bishops of London, Durham and Winchester, and 21 other senior bishops sit in the House of Lords. Clergy of the Church, together with those of the Church of Scotland, the Church of Ireland and the Roman Catholic Church, may not sit in the House of Commons.

The Church has two provinces: Canterbury, comprising 30 dioceses, including the Diocese in Europe; and York, with 14 dioceses. The dioceses are divided into archdeaconries and deaneries, which are in turn divided into about 13,000 parishes, although in practice many of these are grouped together. There are, altogether, about 10,450 full-time stipendiary Church of England clergy—men and women—working within the diocesan structure, excluding mainland Europe. In 1993 an estimated 206,000 people were baptised into the Church in the two provinces, excluding the Diocese in Europe; of these, 160,000 were under one year old, representing 25 per cent of live births. In the same year there were 51,780 confirmations. Attendances at services on a normal Sunday are around 1.1 million. In 1992, 96,828 marriages were solemnised in the Church of England. These accounted for 67 per cent of all marriages with religious ceremonies, and 33 per cent of all marriages in England. Many people who rarely, if ever, attend services still regard themselves as belonging to the Church of England.

The central governing body is the General Synod, which comprises separate houses of bishops, clergy and lay members. Lay people are also concerned with church government in the parishes. The Synod is the centre of an administrative system dealing with such matters as missionary work, inter-church relations, social questions, and recruitment and training for the ministry. It also covers other church work in Britain and overseas, the care of church buildings and their contents, church schools (which are maintained largely from public funds), colleges and institutes of higher education, and voluntary and parish education.

The Church's investment income from historic sources is managed mainly by the Church Commissioners. Most of the remainder of the Church's income is provided by local voluntary donations.

The average annual stipend of a Church of England priest is about £13,450; the average value of additional benefits, including free housing and a non-contributory pension, is estimated to be about £8,322.

In 1992 the General Synod voted in favour of legislation allowing the ordination of women to the priesthood. The measure was subsequently approved by both Houses of Parliament and received the Royal Assent. The first women priests were ordained in 1994 and there are now 800 stipendiary women clergy. The measure also provided for those unable to accept the ordination of women, including the payment of compensation to clergy who feel they have to leave the ministry of the Church. So far nearly 300 clergy have received compensation payments under the measure. Three bishops have been appointed to provide additional pastoral care to those members and parishes of the Church who remain opposed to the ordination of women to the priesthood. Women priests can now be appointed to all offices in the Church except those of archbishop or bishop.

Church of Scotland

The Church of Scotland has a presbyterian form of government, that is, government by church courts, composed of ministers and elders, all of whom are ordained to office, and members of the diaconate. It became the national church following the Scottish Reformation and legislation enacted by the Scottish Parliament. Its status was then consolidated in the Treaty of Union of 1707 and by the Church of Scotland Act 1921, the latter confirming its complete freedom in all spiritual matters. It appoints its own office bearers, and its affairs are not subject to any civil authority.

The adult communicant membership of the Church of Scotland is 715,571; there are about 1,217 ministers serving in parishes. Both men and women may join the ministry. About 1,303 churches are governed locally by Kirk Sessions, consisting of ministers and elders. Above the Kirk Session is the Presbytery. The General Assembly, consisting of elected ministers and elders, meets annually under the presidency of an elected moderator, who serves for one year. The Monarch is normally represented at the General Assembly by the Lord High Commissioner.

There are also a number of independent Scottish Presbyterian churches, largely descended from groups which broke away from the Church of Scotland.

WALES

The Church in Wales became part of the Anglican Church at the Reformation. The Bible was translated into Welsh by Bishop Morgan in 1588. During the 18th and 19th centuries a powerful nonconformist (or Free Church—see below) movement developed throughout Wales: a census of religion in 1851 found that over 80 per cent of those at worship attended a nonconformist chapel. This strength was reflected in the disestablishment of the Church in Wales in 1920. The Church in Wales has around 97,000 members. The Church is responsible for the care of the country's medieval churches and cathedrals; at present only men may join its priesthood.

THE ANGLICAN COMMUNION

The Anglican Communion comprises 36 autonomous Churches in Britain and abroad, and three regional councils overseas with a total membership of about 70 million. In the British Isles there are four Anglican Churches: the Church of England, the Church in Wales, the Scottish Episcopal Church, and the Church of Ireland.

Every ten years the Lambeth Conference meets for consultation between all Anglican bishops. The last Conference was held in Canterbury in 1988. Presided over by the Archbishop of Canterbury, the Conference has no executive authority, but enjoys considerable influence. The Anglican Consultative Council, an assembly of lay people and clergy as well as of bishops, meets every two or three years and is intended to allow consultation within the Anglican Communion. The Primates Meeting brings together the senior bishops from each Church at similar intervals.

FREE CHURCHES

The term 'Free Churches' is often used to describe some of the Protestant churches in Britain which, unlike the Church of England and the Church of Scotland, are not established churches. Free Churches have existed in various forms since the Reformation, developing their own traditions over the years. Their members have also been known as dissenters or nonconformists. All the major Free Churches allow both men and women to become ministers.

The Methodist Church, the largest of the Free Churches, with over 400,000 adult full members and a community of more than 1.2 million, originated in the 18th century following the evangelical revival under John Wesley (1703–91). The present church is based on the 1932 union of most of the separate Methodist Churches. It has 3,600 ministers and 6,950 places of worship.

The Salvation Army was founded in the East End of London in 1865 by William Booth (1829–1912). Within Britain it is second only to the Government as a provider of social services. It is the largest provider of hostel accommodation, offering 3,488 beds every night. Other services include work with alcoholics, prison chaplaincy and a family tracing service which receives 4,935 enquiries each year. The Army in Britain is served by over 1,776 officers (ordained ministers) and runs more than 993 worship centres.

The Baptists first achieved an organised form in Britain in the 17th century. Today they are mainly organised in groups of churches, most of which belong to the Baptist Union of Great Britain (re-formed in 1812), with about 157,000 members, 1,864 ministers and 2,130 places of worship. There are also separate Baptist Unions for Scotland, Wales and Ireland, and other independent Baptist Churches.

The United Reformed Church, with some 106,000 members, 1,800 ministers and 1,800 places of worship, was formed in 1972 following the merger of the Congregational Church in England and Wales (the oldest Protestant minority in Britain, whose origins can be traced back to the Puritans of the 16th century) with the Presbyterian Church of England, many of whose members are descended from Scottish Presbyterians. This was the first union of two different churches in Britain since the Reformation in the 16th century. In 1981 there was a further merger with the Reformed Association of the Churches of Christ.

Among the other Free Churches are the Presbyterian Church in Ireland, the Presbyterian (or Calvinistic Methodist) Church of Wales and the Union of Welsh Independents. There are also groupings of 'Black Majority' Churches.

ROMAN CATHOLIC CHURCH

The formal structure of the Roman Catholic Church in England and Wales, which ceased to exist after the Reformation, was restored in 1850. The Scottish Church's formal structure went out of existence in the early 17th century and was restored in 1878. However, throughout this period Catholicism never disappeared entirely. There are now seven Roman Catholic provinces in Great Britain, each under an archbishop, and 30 dioceses, each under a bishop (22 in England and Wales and eight in Scotland, independently responsible to the Pope). There are almost 3,400 parishes and about 7,000 priests (only men may become priests). Northern Ireland

has six dioceses, some with territory partly in the Irish Republic. About one British citizen in ten claims to be a Roman Catholic. The Pope is represented diplomatically in Britain by an Apostolic Pro-Nuncio.

The Roman Catholic Church attaches great importance to the education of its children and requires its members to try to bring up their children in the Catholic faith. Almost 5 per cent of the teachers in Britain's 2,500 Catholic schools are members of religious orders. These orders also undertake other social work; about 250 Roman Catholic religious orders, congregations and societies are represented in Britain, as are congregations representing about 25 different nationalities who live in Britain. Most Catholic schools are maintained out of public funds.

OTHER CHRISTIAN CHURCHES

Other Protestant Churches include the Unitarians and Free Christians, whose origins are traceable to the Reformation, and the Pentecostalists, whose movement began in the early 20th century. The two main Pentecostalist organisations operating in Britain are the Assemblies of God (approximately 50,000 members) and the Elim Pentecostal Church (approximately 42,000 members). Recently both Pentecostal Churches have applied to join the Free Church Federal Council (see p. 455).

The Religious Society of Friends (Quakers), with about 17,500 adult members in Britain and 450 places of worship, was founded in the middle of the 17th century under the leadership of George Fox (1624–91). Silent worship is central to its life as a religious organisation. Emphasis is also placed on social concern and peace-making.

The Christian Brethren are a Protestant body organised in their present form by J. N. Darby (1800–82). There are two branches: the Open Brethren and the Closed or Exclusive Brethren.

The Christian 'house church' movement (or 'new churches') began in the early 1970s. Services were originally held in private houses but now groups use a variety of hired buildings. These non-denominational congregations may come together as 'streams', of which some of the better known are New Frontiers, Pioneer and Ichthus.

Many Christian communities of foreign origin, including the Orthodox, Lutheran and Reformed Churches of various European countries, and the Coptic Orthodox Church and the Armenian Church, have established their own centres of worship, particularly in London. All these churches operate in a variety of languages. The largest is probably the Greek Orthodox Church, many of whose members are of Cypriot origin. It is represented in many cities throughout Britain.

There are also several other religious organisations in Britain which were founded in the United States in the last century. These include the Jehovah's Witnesses, the Church of Jesus Christ of the Latter-Day Saints (the Mormon Church), the Seventh-Day Adventists, the Christian Scientists and the Spiritualists.

Co-operation among the Churches

The Council of Churches for Britain and Ireland was established in 1990, replacing the former British Council of Churches and taking over its role as the main overall body for the Christian churches in Britain. The Council co-ordinates the work of its 31 member churches, which are also grouped in separate ecumenical bodies for England, Scotland, Wales and Ireland.

The Free Church Federal Council, with 20 member churches, includes most of the Free Churches of England and Wales. It promotes co-operation among the Free Churches (especially in hospital chaplaincy and in education matters) and is a channel for communication with government.

Inter-church discussions about the search for unity now take place through international as well as national bodies. The Roman Catholic, Orthodox and Lutheran Churches are represented on some of these, as are the Anglican and some of the Free Churches. In March 1995 the Church of England and the Methodist Church had an informal meeting to consider moves towards unity.

The Anglican Churches, the Church of Scotland and the main Free Churches are also members of the World Council of Churches. This organisation links some 340 churches in over 100 countries around the world.

OTHER RELIGIONS

The Jewish Community

Jews first settled in England at the time of the Norman Conquest and remained until banished by royal decree in 1290. The present community in Britain dates from 1656, having been founded by those of Spanish and Portuguese origin, known as Sephardim. Later more settlers came from Germany and Eastern Europe; they are known as Ashkenazim.

The present Jewish community in Britain, numbering about 300,000, is the second largest in Western Europe. About 70 per cent are affiliated to synagogues. It is divided into two main groups. Of these, some 77 per cent are Ashkenazi Jews, most of whom acknowledge the authority of the Chief Rabbi. The small Sephardi Orthodox element follow their own spiritual head. The recently established Masorti movement, the Reform movement, founded in 1840, and the Liberal and Progressive movement, established in 1901, account for most of the remaining 23 per cent.

Jewish congregations in Britain number about 350. About one in three Jewish children attend Jewish schools, some of which are supported by public funds. Several agencies care for elderly and handicapped people. The officially recognised representative body is the Board of Deputies of British Jews, which was established in 1760.

The Muslim Community

Figures for the size of the Muslim community in Britain have ranged from three-quarters of a million to 2 million. Recent estimates, based on extrapolations from the 1991 census, suggest the population is around 1.5 million, while estimates from within the Muslim community suggest between 1.5 million and 2 million. The largest number originate from Pakistan and

Bangladesh, while sizeable groups have come from India, Cyprus, the Arab world, Malaysia and parts of Africa. A growing community of British-born Muslims, mainly the children of immigrant parents, includes an increasing number of converts to Islam.

There are over 600 mosques and numerous Muslim prayer centres throughout Britain. Mosques are not only places of worship; they also offer instruction in the Muslim way of life and facilities for educational and welfare activities.

The first mosque in Britain was established at Woking, Surrey, in 1890. Mosques now range from converted houses in many towns to the Central Mosque in Regent's Park, London, and its associated Islamic Cultural Centre, one of the most important Muslim institutions in the Western world. The Central Mosque has the largest congregation in Britain, and during festivals it may number over 30,000. There are also important mosques and cultural centres in Liverpool, Manchester, Leicester, Birmingham, Bradford, Cardiff, Edinburgh and Glasgow.

Many of the mosques are administered by various local Muslim organisations, and both the Sunni and the Shia traditions within Islam are represented among the Muslim community in Britain. Members of some of the major Sufi traditions have also developed branches in British cities. The Ismaili Centre in London provides wide ranging pastoral care and a place of worship for Shi'a Imami Ismaili Muslims, whose current Imam is Prince Karim Aga Khan.

The Sikh Community

A large British Sikh community, of over 300,000, originates mainly from India. The largest groups of Sikhs are in Greater London, Manchester, Birmingham, Nottingham and Wolverhampton. Sikh temples, or gurdwaras, cater for the religious, educational, social welfare and cultural needs of their community. The oldest gurdwara in London was established in 1908 and the largest is in Southall, Middlesex (to the west of London). There are over 140 gurdwaras in Britain.

The Hindu Community

The Hindu community in Britain comprises around 320,000 members and also originates largely from India. The largest groups of Hindus are to be found in Leicester, different areas of London, Birmingham and Bradford. The first Hindu temple, or mandir, was opened in London in 1962 and there are now over 150 mandirs in Britain.

Buddhism

The Buddhist community in Britain consists largely of adherents of British or Western origin. There are well over 400 Buddhist groups and centres, including some 15 monasteries and temples. All the main schools of Buddhism are represented. The Buddhist Society, founded in 1924, promotes the principles of Buddhism; it does not belong to any particular school of Buddhism.

Other Religious Communities

Other religious communities include about 30,000 Jains, whose religion is of ancient Indian origin. A deresar, or Jain temple, opened in Leicester in 1988. The Zoroastrian religion, or Mazdaism, originated in ancient Iran. It is mainly represented in Britain by the Parsi community, who are by origin from the South Asian sub-continent. The Baha'i movement, originating in 19th-century Iran, regards all the major religions as divine in origin; there are an estimated 6,000 Baha'is in Britain.

New Religious Movements

A large number of new religious movements or cults, mainly established since the Second World War and often with overseas origins, are active in Britain. Examples include the Church of Scientology, the Transcendental Meditation movement and the Unification Church (popularly known as the 'Moonies'). In response to public concern about the activities of some of these cults the Government provided start-up funding from

1987 to 1993 for the Information Network Focus on Religious Movements (INFORM), which is a group supported by the main churches. It seeks to provide objective information about new religious movements.

CO-OPERATION BETWEEN FAITHS

A number of organisations exist which seek to develop relations between different religions in Britain. They include the Inter-Faith Network for the United Kingdom, which links a wide range of organisations with an interest in inter-faith relations, including representative bodies from the Baha'i, Buddhist, Christian, Hindu, Jain, Jewish, Muslim, Sikh and Zoroastrian faith communities. Other organisations include the Council of Christians and Jews, which works for better understanding among members of the two religions and deals with issues in the educational and social fields.

Within each faith tradition there are organisations and individuals working to further good relations with other faiths. For example, the Council of Churches for Britain and Ireland (see p. 455) have a Commission on Inter Faith Relations.

Further Reading

Religion. Aspects of Britain series, HMSO, 1992.

Religions in the UK: A Multi-Faith Directory. University of Derby and The Inter-Faith Network for the United Kingdom, 1993.

UK Christian Handbook, 1996–97 ed. Christian Research Association.

28 The Arts

Britain's artistic and cultural life covers a wide range of activities at both professional and amateur level. In 1994 nearly 17 million people attended events in one or more of the major art forms, while Britain's museums and galleries were visited by about 80 million people. In the past ten years cinema admissions have doubled and there has been a steady increase in the popularity of opera.

INTRODUCTION

Britain's artistic and cultural heritage is one of the richest in the world. The origins of English literature, one of the world's most influential bodies of writing, can be traced back to medieval times, while over the centuries Britain has amassed some of the finest collections of works of art. The performing arts also have a long and distinguished history.

London is one of the leading world centres for the arts. Other large cities, including Birmingham, Leeds, Manchester, Edinburgh, Glasgow and Cardiff, have also sustained and developed their reputations as centres of artistic excellence in recent years. Arts festivals attract wide interest. Many British playwrights, craftspeople, composers, film-makers, painters, writers, actors, singers, musicians and dancers enjoy international reputations. They include, for example, Harold Pinter, Sir Colin Davis, Sir Andrew Lloyd Webber, David Hockney, Sir V.S. Naipaul, Vanessa Redgrave and Sir Ian McKellen. Television and radio bring a wide range of arts events

to a large audience. At an amateur level, numerous groups and societies for the arts make use of local talent and resources.

Department of National Heritage

The Secretary of State for National Heritage, who is a member of the Cabinet, is responsible for government policy in support of the arts for England. The Department of National Heritage (see p. 530) determines government policy and administers expenditure on national museums and art galleries in England, the Arts Council of England (see p. 460), the British Library and other national arts and heritage bodies. Other responsibilities include the regulation of the film industry, broadcasting, press regulation, the National Lottery and the export licensing of antiques.

The Secretaries of State for Wales, Scotland and Northern Ireland are responsible for the arts in their countries, including the national museums, galleries and libraries and their respective Arts Councils.

The Government's arts policies aim to:

- develop a high standard of artistic and cultural activity throughout Britain;
- encourage innovation; and
- promote public access to, and appreciation of, the arts, crafts and the cultural heritage.

The Department of National Heritage and the home departments provide funds and advice, and encourage partnership with the private sector, including business sponsorship. National museums and galleries are given an incentive to increase their resources—for example, through trading and other activities. An important concept in funding policy is the 'arm's length' principle, by which government funds are distributed to arts organisations indirectly, through bodies such as the Arts Councils, the British Film Institute and the Scottish Film Council. This principle helps to avoid political influence over funding decisions by ensuring that funds are allocated by those best qualified to do so.

Council of England mainly to support the performing and visual arts; over £80 million goes to the British Library. Grants are also made to the British Film Institute, the Crafts Council, certain other museums and arts bodies, and to the National Heritage Memorial Fund. The Fund helps organisations wishing to acquire, for the public benefit, land, buildings, works of art and other objects associated with the national heritage.

Planned 1995–96 expenditure by the Arts Councils for Scotland, Wales and Northern Ireland is £24.4 million, £14.2 million and £6.6 million respectively. The Scottish Office is providing £45 million for Scotland's National Galleries and Museums and National Library, while the Welsh Office is providing £27 million for Wales's National Museum and National Library. Planned spending by the Department of Education for Northern Ireland on the three major museums there amounts to nearly £9 million in 1995–96.

Local Authorities

Local authorities maintain around 1,000 local museums and art galleries and a network of over 4,000 public libraries. They also support many other arts buildings, arts organisations and artistic events in their areas, providing grant aid for professional and voluntary bodies, including orchestras, theatres, and opera and dance companies. They undertake direct promotions of the arts and contribute to the cost of new or converted buildings for the arts. In England revenue support from local authorities is estimated to be about £190 million a year; arts education in schools, colleges, evening institutes and community centres is the responsibility of central government education departments, in partnership with local education authorities and voluntary bodies. In Scotland revenue support is around £35 million a year.

Finance

Planned central government expenditure through the Department of National Heritage, excluding sport, amounts to £945 million in 1995–96, of which about £191 million is channelled through the Arts

Business Sponsorship

Industrial and commercial companies offer vital sponsorship to a wide range of arts.

Managed by the Association for Business Sponsorship of the Arts (ABSA), the Pairing Scheme aims to encourage businesses in Great Britain to sponsor the arts. Under the scheme, government funding of between £1,000 and £35,000 is awarded to arts organisations to match the sponsorship from private businesses. Launched in 1985, the sponsorship scheme has brought over £87 million into the arts (including a government contribution of £29 million). In 1995–96 the Government is making available £5.5 million to match new sponsorships. A similar scheme exists in Northern Ireland.

Some business sponsorships during 1995 include:
- productions at the English National Opera and Opera Factory in London (British Airways, KPMG and SPERO Communications);

- London City Ballet's *Giselle* (ADT); and
- the National Gallery's Spanish Still Life exhibition (Glaxo).

Among the many business sponsorships that took place around Britain in 1995 were the Cardiff Singer of the World (BP) and Citroën's outdoor concerts at Macclesfield, Warwick Castle, Burghley House (Lincolnshire) and Audley End (Essex).

Under the ABSA's Business in the Arts scheme, the private sector gives part-time management expertise to arts organisations.

Foundation for Sport and the Arts

The Foundation for Sport and the Arts was set up in 1991 by the Pool Promoters Association to channel funds into sport and the arts. About one-third of the £67 million annual revenue is used to benefit the arts and is distributed in the form of awards to a variety of organisations.

National Lottery

The National Lottery (see p. 512) is already beginning to generate substantial funds for the arts and Britain's national heritage. Since the Lottery began in November 1994, grants of over £100 million have been distributed by the Arts Councils and the National Heritage Memorial Fund (see p. 417) to a wide range of arts projects, including:

- £6,640,000 to renovate Cambridge Arts Theatre;

- £40,000 to the Inner Sense Percussion Orchestra (a band specialising in samba, jazz and reggae);

- £609,000 to Isle of Arran Theatre of Arts to convert a church into an arts centre; and

- £135,000 to the Yorkshire Air Museum in Elvington.

Substantial funding is also to be channelled into the British film industry (see p. 469).

Arts Councils

The main channels for government aid to the arts are the independent Arts Councils of England, Scotland, Wales and Northern Ireland.

The aims of the Arts Councils are to:

- develop and improve the knowledge, understanding and practice of the arts;

- make the arts more accessible to the public; and

- advise and co-operate with central government departments, local authorities and other organisations.

The Arts Councils give financial help and advice to organisations ranging from the major arts centres and opera, dance and drama companies to small touring theatre companies and experimental performance groups. They also provide funds for the training of arts administrators and help arts organisations to develop other sources of income, including sponsorship and local authority support. They encourage a variety of art forms, including ballet and contemporary dance, drama, mime, literature, music, opera and photography, and help professional creative writers, dramatists, choreographers, dancers, actors, musicians, composers, artists and photographers. The Councils also promote art exhibitions and tours of arts events and performances, make funds available for some specialist training courses in the arts and promote the work of artists in education. Emphasis is being placed on obtaining funds through partnership arrangements with local authorities and other agencies, and from commercial sources.

Arts Funding

In England the Arts Council and ten Regional Arts Boards comprise the integrated arts funding system. Together, they aim to ensure that a wide range of high-quality arts is accessible to people across the country. The Regional Arts Boards offer financial assistance to artists and arts organisations and advise on, and sometimes help to promote, arts activities. They are financed mainly by the Arts Council of England, with smaller sums from the British Film Institute and Crafts Council, as well as from local authorities. The Boards also concentrate on business development and sponsorship and many have established 'Business in the Arts' schemes in their areas. Through a system of forward planning and budgeting, the Boards are accountable to their national funders. One-third of the members of each Board are nominated by local authorities. Boards also include representatives of the regional business community as well as others with expertise and interest in the arts.

The Boards are responsible for most of the funding of organisations within their region. The Arts Council of England continues to be responsible for the funding of the national companies—Royal Opera, Royal Ballet and the Birmingham Royal Ballet, the English National Opera, the Royal Shakespeare Company, the Royal National Theatre and the South Bank Centre. It is also responsible for touring companies without a regional base and for other arts organisations which have a national strategic role.

Cultural Diversity and Disability

The arts activities undertaken by Britain's diverse communities embrace both traditional and new forms of artistic expression. The Arts Council of England is establishing specialist programmes to make the arts more accessible to specific communities, to develop the knowledge, understanding and practice of diversity in the arts, and to increase involvement in a wide range of arts.

Black and Asian Arts

The Arts Council of England and the Regional Arts Boards jointly support the National Black Arts Network, a group of individuals and agencies which is helping to develop an infrastructure for black and Asian arts across England. The Arts Council also supports other umbrella organisations, including Asian Arts Access and ADiTi, and has helped in the setting up of the Institute of International Visual Arts. This body supports, for example, Afro-Caribbean and Asian music circuits, an education officer in South Asian music, a funding programme for black video and film-makers and the development of black theatre companies.

Arts and Disability

The Arts Council of England has access to experts in disability arts, and all its art-form advisory panels include disabled representatives. The Council has a bulletin on quality of service for disabled people which provides practical information and advice for Council and Regional Arts Boards staff. Funding agreements with arts organisations state that they must have an equal opportunities policy; they are also encouraged to adopt the code of practice on employment issued by the Equal Opportunities Commission (see p. 37).

The National Disability Arts Forum and other national agencies are funded by the Arts Council of England, as are creative organisations, such as Candoco and Graeae. The Council also supports an apprenticeship scheme for disabled people in major arts organisations, such as the Royal Shakespeare Company, which is part of an initiative aimed at increasing employment opportunities in the arts for disabled people.

Other schemes supported by the Arts Council of England include an audit of deaf arts conducted by Deafworks and projects involving disabled artists in schools. The Scottish Arts Council supports Art Link and Project Ability, which provide opportunities for people with disabilities to develop creativity in a range of art forms.

The provision of access for the disabled to arts buildings is a basic criterion for all grants made from the National Lottery (see p. 460).

Arts Centres

Over 200 arts centres in Britain give people the chance of enjoying and taking part in a range of activities, with educational projects becoming increasingly important. Nearly all arts centres are professionally managed and most are supported by volunteer groups. They are assisted mainly by Regional Arts Boards and local authorities, while the Arts Council of England funds two national centres—the South Bank Centre and the Institute of Contemporary Arts. Many theatres and art galleries also provide a focal point for the community by making available facilities for other arts.

The British Council

The British Council (see p. 134) is Britain's international network for culture, development and education, and maintains libraries (including film libraries) in many of the 109 countries in which it is represented. The Visiting Arts Office, an autonomous body administered by the British Council, fosters an appreciation and understanding of the arts of other countries. It acts as a broker between Britain and overseas arts organisations, advises on touring matters and makes awards for projects.

Broadcasting

BBC radio and television and the independent companies (see Chapter 29) broadcast a wide variety of drama, opera, ballet and music, as well as general arts magazine programmes and documentaries. These have won many international awards at festivals such as the Prix Italia and Montreux International Television Festivals. Independent television companies also make grants for arts promotion in their regions.

Broadcasting is a major medium for making the arts available to the public and is a crucial source of work for actors, musicians, writers, composers, technicians and others in the arts world. It has created its own forms—nothing like arts documentaries or drama series, for instance, exists in any other medium. Broadcasters commission and produce a vast quantity of new work. Television and radio provide critical debate, information and education about the arts.

The BBC has six orchestras, which employ many of Britain's full-time professional musicians. Each week it broadcasts about 100 hours of classical and other music (both live and recorded) on its Radio 3 (FM) channel. BBC Radio 1 (FM) broadcasts rock and pop music 24 hours a day, and a large part of the output of BBC Radio 2 (FM) is popular and light music. There are at present two national commercial radio stations which broadcast music:

● Classic FM, which broadcasts mainly classical music; and

● Virgin 1215, which plays broad-based rock music.

Much of the output of Britain's local radio stations consists of popular and light music.

The BBC regularly commissions new music, particularly by British composers, and sponsors concerts, competitions and festivals. Each summer it presents and broadcasts the BBC Promenade Concerts (the 'Proms'), the world's largest music festival, at the Royal Albert Hall.

The Press

Many national and local newspapers devote considerable space to coverage of the arts, and developments in the arts are also covered in periodicals such as the *Spectator* and *New Statesman and Society* (see Chapter 29). Weekly 'listings' magazines, including *Time Out*, provide details of cultural and other events in London and other large cities.

There are also a large number of specialist publications which cover specific aspects of the arts, including *Classical Music*, *Art Monthly*, *Dance Theatre Journal* and *Opera*. A number of publications publish original literature, including the *London Magazine* and *Granta*, which publishes fiction as well as cultural journalism. *New Musical Express (NME)* and *Melody Maker* cover rock and pop music. The newspaper *Stage and Television Today* is directed at professional actors and others in the industry.

Festivals

Some 650 professional arts festivals take place in Britain each year. The annual Edinburgh International Festival, featuring a wide range of arts, is held in August and September and is the largest of its kind in the world. Other festivals held in Edinburgh include the annual International Jazz Festival, the International Film and Television Festivals and the biennial Book Festival. The international arts Mayfest takes place in Glasgow. Some well-known festivals concentrating on music are the Three Choirs Festival, which has taken place annually for more than 260 years in Gloucester, Worcester or Hereford; the Cheltenham International Festival of Music, largely devoted to contemporary British music; and the Aldeburgh festival.

Among other festivals catering for a number of art forms are the Royal National Eisteddfod of Wales, the Royal National Gaelic Mod in Scotland, the Belfast Festival at Queen's University, and the festivals in Brighton, Buxton, Chester, St Davids, Harrogate, Llangollen, Malvern, Perth, and York. Many smaller towns also hold arts festivals. A major event in London is the Notting Hill Carnival, which is largely organised by the Afro-Caribbean community.

Arts 2000

Arts 2000 is an Arts Council initiative which celebrates the approach of the millennium. During each year between 1992 and 2000, a city, town or region in Britain has been nominated to celebrate a particular art form. Manchester was the City of Drama in 1994, while Swansea was the City of Literature in 1995. The Northern Region is the Region of Visual Arts for 1996. Future years have been designated as follows:

- the Eastern Region as the Region of Opera and Musical Theatre for 1997;
- Yorkshire and Humberside as the Region of Photography and the Electronic Image for 1998; and
- Glasgow as the City of Architecture and Design for 1999.

Arts 2000 is a competitive process judged by expert Arts Council selection committees. Winners are offered £350,000 from Arts Council funds, and are expected to match this to create a wide-ranging and imaginative programme with a strong European context.

DRAMA

Britain is one of the world's major centres for theatre, and has a long and rich dramatic tradition. There are many companies based in London and in many other cities and towns; in addition, numerous touring companies visit theatres, festivals and other venues, including arts and sports centres and social clubs. There were more than 250 companies in receipt of Arts Council or Regional Arts Boards subsidies in 1994–95.

Contemporary British playwrights who have received international recognition, with examples of their works, include:

- Harold Pinter—*The Caretaker, The Homecoming*;
- Alan Bennett—*The Madness of George III*;
- Tom Stoppard—*Arcadia, Indian Ink*;
- Caryl Churchill—*Top Girls, The Skriker*; and
- David Hare—*The Absence of War, Skylight*.

The musicals of Sir Andrew Lloyd Webber have been highly successful both in Britain and overseas; his more recent works are *The Phantom of the Opera* and *Sunset Boulevard*.

Among the best-known directors are Sir Peter Hall, Richard Eyre, Nicholas Hytner, Trevor Nunn, Adrian Noble, Jonathan Miller, Deborah Warner and Terry Hands, while the many British performers who enjoy international reputations include Kenneth Branagh, Dame Judi Dench, Albert Finney, Sir John Gielgud, Sir Alec Guinness, Sir Derek Jacobi, Sir Ian McKellen, Helen Mirren, Vanessa Redgrave, Dame Diana Rigg, Dame Maggie Smith and Juliet Stephenson. British stage designers such as John Bury, Ralph Koltai and Carl Toms are internationally acclaimed.

Britain has about 300 theatres intended for professional use which can seat between 200 and 2,300 people. Some are privately owned, but most are owned either municipally or by non-profit-making organisations. Over 40 of these have resident theatre companies receiving subsidies from the Arts Councils and Regional Arts Boards. In summer there are also open air theatres, including one in London's Regent's Park and the Minack Theatre, which is on a clifftop near Land's End in Cornwall.

Most theatres are commercially run and self-financing, relying on popular shows and musicals to be profitable. By contrast, companies funded by the Arts Councils tend to offer a variety of traditional and experimental productions. Experimental or innovative work is often staged in 'fringe' theatres in London and other cities; these are smaller theatres which use a variety of buildings, such as rooms in pubs.

London

London has about 100 theatres, 15 of them permanently occupied by subsidised companies. These include:

- the Royal National Theatre, which stages a wide range of modern and classical plays in its three auditoriums on the South Bank;
- the Royal Shakespeare Company, which presents plays mainly by Shakespeare and his contemporaries as well as some modern work, in Stratford-upon-Avon and in its two auditoriums in the City's Barbican Centre—from 1996 the Company is also to tour other parts of Britain for six months of the year; and
- the English Stage Company at the Royal Court Theatre in Sloane Square, which stages the work of many new playwrights.

The largest concentration of London's commercial theatres is around Shaftesbury Avenue. West End theatre attendance was over 11 million in 1994; over half of these went to musicals.

In 1989 the partial remains of the Globe Theatre, where Shakespeare acted, and the Rose Theatre, where his plays were performed during his lifetime, were excavated on the south bank of the Thames; both have since been listed as ancient monuments. A

Table 28.1: Attendances at West End Theatres, 1993 and 1994

| | Percentage | |
Type of Performance	1993	1994
Modern musicals	48	43
Modern drama	8	10
Traditional musicals	11	14
Classical plays	12	11
Comedy	6	6
Opera/operetta	6	6
Ballet/dance	4	3
Thrillers/others	2	2
Revue/variety	1	2
Children's shows/ pantomimes	1	1

Source: *The Society of London Theatre Box Office Data Report 1994*

modern reconstruction of the Globe Theatre, near its original site, is in progress and is due for completion in 1996.

Regional Theatres

Outside London most cities and many large towns have at least one theatre. Older theatres which have been restored include the Theatre Royal, Newcastle upon Tyne, which dates from the 18th century; the Alhambra, Bradford; the Lyceum, Sheffield; the Theatre Royal, Bristol; and the Grand Opera House, Belfast, all dating from the 19th century. Others, such as the West Yorkshire Playhouse, Leeds, and the Theatre Royal, Plymouth, have been built to modern designs. Edinburgh's rebuilt and restored Empire Theatre, reopened as the Edinburgh Festival Theatre in 1994, provides an international venue for large-scale productions. A custom-built theatre for new writing recently became the new home of the Traverse Theatre in Edinburgh. Several universities have theatres which house professional companies playing to the public.

Most regional repertory companies mount about eight to ten productions a year; several have studio theatres in addition to the main auditorium, where they present new or experimental drama and plays of specialist interest. Repertory theatres also often function as social centres by offering concerts, poetry readings and exhibitions, and by providing restaurants, bars and shops.

Regional theatre companies with major reputations include the Citizens' Theatre, Glasgow; the Royal Exchange, Manchester; Bristol Old Vic; West Yorkshire Playhouse; the Festival Theatre, Chichester; and Nottingham Playhouse, one of the first modern regional theatres. Successful productions from regional theatre companies often transfer to London's West End. In addition, the largest regional theatres receive visits from the Royal National Theatre or the Royal Shakespeare Company, which has three theatres at its base in Stratford-upon-Avon. The Cambridge Theatre Company, Oxford Stage Company and English Touring Theatre Company tour the English regions and worldwide.

Theatre for Young People

Unicorn Theatre for Children and Polka Children's Theatre, both in London, present plays specially written for children; and the Whirligig Theatre tours throughout Britain. The Young Vic Company in London and Contact Theatre Company in Manchester stage plays for young people. Numerous Theatre-in-Education companies perform in schools. Some of these companies operate independently—Theatre Centre, for example, plays in London and tours further afield. Others are attached to regional repertory theatres such as the Wolsey Theatre, Ipswich, and Greenwich Theatre. Most regional repertory theatres also mount productions for younger audiences, and concessionary ticket prices are generally available for those at school, college or university. The first Festival of Theatre for Children and Young People took place in London in 1995.

There has been a marked growth in youth theatres, which number more than 500 in England alone; both the National Youth Theatre in London and the Scottish Youth Theatre in Glasgow offer early acting opportunities to young people.

Dramatic Training

Training for actors, directors, lighting and sound technicians and stage managers is provided mainly in drama schools, among them the Royal Academy of Dramatic Art (RADA), the Central School of Speech and Drama, the London Academy of Music and Dramatic Art, and the Drama Centre (all in London), the Bristol Old Vic School, the Royal Scottish Academy of Music and Drama (Glasgow) and the Welsh College of Music and Drama (Cardiff). Theatre design courses, often based in art schools, are available for people wanting to train as stage designers. A number of universities and colleges offer degree courses in drama.

Amateur Theatre

There are several thousand amateur dramatic societies throughout Britain. They use a variety of buildings, including schools and public halls. Their work is encouraged by a number of organisations, such as the Central Council for Amateur Theatre, the National Drama Conference, the Scottish Community Drama Association and the Association of Ulster Drama Festivals. A nationwide representative body, the Voluntary Arts Network, was established in 1991. Amateur companies sometimes receive financial support from local government and other bodies.

MUSIC

People in Britain are interested in a wide range of music, from classical to different forms of rock and pop music. Jazz, folk and world music, and brass bands also have substantial followings.

The fourth National Music Day took place in June 1995. Over 1,500 separate events were organised, ranging from musical fêtes and marathons to activities involving local churches, schools and charities.

Orchestral and Choral Music

Seasons of orchestral and choral concerts are promoted every year in many large towns and cities. The principal concert halls in central London are the Royal Festival Hall in the South Bank Centre, next to which are the Queen Elizabeth Hall and the Purcell Room, which accommodate smaller scale performances; the Barbican Hall (part of the Barbican Centre for Arts and Conferences in the City of London); the Royal Albert Hall in Kensington; the Wigmore Hall, a recital centre; and St John's, Smith Square. Birmingham has its own recently built concert hall, the Symphony Hall, and a 2,400-seat international concert hall is being erected for Manchester's Hallé Orchestra.

The leading symphony orchestras in London include the London Symphony, the Philharmonia, the London Philharmonic, the Royal Philharmonic and the BBC Symphony. Important regional orchestras include the Royal Liverpool Philharmonic, the Hallé, the City of Birmingham Symphony, the Bournemouth Symphony, the Ulster, and the Royal Scottish National Orchestras and the BBC National Orchestra of Wales. The BBC's six orchestras give broadcast concerts which are often open to the public. There are also chamber orchestras, such as the City of London Sinfonia, the Academy of St Martin-in-the-Fields, Northern Sinfonia, the Bournemouth Sinfonietta and the Scottish Chamber Orchestra. Specialised ensembles include the Orchestra of the Age of Enlightenment, the English Baroque Soloists and the English Concert. The London Sinfonietta and the Birmingham Contemporary Music Group specialise in contemporary music.

British conductors such as Sir Colin Davis, Vernon Handley, Sir Charles Mackerras, John Eliot Gardiner, Andrew Davis, Sir Simon Rattle, Christopher Hogwood, Jane Glover, and Richard Hickox reach a wide audience through their recordings as well as by their performances. The works of living composers such as Sir Michael Tippett, Sir Peter Maxwell Davies and Sir Harrison Birtwistle enjoy international acclaim. Other well-established British composers include Michael Berkeley, John Tavener, Sir Malcolm Arnold, Oliver Knussen, Nicola le Fanu, George Lloyd, David Matthews, Mark Anthony Turnage, John Casken and Judith Weir. The Master of the Queen's Music, Malcolm Williamson, holds an office within the Royal Household with responsibility for organising and writing music for state occasions. Percussionist Evelyn Glennie and clarinettist Emma Johnson are among solo performers currently enjoying great acclaim.

The principal choral societies include the Bach Choir, the Royal Choral Society, the Huddersfield Choral Society, the Cardiff Polyphonic Choir, the Edinburgh International Festival Chorus and the Belfast Philharmonic Society. Almost all the leading orchestras maintain their own choral societies. The English tradition of church singing is represented by choirs such as those of King's College Chapel, Cambridge, and Christ Church Cathedral, Oxford, while other choirs such as the Roman Catholic Westminster Cathedral choir are also well known. There are many male-voice choirs in Wales and in certain parts of England.

Pop and Rock Music

Hundreds of hours of pop and rock music are broadcast through BBC and independent radio stations every week. Television programmes of both live and recorded music also feature pop and rock, which is by far the most popular form of music in Britain. This covers a diversity of styles, ranging from dance to heavy metal.

In the 1960s and 1970s groups such as the Beatles, the Rolling Stones, Led Zeppelin and Pink Floyd achieved international success. British groups continue to be popular throughout the world and are often at the forefront of new developments in music.

The British record industry recognises the most talented British performers at the annual Brit Awards. These were dominated in 1995 by Blur, who won a record four categories, including best British group and best album (*Parklife*). Other winners were Paul Weller (best British male solo artist), Eddi Reader (best British female artist), M People (best dance act) and Oasis (best British newcomer). Other nominated artists included Eternal, Prodigy, Portishead, Des'ree and Lisa Stansfield. Great success has also been achieved in recent years by Take That, Wet Wet Wet and East 17, whose lead singer—Tony Mortimer—won the Ivor Novello Songwriter of the Year Award in 1995.

The pop and rock music industry contributes significantly to Britain's overseas earnings through the sale of recordings, concert tours, and promotional material, including clothing and books. The recording industry in Britain has an estimated annual turnover of £1,000 million.

Jazz

Jazz has a large following in Britain and is played in numerous clubs and pubs. There is also a jazz radio station, Jazz FM, which began broadcasting in 1991. The London Jazz Festival attracts international stars, such as the bandleader Django Bates, saxophonists Pharoah Saunders and Joshua Redman, and the singer Jean Carn. British musicians such as Barbara Thompson, Stan Tracey, Julian Joseph, David Jean Baptiste, Tommy Smith and Courtney Pine have established international reputations. Festivals of jazz music are held throughout Britain, including Cardiff Bay, Brecon, Edinburgh, Glasgow and Birmingham.

Training

Professional training in music is given mainly at colleges of music. The leading London colleges are the Royal Academy of Music, the Royal College of Music, the Guildhall School of Music and Drama, and Trinity College of Music. The City University's music industry course provides training in business practice aimed specifically at musicians and music administrators. Outside London the main centres are the Royal Scottish Academy of Music and Drama in Glasgow, the Royal Northern College of Music in Manchester, the Welsh College of Music and Drama, Cardiff, and the Birmingham Conservatoire. Many universities also offer courses in music.

Other Educational Schemes

Many children learn to play musical instruments at school, and some take the examinations of the Associated Board of the Royal Schools of Music. Music is one of the foundation subjects in the National Curriculum (see p. 435). In Scottish schools music and the expressive arts are also well developed. The National Youth Orchestras of Great Britain, Scotland, Ulster and Wales, and other youth orchestras have established high standards. Nearly a third of the players in the European Community Youth Orchestra come from Britain. There is also a National Youth Jazz Orchestra.

Youth and Music, an organisation affiliated to the international *Jeunesses Musicales*, encourages attendance by young people at opera, dance and concert performances.

OPERA

Interest in opera has been growing markedly in Britain, with an estimated 3 million of the adult population attending opera performances in 1994: some 25 per cent more than in 1986.

A number of British singers—Thomas Allen, Anne Evans, Philip Langridge, Felicity Lott, Ann Murray and Bryn Terfel, for example— have now established themselves in the international opera houses.

> An opera season for which international casts are specially assembled is held every summer at Glyndebourne in East Sussex. This is followed by an autumn tour by Glyndebourne Touring Opera, using casts drawn from the chorus of the festival season. Since 1994 the summer season at Glyndebourne has taken place in a new enlarged 1,200-seat opera house, built at a cost of £33 million. All the funding came from private sources.

Regular seasons of opera are held at the Royal Opera House, Covent Garden, London. The English National Opera stages opera in English at the London Coliseum. Scottish Opera has regular seasons at the Theatre Royal in Glasgow, and tours mainly in Scotland and northern England. Welsh National Opera presents seasons in Cardiff and other cities; Music Theatre Wales has become well known for its contemporary work. Leeds-based Opera North tours primarily in the north of England and has gained an international reputation. Opera Factory in London presents experimental work in opera and music theatre. English Touring Opera takes opera to towns throughout England. Opera Northern Ireland presents seasons at the Grand Opera House, Belfast, and tours the province.

The National Opera Studio provides advanced training for young singers.

DANCE

An estimated 6 million people take part in dance, making it one of Britain's leading participatory activities, and audiences are attracted to a widening range of professional dance.

The Royal Ballet and the Birmingham Royal Ballet, English National Ballet, Northern Ballet Theatre and Rambert

Dance Company rank among the world's leading companies and are supported by professional orchestras.

Subsidised Dance Companies

Subsidised dance companies include the Birmingham (formerly Sadler's Wells) Royal Ballet, which tours widely in Britain and overseas; English National Ballet, which divides its performances between London and the regions; Northern Ballet Theatre, which is based in Halifax and also tours; and Scottish Ballet, based in Glasgow. Other subsidised companies are the Cardiff-based Diversions Dance Company and the Dundee Repertory Dance Company.

The Arts Councils also subsidise a wide range of other companies and dance organisations, including Rambert Dance Company (one of Britain's leading contemporary dance companies), Adzido Pan African Dance Ensemble, Shobana Jeyasingh Dance Company and Richard Alston Dance Company. Also subsidised is Dance Umbrella, which promotes an annual festival of contemporary dance in London. The Arts Councils and the Regional Arts Boards support many smaller companies, such as the Phoenix Dance Company, Adventures in Motion Pictures and the Candoco Dance Company.

Matthew Bourne, Christopher Bruce, Richard Alston, Lloyd Newson, Ashley Page, Shobana Jeyasingh, Siobhan Davies, Neville Campbell and Jonathan Burrows are among the foremost British choreographers. Leading dancers include Darcey Bussell, Marion Tait, Gill Clarke, Adam Cooper and Deborah Bull.

Training

Professional training for dancers and choreographers is provided mainly by specialist schools, which include the Royal Ballet School, the Central School of Ballet, the Northern School of Contemporary Dance (Leeds) and the London Contemporary Dance School; these, with many private schools, have helped in raising British dance to its present standard. Dance is a subject for degree studies at a number of institutions, including the Laban Centre (University of London), the University of Surrey, Dartington College of Arts in Devon and Middlesex University.

Courses for students intending to work with community groups are available at several institutions. The Royal Ballet is running a scheme that aims to widen access to ballet training for children from a broader range of cultural backgrounds.

National Dance Agencies

A network of agencies for professional and amateur dancers has been established in Birmingham, Leeds, Nottingham, London, Newcastle upon Tyne, Swindon and Suffolk. The agencies, which receive Arts Council support, offer classes, provide information and advice, help to co-ordinate activities, and commission dance artists to create work. All ten Regional Arts Board areas have a national dance agency or are preparing to set one up.

Other Educational Schemes

The Arts Council of England runs Taped, a scheme to finance dance videos for use in education, while the Video Place provides a library of videotape documentation of dance performances for viewing by promoters, choreographers, dancers, teachers and students. The Scottish Arts Council supports Dance Base, which offers a range of classes in dance.

All government-funded dance companies provide dance workshops and education activities. Many have won awards for major projects, such as Phoenix Dance Company's 'Urban Exchange' and English National Ballet's 'Striking a Balance'. Ludus Dance Company, based in Lancaster, works mainly with young people; and Scottish Ballet has a programme of work in schools in Scotland. The Performing Arts and Technology School in Croydon, Surrey, offers studies in drama, music and dance to pupils aged from 14 to 18, with the emphasis on the application of technology to the performing arts.

The National Youth Dance Company provides opportunities for young dancers to work with professionals and to create and perform dance. Similar opportunities exist for young people to join youth dance companies throughout the country.

FILMS

British films, actors, and producers as well as the creative and technical services supporting them are widely acclaimed. British performers who enjoy international reputations include Kenneth Branagh, Michael Caine, Sean Connery, Ralph Fiennes, Hugh Grant, Sir Anthony Hopkins, Jeremy Irons, Liam Neeson, Miranda Richardson, Alan Rickman, Greta Scacchi and Emma Thompson. Successful British directors include Alan Parker, Mike Newell, Mike Leigh, Sally Potter and Ken Loach. The award-winning *Four Weddings and a Funeral*, which was released in 1994, has become the most successful British film ever. Funded by Channel 4, it has grossed more than £160 million worldwide.

There are about 1,800 cinema screens in Britain, and estimated attendances are currently running at about 1.9 million a week. Seating capacity in cinemas increased during the late 1980s, due almost entirely to the rise in the number of multi-screen cinema complexes.

Cinema admissions in 1994 were 124 million—twice as many as in 1984. In London and other large cities a number of art or repertory cinemas show films which have not been more widely distributed. These include low-budget films from Britain and abroad; other foreign films, often with English subtitles; and older films which are being shown again, sometimes in a newly edited form. Arts centres often include cinemas, and film societies use a range of buildings including, for example, public libraries.

Animation

The resurgence of interest in animation in Britain is due in part to the pioneering work of British animators, who have created 3D animation and computer animation. British animated films have won four Oscars in recent years, including in 1994 Nick Park's *The Wrong Trousers* (BBC-commissioned) and in 1995 a 'short' by David Fine and Alison Snowdon called *Bob's Birthday* for Channel 4.

Television has proved an important source of production finance. Welsh television channel S4C, for example, funded *Operavox*, a six-part series of half-hour animated films of famous operas sung by Welsh National Opera.

Government Support

An annual government grant of about £17 million is made to the British Film Institute and one of over £1 million to the Scottish Film Council and the Scottish Film Production Fund. Since 1993 Britain has been a member of Eurimages, the Council of Europe's film co-production support scheme, contributing approximately £5.5 million over the first three years of membership. Eurimages aims to develop the European cinema and audio-visual industry by providing financial support for feature-length fiction films, creative documentaries and distribution. Since 1993, 32 productions with British participation have received loans worth about £8 million.

In addition, more than £80 million from the National Lottery (see p. 460) will be provided by the Arts Council of England to support film-making over the next five years.

British Film Commission

The British Film Commission was launched in 1991, with government funding of £3.5 million over four years. The Commission aims to attract film productions from overseas by offering a service to assist film-makers. Fifteen foreign-produced films went into production in Britain in 1994.

The Government is also to contribute funding to help create a London Film Commission. This will complement the work of the British Film Commission and will attempt to attract film productions to the capital.

British Screen Finance

British Screen Finance, a private sector company, provides finance for new film-makers with commercially viable productions who have difficulty in attracting funding. The company, investing its own money together with contributions from the

Government, part-finances the production of low- and medium-budget films involving largely British talent. It encourages the early stages of film project development and the production of short films. The Government funds the company with £2 million a year. British Screen supported 15 films in 1994. Successful films include *Naked*, *Camilla* and *An Awfully Big Adventure*.

European Co-Production Fund

Funded by the Government with £2 million a year, the European Co-Production Fund (ECPF) offers loans of up to 30 per cent of a film's budget, enabling British producers to collaborate in the making of films in Europe. It has invested £6.5 million in 19 feature films. In 1994 the ECPF-funded film *Before the Rain* was the winner at the Venice Film Festival.

British Film Institute

The development of film, video and television as art forms is promoted by the British Film Institute (BFI) and in Scotland by the Scottish Film Council. The BFI offers some direct financial and technical help through its Production Board.

The BFI runs the National Film Theatre in London and the National Film and Television Archive, and has the world's largest library of information on film and television. It holds extensive international collections of books, periodicals, scripts, stills and posters. Its Education Department aims to enable as many people as possible to discover new ways of appreciating film, video and television.

The National Film and Television Archive contains over 200,000 films and television programmes, including newsreels, dating from 1895. BFI South Bank comprises the Museum of the Moving Image, which traces the history of film and television, and the National Film Theatre. The latter has three cinemas showing films of historical, artistic or technical interest, and is unique in offering regular programmes unrestricted by commercial considerations. In November each year it hosts the London Film Festival,

at which some 250 new films from all over the world are screened.

The BFI promotes, and helps to fund, a network of 35 regional film theatres, and is involved in establishing film and television centres with a range of activities and facilities. It also co-operates with the Regional Arts Boards and grant-aids their film work.

The Wales Film Council acts as the BFI's agent in Wales, and also receives funding from the Arts Council of Wales. The BFI's charter extends to Northern Ireland, where the BFI works with the Northern Ireland Film Council (NIFC). The NIFC receives funds from the Arts Council of Northern Ireland.

Scottish Film Council

The Scottish Film Council supports regional film theatres, promotes and provides material for media education and administers the Scottish Film Archive. Financial assistance to develop film scripts is available through the Scottish Film Production Fund. Scottish Screen Locations provides advice to film makers on suitable locations for film-productions in Scotland.

Children's Film

The Children's Film and Television Foundation produces and distributes entertainment films for children, shown largely through video and television.

The Children's Film Unit makes feature films for children (mainly for Channel 4) and runs weekly workshops for children on all aspects of film-making. The Unit caters for about 80 children at any time and has produced 14 feature films.

The Northern Ireland Film Council runs Cinemagic, an award-winning international film festival for young people.

Training in Film Production

The National Film and Television School is financed jointly by the Government and by the film, video and television industries. It offers postgraduate and short course training for directors, editors, camera operators, animators and other specialists. The School enrols about 30 full-time students a year and about 500 on short course programmes. In 1995–96 it is receiving a government grant of £1.85 million. The School is to move from its present location in Buckinghamshire to the BBC film studios at Ealing.

The London International Film School, the Royal College of Art, and some universities and other institutions of higher education also offer training in film production.

Cinema Licensing and Film Classification

Cinemas showing films to the public must be licensed by local authorities, which have a legal duty to prohibit the admission of children under 16 to unsuitable films, and may prevent the showing of any film. In assessing films the authorities normally rely on the judgment of an independent non-statutory body, the British Board of Film Classification (BBFC), to which films must be submitted. The Board was set up on the initiative of the cinema industry to ensure a proper standard in films shown to the public. It does not use any written code of censorship, but can require cuts to be made before granting a certificate; on rare occasions, it refuses a certificate.

Films passed by the Board are put into one of the following categories:

- U (universal)—suitable for all;
- PG (parental guidance), in which some scenes may be unsuitable for young children;
- 12, 15 and 18, for people of not less than those ages; and
- Restricted 18, for restricted showing only at segregated premises to which no one under 18 is admitted—for example, licensed cinema clubs.

Videos

The BBFC is also legally responsible for classifying videos under a system similar to that for films. It is an offence to supply commercially a video which has not been classified or to supply it in contravention of its classification—for example, to sell or hire a video classified 18 to a person under the age of 18.

VISUAL ARTS

State support for the visual arts consists largely of funding for the national museums and galleries, purchase grants for municipal museums and galleries, and funding through local authorities, the Museums and Galleries Commission and the area museum councils. It also includes funding for the production, exhibition and distribution of work by contemporary artists and photographers and for the promotion of art to the public, channelled through the Arts Councils, the Crafts Council and the Regional Arts Boards, and grants towards the cost of art education. The Government encourages high standards of industrial design and craftsmanship through grants to the Design Council (see p. 206).

All national museums and galleries are financed chiefly from government funds. They may charge for entry to their permanent collections and special exhibitions. All the national collections are managed by independent trustees.

Museums and art galleries maintained by local authorities, universities, independent museums and private funds may receive help in building up their collections through grants administered by the Museums and Galleries Commission (for England) and the Museum Councils in Scotland, Wales and Northern Ireland. Support to national and regional public and independent museums and galleries is also given by the Arts Councils and by trusts and voluntary bodies, including the Henry Moore Foundation, the Calouste Gulbenkian Foundation and the National Art Collections Fund. National Lottery proceeds are being distributed in the form of capital grants by the National Heritage Memorial Fund, the Arts Councils and the Millennium Commission.

The National Heritage Memorial Fund also distributes grants for the purchase of works of art and items of national significance. In recent years, for example, the Fund has helped towards the acquisition of masterpieces by Hans Holbein and

Jacques-Louis David (bought by the National Gallery) and by El Greco (the National Gallery of Scotland).

Pre-eminent works of art are accepted by the Government in place of inheritance tax and are allocated to public galleries; items thus acquired in 1994–95 include paintings by Francis Bacon, Marc Chagall and the Elizabethan miniaturist Nicholas Hilliard.

In collaboration with the Regional Arts Boards, the Arts Council of England provides some strategic funding for galleries; educational institutions from art schools and universities to schools; commercial galleries and publishers; artists' agencies; and media centres. It also supports touring exhibitions and the presentation of works of art in a variety of public spaces. The Arts Council of England's unique collection of 20th century British art, with the National Touring Exhibition Service, is managed on its behalf by the South Bank Board, which also runs the Hayward Gallery.

The Council also supports the Institute of Contemporary Art in London and five other independent galleries: the Whitechapel and the Serpentine in London, the Museum of Modern Art in Oxford, Ikon in Birmingham and Arnolfini in Bristol, as well as the Institute of International Visual Arts, based in London. The ten Regional Arts Boards also fund galleries and centres and provide direct support for artists.

Support for galleries is also given by the Arts Councils in Scotland, Wales and Northern Ireland.

British artists, photographers, architects and sculptors with international reputations include David Hockney, Lucian Freud, David Bailey, Sir Richard Rogers and Sir Anthony Caro. Younger artists with a similar standing include Richard Deacon, Tony Cragg and Anish Kapoor.

Museums and Art Galleries

About 80 million people a year, across all social groups, attend more than 2,000 museums and galleries open to the public, which include the major national collections and around 1,100 independent museums, some receiving support from local authorities.

Government provision for the national museums and galleries is £218 million in 1995–96. The Museums and Galleries Improvement Fund, which is jointly financed by the Government and the Wolfson Charities and the Family Charitable Trusts, is providing an annual budget of £4 million over five years from 1991–92 for refurbishment. The Fund is already supporting over 100 projects at national and other museums and galleries, including work in Luton, Newcastle upon Tyne and Ullapool.

The Government takes advice on policy from the Museums and Galleries Commission. The Commission also promotes co-operation between national and regional institutions. Ten area museum councils supply technical services and advice on conservation and the environment, display, documentation and publicity.

The Government encourages the loan of objects from national and regional collections so that works of art can be seen by as wide a public as possible. The Arts Council of England, through a National Collections Training Scheme and the National Training Exhibition Service, is also broadening access to the national collections.

The Museum Training Institute is responsible for developing training standards and programmes within museums; the Arts Council of England supports an MA course

Table 28.2: Visitors to National Museums and Galleries 1994–95 in England	
	(million)
British Museum	6.32
Imperial War Museum	1.23
Museum of London	0.30
National Gallery	4.00
National Maritime Museum	0.54
National Museums and Galleries on Merseyside	1.38
National Portrait Gallery	0.85
Natural History Museum	1.54
Science Museum	2.48
Tate Gallery	2.80
Victoria and Albert Museum	1.60
Wallace Collection	0.16

Source: *Department of National Heritage Annual Report 1994*

472

at the Royal College of Art for curating and commissioning contemporary art, and promotes professional practice among artists and curators.

Museums Association

The independent Museums Association, to which many museums and art galleries and their staffs belong, and which has many overseas members, facilitates exchange of information and discussion of matters relating to museums and galleries. It provides training, seminars and research; its publications include the monthly *Museums Journal* and a new technical periodical, *Museums Practice*.

National Collections

The national museums and art galleries, many of them located in London, contain some of the world's most comprehensive collections of objects of artistic, archaeological, scientific, historical and general interest. They are:

- the British Museum (including the ethnographic collections of the Museum of Mankind);
- the Natural History Museum;
- the Victoria and Albert Museum (the V&A, which displays fine and decorative arts);
- the Science Museum and its two regional institutes—the National Railway Museum (York) and the National Museum of Photography, Film and Television (Bradford);
- the National Gallery (which houses western painting from around 1260 to 1920);
- the Tate Gallery, London (British painting and modern art);
- the Tate Gallery, Liverpool;
- the Tate Gallery, St Ives (St Ives School and contemporary art);
- the National Portrait Gallery;
- the Imperial War Museum;
- the National Army Museum;

- the Royal Air Force Museum;
- the National Maritime Museum;
- the Wallace Collection (which includes paintings, furniture, arms and armour; and objets d'art); and
- the National Museums and Galleries on Merseyside.

The Sainsbury Wing of the National Gallery provides a venue for major international touring exhibitions and other events. London is to be the location of the Tate's new museum of modern art.

In Scotland the national collections are held by the National Museums of Scotland and the National Galleries of Scotland. The former include the Royal Museum of Scotland, the National Museum of Antiquities of Scotland, the Scottish United Services Museum and the Scottish Agricultural Museum, in Edinburgh; the Museum of Flight, near North Berwick; and the Museum of Costume at Shambellie House near Dumfries. A new Museum of Scotland is being built next to the Royal Museum to house the National Museums' Scottish collection.

The National Galleries of Scotland comprise the National Gallery of Scotland, the Scottish National Portrait Gallery and the Scottish National Gallery of Modern Art. In 1994–95 the National Museums of Scotland attracted 1.5 million visitors and the National Galleries of Scotland some 900,000.

The National Museum of Wales, which has opened new galleries at its main building in Cardiff, has a number of branches, including the Welsh Folk Museum at St Fagans and the Industrial and Maritime Museum in Cardiff's dockland.

Northern Ireland has two national museums: the Ulster Museum in Belfast and the Ulster Folk and Transport Museum in County Down.

Other Collections

Other important collections in London include the Museum of London; Sir John Soane's Museum; the Courtauld collection; and the London Transport Museum. The Queen's Gallery in Buckingham Palace has exhibitions of pictures from the extensive royal collection. The Royal Armouries, Britain's oldest museum, has been housed in the Tower of London for 900 years. A new headquarters for the collection is being built in Leeds. Due to open in 1996, the project is a pioneering joint public and private sector venture.

Most cities and towns have museums devoted to art, archaeology and natural history, usually administered by the local authorities but sometimes by local learned societies or by individuals or trustees. Both Oxford and Cambridge are rich in museums. Many are associated with their universities, such as the Ashmolean Museum in Oxford and the Fitzwilliam Museum in Cambridge.

Many private collections of art and antiques in historic family mansions, including those owned by the National Trusts and English Heritage (see p. 357), are open to the public.

An increasing number of open air museums depict the regional life of an area or preserve early industrial remains. These include the Weald and Downland Museum in West Sussex, and the Ironbridge Gorge Museum in Shropshire. Skills of the past are revived in a number of 'living' museums, such as the Gladstone Pottery Museum near Stoke-on-Trent and the Quarry Bank Mill at Styal in Cheshire.

Among recently opened museums are:

- the Museum of Science and Industry in Manchester;

- the Mary Rose Museum in Portsmouth, housing the restored wreck of the flagship of Henry VIII;

- the St Mungo Museum of Religious Life and Art in Glasgow, containing artefacts representing the world's major religions; and

- Eureka!, the first museum designed specifically for children, in Halifax, West Yorkshire.

The Burrell Collection in Glasgow houses world-famous tapestries, paintings and objets d'art. The Design Museum in London's Docklands contains a collection of 20th-century mass-produced consumer objects.

There are also a number of national art exhibiting societies, the most famous being the Royal Academy of Arts at Burlington House in London. The Academy holds an annual

Summer Exhibition and other important exhibitions during the rest of the year. The Summer Exhibition is the world's largest open contemporary art exhibition and brings together a wide range of work by established artists and by others exhibiting for the first time. The Royal Scottish Academy holds annual exhibitions in Edinburgh. There are also children's exhibitions, including the National Exhibition of Children's Art.

Crafts

The crafts in Britain have an annual turnover estimated at £400 million. Government aid for the crafts, amounting to an estimated £3.2 million in 1995–96, is administered in England and Wales by the Crafts Council. The Council supports craftspeople by promoting public interest in their work, and encouraging the creation of works of contemporary craftsmanship. Grants are available to help with setting up workshops and acquiring equipment. The Crafts Council runs the national centre for crafts in London, which houses a gallery, reference and picture libraries, and a gallery shop. It organises the annual Chelsea Crafts Fair, and co-ordinates British groups at international trade fairs. Crafts Council exhibitions tour nationally and internationally, and grants are made to encourage exhibitions, projects and organisations.

Funding is given to the Regional Arts Boards and the Arts Council of Wales for the support of crafts, and to Contemporary Applied Art, a membership organisation that holds exhibitions and sells work through its London gallery.

Craftworks, an independent company, is the crafts development agency for Northern Ireland, providing training, marketing and business counselling for the crafts sector. The Arts Council of Northern Ireland also funds crafts promotion, as does the Scottish Office through the Scottish Arts Council.

Training in Art and Design

Most practical education in art and design is provided in the art colleges and fine and applied art departments of universities: these include the Slade School of Art and Goldsmith's College of Art, London; and in further education colleges and private art schools. Many of these institutions award degrees at postgraduate level. Art is also taught at an advanced level at the four Scottish Central (Art) Institutions.

Courses at universities concentrate largely on academic disciplines, such as the history of art. The leading institutions include the Courtauld and Warburg Institutes of the University of London and the Department of Classical Art and Archaeology at University College, London. The Open University also offers courses in art history and theory of art. Art is one of the foundation subjects in the National Curriculum. The Society for Education through Art encourages, among other activities, the purchase by schools of original works of art by organising an annual Pictures for Schools exhibition.

The Open College of the Arts offers correspondence courses in art and design, painting, sculpture, textiles, photography and creative writing to people wishing to study at home.

Export Control of Works of Art

London is a major centre for the international art market, and sales of works of art take place in the main auction houses (two of the longest established being Sotheby's and Christie's), and through private dealers. Certain items are covered by export control. These are:

- works of art and collectors' items over 50 years old and worth £20,000 or more (£5,000 or more in the case of British historical portraits);

- photographic material over 50 years old and valued at £500 or more an item; and

- documents, manuscripts and archives over 50 years old, irrespective of value.

A licence from the Department of National Heritage is required before such items can be exported. If the Department's advisers recommend withholding a licence, the matter is referred to the Reviewing Committee on the Export of Works of Art. If the Committee considers a work to be of national importance, it can advise the Government to withhold the export licence for a specified time to give a public museum, art gallery, or private collector an opportunity to buy at a fair price.

LITERATURE AND LIBRARIES

A number of literary activities receive public subsidy through the Arts Councils. In 1995, for example, there was continued support for a programme of tours by writers from other countries, for innovative broadcasting projects promoting reading and writing, and for literary magazines and independent publishers.

There are free public libraries throughout Britain (see p. 477), private libraries and several private literary societies. Book reviews are featured in the press and on television and radio, and numerous periodicals concerned with literature are published (see p. 462). Recognition of outstanding literary merit is provided by a number of awards, some of the most valuable being the Booker and Whitbread prizes. The 1994 Booker Prize was won by James Kelman for *How Late it Was, How Late*.

In 1995 Harold Pinter was awarded the second David Cohen British Literature Prize for a lifetime's achievement by a living British writer. A part of the £40,000 prize, which is awarded every two years, enables winners to commission new works from younger writers. Other awards to encourage young authors include those of the Somerset Maugham Trust Fund and the E.C. Gregory Trust Fund.

Many writers from overseas, often from Commonwealth countries, also live and work in Britain, writing books in English which have a wide circulation in Britain and overseas.

Distinguished British poets include Ted Hughes (the Poet Laureate), James Berry, Gillian Clarke, Carol Ann Duffy, Gavin Ewart, Alison Fell, Tony Harrison, Geoffrey Hill, Elizabeth Jennings and Carol Rumens. As the Poet Laureate, Ted Hughes is a member of the Royal Household and receives an annual stipend from the Civil List—see p. 47. His most recent commemorative verse was written on the occasion of the Queen Mother's 95th birthday.

Many British writers are internationally recognised. Well-known living novelists, with examples of their works, include:

- Martin Amis—*London Fields, Money, The Information*;
- Dame Muriel Spark—*The Prime of Miss Jean Brodie, Memento Mori*;
- Julian Barnes—*Talking it Over, The Porcupine*; and
- P.D. James—*The Children of Men, Original Sin*.

English literature is taught extensively at schools, colleges and universities throughout Britain. Creative writing is also taught at a wide variety of institutions; one of the best known is the University of East Anglia, in Norwich, where writers such as Ian McEwan and Kazuo Ishiguro have studied. The University also houses the British Centre for Literary Translation.

Authors' Copyright and Performers' Protection

Original literary, dramatic, musical or artistic works, films, sound recordings and broadcasts are automatically protected by copyright in Britain. This protection is also given to works from countries party to international copyright conventions. The copyright owner has rights against unauthorised reproduction, public performance, broadcasting and issue to the public of his or her work; and against dealing in unauthorised copies. In most cases the author is the first owner of the copyright, and the term of copyright is the life of the author and a period of 50 years after death (50 years from the year of release for films and sound recordings and 50 years from the year of broadcast for broadcasts).

The Copyright, Designs and Patents Act 1988 reformed copyright law and introduced the concept of moral rights, whereby authors have the right to be identified on their works and to object to derogatory treatment of them. The Act also updated the rights which protect performers against making and trading in unauthorised recordings of live performances, the term of protection for these rights then being 50 years from the year in which the performance was given. From July 1995 that protection was extended to 70 years.

Literary and Philological Societies

Societies to promote literature include the English Association and the Royal Society of Literature. The leading society for studies in the humanities is the British Academy for the Promotion of Historical, Philosophical and Philological Studies (the British Academy).

Other specialist societies are the Early English Text Society, the Bibliographical Society and several societies devoted to particular authors, the largest of which is the Dickens Fellowship. Various societies, such as the Poetry Society, sponsor poetry readings and recitals.

Libraries

The British Library

The British Library, the national library of Britain, is one of the world's greatest libraries, with a collection of more than 150 million separate items. These include books, journals, manuscripts, newspapers, stamps, maps and recorded sound. Publishers must deposit in the Library a copy of everything published.

A new building for the British Library's reference collections is being constructed at St Pancras, London, at a cost of £496 million; it is due to be completed at the end of 1996. The St Pancras building will offer, for the first time, a purpose-built home for the national library with environmentally controlled storage, increased reader space and seating and greatly improved public facilities, including three exhibition galleries, an auditorium and a bookshop.

The Library's collection grows by about five shelf miles a year and consists of bequests, donations and purchases collected over a period of more than 200 years. It is also the guardian of treasures such as the Magna Carta and Shakespeare's First Folio. Some 450,000 reader visits are made to the Library each year; admission to all reading rooms is free of charge.

The Library's Document Supply Centre at Boston Spa (West Yorkshire) is the national centre for inter-library lending within Britain and between Britain and countries overseas. It dispatches over 4 million documents a year.

The Research and Development Department is a major source of funding for research and development in library and information services.

Other Libraries

The National Libraries of Scotland and Wales, the Bodleian Library of Oxford University and the Cambridge University Library can also claim copies of all new British publications under legal deposit. The first phase of a new building for the National Library of Scotland was opened in 1989, accommodating a map library, lending services and the Scottish Science Library. The second stage was opened in May 1995. A major extension of the National Library of Wales was completed in 1995.

Some national museums and government departments have important libraries.

- The Public Record Office in London and in Kew, Surrey, houses the records of the superior courts of law of England and Wales and of most government departments, as well as famous historical documents. The Office has many millions of documents, dating from the time of the Norman Conquest to the present day. Public records, with few exceptions, are available for inspection by members of the public 30 years after the end of the year in which they were created.

- The Scottish Record Office in Edinburgh and the Public Record Office of Northern Ireland, Belfast, serve the same purpose.

Besides a number of great private collections, such as that of the London Library, there are the libraries of the learned societies and institutions, such as the Royal Institute of International Affairs, the Royal Geographical Society and the Royal Academy of Music. The Poetry Library in the South Bank Centre, owned by the Arts Council of England, is a collection of 20th-century poetry written in or translated into English; the library houses about 60,000 volumes.

University Libraries

The university libraries of Oxford and Cambridge are unmatched by those of the more recent foundations. However, the combined library resources of the colleges and institutions of the University of London total 9 million volumes, the John Rylands University Library of Manchester contains 3.5 million volumes, Edinburgh 2.5 million, Leeds 2.3 million, and Birmingham, Glasgow, Liverpool and Aberdeen each have over 1 million volumes. Many universities have important research collections in special subjects—the Barnes Medical Library at Birmingham and the British Library of Political and Economic Science at the London School of Economics, for example. University libraries also have on-line access to library information worldwide.

Special Libraries

Numerous associations and commercial and industrial organisations run library and information services. Although most are intended primarily for use within the organisation, many can be used, by arrangement, by people interested in the area covered, and the specialist publications held are often available for inter-library lending.

Public Libraries

Local authorities in Great Britain and education and library boards in Northern Ireland have a duty to provide a free lending and reference library service, and Britain's network of about 4,100 public libraries has a total stock of over 130 million books. Public libraries issue an average of ten books a year for every person in Britain. Of these, 58 per cent are works of fiction. Over half of the total population are members of public libraries. Some areas are served by mobile libraries, and domiciliary services cater for people unable to visit a library.

Many libraries have collections of compact discs, records, audio- and video-cassettes, and musical scores for loan to the public, while a number also lend from collections of works of art, which may be originals or reproductions. Most libraries hold documents on local history, and nearly all provide children's departments, while reference and information sections and art, music, commercial and technical departments meet the growing demands in these fields. The information role is one of increasing importance for many libraries, and greater use is being made of information technology, including microcomputers and reference databases.

The Government remains committed to providing a free basic library service—the borrowing and consultation of printed materials—but believes there is scope for greater private sector involvement.

Public libraries charge for some services, such as research services and the lending of non-printed materials.

The Government is advised by the Library and Information Commission, which is a forum for policy on library and information provision in general, and the Advisory Council on Libraries, which advises Government on public libraries in England. The Commission also advises the Government on Britain's representation abroad and research strategy.

The Government is reviewing the scope and value of services provided by public libraries in England and the feasibility of contracting out the delivery of some parts of their service.

The Library Association

The Library Association is the principal professional organisation for those engaged in library and information services. Founded in 1877, the Association has 25,000 members. It maintains a Register of Chartered Librarians and publishes books, pamphlets and an official journal.

The Library Association is the designated authority for the recognition of qualifications gained in other EU member states.

Public Lending Right Scheme

The Public Lending Right Scheme gives registered authors the right to receive payment from a central fund (totalling £4.9 million in 1995–96) for the loans made of their books from public libraries in Britain. Payment is made in proportion to the number of times the authors' books are lent out. In 1994–95, 110 authors received the maximum payment of £6,000 and altogether about £4.3 million was distributed among 19,000 authors.

Books

In 1994 British publishers issued about 88,700 separate titles. The British publishing industry devotes much effort to developing overseas markets, and in 1994 the estimated value of exports of British books amounted to £700 million.

Among the leading organisations representing publishing and distribution interests are the Publishers Association, which has 200 members; and the Booksellers' Association, with 3,300 members. The Publishers Association, through its International Division, promotes the export of British books. The Welsh Book Council supports the production of books in the Welsh language.

Historical Manuscripts

The Royal Commission on Historical Manuscripts locates, reports on, and gives information and advice about historical papers outside the public records. It also advises private owners, grant-awarding bodies, record offices, local authorities and the Government on the acquisition and maintenance of manuscripts. In addition, the Commission maintains the National Register of Archives (the central collecting point for information about British historical manuscripts) and the Manorial Documents Register, which are available to researchers.

29 The Media

The media have an increasingly central role in Britain's democratic and cultural life. The public interest requires the protection of media plurality and diversity; it also requires a healthy and growing media industry. To that end, the Government has announced new proposals to regulate media ownership into the next century (see p. 501) which, while avoiding interference in the dynamics of the market, aim to ensure that no organisation is allowed to dominate and unduly influence the media.

Television and Radio

Broadcasting in Britain has traditionally been based on the principle that it is a public service accountable to the people through Parliament. While retaining the essential public service element, it now embraces the principles of competition and choice.

Three public bodies have the main responsibility for television and radio services to which nearly everyone has access:

- the BBC (British Broadcasting Corporation) broadcasts television and radio programmes;

- the ITC (Independent Television Commission) licenses and regulates non-BBC television services, including cable and satellite services; and

- the Radio Authority licenses and regulates all non-BBC radio services, including cable and satellite.

These authorities work to broad requirements and objectives defined by Parliament, but are otherwise independent in their day-to-day conduct of business.

The government department responsible for overseeing the broadcasting system is the Department of National Heritage. The Secretary of State for National Heritage is answerable to Parliament on broad policy questions.

Television

Television viewing is by far Britain's most popular leisure pastime: 96 per cent of households have a colour television set and 73 per cent a video recorder. People spend an average of over three and a half hours a day watching television, including video playbacks.

There are currently four terrestrial television channels (a fifth is planned—see p. 484), offering a mixture of drama, light entertainment, films, sport, educational, children's and religious programmes, news and current affairs, and documentaries.

The BBC provides two complementary national networks—BBC 1 and BBC 2—which are financed predominantly by a licence fee. The ITC regulates two television services—ITV (Channel 3) and Channel 4—which complement each other and are largely funded by advertising. In Wales, S4C (Sianel Pedwar Cymru) broadcasts programmes on the fourth channel. All four channels broadcast on 625 lines UHF (ultra-high frequency) and over 99 per cent of the population live within range of transmission.

British television productions continue to win many international awards, and in 1994 film and television companies received £185 million in export earnings.

Radio

Practically every home has a radio, and the widespread ownership of portable sets (including personal stereos) and car radios means that people can listen to radio throughout the day. About 70 per cent of the population listen to the radio on a normal day and more than 85 per cent do so over the week.

The BBC has five national networks, which together transmit all types of music, news, current affairs, drama, education, sport and a range of features programmes. The Radio Authority regulates three national commercial radio stations—Classic FM, Virgin 1215 and Talk Radio UK (see p. 485).

There are 37 BBC local radio stations serving England and the Channel Islands, and regional and community radio services in Scotland, Wales and Northern Ireland. About 180 independent local radio (ILR) services are also in operation. Stations supply a comprehensive service of local news and information, sport, music and other entertainment, education and consumer advice. 'Phone-in' programmes allowing listeners to express their views on air are popular.

GOVERNMENT ROLE

In recent years broadcasting in Britain has seen radical changes. The availability of more radio frequencies, together with satellite, cable and microwave transmissions, has made a greater number of local, national and international services possible. Moreover, the technical quality of sound and pictures is improving.

In response to rapidly developing technology and rising public demand for a wide choice of programmes and services, the Broadcasting Act 1990 was passed with the aim of making the regulatory framework for broadcasting more flexible and efficient, and giving viewers and listeners access to a greater range of services. At the same time the Act aimed to promote competition and to maintain high standards of taste and decency.

Changes under the Broadcasting Act 1990

The Broadcasting Act 1990 overhauled the regulation of independent television and radio and opened the way for many more services.

In 1991 the IBA (Independent Broadcasting Authority) was replaced by the ITC (Independent Television Commission), the Radio Authority and a transmission and engineering company, National Transcommunications Limited (NTL—see below). At the same time the Cable Authority was made part of the ITC and the Radio Authority.

The ITC and the Radio Authority issue licences to commercial broadcasters and enforce rules to ensure diversity of ownership. The 1990 Act made provision for setting up a new national independent television station—Channel 5—and three national commercial radio stations, with opportunities for launching hundreds of independent local radio and television channels.

In 1991 the IBA networks and other facilities were transferred to National Transcommunications Limited, a public company. NTL was then sold for £70 million to a company formed for the purpose by Mercury Asset Management. NTL transmits television services for the independent television companies, Channel 4, S4C, and radio services for about 100 independent local radio stations.

For the Act's provisions on media ownership see p. 501.

Programming Obligations

Licence-holders of the independent television Channel 3 (and the proposed Channel 5) need to pass demanding quality tests (see p. 484). ITC regulations place a limit on the proportion of non-European material broadcast. Since 1993 both the BBC and commercial television licensees have been required to ensure that at least 25 per cent of their original programming comes from independent producers. This percentage does not include news and news-related daily current affairs programmes.

Programme Standards

Recognising that broadcasting is an extremely powerful medium with the potential to offend, exploit and cause harm, the Broadcasting Act 1990 contained guarantees on programme standards which are extended to all British-based broadcasters. These guarantees cover taste, decency, accuracy and balance. The Government can proscribe unacceptable foreign satellite services receivable in Britain, and anyone in Britain supporting such a service can be prosecuted.

THE BBC

The constitution, finances and obligations of the BBC are governed by a Royal Charter and by a Licence and Agreement. The Corporation's board of 12 governors, including the chairman, vice-chairman and a national governor each for Scotland, Wales and Northern Ireland, is appointed by the Queen on the advice of the Government. The board of governors is ultimately responsible for all aspects of broadcasting by the BBC. The governors appoint the Director-General, the Corporation's chief executive officer, who heads the board of management—the body in charge of the daily running of the Corporation.

The BBC has a regional structure throughout Britain. The three English regions—BBC North, BBC Midlands & East and BBC South—and BBC Scotland, Wales and Northern Ireland make programmes for their local audiences as well as contributing to the national network.

The National Broadcasting Councils for Scotland, Wales and Northern Ireland advise on the policy and content of television and radio programmes intended mainly for reception in their areas. Ten Regional Councils in England advise the board of governors on the needs and concerns of audiences.

Finance

The domestic services of the BBC are financed predominantly from the sale of television licences. Households with a television must buy an annual licence costing £86.50 for colour and £28.50 for black and white. Nearly 20.8 million licences were current on 31 July 1995; of these, 20 million were for colour.

Licence income is supplemented by profits from trading activities, such as television programme exports, sale of recordings, publications and other merchandise connected with BBC programmes, hire and sale of educational films, film library sales, and exhibitions based on programmes. The BBC World Service's radio broadcasting operations (see p. 489) are financed by a grant-in-aid from the Foreign & Commonwealth Office (£136 million in 1995–96), while BBC Worldwide Television (see p. 489) is self-financing.

TV Licensing, a subsidiary company of the Post Office, undertakes the licence administration on behalf of the BBC. Since 1988 annual rises in the licence fee have been linked to the rate of inflation, and will continue to be until the end of 1996; this is intended to improve the BBC's efficiency even further and encourage it to continue to develop alternative sources of revenue.

Future of the BBC

A government White Paper, entitled *The Future of the BBC: Serving the Nation, Competing Worldwide*, was published in July 1994. It considered the BBC's future after the expiry of its current Royal Charter at the end of 1996 and proposed that:

- the BBC should remain a public service broadcaster, maintaining its current radio and television services, and this should be its main role. A new Royal Charter and Agreement should provide the framework for the BBC's activities for ten years from 1997;

- the BBC should be more accountable and responsive to its audiences, publishing objectives for its programmes and services;

- a reasonable proportion of the BBC's network programmes should be made in Scotland, Wales, Northern Ireland and the English regions;

- the licence fee should be the main source of income for the BBC's public services in Britain until at least 2001;

- World Service Radio should continue, funded by grant-in-aid;

- the BBC should develop its commercial activities in Britain and abroad, in partnership with the private sector, and should evolve into an international multimedia organisation. These commercial activities should be distinct from its public services, and should not be subsidised from the licence fee; and

- the Government and the BBC would explore options for injecting private finance into the Corporation's transmission services. Privatisation, either in whole or in part, would be among the options under consideration.

BBC Television

The two domestic channels are BBC 1 and BBC 2:

- BBC 1, the channel of broad appeal, broadcasts news and current affairs, major documentaries, sport, popular drama and light entertainment, and children's programmes;

- BBC 2 is more innovatory. Its programmes complement those on BBC 1 and cater for minorities within the general audience, embracing music and the arts, comedy and challenging drama, as well as education, community and special needs programmes.

Together, BBC 1 and BBC 2 transmit over 18,000 hours of programmes a year for national and regional audiences.

Programmes are made by, commissioned from, or acquired through London-based production departments and six BBC regions. BBC Television departments throughout Britain commission a wide range of programmes from independent producers. Feature films, mini-series, children's series, cartoons and overseas sport are also acquired from other organisations around the world.

In April 1994 the BBC pledged to increase the proportion of network television and radio programmes produced outside London from one-fifth to broadly one-third by 1997–98. The BBC enters into agreements with overseas television corporations in order to share the cost of some new programmes.

BBC Focus

BBC Focus is the Corporation's specialist night-time television service. It is a unit within the BBC's Education Directorate and broadcasts education, training, and professional information and updating programmes as part of BBC 2's night-time service, The Learning Zone.

BBC Focus does not make any of the programmes that it broadcasts, but works with a variety of public bodies and charities to enable them to communicate with specific audiences as part of the BBC's educational service. All programmes are 'open access' and free. They are designed for recording on video and viewing at a later date.

BBC Network Radio

BBC Network Radio serves an audience of 28 million a week in Britain, broadcasting around 38,000 hours of programmes each year on its five networks:

- BBC Radio 1 FM broadcasts pop music, as well as live concerts, social action campaigns and comedy, 24 hours a day;

- BBC Radio 2 transmits popular music and light entertainment, also for 24 hours a day;

- BBC Radio 3 broadcasts mainly classical music, but presents jazz, drama, poetry, documentaries and school programming as well;

- BBC Radio 4 (broadcast with some differences on FM and LW) provides news and current affairs coverage, together with drama, comedy, documentaries and panel games; it also carries parliamentary coverage, and cricket in season on LW; and

- BBC Radio 5 Live, which superseded Radio 5 in March 1994, is a 24-hour news and sport network.

INDEPENDENT BROADCASTING

Independent Television Commission

Like the Radio Authority and S4C, the ITC's constitution and finances are governed by the Broadcasting Act 1990. The ITC is responsible for licensing and regulating non-BBC television services operating in or from Britain. These include:

- ITV (Channel 3);

- Channel 4;

- the proposed Channel 5;

- cable and other local delivery services;

- independent teletext services; and

- satellite services transmitted from Britain.

The ITC monitors the licences and licence conditions but is not involved in detailed scheduling of programmes. It is advised by committees on educational broadcasting, religious broadcasting, charitable appeals and advertising. Ten viewer consultative councils also comment on the commercial services' programmes.

ITV Programmes

The first regular ITV programmes began in London in 1955. ITV programmes are broadcast 24 hours a day throughout the country. About one-third of the output comprises informative programmes—news, documentaries, and coverage of current affairs, education and religion. The remainder covers sport, comedy, drama, game shows, films, and a range of other programmes with popular appeal. Over half the programmes are produced by the programme companies and ITN (Independent Television News—see below).

ITV (Channel 3) Programme Companies

ITV is made up of 15 regionally based television companies which are licensed to supply programmes in the 14 independent television geographical regions. There are two licences for London, one for weekdays and the other for the weekend. An additional ITC licensee provides a national breakfast-time service, transmitted on the ITV network.

The licensees operate on a commercial basis, deriving most of their revenue from selling advertising time. The financial resources, advertising revenue and programme production of the companies vary considerably, depending largely on the population of the areas in which they operate. Although newspapers may acquire an interest in programme companies, safeguards exist to ensure against concentration of media ownership (see p. 501).

Each programme company plans the content of the programmes to be broadcast in its area. These are produced by the company itself, or by other programme companies, or are bought from elsewhere.

A common news service is provided by ITN. ITN has been appointed to supply a service of national and international news to the ITV network for a ten-year period from January 1993.

ITV Network Centre

The ITV Network Centre, which is wholly owned by the ITV companies, independently commissions and schedules those television programmes which are shown across the ITV network. Programmes are commissioned from the ITV companies as well as from independent producers. The Centre also promotes the ITV network and co-ordinates developments in technology and training.

Licences

The ITV licences for Channel 3, which came up for renewal at the end of 1992, were awarded by the ITC in October 1991. Channel 3 licences are awarded for a ten-year period by competitive tender to the highest bidder who has passed a quality threshold. In exceptional cases a lower bid can be selected, for instance, where an applicant is able to offer a significantly better quality of service than that offered by the highest bidder.

There are safeguards for quality programming, with licensees being required to provide a diverse programme service calculated to appeal to a wide variety of tastes and interests. They also have to show high quality news and current affairs programmes and a reasonable proportion of other programmes of high quality. There is a statutory duty to present programmes made in and about the region. There is also a requirement for district and regional programming to be aimed at different areas within regions. Channel 3 licensees are obliged to operate a national programme network. Networking arrangements are subject to the approval of the ITC and the Director General of Fair Trading so that anti-competitive practices are avoided.

Channel 4 and S4C

Channel 4, which began broadcasting in 1982, provides a national television service throughout Britain, except in Wales, which has a corresponding service—S4C (Sianel Pedwar Cymru). In January 1993 Channel 4 became a public corporation, licensed and regulated by the ITC, and funded by selling its own advertising time. It was previously a public limited company owned by the ITC.

Channel 4's remit is to provide programmes with a distinctive character and to appeal to tastes and interests not generally catered for by Channel 3. It must present a suitable proportion of educational programmes and encourage innovation and experiment. Channel 4 commissions programmes from the ITV companies and independent producers and buys programmes from overseas. It broadcasts for around 139 hours a week, about half of which are devoted to informative programmes.

In Wales programmes on the fourth channel are run and controlled by S4C. Its members are appointed by the Government. S4C is required to see that a significant proportion of programming, in practice about 23 hours a week, is in the Welsh language and that programmes broadcast between 18.30 and 22.00 hours are mainly in Welsh. At other times S4C transmits national Channel 4 programmes.

Like Channel 4, S4C has sold its own advertising since January 1993. S4C is expected to cover only 10 per cent of its costs from advertising, with the remainder financed by the Government.

Gaelic TV Fund

The Gaelic Television Committee, appointed by the ITC, was set up under the Broadcasting Act 1990 to administer government finance for making television programmes in Gaelic. The Gaelic Television Fund was created and programmes thus financed came on screen from January 1993. In 1994 the Government paid £8.4 million to the ITC, which was credited to the Fund. The Fund has increased the output of Gaelic television programmes from 100 to about 300 hours each year.

Channel 5

A new national terrestrial television channel—Channel 5—was originally intended to come into operation in late 1994, financed through advertising, subscription or sponsorship. The ten-year licence was to be awarded by competitive tender. However, in 1992 the ITC rejected the single bid it had received, and in September 1994 announced that it was again inviting applications for the licence; by the closing date of 1 May 1995, four consortia had submitted bids.

In July 1994, the Government announced new frequency allocations for Channel 5 and for up to 12 digital terrestrial television services.

Local Television

Under the Broadcasting Act 1990 licences for the delivery of local television services are awarded by competitive tender; there is no quality threshold. ITC licence-holders can supply national and local television channels using both cable and microwave transmission systems.

The Radio Authority

Independent local radio (ILR) is based on principles similar to those of ITV. The programme companies operate under licence to the Radio Authority and are financed mainly by advertising revenue. The Radio Authority is required to ensure that licensed services, taken as a whole, are of a high quality and offer a range of programmes calculated to appeal to a variety of tastes and interests.

The Authority awards national radio licences by competitive tender to the highest bidder. There are three independent national services:

- Classic FM, which broadcasts mainly classical music, together with news and information, came on air in September 1992;
- Virgin 1215, which plays broad-based rock music, came on air in April 1993; and
- Talk Radio UK, which is a speech-based service, came on air in February 1995.

Since the early 1990s more local radio stations have continued to come on the air, some of which are neighbourhood and 'community of interest' stations. The Authority has awarded 54 new local radio licences since it came into operation in 1991. Local radio licences are not allocated by competitive tender; the success of licence applications is in part determined by the extent to which applicants meet the needs and interests of the people living in the area and in part by whether they have the necessary financial resources to sustain programme plans for the eight-year licence period.

Some of the locations have been selected with small-scale 'community radio' in mind. As part of its brief to develop a wide range of radio services, the Authority is establishing a number of more specialist stations.

The Radio Authority also issues restricted service licences. These are issued at the discretion of the Authority (subject to certain conditions and frequency availability), usually for a maximum of 28 days. They enable local events—such as sports events, arts festivals and conferences—to be covered by a temporary radio service in a limited area, for example, part of a city or town or an arena.

TELETEXT, CABLE AND SATELLITE SERVICES

Teletext

The BBC and independent television each operate a teletext service, offering constantly updated information on a variety of subjects, including news, sport, travel, weather conditions and entertainment. The teletext system allows the television signal to carry additional information which can be selected and displayed as 'pages' of text and graphics on receivers equipped with the necessary decoders. Both the BBC and Channels 3 and 4 provide subtitling for certain programmes for people with hearing difficulties. Channel 3 and Channel 4 are required to offer subtitling services for at least 50 per cent of their programmes by 1998. Around 50 per cent of households in Britain with television have teletext sets.

Licences

The Broadcasting Act 1990 introduced a regulatory system for licensing spare capacity within the lines of the television signal. This allows more varied use of the capacity—data transfer, for instance—but the position of teletext and subtitling on commercial television is safeguarded.

In 1991 the ITC advertised three teletext licences. These ten-year licences are awarded by competitive tender, with applicants having to satisfy certain statutory requirements before their cash bid can be considered. The ITC awarded the main teletext licence to Teletext Ltd, which replaced Oracle in January 1993, and awarded one of the additional commercial service licences on Channel 3 to the only bidder, Data Broadcasting International. The other additional commercial service licence on Channel 4/S4C was readvertised in June 1994 and awarded in October 1994 to SimpleActive Ltd.

Cable Services

Cable services are delivered to consumers through underground cables and are paid for by subscription. The franchising of cable systems and the licensing of cable television services are carried out by the Cable and Satellite Division of the ITC, while the Radio Authority issues cable radio licences.

'Broadband cable', the cable systems currently being designed and built, can carry between 30 and 45 television channels, including terrestrial broadcasts, satellite television, and channels delivered to cable operators by video. Cable systems usually carry a local channel.

Interactive services such as home shopping, home banking, security and alarm services, electronic mail and remote meter readings are also possible. BBC Worldwide Television (see p. 489) has provided 450 hours of BBC programming for a BT interactive television trial involving 2,500 customers in the towns of Colchester and Ipswich, beginning in August 1995. It is involved with another ten trials around the world.

Cable franchises have already been granted covering areas which include two-thirds of all homes and nearly all urban areas in Britain. By April 1995 there were 86 broadband cable franchises in operation in Britain, 21 of which had been set up within the previous year. Regulation is as light as possible to encourage the development of a wide range of services, and flexible enough to adapt to new technology. The ITC awards only one broadband cable franchise in each area so that the new franchisee is protected from direct competition in the early stages. At present there are nearly 4.5 million homes able to receive broadband cable services and there are over 964,000 subscribers.

ITC licences are required for systems capable of serving more than 1,000 homes. They are awarded for each area on the basis of competitive tendering. Systems extending beyond a single building and up to 1,000 homes require only an individual licence from OFTEL (see p. 311). Cable investment must be privately financed.

There are no quality controls on cable services. However, if cable operators also provide their own programme content as opposed to just conveying services, they require a programme services licence from the ITC, which includes consumer protection requirements.

Direct Broadcasting by Satellite

Direct broadcasting by satellite (DBS), by which television is transmitted directly by satellite into people's homes, has been available throughout Britain since 1989. The signals from satellite broadcasting are received through specially designed aerials or 'dishes'.

Several British-based satellite television channels have been set up to supply programmes to cable operators and viewers with dishes in Britain and, in some cases, throughout Europe. While some offer general entertainment, others concentrate on specific areas of interest, such as sport, music and children's programmes.

Licences are granted, on a non-competitive basis, to programme services which are likely to meet consumer protection standards and are run by suitably qualified people.

The largest satellite programmer is BSkyB (British Sky Broadcasting), which provides nine channels devoted to light entertainment, news, feature films, sport and home shopping transmitted from the Astra satellite.

Other satellite channels available to British viewers include Eurosport (sport), CNN (news), MTV (pop videos), and TV Asia (for Asian viewers). The choice available to viewers is expanding steadily.

BBC Worldwide Television (see p. 489) is a shareholder in an entertainment satellite channel—UK Gold—on the Astra satellite. Programmes include drama, soaps, comedy, children's television and quizzes.

OTHER ASPECTS

Educational Broadcasting

Both the BBC and Channel 4 broadcast educational programmes for schools and Continuing Education programmes for adults. Broadcasts to schools deal with all subjects of the National Curriculum (see p. 435), while programmes for adults cover many areas of learning and vocational training. Books, pamphlets, computer software, and audio and video cassettes are produced to supplement the programmes. Ninety-seven per cent of primary schools and 95 per cent of secondary schools in Britain use BBC schools television; 80 per cent of primary schools use BBC schools radio. The ITC has a duty to ensure that schools programmes are presented on independent television.

During 1994 the BBC broadcast 447 hours of radio and 660 hours of television on behalf of the Open University (see p. 445).

Advertising and Sponsorship

The BBC may not obtain revenue or any consideration in kind from the broadcasting of advertisements or from commercial sponsorship of programmes. Its policy is to avoid giving publicity to any firm or organised interest except when this is necessary in providing effective and informative programmes. It does, however, cover sponsored sporting and artistic events.

Advertising and sponsorship are allowed on independent television and radio subject to controls. The ITC and the Radio Authority operate codes of advertising standards and programme sponsorship.

Advertisements on independent television and radio are broadcast between programmes as well as in breaks during programmes. Advertisers are not allowed to influence programme content. Advertisements must be distinct and separate from programmes. The time given to them must not be so great as to detract from the value of the programmes as a medium of information, education or entertainment. Television advertising is limited to an average of seven minutes an hour during the day and seven and a half minutes in the peak evening viewing period. Advertising is prohibited in broadcasts of religious services and in broadcasts to schools. The service provided by Teletext Ltd (see p. 485) carries advertisements.

The ITC and the Radio Authority's codes governing standards and practice in advertising give regulations on the forms of advertisement which are prohibited, alongside rules and guidance on scheduling and creative matters.

Political advertising and advertisements for betting (other than the National Lottery and the football pools) are prohibited. All tobacco advertising is banned on television and cigarette advertisements are banned on radio.

Religious advertisements may be broadcast on commercial radio and television, provided they comply with the guidelines issued by the ITC and the Radio Authority.

Both the ITC and the Radio Authority can impose severe penalties on any television or radio company failing to comply with their codes.

Sponsorship in Independent Broadcasting

In Britain sponsorship is a relatively new way of helping to finance commercial broadcasting, although the practice has long been established in other countries. In return for their financial contribution, sponsors receive a credit associating them with a particular programme.

The ITC's Code of Programme Sponsorship and the Radio Authority's Advertising and Sponsorship Code aim to ensure that sponsors do not exert influence on the editorial content of programmes and that sponsorships are made clear to viewers. News and current affairs programmes may not be sponsored. Potential sponsors for other categories of programme may be debarred if their involvement could constrain the editorial independence of the programme maker in any way. References to sponsors or their products must be confined to the beginning and end of a programme and around commercial breaks; they must not appear in the programme itself. All commercial radio programmes other than news bulletins may be sponsored.

Government Publicity

Government publicity material to support non-political campaigns may be broadcast on independent television and radio. This is paid for on a normal commercial basis. The Central Office of Information (COI) produces short public service items, concerning health, safety and welfare, for free transmission by the BBC and independent television and radio. All government advertisements and public service information films are subtitled via electronic text to support people with hearing difficulties.

Broadcasting Standards

The independence enjoyed by the broadcasting authorities carries with it certain obligations over programme content. Programmes must display, as far as possible, a proper balance and wide range of subject matter, impartiality in matters of controversy and accuracy in news coverage, and must not offend against good taste. Broadcasters must also comply with legislation relating to obscenity and incitement to racial hatred.

The BBC, the ITC and the Radio Authority apply codes providing guidance on violence and standards of taste and decency in television programmes, particularly during hours when children are likely to be viewing.

The BBC opened its own Programme Complaints Unit in early 1994 to investigate serious complaints about BBC television or radio programmes.

Broadcasting Standards Council

The Broadcasting Standards Council (BSC) acts as a focus for public concern about the portrayal of violence and sex, and about standards of taste and decency. Its remit covers television and radio programmes and broadcast advertisements, and includes monitoring programmes broadcast into Britain from abroad.

The Council has statutory powers requiring the codes of practice of the BBC and other broadcasting regulatory bodies to reflect the BSC's own code. The BSC monitors programmes, examines complaints from the public and undertakes research. In 1994–95 a total of 2,032 complaints falling within the Council's remit were received. Of these, 303 were upheld in full or in part.

Broadcasting Complaints Commission

The Broadcasting Complaints Commission, an independent statutory body, deals with complaints of unfair treatment in broadcast programmes and of unwarranted infringement of privacy in programmes or in their preparation. In 1994–95 the Commission received 1,135 complaints of unfair or unjust treatment in broadcast programmes.

The White Paper on the future of the BBC (see p. 481) proposed that the Broadcasting Standards Council and the Broadcasting Complaints Commission be merged in order to simplify the system of broadcasting regulation. Detailed proposals for a merger, requiring legislation, are being developed by the Department of National Heritage.

Parliamentary and Political Broadcasting

The proceedings of both Houses of Parliament may be broadcast on television and radio, either live, or more usually in recorded and edited form on news and current affairs programmes.

The BBC and the commercial services provide time on radio and television for an annual series of party political broadcasts. Party election broadcasts are arranged following the announcement of a general election. In addition, the Government may make ministerial broadcasts on radio and television, with opposition parties also being allotted broadcast time.

Audience Research

Both the BBC and the independent sector are required to keep themselves informed on the state of public opinion about the programmes and advertising that they broadcast. This is done through the continuous measurement of the size and composition of audiences and their opinions of programmes. For television, this work is undertaken through BARB (the Broadcasters' Audience Research Board), owned jointly by the BBC and the ITV Network Centre. For radio, joint research is undertaken for BBC radio and for commercial radio by RAJAR (Radio Joint Audience Research).

Both the BBC and the independent sector conduct regular surveys of audience opinion on television and radio services. Public opinion is further assessed by the

BBC and ITC through the work of their advisory committees, councils and panels. Regular public meetings are also held to debate services, and consideration is given to letters and telephone calls from listeners and viewers.

Training

All ITV (Channel 3) licensees are obliged to provide training. Channel 4 also provides a range of training for staff and for the independent production sector.

The BBC Centre for Broadcast Skills Training (part of BBC Resources) operates on a commercial basis and provides a full programme of courses on all technical aspects of broadcasting, including craft skills. Courses can be mounted specially to meet particular requirements.

In addition BBC World Service Training runs courses for radio and television broadcasters and their managers from all over the world. The department is working with some 25 countries in Eastern Europe, the Arabic-speaking world, Asia and Africa. Courses and training programmes are tailor-made and carried out both in Britain and in the countries concerned.

The Government finances overseas students on broadcasting training courses at the BBC, the British Council and the Thomson Foundation; the Foundation also conducts courses overseas in broadcast journalism, media management, radio and television production, and technology.

INTERNATIONAL SERVICES

The BBC

In May 1994 the Corporation announced a new organisational structure—BBC Worldwide—for the development of its international and commercial strategy. It focuses the activities into three separate divisions—BBC World Service, BBC Worldwide Television and BBC Worldwide Publishing—operating across six distinct regions of the world: Europe, the Americas, Africa and the Middle East, South Asia, Asia-Pacific, and the former Soviet Union and South West Asia.

BBC World Service

BBC World Service broadcasts by radio in English and 40 other languages worldwide, and also produces the television news programming for BBC Worldwide Television (see below). It has a measured global audience of 133 million regular listeners. The core programming of news, current affairs, business and sports reports is complemented by a wide range of cultural programmes, including drama, literature and music.

BBC World Service programmes in English and many other languages are made available by satellite for rebroadcasting by agreement with local or national radio stations, networks and cable operators. BBC World Service Radio International sells recorded programmes to other broadcasters in over 100 countries.

BBC English specialises in teaching the English language on radio and television, and through associated publications, audio and video cassettes, reaching audiences in more than 120 countries.

BBC MPM—Marshall Plan of the Mind—was set up in 1992 to provide a range of business, economic and associated political programmes to the countries of the former Soviet Union. It is mainly funded by the British Government's Know How Fund (see p. 124).

BBC Monitoring, the international media monitoring arm of BBC World Service, provides transcripts of radio and television broadcasts from over 140 countries. As well as providing a vital source of information to the BBC, this service is also used by other media organisations, government departments, the commercial sector and academic institutions.

BBC Worldwide Television

BBC Worldwide Television was created in May 1994 by the merger of the television activity of BBC Enterprises and the channel businesses of BBC World Service Television.

BBC Worldwide Television has two major areas of operation:
● Programme Licensing to international broadcasters and the generation of co-production business; and

- Channel Activity, led by the development of BBC branded satellite and cable channels around the world.

> In 1994–95 BBC Worldwide Television licensed more than 14,500 hours of programming to over 80 countries around the world, making the BBC Europe's largest exporter of television programmes. It also invests in programming; in 1994–95 a total of 111 co-production agreements were made with broadcasting organisations in 14 countries.
>
> The BBC and Pearson plc have established a strategic global alliance under which joint venture companies will distribute a range of BBC branded channels.

BBC World, the BBC's 24-hour international news and information channel, is available to more than 40 million homes across Africa, Asia, Australia, Canada, Europe and the Middle East.

BBC Prime, a 24-hour entertainment channel, is broadcast to three million subscribers across continental Europe. It is marketed and distributed by a joint venture company, European Channel Management, which is owned by the BBC, Thames Television (wholly owned by Pearson plc) and Cox Communications.

BBC Arabic Television, an Arabic language news and information channel, is produced at Television Centre in London and supplied to Orbit, a subscription-funded network broadcasting throughout the Middle East and North Africa.

BBC Worldwide Publishing

BBC Worldwide Publishing produces a wide range of books, spoken word audio tapes, videos, magazines and language learning materials linked to BBC programme output, which are marketed and distributed internationally. It also handles the licensing of BBC properties and brands for all forms of merchandising. From 1996 the multimedia division will be marketing CD-ROMs and on-line services.

COI Overseas Radio and Television Services

The Central Office of Information, which provides publicity material and other information services on behalf of government departments and other public agencies, produces radio programmes for overseas. Recorded material is sent to radio stations all over the world. COI television services also distribute material such as documentary and magazine programmes, commissioned and purchased by the Foreign & Commonwealth Office, or acquired from television broadcasters.

News Agencies

WTN (Worldwide Television News), owned by ITN, ABC (the American Broadcasting Corporation) and Channel 9 in Australia, supplies news and a wide range of television services to about 1,000 broadcasters in over 90 countries, as well as to governments and international corporations. It also produces British Satellite News, an international satellite news service, for the Foreign & Commonwealth Office. The service, under FCO editorial control, transmits programmes five days a week. These are distributed, mainly by satellite, free to television stations throughout Eastern Europe, the Middle East and Southern Africa for use in news bulletins. WTN provides services through the Eurovision network (see below) and by satellite.

For details of Reuters Television, see p. 497.

International Relations

European Agreements

Britain has implemented two important European agreements on cross-border broadcasting: the European Community Directive on Broadcasting and the Council of Europe Convention on Transfrontier Television. Under these, countries have to remove restrictions on the retransmission of programmes originating from other participating countries. They must also

CERAMICS

A Jasper Snake-Handled Vase, part of a commemorative collection marking the bicentenary of Josiah Wedgwood's death. Wedgwood is now an internationally renowned company employing 6,000 people, and accounts for a quarter of Britain's ceramic tableware exports.

Mary Rose Young lives and works from her house in the Forest of Dean, Gloucestershire. She employs 12 people and sells her colourful pottery to Europe, North America and the Far East; her designs also feature in private collections throughout the world.

PARKS AND GARDENS

Alexander Gardens, at the
heart of the Civic Centre in
Cardiff, Wales.

Inside the Warm Temperate
Aquatic House at the Royal
Botanic Garden, Edinburgh,
which is internationally
renowned as a centre for the
scientific study and
conservation of plants.

The gardens at Alton Towers, Staffordshire, were designed by the 18th century landscaper and architect Robert Abraham, who also designed the pagoda, pictured here.

The Time Garden at Carnfunnock Country Park, County Antrim, Northern Ireland, features a number of different sundials, demonstrating the techniques that have been used through the ages to measure time.

MUSIC TECHNOLOGY

Saxophonist Paul Hodgson has developed a software programme to help musicians and students understand more about how melodic improvisations can be added to musical compositions.

Students studying for a degree in Music Technology at London's Guildhall University making instruments in one of the university's workshops.

ensure that their own broadcasters observe certain minimum standards on advertising, sponsorship, taste and decency and the portrayal of sex and violence on television.

European Broadcasting Union

The BBC and the Radio Authority are members of the European Broadcasting Union, which manages Eurovision, the international network of television news and programme exchange. The Union is responsible for co-ordinating the exchange of programmes and news over the Eurovision network and intercontinental satellite links. It also maintains a technical monitoring station where frequency measurements and other observations on broadcasting stations are carried out. The Union provides a forum linking the major public services and national broadcasters of Western Europe and other parts of the world, and co-ordinates joint operations in radio and television.

International Telecommunications Union

The BBC takes part in the work of the International Telecommunications Union, the United Nations agency responsible for regulating and controlling all international telecommunications services, including radio and television. The Union also allocates and registers all radio frequencies, and promotes and co-ordinates the international study of technical problems in broadcasting.

Other International Bodies

The BBC is an associate member of the Asia-Pacific Broadcasting Union and also belongs to the Commonwealth Broadcasting Association, which meets every two years to discuss public service broadcasting issues.

TECHNICAL DEVELOPMENTS

The introduction of computer-based digital production equipment for both television and radio is one of the most significant technical advances in recent years affecting the broadcasting industry in Britain. It allows programmes to be made more quickly and more effectively, with the sound and vision information being held and manipulated on computer disc storage units. A significant proportion of programmes produced by the BBC and independent companies is edited on this type of equipment.

Other recent advances include:

- the introduction of 'all-digital' studios (including digital video recorders and control desks) at both the BBC and independent companies;

- the introduction of digital transmission links, mainly based on optical fibre technology, between studios and from studios to the transmitters;

- the use of miniature cameras and transmitters;

- the increased use of remote controlled cameras in studios and at remote locations; and

- an increasing use by radio broadcasters of digital sound links using 'dial-up' ISDN lines.

The BBC and the ITC also undertake long-term research into broadcast technology. The key topics under investigation include:

- digital television transmission;

- the transmission of digital radio broadcasting from terrestrial transmitters and by satellite;

- digital widescreen and high definition television (HDTV), and its associated surround sound;

- audio descriptive systems for delivering additional television sound channels that can be used to describe the programme for people with impaired sight; and

- realistic computer-generated 3D 'virtual' sets for television production.

Digital Terrestrial Broadcasting

In August 1995 the Government published a policy document on digital terrestrial television and radio in Britain (see Further Reading, p. 501). Its main proposals include:

- six frequency channels ('multiplexes') for digital terrestrial television would be available initially, each able to carry at least three television channels, with potential coverage ranging from 60 to over 90 per cent of the population; and
- seven radio frequency channels, each with capacity to offer at least six digital stereo programme services (one of these has already been allocated to the BBC for its national services and another will be allocated for independent national radio).

In addition:

- the ITC and the Radio Authority would be responsible for awarding licences to operate multiplexes;
- existing national television and radio broadcasters, including the Channel 3 and Channel 5 licence holders, would be offered a guaranteed place on a multiplex; and
- ownership regulations for digital terrestrial television and radio would be broadly in line with those for analogue. However, in recognition of the potentially larger number of television channels available, companies would be able to control any number of digital terrestrial television licences subject to a ceiling of 25 per cent of the available digital terrestrial capacity (provided they remain within a limit of 15 per cent share of total television audience).

The Press

More daily newspapers, national and regional, are sold for every person in Britain than in most other developed countries. On an average day 60 per cent of people over the age of 15 read a national morning newspaper; about 70 per cent read a Sunday newspaper.

National papers have an average total circulation of over 14 million on weekdays and about 16 million on Sundays, although the total readership is considerably greater. Men are more likely to read newspapers than women, and more people in the 45–64 age group read a daily newspaper than in any other age group.

There are about 1,400 regional and local newspaper titles and over 7,700 periodical publications.

Several newspapers have had very long and distinguished histories. The *Observer*, for example, first published in 1791, is the oldest national Sunday newspaper in the world, and *The Times*, Britain's oldest daily national newspaper, began publication in 1785. The weekly *Berrow's Worcester Journal*, established in 1690, claims to be the world's oldest newspaper in continuous circulation.

The press caters for a range of political views, interests and levels of education. Newspapers are almost always financially independent of any political party. Where they express pronounced views and show obvious political leanings in their editorial comments, these derive from proprietorial and other non-party influences. Nevertheless, during General Election campaigns many newspapers recommend their readers to vote for a particular political party. Even newspapers which adopt strong political views in their editorial columns include feature and other types of articles by authors of different political persuasions.

In order to preserve their character and traditions, some newspapers and periodicals are governed by trustee-type arrangements. Others have management arrangements that ensure their editors' authority and independence.

In recent years working practices throughout the newspaper industry have undergone major changes in response to the challenges posed by computer-based technology and the need to contain costs. Newsprint, about three-quarters of which is imported, forms about a quarter of average national newspaper costs; labour represents over half. In addition to sales, many newspapers and periodicals earn considerable amounts from their advertising. Total yearly spending of around £5,600 million on press advertising makes the press by far the largest advertising medium in Britain. Unlike most of its European counterparts the British press receives no subsidies and relatively few tax and postal concessions.

New Printing Technology

Publishers have been able to reduce production costs in recent years by using advanced computer systems for editing and production processes. The 'single keying' system, for example, allows journalists and advertising staff to input copy directly into a computer terminal, and then to transfer it electronically into columns of type. Many newspapers arrange page layouts on screen and output full pages to photographic paper bromides or film which are then used to make plates for the printing press. A number of newspapers still output columns in bromide format from the computerised typesetting operation; these are then pasted up into pages before being sent to the camera room for negatives to be produced from which the plates are made.

News International, publisher of three daily and two Sunday papers, has at its London Docklands headquarters more than 500 computer terminals, one of the largest systems installed at one time anywhere in the world. The *Financial Times* runs its printing plant in Docklands with about 170 production workers, compared with the 600 formerly employed in the City of London. Associated Newspapers, at its Docklands plant, is the only newspaper company to use flexography, an advanced printing process. Most other newspapers print by offset lithography, a method whereby the printed image is transferred, or offset, from the printing plate to a rubber blanket (cylinder) and then on to the paper. A number of the national newspapers print their regional and northern editions on regional newspaper presses.

There has been a tendency within Britain's regional and local press in recent years for weekly newspapers to close ageing press plants and contract out the printing of their titles to larger groups. Many of these groups have invested heavily in state-of-the-art full colour printing plants to meet their own requirements and those of a growing number of contract customers.

NATIONAL AND REGIONAL TITLES

Ownership of the national, London and regional daily newspapers lies in the hands of a number of large press publishing groups.

Although most enterprises are organised as limited liability companies, individual and partner proprietorship survives. The large national newspaper and periodical publishers are major corporations; many are involved in the whole field of publishing and communications.

The National Press

The national press consists of 11 morning daily papers and nine Sunday papers (see Table 29.1). Formerly they were produced in or near Fleet Street in central London with, in some cases, northern editions being printed in Manchester. All the national papers have now moved their editorial and printing facilities to other parts of London or away from the capital altogether; some use contract printing. The *Independent*, for example, is printed in Bradford, Northampton and Portsmouth. Scottish editions of the *Sun*, *Today*, the *News of the World* and the *Sunday Times* (Scottish Section) are printed in Glasgow.

In order to improve distribution and sales overseas, editions of the *Financial Times* are printed in Frankfurt, Roubaix (northern France), New Jersey and Tokyo, while the *Guardian* prints an international edition in Frankfurt. The *European*, a weekly English-language international newspaper, is printed in Britain, France, Germany and Hungary.

National newspapers are often described as either 'quality', 'popular' or 'mid-market' papers on the basis of differences in style and content. Five dailies and four Sundays are usually described as 'quality' newspapers, which are directed at readers who want full information on a wide range of public matters. Popular newspapers appeal to people wanting news of a more entertaining character, presented more concisely. 'Mid-market' publications cover the intermediate market. Quality papers are normally broadsheet (large-sheet) in format and mid-market and popular papers tabloid (small-sheet).

Many newspapers are printed in colour and most produce colour supplements as part of the Saturday or Sunday paper, with articles on travel, food and wine, and other leisure topics.

The leading Scottish papers, *The Scotsman*

Table 29.1: National Newspapers

Title and foundation date	Controlled by	Circulation[a] average February–July 1995
National dailies		
'Populars'		
Daily Mirror (1903)	Mirror Group plc	2,535,998
Daily Star (1978)	United Newspapers	658,690
The Sun (1964)	News International plc	4,060,409
'Mid market'		
Daily Mail (1896)	Associated Newspapers Ltd	1,788,100
Daily Express (1900)	United Newspapers	1,273,230
Today (1986)	News International plc	557,955
'Qualities'		
Financial Times (1888)	Pearson	294,917
The Daily Telegraph (1855)	The Telegraph plc	1,064,906
The Guardian (1821)	Guardian Media Group plc	397,234
The Independent (1986)	Mirror Group consortium[b]	295,490
The Times (1785)	News International plc	650,067
National Sundays		
'Populars'		
News of the World (1843)	News International plc	4,722,306
Sunday Mirror (1963)	Mirror Group plc	2,570,280
The People (1881)	Mirror Group plc	2,062,729
'Mid market'		
The Mail on Sunday (1982)	Associated Newspapers Ltd	1,962,425
Sunday Express (1918)	United Newspapers	1,394,456
'Qualities'		
Sunday Telegraph (1961)	The Telegraph plc	697,926
The Independent on Sunday (1990)	Mirror Group consortium[b]	328,893
The Observer (1791)	Guardian Media Group plc	458,171
The Sunday Times (1822)	News International plc	1,246,344

[a]Circulation figures are those of the Audit Bureau of circulations (consisting of publishers, advertisers and advertising agencies) and are certified average daily or weekly net sales for the period.

[b]The consortium comprises Mirror Group plc, Promotora de Informaciones and Espresso International Holding.

and the *Herald*, have considerable circulations outside Scotland.

There is a growing market for news and information in the electronic media, and quality papers such as the *Financial Times* and the *Daily Telegraph* provide material for use on databases and videotext services.

Regional Newspapers

There are about 100 daily (Monday to Saturday) and Sunday newspapers, and about 1,300 weekly paid-for and free newspapers (not including business, sporting and religious newspapers). It is estimated that 88 per cent of adults read a regional or local newspaper.

England

Of the morning papers the *Yorkshire Post* (Leeds), the *Northern Echo* (Darlington) and the *Eastern Daily Press* (Norwich), each has a circulation of approximately 78,000, and two provincial Sunday papers—the *Sunday Mercury* (Birmingham) and the *Sunday Sun* (Newcastle upon Tyne)—sell 146,500 and 127,700 copies respectively. Circulation figures of evening papers start at about 10,000 and most are in the 20,000 to 100,000 range. Those with much larger sales include the *Manchester Evening News* (194,000), Wolverhampton's *Express and Star* (210,000) and the *Birmingham Evening Mail* (201,000). Paid-for weekly papers have a mainly local appeal and most have circulations in the 5,000 to 60,000 range.

London has one paid-for evening paper, the *Evening Standard*, with a circulation of 462,000. It covers national and international news as well as local affairs. A number of evening papers are published in the outer metropolitan area. Local weeklies include papers for every district in Greater London, which are often different local editions of one centrally published paper.

Wales

Wales has one daily morning newspaper, the *Western Mail*, with a circulation of 64,600, and *Wales on Sunday*, with a circulation of 61,000. Both are published in Cardiff. Evening papers published in Wales are the *South Wales Echo*, Cardiff; the *South Wales Argus*, Newport; the *South Wales Evening Post*, Swansea; and the *Evening Leader*, Wrexham. Circulations range from 32,000 to 80,000. North Wales is also served by the *Daily Post*, published in Liverpool, and the *Liverpool Echo*.

The weekly press (83 publications) includes English-language papers, some of which carry articles in Welsh; bilingual papers; and Welsh-language papers. Welsh community newspapers receive an annual grant as part of the Government's wider financial support for the Welsh language.

Scotland

The daily morning papers, with circulations of between 8,500 and 750,000, are *The Scotsman* (published in Edinburgh); the *Herald*, (published in Glasgow); the *Daily Record* (sister paper of the *Daily Mirror*); the Scottish *Daily Express*; the Scottish edition of the *Sun*; the *Dundee Courier and Advertiser*; the *Aberdeen Press and Journal*; and the *Paisley Daily Express*. The daily evening papers have circulations in the range of 20,000 to 140,000 and include the Edinburgh *Evening News*, Glasgow's *Evening Times*, Dundee's *Evening Telegraph*, Aberdeen's *Evening Express* and the *Greenock Telegraph*. Local weekly newspapers number about 140.

The Sunday papers are the *Sunday Mail*, the *Sunday Post* and a quality broadsheet paper, *Scotland on Sunday*. The national *Sunday Express* has a Scottish edition (printed in Manchester) and the *Observer* and the *Sunday Times* carry Scottish supplements.

Northern Ireland

Northern Ireland has two morning newspapers, one evening and two Sunday papers, all published in Belfast, with circulations ranging from 44,000 to 133,000. They are the *News Letter* (unionist), the *Irish News* (nationalist), the evening *Belfast Telegraph*, *Sunday Life* and *Sunday World* (Northern Ireland edition).

There are about 50 weeklies. Newspapers from the Irish Republic, as well as the British national press, are widely read in Northern Ireland.

Free Distribution Newspapers

About 800 free distribution newspapers, mostly weekly and financed by advertising, are published in Britain; over half are produced by established newspaper publishers. They have enjoyed rapid growth in recent years and now have an estimated total weekly circulation of about 33 million.

Ethnic Minority Publications

Many newspapers and magazines in Britain are produced by members of ethnic minorities. Most are published weekly, fortnightly or monthly. A Chinese newspaper, *Sing Tao*, the Urdu *Daily Jang* (see below) and the Arabic *Al-Arab*, however, are dailies.

Afro-Caribbean newspapers include the *Gleaner* and *West Indian Digest*. The *Voice* and *Caribbean Times*, both weeklies, are aimed at the black population in general. The *Weekly Journal*, the first 'quality' broadsheet aimed at Britain's black community, was launched in 1992.

The *Asian Times* is an English language weekly for people of Asian descent; the *Sikh Courier* is produced quarterly. Examples of ethnic language newspapers include the Urdu *Daily Jang*, an offshoot of the largest circulation paper in Pakistan, and the weeklies *Garavi Gujarat* and *Gujarat Samachar*. Publications also appear in Bengali, Hindi and Punjabi. The fortnightly *Asian Trader* and *Asian Business* are both successful ethnic business publications, while *Cineblitz International* targets those interested in the Asian film industry.

Many provincial papers print special editions for their local populations. The *Leicester Mercury*, for example, publishes a daily Asian edition, incorporating news from the South Asian sub-continent.

THE PERIODICAL PRESS

The 7,700 periodical publications are classified as 'consumer general interest', 'special interest' and 'business-to-business'. There are also several hundred 'house magazines' produced by businesses or public services for their employees and/or clients. Directories and similar publications number more than 2,000. The 'alternative' press comprises a large number of titles, many of them devoted to radical politics, community matters, religion, the occult, science or ecology.

Consumer general and specialist periodicals comprise magazines for a wide range of interests. These include women's magazines; publications for children; religious periodicals; fiction magazines; magazines dealing with sport, motoring, gardening, youth interests and music; humour; retirement; and computer magazines. Learned societies, trade unions, regiments, universities and other organisations also produce publications.

Weekly periodicals with the highest sales are those which carry full details of the forthcoming week's television and radio programmes, including the satellite schedules *What's on TV* has a circulation figure of over 1.6 million, followed by the *Radio Times* with 1.4 million and *TV Times* with 1 million.

Woman's Weekly, *Woman's Own*, *Woman*, *Weekly News* (which sells mainly in Scotland), *Woman's Realm* and *My Weekly* have circulations in the 293,000 to 790,000 range. In recent years several women's magazines owned by overseas publishing houses have achieved large circulations: *Prima* and *Best*, for instance, each sell over 550,000 copies, while *Bella* and *Hello!* are also widely read. There is a growing market for men's general interest magazines—for example, *GQ*, *Esquire* and *Loaded*, with circulations ranging from about 92,000 to 115,000. *Focus* and *Arena* are also popular titles.

Smash Hits, with a circulation of 275,000, is a fortnightly magazine dealing with pop music and teenage lifestyles. *Viz*, a cartoon comic aimed at young adults, sells 558,000 copies. Of monthly magazines, *Reader's Digest* has the highest circulation (1.7 million).

The leading journals of opinion include *The Economist*, an independent conservative publication covering a wide range of topics. *New Statesman and Society* reviews social issues, politics, literature and the arts from an independent socialist point of view, and the *Spectator* covers similar subjects from an independent conservative standpoint.

New Scientist reports on science and technology in terms that the non-specialist reader can understand. *Private Eye*, a satirical fortnightly, also covers public affairs. Weekly 'listings' magazines, such as *Time Out*, provide details of cultural and other events in London and other large cities.

Literary and political journals, and those specialising in international and Commonwealth affairs, appear monthly or quarterly, and generally appeal to a more academic readership. Many of the business, scientific and professional journals, whose publication ranges from twice weekly to quarterly, have a considerable circulation overseas.

NEWS AGENCIES

The principal news agencies in Britain are Reuters, based in London, the Press Association and FT Extel/AFP-Extel News Ltd.

Reuters

Reuters is a publicly owned company, employing over 14,000 staff in 91 countries. It has more than 1,800 staff journalists, photographers and cameramen in 138 news bureaux. The company serves subscribers in 150 countries, including financial institutions; commodities houses; traders in currencies, equities and bonds; major corporations; government agencies; news agencies; newspapers; and radio and television stations.

Reuters has developed the world's largest privately leased communications network to transmit its services. It provides the media with a wide range of news, news video, news pictures and graphics. Services for business clients comprise constantly updated financial news, historical information, facilities for computerised trading, and the supply of communications and other equipment for financial dealing rooms. Information is distributed electronically. Reuters wholly owns Reuters Television (RTV), the largest international television news agency in the world. RTV supplies news video to over 200 broadcasters and their networks in 84 countries.

The Press Association

The Press Association operates through three companies—PA News, PA Sport and PA Data Design—as the national news agency for Britain and the Irish Republic. It offers newspapers and broadcasters a comprehensive range of news and information services.

PA News provides editorial and photographic coverage of the nation's news to the media via satellite, and supplies the news and sports pages broadcast by Teletext on ITV and Channel 4. It also offers an on-line news and sport information service—NewsFile—as well as extensive news cuttings and picture libraries.

PA Sport distributes full coverage of national sport, complemented by a fast results service.

PA Data Design creates camera-ready complete pages of sports results, share prices, racecards, TV listings and weather reports for printing by newspapers. The company is an authority on Internet[1] publishing and was one of the first commercial organisations in Britain to connect its network to the Internet.

FT Extel/AFP-Extel News Ltd

AFX News Ltd, a joint venture of Agence France-Presse and FT Information, supplies information and services to financial and business communities throughout the world. Based in London, and now part of the Financial Times Group, FT Extel has a network of offices in Europe, the United States and in the Asia Pacific region. Data is collected from all the world's major stock exchanges, companies and the international press. FT Extel is a major source of reference material on companies and on securities and taxation data, and supplies up-to-the-minute business and company news.

Other Agencies

News services are also provided by Associated Press and United Press International, which are British subsidiaries of United States news agencies, and UK News. A number of other agencies and news services have offices in London, and there are minor agencies in other cities. Syndication of

---

[1] The Internet is a global, on-line computer network connecting governments, companies, universities, and many other networks and users.

features is not as common in Britain as in some countries, but a few agencies specialise in this type of work.

PRESS INSTITUTIONS

Trade associations include the Newspaper Publishers Association, whose members publish national newspapers, and the Newspaper Society, which represents regional and local newspapers in England, Wales and Northern Ireland. The Scottish Daily Newspaper Society represents the interests of daily and Sunday newspapers in Scotland; the Scottish Newspaper Publishers' Association acts on behalf of the owners of weekly newspapers in Scotland; and Associated Northern Ireland Newspapers is made up of proprietors of weekly newspapers in Northern Ireland. The membership of the Periodical Publishers Association includes most independent publishers of business, professional and consumer journals.

Organisations representing journalists are the National Union of Journalists, with around 25,000 members, and the Chartered Institute of Journalists, with about 1,500 members. The main printing union is the Graphical, Paper and Media Union, with a membership of around 270,000.

The Foreign Press Association was formed in 1888 to help the correspondents of overseas newspapers in their work by arranging press conferences, tours, briefings, and other services and facilities.

The Guild of Editors is the officially recognised professional body for newspaper editors and their equivalents in radio and television. It has approximately 420 members and exists to defend press freedom and to promote high editorial standards. The British Association of Industrial Editors is the professional organisation for editors of house journals. The Association of British Editors represents the whole range of media, including radio, television, newspapers and magazines.

TRAINING AND EDUCATION

The National Council for the Training of Journalists (NCTJ), which represents many regional newspaper publishers, sets and conducts examinations, and organises short training courses for journalists.

The two main methods of entry into newspaper journalism are selection for NCTJ pre-entry courses at a college of further or higher education or direct recruitment by a regional or local newspaper. Both types of entrant take part in 'on-the-job' training. Similar courses exist for press photographers.

The first undergraduate courses in journalism in Britain started in 1991 at City University, London, at the University of Central Lancashire and at the London College of Printing, which also provides GCE (General Certificate of Education) Advanced (A) level courses in journalism. Postgraduate courses in journalism are available at the University of Wales, Cardiff; City University, London; the London College of Printing; Strathclyde University/Glasgow Caledonian University; and the Universities of Central Lancashire and Bournemouth.

Courses for regional newspapers in such subjects as newspaper sales, advertising, and management are provided by the Newspaper Society's training service. Some newspaper publishers carry out journalist training independently of the NCTJ, awarding their own certificates or diplomas. National Vocational Qualifications (see p. 442) are now available in newspaper journalism.

Specialist training courses for journalists and broadcasters from developing countries and from Eastern Europe are offered by the Thomson Foundation in Cardiff. The Foundation runs training courses overseas and provides consultants to assist newspapers and news agencies in editorial advertising as well as broadcast management.

Newspapers in Education, a worldwide scheme using newspapers to improve standards of literacy among young people, is run in Britain by the Newspaper Society. The scheme involves using newspapers in schools for teaching a wide range of subjects at all levels of education. The scheme has over 600 projects operated by regional newspapers in partnership with local schools.

Through its charitable trust—the Reuter Foundation—Reuters offers assistance to overseas journalists to study and train in

Britain and other parts of the world. The Foundation awards fellowships to overseas journalists to spend up to one year at Oxford University. It also runs shorter practical training programmes in London for journalists from the former communist countries of Eastern Europe and Central Asia.

The Periodicals Training Council is the official training organisation in periodical publishing. It offers a range of short courses covering management, editorial work, advertisement sales and circulation sales. It has special responsibility for editorial training and administers an editorial training scheme for those already in employment.

PRESS CONDUCT AND LAW

The Press Complaints Commission

The Press Complaints Commission, a non-statutory body, was established in 1991 following recommendations in a report on privacy and related matters by a government-appointed independent committee. The Commission was set up by the newspaper and periodical industry in a final attempt to make self-regulation of the press work properly. It is funded by PRESSBOF (the Press Standards Board of Finance), which co-ordinates and promotes self-regulation within the industry. These measures were prompted by growing criticism of press standards, with allegations of unjustified invasion of privacy and inaccurate and biased reporting, among other abuses, resulting in calls for government regulation of the press.

In its White Paper (*Privacy and Media Intrusion: The Government's Response*) published in July 1995, the Government rejected proposals for statutory regulation of the press, and for legislation to give protection to privacy. Instead, it endorsed self-regulation under the Commission, and recommended further measures to make self-regulation more effective.

The Commission's membership is drawn from newspaper and magazine editors and from people outside the industry. It deals with complaints by members of the public about the contents and conduct of newspapers and magazines, and advises editors and journalists. It operates a code of practice agreed by editors governing respect for privacy, opportunity to reply, corrections, journalists' behaviour, references to race and religion, payments to criminals for articles, protection of confidential sources and other matters. The Commission publishes regular reports of its findings.

The industry and the Press Complaints Commission have reinforced voluntary regulation through, for example:

- measures to increase the number of independent members of the Commission to ensure a lay majority;

- a strengthening of the code of practice, and the incorporation of the code into the contracts of employment of most editors and journalists;

- the setting up of a helpline service for members of the public who fear the code of practice has been, or is about to be, breached; and

- the appointment of a Privacy Commissioner with special powers to investigate complaints about privacy.

The Press and the Law

There is no state control or censorship of the newspaper and periodical press, and newspaper proprietors, editors and journalists are subject to the law in the same way as any other citizen. However, certain statutes include sections which apply to the press.

There are laws governing:

- the extent of newspaper ownership in television and radio companies (see p. 501);

- the transfer of newspaper assets; and

- the right of press representatives to be supplied with agenda and reports for meetings of local authorities and reasonable facilities for taking notes and telephoning reports.

There is a legal requirement to reproduce 'the printer's imprint' (the printer's name and address) on all publications, including newspapers. Publishers are legally obliged to deposit copies of newspapers and other publications at the British Library (see p. 476).

Publication of advertisements is governed by wide-ranging legislation, including public health, financial services and fraud legislation. Legal restrictions are imposed on certain types of prize competition; copyrights come under various copyright laws.

Laws on contempt of court, official secrets and defamation are also relevant to the press. A newspaper may not publish comments on the conduct of judicial proceedings which are likely to prejudice the reputation of the courts for fairness before or during the actual proceedings, nor may it publish before or during a trial anything which might influence the result. The unauthorised acquisition and publication of official information in such areas as defence and international relations, where such unauthorised disclosure would be harmful, are offences under the Official Secrets Acts 1911 to 1989. However, these are restrictions on publication—that is, on dissemination to the public by any means—not just through the printed press.

Most legal proceedings against the press are libel actions brought by private individuals.

Defence Advisory Notices

Government officials and representatives of the media form the Defence, Press and Broadcasting Advisory Committee, which has agreed that in some circumstances the publication of certain categories of information might endanger national security. Details of these categories are contained in Defence Advisory Notices (DA Notices) circulated to the media, whose members are asked to seek advice from the Secretary of the Committee, a retired senior military officer, before publishing information in these areas. Compliance with any advice offered by the Secretary is expected but there is no legal force behind it and the final decision on whether to publish rests with the editor, producer or publisher concerned.

The Notices were published for the first time in July 1993 to promote a better understanding of the system and to contribute to greater openness in government.

Advertising Practice

Advertising in all non-broadcast media, such as newspapers, magazines, posters, sales promotions, cinema and direct mail, is regulated by the Advertising Standards Authority, an independent body funded by a levy on display advertising expenditure. The Authority aims to promote and enforce the highest standards of advertising in the interests of the public through its supervision of the British Codes of Advertising and Sales Promotion.

The Codes' basic principles are to ensure that advertisements:

- are legal, decent, honest and truthful;

- are prepared with a sense of responsibility to the consumer and society; and

- conform to the principles of fair competition as generally accepted in business.

The Authority monitors advertisements to ensure their compliance with the Codes and investigates any complaints received.

The advertising industry has agreed to abide by the Codes and to support them with effective sanctions. Free and confidential pre-publication advice is offered to assist publishers, agencies and advertisers. The Authority's main sanction is to recommend that advertisements considered to be in breach of the Code should not be published. This is normally sufficient to ensure that an advertisement is withdrawn or amended. The Authority also publishes monthly reports on the results of its investigations.

The Authority is recognised by the Office of Fair Trading as the established means of controlling non-broadcast advertising. It can refer misleading advertisements to the Director General of Fair Trading, who has the power to seek an injunction to prevent their publication.

Media Ownership

Existing Rules

The Broadcasting Act 1990 established rules designed to enable the ITC and Radio Authority to keep ownership of the broadcasting media widely spread and to prevent undue concentrations of single and cross-media ownership. Ownership of broadcasters by companies based outside the European Union is largely prohibited. Newspapers are allowed relatively small stakes in Channels 3 (and 5), and national and local radio, but are not restricted in non-domestic satellite broadcasters. Public telecommunications operators are not allowed to have controlling interests in any Channel 3, Channel 5, national radio or domestic satellite licence; and political bodies and local authorities are barred from holding licences.

Following a limited relaxation of the ITV (independent television) ownership rules at the beginning of 1994, a company may hold any two regional licences (except in London), a 20 per cent stake in a third company, and 5 per cent in any further licences. A local newspaper can own a local radio station if the station does not serve an area overlapping that served by the newspaper.

Government consent is needed to transfer a newspaper or newspaper assets to a proprietor whose newspapers have an average daily circulation amounting, with that of the newspaper to be taken over, to 500,000 or more copies. Except in certain limited cases, consent may be given only after the President of the Board of Trade has referred the matter to the Monopolies and Mergers Commission and received its report.

Policy Document

Following a review of media ownership regulation, the Government issued a policy document in May 1995. This concludes:

- that there is a continuing case for specific regulations governing media ownership, beyond those which are applied by the general competition law; but

- that there is a need to liberalise the existing ownership regulations both within and across different media sectors.

The Government intends to enact legislation which would, among other things:

- allow newspaper groups with less than 20 per cent of national newspaper circulation to apply to control television broadcasters constituting up to 15 per cent of the total television market;

- give an independent regulator the power to disallow such control when it is not in the public interest; and

- prevent the development of local media monopolies by disallowing newspaper groups from controlling any regional Channel 3 or local radio licence in areas where the newspaper group has more than 30 per cent of regional or local newspaper circulation.

Further Reading

The Future of the BBC: Serving the Nation, Competing Worldwide. Cm 2621. HMSO, 1994.

Broadcasting. Aspects of Britain series, HMSO, 1993.

Media Ownership: The Government's Proposals. Cm 2872. HMSO, 1995.

Privacy and Media Intrusion: The Government's Response. Cm 2918. HMSO, 1995.

Digital Terrestrial Broadcasting: the Government's Proposals. Cm 2946. HMSO, 1995.

30 Sport and Active Recreation

Over 100 British sportsmen and women currently hold world championship titles in sports ranging from athletics to windsurfing. The most popular participation sports include swimming, cycling and keep fit/yoga. More than half the population of Britain regularly takes part in some form of sporting activity.

PARTICIPATION

Improvements in facilities and growing awareness of the importance of regular exercise for good health have contributed to increasing levels of participation in sport.

It is estimated that 29 million people over the age of 16 regularly take part in sport or exercise. The *1993 General Household Survey* found that almost two-thirds of those interviewed had taken part in at least one sporting activity during the previous four weeks. The most popular participation sports or activities are walking (including rambling and hiking), swimming, snooker/pool, keep fit/yoga and cycling.

Men were more likely than women to have participated in a sporting activity, with 72 per cent of men claiming to have taken part in at least one sport during the previous four weeks compared with 57 per cent of women.

Sport: Raising the Game

The Government aims to encourage greater participation in sport from an early age. In July 1995 it published a policy statement on sport—*Sport: Raising the Game*—which sets out its proposals for providing the highest standards of sporting provision and facilities from grass roots through to international level. The main proposals include:

- increased investment in coaching schemes for teachers with the opportunity for them to acquire coaching qualifications;

- a further £1 million to be provided by the Sports Councils (see p. 505) for coaching opportunities via the National Coaching Foundation (see p. 506) and the governing bodies of sport;

- a new £2 million challenge fund for promoting links between schools and clubs;

- the setting up of a working group to advise on increasing sports scholarships in higher education; and

- the establishment of a British Academy of Sport as the focal point of a national network of centres of excellence.

The Government envisages that the Academy would be funded by the National Lottery (see p. 512) and would offer a wide range of services and facilities for sportsmen and women and their coaches. These would include sports medicine and science services and financial support for individual athletes in the form of scholarships. The proposals are to be developed by the Sports Council.

A parallel paper—*Scotland's Sporting Future: A New Start*—tailored to the specific needs and circumstances in Scotland was also launched in July 1995.

Women and Sport

Efforts to narrow the gap between men's and women's participation in sporting activities have resulted in an increase in the number of women taking part in sport. This includes traditionally male dominated sports, such as football, rugby and snooker. Emphasis has now switched to encouraging women to adopt leadership roles—as coaches, officials and administrators, for example. Projects to promote coaching opportunities have been established by the Sports Councils in partnership with the National Coaching Foundation and the Women's Sports Foundation (WSF).

The WSF is a voluntary organisation promoting the interests of women and girls in sport and active recreation. With Sports Council funding, the WSF encourages the establishment of women's sports groups throughout Britain and organises a wide range of events and activities. It runs both the Sportswomen of the Year Awards and an annual nationwide awards scheme for girls and young women between the ages of 11 and 19.

Sport for People with Disabilities

The governing bodies of sport are increasingly taking responsibility for people with disabilities. Close liaison takes place with the Sports Council, which provides advice to governing bodies on encouraging the integration of people with disabilities.

The key organisations for people with disabilities are the British Sports Association for the Disabled (BSAD), the United Kingdom Sports Association for People with Learning Disability (UKSAPLD), the British Paralympic Association (BPA—see p. 506) and a range of bodies concerned with individual disabilities and single sports. These include the Riding for the Disabled Association, which caters for some 25,000 riders.

The BSAD is a national body working across all the disabilities. It organises regional and national championships in a wide range of sports and also runs training courses, coaching courses and development days. The Scottish and the Welsh Sports Associations for the Disabled and Disability Action (Northern Ireland) have similar co-ordinating roles.

The UKSAPLD is a co-ordinating body with a membership of over 20 national organisations. It promotes and develops opportunities in sport and recreation for people with learning disability throughout Britain. It is also responsible, in partnership with the BPA, for the training and preparation of the Great Britain team in the Paralympics.

There are five national disability sports organisations concerned with individual disabilities. These organisations provide coaching and help to organise national competitions in conjunction with the national governing bodies of sport and the BSAD. They comprise:

- the British Amputee and Les Autres Sports Association;
- British Blind Sport;
- the British Deaf Sports Council;
- the British Wheelchair Sports Foundation; and
- Cerebral Palsy Sport.

Young People

Special programmes of activity for young people are run by the governing bodies of individual sports. In addition, the four Sports Councils (see p. 505) help to organise local and national initiatives to encourage more young people to take part in sport. Young people also have the opportunity to take part in a wide variety of sports in school (see p. 504).

SPORT IN SCHOOLS

All schools (except those solely for infants) are expected to have a playing field or the use of one, and most secondary schools have a gymnasium. Some have other amenities, such as swimming pools, sports halls and halls designed for dance and movement.

National Curriculum

The Government believes that all young children should have the opportunity to learn basic sports skills. It has therefore made physical education (PE), which includes sport, a compulsory subject in the National Curriculum (see p. 435) for all pupils aged 5 to 16 in state-maintained schools in England and Wales.

A revised National Curriculum introduced in August 1995 places a greater emphasis on traditional team games and competitive sports. The Curriculum also states that all pupils should be able to swim at least 25 metres by the age of 11.

In Scotland the Secretary of State for Scotland has issued National Guidelines which contain programmes of study and attainment targets for physical activity for pupils aged 5 to 14.

Sportsmark

The Government has announced that it intends to establish a Sportsmark scheme to recognise schools that have effective policies for promoting sport, with additional 'Gold Star' awards for the most innovative. The scheme sets the target of four hours of sporting provision a week outside formal lessons and will be managed by the Sports Council.

Accountability and Inspection

The Government is to require schools to include in their annual prospectuses details of their sporting aims and the provision for sport and to record in their annual governors' reports how they have met these aims. In addition, the Government is to ask OFSTED (see p. 439) to inspect the quality and range of games offered by schools and to report annually to Parliament on its findings.

Partnerships with the Local Community

The Government is encouraging stronger links between schools and the wider community to ensure that children have access to the sports amenities which clubs and associations can make available outside school hours. Efforts to strengthen these links have been promoted by schemes such as 'Team Sport Scotland', which aims to promote the development of school-aged team sport, with support from The Scottish Office.

> Since its inception in 1991, Team Sport Scotland has provided significant opportunities for coach education and in-service training of teachers, covering 700 courses involving over 10,000 participants. It has also organised almost 1,500 events attracting over 100,000 school-aged participants. The initiative has now been extended to include non-team sports, such as athletics and swimming, as well as sport for people with disabilities.

The Government wants to increase business sponsorship in schools by encouraging the private sector to sponsor school teams, adopt a sporting facility or sponsor inter-school competitions.

ORGANISATION AND ADMINISTRATION

Responsibility for government policy on sport and active recreation in England rests with the Secretary of State for National Heritage. The Secretaries of State for Wales, Scotland and Northern Ireland are responsible for sport in their countries.

Responsibility for the organisation and promotion of sport is largely decentralised, and many sport and recreation facilities are provided by local authorities. The main mechanism by which the Government directly channels financial assistance to sport is through the Sports Councils.

Sports Councils

The Sports Councils, appointed and directly funded by the Government, are the Government's principal advisers on sporting matters. The Government works closely with them in implementing its sports policies.

There are currently four Councils:

- the Sports Council—for general matters affecting Great Britain and specifically English matters;

- the Sports Council for Wales;

- the Scottish Sports Council; and

- the Sports Council for Northern Ireland.

The Councils make grants for sports development, coaching and administration to the governing bodies of sports and other national organisations, and administer the National Sports Centres (see p. 507). Grants and loans are also made to voluntary organisations, local authorities and commercial organisations to help them provide sports facilities. In 1994–95 the Councils received government funds of approximately £67 million.

Facilities receiving support from the Sports Councils include sports halls, indoor swimming pools, intensive-use pitches, indoor tennis halls and school facilities.

Development of Sport

Strategies for the development of sport have been drawn up by the four Sports Councils. The aims are broadly to ensure that:

- all young people have the opportunity to acquire basic sports skills;

- everyone has the opportunity to take part in the sports or active recreation of their choice; and

- everyone with the interest and the ability has the opportunity to improve their standard of performance in sport and fulfil their potential.

The Sports Councils are increasingly focusing resources on young people and the development of excellence.

Restructuring

The Sports Council will be replaced in January 1996 by two new bodies: the United Kingdom Sports Council (UKSC) and the Sports Council for England.

The UKSC will have ten members: an independent chairman; the chairmen of the four other Sports Councils; the chairman of the British Olympic Association; and representatives of amateur and professional sport. It will represent Britain and seek to increase its influence in international sport, with a co-ordinating role for bringing major international events to Britain. The UKSC will not have a supervisory role, but instead will co-ordinate matters where the Government considers that there is a need for a policy covering the whole of Britain. These include doping control, sports science, sports medicine and coaching.

The Sports Council for England will concentrate its resources on an increased programme of direct support to governing bodies to help the 'grass roots' of sport, and on services in support of sporting excellence, such as the National Sports Centres in England. The new council will give particular support to the pursuit of high standards of sporting achievement, concentrating a greater proportion of its funding on fewer sports than at present. Governing bodies will be required to prepare plans with specific targets for the development of their sports, from the grass roots to the highest competitive levels.

Local Authorities

Local authorities are the main providers of basic sport and recreation facilities for the local community. In England local authorities manage over 1,500 indoor centres, largely built in the last 20 years, as well as numerous outdoor amenities. The facilities include parks, lakes, playing fields, sports halls, tennis courts, golf courses, swimming pools, gymnasiums and sports centres catering for a wide range of activities.

There has been a rapid growth in the provision of artificial pitches—largely for hockey—and a similar increase in the number of leisure pools, which offer wave machines, waterfalls, jacuzzis and other leisure equipment. Gross annual expenditure by local authorities on sport and recreation amounts to some £900 million in England alone.

National Sports Associations

The Central Council of Physical Recreation (CCPR) is the largest sport and recreation federation in the world. It comprises 202 British bodies and 66 English associations, most of which are governing bodies of sport. Similar associations in Scotland, Wales and Northern Ireland are the Scottish Sports Association, the Welsh Sports Association and the Northern Ireland Council of Physical Recreation (NICPR). Their primary aim is to represent the interests of their members to the appropriate national and local authorities, including the Sports Councils, from which they receive funding. Award schemes run by the associations include the CCPR's Community Sports Leaders Award scheme and the NICPR's Service to Sport Awards.

British Olympic Association

The British Olympic Association (BOA) is the National Olympic Committee for Britain and comprises representatives of the 33 governing bodies of Olympic sports. Its primary function is to organise the participation of British teams in the Olympic Games, but it is also responsible for nominating British cities for staging the Olympics.

The BOA determines the size of British Olympic teams and sets standards for selection, raises funds and makes all necessary arrangements for Britain's participation in the Olympics. It also makes important contributions to the preparation of competitors in the period between Games. The Association's British Olympic Medical Centre at Northwick Park Hospital in north London supplies a medical back-up service for competitors before and during the Olympic Games. The BOA is supported by sponsorship and by donations from the private sector and the public.

The BOA is investigating whether a British city could submit a viable bid for the 2008 Olympic Games. The Sports Council's choice of venue for Britain's new national stadium is likely to influence the BOA's decision.

British Paralympic Association

Britain's participation in the Paralympics is organised by the BPA, which liaises closely with the BOA. The BPA assists in the preparation and training of Paralympic and other international teams, and advises the Sports Council on the distribution of grants for all international disabled sports events.

Sports Governing Bodies

Individual sports are run by over 400 independent governing bodies, whose functions include drawing up rules, holding events, regulating membership, and selecting and training national teams. Governing bodies receiving funding from the Sports Councils are required to produce four-year development plans which should include their proposals for young people. There are also organisations representing people who take part in more informal physical recreation, such as walking and cycling. The majority of the sports clubs in Britain belong to the appropriate governing body.

National Coaching Foundation

The National Coaching Foundation (NCF) works closely with national governing bodies of sport, local authorities, and higher and further education. Supported by the Sports Councils, it provides a comprehensive range of coach education and coaching development services for coaches in all sports. The NCF network has ten regional offices in England.

The NCF also runs Champion Coaching, a programme which provides after-school coaching in a wide variety of sports in England, Wales and Northern Ireland for those aged 11 to 14. In 1995–96 there will be 76 schemes, with about 55,000 children and 6,000 coaches participating.

Sports Clubs

A wide variety of recreational facilities are provided by local sports clubs. Some cater for indoor recreation, but more common are those providing sports grounds, particularly for cricket, football, rugby, hockey, tennis and golf. It is estimated that there are over 150,000 voluntary sports clubs affiliated to the national governing bodies of sport. Many clubs linked to business firms cater for sporting activities. Commercial facilities include tenpin bowling centres, ice and roller-skating rinks, squash courts, golf courses and driving ranges, riding stables, marinas and, increasingly, fitness centres.

Countryside Bodies

The Countryside Commission (for England), the Countryside Council for Wales and Scottish Natural Heritage are responsible for conserving and improving the natural beauty of the countryside, and for encouraging the provision of facilities for open-air recreation. They are also responsible for designating National Parks, 'areas of outstanding natural beauty', heritage coasts and National Scenic Areas (see p. 363).

In Northern Ireland the Ulster Countryside Committee advises the Department of the Environment on the preservation of amenities and the designation of 'areas of outstanding natural beauty'.

British Waterways

British Waterways is a publicly owned body responsible for managing and developing much of Great Britain's inland waterways. Many leisure and recreational pursuits, such as angling and various types of sailing and boating, are enjoyed on waterways and reservoirs. British Waterways, which is responsible for approximately 2,000 miles (3,220 km) of canals and water navigations, actively promotes water safety and organises community activities.

National Playing Fields Association

The National Playing Fields Association (NPFA) is a registered charity which aims to ensure that there are adequate playing fields and playspace available for use by the community. There are affiliated associations in the English and Welsh counties and independent organisations in Scotland and Northern Ireland.

A major study of England's recreational land was completed in 1993 as part of a strategy to safeguard playing fields. It revealed that England has over 73,000 pitches on about 24,000 sites, about half of which are owned by education authorities. The Government intends to take action to prevent the future loss of any playing fields.

Commonwealth Games in Manchester

Manchester is bidding to stage the Commonwealth Games in 2002. As the sole bidder, Manchester should be confirmed as the host city in a formal announcement by the Commonwealth Games Federation in November 1995. It will be the first time Britain has staged the Games since 1986, when they were hosted by Edinburgh.

Preparations for the Games are already under way. This includes the construction of a £55 million indoor arena with seating for 7,500 and a 3,500-capacity velodrome (see p. 508), which was opened in 1994. The two facilities were assisted by a government grant of some £43 million.

Manchester is also planning to build an 80,000-capacity stadium at a cost of £115 million on the eastern outskirts of the city. The site has already been purchased and cleared with the help of a government grant of £30 million originally provided for Manchester's Olympic bids.

NATIONAL SPORTS CENTRES

The four Sports Councils operate a total of 13 National Sports Centres, which provide world-class facilities for training and competition at the highest level. First priority at the Centres is given to the governing bodies of sport for national squad training and for the training of coaches. However, the Centres also make their facilities available to top sportsmen and women for individual training and to the local community. Most of the Centres provide residential facilities.

England

In England the Sports Council operates five major National Centres and a minor National Centre for climbers at Harrison's Rocks in Kent.

Crystal Palace in London is a leading competition venue for a wide range of sports and a major training centre for national squads, clubs, schools and serious enthusiasts. Its facilities are used by over 20 separate governing bodies, and the Centre is a regional centre of excellence for athletics, netball, weightlifting and swimming. Crystal Palace stadium is Britain's major international athletics venue, with capacity for 17,000 spectators. Other facilities include an Olympic-size swimming pool and a sports injury centre.

Bisham Abbey in Berkshire caters for a number of sports, including tennis, football, hockey, weightlifting, squash, rugby and golf. The England football, rugby and hockey squads train at the Centre. Bisham Abbey has long-standing partnerships with the British Amateur Weightlifters Association and the Lawn Tennis Association, which has helped to develop the Abbey as the National Tennis Training Centre.

Lilleshall National Sports Centre in Shropshire offers extensive sports facilities, which are used by a variety of national teams. Facilities include a world-class gymnastic training centre, regularly used by the British gymnastic squads, and extensive playing fields for football and hockey. The Football Association (FA) uses Lilleshall as its base for major coaching activities and has established a training school there. Founded in 1984, the school has 32 places for boys aged 15 and 16, who each take up a two-year residency funded by an FA scholarship.

The National Watersports Centre at Holme Pierrepont in Nottinghamshire is one of the most comprehensive water sports centres in the world, with facilities for rowing, canoeing, water-skiing, powerboating, ski-racing, angling and sailing. Its main feature is a 2,000-metre regatta course.

England's fifth major National Sports Centre—the National Cycling Centre—was opened in Manchester in September 1994. It is Britain's first indoor velodrome and will be the venue for cycling's 1996 World Cup. Its construction was assisted by a government grant of £8 million.

Wales

The Sports Council for Wales runs two National Sports Centres: the Welsh Institute of Sport and the National Watersports Centre. A further Centre—Plas y Brenin—is run by the Sports Council.

The Welsh Institute of Sport in Cardiff is the country's premier venue for top-level training and for competition in a large number of sports. Facilities include a world-standard gymnastics hall, a sports science laboratory and a sports injury clinic.

The National Watersports Centre at Plas Menai in north Wales is primarily a centre of excellence for sailing and canoeing, with an extensive range of activities including dinghy and catamaran sailing, offshore cruising and powerboat training.

Plas y Brenin National Mountain Centre, situated in Snowdonia National Park in north Wales, offers a variety of courses in rock climbing, mountaineering, sea and river canoeing, orienteering, skiing and most other mountain-based activities.

Scotland

Scotland has three National Sports Centres, which are operated by the Scottish Sports Council.

The National Outdoor Training Centre at Glenmore Lodge near Aviemore caters for a wide range of activities, including hill walking, rock climbing, mountaineering, skiing, kayaking and canoeing. Its main purpose is to provide top-quality training for those who intend to lead or instruct others in outdoor activities. The Scottish Sports Council invested nearly £500,000 in Glenmore Lodge in 1994 for the redevelopment and provision of training courses. A purpose-built biathlon and cross-country skiing facility was opened in the same year.

The Inverclyde National Sports Training Centre at Largs has a large number of facilities, including a gymnastics hall, a golf training facility and a laboratory for fitness assessment. The Centre also acts as an important competition venue for major national and international championships. Inverclyde was used by 26 governing bodies of sport in 1994, many of them using it as their national training base.

The Cumbrae National Water Sports Training Centre on the island of Great Cumbrae in the Firth of Clyde offers an extensive range of courses catering for all levels of ability. The Centre has a comprehensive range of modern craft for a wide variety of sailing activities, as well as sub-aqua diving equipment. Cumbrae regularly hosts major sailing championships.

Northern Ireland

The Northern Ireland Centre for Outdoor Activities at Tollymore in County Down, run by the Sports Council for Northern Ireland, offers courses in mountaineering, rock climbing, canoeing and outdoor adventure. Leadership and instructor courses leading to nationally recognised qualifications are also available.

A new Northern Ireland Sports Centre is being built at Upper Malone, Belfast, with the assistance of a £1 million grant from the Foundation for Sport and the Arts (see p. 511). The Centre's first facilities will be a number of synthetic pitches.

SPORTS MEDICINE AND SCIENCE

Sports Medicine

The National Sports Medicine Institute, set up by the Sports Council, provides clinical services aimed at assessing and improving fitness as well as treating and preventing sports injuries. Based at St Bartholomew's Hospital, London, its facilities include a physiology laboratory and an information centre.

Work is in progress to develop a network of regional centres to provide both clinical and educational services, which will be linked with new support services at the National Sports Centres. The Sports Council has allocated £566,000 towards sports medicine

for 1995–96. In Scotland a network of 33 sports medicine centres provide specialist help with sports injuries.

In 1994 the Scottish Sports Council developed a partnership with the Universities of Strathclyde and Aberdeen to create the Scottish Institute of Sports Medicine and Sports Science.

Sports Science

The development of sports science support services for the national governing bodies of sport is being promoted by the Sports Councils, in collaboration with the BOA and the NCF (see p. 506), in an effort to raise the standards of performance of national squads. Some 27 governing bodies are involved in the Sports Council's Sports Science Support Programme. In 1995–96 the Sports Council is contributing £635,000 in support of sports science studies. The Sports Council for Wales has established a sports science service at the Welsh Institute of Sport with support from the Welsh Office (see p. 533).

Drug Abuse in Sport

The Sports Council's independent drugs-testing regime provides for random testing in and out of competition by independent sampling officers, and the publication of adverse findings. The Council also funds an international laboratory, accredited by the International Olympic Committee, at King's College, University of London, which carries out analysis and research into methods of detection for new drugs which unfairly aid performance.

The Sports Councils have intensified their drugs-testing programmes, with greater emphasis being placed on out-of-competition tests. In 1994–95 the Sports Council carried out 4,374 tests in 50 sports, with 1.5 per cent proving positive. Funding in Britain by the four Sports Councils for the programme exceeded £900,000 in 1994–95.

The Home Secretary is planning to introduce greater penalties for supplying anabolic steroids in an attempt to curb their use in sport.

Britain has fully implemented the provisions of the Council of Europe's Anti-doping Convention, which aims to provide an international framework within which national anti-doping campaigns can work effectively.

SPECTATOR SAFETY

Safety at sports grounds is governed by legislation. The main instrument of control is a safety certificate which is issued by the relevant local authority. When determining the conditions of a safety certificate, the local authority is expected to comply with the *Guide to Safety at Sports Grounds* produced by the Home Office and The Scottish Office. This was revised in 1990 to include the relevant safety recommendations of the Taylor Report on the Hillsborough stadium disaster in Sheffield in 1989, which resulted in the death of 96 spectators.

The Taylor Report

The Taylor Report, published in 1990, contained 76 recommendations for promoting better and safer conditions at all sports grounds. Its major recommendation was that standing accommodation should be eliminated at all grounds designated under the Safety of Sports Grounds Act 1975. The Government accepted the report but limited the all-seating requirement to football in view of the particular problems of safety and crowd control in that sport. It also set a timetable for all-seater football stadiums.

Following a review in 1992, the timetable was modified. In addition, clubs in the Second and Third Divisions of the Football League are permitted to keep some standing accommodation, providing that the terracing is safe. In England and Wales the all-seater policy is being enforced through licences issued by the Football Licensing Authority. Conditions in these licences require all Premier League and First Division clubs to have all-seater grounds; these conditions have now largely been satisfied.

In Scotland the all-seating policy is being implemented through a voluntary agreement under the direction of the Scottish football authorities.

The Football Trust

Founded in 1990 by the football pools companies, the Football Trust provides grant aid to help football clubs at all levels. Its income is about £36 million a year and it is funded partly by the pools companies from their spot-the-ball competition and partly from a 2.5 per cent reduction in pool betting duty. This concession has provided over £136 million to football to assist clubs in the Premier League, the Football League and the Scottish Football League to finance projects to improve the comfort and safety of spectators in line with the Taylor Report recommendations.

In 1995 the betting duty concession was extended for a further five years in order to help clubs in the lower divisions of the Football League and the Scottish Football League to meet the safe terracing requirements.

The Government has given the Football Trust a new wider role to enable it to fund up to £8 million a year of safety work at rugby league, rugby union, cricket and non-league football grounds. The work will be financed through the Foundation for Sport and the Arts (see p. 511).

Crowd Control

The Government has worked closely with the police, football authorities and the governments of other European countries to implement crowd control measures.

Legislation has made it an offence in England and Wales to throw objects at football matches, run onto the playing area or chant indecent or racist abuse. There are also controls on the sale and possession of alcohol at football grounds and on transport to and from grounds.

Courts in England and Wales have the power to prohibit convicted football hooligans from attending football matches. They also have powers to impose restriction orders on convicted football hooligans to prevent them travelling abroad to attend specified matches. The National Criminal Intelligence Service Football Unit co-ordinates police intelligence about football hooligans and liaises with overseas police forces.

SPONSORSHIP AND OTHER FUNDING

Sport is a major industry in Britain. In addition to professional sportsmen and women, over 450,000 people are employed in the provision of sports clothing, publicity, ground and club maintenance and other activities connected with sport. In total an estimated £9,750 million is spent on sport annually in Britain. The private sector makes a substantial investment in sports sponsorship, contributing over £265 million a year. This involves more than 2,000 British companies.

Sponsorship may take the form of financing specific events or championships, such as horse races or football/cricket leagues, or of grants to sports organisations or individual performers. Motor sport and football receive the largest amounts of private sponsorship.

Sponsorship of sport is encouraged by a number of bodies, including:

- the Institute of Sports Sponsorship, set up by the CCPR (see p. 506) to develop sponsorship at local, national and international level. It currently comprises some 80 British companies involved in the sponsorship of sport;
- the Sports Sponsorship Advisory Service, administered by the CCPR and funded by the Sports Council, which has helped sporting bodies to raise over £1 million in England over the last three years;
- the Scottish Sports Council's Sponsorship Advisory Service, which raised £300,000 for Scottish sport in 1993–94; and
- the Sports Council for Wales's Sponsorship Advisory Service, which generated more than £190,000 for Welsh sport in 1993–94.

Successive governments have negotiated voluntary agreements with the tobacco industry to regulate tobacco companies' sponsorship of sport.

Sportsmatch

Launched by the Government in 1992, Sportsmatch is a business sponsorship incentive scheme which aims to increase the amount of business sponsorship going into 'grass roots' sport and physical recreation. The scheme offers matching funding for new sponsorships and extension of existing sponsorships. In England funding is subject to a minimum of £1,000 and a maximum of £75,000; in Scotland and Wales the minimum is £500 and in Wales the maximum is £25,000. Priority is given to projects involving groups such as the young, disabled people and ethnic minorities and to projects in deprived areas. Recent awards include a grant of £63,000 to help set up a new British football league for people with learning disabilities.

In England the Institute of Sports Sponsorship runs the scheme on behalf of the Department of National Heritage. Since its inception, Sportsmatch has approved over 1,000 awards in England, totalling nearly £9 million. In Scotland and Wales the scheme is managed by the appropriate Sports Council's Sponsorship Advisory Service. Between April 1993 and August 1994 the Scottish Awards Panel approved some 200 awards totalling nearly £700,000. In Wales some 120 awards were allocated in 1993–94 totalling more than £200,000. Northern Ireland has its own sports sponsorship incentive scheme, which is currently being reviewed.

Sportsmatch is to set aside £1 million specifically for schools projects, to be matched by £1 million of commercial sponsorship.

Sports Aid Foundation

The Sports Aid Foundation raises and distributes funds from industry, commerce and private sponsors in order to assist the training of talented individuals. Grants are awarded on the recommendation of the appropriate governing bodies to British competitors who need help preparing for Olympic, World and European championships. The Scottish and Welsh Sports Aid Foundations and the Ulster Sports and Recreation Trust have similar functions.

Foundation for Sport and the Arts

The Foundation for Sport and the Arts was set up by the football pools promoters in

1991 to channel funds into sport and the arts. The pools promoters are providing the Foundation with some £45 million a year. A further £22.5 million a year is received as a result of the 2.5 per cent reduction in pool betting duty announced in the 1990 Budget. This was extended for a further five years in the 1994 Budget. About £41 million a year is available for sport. Since its launch, the Foundation has made some 8,300 awards to schemes benefiting over 100 sports and totalling over £150 million.

Horserace Betting Levy

Most betting in Britain takes place on horse racing and greyhound racing. Bets may be made at racecourses and greyhound tracks, or through over 9,000 licensed off-course betting offices, which take about 90 per cent of the money staked. A form of pool betting—totalisator betting—is organised on racecourses by the Horserace Totalisator Board (the Tote). Racecourse bets may also be placed with independent on-course bookmakers.

Bookmakers and the Tote contribute an annual levy—a fixed proportion of their turnover—to the Horserace Betting Levy Board. The amount of levy payable is decided by the racing and bookmaking industries or, in cases where agreement cannot be achieved, by the Home Secretary. The Levy Board promotes the improvement of horse breeds, advancement of veterinary science and the improvement of horse racing.

In 1993–94 the total money staked in all forms of gambling, excluding gaming machines, was estimated at £10,319 million.

National Lottery

Launched in November 1994, the National Lottery is providing significant new funding for five good causes: sport, charities, the arts, heritage and projects to mark the millennium. Each receives one-fifth of the money generated for good causes. Funds are being distributed to a wide range of schemes by the Sports Councils, the Charities Board, the Arts Councils, the National Heritage Memorial Fund and the Millennium Commission. By September 1995 the amount raised for good causes amounted to some £1,000 million.

About 28 per cent of the Lottery's net proceeds is being distributed to good causes. The remainder is divided between prizes (50 per cent), tax (12 per cent), retailers' commission (5 per cent) and operating costs and profit (5 per cent). The Lottery is run by a private sector company—Camelot Group plc—and regulated by the Director General of the National Lottery.

It is estimated that three-quarters of all households in Britain regularly play the Lottery, which has an average weekly jackpot of £8 million. The average spent on tickets is £2.10 a week per household.

The first awards of National Lottery money for sport were announced in spring 1995. Schemes in England, Scotland and Northern Ireland received £3 million, £1.8 million and £440,000 respectively. Further grants are being awarded on a monthly basis. By September 1995 the Sports Council had distributed awards totalling £95.9 million to 520 schemes in England in 45 sports.

TELEVISED SPORT

Major sporting events receive extensive television coverage and are watched by millions of viewers. In 1994 some of the highest viewing figures were achieved by:

- horse racing: the Grand National (17 million viewers);
- football World Cup finals (13.5 million); and
- the FA Cup Final (12 million).

The largest ever audience for a sporting event shown on one channel was achieved by Jayne Torvill and Christopher Dean, who attracted 23 million viewers for their performance in the ice dance competition at the 1994 Winter Olympics.

The advent of satellite television and the greater availability of cable have increased substantially the amount of sport on television, including a number of minority sports. On terrestrial television the sports which receive the most coverage are football, horse racing, snooker and cricket.

Certain important sporting events are not

permitted to be shown on television on pay-per-view terms. These 'listed' events comprise:

- the football World Cup Finals;
- the FA Cup Final;
- the Scottish FA Cup Final;
- the finals of the Wimbledon Tennis Championships;
- the Olympic Games;
- the Grand National;
- the Derby; and
- Test matches in England.

The Secretary of State for National Heritage keeps this list under review and can alter it at any time.

A TO Z OF POPULAR SPORTS

Some of the major sports in Britain, many of which were invented by the British, are described below. Additional information on these and other sports not covered here can be found in *A Digest of Sports Statistics for the UK*, published by the Sports Council.

Angling

One of the most popular countryside sports is angling, of which there are three main types: coarse, game and sea.

Angling is an overwhelmingly male sport, with an estimated ten times as many male as female participants among Britain's 4 million anglers. Many fish for salmon and trout, particularly in the rivers and lochs of Scotland and in Wales. In England and Wales the most widely practised form of angling is for coarse fish. Separate organisations represent game, coarse and sea fishing clubs in England, Wales, Scotland and Northern Ireland.

The National Federation of Anglers in England organises national championships for coarse fishing and enters a team in the world angling championships.

Athletics

Athletics is governed in Britain by the British Athletic Federation (BAF), which is affiliated to the International Amateur Athletic Federation. The BAF is responsible for the selection of British teams for international events, and also administers coaching schemes. For the Olympic Games and the World and European championships one team represents the whole of Britain.

Athletics is attracting increasing numbers of participants. In recent years there has been a significant growth in mass participation events, such as marathons and half marathons. The London Marathon, which takes place every spring, regularly attracts over 25,000 runners.

At the 1995 World Athletics Championships in Gothenburg Jonathan Edwards won a gold medal in the triple jump with a new world record. In so doing, he became the first man to jump beyond 18 metres.

In February 1995 Linford Christie set a new indoor world record in the 200 metres at Lievin, France.

Badminton

Badminton takes its name from the Duke of Beaufort's country home, Badminton House, where the sport was first played in the 19th century. The game is organised by the Badminton Association of England and the Scottish, Welsh and Irish (Ulster branch) Badminton Unions. Around 5 million people play badminton in Britain and there are over 5,000 clubs. The All England Badminton Championships, held at the National Indoor Arena in Birmingham, is the premier tournament in the world grand prix circuit.

A mini version of the game—Short Badminton—and badminton for the disabled have been introduced in recent years.

Basketball

In Britain over 3 million people participate in basketball. The English Basket Ball Association is the governing body in England, and there are similar associations in Wales, Scotland and Northern Ireland. All the associations are represented on the British and Irish Basketball Federation, which acts as the co-ordinating body for Britain and the Irish Republic.

The leading clubs play in the National Basketball Leagues. Mini-basketball and micro-basketball are versions of the game which have been developed for players under the age of 13.

Wheelchair basketball is played under the same rules, with a few basic adaptations, and on the same court as the running game. Over 30 teams play in the National League.

In 1995 the English Basket Ball Association started a new coaching scheme for schoolchildren which aims to increase participation and improve the quality of basketball throughout England. The scheme has received a £75,000 Sportsmatch award (see p. 511).

Bowls

The two main forms of bowls are lawn (flat green and crown green) and indoor bowls. The game is increasingly enjoyed by adults of all ages. In recent years the most notable increases have been in the number of women taking part. Bowls is also popular among people with disabilities.

About 4,000 lawn bowling clubs are affiliated to the English, Scottish, Welsh and Irish Bowling Associations, which, together with Women's Bowling Associations for the four countries, play to the rules of the World Bowls Board. Crown green bowls and indoor bowls have their own separate associations.

In 1995 Andy Thomson won the world indoor singles championships for the second year in succession.

Boxing

Boxing in its modern form is based on the rules established by the Marquess of Queensberry in 1865. In Britain boxing is both amateur and professional, and in both strict medical regulations are observed.

All amateur boxing in England is controlled by the Amateur Boxing Association of England. There are separate associations in Scotland and Wales, and boxing in Northern Ireland is controlled by the Irish Boxing Association. The associations organise amateur boxing championships as well as training courses for referees, coaches and others. The wearing of headguards is now compulsory in all British amateur competitions.

Professional boxing is controlled by the British Boxing Board of Control. The Board appoints inspectors, medical officers and representatives to ensure that regulations are observed and to guard against overmatching and exploitation. Britain currently has four world champions: Frank Bruno (World Boxing Council—WBC—heavyweight), Nigel Benn (WBC super-middleweight), Naseem Hamed (World Boxing Organisation—WBO—featherweight) and Eamonn Loughran (WBO welterweight).

Cricket

The basic rules for cricket were drawn up in 1835 by the Marylebone Cricket Club (MCC), which still frames the laws of the game today. The MCC and the Test and County Cricket Board (TCCB), which represents first-class cricket in England, are both based at Lord's cricket ground in north London, the administrative centre of the English game. Men's cricket in Britain is governed by the Cricket Council, consisting of representatives of the TCCB, the National Cricket Association (NCA—representing club and junior cricket), the Minor Counties Cricket Association and the MCC.

The TCCB is likely to be replaced before the end of 1996 by an English Cricket Board, which will govern all domestic cricket. The Board is expected to undertake a fundamental review of English cricket and to submit proposals on the future funding of the domestic game.

Cricket is played in schools, colleges and universities, and amateur teams play weekly games in cities, towns and villages. Throughout Britain there is a network of cricket consisting of first class, minor counties and club games with a variety of leagues.

The main competition in professional cricket is the Britannic Assurance County Championship, played by 18 first-class county teams in four-day matches. There are also three one-day competitions: the Benson and Hedges Cup, the National Westminster Trophy and the AXA Equity & Law Sunday League.

Every year there is a series of five-day Cornhill Insurance Test matches played between England and one or more touring teams from Australia, India, New Zealand, Pakistan, South Africa, Sri Lanka, the West Indies or Zimbabwe. A team representing England usually tours one or more of these countries in the British winter. A World Cup limited-over competition takes place every four years. In 1996 this will be held in India, Pakistan and Sri Lanka.

The governing body of cricket for women and girls is the Women's Cricket Association. Women's cricket is played at local, county and international level. In 1993 England won the Women's World Cup for the second time.

Cycling

Cycling, one of Britain's fastest growing outdoor activities, includes road and track racing, time-trialling, cyclo-cross (cross country racing), touring and bicycle moto cross (BMX). All-terrain or mountain bikes have grown significantly in popularity.

The British Cycling Federation has 17,360 members and is the governing body for cycling as a sport. The Cyclists' Touring Club (CTC), with 40,000 members, is the representative body for recreational and urban cycling. Scotland and Wales have their own Cyclists' Unions. Northern Ireland has two separate Cycling Federations.

In recent years three British cyclists—Chris Boardman, Graeme Obree and Yvonne McGregor—have broken the one-hour world record; in 1993 Chris Boardman became the first man to break through 52 km. Yvonne McGregor broke the women's one-hour world record in Manchester in June 1995, covering 47.4 km. Graeme Obree regained his world 4,000 metres pursuit title in Bogota, Colombia, in September 1995.

Major cycling events taking place each year in Britain include the Tour of Britain and the CTC rally at York. In July 1994 Britain hosted two stages of the Tour de France around Dover and Portsmouth. Britain's first indoor velodrome was opened in 1994 (see p. 508).

Equestrianism

Equestrian activities include recreational riding, dressage, endurance riding, carriage driving, one- and three-day eventing and show jumping.

The arts of riding and driving are promoted by the British Horse Society, which is concerned with the welfare of horses, road safety, riding rights of way and training. It runs the British Equestrian Centre at Stoneleigh in Warwickshire. With some 62,500 members, the Society is the parent body of the Pony Club and the Riding Club movements, which hold rallies, meetings and competitions culminating in annual national championships.

Leading horse trials, comprising dressage, cross-country and show jumping, are held every year at a number of locations, including Badminton (Avon) and Gatcombe Park (Gloucestershire). In July 1994 the British team of Charlotte Bathe, Karen Dixon, Kristina Gifford and Mary Thomson won the three-day event team title at the World Equestrian Games in The Hague.

Show jumping is regulated and promoted by the British Show Jumping Association. The major show jumping events each year include the Royal International Horse Show at Hickstead (West Sussex) and the Horse of the Year Show at Wembley in London.

The authority responsible for equestrian competitions (other than racing) at international and Olympic level is the British Equestrian Federation, which co-ordinates the activities of the British Horse Society and the British Show Jumping Association.

Football

Association football is controlled by separate football associations in England, Wales, Scotland and Northern Ireland. In England 340 clubs are affiliated to the Football Association (FA) and more than 42,000 clubs to regional or district associations. The FA, founded in 1863, and the Football League, founded in 1888, were both the first of their kind in the world.

A new FA Premier League was started in England and Wales in 1992, comprising 22 clubs. This was reduced to 20 clubs in 1995–96. The remaining 72 full-time professional clubs play in three main divisions run by the Football League. During the season, which lasts from August until May, over 2,000 English League matches are played. Stan Collymore became Britain's most expensive footballer when he was transferred from Nottingham Forest to Liverpool for £8.5 million in June 1995.

Three Welsh clubs play in the Football League, while the National League of Wales contains 20 semi-professional clubs. In Scotland the Scottish Football League was increased in 1994–95 to 40 clubs, equally divided into four divisions. These include one English club—Berwick Rangers. In Northern Ireland, 16 semi-professional clubs play in the Irish Football League.

The major annual knock-out competitions are the FA Cup and the Coca-Cola Cup (the League Cup) in England, the Tennents Scottish Cup, the Coca-Cola Cup (the Scottish League Cup), the Irish Cup and the Welsh FA Cup. England is to host the European Championship finals in June 1996.

Gaelic Games

Gaelic Games, increasingly popular in Northern Ireland, cover the sports of Gaelic football, hurling, handball, camogie (a modified form of hurling) and rounders. There are over 700 clubs in Northern Ireland affiliated to the Gaelic Athletic Association, the official governing body responsible for Gaelic Games.

Golf

Golf originated in Scotland and is ruled by the Royal and Ancient Golf Club (R & A), which is situated at St Andrews on the east coast of Scotland. The Golfing Union of Ireland and parallel unions in Wales, Scotland and England are the national governing bodies for men's amateur golf. These bodies are affiliated to the R & A and are represented on the Council of National Golf Unions, which is the British co-ordinating body responsible for handicapping and organising home international matches. Women's amateur golf is governed by the Ladies' Golf Union. Club professional golf is governed by the Professional Golfers' Association (PGA) and tournament golf by the European PGA Tour and the Women's PGA Tour.

The main event of the British golfing year is the Open Championship, one of the world's leading tournaments. Other important events include the Walker Cup and Curtis Cup matches for amateurs, played between Great Britain and Ireland and the United States, and the Ryder Cup match for professionals, played every two years between Europe and the United States. In September 1995 Europe regained the Ryder Cup at Oak Hill in the United States.

There are about 1,900 golf courses in Britain. Some of the most famous include St Andrews (which hosted the 1995 British Open Championship), Muirfield and Royal Birkdale. Nick Faldo and Colin Montgomerie are both in the top ten in the world rankings. In the women's game Laura Davies is currently ranked number one in the world.

Greyhound Racing

Greyhound racing is one of Britain's most popular spectator sports and takes place at 37 major tracks. Meetings are usually held three times a week at each track, with at least ten races a meeting. The main event of the year is the Greyhound Derby, run in June at Wimbledon Stadium, London. There are also about 50 mainly small tracks which operate independently. Like the major tracks, they are licensed by local authorities. The first Sunday greyhound race meetings took place in January 1995 at Canterbury, Hove, Peterborough, Powderhall (Edinburgh) and Wembley.

The rules for the sport are drawn up by the National Greyhound Racing Club, the sport's judicial and administrative body. The representative body is the British Greyhound Racing Board.

Gymnastics

Gymnastics is divided into four main disciplines: artistic (or Olympic) gymnastics, rhythmic gymnastics, sports acrobatics and general gymnastics.

The governing body for the sport is the British Amateur Gymnastics Association (BAGA). Over the past decade the number of clubs affiliated to the BAGA has nearly doubled. The sport is particularly popular with schoolchildren and young adults, and it is estimated that between 3 and 4 million schoolchildren take part in some form of gymnastics every day.

Highland Games

Scottish Highland Games cover a wide range of athletic competitions in addition to activities such as dancing and piping competitions. The main events include running, cycling, throwing the hammer, tossing the caber and putting the shot.

Over 70 gatherings of various kinds take place throughout Scotland, the most famous of which is the annual Braemar Gathering.

The Scottish Games Association is the official governing body responsible for athletic sports and games at Highland and Border events in Scotland.

Hockey

The modern game of hockey was started by the Hockey Association (of England), which was founded in 1886 and acts as the governing body for men's hockey. The controlling body of women's hockey in England is the All England Women's Hockey Association; separate associations regulate the sport in Scotland, Wales and Ireland. Cup competitions and leagues exist at national, divisional or district, club and school levels, both indoors (six-a-side) and outdoors, and there are regular international matches and tournaments.

A National Hockey Centre in Milton Keynes will be the venue for all major hockey matches in England from the start of 1996.

Horse Racing

Horse racing takes two forms—flat racing and National Hunt (steeplechasing and hurdle) racing. The main flat race season runs from late March to early November, but all-weather flat racing and National Hunt racing take place throughout the year.

The Derby, run at Epsom, is the outstanding event in the flat racing calendar. Other classic races are: the 2,000 Guineas and the 1,000 Guineas, both run at Newmarket; the Oaks (Epsom); and the St Leger (Doncaster). Floodlit racing takes place at Wolverhampton all-weather racecourse. Britain has 59 racecourses and about 13,000 horses currently in training.

The most important National Hunt meeting is the National Hunt Festival held at Cheltenham in March, which features the Gold Cup and the Champion Hurdle. The Grand National, run at Aintree, near Liverpool, is the world's best-known steeplechase and dates from 1839.

Sunday racing with on- and off-course betting was introduced in 1995. A total of 24 Sunday race meetings are being held on 12 Sundays throughout the year. The first two took place at Salisbury and Newmarket on 7 May 1995, when the 1,000 Guineas became the first British classic to be run on a Sunday.

The British Horseracing Board is the governing authority for racing in Britain. Its responsibilities include the fixture list, race programmes, relations with the Government and the betting industry, and central marketing. The Jockey Club, as the regulatory authority, remains responsible for licensing, discipline and security.

Ice Skating

Ice skating takes four main forms: figure skating (solo and pairs), ice dancing, speed-skating (indoor and outdoor) and precision skating. The governing body is the National Ice Skating Association of United Kingdom.

Participation in ice skating is concentrated among the under-25s, and is one of the few sports that attracts more female than male participants as individuals. There are over 70 rinks in Britain; almost half have opened since 1985.

British couples have won the world ice dance championship 17 times, the most recent being Jayne Torvill and Christopher

Dean, who won four consecutive world championships between 1981 and 1984. The couple returned to amateur competition in 1994 and won a gold medal at the 1994 European Championships in Copenhagen.

Britain won two bronze medals at the 1994 Winter Olympics in Lillehammer, Norway: Nicky Gooch (indoor speed skating) and Torvill and Dean (ice dance).

In 1995 Britain hosted the World Figure Skating Championships at the National Arena in Birmingham.

Judo

Judo is popular not only as a competitive sport and self-defence technique, but also as a means of general fitness training. An internationally recognised grading system is in operation through the sport's governing body, the British Judo Association.

Britain has won medals for judo at every Olympic Games since 1972. This includes four at the 1992 Olympics, where women's judo was included for the first time.

At the 1995 European Championships, which were held in Birmingham's Indoor Arena, Britain had two gold medallists (Nicola Fairbrother and Nigel Donohue) and finished second in the medals table.

Keep Fit

Keep fit encompasses various forms of movement and exercise activities. In March 1994 the Sports Council launched the Exercise Association of England as an impartial advisory authority for the organisations involved in these activities.

The Keep Fit Association, one of the largest governing bodies in England, receives funding from the Sports Council to promote physical fitness and a positive attitude to health in England. Its national certificated training scheme for keep fit teachers is recognised by local education authorities throughout Britain. Autonomous associations serve Scotland, Wales and Northern Ireland.

Martial Arts

A broad range of martial arts, mainly derived from the Far East, has been introduced into Britain during the 20th century. There are recognised governing bodies responsible for their own activities in karate, ju-jitsu, aikido, Chinese martial arts, kendo, taekwondo and tang soo do. The most popular martial art is karate, with over 100,000 participants.

Motor-car Sports

The main four-wheeled motor sports include motor racing, autocross, rallycross, rallying and karting. In motor racing the Grand Prix Formula 1 World Championship is the major form of the sport.

The governing body for four-wheeled motor sport in Britain is the RAC (Royal Automobile Club) Motor Sports Association. The Association issues licences for a variety of motoring competitions. It also organises the Network Q RAC Rally, an event in the contest for the World Rally Championship, and the British Grand Prix, which is held at Silverstone as part of the Formula 1 World Championship.

Britain has had more Formula 1 world champions than any other country, the latest being Nigel Mansell in 1992. The following year Nigel Mansell became the first person to win the IndyCar World Series Championship in his debut year. In 1994 Damon Hill was runner-up in the Formula 1 World Championship.

Three out of the seven British drivers who competed in the 1995 Formula 1 World Championship recorded Grand Prix victories: Damon Hill, Johnny Herbert and David Coulthard.

British car constructors, including McLaren and Williams, have enjoyed outstanding success in Grand Prix racing and many other forms of racing.

Motor-cycle Sports

Motor-cycle sports include road racing, moto-cross, grass track, speedway, trials, drag racing and sprint. It is estimated that there are between 40,000 and 50,000 competitive motor cyclists in Britain.

The governing bodies of the sport are the Auto-Cycle Union in England and Wales, the

Scottish Auto-Cycle Union and the Motor Cycle Union of Ireland (in Northern Ireland). The major events of the year include the Isle of Man TT races and the British Road Race Grand Prix. The Auto-Cycle Union also provides off-road training by approved instructors for riders of all ages.

Mountaineering

All forms of mountaineering, which includes mountain walking and rock-climbing, are growing in popularity. A recent survey estimated that there were 700,000 climbers in Britain.

The representative body is the British Mountaineering Council, which works closely with the Mountaineering Councils of Scotland and Ireland. The main areas of work include access and conservation. There are over 300 mountaineering and climbing clubs in Britain, and four National Centres for mountaineering activities run by the Sports Councils (see p. 505). Organisations such as the Scottish Mountain Safety Group help to promote the safe enjoyment of the hills.

British mountaineers have played a leading role in the exploration of the world's great mountain ranges. The best-known is Chris Bonington, who has climbed Everest and led many other successful expeditions. Some of the world's hardest rock climbs are found on cliffs in Britain, and leading British climbers, such as Jerry Moffat and Ben Moon, have set new standards of difficulty on cliffs overseas.

In May 1995 Alison Hargreaves became the first woman to climb Everest unaided and without additional oxygen; she achieved the same feat on K2 in August 1995, where she met her death on descending the mountain.

Netball

More than 60,000 adults play netball regularly in England and a further 1 million participants play in schools. The sport is played almost exclusively by women and girls both indoors and outdoors.

The All England Netball Association is the governing body in England, with Scotland, Wales and Northern Ireland having their own governing bodies. The number of clubs affiliated to the All England Association has grown steadily in recent years and currently stands at 3,750. The biggest growth has been in the youth development programme. National competitions are staged annually for all age groups.

The 1995 World Netball Championships were held at the National Indoor Arena in Birmingham.

Rowing

Rowing is taught in many schools, universities and rowing clubs throughout Britain. The main types of boats are single, pairs and double sculls, fours and eights. The governing body in England is the Amateur Rowing Association; similar bodies regulate the sport in Scotland, Wales and Northern Ireland.

The University Boat Race, between eight-oared crews from Oxford and Cambridge, has been rowed on the Thames almost every spring since 1836. The Head of the River Race, also on the Thames, is the largest assembly of racing craft in the world, with more than 420 eights racing in procession. At the Henley Regatta in Oxfordshire crews from all over the world compete each July in various kinds of race over a straight course of 1 mile 550 yards (about 2.1 km).

At the 1995 World Rowing Championships in Tampere, Finland, Britain won two gold medals: the coxless pairs (Steven Redgrave and Matthew Pinsent) and the lightweight single sculls (Peter Haining). Overall, Britain recorded its best tally in a world championships, winning a total of six medals.

Rugby League

Rugby league (a 13-a-side game) originated in 1895 following the breakaway from rugby union (see p. 520) of a number of clubs in the north of England. Rugby league has kept many of the features of the union game but has its own distinct set of rules and is concentrated in the north of England.

The governing body of the professional game is the Rugby Football League while the amateur game is governed by the British Amateur Rugby League Association. The major club match of the season is the Challenge Cup Final, which is played at Wembley Stadium in London. In 1995 the Cup was won by Wigan for the eighth year in succession. Rugby league's centenary world cup took place in England and Wales in October 1995. A Great Britain team will tour Australia and New Zealand in autumn 1996.

> Rugby league is to be revolutionised in 1996 with the creation of a summer Super League. This will consist of 12 clubs: ten from the north of England, one from London and one representing Paris. Matches will be played in a season lasting from March to October. In the autumn the top four Super League clubs will have play-offs against the top four teams in the Australasian Super League. Under the new format, there will also be a First Division of 11 clubs and a Second Division of 10.

Rugby Union

Rugby union football (a 15-a-side game) is thought to have originated at Rugby School in the first half of the 19th century.

The sport is played under the auspices of the Rugby Football Union in England and parallel bodies in Wales, Scotland and Ireland. Each of the four countries runs separate national league and knock-out competitions for its domestic clubs.

An annual Five Nations Championship is contested by England, Scotland, Wales, Ireland and France. In 1995 England won the Grand Slam (defeating all its opponents) for the third time in five years. Overseas tours are undertaken by the national sides and by the British Lions, a team representing Great Britain and Ireland. Tours are also made to Britain by teams representing the major rugby-playing nations.

The Rugby World Cup, which is held every four years, was hosted and won by South Africa in 1995. Among the home nations, England achieved the most success by reaching the semi-finals. The Women's World Cup was won in April 1994 by England.

Wales has been selected by the International Rugby Board to host the finals of the 1999 World Cup. Other matches in the competition will be shared among England, Scotland, Ireland and France.

Tournaments of seven-a-side rugby union include the Middlesex Sevens, which is held every year at Twickenham. An inaugural World Cup Sevens, held in Edinburgh in 1993, was won by England.

The sport of rugby union abandoned its amateur status in 1995, when the International Rugby Board repealed the sport's amateur regulations and replaced them with a new dispensation ending any prohibition on payment or material benefit for anyone involved as a player or official at any level of the game.

Skiing

Skiing takes place in Scotland from December to May and also at several English locations when there is sufficient snow. The five established winter sports areas in Scotland are Cairngorm, Glencoe, Glenshee, the Lecht and Nevis Range, all of which have a full range of ski-lifts, prepared ski runs and professional instructors.

There are over 115 artificial or dry ski-slopes located throughout Britain, and it is estimated that 1.5 million people in Britain take part in the sport. The sport's governing body is the British Ski Federation.

Snooker and Billiards

Snooker was invented by the British in India in 1875 and is currently played by approximately 7 million people in Britain. British players have an outstanding record in the game and have dominated the major professional championships. The main tournament is the annual Embassy World Professional Championship, held in Sheffield. In the 1980s Steve Davis won the world title six times and in 1995 Stephen Hendry became world champion for the fifth time.

The controlling body for the non-professional game in England is the English Association for Snooker and Billiards. Scotland, Wales and Northern Ireland have separate associations. The World Professional Billiards and Snooker Association is responsible for professional players, organises all world-ranking professional events and holds the copyright for the rules.

A growing number of women play snooker and billiards. Their representative body is the World Ladies' Billiards and Snooker Association, with around 250 members. A women's world snooker championship is played every year in London. The Embassy World Professional Championship was opened to women in 1992.

Squash

Squash derives from the game of rackets, which was invented at Harrow School in the 1850s. The governing body for squash in England is the Squash Rackets Association; there are separate governing bodies in Wales, Scotland and Northern Ireland. The British Open Championships is one of the major world events in the sport.

The number of players in Britain is estimated at over 2 million, of whom more than 500,000 compete regularly in inter-club league competitions. There are nearly 9,000 squash courts in England. The main providers of facilities are member clubs, commercial organisations and local authorities.

England won both the men's and women's finals in the European Team Championships in Amsterdam in April 1995.

Swimming

Swimming is enjoyed by millions of people with a wide range of abilities from all age groups. All forms of competitive swimming are governed by the Amateur Swimming Association (ASA) in England and by similar associations in Scotland and Wales. These three associations combine to form the Amateur Swimming Federation of Great Britain, which acts as the co-ordinating body for the selection of Great Britain teams and the organisation of international competitions. Northern Ireland forms part of the Irish Amateur Swimming Association. Instruction and coaching are provided by qualified teachers and coaches who hold certificates awarded mainly by the ASA.

Mark Foster set a new short course world record in the 50 metres butterfly at a World Cup meeting in Sheffield in February 1995.

Table Tennis

Table tennis developed in Britain in the second half of the 19th century. It is popular with all sections of the community and widely played in a variety of venues. The sport is also a major recreational and competitive activity for people with disabilities.

The governing body in England is the English Table Tennis Association. There are separate governing bodies in Scotland, Wales and Northern Ireland.

England is to host the 1997 World Table Tennis Championships at the Indoor Arena in Manchester.

Tennis

The modern game of tennis originated in England in 1872 and the first championships were played at Wimbledon in 1877. The governing body for tennis in Great Britain is the Lawn Tennis Association (LTA), to which the Welsh and Scottish LTAs are affiliated. Tennis in Northern Ireland is governed by Tennis Ireland.

The Wimbledon Championships, held within the grounds of the All England Club, are one of the four tennis 'Grand Slam' tournaments. Prize money totalled over £6 million in 1995. An extensive redevelopment of the All England Club is taking place. The first phase, a new No 1 Court, is due to be opened in 1997.

Since 1981 the Championships have generated over £125 million for British tennis. This has been used for schemes such as the Indoor Tennis Initiative, which since 1986 has produced 35 public centres throughout Britain.

Club players take part in national and county championships. To encourage younger people to play tennis, national competitions are organised for boys' and girls' schools, and short tennis has been introduced for children aged five and over. The game is played in over 3,000 schools and in leisure centres. In all, about 3 million people play tennis in Britain.

Tenpin Bowling

It is estimated that about 4.8 million people take part in tenpin bowling every year in Britain. There are over 200 national tournaments and an annual National Championship.

Britain has over 200 indoor bowling centres, the first having opened in 1960. More than 30,000 people belong to the sport's governing body, the British Tenpin Bowling Association.

Volleyball

The English Volleyball Association and parallel associations in Scotland, Wales and Northern Ireland act as the sport's governing bodies. To encourage more children to play volleyball, the Association organises national, regional and area championships for a variety of ages, from under 13s to under 19s. Mini-Volley is a three-a-side version of the game adapted for children under 13.

Grass and beach volleyball tournaments are proving very popular with children and are leading to an increase in the number of schools playing volleyball.

Yachting

Yachting comprises sailing, powerboating and windsurfing on both inland and offshore waters. Racing in sailing boats takes place between one-design classes or under handicap, which provides level racing for boats of different size and shape. The most well-known ocean races include the Whitbread Round The World Yacht Race and the Fastnet Race. A new round-the-world yacht race is to take place in 1996–97. The Grand Mistral Race will be held in identical boats, putting the emphasis on sailing skills rather than design and technology.

Powerboat racing has two main forms: inland circuit racing and offshore racing. Events take place at many locations, including Liverpool and Cardiff docks.

The Royal Yachting Association is the governing body for all yachting in Britain. It is estimated that about 3 million people participate in the sport.

Further Reading

Sport: Raising the Game. Department of National Heritage.
Scotland's Sporting Future: A New Start. The Scottish Office.
Sport and Leisure. Aspects of Britain series. HMSO, 1994.

Appendices
and Index

Government Departments and Agencies

An outline of the principal functions of the main government departments and executive agencies (see p. 64) is given below.

Cabinet ministries are indicated by an asterisk. Executive agencies for which the Secretaries of State for Northern Ireland, Scotland or Wales are responsible appear in italics. Executive agencies are normally listed under the relevant department, although in some cases they are included within the description of the department's responsibilities.

The work of many of the departments and agencies listed below covers Britain as a whole. Where this is not the case, the following abbreviations are used:

- (GB) for functions covering England, Wales and Scotland;
- (E,W & NI) for those covering England, Wales and Northern Ireland;
- (E & W) for those covering England and Wales; and
- (E) for those concerned with England only.

The principal address and telephone number of each department are given. For details of the addresses of executive agencies see the *Civil Service Year Book*.

The Cabinet Office and the responsibilities of the Office of Public Service—OPS—are described on p. 62.

Cabinet Office (Office of Public Service)
70 Whitehall, London SW1A 2AS
Tel: 0171 270 1234

Executive Agencies

Chessington Computer Centre
Civil Service College
Civil Service Occupational Health Service
Recruitment and Assessment Services Agency

Two further agencies report to the Chancellor of the Duchy of Lancaster but are departments in their own right rather than part of OPS. They are:

Central Office of Information (see p. 530)

HMSO (Her Majesty's Stationery Office—see p. 530)

ECONOMIC AFFAIRS

*Ministry of Agriculture, Fisheries and Food
3–8 Whitehall Place, London SW1A 2HH Tel: 0171 270 3000

Policies for agriculture, horticulture, fisheries and food; responsibilities for related environmental and rural issues (E); food policies.

Executive Agencies

ADAS (Food, Farming, Land and Leisure)
Central Science Laboratory
Central Veterinary Laboratory
Intervention Board
Pesticides Safety Directorate
Veterinary Medicines Directorate

*Department of Employment

See under Department of Education and Employment on p. 529

*Department of Trade and Industry
1–19 Victoria Street, London SW1H OET
Tel: 0171 215 5000

Industrial and commercial affairs; science and technology; promotion of new enterprise and competition; information about new business methods and opportunities; investor protection and consumer affairs. Specific responsibilities include innovation policy; regional industrial policy and inward investment promotion; small businesses; management best practice and business/education links; industrial relations and employment legislation; deregulation; international trade policy; commercial relations and export promotion; competition policy; company law; insolvency; radio regulation; patents and copyright protection (GB); the development of new sources of energy; and the Government's relations with the energy industries.

Executive Agencies

Companies House
The Insolvency Service
Laboratory of the Government Chemist
NEL (National Engineering Laboratory)
National Physical Laboratory
National Weights and Measures Laboratory
Patent Office
Radiocommunications Agency

*Department of Transport
2 Marsham Street, London SW1P 3EB
Tel: 0171 276 3000

Land, sea and air transport; domestic and international civil aviation; international transport agreements; shipping and the ports industry; marine pollution; regulation of drivers and vehicles (including road safety); regulation of the road haulage industry; transport and the environment. Motorways and trunk roads; oversight of local authority transport (E). Sponsorship of London Transport (E), British Rail; Railtrack (GB) and the Civil Aviation Authority.

Executive Agencies

Coastguard Agency
Driver and Vehicle Licensing Agency
Driving Standards Agency
Highways Agency
Marine Safety Agency
Transport Research Laboratory
Vehicle Certification Agency
Vehicle Inspectorate

*HM Treasury
Parliament Street, London SW1P 3AG
Tel: 0171 270 3000

Oversight of tax and monetary policy; planning and control of public spending; international financial relations; supervision of the financial system; and responsibility for a range of Civil Service management issues.

HM Customs and Excise
New King's Beam House, 22 Upper Ground, London SE1 9PJ Tel: 0171 620 1313

Collecting and accounting for Customs and Excise revenues, including value added tax; agency functions, including controlling certain imports and exports, policing prohibited goods, and compiling trade statistics.

ECGD (Export Credits Guarantee Department)
2 Exchange Tower, Harbour Exchange Square, London E14 9GS Tel: 0171 512 7000

Access to bank finance and provision of insurance for British project and capital goods exporters against the risk of not being paid for goods and services; insurance cover for new British investment overseas; reinsurance to British-based private sector insurance companies offering insurance for consumer-type exports.

Inland Revenue
Somerset House, London WC2R 1LB
Tel: 0171 438 6622

Administration and collection of direct taxes; valuation of property (GB).

Executive Agency

Valuation Office

PAYMASTER: The Office of HM Paymaster General

Sutherland House, Russell Way, Crawley, West Sussex RH10 1UH Tel: 01293 560999

An executive agency providing banking services for government departments other than the Boards of Inland Revenue and Customs and Excise, and the administration and payment of public service pensions.

Royal Mint

Llantrisant, Pontyclun, Mid Glamorgan CF7 8YT Tel. 01443 222111.

An executive agency responsible for producing and issuing coinage for Britain. It also produces, among other things, ordinary circulation coins and coinage blanks for around 100 countries as well as special proof and uncirculated quality collectors' coins, commemorative medals, and royal and official seals.

Central Statistical Office

Great George Street, London SW1P 3AQ Tel: 0171 270 3000

Preparing and interpreting key economic statistics needed for government policies; collecting and publishing business statistics; publishing annual and monthly statistical digests.

From 1 April 1996 the Central Statistical Office will merge with the Office of Population Censuses and Surveys (see p. 531) to form a new executive agency called the **Office for National Statistics**. The new agency, which will be accountable to the Chancellor of the Exchequer, will take on the existing functions of the Central Statistical Office and the Office of Population Censuses and Surveys. It will also be responsible for establishing and maintaining a central database of key economic statistics produced to common definitions and standards.

REGULATORY BODIES

Office of Electricity Regulation (OFFER)

Hagley House, Hagley Road, Birmingham B16 8QG Tel: 0121 456 2100

Regulating and monitoring the electricity supply industry; promoting competition in the generation and supply of electricity; ensuring that companies comply with the licences under which they operate; protecting customers' interests (GB).

Office of Gas Supply (OFGAS)

Stockley House, 130 Wilton Road, London SW1V 1LQ Tel: 0171 828 0898

Regulating and monitoring British Gas to ensure value for money for customers, and granting authorisations to other suppliers of gas through pipes; enabling development of competition in the industrial and domestic markets.

Office of the National Lottery (OFLOT)

PO Box 4465, London SW1Y 5XL Tel: 0171 240 4624

Responsible for the grant, variation and enforcement of licences to run the National Lottery and promote lotteries as part of it.

Office for Standards in Education (OFSTED)

29–33 Kingsway, London WC2B 6SE Tel: 0171 925 6800

Monitoring standards in English schools; regulating the work of independent registered schools inspectors (E).

Office of Telecommunications (OFTEL)

50 Ludgate Hill, London EC4M 7JJ Tel: 0171 634 8700

Monitoring telecommunications operators' licences; enforcing competition legislation; representing users' interests.

Office of Water Services (OFWAT)
Centre City Tower, 7 Hill Street,
Birmingham B5 4UA Tel: 0121 625 1300

Monitoring the activities of companies
appointed as water and sewerage undertakers
(E & W); regulating prices, promoting
economy and efficiency, protecting
customers' interests and facilitating
competition. Ten regional customer service
committees represent customer interests and
investigate complaints from customers.

LEGAL AFFAIRS

*The Lord Chancellor's Department
Trevelyan House, 30 Great Peter Street,
London SW1P 2BY Tel: 0171 210 8500

Responsibility, through the Court Service, for
the administration of the Supreme Court,
county courts and a number of tribunals.
Also oversees the locally administered
magistrates' courts and the Official Solicitor's
Department. All work relating to judicial and
quasi-judicial appointments (see p. 105).
Overall responsibility for civil and criminal
legal aid, for the Law Commission and for
the promotion of general reforms in the civil
law. Lead responsibility for private
international law. The Legal Services
Ombudsman and the Advisory Committee on
Legal Education and Conduct are
independent of the Department but report to
the Lord Chancellor. The Lord Chancellor
also has responsibility for the Northern
Ireland Court Service; national archives
(maintained by the Public Record Office—
see below); and the Public Trust Office.
Except for the Northern Ireland Court
Service, the Lord Chancellor's remit covers
England and Wales only.

Executive Agencies

The Court Service
HM Land Registry
Public Record Office
Public Trust Office

Crown Prosecution Service
50 Ludgate Hill, London EC4M 7EX
Tel: 0171 273 8000

An independent organisation responsible for
the prosecution of criminal cases resulting
from police investigations, headed by the
Director of Public Prosecutions and
accountable to Parliament through the
Attorney General, superintending Minister
for the service (E & W).

Legal Secretariat to the Law Officers
Attorney General's Chambers, 9 Buckingham
Gate, London SW1E 6JP Tel: 0171 828 7155

Supporting the Law Officers of the Crown
(Attorney General and Solicitor General) in
their functions as the Government's principal
legal advisers (E, W & NI).

The Attorney General, who is also
Attorney General for Northern Ireland, is the
Minister responsible for the Treasury
Solicitor's Department (see below), and has a
statutory duty to superintend the Director of
Public Prosecutions and the Director of the
Serious Fraud Office (see below), and the
Director of Public Prosecutions for Northern
Ireland.

Parliamentary Counsel
36 Whitehall, London SW1A 2AY Tel: 0171
210 6633

Drafting of government Bills (except those
relating exclusively to Scotland); advising
departments on parliamentary procedure (E,
W & NI).

**HM Procurator General and Treasury
Solicitor's Department**
Queen Anne's Chambers, 28 Broadway,
London SW1H 9JS Tel: 0171 210 3000

Provision of legal services to a large number of
government departments, agencies, and public
and quasi-public bodies. Services include
litigation; giving general advice on interpreting
and applying the law; instructing Parliamentary
Counsel on Bills and drafting subordinate
legislation; and, through an executive agency,
providing conveyancing services and property
related legal work (E & W).

Executive Agency

Government Property Lawyers

Lord Advocate's Department and Crown Office (see p. 532)

Serious Fraud Office
Elm House, 10–16 Elm Street, London
WC1X 0BJ Tel: 0171 239 7272

Investigating and prosecuting serious and complex fraud under the superintendence of the Attorney General (E, W & NI).

EXTERNAL AFFAIRS AND DEFENCE

*Ministry of Defence
Main Building, Whitehall, London SW1A
2HB Tel: 0171 218 9000

Defence policy and control and administration of the armed services.

Defence Agencies

Army Base Repair Organisation
Army Base Storage and Distribution Agency
Army Technical Support Agency
Defence Accounts Agency
Defence Analytical Services Agency
Defence Animal Centre
Defence Bills Agency
Defence Clothing and Textiles Agency
Defence Evaluation and Research Agency
Defence Postal and Courier Services
Defence Transport and Movements
  Executive
Disposal Sales Agency
Duke of York's Royal Military School
Hydrographic Office
Logistic Information Systems Agency
Meteorological Office
Military Survey
Naval Aircraft Repair Organisation
Naval Recruiting and Training Agency
Queen Victoria School
RAF Maintenance Group
RAF Signals Engineering Establishment
RAF Training Group Defence Agency
Service Children's Schools (North West
  Europe)

*Foreign & Commonwealth Office
Downing Street, London SW1A 2AL Tel:
0171 270 1500

Conduct of Britain's overseas relations, including advising on policy, negotiating with overseas governments and conducting business in international organisations, promoting British exports and trade generally; administering aid (see below). Presenting British ideas, policies and objectives to the people of overseas countries; administering the remaining dependent territories; and protecting British interests abroad, including the welfare of British citizens.

Executive Agency

Wilton Park Conference Centre

Overseas Development Administration
94 Victoria Street, London SW1E 5JL
Tel: 0171 917 7000

Responsibility for Britain's overseas aid to developing countries, for global environmental assistance, and also for the joint administration, with the Foreign & Commonwealth Office, of assistance to Eastern Europe and the countries of the former Soviet Union. Responsibility for overseas superannuation.

Executive Agency

Natural Resources Institute

SOCIAL AFFAIRS, THE ENVIRONMENT AND CULTURE

*Department for Education and Employment
Sanctuary Buildings, Great Smith Street,
London SW1P 3BT Tel: 0171 925 5000

Overall responsibility for school, college and university education (E). The Careers Service (E); Employment Service; youth and adult training policy and programmes; sponsorship of training and enterprise councils; European social policies and programmes; co-ordination of government policy on women's issues and equal opportunities issues in employment (GB).

Executive Agencies

Employment Service
Teachers' Pensions Agency

*Department of the Environment
2 Marsham Street, London SW1P 3EB
Tel: 0171 276 3000

Policies for local government finance and structure; land use planning; housing; construction industry; energy efficiency; environmental protection; water industry and the British Waterways Board; urban and rural regeneration; countryside and wildlife protection (E); and the management of the Government estate, through Property Holdings (GB).

Executive Agencies

Building Research Establishment
The Buying Agency
Planning Inspectorate
Queen Elizabeth II Conference Centre
Security Facilities Executive

*Department of Health
Richmond House, 79 Whitehall, London SW1A 2NS Tel: 0171 210 3000

National Health Service; personal social services provided by local authorities; and certain aspects of public health, including hygiene (E).

Executive Agencies

Medicines Control Agency
Medical Devices Agency
NHS Estates
NHS Pensions Agency

*Home Office
50 Queen Anne's Gate, London SW1H 9AT
Tel: 0171 273 3000

Administration of justice; criminal law; treatment of offenders, including probation and the prison service; the police; crime prevention; fire service and emergency planning; licensing laws; regulation of firearms and dangerous drugs; electoral matters and local legislation (E & W). Gaming (GB). Passports, immigration and nationality; race relations; royal matters. Responsibilities relating to the Channel Islands and the Isle of Man.

Executive Agencies

Fire Service College
Forensic Science Service
HM Prison Service
United Kingdom Passport Agency

*Department of National Heritage
2-4 Cockspur Street, London SW1Y 5DH
Tel: 0171 211 6000.

The arts; public libraries; national museums and galleries; tourism; sport; heritage, including listing and scheduling buildings, and royal parks and palaces (E); broadcasting; press regulation; film industry; export licensing of antiques; the National Lottery.

Executive Agencies

Historic Royal Palaces Agency
Royal Parks Agency

*Department of Social Security
Richmond House, 79 Whitehall, London SW1A 2NS Tel: 0171 210 3000

The social security system (GB).

Executive Agencies

Benefits Agency
Child Support Agency
Contributions Agency
Information Technology Services Agency
Resettlement Agency
War Pensions Agency

Central Office of Information
Hercules Road, London SE1 7DU
Tel: 0171 928 2345

An executive agency procuring publicity material and other information services on behalf of government departments and publicly funded organisations.

HMSO (Her Majesty's Stationery Office)
St Crispins, Duke Street, Norwich NR3 1PD
Tel: 01603 622211

An executive agency providing stationery,

office machinery and furniture, printing and related services to Parliament, government departments and other public bodies. Publishing and selling government documents.

Ordnance Survey

Romsey Road, Southampton SO16 4GU Tel: 01703 792000

An executive agency which reports to the Secretary of State for the Environment, providing official surveying, mapping and associated scientific work covering Great Britain and some overseas countries.

Office of Population Censuses and Surveys

St Catherine's House, 10 Kingsway, London WC2B 6JP Tel: 0171 242 0262

A department responsible for administration of the marriage laws and local registration of births, marriages and deaths; provision of population estimates and projections and statistics on health and other demographic matters; Census of Population (E & W). Surveys for other government departments and public bodies (GB).

See entry under Central Statistical Office on p. 527 for details of planned merger in April 1996.

NORTHERN IRELAND

*Northern Ireland Office

Stormont Castle, Belfast BT4 3ST Tel: 01232 520700
Whitehall, London SW1A 2AZ
Tel: 0171 210 3000

Department of Agriculture for Northern Ireland

Development of agri-food, forestry and fisheries industries; veterinary, scientific and development services; food and farming policy; agri-environment policy and rural development.

Department of Economic Development for Northern Ireland

Promotion of inward investment and development of larger home industry (Industrial Development Board); promotion of enterprise and small business (Local Enterprise Development Unit); training and employment through the *Training and Employment Agency (Northern Ireland);* promotion of industrially relevant research and development and technology transfer (Industrial Research and Technology Unit); promotion and development of tourism (Northern Ireland Tourist Board); energy; mineral development; company regulation; consumer protection; health and safety at work; industrial relations; and equal opportunity in employment.

Department of Education for Northern Ireland

Control of the five education and library boards and education from nursery to further and higher education; youth services; sport and recreation; the arts and culture (including libraries); and the development of community relations within and between schools.

Department of the Environment for Northern Ireland

Environmental protection; housing; planning; roads; transport and traffic management; vehicle licensing and taxation (including *Driver and Vehicle Licensing Northern Ireland* and *the Driver and Vehicle Testing Agency*); harbours, water and sewage; *Ordnance Survey of Northern Ireland*; maintenance of public records; certain controls over local government; and the *Rate Collection Agency*.

Department of Finance and Personnel

Control of public expenditure; liaison with HM Treasury and the Northern Ireland Office on financial matters and economic and social research and analysis; EC co-ordination; charities; *Valuation and Lands Agency*; policies for equal opportunities and personnel management; and management and control of the Northern Ireland Civil Service.

Department of Health and Social Services for Northern Ireland

Health and personal social services and social legislation. Responsibility for the *Northern Ireland Child Support Agency*. The *Northern Ireland Social Security Agency* has responsibility for the administration of all social security benefits and the collection of National Insurance contributions.

SCOTLAND

*The Scottish Office

St Andrew's House, Edinburgh EH1 1DG
Tel: 0131 556 8400
Dover House, Whitehall, London SW1A
2AU Tel: 0171 270 3000

Scottish Office Agriculture, Environment and Fisheries Department

Promotion and regulation of the agricultural and fishing industries; safeguarding public, food, plant and animal health and welfare; enforcement of fisheries laws and regulations through the *Scottish Fisheries Protection Agency*. Responsibility for the *Scottish Agricultural Science Agency*. Land use and forestry, livestock subsidies and commodities.

Environment, including environmental protection, nature conservation and the countryside; land-use planning; water supplies and sewerage; local government, including finance; housing; building control; protection and presentation to the public of historic buildings and ancient monuments through *Historic Scotland*.

Scottish Office Development Department

Industrial and regional economic development matters; housing and urban regeneration; new towns; local government; transport and local roads, Roads Directorate, exports, publicity and technology; co-ordination of Scottish Office European interests; training; Highlands and Islands co-ordination.

Scottish Office Education and Industry Department

Enterprise and tourism; industrial expansion; co-ordination of Scottish Office European interests; energy; training; education; student awards (through the *Student Awards Agency for Scotland*); Scottish Higher Education Funding Council; the arts, libraries, museums and galleries, Gaelic language; sport and recreation. Responsibility for *The Scottish Office Pensions Agency*.

Scottish Office Health Department

National Health Service; Chief Scientist's Office.

Scottish Office Home Department and Scottish Courts Administration

Central administration of law and order (includes police service, criminal justice and licensing, legal aid, the *Scottish Courts Service* and the *Scottish Prison Service*) fire, home defence and civil emergency services; social work services.

Central Services

Services to the five Scottish departments. These include the Solicitor's Office to the Secretary of State, The Scottish Office Information Directorate, Administrative Services and the Personnel Group.

The following departments are directly responsible to the Law Officers and are not part of The Scottish Office.

Lord Advocate's Department

2 Carlton Gardens, London SW1Y 5AA.
Tel: 0171 210 1010

Provision of legal advice to the Government on issues affecting Scotland; responsibility for drafting government primary legislation relating to Scotland and adapting for Scotland other primary legislation. Provision of advice in matters of parliamentary procedure affecting Scotland.

Crown Office

25 Chambers Street, Edinburgh EH1 12A
Tel: 0131 226 2626

Control of all prosecutions in Scotland.

WALES

*Welsh Office

Cathays Park, Cardiff CF1 3NQ
Tel: 01222 825111
Gwydyr House, Whitehall, London SW1A
2ER Tel: 0171 270 3000

Many aspects of Welsh affairs, including health, community care and personal social services; education, except for terms and conditions of service, student awards and the University of Wales; Welsh language and culture; agriculture and fisheries; forestry; local government; housing; water and sewerage; environmental protection; sport; land use, including town and country planning; countryside and nature conservation; new towns; and ancient monuments and historic buildings (through *CADW:Welsh Historic Monuments*).

The Department's responsibilities also include roads; tourism; enterprise and training; selective financial assistance to industry; the Urban Programme and urban investment grants in Wales; the operation of the European Regional Development Fund in Wales and other European Union matters; women's issues; non-departmental public bodies; civil emergencies; all financial aspects of these matters, including Welsh revenue support grant; and oversight responsibilities for economic affairs and regional planning in Wales.

Britain's Economy: Statistical Annex

All the following statistics, apart from some relating to the labour market and retail sales, cover England, Wales, Scotland and Northern Ireland. Some figures may be subject to revision at a later stage.

Gross Domestic Product (GDP)				
				£ million
	1987	1992	1993	1994
GDP at market prices[a]	423,381	597,242	630,707	668,866
GDP at factor cost[b]	360,675	516,458	546,733	579,140
GDP at factor cost at 1990 prices	443,817	466,456	476,946	495,719
Value indices at current prices —GDP at factor cost (1990 = 100)	75.3	107.8	114.2	120.9
Percentage change since previous year	*+9.9*	*+4.1*	*+5.9*	*+5.9*
Volume indices at 1990 prices—GDP at factor cost	92.7	97.4	99.6	103.5

[a] Market prices are the prices people pay for goods and services.
[b] Factor cost is the cost of goods and services before adding taxes and subtracting subsidies.

Output				
	1987	1992	1993	1994
Output of production[a] industries (1990 = 100)	93.7	96.2	98.1	103.1
Output per person employed (1990 = 100)				
Whole economy	98.8	102.5	105.9	109.7
Percentage change since previous year	*n.a.*	*+1.9*	*+3.3*	*+3.6*
Manufacturing	88.5	108.3	113.4	118.8
Percentage change since previous year	*n.a.*	*+5.7*	*+4.7*	*+4.8*

[a] Consists of the mining and quarrying, manufacturing and electricity, gas and water supply industries.

Labour Market[a]

Thousands

	1990	1993	1994	June 1995
Employees in employment	22,909	21,588	21,639	21,889
Self-employed	3,551	3,178	3,288	3,346
Unemployment	1,661	2,901	2,619	2,314
Percentage of workforce	5.8	10.3	9.4	8.3
Percentage increase in earnings on previous year	n.a.	n.a.	+4.0	+3.1

[a] Figures for employees in employment and self-employment are for June each year and are seasonally adjusted. Other figures are annual averages, except for June 1995. The figures for unemployment are seasonally adjusted, while those for earnings are not seasonally adjusted and are for Great Britain.
n.a. = not available.

Retail Sales in Great Britain

	1991	1992	1993	1994
Volume index (average 1990 prices) 1990 =100	98.7	99.4	102.4	106.2
Percentage change since previous year	*−1.3*	*+0.7*	*+3.0*	*+3.7*
Value in current prices (1990 = 100)	104.5	108.6	114.3	119.6
Percentage change since previous year	*+4.5*	*+3.9*	*+5.2*	*+4.6*

Prices[a]

(Jan 1987 = 100)	1991	1992	1993	1994	June 1995
Retail Prices Index (RPI)	133.5	138.5	140.7	144.1	149.8
Percentage change since previous year	*+5.9*	*+3.7*	*+1.6*	*+2.4*	*+3.5*
RPI excluding mortgage interest payments	130.3	136.4	140.5	143.8	148.5
Percentage change since previous year	*+6.7*	*+4.7*	*+3.0*	*+2.3*	*+2.8*

[a] Annual averages, except for June 1995.

Sources

The following Central Statistical Office publications:
United Kingdom National Accounts 1995 Edition
Monthly Digest of Statistics
CSO press notice
Employment Gazette (jointly with the Department for Education and Employment)

Recent Legislation

The public Acts of Parliament passed since autumn 1994 are listed below. Eighteen Acts were introduced by private members; these are indicated by asterisks. All are available from HMSO.

1994

Consolidated Fund (No 2) Act 1994.
Ch 41. 60p.

Criminal Justice and Public Order Act 1994.
Ch 33. £18.

Deregulation and Contracting Out Act 1994.
Ch 40. £13.

Drug Trafficking Act 1994. Ch 37. £8.40.

European Union (Accessions) Act 1994.
Ch 38. 60p.

Law of Property (Miscellaneous Provisions) Act 1994. Ch 36. £3.80.

Local Government etc (Scotland) Act 1994.
Ch 39. £19.70.

*Marriage Act 1994. Ch 34. £1.50.

*Sale of Goods (Amendment) Act 1994.
Ch 32. 60p.

*Sale and Supply of Goods Act 1994.
Ch 35. £4.30.

1995

*Activity Centres (Young Persons' Safety) Act 1995. Ch 15. £1.10.

Agricultural Tenancies Act 1995. Ch 8. £6.30.

Appropriation Act 1995. Ch 19. £7.

*Building Societies (Joint Account Holders) Act 1995. Ch 5. £1.10.

*Carers (Recognition and Services) Act 1995.
Ch 12. £1.10.

Child Support Act 1995. Ch 34. £6.30.

Children (Scotland) Act 1995. Ch 36. £13.

*Civil Evidence (Family Mediation) (Scotland) Act 1995. Ch 6. £1.50.

Commonwealth Development Corporation Act 1995. Ch 9. £1.10.

Consolidated Fund Act 1995. Ch 2. 65p.

Criminal Appeal Act 1995. Ch 35. £6.30.

Criminal Justice (Scotland) Act 1995.
Ch 20. £16.40.

Crown Agents Act 1995. Ch 24. £2.85.

Environment Act 1995. Ch 25. £25.90.

European Communities (Finance) Act 1995.
Ch 1. 65p.

Finance Act 1995. Ch 4. £25.

*Geneva Conventions (Amendment) Act 1995.
Ch 27. £8.40.

Goods Vehicle (Licensing of Operators) Act 1995. Ch 23. £9.25.

Health Authorities Act 1995. Ch 17. £7.70.

*Home Energy Conservation Act 1995.
Ch 10. £1.10.

*Insurance Companies (Reserves) Act 1995.
Ch 29. £1.10.

Jobseekers Act 1995. Ch 18. £7.70.

*Land Registers (Scotland) Act 1995.
Ch 14. 65p.

*Landlord and Tenant (Covenants) Act 1995.
Ch 30. £4.85.

Licensing (Sunday Hours) Act 1995.
Ch 33. £1.10.

Merchant Shipping Act 1995. Ch 21. £19.95.

*National Health Service (Amendment) Act
1995. Ch 31. £3.30.

*Olympic Symbol etc (Protection) Act 1995.
Ch 32. £3.30.

Pensions Act 1995. Ch 26. £16.40.

*Prisoners (Return to Custody) Act 1995.
Ch 16. 65p.

Proceeds of Crime Act 1995. Ch 11. £4.85.

*Requirements of Writing (Scotland) Act 1995.
Ch 7. £7.

*Road Traffic (New Drivers) Act 1995.
Ch 13. £3.30.

*Sale of Goods (Amendment) Act 1995.
Ch 28. £1.10.

Shipping and Trading Interests (Protection) Act
1995. Ch 22. £3.30.

South Africa Act 1995. Ch 3. £1.10.

The Citizen's Charter Initiative

A detailed account of the Citizen's Charter initiative is given on pp. 66–8. The publications which launched the initiative and the most recent follow-up report are:

- *The Citizen's Charter. Raising the Standard.* Cm 1599. HMSO, 1991, £8.50. (See p. 66.)
- *The Citizens' Charter for Northern Ireland.* HMSO, 1992, £8.50.
- *The Citizen's Charter: The Facts and Figures: A Report to Mark Four Years of the Charter Programme.* Cm 2970. HMSO, £13.50.

A White Paper on Open Government was published in July 1993—see p. 67. (*Open Government.* Cm 2290. HMSO, £11.)

INDIVIDUAL CHARTERS

The 40 Charters for individual public services, published as part of the Citizen's Charter initiative, with the name of the department or organisation responsible in brackets,[1] are:

Britain

Taxpayer's Charter—see p. 166 (Inland Revenue)
Taxpayer's Charter (HM Customs and Excise)
Travellers' Charter (HM Customs and Excise)

England, Scotland and Wales only

Benefits Agency Customer Charter (Social Security Benefits Agency)

Child Support Agency Charter (Child Support Agency)
Contributors' Charter (Social Security Contributions Agency)
Employers' Charter (Social Security Contributions Agency)
Jobseeker's Charter—see p. 187 (Employment Service)
Passenger's Charter—see p. 301 (British Rail)
Redundancy Payments Service Charter (Department of Employment)

England and Wales only

Charter for Court Users—see p. 90 (Lord Chancellor's Department, Home Office, Crown Prosecution Service)

England only

Charter for Further Education—see p. 440 (Department for Education)
Charter for Higher Education—see p. 440 (Department for Education)
Council Tenant's Charter (Department of the Environment)
London Bus Passenger's Charter (London Transport)
London Underground's Customer Charter—see p. 303 (London Underground Ltd)
Parent's Charter—see p. 432 (Department for Education)
Patient's Charter—see p. 382 (Department of Health)
Road Users' Charter—see p. 294 (Highways Agency)

---

[1]The addresses and telephone numbers of government departments are given on pp. 525-33.

Northern Ireland only

Bus Passenger's Charter (Ulsterbus/Citybus)

Charter for Patients and Clients (Northern Ireland Office—Department of Health and Social Services)

Social Security Agency Charter (Northern Ireland Social Security Agency)

Child Support Agency Charter (Northern Ireland Child Support Agency)

Council Tenant's Charter (Northern Ireland Housing Executive)

Courts Charter (Northern Ireland Courts Service)

Parent's Charter—see p. 432 (Northern Ireland Office—Department of Education)

Railway Passenger's Charter—see p. 302 (Northern Ireland Railways)

RUC Charter (Royal Ulster Constabulary)

Training and Employment Agency Customer's Charter (Training and Employment Agency, Northern Ireland)

Scotland only

Charter for Further and Higher Education (see p. 440)

Justice Charter (see p. 91)

Parent's Charter (see p. 432)

Patient's Charter

Council Tenant's Charter

(All published by The Scottish Office)

Wales only

Charter for Further Education (see p. 440)

Charter for Higher Education (see p. 440)

Council Tenant's Charter

Parent's Charter (see p. 432)

Patient's Charter

(All published by the Welsh Office in English and Welsh)

Further Information

Information about the charters, including telephone numbers and addresses, can be obtained by calling 0345 223242 (all calls are charged at local rates). The service is available 24 hours a day. For copies of the guide to the Charter Mark awards (see p. 67), ring 0171 270 6304.

Obituaries

Sir Kingsley Amis, CBE
Writer, winner of the 1986 Booker prize
Born 1922, died October 1995

Lord Benson, GBE
Chartered accountant and former adviser to
the Governor of the Bank of England
Born 1909, died March 1995

Professor Raymond Beverton, CBE, FRS
Marine biologist
Born 1922, died August 1995

Robert Bolt, CBE
Dramatist and screenwriter
Born 1924, died February 1995

William Boon
Biochemist, discoverer of paraquat
Born 1911, died October 1994

Brigid Brophy
Writer and campaigner for public lending
right
Born 1929, died August 1995

Peter Cook
Comic writer and entertainer
Born 1937, died January 1995

Susie Cooper, OBE
Ceramics designer
Born 1902, died July 1995

Stuart Davies, CBE
Aircraft designer
Born 1906, died January 1995

Gerald Durrell, OBE
Naturalist and writer
Born 1925, died January 1995

Stephen Dykes Bower
Church architect
Born 1903, died November 1994

Sir Alexander Gibson, CBE
Conductor and founder of Scottish Opera
Company
Born 1936, died January 1995

Carl Giles, OBE ('Giles')
Cartoonist
Born 1916, died August 1995

Lord Goodman, CH
Lawyer
Born 1913, died May 1995

Bert Hardy
Photographer
Born 1913, died July 1995

Alison Hargreaves
Mountaineer
Born 1962, died August 1995

Professor Harold Hopkins
Physicist; developed the zoom lens and the
endoscope
Born 1918, died October 1994

Sir Michael Hordern, CBE
Stage and screen actor
Born 1911, died May 1995

Lord Home of the Hirsel
Conservative Prime Minister, 1963–64;
Foreign Secretary, 1960–63 and 1970–74
Born 1903, died October 1995

Harold Larwood, MBE
Cricketer
Born 1904, died July 1995

**Lord Lever of Manchester (formerly
Harold Lever)**
Labour MP 1945–79 and Cabinet minister in
two Labour governments
Born 1949, died August 1995

Dame Elizabeth Maconchy, DBE
Composer
Born 1907, died November 1994

The Rev Gordon Moody, MBE
Founder of Gamblers Anonymous
Born 1912, died September 1994

Jean Muir, CBE
Fashion designer
Born July 1928, died May 1995

John Osborne
Playwright and actor
Born 1929, died December 1994

Fred Perry
Tennis player
Born 1909, died February 1995

Sir Alastair Pilkington, FRS
Inventor of the float glass process
Born 1920, died May 1995

Lord Pitt of Hampstead
Medical practitioner, politician, campaigner
Born 1913, died December 1994

Donald Pleasence, OBE
Actor
Born 1919, died February 1995

Dilys Powell
Film critic
Born 1901, died June 1995

Dame Lucie Rie, DBE
Potter
Born 1902, died April 1995.

Sir Stephen Spender, CBE
Poet and critic
Born 1909, died July 1995

Edwin Stevens, CBE
Pioneer in developing hearing aids
Born 1905, died January 1995

J.I.M. Stewart ('Michael Innes')
Writer and scholar
Born 1906, died November 1994

Group Captain Peter Townsend, CVO, DSO, DFC and Bar
Battle of Britain pilot and former equerry to George VI and to Elizabeth II
Born 1914, died June 1995

Ernest Walton
Nuclear physicist, winner of the Nobel Prize for Physics, 1951
Born 1903, died June 1995

Lord White of Hull, KBE
Co-founder of the Hanson Trust and chairman of Hanson Industries
Born 1923, died August 1995

James Wight, OBE ('James Herriot')
Writer and veterinary surgeon
Born 1916, died February 1995

Sir Edgar Williams, CB, CBE, DSO, DL
Secretary of the Rhodes Trust and former editor of the DNB
Born 1912, died June 1995

Lord Wilson of Rievaulx, KG, OBE, PC, FRS (formerly Harold Wilson)
Labour MP 1945–83; Prime Minister, 1964–70 and 1974–76
Born 1916, died May 1995

Principal Abbreviations

ACAS: Advisory, Conciliation and Arbitration Service

BBC: British Broadcasting Corporation

BR: British Rail

BT: British Telecommunications plc

CAA: Civil Aviation Authority

CAP: Common Agricultural Policy

CBI: Confederation of British Industry

CCW: Countryside Council for Wales

CO$_2$: carbon dioxide

CPS: Crown Prosecution Service

DFEE: Department for Education and Employment

DTI: Department of Trade and Industry

EC: European Community

ECGD: Export Credits Guarantee Department

EEA: European Economic Area

ESAs: Environmentally Sensitive Areas

EU: European Union

FCO: Foreign & Commonwealth Office

GATT: General Agreement on Tariffs and Trade

GDP: gross domestic product

GNP: gross national product

GPs: general practitioners

HMIP: Her Majesty's Inspectorate of Pollution

HMSO: Her Majesty's Stationery Office

HSE: Health and Safety Executive

IPC: integrated pollution control

ITC: Independent Television Commission

ITV: independent television

LEAs: local education authorities

LECs: Local Enterprise Companies

LT: London Transport

MAFF: Ministry of Agriculture, Fisheries and Food

MFA: Multi-Fibre Arrangement

MP: Member of Parliament

NATO: North Atlantic Treaty Organisation

NHS: National Health Service

NO$_x$: oxides of nitrogen

NRA: National Rivers Authority

ODA: Overseas Development Administration

OECD: Organisation for Economic Co-operation and Development

OPS: Office of Public Service

plc: public limited company

PSBR: public sector borrowing requirement

RAF: Royal Air Force

R & D: research and development

RPI: Retail Prices Index

SIB: Securities and Investments Board

SNH: Scottish Natural Heritage

SO$_2$: sulphur dioxide

TECs: Training and Enterprise Councils

TUC: Trades Union Congress

TWh: terawatt hours

UKCS: United Kingdom Continental Shelf

UN: United Nations

VAT: value added tax

WEU: Western European Union

WTO: World Trade Organisation

Calendar of Events 1996

JANUARY

1: New Year Public Holiday in England, Northern Ireland, Scotland and Wales.
2: New Year Public Holiday in Scotland only.
20: start of Five Nations Rugby Championship.

FEBRUARY

3: Five Nations Rugby Championship fixtures; Blessing of Throats, St Ethelreda's Church, Holborn, London.
17: Five Nations Rugby Championship fixtures.
17–25: Boat, Caravan and Leisure Show, National Exhibition Centre, Birmingham.
18: Chinese New Year celebrations, Soho, London.
21: Shrove Tuesday/Pancake Day—pancake races at various venues, including Westminster School; Royal Ulster Agricultural Show, Belfast.

MARCH

1: St David's Day. (St David is the patron saint of Wales.)
12–14: Cheltenham Gold Cup, Cheltenham Racecourse, Prestbury, Gloucestershire.
14: start of Ideal Home Exhibition, Earl's Court, London.
14–17: Crufts Dog Show, National Exhibition Centre, Birmingham.
15–17: Liberal Democrat Spring Party Conference, Nottingham.
16: Five Nations Rugby Championship final.
17: St Patrick's Day. (St Patrick is the patron saint of the island of Ireland.)
18: St Patrick's Day Public Holiday, Northern Ireland only.
24: Coca Cola Cup Final, Wembley.
25: distribution of the Tichborne Dole (a measure of flour to all parishioners), Tichborne, Hampshire.
29: start of Edinburgh International Science Festival, various venues throughout the city.
30: Grand National steeplechase, Aintree, Liverpool.

APRIL

1–11: Ideal Home Exhibition, Earl's Court, London.
1–16: Edinburgh International Science Festival, various venues throughout the city.
4: Maundy Thursday, distribution of Maundy money by the Queen at Norwich Cathedral.
5: Good Friday Public Holiday in England, Northern Ireland, Scotland and Wales.
8: Easter Monday Public Holiday in England, Northern Ireland and Wales.
20: start of World Professional Snooker Championship, Crucible Theatre, Sheffield.
21: London Marathon, starts in Greenwich/Blackheath and ends in the Mall.
23: St George's Day. (St George is the patron saint of England.)
27: Rugby League Challenge Cup Final, Wembley.

MAY

1: May Day celebrations at various venues, including the Padstow 'Obby 'Oss at Padstow, Cornwall.
2–5: Badminton Horse Trials, Badminton, Avon.
**6: May Day Public Holiday in England, Northern Ireland and Wales;
Spring Public Holiday in Scotland.**
11: F.A. Cup Final, Wembley.
18: Scottish Cup Final, Hampden Park, Glasgow.
21–24: Chelsea Flower Show, Royal Hospital, Chelsea.
26: start of Royal Academy Summer Exhibition, Burlington House, Piccadilly, London.
**27: Spring Public Holiday in England, Northern Ireland and Wales;
May Day Public Holiday in Scotland.**
29: Oak Apple Day, Worcester.

JUNE

5,7,8: Derby (horseracing), Epsom, Surrey.
8–30: European Football Championship, various venues throughout England.
10–16: Queen's Club Tennis Championships, London.
15: Trooping the Colour, Horse Guards Parade, Westminster, London.
17: Garter Procession, St George's Chapel, Windsor.
18–21: Royal Ascot (horseracing), Ascot, Berkshire.
20–23: Royal Highland Show, Newbridge, Edinburgh.
24: start of All England Tennis Championship, Wimbledon.
28–30: Upton-upon-Severn Jazz Festival.

JULY

1–4: Royal International Agricultural Show, Stoneleigh, Warwickshire.
1–7: second week of All England Tennis Championship, Wimbledon.
1–16: Chichester Festival, Chichester Festival Theatre and other venues in Chichester.
3–7: Henley Regatta, Henley-on-Thames, Oxfordshire.
6–7: Junior Athletics, Stanley Park, Blackpool.
9–14: International Music Eisteddfod, Llangollen, Clwyd, Wales.
12: Battle of the Boyne Public Holiday in Northern Ireland.
12–14: British Grand Prix (motor racing), Silverstone Circuit, Towcester, Northamptonshire.
13: Durham Miners' Gala.
9–20: Royal Tournament, Earl's Court, London.
18–21: Golf Open Championship, Royal Lytham St Anne's, Lancashire.
19: start of Henry Wood Promenade Concerts, various venues in London.
20: start of King's Lynn Festival, King's Lynn, Norfolk.
22–25: Royal Welsh Show, Builth Wells, Powys.
*25: Whitstable Oyster Festival, Reeves Beach, Whitstable, Kent.
25–27: Cambridge Folk Festival, Cherry Hinton Hall, Cambridge.

AUGUST

1–11: last days of Royal Academy Summer Exhibition.
2–24: Edinburgh Tattoo, Edinburgh Castle, Scotland.

3–10: National Eisteddfod, Llandeilo, Wales.
3–10: Cowes Regatta, Isle of White.
5: Summer Public Holiday in Scotland.
11–31: Edinburgh Festival (arts), various venues in and around the city.
12–16: Tour of Britain (cycling), route to be announced.
15–18: Women's British Open (golf), Woburn Golf and Country Club, Bedfordshire.
17–24: Three Choirs Festival, Worcester.
25–26: Notting Hill Carnival, London.
26: Summer Public Holiday in England, Northern Ireland and Wales.
30: start of Blackpool Illuminations, The Promenade, Blackpool, Lancashire.

SEPTEMBER

1–4: last fortnight of Henry Wood Promenade Concerts, various venues in London.
7: Braemar Highland Gathering, Braemar, Grampian, Scotland.
7–13: British Association for the Advancement of Science Conference, Birmingham.
9–13: Trades Union Conference, Winter Gardens, Blackpool, Lancashire.
26: start of Soho Jazz Festival, London.
26–28: Liberal Democrat Autumn Party Conference, Brighton.
26–29: Plaid Cymru Conference, Llandudno, Gwynedd, Wales.
30: start of Labour Party Conference, Winter Gardens, Blackpool, Lancashire.

OCTOBER

1–3: completion of Labour Party Conference, Winter Gardens, Blackpool, Lancashire.
2–6: Horse of the Year Show, Wembley.
4–6: Nottingham Goose Fair.
8–11: Conservative Party Conference, Bournemouth.
10–20: Norfolk and Norwich Festival, various venues around the county.
*13 or 20: World Matchplay Golf Tournament, Wentworth Golf Club, Surrey.
18–27: British International Motor Show, National Exhibition Centre, Birmingham.

NOVEMBER

3: end of illuminations at Blackpool.
5: Guy Fawkes Night, bonfires and fireworks in parks and other open spaces throughout Britain.
10: Remembrance Sunday, memorial services in churches throughout Britain and wreath-laying ceremony at the Cenotaph, Whitehall, London.
13: Lord Mayor's Show, London.

DECEMBER

25: Christmas Day Public Holiday.
26: Boxing Day Public Holiday.
26–31: start of sales in department stores, chain stores and many other shops throughout Britain.

* indicates a provisional date.

This calendar of events has been included in the *Handbook* for the first time, in response to requests from users of the book. Inevitably, it is not exhaustive, but we would be pleased to hear from any individuals or organisations who can provide information on events that have not appeared this year, so that we can include them next year.

Index

Acknowledgments for photographs

50 Years of Photographs at COI (photographs listed top to bottom and left to right): London News Agency, COI Pictures, Press Association, COI Pictures, United Press International, COI Pictures; **50th Anniversary of VE Day**: COI Pictures; **Britain in Europe**: European School at Culham, European Parliament, CERN, Jonty Wilson, European Youth Orchestra; **Northern Ireland Peace Process**: COI Pictures, Press Association; **City Livery Companies**: COI Pictures; **The Electricity Supply Industry**: Scottish Hydroelectric, Nuclear Electric, Wellman Process Engineering, National Grid Company; **Textiles**: COI Pictures; **Construction**: COI Pictures; **Science and Technology**: COI Pictures, BT Laboratories, COI Pictures; **Transport Design and Safety**: COI Pictures; **Horticulture**: COI Pictures; **British Newspaper Library**: COI Pictures; **Developments in Sport**: COI Pictures; **Social Services**: Sally and Richard Greenhill; **Leisure**: PA Photo Library, Trevor Jones; **Ceramics**: COI Pictures; **Parks and Gardens**: Wales Tourist Board, COI Pictures, Northern Ireland Tourist Board, COI Pictures; **Music Technology**: COI Pictures.

Cover

Leighton Moss, Lancashire, a Special Protection Area under the European Community Birds Directive. Jonty Wilson.

Printed in the United Kingdom for HMSO
Dd 301598   C210   12/95   56-8908   43311

Main railway passenger routes

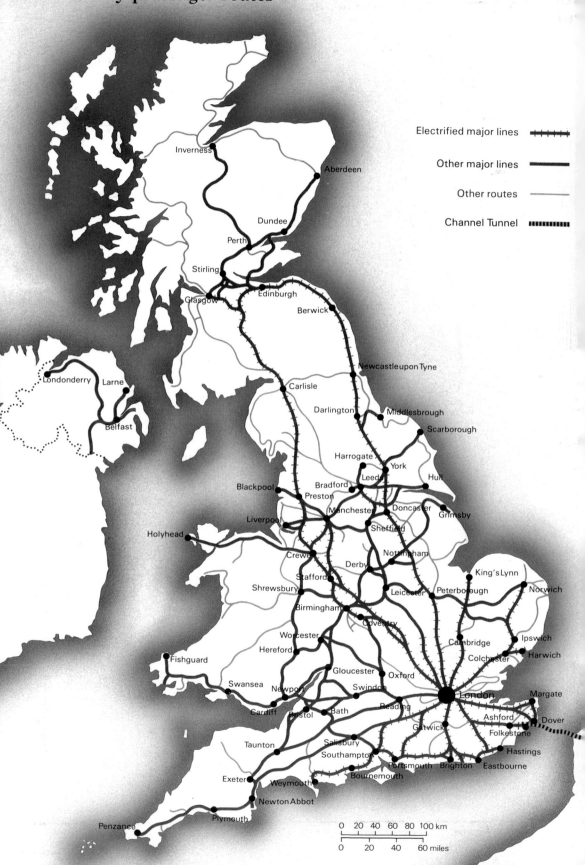

Legend:

- Electrified major lines
- Other major lines
- Other routes
- Channel Tunnel

Inverness
Aberdeen
Dundee
Perth
Stirling
Glasgow
Edinburgh
Berwick
Newcastle upon Tyne
Carlisle
Darlington
Middlesbrough
Scarborough
Harrogate
York
Hull
Bradford
Leeds
Blackpool
Preston
Manchester
Doncaster
Grimsby
Liverpool
Sheffield
Holyhead
Nottingham
Crewe
Derby
Stafford
King's Lynn
Shrewsbury
Leicester
Peterborough
Norwich
Birmingham
Coventry
Worcester
Ipswich
Hereford
Cambridge
Colchester
Harwich
Fishguard
Gloucester
Oxford
Swansea
Newport
Swindon
London
Margate
Cardiff
Bristol
Bath
Reading
Ashford
Dover
Gatwick
Folkestone
Taunton
Salisbury
Hastings
Southampton
Portsmouth
Brighton
Eastbourne
Exeter
Weymouth
Bournemouth
Newton Abbot
Penzance
Plymouth

Londonderry
Larne
Belfast

0 20 40 60 80 100 km

0 20 40 60 miles